Lecture Notes in Artificial Intelligence 13654

Subseries of Lecture Notes in Computer Science

Series Editors

Randy Goebel
University of Alberta, Edmonton, Canada

Wolfgang Wahlster
DFKI, Berlin, Germany

Zhi-Hua Zhou
Nanjing University, Nanjing, China

Founding Editor

Jörg Siekmann
DFKI and Saarland University, Saarbrücken, Germany

More information about this subseries at https://link.springer.com/bookseries/1244

João Carlos Xavier-Junior ·
Ricardo Araújo Rios (Eds.)

Intelligent Systems

11th Brazilian Conference, BRACIS 2022
Campinas, Brazil, November 28 – December 1, 2022
Proceedings, Part II

 Springer

Editors
João Carlos Xavier-Junior (iD)
Federal University of Rio Grande do Norte
Natal, Brazil

Ricardo Araújo Rios (iD)
Federal University of Bahia
Salvador, Brazil

ISSN 0302-9743   ISSN 1611-3349 (electronic)
Lecture Notes in Artificial Intelligence
ISBN 978-3-031-21688-6   ISBN 978-3-031-21689-3 (eBook)
https://doi.org/10.1007/978-3-031-21689-3

LNCS Sublibrary: SL7 – Artificial Intelligence

This Springer imprint is published by the registered company Springer Nature Switzerland AG
The registered company address is: Gewerbestrasse 11, 6330 Cham, Switzerland

Preface

The 11th Brazilian Conference on Intelligent Systems (BRACIS 2022) was one of the most important events in Brazil for researchers interested in publishing significant and novel results related to Artificial and Computational Intelligence. The Brazilian Conference on Intelligent Systems (BRACIS) originated from the combination of the two most important scientific events in Brazil in Artificial Intelligence (AI) and Computational Intelligence (CI): the Brazilian Symposium on Artificial Intelligence (SBIA, 21 editions), and the Brazilian Symposium on Neural Networks (SBRN, 12 editions). The event is supported by the Brazilian Computer Society, the Special Committee of Artificial Intelligence (CEIA), and the Special Committee of Computational Intelligence (CEIC).

The conference aims to promote theoretical aspects and applications of Artificial and Computational Intelligence, as well as the exchange of scientific ideas among researchers, practitioners, scientists, and engineers.

This year, BRACIS was held in Campinas, Brazil, from November 28 to December 1, 2022, in conjunction with five other events: the National Meeting on Artificial and Computational Intelligence (ENIAC), the Symposium on Knowledge Discovery, Mining and Learning (KDMiLe), the Concurso de Teses e Dissertações em Inteligência Artificial e Computacional (CTDIAC), the Brazilian competition on Knowledge Discovery in Databases (KDD-BR) and the Workshop of the Brazilian Institute of Data Science (WBIOS).

BRACIS 2022 received 225 submissions. All papers were rigorously double-blind peer-reviewed by an international Program Committee (with an average of three reviews per submission), which was followed by a discussion phase for conflicting reports. After the review process, 89 papers were selected for publication in two volumes of the Lecture Notes in Artificial Intelligence series (an acceptance rate of 39.5%).

The topics of interest included, but were not limited to, the following:

- Agent-based and Multi-Agent Systems
- Cognitive Modeling and Human Interaction
- Constraints and Search
- Foundations of AI
- Distributed AI
- Information Retrieval, Integration, and Extraction
- Knowledge Representation and Reasoning
- Knowledge Representation and Reasoning in Ontologies and the Semantic Web
- Logic-based Knowledge Representation and Reasoning
- Natural Language Processing
- Planning and Scheduling
- Evolutionary Computation and Metaheuristics
- Fuzzy Systems
- Neural Networks

- Deep Learning
- Machine Learning and Data Mining
- Meta-learning
- Reinforcement Learning
- Molecular and Quantum Computing
- Pattern Recognition and Cluster Analysis
- Hybrid Systems
- Bioinformatics and Biomedical Engineering
- Combinatorial and Numerical Optimization
- Computer Vision
- Education
- Forecasting
- Game Playing and Intelligent Interactive Entertainment
- Intelligent Robotics
- Multidisciplinary AI and CI
- Foundation Models
- Human-centric AI
- Ethics

We would like to thank everyone involved in BRACIS 2022 for helping to make it a success.

November 2022

João C. Xavier Júnior
Ricardo A. Rios

Organization

General Chairs

João M. T. Romano	UNICAMP, Brazil
Leonardo T. Duarte	UNICAMP, Brazil

Program Committee Chairs

João C. Xavier Júnior	UFRN, Brazil
Ricardo A. Rios	UFBA, Brazil

Organizing Committee

João M. T. Romano	UNICAMP, Brazil
Leonardo T. Duarte	UNICAMP, Brazil
Gisele Baccaglini	UNICAMP, Brazil
Cristiano Torezzan	UNICAMP, Brazil
Denis Gustavo Fantinato	UFABC, Brazil
Henrique N. de Sá Earp	UNICAMP, Brazil
Ricardo Suyama	UFABC, Brazil
Rodolfo de C. Pacagnella	UNICAMP, Brazil
João B. Florindo	UNICAMP, Brazil
Jurandir Z. Junior	UNICAMP, Brazil
Leandro Tessler	UNICAMP, Brazil
Luiz Henrique A. Rodrigues	UNICAMP, Brazil
Priscila P. Coltri	UNICAMP, Brazil
Renato Machado	ITA, Brazil
Renato da R. Lopes	UNICAMP, Brazil
Rosângela B.	UNICAMP, Brazil

Program Committee

Adenilton da Silva	UFPE, Brazil
Adrião D. Dória Neto	UFRN, Brazil
Alexandre Falcao	UNICAMP, Brazil
Alexandre Ferreira	UNICAMP, Brazil
Aline Neves	UFABC, Brazil
Aline Paes	UFF, Brazil

Alneu Lopes	USP, S.Carlos, Brazil
Aluizio Araújo	UFPE, Brazil
Ana Bazzan	UFRGS, Brazil
Ana Carolina Lorena	ITA, Brazil
Ana C. B. Kochem Vendramin	UTFPR, Brazil
Anderson Soares	UFG, Brazil
André Britto	UFS, Brazil
André Ponce de Leon F. de Carvalho	USP, S.Carlos, Brazil
André Rossi	UNESP, Brazil
André Takahata	UFABC, Brazil
Andrés Eduardo Coca Salazar	UTFPR, Brazil
Anna Helena Reali Costa	USP, Brazil
Anne Canuto	UFRN, Brazil
Araken Santos	UFERSA, Brazil
Ariane Machado-Lima	USP, Brazil
Aurora Pozo	UFPR, Brazil
Bruno Masiero	UNICAMP, Brazil
Bruno Nogueira	UFMS, Brazil
Bruno Pimentel	UFAL, Brazil
Carlos Ribeiro	ITA, Brazil
Carlos Silla	PUCPR, Brazil
Carlos Thomaz	FEI, Brazil
Carolina Paula de Almeida	UNICENTRO, Brazil
Celia Ralha	UnB, Brazil
Cephas A. S. Barreto	UFRN, Brazil
Claudio Bordin Jr.	UFABC, Brazil
Claudio Toledo	USP, Brazil
Cleber Zanchettin	UFPE, Brazil
Cristiano Torezzan	UNICAMP, Brazil
Daniel Dantas	UFS, Brazil
Danilo Sanches	UTFPR, Brazil
Debora Medeiros	UFABC, Brazil
Denis Fantinato	UFABC, Brazil
Denis Mauá	USP, Brazil
Diana Adamatti	FURG, Brazil
Diego Furtado Silva	USP, Brazil
Edson Gomi	USP, Brazil
Edson Matsubara	UFMS, Brazil
Eduardo Borges	FURG, Brazil
Eduardo Costa	Corteva, Brazil
Eduardo Palmeira	UESC, Brazil

Eduardo Spinosa	UFPR, Brazil
Edward Hermann Haeusler	PUC-Rio, Brazil
Elaine Faria	UFU, Brazil
Elizabeth Goldbarg	UFRN, Brazil
Emerson Paraiso	PUCPR, Brazil
Eraldo Fernandes	UFMS, Brazil
Eric Araújo	UFLA, Brazil
Fabiano Silva	UFPR, Brazil
Fábio Cozman	USP, Brazil
Fernando Osório	USP, Brazil
Flavia Bernardini	UFF, Brazil
Flávio Soares Corrêa da Silva	USP, Brazil
Francisco Chicano	UMA, ES
Francisco De Carvalho	UFPE, Brazil
Gabriel Ramos	UNISINOS, Brazil
George Cavalcanti	UFPE, Brazil
Gerson Zaverucha	UFRJ, Brazil
Giancarlo Lucca	FURG, Brazil
Gisele Pappa	UFMG, Brazil
Gracaliz Dimuro	FURG, Brazil
Guilherme Coelho	UNICAMP, Brazil
Guilherme Derenievicz	UFPR, Brazil
Guilherme Dean Pelegrina	UNICAMP, Brazil
Gustavo Giménez-Lugo	UTFPR, Brazil
Gustavo Paetzold	USH, UK
Helena Caseli	UFSCar, Brazil
Heloisa Camargo	UFSCar, Brazil
Huei Lee	UNIOESTE, Brazil
Islame Felipe da Costa Fernandes	UFBA, Brazil
Ivandré Paraboni	USP, Brazil
Ivette Luna	UNICAMP, Brazil
João Balsa	ULisboa, Portugal
João Bertini	UNICAMP, Brazil
João Papa	UNESP, Brazil
João Paulo Canário	Stone Co., Brazil
Jomi Hübner	UFSC, Brazil
Jonathan Andrade Silva	UFMS, Brazil
Jose Eduardo Ochoa Luna	UCSP, Peru
Julio Nievola	PUCPR, Brazil
Karliane Vale	UFRN, Brazil
Kenji Nose Filho	UFABC, Brazil
Leliane Nunes de Barros	USP, Brazil

Renato Ishii	UFMS, Brazil
Renato Krohling	UFES, Brazil
Renato Tinos	USP, Brazil
Ricardo Cerri	UFSCar, Brazil
Ricardo Dutra da Silva	UTFPR, Brazil
Ricardo Marcacini	USP, Brazil
Ricardo Prudêncio	UFPE, Brazil
Ricardo Suyama	UFABC, Brazil
Robson Cordeiro	USP, Brazil
Rodrigo Barros	PUCRS, Brazil
Rodrigo Wilkens	UCLouvain, Belgium
Ronaldo Prati	UFABC, Brazil
Rosangela Ballini	UNICAMP, Brazil
Sandra Avila	UNICAMP, Brazil
Sandra Venske	UNICENTRO, Brazil
Sarajane Peres	USP, Brazil
Sílvio Cazella	UFCSPA, Brazil
Solange Rezende	USP, Brazil
Sylvio Barbon Junior	UniTS, Italy
Tatiane Nogueira	UFBA, Brazil
Thiago Covoes	Wildlife Studios, Brazil
Thiago Pardo	USP, Brazil
Tiago Almeida	UFSCar, Brazil
Valerie Camps	UTO, France
Valmir Macario	UFRPE, Brazil
Vasco Furtado	UNIFOR, Brazil
Vítor Santos Costa	U.Porto, Portugal
Vinicius Souza	PUCPR, Brazil
Vladimir Rocha	UFABC, Brazil
Wagner Meira Jr.	UFMG, Brazil

Contents – Part II

Contents – Part I

A Sequential Recommender System with Embeddings Based on GraphSage Aggregators

Anderson Bottega da Silva[✉] and Eduardo J. Spinosa

Universidade Federal do Paraná, Curitiba, PR, Brazil
andersonbottegas@hotmail.com, spinosa@inf.ufpr.br

Abstract. Recommender systems help users by filtering a large amount of content to which they are exposed daily, in order to recommend products in e-commerce, music, movies, people on social networks and others in a personalized way, thus being a complex task. Currently, sequential recommender systems have been increasingly used in these tasks. They receive behavior trajectories as input, that is, items accessed during a given time, and use recommendation algorithms to suggest the next item. In a graph-based representation of these sequences, an initial step involves learning representations for the items, vectors of real numbers called embeddings. In this work we propose to change the module responsible for building these item representations, which originally employs the GGNN technique in the SR-GNN Sequential Recommendation System, by the Graph-Sage technique with its aggregators: Mean, Maxpooling and LSTM. We validated our proposal with the datasets: yoochoose, diginetica, aotm and 30music. The results indicate that, with the Mean aggregator, it is possible to reduce the execution time in all tested scenarios, maintaining the original effectiveness.

Keywords: Sequential Recommender Systems · GraphSage · SR-GNN

1 Introduction

Recommender System aims to filter the content to which a user is exposed, so these systems try to predict user's preference based on the content of their search. To carry out this recommendation, the system needs to learn the user's content consumption pattern through past data, therefore, in these cases the search history is stored and associated with a specific user. More traditional Recommender Systems are based on collaborative filtering, that is, they usually employ user's long-term history to try to learn their preferences and target the most appropriate content possible, however, only the long-term history may not exactly match what the user is looking for at that moment and the recommendations become inappropriate [1].

Due to these limitations, Sequential Recommender Systems emerged. They refer to a system that learns the consumption pattern through sessions. A session consists of a few clicks on products in a short time. A session does not depend

J. C. Xavier-Junior and R. A. Rios (Eds.): BRACIS 2022, LNAI 13654, pp. 1–15, 2022.
https://doi.org/10.1007/978-3-031-21689-3_1

on the identification of a specific user, the clicks should only be performed in sequence over a short period of time and for this reason, sessions are usually small. In this way, there are no records of consumption over long periods of time, nor the need to store them and associate them with a user, which is an advantage in some scenarios, where the user login is not performed. Another advantage is that the click sequence can be easily modeled using graphs [16].

With the modeling of sequences in the form of graphs, the need arose to build representations for the items of the graphs. The representations are low-dimensional vectors of real numbers, called embeddings. Their purpose is to provide data about an item (node), so that the similarity between the representations is easily calculated by a Sequential Recommendation System. For the construction of these representations, several Deep Learning (DL) techniques were shown to be promising and were used [2], such as: Recurrent Neural Network (RNN) [13], Graph Convolutional Network (GCN) [14], Gated Graph Neural Network (GGNN) [15], Graph Attention Network (GAT) [17] and Graph-Sage [10], the latter being the focus of this work. These techniques use different strategies to generate representations of items. Although mentioned techniques use different strategies, their objective is the same: build representations for the different input items of a Sequential Recommender System, so when an item looks like another item, more similar their embeddings will be. Thus, the matrix of representations acquired through these techniques reflects the structure of the input graph of the Sequential Recommender System.

To identify the relationship between items, the most common strategy of these techniques is to extract characteristics of the graph structure generated from the sequences modeled through directed graphs. The relationships can be connections between nodes of the graphs, node degrees, among others. In addition to the relationships present in the graph structure, we can use images, textual descriptions and user ratings for the items, making representations rich in information. Such information used as input, before processing by deep learning techniques, are called features.

We found in the literature several Sequential Recommender Systems that perform the construction of these embeddings in different ways, so we performed some preliminary experiments to analyze their behavior, including the following methods: NARM [6], STAMP [7], SR-GNN [3], MGNN-SPred [8] and FGNN [9].

Motivated by several researches in the area of Sequential Recommender Systems and the study of the mentioned methods, the focus of this work is on how the construction of item representations can influence the efficiency of a Sequential Recommender System. To verify these results, we propose a modification in the general structure of the SR-GNN method, where we replace the GGNN module, responsible for building the representations, by GraphSage, which in this case will also be responsible for building the item representations. In addition to inserting GraphSage into the SR-GNN method, we also evaluate different aggregators, based on Average, Max-pooling and LSTM. Thus, given the input in the form of a session graph, this work evaluates the effectiveness and efficiency of the original method (SR-GNN) and the proposed method with three aggregators for the recommendation of items.

2 Related Work

2.1 GraphSage

Convolutional graph networks were only applied in transductive scenarios with fixed graphs, where a transductive scenario means that all nodes of the graph were needed during training to build embeddings. GraphSage proposes a framework that generalizes the GCN [14] approach, using aggregation functions instead of performing convolutions. This method takes a graph as input and is able to extract features from the graph structure such as node connections, node degree, among others. It is also possible to extract features from data such as textual description and product and movie reviews. Embeddings generated with this data are low-dimensional vectors that represent the nodes of the graph. To arrive at these vectors, dimensionality reduction techniques are used to filter the high-dimensional information (features) [10].

The advantage of GraphSage is in the ease of dealing with large graphs and with many features, because instead of training the embeddings for all nodes of the graph, it learns a function to generate embeddings through sampling and feature aggregation functions. The generation of embeddings aggregates information about the neighbors of each node and uses a set of weight matrices denoted by $\mathbf{W}^k, \forall k \in \{1, ..., K\}$, where k is the depth of the layer (distance from the graph). These matrices are used to propagate information between layers of the model.

Hamilton et al. [10] defines the algorithm of Fig. 1 as the embedding generation process. This algorithm has the function of performing the aggregation of information from neighbors of the nodes of the graph $G = (\nu, \varepsilon)$ and its features $x_v, \forall v \in \nu$ in the current node, as the iterations pass, so nodes gain information further away from the graph. The aggregation function is defined by $AGGREGATE_k, \forall k \in \{1, ..., K\}$, h_v^0 is the initialization of the features, $h_{N(v)}^k$ stores the output of the aggregation function, h_v^k stores multiplication of the weight matrix $\mathbf{W}^k$ with the concatenation of the feature from the previous layer with the new feature generated by aggregation function. Finally, z_v stores the embeddings $h_v^K, \forall v \in \nu$.

Algorithm 1: GraphSAGE embedding generation (i.e., forward propagation) algorithm

Input : Graph $\mathcal{G}(\mathcal{V}, \mathcal{E})$; input features $\{x_v, \forall v \in \mathcal{V}\}$; depth K; weight matrices
$\mathbf{W}^k, \forall k \in \{1 ..., K\}$; non-linearity σ; differentiable aggregator functions
$AGGREGATE_k, \forall k \in \{1, ..., K\}$; neighborhood function $\mathcal{N} : v \to 2^{\mathcal{V}}$

Output : Vector representations z_v for all $v \in \mathcal{V}$

1 $h_v^0 \leftarrow x_v, \forall v \in \mathcal{V}$;
2 **for** $k = 1...K$ **do**
3   **for** $v \in \mathcal{V}$ **do**
4        $h_{\mathcal{N}(v)}^k \leftarrow AGGREGATE_k(\{h_u^{k-1}, \forall u \in \mathcal{N}(v)\})$;
5        $h_v^k \leftarrow \sigma\left(\mathbf{W}^k \cdot CONCAT(h_v^{k-1}, h_{\mathcal{N}(v)}^k)\right)$
6   **end**
7     $h_v^k \leftarrow h_v^k / \|h_v^k\|_2, \forall v \in \mathcal{V}$
8 **end**
9 $z_v \leftarrow h_v^K, \forall v \in \mathcal{V}$

Fig. 1. Embedding generation process [10].

Aggregation function $AGGREGATE_k, \forall k \in \{1, ..., K\}$ can be performed by different algorithms. These aggregators, unlike machine learning, operate on an unordered set of vectors. Hamilton et al. [10] propose three aggregators: mean, pooling and LSTM.

The mean aggregator is the element-by-element average of the vectors of embeddings. This operation is defined by the Eq. 1. To use this aggregator, Hamilton et al. [10] replace this function with lines four and five of the algorithm in Fig. 1. This aggregator is called convolutional and its most important difference from other aggregators is that it does not use line five of the algorithm responsible for the concatenation operation.

$$h_v^k \leftarrow \sigma(\mathbf{W} \cdot MEAN(\{h_v^{k-1}\}) \cup \{h_u^{k-1}, \forall u \in N(v)\}) \tag{1}$$

The LSTM aggregator is based entirely on the LSTM architecture proposed by Hochreiter and Schmidhuber [5].

Finally, the pooling aggregator feeds each neighbor's vector independently through a fully connected neural network, then an elementwise max-pooling operation is applied to the entire neighbor set. The max-pooling operation is defined by the Eq. 2. Before max-pooling, a multilayer perceptron (MLP) function can be applied, responsible for using a set of functions that calculate the features of each representations of neighboring nodes, so that max-pooling is able to obtain different aspects of these nodes from the neighborhood.

$$AGGREGATE_k^{pool} = max(\{\sigma(\mathbf{W}_{pool}h_{u_i}^k + \mathbf{b}), \forall u_i \in N(v)\}) \tag{2}$$

In addition to GraphSage, other techniques can be applied to build the representation of items in a Sequential Recommender System. Some of these techniques are: A Recurrent Neural Network (RNN) [13] which use recursive neural networks to build representations of items, Graph Convolutional Network (GCN) [14] using convolutional networks in graphs, Gated Graph Neural Network (GGNN) that uses ports based on the GRU network (Gated Recurrent Unit), Graph Attention Network (GAT) [17] based on attention mechanisms, among other techniques.

2.2 Sequential Recommender System Methods

Several works have been carried out on Recommender Systems and Sequential Recommender Systems. RNN-based works such as NARM [6] and STAMP [7], were able to overcome the state-of-the-art in the context of sequential recommendation. Still in the search for improvements in algorithms used for sequential recommendation, some authors employed GNNs. According to Wu et al. [16], the main motivations for using them is that most of the data from recommender systems has a graph structure, in addition, GNNs can be effective in capturing connections between nodes and extracting relationships between items.

Wu et al. [16] reviewed several types of Recommender Systems and presented a classification of works based on sequential recommendation 1. In the column *GNN Framework* we have the technique used to create the representation of items, where we can see that most of the methods use variations of GGNN, two methods using GraphSage, two methods using variations of GraphSage and finally, two methods using the GAT.

Table 1. Recommender systems based on sequence [16].

Information	Graph	Model	Venue	Year	GNN Framework
	Seq	SR-GNN [136]	AAAI	2019	variant of GGNN (in & out adjacent matrices)
	Seq	GC-SAN [141]	IJCAI	2019	variant of GGNN (in & out adjacent matrices)
	Seq	NISER [26]	CIKM	2019	variant of GGNN (in & out adjacent matrices)
	Seq	TAGNN [146]	SIGIR	2020	variant of GGNN (in & out adjacent matrices)
	Seq	FGNN [82]	CIKM	2019	variant of GAT
	Seq	A-PGNN [137]	TKDE	2019	variant of GGNN (in & out adjacent matrices)
Sequence	Seq	MA-GNN [73]	AAAI	2020	GraphSage
(Seq)	Seq	MGNN-Spred [116]	WWW	2020	variant of GraphSage (sum updater)
	Seq	HetGNN [116]	WWW	2020	variant of GraphSage (sum updater)
	Seq	GAG [83]	SIGIR	2020	variant of GGNN (in & out adjacent matrices)
	Seq	SGNN-HN [80]	CIKM	2020	variant of GGNN (in & out adjacent matrices)
	Seq	LESSR [11]	KDD	2020	-
	Seq	GCE-GNN [126]	SIGIR	2020	variant of GAT
	Seq	ISSR [65]	AAAI	2020	GraphSage
	Seq	DGTN [160]	arxiv	2020	mean-pooling

SR-GNN [3] is a method that employs GGNN to explore transitions between items and generates embeddings of these items for recommendation. Initially, graphs directed to each session are constructed and the session sequences are treated as a subgraph, then each subgraph is processed by a variation of the GGNN and embeddings are obtained for all nodes of the constructed graphs. The construction of these embeddings takes place through the equations of the GRU propagation model. After this process, the node embeddings are represented by two vectors, a global preference (s_g) and a local preference (s_l). Both vectors are constructed through an attention mechanism proposed by [11], which is called soft attention.

Global preference vector represents sessions. It contains all the items of the session and is obtained through Eq. 3 and 4. The local vector represents the user's interest in that session, being composed of the last item clicked, therefore, $S_l = v_n$ and v_n represent the last item that the user clicked. Having these two vectors, the vector s_h is generated, which is the concatenation performed through Eq. 5, where variables $\mathbf{q}$, $\mathbf{W}_1$, $\mathbf{W}_2$ and $\mathbf{c}$ are weight matrices.

$$\alpha_i = \mathbf{q}^\top \sigma(\mathbf{W}_1 v_n + \mathbf{W}_2 v_i + \mathbf{c}) \tag{3}$$

$$s_g = \sum_{i=1}^{n} \alpha_i v_i \tag{4}$$

$$s_h = \mathbf{W}_3[s_l; s_g] \tag{5}$$

In Eq. 5, $\mathbf{W}_3$ is a matrix that compresses the two vectors into a space R^d. Finally, with the representation of the s_h session constructed, we calculated the score of each of the items through Eq. 6. The probability of each item being the next click is calculated by Eq. 7.

$$\hat{z}_i = s_h^\top v_i \qquad (6)$$

$$\hat{y} = softmax(\hat{z}) \qquad (7)$$

Gupta et al. [18] realized that SR-GNN tends to recommend the most popular items, so NISER was proposed to try to solve this problem. NISER maps all items to a vector of dimension d and then normalizes them, after which it employs a variation of GGNN, as does SR-GNN to take as input the adjacency matrices (corresponding to the input and output edges of the graph of items and sessions) and the normalized item embeddings, so it returns updated embeddings. S is a linear transformation of the concatenation of the session embeddings and finally the transformation is normalized again.

GC-SAN (Graph Contextualized Self-Attention) [12], uses the technique of Self-Attention Network (SAN) and graphs to overcome some problems such as the lack of local information. The beginning of the GC-SAN structure is identical to the SR-GNN, where a variation of the GGNN generates the embeddings through the items graph to feed the attention layer, responsible for capturing global preference. Then, the Point-Wise Feed-Forward network is responsible for considering the interactions between different dimensions. Then Residual Connection is added to cover losses in previous operations. Finally, the Prediction Layer module combines global and local preferences.

3 Proposed Method and Implementation

3.1 Proposed Method

As seen in the Sect. 2.2, SR-GNN [3] is a method that uses a GGNN in its structure to create representations (embeddings) from the graph, such as the node degree. The GGNN generates the embeddings for all nodes of the graph and they become the input of an attention mechanism, which is responsible for extracting the global information. Also, this method uses the embedding of the last item in the session as the local representation. In this way, it can build long-term and short-term embeddings respectively.

Another relevant point related to recommender systems is scalability, which according to Wu et al. [16], is fundamental. So, to deal with large graphs, current works adopt sampling methods, which can use, for example, the random walk strategy or the shortest path algorithm to obtain the neighborhood and perform the construction of the subgraphs. The GraphSage [10] is able to handle these large graphs in a scalable way. Such strategies can change the efficiency and effectiveness of the method.

We observed two interesting aspects: the first one is that the methods that extract features from description texts or item evaluation usually employ the GraphSage technique and this is related to its ease in dealing with very large and information-rich graphs, since its approach does not need to traverse all nodes in the neighborhood. The second aspect is that the SR-GNN method has its structure used in several later works, such as the GC-SAN [12], the KV-MN [4], the NISER [18], among others, suggesting that it became a basis for new methods.

In this work we propose to replace the GGNN module of the SR-GNN structure by GraphSage. GraphSage will be responsible for generating embeddings for all nodes, and can be used with different aggregators, as described in Sect. 2.1.

From this point on, the proposal will be the same as the SR-GNN, given that the attention module manages to balance global and local information, so the embeddings generated by GraphSage will be inputs to the attention mechanism that will extract the vector of global embeddings (S_g).

The vector of local embeddings (S_l) will continue to be exactly the embedding of the last clicked item in each session, also generated by the GraphSage aggregator. Then a linear transformation is performed in the concatenation of the global vector with the local vector, called S_h and finally, a softmax function will be applied to S_h.

With this proposed structure, we hope to aggregate features in different ways, taking advantage of GraphSage's efficiency in large graphs. In Fig. 2 we can see how the proposed structure will look, where the nodes in red represent a session. The red dotted line rectangle indicates where there has been no change to the original SR-GNN structure.

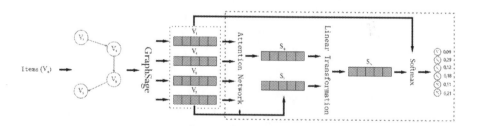

Fig. 2. Proposed approach.

3.2 Implementation

SR-GNN [3] uses the Python language and the PyTorch in its implementation. Pytorch is a library used for machine learning and was designed with the objective of loading the information of all the operations carried out within its tensors, which can be processed by the CPU or the GPU. Tensors are like arrays, being distinguished by their ability to store the history of mathematical operations. Its application is mainly in computer vision and natural language processing.

For the implementation of this work, we used a re-implementation of SR-GNN that uses the PyTorch Geometric. This library was built from PyTorch, but specific for training through Graph Neural Networks. The decision to continue using these libraries when implementing the proposal for this work was due to the ease of access to their open source code and the ease of finding the necessary documentation for understanding the code.

Implementation of the new model allows us to run SR-GNN with its GGNN module or GraphSAGE and its aggregators just by changing a hyperparameter. Aggregators were proposed by Hamilton et al. [10]. The implementations of these aggregators based on the PyTorch library are available in different places: the Mean Aggregator is available in the documentation of the official PyTorch Geometric website, the Maxpooling Aggregator is available on the website towardsdatascience.com and for the LSTM Aggregator, we use the original LSTM implementation available on the official PyTorch website. To use these aggregators together with the implementation of SR-GNN, some adaptations and modifications were necessary in all codes: SR-GNN, Mean Aggregator, Maxpooling Aggregator and LSTM Aggregator. The code proposed in this work and the links of the used aggregators are available on github[1].

4   Experiments and Analysis

4.1   Databases

To evaluate the selected methods, we used four databases: yoochoose obtained from *RecSys Challenge 2015*, diginetica obtained from the *CIKM Cup 2016*, the aotm and 30music. The yoochoose and diginetica databases were created through user clicks in an online product sales site. Aotm is a playlist of songs, just like 30music.

The proposed method requires pre-processing in the datasets. This preprocessing was defined by Wu et al. [3]. It removes sessions with size one and sessions that contain items that appear five times or less in the entire dataset. We can observe some statistics of the datasets used through in Table 2.

Table 2. Statistics of the datasets.

Statistics	yoochoose1_64	Diginetica	Aotm	30music
Number of training sessions	369.859	719.470	814.263	1.794.929
Number of test sessions	55.898	60.858	72.265	179.560
Number of items	16.766	43.097	53.948	137.999
Average sessions size	6,16	4,85	11,48	12,94

4.2   Methodology

Hyperparameters in Table 3 were applied to evaluate the performance, with focus on the impact of the size of the embeddings, represented by hidden_layers The

---

[1] https://github.com/AndersonBottega/SRGNN-GraphSage.

number of epochs was defined after carrying out some initial experiments, which demonstrated that after the 15th epoch the results did not vary. In this way, it was decided to use 20 epochs to ensure that all methods are able to converge. We tested the other hyperparameters empirically, through experiments, where it was noticed that the changes did not contribute to improvements in the performance of the methods, in this way, it was decided to assign the hyperparameters suggested by Wu et al. [3]. We performed these methods on a computer with the following configurations: Intel processor - 3.0 GHz, 196 GB RAM and Linux Mint 19.1 Tessa operating system.

Table 3. Hyperparameter settings.

Hyperparameter	Settings
learning_rate	0,001
hidden_layers	(20, 50, 80)
batch_size	100
Epochs	20

Metrics: We use the HR@k and MRR@k metrics to measure the effectiveness of the methods. The HR@k (Hit Rate) checks if the item that should be recommended is in the recommendation list of size k that the method generated. For each correct item, a hit is scored. To calculate the HR we must divide the number of hits by the total number of tests. Like HR, it checks if the item that should be recommended is in the recommendation list of size k that the method generated, however, it does not only score a hit whenever the item is in the list, but assigns different weights to each position in which the item is and the further to the top, the higher the score the item will receive [20].

In addition to effectiveness, measured by the HR@k and MRR@k metrics, we measured the training and testing runtime for each of the methods. We used the Kruskal-Wallis and Conover-Iman statistical tests, with threshold $\alpha = 0.05$ to determine the existence of statistical difference.

4.3   Results and Analysis

This section presents the results and analysis of the experiments performed. The original SR-GNN method is denoted as GGNN. The proposed approach based on GraphSage with each of the three aggregators Mean, Maxpooling and LSTM are denoted as Mean, Max and LSTM respectively. We use $k = 20$ for the recommended items list size, so our metrics are represented as HR@20 and MRR@20. Tables 4, 5, 6 and 7 show the mean and standard deviation of five runs performed in each dataset, as well as their average execution time. The highlighted values indicate statistical superiority or inferiority in relation to GGNN method.

Analyzing Table 4 we can see a pattern, where the Mean method has a slightly higher hit rate than the other methods in all sizes of embeddings, followed by the

Table 4. Performance of the GGNN, Mean, Max and LSTM methods for the yoo-choose1_64 dataset. Mean of metrics in %, followed by the standard deviation after ±. Time is measured in minutes.

| Methods | Embedding and hidden_layer 20 | | |
	HR@20	MRR@20	Time
GGNN	$65,4910 \pm 0,2348$	$27,0213 \pm 0,1352$	$254 \pm 0,0054$
Mean	$\mathbf{66,5397} \pm 0,1878$	$\mathbf{27,7082} \pm 0,0935$	$\mathbf{230} \pm 0,0039$
Max	$65,0441 \pm 0,2760$	$26,7996 \pm 0,1624$	$\mathbf{230} \pm 0,0039$
LSTM	$\mathbf{58,1054} \pm 0,7154$	$\mathbf{22,2251} \pm 0,4879$	$\mathbf{455} \pm 0,0077$
Methods	Embedding and hidden_layer 50		
	HR@20	MRR@20	Time
GGNN	$69,1574 \pm 0,1864$	$29,2815 \pm 0,0265$	$296 \pm 0,0103$
Mean	$69,4685 \pm 0,0868$	$\mathbf{29,3802} \pm 0,0482$	$\mathbf{256} \pm 0,0078$
Max	$\mathbf{68,5122} \pm 0,1692$	$28,8819 \pm 0,0656$	$\mathbf{271} \pm 0,0086$
LSTM	$\mathbf{66,9605} \pm 0,3039$	$27,9310 \pm 0,2629$	$\mathbf{542} \pm 0,0191$
Methods	Embedding and hidden_layer 80		
	HR@20	MRR@20	Time
GGNN	$69,7863 \pm 0,0887$	$29,8021 \pm 0,0905$	$393 \pm 0,0076$
Mean	$69,7888 \pm 0,1303$	$29,8836 \pm 0,0587$	$\mathbf{293} \pm 0,0058$
Max	$\mathbf{69,2686} \pm 0,0542$	$\mathbf{29,4441} \pm 0,0664$	$\mathbf{316} \pm 0,0008$
LSTM	$\mathbf{68,4940} \pm 0,1255$	$\mathbf{28,7388} \pm 0,0880$	$\mathbf{807} \pm 0,0531$

GGNN and Max methods, respectively. With the statistical analysis, we noticed that Mean method is superior at times for the hit rate and Max method is statistically inferior or equivalent to GGNN method. The largest difference is in relation to the LSTM method, which has the lowest hit rates, being statistically lower than GGNN method. Another relevant point that we can observe is how the size of the embedding affects the results. For size 20, HR@20 and MRR@20 metrics do not reach the values obtained with the embeddings of size 50 and when we increase this size to 80, we do not notice any difference in these same metrics in relation to size 50. Then conclude that the size 20 for the representation of the items is not enough for the tested methods to achieve their best performance within the HR@20 and MRR@20 metrics in these experiments.

When it comes to average execution time, the most efficient method is Mean, being 14% faster than GGNN for the size 50 embedding, followed by the Max method with approximately 9% faster than GGNN. As expected, the LSTM method is the least efficient, being approximately 83% slower than GGNN for embedding size 50, which is due to its structure that uses long-term memory, causing the longest execution time. The Mean and Max methods are statistically superior to GGNN method at runtime, while LSTM method is statistically inferior. This pattern is observed in all three embeddings sizes and as expected, the execution time increases as the size of the embedding increases.

Table 5. Performance of the GGNN, Mean, Max and LSTM methods for the diginetica dataset. Mean of metrics in %, followed by the standard deviation after ±. Time is measured in minutes.

Methods	Embedding and hidden_layer 20		
	HR@20	MRR@20	Time
GGNN	$47,8836 \pm 0,3958$	$15,9059 \pm 0,1494$	$500 \pm 0,0116$
Mean	$\mathbf{49,1327} \pm 0,2592$	$\mathbf{16,6220} \pm 0,0417$	$\mathbf{444} \pm 0,0100$
Max	$47,4593 \pm 0,4456$	$15,6365 \pm 0,2185$	$\mathbf{453} \pm 0,0095$
LSTM	$\mathbf{44,1394} \pm 2,3341$	$\mathbf{14,3732} \pm 1,0325$	$\mathbf{835} \pm 0,0109$
Methods	Embedding and hidden_layer 50		
	HR@20	MRR@20	Time
GGNN	$51,5817 \pm 0,1986$	$17,7342 \pm 0,0726$	$570 \pm 0,0204$
Mean	$51,8474 \pm 0,0819$	$17,8952 \pm 0,0611$	$\mathbf{488} \pm 0,0099$
Max	$\mathbf{50,5619} \pm 0,2227$	$\mathbf{16,9627} \pm 0,0888$	$\mathbf{503} \pm 0,0069$
LSTM	$\mathbf{50,5751} \pm 0,1074$	$\mathbf{17,0659} \pm 0,0265$	$\mathbf{934} \pm 0,0320$
Methods	Embedding and hidden_layer 80		
	HR@20	MRR@20	Time
GGNN	$51,5209 \pm 0,1272$	$17,7396 \pm 0,0884$	$676 \pm 0,0133$
Mean	$51,5935 \pm 0,1079$	$17,7673 \pm 0,0313$	$\mathbf{525} \pm 0,0090$
Max	$\mathbf{50,9020} \pm 0,1646$	$\mathbf{17,1588} \pm 0,0856$	$\mathbf{553} \pm 0,0116$
LSTM	$\mathbf{50,9109} \pm 0,1282$	$\mathbf{17,1863} \pm 0,0370$	$\mathbf{1317} \pm 0,0125$

Table 5 shows the average of the results obtained for the diginetica dataset, in which we can observe the same pattern obtained for the yoochoose1_64 dataset, where the Mean method has the highest percentage of correct answers in relation to the other methods, although not all are statistically superior to GGNN. The GGNN and Max methods, on the other hand, occupy the second and third highest hit rates, respectively. The largest difference remains in relation to the LSTM method, having the lowest hit rates. The size of the embeddings also affect the results in the same way as the previous dataset.

For the runtime we have the following order: Mean, Max, GGNN and LSTM, from the most efficient to the least efficient. Considering the embedding size 50, the Mean method is approximately 14% more efficient than GGNN, followed by the Max method with approximately 12% faster than GGNN. LSTM is approximately 64% less efficient than the original method, GGNN.

For the aotm and 30music datasets, the LSTM aggregator was not included in the experiments, as through empirical testing we realized that it maintains the same pattern as the yoochoose1_64 and diginetica datasets. As there were no significant changes with size 80 embeddings compared to size 50, experiments with size 80 were not performed. For 30music, we also did not perform the experiments with size 50 embeddings, as the execution time was prohibitive.

Table 6 shows the average of the results obtained for the aotm dataset, in which we can observe that the Mean method has the highest percentage of

Table 6. Performance of the GGNN, Mean, Max and LSTM methods for the aotm dataset. Mean of metrics in %, followed by the standard deviation after $\pm$. Time is measured in minutes.

Methods	Embedding and hidden_layer 20		
	HR@20	MRR@20	Time
GGNN	$2,9679 \pm 0,1479$	$0,6624 \pm 0,0329$	$655 \pm 0,0146$
Mean	$3,2369 \pm 0,1774$	$\mathbf{0,7370} \pm 0,0359$	$\mathbf{597} \pm 0,0062$
Max	$2,8203 \pm 0,1267$	$0,6352 \pm 0,0334$	$\mathbf{607} \pm 0,0130$
Methods	Embedding and hidden_layer 50		
	HR@20	MRR@20	Time
GGNN	$4,5463 \pm 0,1546$	$1,0952 \pm 0,0505$	$960 \pm 0,0137$
Mean	$4,6849 \pm 0,1061$	$1,1277 \pm 0,0336$	$\mathbf{778} \pm 0,0497$
Max	$4,5986 \pm 0,1201$	$1,0972 \pm 0,0253$	$\mathbf{841} \pm 0,0181$

correct answers in relation to the other methods for size 20. The GGNN and Max methods occupy the second and third highest hit rates, respectively. The execution times were close, where the Mean method was the most efficient, followed by the Max method, which was on average 10 min less efficient than the Mean method and finally, with a small difference, we have the GGNN. With statistical analysis, we cannot confirm that the Mean method is statistically superior in all scenarios in the hit rate, while for the runtime the Mean and Max method are statistically superior to GGNN method.

For size 50, we can notice that the HR and MRR metrics of the GGNN and Max methods obtained a very small difference, with the rates of the Mean method slightly higher, therefore, we can say that they are statistically equivalent. For the runtime, we have the same scenario, although the difference between the times is greater and the Mean and Max methods are statistically superior than GGNN.

Table 7. Performance of the GGNN, Mean, Max and LSTM methods for the 30music dataset. Mean of metrics in %, followed by the standard deviation after $\pm$. Time is measured in minutes.

Methods	Embedding and hidden_layer 20		
	HR@20	MRR@20	Time
GGNN	$31,6328 \pm 0,3805$	$11,3683 \pm 0,2419$	$2556 \pm 0,0894$
Mean	$\mathbf{33,8550} \pm 0,2916$	$\mathbf{12,9559} \pm 0,3468$	$\mathbf{2326} \pm 0,0610$
Max	$31,1667 \pm 0,1572$	$\mathbf{12,2107} \pm 0,2619$	$2493 \pm 0,0709$

Table 7 displays the average of the results obtained with the 30music dataset. We can observe that the Mean method has the highest percentage of correct answers in relation to the other methods. The GGNN and Max methods, on the other hand, occupy the second and third highest hit rates, respectively for the HR metric, different from the MRR metric in which the Max method obtained a higher rate than the GGNN. The execution times were close, and like the other datasets, the Mean method was the most efficient, followed by the Max method and the GGNN method, although for the first time in our experiments, the Max method was not statistically superior to GGNN method.

4.4   Synthesis

As already mentioned, there are indications that Graphsage is more efficient in large graphs with many representations, which may explain the small difference obtained in the efficiency of the Mean and Max methods in relation to GGNN, since the datasets used in these experiments have small graphs with only one type of representation for the items, not fully exploring the best feature that this technique can offer. When considering the execution time, the Mean and Max methods may have been more efficient due to the simplicity of their aggregation calculations, given that the GGNN uses about six equations to build the representations and several weight matrices, while these two methods of aggregation use only one. Another point that we can notice is that in all datasets with embedding size 20, the Mean method obtained significantly better results than the other methods in the HR and MRR metrics, giving us indications that it is capable of creating better representations than the GGNN, Max and LSTM methods with less information.

We expected that although the LSTM method would be the least efficient, it would be as effective as the other methods or better, as this method deals well with long-term memory, in this case, the user's search history. Its inferiority in hit rates compared to other methods may have occurred because the size of the embeddings may not be sufficient. Observing the average values of the HR and MRR rates in the yoochoose1_64 and diginetica datasets, it is possible to notice that there was an increase in the percentage of correct answers, as the size of the embeddings increased.

We can conclude then Mean and Max methods are superior in execution time in relation to GGNN, and that the Mean method is the most efficient among them. Regarding the hit rates, the Mean method is statistically superior then the GGNN method, while the Max method is inferior at times.

5   Conclusions

Through the results obtained, we can see that the Mean aggregator was superior to the other methods in all scenarios in the execution time and was slightly superior to the GGNN method in the hit rates. The Max method, on the other hand, was able to be more efficient than GGNN, even though it achieved lower hit rates in several cases. The LSTM method achieved a significantly worse performance, not being possible to reach an efficiency close to the other aggregators and the original method. Also, its execution time was the highest.

There are some limitations in the studies of Sequential Recommender Systems and in the analyzes performed. In relation to this study, we can conclude that it is difficult to recommend a new item and obtain actual feedback related to recommendation, such as the usefulness of the item for the user who received the recommendation; if the purchase has been made; between others. Another point is that for datasets with the historical of sessions that have already been carried out, we are not actually recommending a new item for the session, but making a prediction, that is, we are checking if the recommended item Sequential Recommendation System is the same item that is already in the evaluated sessions. One way to carry out the recommendation would be to apply the methods in a real scenario. Regarding the evaluations, to calculate the real impact on the execution time of each method, it is necessary to perform a complexity analysis of their algorithms.

As future works we can suggest: use the item graph of all sessions to generate representations; apply the proposed approach to a method other than SR-GNN; consider other sources of representations such as images and textual descriptions, as representations of the items; Remove and replace SR-GNN's attention module to evaluate the performance impact.

Acknowledgements. The authors thank CNPq for the financial support.

References

1. Zhang, S., Yao, L., Sun, A., Tay, Y.: Deep learning for sequential recommendation: algorithms, influential factors, and evaluations. ACM Trans. Inf. Syst. **39**(1), 1–41 (2020)
2. LeCun, Y., Bengio, Y., Hinton, G.: Deep learning. Nature **521**, 436–444 (2015)
3. Wu, S., Tang, Y., Zhu, Y., Wang, L., Xie, X., Tan, T.: Session-based recommendation with graph neural networks. In: Proceedings of the AAAI Conference on Artificial Intelligence, vol. 33(1), pp. 346–353 (2019)
4. Wang, B., Cai, W.: Knowledge-enhanced graph neural networks for sequential recommendation. Information **11**(8) (2020)
5. Hochreiter, S., Schmidhuber, J.: Long short-term memory. Neural Comput. **9**(8), 1735–1780 (1997)
6. Li, J., Ren, P., Chen, Z., Ren, Z., Lian, T., Ma, J.: Neural attentive session-based recommendation. In: Proceedings of the 2017 ACM on Conference on Information and Knowledge Management, pp. 1419–1428. ACM, New York (2017)
7. Liu, Q., Zeng, Y., Mokhosi, R., Zhang, H.: STAMP: short-term attention/memory priority model for session-based recommendation. In: Proceedings of the 24th ACM SIGKDD International Conference on Knowledge Discovery & Data Mining, pp. 1831–1839. ACM, New York (2018)
8. Wang, W., et al.: Beyond clicks: modeling multi-relational item graph for session-based target behavior prediction. In: Proceedings of the Web Conference 2020, New York, pp. 3056–3062 (2020)
9. Qiu, R., Li, J., Huang, Z., Yin, H.: Rethinking the item order in session-based recommendation with graph neural networks. In: Proceedings of the 28th ACM International Conference on Information and Knowledge Management, pp. 579–588. ACM, New York (2019)

10. Hamilton, W.L., Ying, R., Leskovec, J.: Inductive representation learning on large graphs. In: Proceedings of the 31st International Conference on Neural Information Processing Systems, pp. 1025–1035. Red Hook, USA (2017)
11. Xu, K., et al.: Show, attend and tell: neural image caption generation with visual attention. In: Proceedings of the 32nd International Conference on Machine Learning, pp. 2048–2057. Lille, France (2015)
12. Chengfeng, X., et al.: Graph contextualized self-attention network for session-based recommendation. In: Proceedings of the 38th International Joint Conference on Artificial Intelligence, pp. 3940–3946. (2019)
13. Medsker, L.R., Jain, L.C.: Recurrent Neural Networks Desing and Applications, 1ft edn. CRC Press (1999)
14. Kipf, T.N., Welling, M.: Semi-supervised classification with graph convolutional networks. https://arxiv.org/abs/1609.02907. Accessed 09 June 2022
15. Li, Y., Tarlow, D., Brockschmidt, M., Zemel, R.: Gated graph sequence neural networks. https://arxiv.org/abs/1511.05493. Accessed 09 June 2022
16. Wu, S., Zhang, W., Sun, F., Cui, B.: Graph neural networks in recommender systems - a survey. https://arxiv.org/abs/2011.02260. Accessed 09 June 2022
17. Cucurull, G., Veličković, P., Casanova, A., Romero, A., Liò, P., Bengio, Y.: Graph attention networks. https://arxiv.org/abs/1710.10903. Accessed 09 June 2022
18. Gupta, P., Garg, D., Malhotra, P., Vig, L., Shroff, G.: NISER: normalized item and session representations to handle popularity bias. https://arxiv.org/abs/1909.04276. Accessed 09 June 2022
19. Liu, F., Liu, W., Li, X., Ye, Y.: Inter-sequence enhanced framework for personalized sequential recommendation. https://arxiv.org/abs/2004.12118. Accessed 09 June 2022
20. Wang, B.: Ranking evaluation metrics for recommender systems. https://towardsdatascience.com/ranking-evaluation-metrics-for-recommender-systems-263d0a66ef54. Accessed 09 June 2022

Least-Squares Linear Dilation-Erosion Regressor Trained Using a Convex-Concave Procedure

Angelica Lourenço Oliveira$^{(\boxtimes)}$ [ID] and Marcos Eduardo Valle [ID]

University of Campinas, Campinas – São Paulo, Brazil
{ra211686,valle}@ime.unicamp.br

Abstract. This paper presents a hybrid morphological neural network for regression tasks called linear dilation-erosion regressor (ℓ-DER). An ℓ-DER is given by a convex combination of the composition of linear and morphological operators. They yield continuous piecewise linear functions and, thus, are universal approximators. Besides introducing the ℓ-DER model, we formulate their training as a difference of convex (DC) programming problem. Precisely, an ℓ-DER is trained by minimizing the least-squares using the convex-concave procedure (CCP). Computational experiments using several regression tasks confirm the efficacy of the proposed regressor, outperforming other hybrid morphological models and state-of-the-art approaches such as the multilayer perceptron network and the radial-basis support vector regressor.

Keywords: Morphological neural network · Continuous piecewise linear function · Regression · DC optimization

1 Introduction

Dilations and erosions are the elementary operations of mathematical morphology, a non-linear theory widely used for image processing and analysis [11,27]. In the middle 1990s,s, Ritter et al. proposed the first morphological neural networks whose processing units, the morphological neurons, perform dilations and erosions [22,23]. Morphological neurons are obtained by replacing the usual dot product with either the maximum or minimum of sums. Because of the maximum and minimum operations, morphological neural networks are usually cheaper than traditional models. However, training morphological neural networks are often a big challenge because of the non-differentiability of the maximum and minimum operations [21]. This paper addresses this issue by proposing a different method for training a hybrid morphological neural network for regression tasks. Precisely, we focus on training the so-called linear dilation-erosion perceptron using a difference of convex (DC) optimization method.

This work was supported in part by CNPq under grant no. 315820/2021-7, FAPESP under grant no. 2022/01831-2, and Coordenação de Aperfeiçoamento de Pessoal de Nível Superior - Brasil (CAPES) - Finance Code 001.

J. C. Xavier-Junior and R. A. Rios (Eds.): BRACIS 2022, LNAI 13654, pp. 16–29, 2022.
https://doi.org/10.1007/978-3-031-21689-3_2

A dilation-erosion perceptron (DEP) is a hybrid morphological neural network obtained by a convex combination of dilations and erosions [3]. Despite its application in regression tasks such as time-series prediction and software development cost estimation [2,3], the DEP model has an inherent drawback: as an increasing operator, it implicitly assumes an ordering relationship between inputs and outputs [32]. Fortunately, one can circumvent this problem by adding neurons that perform anti-dilations or anti-erosions [30]. For example, considering the importance of dendritic structures, Ritter and Urcid presented a single morphological neuron that circumvents the limitations of the DEP model [24].

Alternatively, Valle proposed the reduced dilation-erosion perceptron (r-DEP) using concepts from multi-valued mathematical morphology [32]. In a few words, an r-DEP is obtained by composing an appropriate transformation with the DEP model, i.e., the inputs are transformed before they are fed to the DEP model. However, choosing the proper transformation is challenging in designing an efficient r-DEP model. As a solution, Oliveira and Valle proposed the so-called linear dilation-erosion perceptron (ℓ-DEP) by considering linear mappings instead of arbitrary transformations [19]. Interestingly, the linear dilation-erosion perceptron is equivalent to a maxout network with two hidden units [8]. The ℓ-DEP model is also closely related to one of two hybrid morphological neural networks investigated by Hernández et al. for big data classification [12].

From a mathematical point of view, the ℓ-DEP yields a continuous piecewise linear function. Thus, like many traditional neural networks, they are universal approximators; that is, an ℓ-DEP model can approximate a continuous function within any desired accuracy in a compact region in a Euclidean space [33]. Besides the models mentioned above, the morphological/linear perceptron [29] and the hybrid multilayer morphological network [18] also exhibit universal approximation capability. However, all these hybrid morphological networks differ significantly in the training rule.

Like traditional neural networks, maxout and hybrid multilayer morphological networks can be trained using the stochastic gradient descent (SGD) method [8,18]. Despite the non-differentiability of morphological operators, Henández et al. also used the SDG method for training their hybrid morphological neural networks [12]. In contrast, Sussner and Campiotti circumvented the non-differentiability of the morphological operators using an extreme learning machine approach to train the morphological/linear perceptron [29]. Apart from the hybrid morphological/linear network literature, Ho et al. formulated the learning of a continuous piecewise linear function as a difference of convex functions (DC) programming problem [14]. Because the ℓ-DEP model can be identified with continuous piecewise linear functions, it can also be trained using DC programming. Indeed, this paper uses the concave-convex procedure (CCP) for training the ℓ-DEP model for regression tasks. Interestingly, the CCP results in more straightforward optimization problems than the approach of Ho et al.. Computational experiments with many regression tasks confirm the advantage of the proposed ℓ-DEP model against the hybrid morphological/linear methods from the literature and the approach based on the DC optimization of Ho et al.

The paper is organized as follows. The following section reviews some basic concepts regarding DC optimization, including definitions and the CCP optimization technique. Section 3 presents the ℓ-DEP model for regression tasks while the training based on CCP is addressed in Sect. 4. Computational experiments using several regression problems from the literature are detailed in Sect. 5. The paper finishes with some remarks in Sect. 6.

2   Difference of Convex Optimization and the Convex-Concave Procedure

The difference of convex (DC) functions results non-convex functions that enjoy interesting and useful properties [9,31]. DC optimization aims to optimize such kinds of functions. Applications of DC optimization programs include signal processing, machine learning, computer vision, and statistics [16,26]. This section presents some basic concepts of DC optimization. This section also addresses the convex-concave procedure proposed by Yuille and Rangarajan for constrained DC optimization problems [35]. The convex-concave procedure will be used in Sect. 4 for training the linear dilation-erosion perceptron for regression tasks.

2.1   Basic Concepts of DC Optimization

Consider a real-valued function $f : \mathcal{C} \to \mathbb{R}$ defined in a convex set $\mathcal{C} \subseteq \mathbb{R}^n$. We say that f is a DC function if there are convex functions $g, h : \mathcal{C} \to \mathbb{R}$ such that

$$f(\boldsymbol{\alpha}) = g(\boldsymbol{\alpha}) - h(\boldsymbol{\alpha}), \quad \forall \alpha \in \mathcal{C}. \tag{1}$$

Recall that a function is convex if the line joining two points on its graph is below the graph [17]. The functions g and h are called the DC components of f and the identity in (1) is is the DC decomposition of f.

In a DC optimization problem, the objective and constraints are DC functions. In this paper, we focus on the following constrained DC optimization problem:

$$\begin{cases} \underset{\boldsymbol{\alpha} \in \mathbb{R}^n}{\text{minimize}} & f_0(\boldsymbol{\alpha}) = g_0(\boldsymbol{\alpha}) - h_0(\boldsymbol{\alpha}) \\ \text{subject to} & f_i(\alpha) = g_i(\boldsymbol{\alpha}) - h_i(\boldsymbol{\alpha}) \le 0, \quad i = 1, \ldots, m, \end{cases} \tag{2}$$

where $g_i : \mathbb{R}^n \to \mathbb{R}$ and $h_i : \mathbb{R}^n \to \mathbb{R}$ are convex functions for all $i = 0, 1, \ldots, m$.

In general terms, DC optimization methods take advantage of the convexity of the DC components g_i and h_i of f_i. For example, many methods approximate the convex terms h_i of the DC decomposition of f_i an affine function, resulting in convex optimization subproblems that are solved more effectively than the original DC problem [14,16,31]. This paper uses the convex-concave procedure (CCP) proposed by Yuille and Rangarajan [35] for solving DC optimization problems given by (2).

Algorithm 1: CCP

Input   : Convex functions: $g_0, \ldots, g_m$ and $f_0, \ldots, f_m$.
Output : $\boldsymbol{\alpha}^*$ (Solution)
Initialize: a feasible $\boldsymbol{\alpha}_0 \in \mathbb{R}^n$ and $k = 0$.
repeat

> Compute a subgradient $\boldsymbol{\beta}_i$ of h_i at $\boldsymbol{\alpha}_k$, for all $i = 0, \ldots, m$.
> Solve the convex problem:
> $$\begin{cases} \boldsymbol{\alpha}_{k+1} = \underset{\alpha \in \mathbb{R}^n}{\operatorname{argmin}} \quad g_0(\boldsymbol{\alpha}) - h_0(\boldsymbol{\alpha}_k) - \langle \boldsymbol{\beta}_0, \boldsymbol{\alpha} - \boldsymbol{\alpha}_k \rangle \\ \qquad\quad \text{s.t.} \qquad g_i(\boldsymbol{\alpha}) \le h_i(\boldsymbol{\alpha}_k) + \langle \boldsymbol{\beta}_i, \boldsymbol{\alpha} - \boldsymbol{\alpha}_k \rangle, \quad i = 1, \ldots, m. \end{cases}$$
> $k = k + 1$

until *converge*;
return $\boldsymbol{\alpha}^* = \boldsymbol{\alpha}_k$

2.2 Convex-Concave Procedure

The convex-concave procedure (CCP), also called concave-convex procedure [35], is a majorization-minimization methodology that uses convex optimization tools to find a local optimum for DC problems through of a sequence of convex subproblems. Briefly, the CCP method solves a constrained DC problem sequentially as follows: Given a feasible approximation $\boldsymbol{\alpha}_k \in \mathbb{R}^n$, the convex component $h_i : \mathbb{R}^n \to \mathbb{R}$ is approximated by

$$\tilde{h}_i(\boldsymbol{\alpha}) = h_i(\boldsymbol{\alpha}_k) + \langle \boldsymbol{\beta}_i, \boldsymbol{\alpha} - \boldsymbol{\alpha}_k \rangle, \quad \forall i = 0, 1, \ldots, m, \tag{3}$$

where $\boldsymbol{\beta}_i$ is a subgradient of h_i at $\boldsymbol{\alpha}_k$. In particular, $\boldsymbol{\beta}_i = \nabla h_i(\boldsymbol{\alpha}_k)$ if the function h_i is differentiable at $\boldsymbol{\alpha}_k$. Replacing h_i by $\tilde{h}_i$ results the convex optimization problem

$$\begin{cases} \underset{\alpha \in \mathbb{R}^n}{\text{minimize}} \quad g_0(\boldsymbol{\alpha}) - h_0(\boldsymbol{\alpha}_k) - \langle \boldsymbol{\beta}_0, \boldsymbol{\alpha} - \boldsymbol{\alpha}_k \rangle \\ \text{subject to} \quad g_i(\boldsymbol{\alpha}) - h_i(\boldsymbol{\alpha}_k) - \langle \boldsymbol{\beta}_i, \boldsymbol{\alpha} - \boldsymbol{\alpha}_k \rangle \le 0, \; i = 1, \ldots. \end{cases} \tag{4}$$

The solution of (4) is a new feasible approximation $\boldsymbol{\alpha}_{k+1}$, and the process is repeated. The sequence $\{\boldsymbol{\alpha}_k\}$ obtained solving (4) recursively is convergent and $\{f(\boldsymbol{\alpha}_k)\}$ is non-increasing. Further details on the convergence of the sequence $\{\boldsymbol{\alpha}_k\}_{k \ge 0}$ can found at [16]. Algorithm 2 summarizes the CCP method.

3 Linear Dilation-Erosion Regressor

Predictive classification models categorize information based on a set of historical data. Predictive regression models are used to solve curve-fitting problems whose goal is to find a function that best fits a given data set. The adjusted mapping can be used for forecasting or predictions outside the data set.

Recently, [19] introduced the linear dilation-erosion perceptron (ℓ-DEP) for classification tasks. A linear dilation-erosion perceptron is given by a convex combination of the composition of linear transformations and two elementary operators from mathematical morphology [3, 22]. Let us review the main concepts from mathematical morphology and the ℓ-DEP model. We will subsequently present the linear dilation-erosion regressor, the predictive model of the regression type corresponding to the ℓ-DEP regressor.

Mathematical morphology is mainly concerned with non-linear operators defined on complete lattices [11,27]. Complete lattices are partially ordered sets with well-defined supremum and infimum operations [4]. Dilations and erosions are the elementary operators from mathematical morphology. Given complete lattices $\mathbb{L}$ and $\mathbb{M}$, a dilation $\delta : \mathbb{L} \to \mathbb{M}$ and an erosion $\varepsilon : \mathbb{L} \to \mathbb{M}$ are operators such that

$$\delta\left(\sup X\right) = \sup\{\delta(\mathbf{x}) : \mathbf{x} \in X\} \quad \text{and} \quad \varepsilon\left(\inf X\right) = \inf\{\varepsilon(\mathbf{x}) : \mathbf{x} \in X\}, \quad (5)$$

for all $X \subseteq \mathbb{L}$ [11]. For example, consider the complete lattices $\mathbb{L} = \bar{\mathbb{R}}^n$ and $\mathbb{M} = \bar{\mathbb{R}}$, where $\bar{\mathbb{R}} = \mathbb{R} \cup \{-\infty, +\infty\}$. Given vectors $\mathbf{a}, \mathbf{b} \in \mathbb{R}^n$, the operators $\delta_{\mathbf{a}}, \varepsilon_{\mathbf{b}} : \bar{\mathbb{R}}^n \to \bar{\mathbb{R}}$ defined by

$$\delta_{\mathbf{a}}(\mathbf{x}) = \max_{j=1:n}\{x_j + a_j\} \quad \text{and} \quad \varepsilon_{\mathbf{b}}(\mathbf{x}) = \min_{j=1:n}\{x_j - b_j\}, \quad \forall \mathbf{x} \in \bar{\mathbb{R}}^n, \quad (6)$$

are respectively a dilation and an erosion [30]. Note that dilations and erosions given by (6) satisfy the duality identity $\varepsilon_{\mathbf{b}}(-\mathbf{x}) = -\delta_{\mathbf{b}}(\mathbf{x})$, for all $\mathbf{x} \in \bar{\mathbb{R}}^n$.

A dilation-erosion perceptron (DEP) is given by a convex combination of a dilation and an erosion defined by (6). The reduced dilation-erosion perceptron (r-DEP) proposed by Valle is an improved version of the DEP model obtained using concepts from vector-valued mathematical morphology [32]. The ℓ-DEP model is a particular but powerful r-DEP classifier [19]. Formally, given a one-to-one mapping σ from the set of binary class labels $\mathbb{C}$ to $\{+1, -1\}$, an ℓ-DEP classifier is defined by the equation $y = \sigma^{-1}f\tau^{\ell}(\mathbf{x})$, where $f : \mathbb{R} \to \{-1, +1\}$ is a threshold function and $\tau^{\ell} : \mathbb{R}^n \to \mathbb{R}$ is the decision function given by

$$\tau^{\ell}(\mathbf{x}) = \delta_{\mathbf{a}}(W\mathbf{x}) - \delta_{\mathbf{b}}(M\mathbf{x}), \quad (7)$$

where $W \in \mathbb{R}^{r_1 \times n}$, $M \in \mathbb{R}^{r_2 \times n}$, $\mathbf{a} \in \mathbb{R}^{r_1}$, and $\mathbf{b} \in \mathbb{R}^{r_2}$. We would like to point out that the erosion has been replaced by minus a dilation in (7) using the duality identity. Equivalently, the decision function τ^{ℓ} satisfies

$$\tau^{\ell}(\mathbf{x}) = \max_{i=1:r_1}\{\langle\mathbf{w}_i, \mathbf{x}\rangle + a_i\} - \max_{j=1:r_2}\{\langle\mathbf{m}_j, \mathbf{x}\rangle + b_j\}, \quad (8)$$

where $\mathbf{a} = (a_1, \ldots, a_{r_1}) \in \mathbb{R}^{r_1}$ and $\mathbf{b} = (b_1, \ldots, b_{r_2}) \in \mathbb{R}^{r_2}$, and $\mathbf{w}_i \in \mathbb{R}^n$ and $\mathbf{m}_i \in \mathbb{R}^n$ are rows of $W \in \mathbb{R}^{r_1 \times n}$ and $M \in \mathbb{R}^{r_2 \times n}$, respectively. From the last identity, we can identify τ^{ℓ} with a piece-wise linear function [33]. Moreover, from Theorem 4.3 in [8], the decision function τ^{ℓ} is an universal approximator, i.e., it is able to approximate any continuous-valued function from a compact set on $\mathbb{R}^n$ to $\mathbb{R}$ [8,28]. Consequently, an ℓ-DEP model can theoretically solve any binary classification problem. In addition, the decision function τ^{ℓ} can be identified with a maxout network with two hidden units [8].

Because the decision function of an ℓ-DEP model is a universal approximator, τ^{ℓ} given by (7) can also be used as a predictive model for regression tasks. In other words, it is possible to use the mapping τ^ℓ as the prediction function that maps a set of independent variables in $\mathbb{R}^n$ to a dependent variable in $\mathbb{R}$. In this case, we refer to the operator $\tau^\ell : \mathbb{R}^n \to \mathbb{R}$ given by (7), as a linear dilation-erosion regressor (ℓ-DER). In this paper, the parameters $(\mathbf{w}_i^T, a_i) \in \mathbb{R}^{n+1}$ and $(\mathbf{m}_j^T, b_j) \in \mathbb{R}^{n+1}$, for $i = 1, \ldots, r_1$ and $j = 1, \ldots, r_2$, are determined by minimizing the squares of the difference between the predicted and desired values. The following section addresses an approach for training an ℓ-DER model.

4 Training the ℓ-DER Using CCP

In this section, we present approaches for training an ℓ-DER model using a set $\mathcal{T} = \{(\mathbf{x}_i, y_i) : i = 1 : m\} \subset \mathbb{R}^n \times \mathbb{R}$, called training set. The goal is to find the parameters of an ℓ-DER model such that the estimate $\tau^\ell(\mathbf{x}_i)$ approaches the desired output y_i according to some loss function. Recall that the parameters of an ℓ-DEP regressor are the matrices $W \in \mathbb{R}^{r_1 \times n}$ and $M \in \mathbb{R}^{r_2 \times n}$ as well as the vectors $\mathbf{a} = (a_1, \ldots, a_{r_1}) \in \mathbb{R}^{r_1}$ and $\mathbf{b} = (b_1, \ldots, b_{r_2}) \in \mathbb{R}^{r_2}$. To simplify the exposition, the parameters of an ℓ-DER are arranged in a vector

$$\boldsymbol{\alpha} = (\mathbf{w}_1, a_1, ..., \mathbf{w}_{r_1}, a_{r_1}, \mathbf{m}_1, b_1, ..., \mathbf{m}_{r_2}, b_{r_2}) \in \mathbb{R}^{(r_1+r_2)(n+1)}, \qquad (9)$$

where $\mathbf{w}_i$ and $\mathbf{m}_i$ denote rows of $W \in \mathbb{R}^{r_1 \times n}$ and $M \in \mathbb{R}^{r_2 \times n}$, respectively. During the training, an ℓ-DER is interpreted as a function of its parameters, that is, $\tau^\ell(\mathbf{x}) \equiv \tau^\ell(\mathbf{x}; \boldsymbol{\alpha})$.

In this paper, the mean squared error (MSE) defined as follows using the training set $\mathcal{T} = \{(\mathbf{x}_i, y_i) : i = 1, \ldots, m\} \subset \mathbb{R}^n \times \mathbb{R}$ is considered as the loss function:

$$\text{MSE}(\mathcal{T}, \boldsymbol{\alpha}) = \frac{1}{m} \sum_{i=1}^{m} (y_i - \tau^\ell(\mathbf{x}_i; \boldsymbol{\alpha}))^2, \qquad (10)$$

As a consequence, the parameters of the ℓ-DER are determined by solving the optimization problem

$$\underset{\boldsymbol{\alpha}}{\text{minimize}} \frac{1}{m} \sum_{i=1}^{m} (y_i - \tau^\ell(\mathbf{x}_i; \boldsymbol{\alpha}))^2. \qquad (11)$$

4.1 Training Based on the Convex-Concave Programming

Inspired by the methodology developed by Charisopoulos and Maragos for training morphological perceptrons [6], we reformulate the unrestricted optimization problem (11) as a constrained DC problem. Precisely, by setting $\xi_i = y_i - \tau^\ell(\mathbf{x}_i)$, the unrestricted problem (11) corresponds to

$$\begin{cases} \underset{W, \mathbf{a}, M, \mathbf{b}, \xi}{\text{minimize}} & \frac{1}{m} \sum_{i=1}^{m} \xi_i^2 \\ \text{subject to} & \tau^\ell(\mathbf{x}_i) = y_i - \xi_i, \quad i = 1, ..., m. \end{cases} \qquad (12)$$

In other words, the ℓ-DER can be trained by solving the following problem

$$\begin{cases} \underset{W,\mathbf{a},M,\mathbf{b},\xi}{\text{minimize}} & \dfrac{1}{m}\sum_{i=1}^{m}\xi_i^2 \\ \text{subject to} & \delta_{\mathbf{a}}(W\mathbf{x}_i) + \xi_i = \delta_{\mathbf{b}}(M\mathbf{x}_i) + y_i, \quad i = 1,...,m. \end{cases} \tag{13}$$

Note that the objective function in (13) is a convex quadratic function. Moreover, the functions at both sides of the equality constraints are convex. Thus, we can view the constraints as DC functions, and the optimization problem (13) can be solved using Algorithm 1 by dealing appropriately with the equality constraints.

We first transform each of the equality constraints into two inequality constraints:

$$\delta_{\mathbf{a}}(W\mathbf{x}_i) + \xi_i \le \delta_{\mathbf{b}}(M\mathbf{x}_i) + y_i \quad \text{and} \quad \delta_{\mathbf{b}}(M\mathbf{x}_i) + y_i \le \delta_{\mathbf{a}}(W\mathbf{x}_i) + \xi_i, \tag{14}$$

for all $i = 1,\ldots,m$. Because a majorant of a set is also a majorant of each of its elements and recalling that

$$\delta_{\mathbf{a}}(W\mathbf{x}_i) = \max_{j=1:r_1}\{\langle \mathbf{w}_j, \mathbf{x}_i\rangle + a_j\} \quad \text{and} \quad \delta_{\mathbf{b}}(M\mathbf{x}_i) = \max_{j=1:r_2}\{\langle \mathbf{m}_j, \mathbf{x}_i\rangle + b_j\}, \tag{15}$$

the two inequalities in (14) yield

$$\langle \mathbf{w}_l, \mathbf{x}_i\rangle + a_l + \xi_i \le \delta_{\mathbf{b}}(M\mathbf{x}_i) + y_i, \quad i \in \mathcal{I}, l \in \mathcal{L}_1, \tag{16}$$

$$\langle \mathbf{m}_l, \mathbf{x}_i\rangle + b_l + y_i \le \delta_{\mathbf{a}}(W\mathbf{x}_i) + \xi_i, \quad i \in \mathcal{I}, l \in \mathcal{L}_2, \tag{17}$$

where $\mathcal{I} = \{1,\ldots,m\}$, $\mathcal{L}_1 = \{1,\ldots,r_1\}$, and $\mathcal{L}_2 = \{1,\ldots,r_2\}$. Thus, (13) can be equivalently written as

$$\begin{cases} \underset{W,\mathbf{a},M,\mathbf{b},\xi}{\text{minimize}} & \dfrac{1}{m}\sum_{i=1}^{m}\xi_i^2 \\ \text{subject to} & (\langle \mathbf{w}_l, \mathbf{x}_i\rangle + a_l + \xi_i - y_i) - \delta_{\mathbf{b}}(M\mathbf{x}_i) \le 0, \ i \in \mathcal{I}, l \in \mathcal{L}_1, \\ & (\langle \mathbf{m}_l, \mathbf{x}_i\rangle + b_l - \xi_i + y_i) - \delta_{\mathbf{a}}(W\mathbf{x}_i) \le 0, \ i \in \mathcal{I}, l \in \mathcal{L}_2. \end{cases} \tag{18}$$

Note that (18) can be identified with a DC optimization problem (2). Furthermore, the convex functions

$$h_{i1}(\boldsymbol{\alpha}) = \delta_{\mathbf{b}}(M\boldsymbol{x}_i) \quad \text{and} \quad h_{i2}(\boldsymbol{\alpha}) = \delta_{\mathbf{a}}(M\boldsymbol{x}_i), \tag{19}$$

can be approximated by the affine functions

$$\tilde{h}_{i1}(\boldsymbol{\alpha}) = \langle \mathbf{m}_{j_{i1}}, \mathbf{x}_i\rangle + b_j \quad \text{and} \quad \tilde{h}_{i2}(\boldsymbol{\alpha}) = \langle \mathbf{w}_{j_{i2}}, \mathbf{x}_i\rangle + a_j, \tag{20}$$

where

$$j_{i1} = \underset{j=1,\ldots,r_2}{\arg\max}\{\langle \mathbf{m}_j, \mathbf{x}_i\rangle + b_j\} \quad \text{and} \quad j_{i2} = \underset{j=1,\ldots,r_1}{\arg\max}\{\langle \mathbf{w}_j, \mathbf{x}_i\rangle + a_j\}, \tag{21}$$

for all $i \in \mathcal{I}$.

Using the affine approximations of the convex components h_{i1} and h_{i2} of the constraints, we obtain the following quadratic problem which is solved at each iteration of the CCP method used for training an ℓ-DER model:

$$
\begin{cases}
\underset{W,\mathbf{a},M,\mathbf{b},\boldsymbol{\xi},\mathbf{p},\mathbf{q}}{\text{minimize}} & \dfrac{1}{m}\sum_{i=1}^{m}\xi_i^2 \\
\text{subject to} & \langle \mathbf{w}_l - \mathbf{m}_{j_{i1}}, \mathbf{x}_i \rangle + a_l - b_{j_{i1}} \leq y_i - \xi_i,\ i \in \mathcal{I}, l \in \mathcal{L}_1 \\
& \langle \mathbf{m}_l - \mathbf{w}_{j_{i2}}, \mathbf{x}_i \rangle + b_l - a_{j_{i2}} \leq \xi_i - y_i,\ i \in \mathcal{I}, l \in \mathcal{L}_2
\end{cases}
\tag{22}
$$

The iterations are performed until a maximum number of iterations is reached or when the difference of the objective function at two consecutive iterations is less than a tolerance ϵ. Algorithm 2 summarizes the training of the ℓ-DER model with the CCP method.

For our models, the starting point for the optimization problems was produced using a deterministic strategy presented in [13]. Roughly speaking, we first use the KKZ method to find a subset of centroids of the training data [15]. The training data is then grouped using Voronoi partitions. Finally, the starting point of the DC optimization method is obtained by (traditional) linear least squares data-fit on the Voronoi regions.

Algorithm 2: ℓ-CCP

Input   : Training set $\mathcal{T} = \{(\mathbf{x}_i, y_i) : i \in \mathcal{I}\}$ and the parameters k_{max} and ϵ.
Output : $\{W, \mathbf{a}, M, \mathbf{b}\}$
Initialize: W, $\mathbf{a}$, M, $\mathbf{b}$, $\boldsymbol{\xi}$ and $k = 0$
repeat
   | Determine the indexes j_{i1} and j_{i2} using (21)
   | Compute W, $\mathbf{a}$, M, $\mathbf{b}$, $\boldsymbol{\xi}$ for $i = 1, \ldots, m$ solving (22)
   | $k = k + 1$
until $k \geq k_{max}$ *or* the difference in the objective function is less than an ϵ;
return $W, \mathbf{a}, M, \mathbf{b}$

---

5   Computational Experiments

This section presents some computational experiments to evaluate the performance of the proposed ℓ-DER model trained using the CCP method for regression tasks. Furthermore, we compare the ℓ-DER model with other models from the literature. Namely, we consider the multilayer perceptron (MLP) [10], the support vector regressor (SVR) [25], the hybrid linear/morphological extreme learning machine (HLM-ELM) [29], the morphological dense network (MDN) [18], and the maxout network [8]. Because the ℓ-DER yields a continuous piecewise linear function, we also compare it with the regressor trained by the difference of convex algorithm (DCA) proposed by Ho et al. [14].

We evaluated the performance of the proposed ℓ-DER and the other models from the literature using regression datasets from the Penn Machine Learning

Table 1. Hyper-parameters for the datasets.

Model	Parameters
MLP	Default Sklearn
SVR	Default Sklearn
HLM-ELM	linear neurons=132
	Morfological neurons=141
MDN	$(r_1^1, r_2^1, \mathrm{out}^1) = (100, 100, 100)$
	$(r_1^2, r_2^2, \mathrm{out}^2) = (100, 100, 1)$
MAXOUT	$(r_1, r_2) = (3, 3)$
DCA	$(r_1, r_2) = (3, 2)$
ℓ-**DER**	$(r_1, r_2) = (3, 2)$

Benchmarks (PMLB), a significant benchmark suite for machine learning evaluation and comparison [20]. The chosen datasets are listed in Table 2. Note that we considered small and medium-sized datasets. We would like to point out that we handled possible missing data using sklearn's SimpleImputer command. Furthermore, we partitioned the data set into training and test sets using the sklearn's KFold, with the default number of splits (n_splits=5).

We trained the ℓ-DER model using the CVXPY package [7] with the MOSEK solver [1]. Because the ℓ-DER is equivalent to a continuous piecewise linear function, we adopt the same hyperparameters $r_1 = 3$ and $r_2 = 2$ as Ho et al. for all datasets [14]. For a fair comparision between the continuous piecewise linear models, we consider $r_1 = r_2 = 3$ for the maxout network [8]. Finally, the other models' hyperparameters are set to the default value of the sklearn or as far as possible to values reported in the literature [5,18,29]. Table 1 summarizes the hyperparameters used in our computational experiment.

We evaluated the performance of the regression models quantitatively using the well-known mean squared error (MSE) and the fraction of variance unexplained (FVU) given by the following equations:

$$\text{MSE} = \frac{1}{m} \sum_{i=1}^{m} (y_i - f(\mathbf{x}_i))^2 \quad \text{and} \quad \text{FVU} = \frac{\sum_{i=1}^{m} (y_i - f(\mathbf{x}_i))^2}{\sum_{i=1}^{m} (y_i - \bar{y})^2}, \qquad (23)$$

where $f : \mathbb{R}^n \to \mathbb{R}$ denotes the regressor and $\bar{y} = \dfrac{1}{m} \sum_{i=1}^{m} y_i$ is the average of the output values. Note that the FVU is the ratio between the MSEs produced by the regressor and a dummy model, which consistently predicts the average output values. The less the MSE and the FVU scores, the better is the regressor f. Table 3 contains the average and the standard deviation of the FVU score obtained from the regressors using 5-fold cross-validation on the considered datasets. The best outcome for each dataset has been typed using boldface numbers. The boxplots shown in Fig. 1 summarize the MSE and FVU scores and

Table 2. Information about the datasets of PMLB for regression tasks.

Dataset	Name	Instances	Feature	PMLB Code
D1	ANALCATDATA_VEHICLE	48	4	485_analcatdata_vehicle
D2	BODYFAT	252	14	560_bodyfat
D3	CHSCASE_GEYSER1	222	2	712_chscase_geyser1
D4	CLOUD	108	5	210_cloud
D5	CPU	209	7	561_cpu
D6	ELUSAGE	55	2	228_elusage
D7	MACHINE_CPU	209	6	230_machine_cpu
D8	PM10	500	7	522_pm10
D9	PWLINEAR	200	10	229_pwLinear
D10	RABE_266	120	2	663_rabe_266
D11	RMFTSA_LADATA	508	10	666_rmftsa_ladata
D12	SLEUTH_CASE1202	93	6	706_sleuth_case1202
D13	SLEUTH_EX1605	62	5	687_sleuth_ex1605
D14	VINEYARD	52	2	192_vineyard
D15	VINNIE	380	2	519_vinnie
D16	VISUALIZING_ENVIRONMENTAL	111	3	678_visualizing_environmental
D17	VISUALIZING_GALAXY	323	4	690_visualizing_galaxy

the execution time (in seconds) taken for training the regressors in the sixteen datasets.

From the boxplot shown in Fig. 1, the ℓ-DER trained with the CCP procedure achieved the best performance (concerning both MSE and FVU) together with the maxout network and the continuous piecewise linear regressor trained using the DCA algorithm. The HLM-ELM and MLP networks presented the worst performance according to both MSE and FVU scores.

Table 3. Average and standard deviation of the FVU scores on datasets in Table 2.

Dataset	MLP	SVR	HLM-ELM	MDN	MAXOUT	DCA	ℓ-DER
D1	2.490 ± 0.233	1.091 ± 0.087	0.656 ± 0.394	1.154 ± 0.242	0.299 ± 0.199	**0.315 ± 0.185**	0.379 ± 0.183
D2	1.277 ± 0.414	0.209 ± 0.058	0.225 ± 0.103	0.904 ± 1.010	0.043 ± 0.030	0.028 ± 0.029	**0.027 ± 0.037**
D3	2.6e1 ± 4.539	0.265 ± 0.016	2.3e1 ± 2.4e1	1.228 ± 0.541	0.251 ± 0.050	0.236 ± 0.032	**0.234 ± 0.034**
D4	0.235 ± 0.182	0.361 ± 0.174	1.724 ± 1.005	0.307 ± 0.124	0.247 ± 0.133	0.529 ± 0.532	**0.202 ± 0.108**
D5	1.215 ± 0.200	1.013 ± 0.060	7.5e1 ± 1.1e2	0.556 ± 0.227	**0.037 ± 0.022**	0.166 ± 0.300	0.099 ± 0.062
D6	3.506 ± 0.883	0.703 ± 0.233	1.896 ± 0.754	**0.340 ± 0.175**	0.409 ± 0.259	0.367 ± 0.131	0.344 ± 0.133
D7	1.255 ± 0.174	1.017 ± 0.063	1.1e4 ± 1.7e4	0.511 ± 0.191	**0.129 ± 0.064**	0.229 ± 0.129	0.148 ± 0.090
D8	0.868 ± 0.053	**0.724 ± 0.033**	2.544 ± 0.572	0.977 ± 0.112	0.886 ± 0.056	0.895 ± 0.160	0.854 ± 0.040
D9	0.221 ± 0.054	0.353 ± 0.069	0.421 ± 0.093	0.776 ± 0.150	**0.181 ± 0.014**	0.299 ± 0.137	0.237 ± 0.055
D10	1.477 ± 0.279	0.633 ± 0.101	0.005 ± 0.002	0.524 ± 0.339	0.004 ± 0.001	**0.002 ± 0.001**	0.010 ± 0.010
D11	0.609 ± 0.238	0.511 ± 0.096	1.459 ± 0.704	0.607 ± 0.236	0.467 ± 0.146	**0.423 ± 0.134**	0.483 ± 0.170
D12	1.945 ± 0.238	1.074 ± 0.176	1.746 ± 0.968	1.126 ± 0.366	0.482 ± 0.193	0.446 ± 0.149	**0.376 ± 0.094**
D13	5.3e1 ± 3.0e1	1.025 ± 0.118	1.295 ± 0.510	8.230 ± 7.666	1.010 ± 0.637	1.504 ± 1.544	**0.576 ± 0.313**
D14	1.0e1 ± 8.189	0.628 ± 0.168	1.734 ± 1.448	5.702 ± 3.840	1.961 ± 3.015	0.588 ± 0.438	**0.529 ± 0.394**
D15	0.278 ± 0.027	0.279 ± 0.042	0.352 ± 0.043	0.314 ± 0.064	0.257 ± 0.015	0.264 ± 0.026	**0.254 ± 0.022**
D16	1.576 ± 0.407	0.728 ± 0.111	4.732 ± 1.608	1.250 ± 0.201	0.716 ± 0.065	0.690 ± 0.033	**0.652 ± 0.092**
D17	2.5e2 ± 2.8e1	0.513 ± 0.015	2.6e3 ± 3.7e3	2.5e1 ± 6.141	0.157 ± 0.079	**0.052 ± 0.014**	0.097 ± 0.010
Average	2.2e1 ± 6.5e1	0.655 ± 0.296	7.8e2 ± 2.5e3	2.917 ± 5.911	0.443 ± 0.473	0.414 ± 0.357	**0.324 ± 0.227**

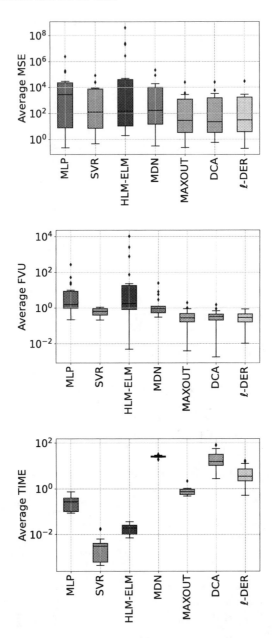

Fig. 1. Boxplots of the MSE and FVU scores and average time required to train the machine learning regressors.

The Hasse diagrams depicted in Fig. 2 illustrate the outcome of Wilcoxon's nonparametric statistical test with a confidence level of 95% for the MSE and FVU scores [34]. In the Hasse diagram depicted in Fig. 2, an edge means that

a) Mean square error (MSE)   b) Fraction of variance unexplained (FVU)

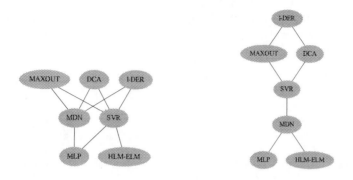

Fig. 2. Hasse diagram of Wilcoxon hypothesis test using the MSE and FVU scores.

the model on top statistically outperformed the one below. Thus, the topmost models are the best-performing models. Moreover, transitivity is valid in the Hasse diagram. Note from Fig. 2 that the ℓ-DER achieved the best performance in terms of FVU score. The maxout network and the model trained using DCA are competitive but superior to the remaining models for the FVU. In terms of the MSE score, the ℓ-DER, maxout network, and the model trained using DCA are all competitive and superior to the other models in these regression tasks.

Finally, note that training the ℓ-DER model using the CCP method is, on average, faster than the DCA model. Indeed, the ℓ-DER model's processing time is approximately 21% of the time the DCA model spends on training. The slowness of DCA probably follows because it requires solving more complex optimization problems than the ones obtained using CCP.

6 Concluding Remarks

This paper introduced the linear dilation-erosion regressor (ℓ-DER), which is given by a convex combination of the composition of linear transformations and elementary morphological operators. Precisely, an ℓ-DER is defined by the DC function τ^ℓ given by (7). Because τ^ℓ is a continuous piecewise linear function, an ℓ-DER is a universal approximator [33].

An ℓ-DER model can be trained by minimizing the mean square error given by (11) using a training set $\mathcal{T} = \{(\mathbf{x}_i, y_i) : i = 1 : m\} \subset \mathbb{R}^n \times \mathbb{R}$. This paper proposed to train an ℓ-DER τ^ℓ using DC optimization. The approach solves a constrained DC problem using the CCP method [16].

We compared the ℓ-DER trained using CCP with other approaches from the literature using several regression tasks. According to the preliminary computational experiments, the ℓ-DER trained using CCP is competitive with state-of-the-art methods like the SVR. Furthermore, regarding the computational complexity of training the ℓ-DER, solving the quadratic optimization subproblems incurs the highest cost.

In the future, we plan to investigate further the performance of the ℓ-DER model trained by the CCP method. In particular, we intend to study the effects of the hyper-parameters – such as the shape of the matrices W and M – on the curve fitting capability of the ℓ-DER.

References

1. ApS, M.: MOSEK Optimizer API for Python (2020). release 9.3.10
2. Araújo, R.d.A., Oliveira, A.L., Soares, S., Meira, S.: An evolutionary morphological approach for software development cost estimation. Neural Netw. **32**, 285–291 (2012). https://doi.org/10.1016/j.neunet.2012.02.040
3. Araújo, R.A.: A class of hybrid morphological perceptrons with application in time series forecasting. Knowl. Based Syst. **24**(4), 513–529 (2011). https://doi.org/10.1016/j.knosys.2011.01.001
4. Birkhoff, G.: Lattice Theory, 3rd edn. American Mathematical Society, Providence (1993)
5. Buitinck, L., et al.: API design for machine learning software: experiences from the scikit-learn project. In: ECML PKDD Workshop: Languages for Data Mining and Machine Learning, pp. 108–122 (2013)
6. Charisopoulos, V., Maragos, P.: Morphological perceptrons: geometry and training algorithms. In: Angulo, J., Velasco-Forero, S., Meyer, F. (eds.) ISMM 2017. LNCS, vol. 10225, pp. 3–15. Springer, Cham (2017). https://doi.org/10.1007/978-3-319-57240-6_1
7. Diamond, S., Boyd, S.: CVXPY: A Python-Embedded Modeling Language for Convex Optimization, June 2016
8. Goodfellow, I., Warde-Farley, D., Mirza, M., Courville, A., Bengio, Y.: Maxout Networks. In: International Conference on Machine Learning, pp. 1319–1327 (2013)
9. Hartman, P.: On functions representable as a difference of convex functions. Pacific J. Math. **9**(3), 707–713 (1959)
10. Haykin, S.: Neural Networks and Learning Machines, 3rd edn. Prentice Hall, New York (2008)
11. Heijmans, H.J.A.M.: Mathematical morphology: a modern approach in image processing based on algebra and geometry. SIAM Rev. **37**(1), 1–36 (1995)
12. Hernández, G., Zamora, E., Sossa, H., Téllez, G., Furlán, F.: Hybrid neural networks for big data classification. Neurocomputing. **390**, 327–340 (2020). https://doi.org/10.1016/j.neucom.2019.08.095
13. Ho, V.T., Le Thi, H.A., Pham Dinh, T.: DCA with successive DC decomposition for convex piecewise-linear fitting. In: Le Thi, H.A., Le, H.M., Pham Dinh, T., Nguyen, N.T. (eds.) ICCSAMA 2019. AISC, vol. 1121, pp. 39–51. Springer, Cham (2020). https://doi.org/10.1007/978-3-030-38364-0_4
14. Ho, V.T., Le Thi, H.A., Pham Dinh, T.: DCA-based algorithms for DC fitting. J. Comput. Appl. Math. **389**, 113353 (2021). https://doi.org/10.1016/j.cam.2020.113353
15. Katsavounidis, I., Jay Kuo, C.C., Zhang, Z.: A new initialization technique for generalized Lloyd iteration. IEEE Signal Process. Lett. **1**(10), 144–146 (1994). https://doi.org/10.1109/97.329844
16. Lipp, T., Boyd, S.: Variations and extension of the convex–concave procedure. Optim. Eng. **17**(2), 263–287 (2015). https://doi.org/10.1007/s11081-015-9294-x

17. Luenberger, D.G.: Linear and Nonlinear Programming, 2nd edn. Addison-Wesley, Boston (1984)
18. Mondal, R., Mukherjee, S.S., Santra, S., Chanda, B.: Morphological Network: How Far Can We Go with Morphological Neurons? Technical report. arXiv:1901.00109. December 2020
19. Oliveira, A.L., Valle, M.E.: Linear dilation-erosion perceptron trained using a convex-concave procedure. In: Abraham, A., et al. (eds.) SoCPaR 2020. AISC, vol. 1383, pp. 245–255. Springer, Cham (2021). https://doi.org/10.1007/978-3-030-73689-7_24
20. Olson, R.S., La Cava, W., Orzechowski, P., Urbanowicz, R.J., Moore, J.H.: PMLB: a large benchmark suite for machine learning evaluation and comparison. BioData Mining **10**(1), 36 (2017). https://doi.org/10.1186/s13040-017-0154-4
21. Pessoa, L.F.C., Maragos, P.: Neural networks with hybrid morphological/rank/linear nodes: a unifying framework with applications to handwritten character recognition. Pattern Recogn. **33**, 945–960 (2000)
22. Ritter, G.X., Sussner, P.: An introduction to morphological neural networks. In: Proceedings of the 13th International Conference on Pattern Recognition, pp. 709–717. Vienna, Austria (1996)
23. Ritter, G.X., Sussner, P., Diaz-De-Leon, J.L.: Morphological associative memories. IEEE Trans. Neural Netw. **9**(2), 281–293 (1998). https://doi.org/10.1109/72.661123
24. Ritter, G.X., Urcid, G.: Lattice algebra approach to single-neuron computation. IEEE Trans. Neural Netw. **14**(2), 282–295 (2003)
25. Schölkopf, B., Smola, A.: Learning with Kernels: Support Vector Machines, Regularization, Optimization, and Beyond. MIT Press, Cambridge (2002)
26. Shen, X., Diamond, S., Gu, Y., Boyd, S.: Disciplined convex-concave programming. In: 2016 IEEE 55th Conference on Decision and Control (CDC), pp. 1009–1014 (2016). https://doi.org/10.1109/CDC.2016.7798400
27. Soille, P.: Morphological Image Analysis: Principles and Applications, 2nd edn. Springer Verlag, Berlin (1999). https://doi.org/10.1007/978-3-662-05088-0
28. Stone, M.H.: The generalized Weierstrass approximation theorem. Math. Mag. **21**(4), 167–184 (1948). https://doi.org/10.2307/3029750
29. Sussner, P., Campiotti, I.: Extreme learning machine for a new hybrid morphological/linear perceptron. Neural Netw. **123**, 288–298 (2020). https://doi.org/10.1016/j.neunet.2019.12.003
30. Sussner, P., Esmi, E.L.: Morphological perceptrons with competitive learning: lattice-theoretical framework and constructive learning algorithm. Inf. Sci. **181**(10), 1929–1950 (2011). https://doi.org/10.1016/j.ins.2010.03.016
31. Tuy, H.: DC functions and DC sets. In: Convex Analysis and Global Optimization. SOIA, vol. 110, pp. 103–123. Springer, Cham (2016). https://doi.org/10.1007/978-3-319-31484-6_4
32. Valle, M.E.: Reduced dilation-erosion perceptron for binary classification. Mathematics **8**(4), 512 (2020). https://doi.org/10.3390/math8040512
33. Wang, S.: General constructive representations for continuous piecewise-linear functions. IEEE Trans. Circuits Syst. I Regul. Pap. **51**(9), 1889–1896 (2004). https://doi.org/10.1109/TCSI.2004.834521
34. Weise, T., Chiong, R.: An alternative way of presenting statistical test results when evaluating the performance of stochastic approaches. Neurocomputing **147**, 235–238 (2015). https://doi.org/10.1016/j.neucom.2014.06.071
35. Yuille, A.L., Rangarajan, A.: The concave-convex procedure. Neural Comput. **15**(4), 915–936 (2003). https://doi.org/10.1162/08997660360581958

Exploration Versus Exploitation in Model-Based Reinforcement Learning: An Empirical Study

Ângelo Gregório Lovatto(iD), Leliane Nunes de Barros(iD),
and Denis D. Mauá$^{(\boxtimes)}$ (iD)

Instituto de Matemática e Estatística, Universidade de São Paulo, São Paulo, Brazil

Abstract. Model-based Reinforcement Learning (MBRL) agents use data collected by exploration of the environment to produce a model of the dynamics, which is then used to select a policy that maximizes the objective function. Stochastic Value Gradient (SVG) methods perform the latter step by optimizing some estimate of the value function gradient. Despite showing promising empirical results, many implementations of SVG methods lack rigorous theoretical or empirical justification; this casts doubts as to whether good performance are in large part due to the benchmark-overfitting. To better understand the advantages and shortcomings of existing SVG methods, in this work we carry out a fine-grained empirical analysis of three core components of SVG-based agents: (i) the gradient estimator formula, (ii) the model learning and (iii) the value function approximation. To this end, we extend previous work that proposes using Linear Quadratic Gaussian (LQG) regulator problems to benchmark SVG methods. LQG problems are heavily studied in optimal control literature and deliver challenging learning settings while still allowing comparison with ground-truth values. We use such problems to investigate the contribution of each core component of SVG methods to the overall performance. We focus our analysis on the model learning component, which was neglected from previous work, and we show that overfitting to on-policy data can lead to accurate state predictions but inaccurate gradients, highlighting the importance of exploration also in model-based methods.

Keywords: Reinforcement learning · Model-based reinforcement learning · Optimal control · Gradient optimization methods

1 Introduction

Reinforcement Learning (RL) is a framework for automatically generating desirable agent behavior for sequential decision making while interacting with the environment [23,24]. The typical RL setting considers a series of discrete timesteps in which the agent selects an *action*, causing the environment to transition a new *state* and generating a (perceived) *reward*. The main challenge of

J. C. Xavier-Junior and R. A. Rios (Eds.): BRACIS 2022, LNAI 13654, pp. 30–44, 2022.
https://doi.org/10.1007/978-3-031-21689-3_3

RL is to learn a *policy* function mapping states to actions that maximizes the expected sum of rewards (*return*) using as few interactions with the environment as possible, and with limited computational resources. That is certainly no easy feat.

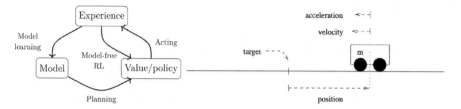

Fig. 1. The left figure shows a general schema of model-based and model-free RL agents (extracted from [7]). The right figure contains a graphical depiction of a simple RL setting that can be formalized as a Linear Quadratic Gaussian environment: the agent's policy sets the car's acceleration in order to reach a target position while minimizing energy consumption and time.

In response to what appeared being the start of a golden age in RL, several researchers have expressed concern about the generalization of the good empirical performance obtained in controlled settings [2,10,12]. In fact, recent studies have shown that code-level optimizations are often the deciding factor of a RL algorithm's performance [6,13]. Additionally, the theoretical justification of many RL methods rely on unrealistic best-case scenarios and low estimation errors. In spite of that, such methods often exhibit good performance even when their theoretical assumptions are violated. For example, [11] showed that although Policy Gradient algorithms often fail to produce good estimates of the gradient, a core tenet of policy gradient theory, they still succeed in finding good policies.

Model-Based Reinforcement Learning (MBRL) methods seek to minimize interaction with the environment (in comparison to Model-Free methods) by maintaining an accurate representation of the environment dynamics, saving costly and potentially dangerous trial-and-error experimentation in the real world [17,18]. MBRL methods present even more challenges to rigorous analysis due to their higher number of moving parts, as shown in the left picture in Fig. 1. For instance, while model-free algorithms often have two interdependent learning components, the policy and value function (return) estimator, MBRL algorithms introduce yet another two components, the state dynamics and reward models, that directly affect the quality of the policy and value function obtained. This additional complexity makes it very difficult to design MBRL algorithms from first principles, as theoretically promising MBRL algorithms may fail in practice [14] without one being able to exactly pinpoint the root of the problem. Moreover, even when MBRL do present good performance, it is hard to show how each component has contributed to such result.

In [15], the authors suggested using a diverse set of synthetic Linear Quadratic Gaussian (LQG) environments to analyze the contribution of value gradient estimation to the overall performance of MBRL algorithms, and in particular to Stochastic Value Gradient (SVG) algorithms. LQG environments are extensively studied sequential decision making problems in the Optimal Control literature [26,27], due to their amenable mathematical treatment and important applications. Notably, LQG solutions (i.e., an optimal policy) can be obtained analytically by mere matrix manipulations. Moreover, several components of SVG algorithms, such as value function estimation and its gradient, can be obtained exactly numerically. This allows one not only to isolate the performance of SVG algorithm's components, but to investigate their interaction contributes to the final outcome. The right picture in Fig. 1 shows diagrammatic explication of an example of a LQG environment, better known as the double integrator. Despite the apparent simplicity, LQG problems offer several challenges to RL algorithms [19].[1]

The authors of [15], however, focused their investigation on the importance of value function gradient estimation to overall performance. Among other things, they concluded that in low-sample regimes Model-Based Actor Critic (MAAC) methods [4], that are (theoretically) known to produce biased estimates of gradient estimation, outperform unbiased estimates of Deterministic Policy Gradient (DPG) methods [22] due to a reduced variance (a special case of the known Bias-Variance trade-off in machine learning theory). Importantly, their analysis was carried out using fixed and ideal models of the dynamics. Since learning accurate models is challenging, this limits the practical implications of the work.

In this work, we extend the analysis initiated by [15] to include also the contribution of model learning components on the overall performance of SVG methods for MBRL. We use the same LQG framework to obtain a rich and diverse set of RL environments with available exact estimates of the core components, which we use to evaluate MAAC and DPG methods for MBRL. To the best of our knowledge, this is the first work to make a complete investigation about exploration versus exploitation for Model-Based Reinforcement Learning (MBRL).

Our results show that data-collection has a major impact on the quality of (model-based) value function gradient estimates, and that using off-policy data is crucial to improving the accuracy of gradient estimators (over model-free approaches). We also observed that model-free estimation produces more stable (less variance) but less accurate estimates of the value gradient, corroborating the results in [5]. In opposition to the statements in [1], our experiments suggest that off-policy model learned can in fact help to accelerate policy improvement without increasing risk of failure.

The rest of this paper is organized as follows. We start in Sect. 2 by revisiting background theory on RL, SVG methods and LQG. Section 3 contains the main contribution of this paper: how to generate a diverse and interesting set of LQG problem instances; the empirical analysis; and a discussion of the results. Final remarks are laid out in Sect. 4.

---

[1] Unlike the RL setting, in the Optimal Control literature it is often assumed that one has access to the true environment dynamics and reward models.

2 Background

2.1 Reinforcement Learning Agent

We consider the agent-environment interaction modeled as an episodic, discrete-time, continuous state and action space Markov Decision Process (MDP) specified by a state space $\mathcal{S} \subseteq \mathbb{R}^n$, an initial state density ρ, an action space $\mathcal{A} \subseteq \mathbb{R}^d$, a reward function $R : \mathcal{S} \times \mathcal{A} \to \mathbb{R}$, a transition probability kernel (also called the dynamics model) p^*, and a time horizon H [24]. Accordingly, an episode consists of a sequence of state and actions ending after H timesteps. Each episode starts from an initial state $\mathbf{s}_0$ sampled according to the initial state distribution ρ. At each timestep $t = 0, 1, \ldots, H - 1$, the agent observes the current state $\mathbf{s}_t$ and selects an action $\mathbf{a}_t$ using its policy $\mu(\mathbf{s}_t)$ This causes a change in the environment from current state to next state s_{t+1} governed by the transition probability kernel, that is, $\mathbf{s}_{t+1} \sim p^*(\cdot \,|\, \mathbf{s}_t, \mathbf{a}_t)$, and the emission of a reward signal $r_{t+1} = R(\mathbf{s}_t, \mathbf{a}_t)$.

The objective of an RL agent is to find a policy μ that produces the highest expected cumulative reward (*return*) without knowledge of the initial and transition kernel densities or the reward function. That is, the agent ought to find μ that maximizes $J(\mu) = \mathbb{E}[\sum_{t=0}^{H-1} r_t]$ by collecting experience data $(\mathbf{s}_t, \mu(\mathbf{s}_t), \mathbf{s}_{t+1}, r_t)$. That leads to the common exploration-exploitation dilemma, where the agent decides between producing data to improve her current model of the world or acting so as to maximize the return given her current model.

The *state-value function* computes the expected return for a given policy μ for an agent that starts at a given state $\mathbf{s}_t$ at timestep t. It can be stated as [24]:

$$V^\mu(\mathbf{s}_t) = \mathbb{E}\left[\sum_{\tau=t}^{H-1} R(\mathbf{s}_\tau, \mu(\mathbf{s}_\tau))\right] = R(\mathbf{s}_t, \mu(\mathbf{s}_t)) + \mathbb{E}[V^\mu(\mathbf{s}_{t+1})]. \tag{1}$$

For many classes of MDPs which include discrete state spaces and LQGs, the value function can be efficiently approximated by recursive application of the equation above, a procedure known as Value Iteration.

2.2 Linear Quadratic Gaussian Environments

Linear Quadratic Gaussian (LQG) environments are episodic, discrete-time and continuous state-action space MDPs whose dynamics model is given by a linear transformation with added Gaussian noise, and whose reward function is a quadratic function of state and action variables [26]:

$$\mathbf{s}_t = \mathbf{F_s}\mathbf{s}_t + \mathbf{F_a}\mathbf{a}_t + \xi, \quad \xi \sim \mathcal{N}(0, \boldsymbol{\Sigma}), \qquad r_t = -\tfrac{1}{2}\left(\mathbf{s}_t^\mathsf{T}\mathbf{C_{ss}}\mathbf{s}_t + \mathbf{a}_t^\mathsf{T}\mathbf{C_{aa}}\mathbf{a}_t\right),$$

where $\mathbf{F_s}$ and $\mathbf{F_a}$ are state and action dependent transitions, $\boldsymbol{\Sigma}$ is a covariance matrix and $\mathbf{C_{ss}}$ and are state and action dependent cost-components (note the minus sign that transforms rewards into costs). Such environments are extensively studied in the Optimal Control literature [26,27], where the initial and transition kernel densities and reward function are assumed given. They often arise as the discretization of a continuous-time dynamics described as linear differential equations. Additionally, LQGs are often substeps in the solution of optimal control problems with non-linear dynamics (by dynamic linearization).

For our purposes, the main advantage of LQG w.r.t. more general and commonly used environments in RL is that for LQGs the ground-truth performance of a given policy can efficiently be obtained numerically. In fact, one can shown that for a LQG the optimal policy can be written as a time-varying *linear policy*: $\mu_\theta(\mathbf{s}_t) = \mathbf{K}_t\mathbf{s}_t + \mathbf{k}_t$, where $\mathbf{K}_t \in \mathbb{R}^{d \times n}$ and $\mathbf{k}_t \in \mathbb{R}^d$ are known as the *dynamic* and *static gains*. Here, θ is the flattened parameter vector corresponding to the collection $\{\mathbf{K}_t, \mathbf{k}_t\}_{t \in \mathcal{T}}$ of function coefficients. For a linear policy, the expectations in Eq. (1) can be computed analytically and the corresponding state-value function can be obtained by *dynamic programming*, much like as in the discrete state and action space case. The solution V^{μ_θ} is itself quadratic and the policy return can also be obtained analytically. An important result from optimal control theory is that a closed-form formula for the optimal (time-varying linear) policy $\mu_\theta^\star$ can be obtained as the pointwise maximization of the right-hand side of Eq. (1), and written and a sequence of matrix multiplications and inversion. LQGs thus constitute one of the few classes of nontrivial continuous control problems which allows us to evaluate RL methods against the theoretical best solutions.

2.3 Stochastic Value Gradient Methods

SVG methods try to find a good policy defined by a set of parameters, i.e., a function mapping the current state and a set of parameters to the action for execution. We call this a parameterized (or parametric) policy. We then reframe the RL problem as searching for the parameters that maximize the expected return of the induced policy. SVG methods use the model to estimate the value gradient: the gradient of the expected return w.r.t. the policy's parameters. With a gradient estimate in hand, we can leverage stochastic optimization methods to update our policy's parameters iteratively. We call this general process *policy optimization*, analogous to how generic parametric functions are updated with gradient-based methods in machine learning.

As function approximation research, specially on deep learning, has advanced, parameterized policies were able to unify perception (processing sensorial input from the environment) and decision-making (choosing actions to maximize return) tasks [16]. To improve such parameterized approximators from data, the workhorse behind many policy optimization methods is SGD [20]. Thus, it is imperative to estimate the gradient of the expected return w.r.t. policy parameters, a.k.a. the *value gradient*, from data (states, actions and rewards) collected via interaction with the environment.

SVG methods build gradient estimates by first using the available data to learn a *model* of the environment, i.e., a function approximator $p_\psi(\cdot \mid \mathbf{s}, \mathbf{a}) \approx p^*(\cdot \mid \mathbf{s}, \mathbf{a})$. A common approach to leveraging the learned model is as follows. First, the agent collects B states via interaction with the environment, potentially with an exploratory policy β (we use $\mathbf{s}_t \sim d^\beta$ to denote sampling from its induced state distribution). Then, it generates short model-based trajectories with the current policy μ_θ, branching off the states previous collected. Finally, it computes the average model-based returns and forms an estimate of the value gradient using backpropagation [9]:

$$\nabla J(\theta) \approx \nabla_\theta \, \mathbb{E}_{\mathbf{s}_t \sim d^\beta} \left[\sum_{l=0}^{K-1} R(\mathbf{s}_{t+l}, \mu_\theta(\mathbf{s}_{t+l})) + \hat{Q}^{\mu_\theta}(\mathbf{s}_{t+K}, \mu_\theta(\mathbf{s}_{t+K})) \right]. \quad (2)$$

Here, $\hat{Q}^{\mu_\theta}$ is an approximation (e.g., a learned neural network) of the policy's *action-value* function $Q^{\mu_\theta}(\mathbf{s}_t, \mathbf{a}_t) = \mathbb{E}_{\mu_\theta}[\sum_{l=t}^{H-1} R(\mathbf{s}_l, \mathbf{a}_l)]$. We refer to Eq. 2 as the MAAC(K) estimator, as it uses K steps of simulated interaction and was featured prominently in [4].[2]

We question, however, if Eq. (2) actually provides good empirical estimates of the true value gradient. To elucidate this matter, we compare MAAC(K) to the value gradient estimator provided by the DPG theorem [22]:

$$\nabla J(\theta) = \mathop{\mathbb{E}}_{\mathbf{s}_t \sim d^{\mu_\theta}} \left[\nabla_\theta \mu_\theta(\mathbf{s}_t) \nabla_\mathbf{a} \, Q^{\mu_\theta}(\mathbf{s}_t, \mathbf{a})|_{\mathbf{a}=\mu_\theta(\mathbf{s}_t)} \right]. \quad (3)$$

Besides the fact that Eq. (3) requires us to use the on-policy distribution of states d^{μ_θ}, more subtle differences with Eq. (2) can be seen by expanding the definition of the action-value function to form a K-step version of Eq. (3), which we call the DPG(K) estimator. Note that DPG(0) is equivalent to Eq. (3).

Equation (2) shows the SCG of the MAAC(K) and DPG(K) estimators [21]. Here, borderless nodes denote input variables; circles denote stochastic nodes, distributed conditionally on their parents (if any); and squares denote deterministic nodes, which are functions of their parents. Because of the $\nabla_\mathbf{a} \, Q^{\mu_\theta}(\mathbf{s}_t, \mathbf{a})|_{\mathbf{a}=\mu_\theta(\mathbf{s}_t)}$ term in Eq. (3), we're not allowed to compute the gradients of future actions w.r.t. policy parameters in DPG(K), hence why only the first action has a link with θ. On the other hand, MAAC(K) backpropagates the gradients of the rewards and value-function through all intermediate actions. Our work aims at identifying the practical implications of these differences and perhaps help explain why MAAC(K) has been used in SVG methods and not DPG(K).

3   Analyzing the Model Learning Component

In our experiments, we follow the same approach as in [15] for sampling LQG instances given the state space dimension (n), action space dimension (d) and time horizon (H). The coefficients $\mathbf{F_s}$ and $\mathbf{F_a}$ (Sect. 2.2) are initialized so that the system may be *unstable*, i.e., with some eigenvalues of $\mathbf{F_s}$ having magnitude greater or equal to 1, but always *controllable*, meaning there is a *dynamic gain* $\mathbf{K}$ such that the eigenvalues of $(\mathbf{F_s}+\mathbf{F_a}\mathbf{K})$ have magnitude less than 1. This ensures

---

[2] Our formula differs slightly from the original in that it considers a deterministic policy instead of a stochastic one.

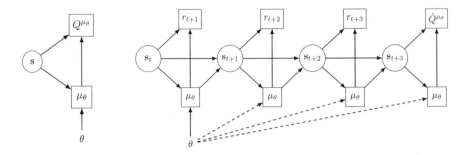

Fig. 2. Stochastic computation graphs for policy gradients. (Left) Model-free DPG. (Right) Model-based DPG: the dashed edges represent the K-step deterministic dependencies of the policy parameters in MAAC(K) for $K = 3$; DPG(K) ignores these dependencies when backpropagating the action gradients.

we are able to emulate real-world scenarios where uncontrolled state variables and costs may diverge to infinity, while ensuring there exists a policy which can stabilize the system [19]. The dynamics is stationary, sharing $\mathbf{F}, \mathbf{f}, \mathbf{\Sigma}$ across all timesteps. We fix the transition bias to $\mathbf{f} = \mathbf{0}$ and we set the Gaussian covariance as the identity matrix, $\mathbf{\Sigma} = I$. The initial state distribution is initialized as a standard Gaussian distribution: $\rho(\mathbf{s}) = \mathcal{N}(\mathbf{s} \mid \mathbf{0}, I)$. The reward parameters, $\mathbf{C_{ss}}$ and $\mathbf{C_{aa}}$, are randomly sampled symmetric positive definite matrices.

Since to analyze the learned model we also need to estimate value gradients for linear policies in LQGs, we define a procedure to generate randomized policies. We start by initializing all dynamic gains $\mathbf{K}_t = \mathbf{K}$ so that $\mathbf{K}$ stabilizes the system. This is done by first sampling target eigenvalues uniformly in the interval $(0, 1)$ and then using the scipy library to compute $\mathbf{K}$ that places the eigenvalues of $(\mathbf{F_s} + \mathbf{F_a}\mathbf{K})$ in the desired targets [25]. This process ensures the resulting policy is safe to collect data in the environment without having state variables and costs diverge to infinity. Last, we initialize static gains as $\mathbf{k}_t = \mathbf{0}$.

Our environment model parameterizes the mean and (diagonal) covariance of a multivariate Gaussian distribution as linear functions of the state and action:

$$p_\psi(\mathbf{s}, \mathbf{a}) \doteq \mathcal{N}(\mu_\psi(\mathbf{s}, \mathbf{a}), \mathrm{diag}(\sigma_\psi(\mathbf{s}, \mathbf{a}))), \tag{4}$$

$$\mu_\psi(\mathbf{s}, \mathbf{a}) = \mathbf{W}_\mu \begin{bmatrix} \mathbf{s} \\ \mathbf{a} \end{bmatrix} + \mathbf{b}_\mu , \tag{5}$$

$$\sigma_\psi(\mathbf{s}, \mathbf{a}) = \mathrm{softplus}(\mathbf{b}_\sigma). \tag{6}$$

where $\mathbf{W}_\mu \in \mathbb{R}^{n \times (n+d)}$ and $\mathbf{b}_\mu, \mathbf{b}_\sigma \in \mathbb{R}^n$ are the model parameters (denoted by ψ) and $\mathrm{softplus}(x) = \log(1 + \exp(x))$ is an element-wise function ensuring the output is positive.

Fitting the model w.r.t the data is very close to system identification in Optimal Control, which also uses linear models. However, a key difference between Eq. (4) and models in system identification is that the latter deterministically maps a state-action pair to a next state using a linear function, i.e., $f(\mathbf{s}, \mathbf{a}) = \mu_\psi(\mathbf{s}, \mathbf{a})$. Linear Least Squares methods are then used to fit these deterministic models to the observed data. We chose Eq. (4) to match other model parameterizations in SVG algorithms, which are stochastic. Besides, MLE with Gaussian models is seen as a generalization of Least Squares optimization [3].

We consider the interplay between the performance in the sub-task of learning a model and the task of predicting accurate gradients. Ultimately, the algorithm's objective is to improve the policy's performance in the environment, so we also consider it in our experiments. Overall, our analysis goals are: (i) to identify the conditions under which model learning fails; and (ii) to evaluate different ways of using the model for gradient estimation.

3.1   Experiment I: Exploration is Crucial for Model-Based Prediction

Ideally, we want to sample performing model-based rollouts from the on-policy state distribution and, as usually, we build a replay buffer of trajectories (on-policy) and use the same data for both, model learning and value gradient estimation for maximum sample-efficiency. So, our in our first experiment we run model-based on our LQG domain with an on-policy approach.

The experimental setup consists of 20 randomly-generated LQGs with $\dim(\mathcal{S}) = \dim(\mathcal{A}) = 2$ and $H = 50$). To isolate the model's influence in the results, we perform our experiment with full access to the ground-truth reward function and the ground-truth value function for bootstrapping. For each environment, we perform a model-based prediction run as follows. We collect 2000 trajectories with a randomly generated, stabilizing policy. Trajectories are split into a training (90%) and a validation (10%) dataset. The training dataset is shuffled before each iteration of model learning (an *epoch*). Model learning fits a dynamics model via MLE: maximizing the likelihood of trajectory segments of length 4 in mini-batches of size 128. After every epoch (implying every data-point in the training set has been used), we compute the model's performance on the validation set, including the: (i) average negative likelihood of all trajectory segments, or *loss*; (ii) empirical Kullback-Leibler (KL) divergence between the model and the environment dynamics; (iii) absolute relative error between the real state-value function and its 4-step expansion with the model (from random states in the dataset); and (iv) gradient accuracy of MAAC(4).

Model Learning with On-Policy Dataset. Figure 3 shows the model's performance metrics during training against the number of epochs for our LQG environment. Each line represents one independent run, each one with 20 sampled environments. Notice how every single run is successful at improving the model's loss, the empirical KL divergence and the 4-step value error, indicating that *the model is predicting states correctly and helping induce a good estimate of the value function. However, the gradient accuracy of the MAAC(4) estimates do not always improve with model learning*, with some ending up worse than with the initial, randomly initialized model.

We also compare the average gradient accuracy of a model-free estimator, MAAC(0) using the ground-truth action-value function, with the model-based

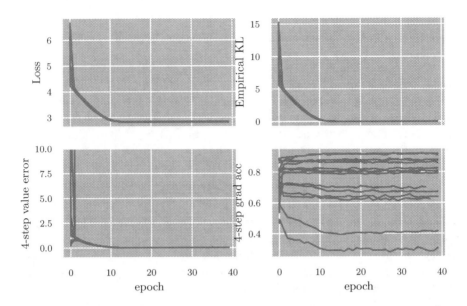

Fig. 3. Loss, empirical KL, value error and gradient accuracy during *model learning from on-policy data*.

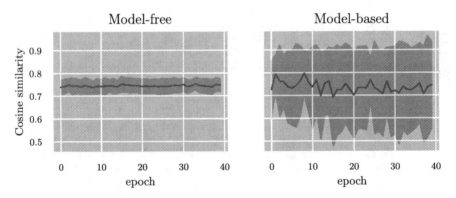

Fig. 4. Comparison of gradient accuracy between (model-free) DPG(0) and MAAC(K) with a *model learned from on-policy data*.

MAAC(4) in Fig. 4, which highlights that, *on average, the estimators have the same accuracy, but the learned model introduces a lot of variance, which is not desirable*.

We try to understand why the above observation happens by analytically inspecting a single instance of model learning in greater detail. Consider the following, simple LQG (randomly generated):

$$p^*(\mathbf{s}, \mathbf{a}) = \mathcal{N}\left(\begin{bmatrix} 1.0689 & 0.0089 & 0.9776 & 0.9827 \\ 0.0089 & 1.0637 & 0.2107 & -0.1850 \end{bmatrix}\begin{bmatrix} \mathbf{s} \\ \mathbf{a} \end{bmatrix}, I\right),\qquad(7)$$

$$R(\mathbf{s}, \mathbf{a}, \mathbf{s}') = \tfrac{1}{2}\mathbf{s}^\mathsf{T}\begin{bmatrix} 0.4530 & -0.2178 \\ -0.2178 & 3.5398 \end{bmatrix}\mathbf{s} + \tfrac{1}{2}\mathbf{a}^\mathsf{T}\begin{bmatrix} 1.3662 & -0.0420 \\ -0.0420 & 0.7659 \end{bmatrix}\mathbf{a},\qquad(8)$$

$$\rho(\mathbf{s}) = \mathcal{N}(\mathbf{0}, I)\qquad\qquad,\qquad(9)$$

where $\dim(\mathcal{S}) = \dim(\mathcal{A}) = 2$ with a horizon of $H = 50$. Policy generation, data collection and model learning are all done as in the experiments of Fig. 3. We stop fitting the model once its loss on the validation set stops improving for 3 consecutive epochs, a technique known as *early stopping* to avoid overfitting the model to training data. Our model learning run found the following parameters:

$$\mathbf{W}_\mu = \begin{bmatrix} -0.1072 & -0.0347 & -0.0238 & 0.0202 \\ 0.0403 & 0.3481 & -0.2826 & 0.3444 \end{bmatrix},$$

$$\mathbf{b}_\mu = [0.0042, -0.0055]^\mathsf{T}, \quad \sigma_\psi = [0.9984, 1.0047]^\mathsf{T}.$$

We can see that the final model correctly predicts the diagonal of the dynamics covariance matrix and its transition bias is close to real one, zero. On the other hand, the transition kernel $\mathbf{W}_\mu$ is much different than the dynamics' kernel. Despite this, the learned model achieves an empirical KL divergence of 0.0004 (on the validation set) with the environment dynamics, implying that its state predictions are very accurate. Indeed, the relative error between the 4-step state-value expansion using this model and the real state-value function is, on average, 0.01. However, the accuracy of the MAAC(4) estimates is, on average over the validation set, approximately -0.806, *meaning that the estimated gradients point in almost the opposite direction of the real value gradient*.

Figure 5 confirms the above analytical result with a visualization of the optimization surface around the policy parameters. The vertical axis corresponds to the policy's value (LQG analytical solution). Each point (x, y) in the horizontal axes correspond to a policy parameter update of $\theta \leftarrow \theta + x\mathbf{u} + y\mathbf{g}$, where $\mathbf{u}$ is a random direction in the parameter space (sampled uniformly at random from the unit sphere) and $\mathbf{g}$ is the normalized gradient estimated with the model. We can see that updating the policy in the direction of the estimated gradient leads to decreasing total value, further confirming that *the model, despite accurate in some metrics, is inadequate for improving the policy*.

To explain these observations, we take a closer look at the model's Jacobians. Specifically, we compare the reparameterized model and environment dynamics when both are fed actions from the target policy:

$$f[*]^\mu(\mathbf{s}, \xi) = f[*](\mathbf{s}, \mu_\theta(\mathbf{s}), \xi), \qquad\qquad f^\mu(\mathbf{s}, \xi) = f(\mathbf{s}, \mu_\theta(\mathbf{s}), \xi).$$

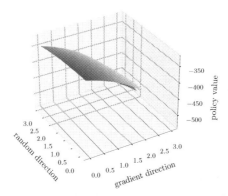

Fig. 5. Optimization surface induced by the SVG estimated with a model fitted to on-policy data through LQG analytical solution.

The noise variable does not affect the Jacobian of these functions, for a given state, since its effect is additive. We sample a random noise variable from a standard Gaussian and a state from the replay buffer and compute the Jacobians w.r.t. to the state inputs (leveraging automatic differentiation), arriving at:

$$\nabla_{\mathbf{s}} f^{\mu}_*(\mathbf{s}, \xi) = \begin{bmatrix} -0.1049 & \approx 0 \\ \approx 0 & 0.7852 \end{bmatrix}, \quad \nabla_{\mathbf{s}} f^{\mu}_{\psi}(\mathbf{s}, \xi) = \begin{bmatrix} -0.1057 & -0.0037 \\ -0.0069 & 0.7887 \end{bmatrix}.$$

We also verify that $\|\nabla_{\mathbf{s}} f^{\mu}_*(\mathbf{s}, \xi) - \nabla_{\mathbf{s}} f^{\mu}_{\psi}(\mathbf{s}, \xi)\| = 0.0086$. Thus, we see that the model obtained mimics the on-policy dynamics in first-order. Indeed, since we collected data exclusively with the target policy, the model was fed a variety of states, but not a variety of actions for each state (only the action that the policy would take). Therefore, we conclude that *the dynamics model learned from on-policy data overfits to the observed action distribution and is not able to correctly estimate the dynamics around for actions that are too different than the ones prescribed by target policy*. Hence, the benefit of MBRL for policy improvement is limited.

Model Learning with Off-Policy Dataset. We then consider collecting data off-policy, using a stochastic behavior policy, for model learning. Ideally, we would also have access to on-policy data for value gradient estimation, however, that would increase the data requirements of an RL agent, which is precisely the opposite of what MBRL proposes to do. Therefore, there needs to be a consideration of how much "off-policy" our data collection is, so as to not hurt either the model learning or SVG estimation subroutines. Since our target policy is deterministic, we borrow from DPG-style algorithms [5,8,22] and use a behavior one that adds white noise to the target policy's actions: $\mu_{\theta}(\mathbf{s}) + \xi$, $\xi \sim \mathcal{N}(\mathbf{0}, 0.3I)$. The rest of the experimental setup is kept the same as used for Fig. 4.

Figure 6 shows the performance metrics for the model against the number of training epochs in the off-policy training dataset. Note that now MAAC(4)

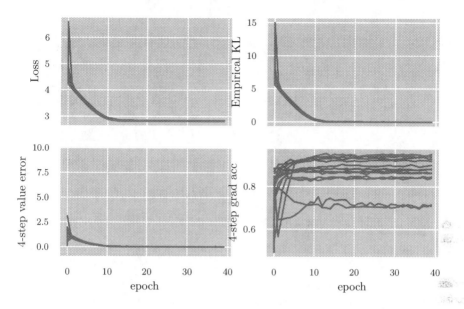

Fig. 6. Loss, empirical KL, value error, and gradient accuracy during *model learning with off-policy data*.

gradient accuracy also improves with model learning, with the exception of one outlier. We aggregate the value gradient accuracy results in Fig. 7, contrasting the model-free MAAC(0) with the model-based MAAC(4). Now, *with a dynamics model trained on off-policy data, we see a benefit in using a model-based estimator over a model-free one*.

3.2 Experiment II: Learning Reward Functions

We also investigate the interplay between exploration and learning the reward function. We use the same function class of the true reward function:

$$R_\psi(\mathbf{s}, \mathbf{a}, \mathbf{s}') = \tfrac{1}{2} \begin{bmatrix} \mathbf{s} \\ \mathbf{a} \end{bmatrix}^\mathsf{T} \mathbf{W}_R \begin{bmatrix} \mathbf{s} \\ \mathbf{a} \end{bmatrix} + \mathbf{w}_R^\mathsf{T} \begin{bmatrix} \mathbf{s} \\ \mathbf{a} \end{bmatrix}. \tag{10}$$

The parameters $\psi = \{\mathbf{W}_R, \mathbf{w}_R\}$ are randomly initialized.

We use a similar experimental setup as in the previous subsection. Here, however, we optimize the reward model to minimize the MSE with the observed environment rewards $\mathbb{E}_{\mathbf{s},\mathbf{a},r\sim}[(R_\psi(\mathbf{s}, \mathbf{a}) - r)^2]$. On the validation set, we monitor two metrics every half an epoch: the cosine similarity between $\nabla_\mathbf{s} R_\psi(\mathbf{s}, \mathbf{a})$ and $\nabla_\mathbf{s} R(\mathbf{s}, \mathbf{a})$, and the same between $\nabla_\mathbf{a} R_\psi(\mathbf{s}, \mathbf{a})$ and $\nabla_\mathbf{a} R(\mathbf{s}, \mathbf{a})$.

Figure 8 shows the validation metrics during reward model learning against the number of epochs. We compare learning on on-policy data (exploration = "None") and off-policy data (exploration = "gaussian"). The latter uses a behavior policy like the one used in the experiments in Figs. 7 and 6. *We can see*

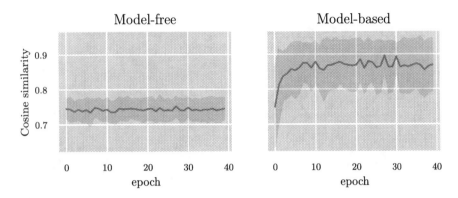

Fig. 7. Estimated SVG accuracy resulting from models fitted from on-policy (left) and off-policy (right) data.

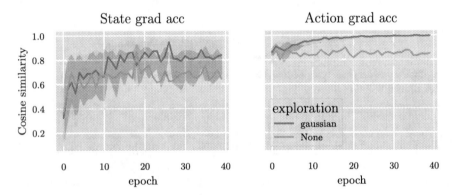

Fig. 8. Reward gradient accuracy during reward model learning. Left: accuracy of reward gradient w.r.t. the state input. Right: accuracy of reward gradient w.r.t. the action input.

that, in general, the learned models approximate the state and action gradients pretty well, with off-policy estimates being superior to on-policy ones, especially for action-gradients.

4   Conclusion

In this paper we extended the previous approach of [15] for studying Model-Based Reinforcement Learning (MBRL) algorithms in Linear Quadratic Gaussian (LQG) environments, and analyzed how the model learning component contributes to the overall performance of methods based on Stochastic Value Gradient (SVG).

Overall, the experiments on the LQG framework help us identify with precision the important issue of data collection for MBRL and its impact on the learned model. Using on-policy data to train a model of the environment dynamics does not improve the quality of value gradient estimator compared to model-free approaches. On the other hand, using off-policy data generated with some exploration strategy improves the quality of gradient estimators. The experiments also serve as a reminder that standard metrics of model quality, such as log-likelihood loss, are not always good indicators of model accuracy for MBRL. Even state-value function error, which requires knowledge of the true value function, can be misleading when using on-policy data. Thus, it remains a future challenge to devise metrics that more adequately measure the quality of learned models for policy improvement in MBRL.

Acknowledgments. This work was partly supported by the CAPES grant #88887.339578/2019-00 (first author), by the joint FAPESP-IBM grant #2019/07665-4 (second and third authors), and CNPq PQx grant #304012/2019-0 (third author).

References

1. Amos, B., Stanton, S., Yarats, D., Wilson, A.G.: On the model-based stochastic value gradient for continuous reinforcement learning. CoRR abs/2008.1 (2020)
2. Chan, S.C.Y., Fishman, S., Korattikara, A., Canny, J., Guadarrama, S.: Measuring the reliability of reinforcement learning algorithms. In: ICLR (2020)
3. Charnes, A., Frome, E.L., Yu, P.L.: The equivalence of generalized least squares and maximum likelihood estimates in the exponential family. J. Am. Stat. Assoc. **71**(353), 169–171 (1976)
4. Clavera, I., Fu, Y., Abbeel, P.: Model-augmented actor-critic: backpropagating through paths. In: ICLR (2020)
5. D'Oro, P., Jaskowski, W.: How to learn a useful critic? Model-based Action-Gradient-Estimator Policy Optimization. In: NeurIPS (2020)
6. Engstrom, L., et al.: Implementation matters in deep RL: a case study on PPO and TRPO. In: ICLR (2020)
7. François-Lavet, V., Henderson, P., Islam, R., Bellemare, M.G., Pineau, J.: An introduction to deep reinforcement learning. Found. Trends Mach. Learn. **11**(3–4), 219–354 (2018)
8. Fujimoto, S., van Hoof, H., Meger, D.: Addressing function approximation error in actor-critic methods. In: ICML. Proceedings of Machine Learning Research, vol. 80, pp. 1582–1591. PMLR (2018)
9. Goodfellow, I.J., Bengio, Y., Courville, A.C.: Deep Learning. Adaptive Computation and Machine Learning. MIT Press, Cambridge (2016)
10. Henderson, P., Islam, R., Bachman, P., Pineau, J., Precup, D., Meger, D.: Deep reinforcement learning that matters. In: AAAI, pp. 3207–3214 (2018)
11. Ilyas, A., et al.: A closer look at deep policy gradients. In: ICLR (2020)
12. Islam, R., Henderson, P., Gomrokchi, M., Precup, D.: Reproducibility of benchmarked deep reinforcement learning tasks for continuous control. CoRR (2017)
13. Liu, Z., Li, X., Kang, B., Darrell, T.: Regularization matters for policy optimization - an empirical study on continuous control. In: International Conference on Learning Representations (2021)
14. Lovatto, A.G., Bueno, T.P., Mauá, D.D., de Barros, L.N.: Decision-aware model learning for actor-critic methods: when theory does not meet practice. In: Proceedings on "I Can't Believe It's Not Better!" at NeurIPS Workshops. Proceedings of Machine Learning Research, vol. 137, pp. 76–86 (2020)

15. Lovatto, Â.G., Bueno, T.P., de Barros, L.N.: Gradient estimation in model-based reinforcement learning: a study on linear quadratic environments. In: Britto, A., Valdivia Delgado, K. (eds.) BRACIS 2021. LNCS (LNAI), vol. 13073, pp. 33–47. Springer, Cham (2021). https://doi.org/10.1007/978-3-030-91702-9_3
16. Mnih, V., et al.: Human-level control through deep reinforcement learning. Nature. **518**(7540), 529–533 (2015)
17. Moerland, T.M., Broekens, J., Jonker, C.M.: Model-based reinforcement learning: a survey. In: Proceedings of the International Conference on Electronic Business 2018-December, pp. 421–429 (2020)
18. Polydoros, A.S., Nalpantidis, L.: Survey of model-based reinforcement learning: applications on robotics. J. Intell. Robot. Syst. **86**(2), 153–173 (2017). https://doi.org/10.1007/s10846-017-0468-y
19. Recht, B.: A Tour of Reinforcement Learning: the view from continuous control. Ann. Rev. Control Robot. Auton. Syst. **2**(1), 253–279 (2019)
20. Ruder, S.: An overview of gradient descent optimization algorithms. CoRR abs/1609.04747 (2016)
21. Schulman, J., Heess, N., Weber, T., Abbeel, P.: Gradient estimation using stochastic computation graphs. In: NIPS, pp. 3528–3536 (2015)
22. Silver, D., Lever, G.: Deterministic policy gradient. In: Proceedings of the 31st International Conference on Machine Learning, vol. 32(1), pp. 387–395, January 2014
23. Sutton, R.S., Barto, A.G.: Reinforcement Learning: An Introduction, 2nd edn. The MIT Press, Cambridge (2018)
24. Szepesvári, C.: Algorithms for reinforcement learning. Synth. Lect. Artif. Intell. Mach. Learn. **4**, 1–3 (2010)
25. Tits, A.L., Yang, Y.: Globally convergent algorithms for robust pole assignment by state feedback. IEEE Trans. Autom. Control **41**(10), 1432–1452 (1996)
26. Todorov, E.: Optimal Control Theory. Bayesian Brain: Probabilistic Approaches to Neural Coding, pp. 269–298. MIT Press, Cambridge (2006)
27. Vinter, R.B., Vinter, R.: Optimal Control. Springer, Boston (2010). https://doi.org/10.1007/978-0-8176-8086-2

BoVW-CAM: Visual Explanation from Bag of Visual Words

Arnaldo Vitor Barros da Silva[(✉)] [iD] and Luis Filipe Alves Pereira[iD]

Universidade Federal do Agreste de Pernambuco, Avenida Bom Pastor, Garanhuns, Pernambuco 55292-270, Brazil
arnaldovitorbarros@gmail.com

Abstract. Classical computer vision solutions were used to extract image features designed by human experts for encoding visual scenes into vectors. Machine learning algorithms were then applied to model such vector space and assign labels to unseen vectors. Alternatively, such space could be composed of histograms generated using the Bag of Visual Words (BoVW) that compute the number of occurrences of clustered handcrafted features/descriptors in each image. Currently, Deep Learning methods automatically learn image features that maximize the accuracy of classification and object recognition. Still, Deep Learning fails in terms of interpretability. To tackle this issue, methods such as Grad-CAM allow the visualization of regions from input images that support the predictions generated by Convolutional Neural Networks (CNNs), *i.e.* visual explanations. However, there is a lack of similar visualization techniques for handcrafted features. This fact obscures the comparison between modern CNNs and classical methods for image classification. In this work, we present the BoVW-CAM that indicates the most important image regions for each prediction given by the BoVW technique. This way, we show a novel approach to compare the performance of learned and handcrafted features in the image domain.

Keywords: Deep Learning · Class Activation Mapping · Image features

1 Introduction

Deep learning has emerged as a new branch of machine learning. It has proven to be very effective in many computer vision tasks such as image classification [15], object detection [25], image segmentation [8], and others. In addition to reporting high accuracy rates, Deep Learning eliminated the requirement for human experts to design feature extractors since convolutional layers of Convolutional Neural Networks (CNNs) are suited for this task.

However, even in the face of all these advantages, Deep Learning used to fail in interpretability [13]. This attribute may be crucial, especially in high misclassification costs. To attack this black box issue, Zhou *et al.* [24] proposed the Class Activation Map (CAM), which highlights the most significant image

J. C. Xavier-Junior and R. A. Rios (Eds.): BRACIS 2022, LNAI 13654, pp. 45–55, 2022.
https://doi.org/10.1007/978-3-031-21689-3_4

regions to produce a prediction by a CNN. This technique modifies the network architecture, replacing the fully connected layers with convolutional layers and a Global Average Pooling (GAP). Then, the channels from the output of the last convolutional layer are weighed by the network parameters that link each element in the GAP output to the neuron of the activated class. As a result, this weighted sum of channels is the final visual explanation provided by CAM. More recently, Selvaraju *et al.* proposed the Grad-CAM [21], this method can be applied to many CNN models without requiring architectural changes. For this, it calculates the gradient of the last convolutional layer concerning the network output, which measures the influence of each cell in the feature map to compose the network prediction.

The huge success of Deep Learning methods currently overshadows classic techniques based on Handcrafted (HC) features for image classification [10]. However, some researchers in the literature suggest a careful comparison between Learned (LN) and HC features. Nanni *et al.* [17] ran an exhaustive comparison between the two approaches in different image domains, from butterfly species classification to cancer detection. Their experiments showed several scenarios where HC features outperformed the LN features in accuracy. In early 2020, Lin *et al.* [12] proposed a random forest to identify Magnetic Resonance (MR) images of livers that are adequate for clinical diagnosis. They reported that HC features outperformed LN features across smaller datasets, *i.e.*, less than 200 images for model training. In 2021, Saba *et al.* [20] investigated the problem of detecting microscopic skin cancer in non-dermoscopic color images. They reported cases where HC features were better than LN features. Finally, in 2022, Silva *et al.* [22] evaluated HC and LN features in the context of violence detection in video frames. Their results showed that LN features can not always be claimed superior since some violent scenes are only detected by HC features.

A widely used image representation technique based on local HC features is the Bag of Visual Words (BoVW) [5]. Concerning the existence of many local descriptors along a single image, a keypoint is referred to as a structure composed of a feature/descriptor vector and an image coordinate to indicate the local region described by such feature/descriptor. The final BoVW image representation is an histogram of the occurrences of clustered handcrafted features/descriptors presented in the given image. Finally, the BoVW histograms may feed a classifier like Support Vector Machine (SVM) [9]. This work proposes a visualization method that allows the interpretation of the most important regions for image classification using BoVW. Several works [12, 17, 20, 22] previously evaluated the accuracy rates obtained by HC and LN features to conclude that they focus on different aspects of the images. However, to the best of our knowledge, such divergence was not demonstrated in the literature at the image domain level.

2   Background

2.1   Keypoints

Keypoints refer to structures for encapsulating the representation of local features along a given image. Therefore, for representing a single image patch, a keypoint has a feature/descriptor vector that holds information about the image *semantics* locally and a coordinate tuple that localize it within the image. The extraction of keypoints is then composed of at least two main steps for retrieving: *(i)* the keypoint localization, and *(ii)* the keypoint feature/descriptor.

On the one hand, a good keypoint localizer identifies local regions that are potentially distinct along the image. Such uniqueness is crucial for representing the image's elements that allow its identification. Example of algorithms for keypoint localization includes FAST [18], BRISK [11], ORB [19], SURF [3], SIFT [14], and KAZE [2]. On the other hand, a good keypoint descriptor faithfully characterizes image local regions. Example of techniques for extracting keypoint descriptors are BRISK [11], FREAK [1], BRIEF [4], SURF [3], ORB [19], SIFT [14], KAZE [2]. Those are all handcrafted techniques, *i.e.* such algorithms are humanly designed and data invariant.

Keypoint Localization. Keypoint localizers generally try to find more representative image patches in relation to their neighbors. This representation can be through aspects such as corners, colors, or brightness. A classic method for locating keypoints is the Harris Corner Detector. From the dx and dy image gradients, a Harris response map is generated by encoding the magnitude of gray level changes in both horizontal and vertical directions for each 3×3 image window. Finally, each pixel in the image whose Harris response exceeds a predefined threshold τ is assigned as a corner.

Another widely used method is the FAST (Features from Accelerated Segment Test). Considering a Bresenham circle of radius three centered at each pixel in the image, the FAST compares the gray value of the central pixel to each intensity along the Bresenham circumference. If an amount of N consecutive pixels of this circumference is brighter or darker than the central point, it is classified as a corner. To speed up the method, it is possible to use a machine learning-based approach for detecting consecutive patterns in a sequence. Then, after extracting these 16-pixel circumferences and their central intensity values, it is possible to train a classifier as a decision tree [16] to decide whether or not this point is a corner.

Other methods like SIFT [14], SURF [3] and KAZE [2] uses multiscale analysis. SIFT algorithm, for instance, computes the Difference of Gaussians (DoG) between different image scales. The local minima and maxima along the DoG are considered keypoint candidates.

Keypoint Descriptors. After the keypoint localization step, it is necessary to associate them with appropriate feature/descriptor vectors that correctly encode their semantics. Such generated descriptors are usually based on histograms of gradients, directions of border orientations, or pixel intensities. For example, using the pixel intensity, we have the BRIEF [4] and FREAK [1] that build the feature/descriptor vectors from the relative intensity of pairs of pixels within the keypoint neighborhood.

Descriptors based on gradients have been more used once they present greater efficiency with lighting variation, resizing, and orientation [2]. In SIFT, for instance, the vectors are constructed within 16 subareas around the keypoint. For each subarea, a histogram of the gradient flow is computed along eight directions. Then, by concatenating the histograms of each subarea, a final feature/descriptor of 128 dimensions is created.

2.2   Bag of Visual Words (BoVW)

The main idea of BoVW is to create new representations of images as histograms. These histograms are relative to the number of occurrences of specific features/descriptor referred to as visual words. To build these histograms, the following steps are necessary: *i)* the features/descriptors of a subset of the data are grouped using some clustering algorithm like K-Means [7], the centroids $\Omega = \{\omega_1, \omega_2, \cdots, \omega_n\}$ resulting from this grouping are then called visual words; *ii)* given the visual dictionary Ω, all features/descriptors extracted within a new image are associated with the visual word closest to them; *iii)* finally, the histogram that will describe this image is generated by computing the number of occurrences of each word in the image. These steps are summarized in Fig. 1.

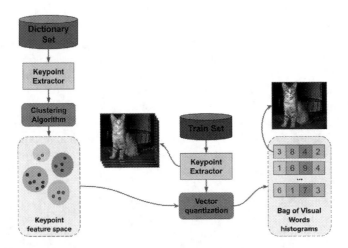

Fig. 1. The Bag of Visual Words (BoVW) working diagram. From a dataset partition (referred to as Dictionary Set), keypoints are localized within all images and their feature/descriptors are extracted. A new vector space of feature/descriptors is then created. By grouping the feature/descriptors using a clustering algorithm, a set of *visual words* $\Omega = \{\omega_1, \omega_2, \cdots, \omega_n\}$ is created in the keypoint feature/descriptors space. Given a new image **x** from the Train Set partition, image keypoints are localized and their feature/descriptors are extracted. Finally, in a vector quantization step, a frequency histogram compute how many keypoints of **x** falls into each word of Ω.

3 Methodology

The proposed Class Activation Mapping (CAM) technique for visualizing significant regions of the image that support the current BoVW prediciton can be divided into three steps: *(i)* generating a correlation matrix between words $\omega_k, 1 \leq k \leq K$ (for K visual words) and labels $c_j, 1 \leq j \leq J$ (for J classes), *(ii)* generating a visual heatmap for highlighting the words along the image domain, and *(iii)* post-processing the BoVW-CAM visualization. These steps are graphically represented in Fig. 2.

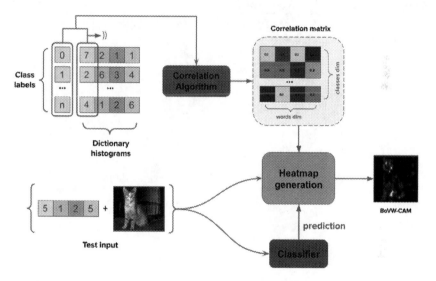

Fig. 2. The BoVW-CAM working diagram. The correlation between each visual word $\omega_k, 1 \leq k \leq K$ (for K visual words) from the dictionary Ω and the classes $c_j, 1 \leq j \leq J$ (for J classes) in the dataset are calculated to generate a $J \times K$ correlation matrix. Finally, given a new test input composed by image, keypoint, BoVW histogram, and class predicted, each keypoint location in the image domain is highlighted according the correlation of its closest visual word and the predicted class to generate a visual explanation accordingly to the BoVW-CAM.

In the first step, using the feature/descriptors ω_k that compose the dictionary Ω of visual words, correlation coefficients between the visual words $\omega_k, 1 \leq k \leq K$ and each problem class $c_j, 1 \leq j \leq J$ are calculated using the Spearman's rank correlation coefficient algorithm [23]. Therefore, a correlation matrix is generated where each column represents a dictionary word ω_k, and each line represents a classification label c_j.

In the second step, an image heatmap is generated from *(a)* an input image, *(b)* its BoVW histogram, *(c)* its keypoints, and *(d)* the predicted label. Then, each keypoint location in the image domain is highlighted according the correlation of its closest visual word and the predicted class to generate a visualization of the most important keypoints.

Finally, in the third step, operations are applied to improve the previous visualization as a heatmap (Fig. 3). First, a MaxPooling2D is used to facilitate the visual identification of image regions densely occupied by keypoints, followed by Gaussian Blur to attenuate the gray value variations to induce a smooth heatmap. Since the MaxPooling2D is an operation that reduces the input dimension, upsampling the image back to the initial size is necessary. Then, we then have the final BoVW-CAM view relative to the target class. The whole method can be seen in details in the Algorithm 1.

Algorithm 1: The BoVW-CAM method

Input: $dict\_hists, class\_labels, kp\_list\_test, img\_test, pred\_test$
Output: $feature\_map$
$corr\_matrix \leftarrow []$
for $each\ label \in class\_labels$ **do**
   $line \leftarrow []$
   for $each\ column \in dict\_hists$ **do**
      $line.add(corr(column, label))$
   end
   $corr\_matrix.add(line)$
end
$feature\_map \leftarrow zeros(img\_test.width, img\_test.height)$
for $each\ kp \in kp\_list\_test$ **do**
   $feature\_map[kp.X][kp.Y] \leftarrow corr\_matrix[pred\_test][kp.Cluster]$
end
$feature\_map \leftarrow max\_pooling(feature\_map)$
$feature\_map \leftarrow gaussian\_blur(feature\_map)$
$feature\_map \leftarrow resize(feature\_map, img\_test.width, img\_test.height)$

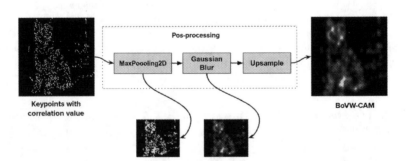

Fig. 3. Scheme for post-processing the visualization of the most important keypoints for generating thee final BoVW-CAM heatmap. The input image goes through a Max-Pooling2D to facilitate the visual identification of image regions densely occupied by keypoints, after that a Gaussian Blur is used to smooth the image gray values to create a smooth heatmap, and finally the image is upsampled to its original size.

4   Experiments

We designed experiments for comparing the most important image regions for classification via Bag of Visual Words and Convolutional Neural Networks (CNNs). To the best of our knowledge, this visual comparison in the image domain is unprecedented in the state-of-the-art.

For the experiments, we used the "Cats vs. Dogs"[1] dataset, which is a standard benchmark for binary image classification. In total, the set is composed of 12,500 images for each class.

4.1   Experimental Parameters

We used SIFT as keypoint extractor, the classifier used with the BoVW was the SVM, and the clustering algorithm was the K-Means. Finally, we used 256 words to construct the dictionary. With respect to the CNN architecture, we used three convolutional layers followed by two fully connected layers. The ReLU activation function was employed in all the layers except for the last one which was activated by Sigmoid. The evaluated architecture can be seen in Fig. 4. The optimization technique was the RMSProp, the loss function was Binary Crossentropy, the learning rate was 0.001, and the training lasted for 20 epochs.

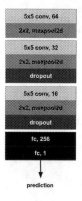

Fig. 4. CNN architecture used in this work.

The database was divided following two distinct approaches: for training the CNN, 70% of the data were used. For training the BoVW, the previous training partition was divided into two folds of the same size, one for building the dictionary and another for training the classifier. The other partitions in both approaches were made in the same proportion, 10% for validation and 20% for testing.

---

5   Results

5.1   Visualization

We generated visual explanations for classifications accordingly the learned features via Grad-CAM [21] and the handcrafted features via the proposed BoVW-CAM in Figs. 5 and 6. It is clear that the two approaches focus on different aspects of the images; the BoVW method seems to cover a larger area of the classified object, while CNN focuses on fewer aspects of the image.

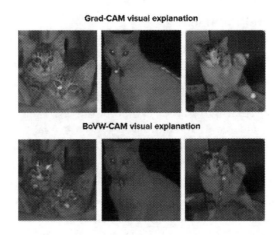

Fig. 5. Visualization for cat class with Grad-CAM and BoVW-CAM methods.

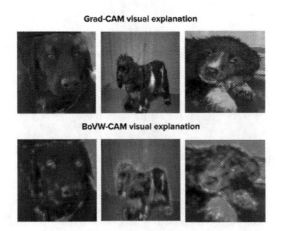

Fig. 6. Visualization for dog class with Grad-CAM and BoVW-CAM methods.

5.2   Venn Diagram

It is also possible to reinforce the hypothesis that learned and handcrafted features are focused on different aspects of the evaluated images by building a Venn Diagram of their predictions. In Fig. 7 we can see that 66.45% of the test set are corrected classified by both methods and the CNN classifies correctly more than BoVW. However, a significant amount of images (523) are misclassified by the CNN while corrected classified by the BoVW. This strengthens the fact that it is not so straightforward that Deep Learning methods can totally replace classical methods based on handcrafted features.

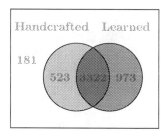

Fig. 7. Number of samples corrected classified by the handcrafted and learned features.

5.3   Dice Score

To measure how big is the difference in the image focus between BoVW and CNN, we transformed the visual explanations of Grad-CAM and BoVW-CAM into binary images for the entire test set for calculating the Dice Score [6] between them. As a result, an average of 0.359 with a standard deviation of 0.138 was obtained. This result confirms that there is a high divergence between the aspects observed by handcrafted and learned features.

6   Conclusion

Based on classification accuracy rates, previous works have suggested that there is a divergence between the aspects that handcrafted and learned features focus on images. In this work, we developed a method capable of generating visual explanations for classification algorithms based on BoVW. Then, we could compare our results with the visual explanations generated by a Grad-CAM on a CNN. In this work, we visually compared the most relevant image regions for classifications based on handcrafted features based on keypoints and learned features. The quantitative evaluation via DICE score confirms that the pixels considered by each classification method highly diverge from each other. Furthermore, despite the Deep Learning method having achieved a higher accuracy rate, we showed a significant amount of test data corrected classified exclusively by the BoVW.

References

1. Alahi, A., Ortiz, R., Vandergheynst, P.: Freak: fast retina keypoint. In: 2012 IEEE Conference on Computer Vision and Pattern Recognition, pp. 510–517. IEEE (2012)
2. Alcantarilla, P.F., Bartoli, A., Davison, A.J.: KAZE features. In: Fitzgibbon, A., Lazebnik, S., Perona, P., Sato, Y., Schmid, C. (eds.) ECCV 2012. LNCS, vol. 7577, pp. 214–227. Springer, Heidelberg (2012). https://doi.org/10.1007/978-3-642-33783-3_16
3. Bay, H., Tuytelaars, T., Van Gool, L.: SURF: speeded up robust features. In: Leonardis, A., Bischof, H., Pinz, A. (eds.) ECCV 2006. LNCS, vol. 3951, pp. 404–417. Springer, Heidelberg (2006). https://doi.org/10.1007/11744023_32
4. Calonder, M., Lepetit, V., Strecha, C., Fua, P.: BRIEF: binary robust independent elementary features. In: Daniilidis, K., Maragos, P., Paragios, N. (eds.) ECCV 2010. LNCS, vol. 6314, pp. 778–792. Springer, Heidelberg (2010). https://doi.org/10.1007/978-3-642-15561-1_56
5. Csurka, G., Dance, C., Fan, L., Willamowski, J., Bray, C.: Visual categorization with bags of keypoints. In: Workshop on Statistical Learning in Computer Vision, ECCV, Prague, vol. 1, pp. 1–2 (2004)
6. Dice, L.R.: Measures of the amount of ecologic association between species. Ecology 26(3), 297–302 (1945)
7. Forgy, E.W.: Cluster analysis of multivariate data: efficiency versus interpretability of classifications. Biometrics 21, 768–769 (1965)
8. Garcia-Garcia, A., Orts-Escolano, S., Oprea, S., Villena-Martinez, V., Garcia-Rodriguez, J.: A review on deep learning techniques applied to semantic segmentation. arXiv preprint arXiv:1704.06857 (2017)
9. Hearst, M.A., Dumais, S.T., Osuna, E., Platt, J., Scholkopf, B.: Support vector machines. IEEE Intell. Syst. App. 13(4), 18–28 (1998)
10. LeCun, Y., Bengio, Y., Hinton, G.: Deep learning. Nature 521(7553), 436–444 (2015)
11. Leutenegger, S., Chli, M., Siegwart, R.Y.: Brisk: Binary robust invariant scalable keypoints. In: 2011 International Conference on Computer Vision, pp. 2548–2555. IEEE (2011)
12. Lin, W., Hasenstab, K., Moura Cunha, G., Schwartzman, A.: Comparison of hand-crafted features and convolutional neural networks for liver MR image adequacy assessment. Sci. Rep. 10(1), 1–11 (2020)
13. Lipton, Z.C.: The mythos of model interpretability: in machine learning, the concept of interpretability is both important and slippery. Queue 16(3), 31–57 (2018)
14. Lowe, D.G.: Distinctive image features from scale-invariant keypoints. Int. J. Comput. Vision 60(2), 91–110 (2004)
15. Lu, D., Weng, Q.: A survey of image classification methods and techniques for improving classification performance. Int. J. Remote Sens. 28(5), 823–870 (2007)
16. Myles, A.J., Feudale, R.N., Liu, Y., Woody, N.A., Brown, S.D.: An introduction to decision tree modeling. J. Chemom. J. Chemom. Soc. 18(6), 275–285 (2004)
17. Nanni, L., Ghidoni, S., Brahnam, S.: Handcrafted vs non-handcrafted features for computer vision classification. Pattern Recogn. 71, 158–172 (2017)
18. Rosten, E., Drummond, T.: Machine learning for high-speed corner detection. In: Leonardis, A., Bischof, H., Pinz, A. (eds.) ECCV 2006. LNCS, vol. 3951, pp. 430–443. Springer, Heidelberg (2006). https://doi.org/10.1007/11744023_34

19. Rublee, E., Rabaud, V., Konolige, K., Bradski, G.: ORB: an efficient alternative to sift or surf. In: 2011 International Conference on Computer Vision, pp. 2564–2571. IEEE (2011)
20. Saba, T.: Computer vision for microscopic skin cancer diagnosis using handcrafted and non-handcrafted features. Microsc. Res. Tech. **84**(6), 1272–1283 (2021)
21. Selvaraju, R.R., Cogswell, M., Das, A., Vedantam, R., Parikh, D., Batra, D.: Grad-CAM: visual explanations from deep networks via gradient-based localization. In: Proceedings of the IEEE International Conference on Computer Vision, pp. 618–626 (2017)
22. da Silva, A.V.B., Pereira, L.F.A.: Handcrafted vs. learned features for automatically detecting violence in surveillance footage. In: Anais do XLIX Seminário Integrado de Software e Hardware, pp. 82–91. SBC (2022)
23. Zar, J.H.: Spearman rank correlation. Encyclop. Biostatist. **7**, 1–7 (2005)
24. Zhou, B., Khosla, A., Lapedriza, A., Oliva, A., Torralba, A.: Learning deep features for discriminative localization. In: Proceedings of the IEEE Conference on Computer Vision and Pattern Recognition, pp. 2921–2929 (2016)
25. Zou, Z., Shi, Z., Guo, Y., Ye, J.: Object detection in 20 years: a survey. arXiv preprint arXiv:1905.05055 (2019)

Using BERT to Predict the Brazilian Stock Market

Arthur Emanuel de Oliveira Carosia[1,2(✉)], Ana Estela Antunes da Silva[2], and Guilherme Palermo Coelho[2]

[1] Federal Institute of Education, Science and Technology of São Paulo (IFSP),
São João da Boa Vista, Brazil
arthuremanuel.carosia@ifsp.edu.br
[2] School of Technology (FT), University of Campinas (Unicamp), Limeira, Brazil
{aeasilva,gpcoelho}unicamp.br

Abstract. Stock market prediction considering financial news is still an open challenge in the literature. Generally, related works consider the sentiment present in news with the following approaches: (1) lexicons; or (2) machine learning algorithms. However, both strategies are subject to errors introduced by human factors. While the lexical approach needs a specific dictionary for the financial domain, algorithms based on machine learning need a database manually labeled by experts. In this sense, this work aims to propose an approach to forecast the Brazilian stock market using news headlines preprocessed through BERT (Bidirectional Encoders Representations from Transformers), stock prices, technical indicators, and a Multilayer Perceptron neural network. Thus, the prediction is carried out directly with the embeddings of the financial news alongside technical analysis indicators and the financial time series, avoiding human intervention in the process. Our results are promising, with the developed approach overcoming the baselines Buy & Hold and Moving Average Crossover, considering both profitability and risk during the investment process.

Keywords: BERT · Stock market prediction · Artificial neural networks

1 Introduction

Investors have long adopted the Efficient Market Hypothesis (EMH) [18], which states that, in an efficient market, the current price of a given stock fully reflects the available information. Thus, past information would already be incorporated into the stock price and future information is immediately incorporated into the future values, resulting in an impossibility of predicting the next movement of the stock market.

On the other hand, there are empirical studies in the literature showing that the stock market can be, at least, partially predicted [2,13]. In fact, the Dow Theory [26] added more information to the stock market field, showing that the

J. C. Xavier-Junior and R. A. Rios (Eds.): BRACIS 2022, LNAI 13654, pp. 56–70, 2022.
https://doi.org/10.1007/978-3-031-21689-3_5

prices of a given asset in the stock market follow trends of different periods. Furthermore, the Adaptive Market Hypothesis (AMH) [17], which combines behavioral economics and psychology, showed that it is possible to exploit weaknesses in the market efficiency to obtain positive returns on a given stock portfolio.

Thus, two different schools of thought about the stock market emerged: Technical Analysis and Fundamental Analysis. Technical Analysis tries to predict the future price of a given asset in the stock market through its past prices and technical indicators. On the other hand, Fundamental Analysis uses financial and macroeconomic factors to decide the investment operation that should be done with a given asset [1, 14].

Furthermore, Fundamental Analysis data are often unstructured (i.e., textual) and it is a challenge to process them computationally. However, recently, Artificial Neural Networks (ANNs), especially deep ANNs, have received considerable attention in applications of Natural Language Processing (NLP). These networks have presented state-of-the-art results in NLP tasks, such as in Sentiment Analysis [22], in which the polarity (positive or negative) of a given document is defined. In addition, another important development in the area occurred in the textual representation of documents for NLP tasks, especially considering the BERT (Bidirectional Encoder Representation from Transformers) model, which was able to achieve state-of-the-art results [7].

Generally, in the literature, studies try to predict the stock market by considering one of the following data sources: (1) historical stock values and their indicators; and (2) news or social network data. However, the ideal way to put these information together for a more accurate prediction model is still an open research topic [16, 24].

While the works of the first category presented above have structured and mathematically defined data, such as the technical indicators, works that incorporate textual data generally use the sentiments associated with a given document to predict the market. These sentiments are typically determined through one of the following approaches: (1) lexical, which usually achieves low accuracy and is dependent on the creation of dictionaries, specialized in each application domain [12]; and (2) machine learning, which requires the creation of a previously labeled database to train a classifier model [30]. Still, sentiments can be subjective to the investor, and they introduce an extra step in the forecasting process that is subject to errors associated with the sentiment classifier model.

Therefore, this work aims to propose an approach to predict the Brazilian stock market incorporating the title of financial news using the BERT model, thus eliminating the usually performed Sentiment Analysis step. Besides, alongside the news, this work also considers the following data: historical stock prices and technical indicators. All the data are used as input to a Multilayer Perceptron neural network, as in [10, 27]. It's worth highlighting that the use of both news and stock prices combines elements of Technical and Fundamental Analysis into a single prediction model.

Experiments were made with news from the Brazilian stock market, related to the Ibovespa index, published from January 2013 to July 2017. Besides, investment simulations considering a period of 6 months were also made, and the proposed model was compared with the Buy & Hold and Moving Averages Crossover baselines. The results showed that the proposed approach obtained a higher return of investment and presented lower risk in the considered period.

This work is organized as follows. Section 2 covers the theoretical and practical aspects of BERT, in addition to the related works. In Sect. 3, we discuss the methodology of this work. Next, in Sect. 4, we present and discuss the results of the experiments considering the Brazilian stock market. Finally, Sect. 5 presents the conclusions and provides suggestions for future work.

2   Theoretical Foundation

The use of the knowledge available on the World Wide Web through Natural Language Processing (NLP) techniques has increased dramatically in the last decade. Among its areas of application, the stock market has become very popular, whether considering social networks, news sites, or other sources of information [4,10,16,20].

Thus, this work presents a proposal to predict the Brazilian stock market through the use of the BERT model applied to financial news, alongside technical indicators and historical stock prices. This section, contains the theoretical foundation necessary for the development of this work. Section 2.1 presents information about the BERT model, while Sect. 2.2 presents the related studies and also highlights the main contributions of this work.

2.1   BERT

The BERT model (Bidirectional Encoder Representation from Transformers) [7], illustrated in Fig. 1, consists of a Natural Language Processing (NLP) model to generate word representations (embeddings), based on transformer encoder. The Transformer architecture is a sequence-to-sequence architecture based on attention mechanisms [29] considering both the encoder and the decoder. Since BERT is not a sequence-to-sequence model, its architecture ignores the decoder network of the Transformer and uses only the transformer encoder [27]. The original BERT model was trained bidirectionally with a large corpus of unlabeled text, including Wikipedia. The bidirectional process allows the model to consider contexts in a sentence. This model represents one of the most successful results in machine learning tasks that use textual data.

In Fig. 1, it is possible to observe that, for each word in a sentence provided to the input layer of the model, is generated its vectorial representation in the output layer. Also, the model contains a series of layers of stacked encoders. Each encoder performs calculations using the attention mechanism through the word representation generated in the previous layer, and transfers it to the next encoder layer. At the beginning of each input sentence an artificial token, namely [CLS], is added. The final vector representation that corresponds to the token [CLS] summarizes the sentence provided to BERT, shown as the blue vector in Fig. 1. This representation is a bundled output that encodes the semantics of the

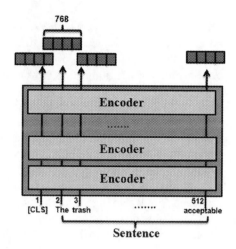

Fig. 1. Representation of the BERT model. The inputs are given at the bottom (each word to be processed and the [CLS] token). The vectorial representation of each input is given at the top, in blue. Adapted from [8]. (Color figure online)

entire input sentence and is usually used for classification tasks. Still, in Fig. 1, it is possible to verify that there is a vectorial output for each input word. This representation can capture the context of each word in the sentence as a whole, being one of the advantages of the BERT model compared to previous models in the literature, such as Word2Vec and FastText [3, 6].

Some works also fine-tune the BERT model to perform text classification considering the token [CLS]. The vectorial representation of this token is used as input to the classification layer, which is generally a common softmax layer.

In addition, BERT presents two pre-trained models based on their processing complexity: BERT-base and BERT-large [7]. The BERT-base model has the following parameters: 12 layers of stacked encoders and a vector representation of 768 dimensions. On the other hand, the BERT-large model features 24 stacked encoders and 1024-dimensional vectors. This work, as in [8], uses: (1) the BERT-base version, taking into account its better efficiency in text processing; and (2) the [CLS] token to represent a sentence encoded by BERT.

In this context, BERT is a suitable tool to extract the semantic resources of news through its bundled output (i.e., the [CLS] token), as well as to be incorporated into the stock market prediction model proposed in this work.

2.2   Related Work

The use of textual data to predict the stock market is a topic of great interest in the literature. The pioneer work of Bollen et al. [4] used the social network Twitter to correlate and predict the stock market. Recent works use sentiment present in news alongside technical indicators to forecast the stock market, as in [24], in which Sentiment Analysis was performed with a financial dictionary and the experiments showed that news improve the stock market prediction. The work [16] presented a stock market forecasting strategy with a Long Short-Term Memory (LSTM) neural network with Sentiment Analysis also applied to financial news through a financial dictionary. However, [16] did not present investment simulations.

Although, the use of the BERT model applied to the financial market domain is recent in the literature, there are some promising works in this context. The most relevant studies among those related to this work are listed below.

The work [27] used the BERT model to perform news Sentiment Analysis to provide information for decision-making in the stock market. The authors performed a manual labeling process of 582 news, and the BERT model led to a 72.5% F-score in the sentiment analysis stage. Furthermore, the results showed that in 69% of the periods between the opening and closing of the stock market, the news' sentiment was consistent with the variation of the Dow Jones Industrial Index (DJI).

In [5], the authors proposed an LSTM neural network to forecast the Thai stock market using inputs from technical indicators and textual information from various online sources. To represent the textual information, the authors used BERT and a hierarchical ANN. The results showed that the use of news can increase up to 6.9% the accuracy of forecasting the market movement.

The work [19] presents a stock trading strategy with ensembles and the use of sentiments, determined through BERT. The results showed that the return of investment can reach up to 21%, surpassing the baselines, considering the CSI 300 index.

Besides, [15] developed Sentiment Analysis according to the point of view of the stock market investor using the BERT model. The textual data were obtained from the Eastern Stock Exchange. The work also investigated the relationship between investor sentiment and stock earnings. The results showed that the investor sentiment has a significant impact on stock returns.

In [21], the authors presented the use of sentiment analysis in economic news using BERT and the baselines VADER, TextBlob, and a Recurrent Neural Network (RNN). The authors used data from Amazon, AMD, Facebook, and Google in their experiments. The results showed that both BERT and the RNN outperformed the baseline models.

The work [8] showed the use of news published on Twitter, using the BERT model, to feed an LSTM neural network to predict the stock market, called BERT-LSTM (BELT). The experiments were performed considering seven stocks, including the Dow Jones Industrial Average. The results showed that BELT is able to predict stock prices more accurately using news information than if only historical prices were used.

Finally, [25] presented an LSTM model to predict the Thai Futures Exchange (TFEX) using Thai economic news headlines, represented with the BERT model. Experimental results showed that the use of news can improve the forecasting performance, outperforming baselines.

The presented review shows that most works still focus on the sentiment analysis stage to predict the stock market using BERT. Besides, the use of BERT in the stock market is recent, and there is still room for improvements. In this sense, the main contributions of this work are: (1) the use of the textual representation (embeddings) obtained with the BERT model as input for an ANN, avoiding the commonly performed Sentiment Analysis step, an error-prone stage since it needs human intervention to manually label the training database; (2) the development of an investment simulation to ensure that the use of BERT in the stock market prediction process can be profitable; (3) the use of the Brazilian stock market as a case study, since most publications are focused on the North American and Asian markets, according to [14,22]; and (4) a new approach to combine news, technical indicators, and stock prices to stock price prediction.

3   Methodology

The methodology proposed in this work, which aims to predict the Brazilian stock market incorporating the BERT model, technical indicators, and historical stock prices, is presented in Fig. 2. This methodology has the following steps:

– **News Processing:** the news used in this work were downloaded from the most relevant Brazilian newspapers and stored locally. Then, the downloaded news were used as input for the BERT model, which generates their word representations. This task is detailed in Sect. 3.1.
– **Stock Price Processing:** the historical stock prices considered in this work were downloaded and stored locally. Then, the technical indicators were calculated. This task is detailed in Sect. 3.2.
– **Artificial Neural Network**: both the results of the News and Stock Price Processing steps are used as input to train an ANN, which aims to predict future stock prices. This task is detailed in Sect. 3.3.
– **Evaluation:** the results of the ANN predictions from the previous task were evaluated in this work considering both typical Machine Learning metrics and the outcomes of an investment simulation. This task is detailed in Sect. 3.4.

3.1   News Processing

Once downloaded, the first step to process the news headlines consists of the removal of symbols, links, and special characters. Second, the text resulting from the previous step is used to generate vectorial representations using the BERT model. This step generates, as output, a representation, called [CLS], which comprises the information of each news headlines and can be used directly for classification purposes.

Considering that this stage was developed for the Portuguese language, we used the adaptation of BERT to Portuguese, called BERTimbau [28]. This approach led to better results in relation to NLP tasks in Portuguese than the

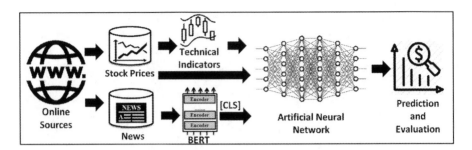

Fig. 2. Representation of the proposed methodology: news and historical stock prices are used as data sources for the ANN's predictions.

multilingual version of BERT. In this work, we use the BASE version of BERT-timbau[1].

Finally, we need to take into account the average information contained in the daily news, since several news about the same asset can be published throughout the day. Therefore, the average vector of daily news representations, taking into account the [CLS] token, is calculated considering all the news published in a day of a given stock. This vector is then used as inputs to the ANN, alongside the historical stock prices and technical indicators, detailed in the next section.

3.2 Stock Price Processing

The historical stock prices consist of the following daily elements: market opening value, high, low, and closing value, in addition to the volume of transactions. The historical stock prices are also used to calculate technical indicators (i.e. indicators often associated with Technical Analysis), which are mathematical indicators calculated by investors in order to comprehend the market behavior.

In this work, besides the news and historical stock values, we also consider several commonly used technical indicators: (1) Moving Averages (MA), with 10, 20, and 30-day periods; (2) Moving Average Convergence and Divergence (MACD), with 12 and 26-day periods for each moving average and a signal moving average considering a 9-day period; (3) Relative Strength Index (RSI), with 6, 12, and 24-day periods; (4) Money Flow Index (MFI) with 14-day period; (5) Bollinger Bands (BB); and (6) On Balance Volume (OBV), which does not need any additional parameters. These indicators were configured by parameters that reflect market trends or fluctuations, according to [1, 16].

3.3 Artificial Neural Network

The prediction step uses a Multilayer Perceptron (MLP) neural network model as in [24]. As presented in [22], ANNs are receiving increasing attention in the literature, due to their ability to outperform classical machine learning models.

---

[1] https://github.com/neuralmind-ai/portuguese-bert.

Also, the same authors indicate that the Multilayer Perceptron is one of the most used ANNs in the literature, including the financial domain, due to its ability to generalize and adapt to different areas of knowledge [11]. The MLP is composed of connected units called artificial neurons, which simulate the behavior of biological neurons. Each layer of an MLP network contains one or more artificial neurons, called *Perceptrons*. Each Perceptron receives the input signals, applies the weights and bias, and, finally, propagates its result to the next layer through an activation function, until the output layer is reached.

In this work, the MLP receives as input the following attributes: (1) historical stock prices, with opening, low, high and closing values alongside with the volume of transactions (totalizing 5 attributes); (2) technical indicators (totalizing 10 attributes); (3) the average [CLS] vector from the daily news (totalizing 768 attributes). The attribute vectors pass through a Min-Max normalization process, to limit the attributes in the interval [0, 1].

The MLP output is the one-day ahead return of the closing price. This value is determined by subtracting the closing price of the current day (d) from the closing price of the next day $(d + 1)$.

The training process of the ANN was performed using the Mean Squared Error (MSE), commonly used for regression tasks [20]. The optimization of the ANN parameters was performed with the *Adam* algorithm, with learning rate defined as 0.001, according to [24]. The activation function was defined as ReLu, since it is simple to calculate and allows faster training convergence [30].

3.4   Evaluation

The evaluation process of the proposed methodology was divided into two stages, considering the approach presented by [24]. First, we evaluate Machine Learning quality metrics, by measuring the model training error, and then we perform an investment simulation to evaluate the quality of the predictions.

To evaluate the investment results, the following financial metrics were used: Return on Investment (ROI), Sharpe Ratio (SR), and Maximum Drawdown (MDD) [24]. The ROI represents the final result of an investment considering a given amount of money at the beginning of the period. The SR represents the risk of the investment, calculated through the average return (R) minus the risk-free rate (r), divided by the volatility or standard deviation of the stock prices in a given period. Finally, the MDD measure is an indicator of the stock's downside risk over a specified period, calculated considering the asset's maximum possible loss from a maximum value to a minimum.

The investment strategy used in this work is defined as follows. First, the ANN predicts the next day's return $(d+1)$. If the predicted value is positive and the investor does not own the stock, a *buy* operation is made. If the investor owns the stock, he/she must keep the current (*bought*) position. If the predicted value is negative, and the investor owns the stock, a *sell* operation is processed. If the investor does not own the asset, he/she must keep the current (*sold*) position.

The investment results obtained by the proposed methodology were compared with two baselines. The first baseline, Buy & Hold, consists of buying an asset at the beginning and selling it in the end of the considered period. The second baseline, Moving Average Crossover, is a commonly used investment strategy that considers two moving averages, long-term (34-day periods) and short-term (17-day periods), to operate the investment strategy [9]. The crossing of each of the moving averages indicates the current market trend. Thus, the strategy addresses that if the short-term moving average exceeds the long-term moving average, there is an indication of an uptrend, which is a *buy* signal to the investor. Otherwise, that is, if the long-term moving average is above the short-term moving average, there is a downtrend, which is a *sell* signal to the investor.

4   Results

This section presents the results of the experiments performed in this work, and is organized as follows: (1) details of the dataset used are presented in Sect. 4.1; (2) evaluation of the proposed ANN model considering Machine Learning metrics are presented in Sect. 4.2; and (3) evaluation of the selected model considering financial metrics is given in Sect. 4.3.

4.1   Database

All data used in this work were collected through scripts developed in Python, considering the period from January 2013 to July 2017. In the experiments, we used historical data and news from the main index of the Brazilian stock exchange, Ibovespa. Unlabeled news were collected from the most significant online Brazilian newspapers, according to the *Associação Nacional de Jornais* (National Association of Newspapers)[2]: G1, Estadão, and Folha de São Paulo. The news download process simulated access to the search pages of each web portal, looking for the following terms: *bovespa*, *ibovespa*, and *bolsa de valores*. The resulting news headlines were stored in textual format files. The historical stock prices of the Ibovespa index were obtained through *Yahoo Finance*[3] and stored locally, in a CSV (*Comma-separated values*) file.

4.2   ANN's Parameters

As previously discussed, the MLP adopted here was configured to receive as input the outcomes of the BERT model, historical stock prices, and technical indicators. Thus, the first step is to evaluate which parameters are most suitable for the ANN, i.e., the parameters that lead to the best prediction. For this, we use a grid-search method, together with an increasing window cross-validation with 3 steps, as presented in [16,24], to find the ideal values among the following ANN parameters:

---

[2] https://www.anj.org.br/.
[3] https://finance.yahoo.com/.

1. Number of hidden layers: 1, 2, 3, and 4;
2. Number of neurons per layer: 10, 25, and 50;
3. Number of epochs: 250 and 500.

To train the ANN, the dataset was divided into different parts. The first one, from January 2013 to December 2016, is the training set; the second, from January 2017 to July 2017, is the test set, never used during the training stage. This stage of the work was developed in Python, together with the libraries *Numpy*, *Scikit-Learn* and *Pandas*.

Table 1 presents the results obtained with the MLP neural network configured with each combination of parameters considering the cross-validation process applied to the training set. The metric considered in this case is the MSE.

The parameter selection results show that an MLP neural network with only 1 hidden layer, 10 neurons, trained with 250 epochs is enough to obtain the lowest average and standard deviation of the MSE. This configuration, therefore, was used in the remaining experiments of this work.

Table 1. Results obtained by the MLP for each combination of parameters. Average and Standard Deviation of the MSE considering the cross-validation process.

Layers	Neurons	Epochs	Average MSE	Standard deviation
1	10	250	**0.1346**	**0.0372**
		500	0.2284	0.0958
	25	250	0.2560	0.0599
		500	0.3021	0.1098
	50	250	0.2230	0.0475
		500	0.3036	0.1086
2	10	250	0.1747	0.0712
		500	0.3482	0.2323
	25	250	0.5177	0.4101
		500	0.3291	0.0346
	50	250	0.4836	0.1068
		500	0.3840	0.1043
3	10	250	0.4727	0.2100
		500	0.1989	0.2089
	25	250	0.6426	0.0866
		500	0.3643	0.1616
	50	250	0.6549	0.2934
		500	1.2941	0.7242
4	10	250	0.1907	0.0486
		500	0.3082	0.1284
	25	250	0.5514	0.1590
		500	0.6155	0.0594
	50	250	0.7621	0.4081
		500	0.7910	0.5764

Table 2. MSE of the best MLP obtained through grid search, applied to the test set.

Layers	Neurons	Epochs	MSE score
1	10	250	0.4602

Table 2 presents the MSE of the previously selected MLP applied to the test set, which was not considered during the training period.

4.3   Investment Simulation

The forecasts obtained with the previously built MLP was used for an investment simulation considering an initial capital of R$100,000.00 and the Ibovespa index forecasts in the period from January to July 2017 (test set). In the experiments, it was also considered an average cost of R$ 2.50 in each buy or sell operation, associated with taxes and brokerage. Table 3 presents the monthly results of

Table 3. Investment simulation results considering an initial value of R$100,000.00. Monthly and average results of the methodology proposed in this work (ML Strat), together with the baselines Buy & Hold (BuyHold) and Moving Average Crossover (Mov Avg) are shown.

Period	Strategy	Final value	Maximum drawdown	Sharpe ratio
01-01-2017 to 01-02-2017	ML Strat	R$ 103,019.00	0.003	0.294
	BuyHold	R$ 105,040.00	1.773	0.316
	Mov Avg	R$ 100,000.00	0.000	0.000
01-01-2017 to 01-03-2017	ML Strat	R$ 104,522.00	0.250	0.275
	BuyHold	R$ 107,031.00	2.184	0.249
	Mov Avg	R$ 98,906.00	2.359	−0.115
01-01-2017 to 01-04-2017	ML Strat	R$ 104,501.00	2.645	0.128
	BuyHold	R$ 105,353.00	5.549	0.112
	Mov Avg	R$ 97,128.00	4.780	−0.104
01-01-2017 to 01-05-2017	ML Strat	R$ 105,393.00	2.645	0.118
	BuyHold	R$ 105,772.00	5.689	0.095
	Mov Avg	R$ 97,128.00	4.780	−0.093
01-01-2017 to 01-06-2017	ML Strat	R$ 105,079.00	2.645	0.083
	BuyHold	R$ 103,080.00	6.813	0.032
	Mov Avg	R$ 94,134.00	8.170	−0.078
01-01-2017 to 01-07-2017	ML Strat	R$ 105,474.00	3.106	0.075
	BuyHold	R$ 103,269.00	7.576	0.030
	Mov Avg	R$ 93,712.00	8.170	−0.077
	ML Strat	R$ 104,664.67	1.88	0.16
Average	BuyHold	R$ 104,924.17	4.93	0.14
	Mov Avg	R$ 96,834.67	4.71	−0.08

this simulation, obtained with the aid of the *Backtrader*[4] library, considering both the model proposed in this work (ML Strat), Buy & Hold (BuyHold), and Moving Average Crossover (Mov Avg).

The simulation results show that, despite the higher monthly average of the Buy & Hold strategy during the 6 months, the technique proposed in this work was capable of obtaining the highest final return during the considered months. In addition, the proposed strategy (ML Strat) obtained the lowest MDD value, both at the end of the considered months and on average. The same happens for the SR metric, where ML Strat presented the highest value in both cases, showing that the proposed methodology also reduces the risk in the considered investment period.

Figures 3, 4 and 5 present the monthly results for each strategy considering the metrics Return, MDD and SR. It is possible to observe that, initially, the Buy & Hold technique presents better performance, but, at the end of the experiment, it is surpassed by the methodology proposed in this work.

Finally, our experiments suggest that there is significant information present in news, indicating that its contents influence the stock market movement and that they can improve the market forecasting process when used alongside with historical stock prices and technical indicators, corroborating related works on this matter [16, 20, 24].

Thus, it is possible to observe that in the proposed strategy, the use of news not only resulted in higher investment return but also in lower investment risk. Our results also indicate that it is highly recommended that investors consider news in their investment strategies. Besides, before performing an investment, we believe that the investor must consider both the return of each approach as well as the risk, observed with the Maximum Drawdown and the Sharpe Ratio metrics.

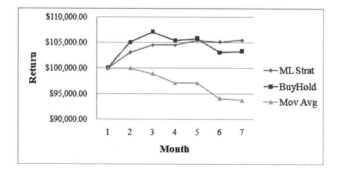

Fig. 3. Monthly Return of investment. Results of the methodology proposed in this work (ML Strat), together with the baselines Buy & Hold (BuyHold) and Moving Average Crossover (Mov Avg) are shown.

---

[4] https://backtrader.com/.

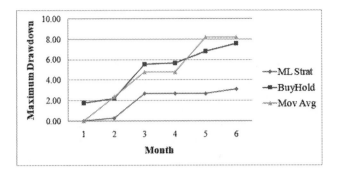

Fig. 4. Monthly Maximum Drawdown. Results of the methodology proposed in this work (ML Strat), together with the baselines Buy & Hold (BuyHold) and Moving Average Crossover (Mov Avg) are shown.

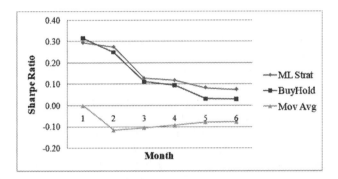

Fig. 5. Monthly Sharpe Ratio. Results of the methodology proposed in this work (ML Strat), together with the baselines Buy & Hold (BuyHold) and Moving Average Crossover (Mov Avg) are shown.

5   Conclusion

This work presented an approach to predict the Brazilian stock market incorporating news, historical stock prices, and technical indicators. Our results showed that incorporating news encoded by BERT into stock market prediction models helps to increase the return of investment as well as to reduce risk.

Furthermore, the main contribution of this work is the use of BERT to extract representations of news, thus avoiding human intervention in the process, considering both the creation of a lexicon and the manual labeling of a training database. Considering works that require lexicons, such lexicons must be built for a specific domain. Besides, the use of BERT to generate representations of news allows the removal of the Sentiment Analysis stage, generally adopted in related works. The process of creating a database labeled by experts (in case of Machine Learning algorithms) requires consensus between different experts, resulting in a time-consuming and costly process.

Finally, our case study of the Brazilian stock market contributes to the lack of papers considering this particular market. The Portuguese language lacks Natural Language Processing resources [23], since the most of the published papers in this area of knowledge focus mainly on North American and Asian markets [14,22].

We believe, therefore, that the proposal of this work can contribute to future developments in this area, mainly considering that the elimination of the Sentiment Analysis step reduces human intervention in the development of the prediction models, which may reduce the associated errors.

As future work, we intend to expand the proposed approach for other Brazilian assets and periods, such as the post pandemic period. Besides, we will also consider other ANNs' models, such as RNNs and CNNs, in order to evaluate their impact in prediction performance. Finally, we will compare our proposal with approaches that explicitly use Sentiment Analysis.

Acknowledgement. This study was financed in part by the Coordenação de Aperfeiçoamento de Pessoal de Nível Superior - Brasil (CAPES) - Finance Code 001. The authors would also like to thank Instituto Federal de São Paulo (IFSP) - for the financial support.

References

1. Achelis, S.B.: Technical Analysis from A to Z. McGraw Hill, New York (2001)
2. Atsalakis, G.S., Valavanis, K.P.: Surveying stock market forecasting techniques-Part II: soft computing methods. Expert Syst. Appl. 5932–5941 (2009)
3. Bojanowski, P., Grave, E., Joulin, A., Mikolov, T.: Enriching word vectors with subword information. Trans. Assoc. Comput. Linguist. 135–146 (2017)
4. Bollen, J., Mao, H., Zeng, X.: Twitter mood predicts the stock market. J. Comput. Sci. **1**, 1–8 (2011)
5. Chiewhawan, T., Vateekul, P.: Explainable deep learning for Thai stock market prediction using textual representation and technical indicators. In: Proceedings of the 8th International Conference on Computer and Communications Management, pp. 19–23 (2020)
6. Church, K.W.: Word2vec. Nat. Lang. Eng. **23**(1), 155–162 (2017)
7. Devlin, J., Chang, M.W., Lee, K., Toutanova, K.: BERT: pre-training of deep bidirectional transformers for language understanding. arXiv preprint arXiv:1810.04805 (2018)
8. Dong, Y., Yan, D., Almudaifer, A.I., Yan, S., Jiang, Z., Zhou, Y.: Belt: a pipeline for stock price prediction using news. In: 2020 IEEE International Conference on Big Data (Big Data), pp. 1137–1146. IEEE (2020)
9. Fang, J., Qin, Y., Jacobsen, B.: Technical market indicators: an overview. J. Behav. Exp. Finance **4**, 25–56 (2014)
10. Hájek, P.: Combining bag-of-words and sentiment features of annual reports to predict abnormal stock returns. Neural Comput. Appl. (7), 343–358 (2018)
11. Haykin, S.: Neural Networks: A Comprehensive Foundation. Prentice Hall PTR, Upper Saddle River (1994)
12. Januário, B.A., Carosia, A.E.O., Silva, A.E.A., Coelho, G.P.: Sentiment analysis applied to news from the Brazilian stock market. IEEE Latin Am. Trans. **100** (2021)

13. Khadjeh Nassirtoussi, A., Aghabozorgi, S., Ying Wah, T., Ngo, D.C.L.: Text mining for market prediction: a systematic review. Expert Syst. Appl. 7653–7670 (2014)
14. Kumbure, M.M., Lohrmann, C., Luukka, P., Porras, J.: Machine learning techniques and data for stock market forecasting: a literature review. Expert Syst. Appl. 116659 (2022)
15. Li, M., Li, W., Wang, F., Jia, X., Rui, G.: Applying BERT to analyze investor sentiment in stock market. Neural Comput. Appl. **33**(10), 4663–4676 (2021)
16. Li, X., Wu, P., Wang, W.: Incorporating stock prices and news sentiments for stock market prediction: a case of Hong Kong. Inf. Process. Manag. (5), 102212 (2020)
17. Lo, A.W.: The adaptive markets hypothesis. J. Portfolio Manag. **5**, 15–29 (2004)
18. Malkiel, B.G., Fama, E.F.: Efficient capital markets: a review of theory and empirical work. J. Financ. **2**, 383–417 (1970)
19. Man, X., Lin, J., Yang, Y.: Stock-uniBERT: a news-based cost-sensitive ensemble BERT model for stock trading. In: 2020 IEEE 18th International Conference on Industrial Informatics (INDIN), vol. 1, pp. 440–445. IEEE (2020)
20. Maqsood, H., et al.: A local and global event sentiment based efficient stock exchange forecasting using deep learning. Int. J. Inf. Manag. 432–451 (2020)
21. Nemes, L., Kiss, A.: Prediction of stock values changes using sentiment analysis of stock news headlines. J. Inf. Telecommun. 1–20 (2021)
22. Ozbayoglu, A.M., Gudelek, M.U., Sezer, O.B.: Deep learning for financial applications: a survey. Appl. Soft Comput. 106384 (2020)
23. Pereira, D.A.: A survey of sentiment analysis in the Portuguese language. Artif. Intell. Rev. **2**, 1087–1115 (2021)
24. Picasso, A., Merello, S., Ma, Y., Oneto, L., Cambria, E.: Technical analysis and sentiment embeddings for market trend prediction. Expert Syst. Appl. 60–70 (2019)
25. Prachyachuwong, K., Vateekul, P.: Stock trend prediction using deep learning approach on technical indicator and industrial specific information. Information **12**(6), 250 (2021)
26. Rhea, R.: The Dow Theory: An Explanation of Its Development and An Attempt to Define Its Usefulness as an Aid in Speculation. Fraser Publishing Company, Flint Hill (1993)
27. Sousa, M.G., Sakiyama, K., de Souza Rodrigues, L., Moraes, P.H., Fernandes, E.R., Matsubara, E.T.: BERT for stock market sentiment analysis. In: 2019 IEEE 31st International Conference on Tools with Artificial Intelligence (ICTAI), pp. 1597–1601. IEEE (2019)
28. Souza, F., Nogueira, R., Lotufo, R.: BERTimbau: pretrained BERT models for Brazilian Portuguese. In: Cerri, R., Prati, R.C. (eds.) BRACIS 2020. LNCS (LNAI), vol. 12319, pp. 403–417. Springer, Cham (2020). https://doi.org/10.1007/978-3-030-61377-8_28
29. Vaswani, A., et al.: Attention is all you need. In: Advances in Neural Information Processing Systems, pp. 5998–6008 (2017)
30. Zhang, L., Wang, S., Liu, B.: Deep learning for sentiment analysis: a survey. Wiley Interdisc. Rev. Data Min. Knowl. Discov. (4), e1253 (2018)

Human Action Recognition Based on 2D Poses and Skeleton Joints

Bruno Belluzzo$^{(\boxtimes)}$ ⓘ and Aparecido Nilceu Marana ⓘ

Faculty of Sciences, UNESP - São Paulo State University, Bauru, SP, Brazil
{bruno.belluzzo,nilceu.marana}@unesp.br

Abstract. With the growing capacity of current technologies to store
and process data at extremely fast speed, video processing and its diverse
applications have been studied and several researches have emerged using
videos as objects of study. One of them is human action recognition,
which seeks to identify in a given video what actions the people present
in it are performing, whether for recreational purposes or for monitoring
public places for people's safety. Being able to extract the necessary
characteristics to perform the action classification is a complex task,
because, unlike traditional image classification problems, the recognition
of human actions requires that the solution works with spatio-temporal
characteristics, which represent a pattern of movements performed by the
person in both the spatial and temporal aspects along the frames that
make up the action. One way to generate information that describes
human movement is to identify the skeleton joints and limbs and use
them to perform the classification, and the extraction of this data can be
done by using 2D pose estimation algorithms, capable of tracking parts
of the human body and returning their coordinates. This paper proposes
a method for human action recognition that uses skeleton joints and limb
information as features and a CNN together with an LSTM network for
classification. The method was assessed on a public dataset (Weizmann
dataset) and obtained superior recognition rates when compared to other
action recognition methods of literature.

Keywords: Human action recognition · Human pose estimation ·
CNN · LSTM · 2D pose

1 Introduction

The recognition of human actions has become a research area with high demand
in the academic environment. Some challenges present in the task of recognizing
these actions are the occlusion of people that the method is tracking the action,
irregular movements, changes in the background of the image, changes in the
viewing angle, etc. [1].

These challenges end up causing current computer vision algorithms to be far
below human performance in action recognition tasks. While most of them work
very well for databases created in laboratories with controlled environments,

J. C. Xavier-Junior and R. A. Rios (Eds.): BRACIS 2022, LNAI 13654, pp. 71–83, 2022.
https://doi.org/10.1007/978-3-031-21689-3_6

the biggest difficulty is in recognizing actions in unfavorable environments in different scenarios and situations of people's daily lives [2].

Features extracted from space-time capture characteristic shapes and motions in the videos and provide scale-independent representations and other complications in the images such as background changes. Feature descriptors seek to capture shape and motion in the vicinity of selected points using image measurements such as spatial or spatiotemporal image gradients and optical flow [3].

Recently, with the emergence of new human pose estimation techniques, such as OpenPose [4] and PifPaf [5], features from the skeletons generated by these technologies have also been used for the recognition of human actions, since they can abstract information from the background of the images and preserve the privacy of those involved in the footage [6].

This article aims to propose and develop a new method for the recognition of human actions in videos based on 2D pose estimation methods and deep machine learning, in particular Convolutional Neural Networks (CNN) and Recurrent Neural Networks (RNN), named Skeleton Joints on Black Background (SJoBB). The main contribution of our method is the use of information obtained from 2D human poses associated with suitable machine learning methods in order to contribute to the advance of the state of the art of automatic recognition methods for human actions in videos. The proposed method was assessed on the Weizmann dataset (described in Sect. 5) and obtained superior recognition rates than other action recognition methods of literature. Those methods use hand-crafted information and work with more traditional machine learning models such as nearest neighbours and support vector machines or using neural networks. The results obtained by our method and by other state-of-the-art methods of literature can be seen in Table 2.

2   Human Pose Estimation

The problem of locating key anatomical points or parts of the body of individuals is known as human pose estimation. Inferring the pose of various people in images presents a set of challenges. First, each image can contain an unknown number of people that can occur in any position or scale. Second, interactions between people induce complex spatial interference, due to contact, occlusion and limb joints, making it difficult to associate the parts. Third, the execution time tends to grow as the number of people in the image grows, making real-time performance a challenge [4].

A common approach is to use person detection algorithms and perform pose estimation of a single person for each detection. These *top-down* approaches directly leverage existing techniques for estimating a person's pose, but suffer from errors in the early stages: if the person detection fails, which is likely to happen when people are close, there is no way to recover the error. Furthermore, the execution times of these top-down approaches are proportional to the number of people: for each detection, a pose is estimated, and the more people there are, the greater the computational cost.

In contrast, *bottom-up* approaches are attractive as they offer robustness to initial activities and have the benefit of decoupling run-time complexity from the number of people in the image. It works by first finding all the joints in the image and then linking those joints together to form the skeletons. However, bottom-up approaches do not directly use global contextual cues from other body parts and other people. In practice, the old bottom-up methods do not retain the efficiencies, as the final analysis requires costly global inferences [4].

With the emergence of new databases focused on computer vision problems and some of them focused on pose estimation, such as Microsoft Objects in Context (COCO) [8], several models to represent 2D poses emerged, within which stand out: MPI [9], COCO [8] and BODY 25 [4]. Figure 1 shows these models.

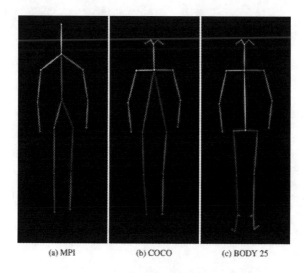

(a) MPI   (b) COCO   (c) BODY 25

Fig. 1. 2D pose models. Source: [10]

2.1   PifPaf

The purpose of the PifPaf method is to estimate human poses in images with many people. The method tries to deal with challenges such as low-resolution images and partially occluded people. Techniques that use the *top-down* approach often fail when people are occluded by others (when the *bounding boxes* overlap). In general, the *bottom-up* methods proposed before PifPaf are *bounding box* free, but they still contain a feature location map. However, the PifPaf method is free from any grid-based constraints of spatial location of joints and can detect multiple poses even when occlusion occurs. The main difference between PifPaf and OpenPose is that PifPaf goes beyond scalar and vector fields to composite fields in the PAF module [5].

Figure 2 shows the architecture of PifPaf, which makes use of a *Residual Network* (ResNet) shared with two other networks: one responsible for predicting the joints of the body (location, reliability and size), which is called *Part Intensity Field* (PIF), and another network that returns the associations between joints, called *Part Association Field* (PAF), thus giving the PifPaf method its name.

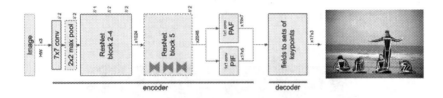

Fig. 2. PifPaf architecture. Source: [5]

The first step of the PifPaf method is the Part Intensity Fields (PIF), which accurately detects and locates human body parts. To merge a confidence map, a regression for keypoint detection is used. As a result of the PIF module, a joint structure is generated including the confidence measure, a vector pointing to the closest body part, and the joint size. Figure 3a, for example, shows the confidence map for the left shoulders in the image. In order to improve the location of the confidence map, a fusion with the vector part of the PIF is performed, as shown in Fig. 3b, forming a high-resolution confidence map.

Fig. 3. PIF module. Source: [5]

Part Association Fields (PAF) is the step to connect joint locations in 2D poses. For each joint, PAF returns: location, confidence measure, two vectors for the two associated parts, and two widths for the spatial precision. Figure 4 shows the PAF that associates the left shoulder with the left hip [5].

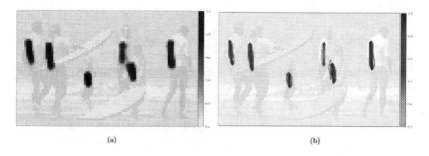

(a)   (b)

Fig. 4. PAF module. Source: [5]

3   Human Action Recognition

Human action recognition systems aim to identify and classify the actions of one or more individuals in a given context. In the scope of computer vision, there are several tasks to be done in order to achieve this goal, which start with capturing images, segmentation, identification and tracking of objects, and finally their respective classification. An action can be considered as a sequence of movements of the human body that can involve several parts simultaneously, and the recognition of this action is to assimilate the observation of what is happening in the video with previously defined patterns and thus label that action [15].

Depending on the recognition complexity, there are different classes into which we can group human actions, according to [16]:

Gesture: Sequence of movements associated with meaning, made by limbs, head or face, such as stretching the arm, smiling, bending the leg;

Action: Sequence of various gestures made by a person, for example, walking, running or swimming;

Interaction: Sequence where a human interacts with another object, this can be another human or an actual object, such as two people fighting or someone holding a knife;

Group activity: Activities performed by more than one person and/or objects, such as a soccer game.

Complementing this categorization, [17] proposed two other classes of human activities, behaviours and events. The first one refers to physical actions that are associated with some emotion or personality of the individual. Events represent a social activity and indicate a person's social intention. The representation of the classes defined in [17] is illustrated in Fig. 5, where the actions above represent greater complexity, whilst those below are simpler.

Fig. 5. Categorization of human actions. Source: [10]

To perform action recognition, the process generally follows two main components: action representation and action classification. The first is responsible for transforming a given action performed in a video into a vector of features, or a series of vectors. The second component uses this generated vector to classify the action. Recent studies have shown deep networks, such as convolutional neural networks, unifying these two steps, causing a gain in performance in general [18].

Considering the possibility of using neural networks to solve the action recognition problem, the techniques to solve this type of problem are divided into two groups: *handcrafted*, which are techniques where the features are extracted with a pre-defined algorithm based on knowledge of the problem, and *deep learning* techniques, whose purpose is to extract *features* derived from an image database by training a CNN [19].

4 Proposed Method

The method proposed in this work for the recognition of human actions is composed of a feature extraction module using pose estimation and an action recognition module using neural networks containing convolutional and recurrent layers.

4.1 Feature Extraction Module

The feature extraction module is responsible for, from an input image, extracting information about the person's pose, and capturing information about his joints and limbs to generate images that show these characteristics that will be used by the action recognition module.

In this feature extraction step based on pose estimation, a method for estimating 2D poses is used, such as PifPaf [5]. Initially, the input video is submitted to the 2D pose estimation process by the PifPaf method, which generates the following data: the skeleton (pose) of the person, the coordinates of the skeleton joints and a heat map of the skeleton joints. These data are used to generate the feature vectors that will be used in the human actions recognition module.

In order to generate the feature vectors, a preprocessing step is necessary, in which the images generated by PifPaf are cropped in such a way that the skeleton and the heat map of the joints are centered in the images. All images generated in this preprocessing step have the same dimension and contain only the skeleton or heatmap centered on the image. Figure 6 shows examples of the images generated by this preprocessing step.

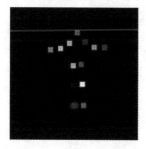 

Fig. 6. Images of joint (left) and skeleton (right) coordinates generated by the PifPaf method, after the preprocessing step. Source: Prepared by the author.

4.2   Recognition Module

This module is responsible for identifying the action being performed in the video through the extracted images *frame by frame*. The identification is performed using a classifier whose objective is to recognize the action that the person is performing, among a set of previously defined actions.

In order to use spatio-temporal information, a Recurrent Neural Network with convolutional layers is used, in this way the network can learn how an action behaves over time, receiving several frames as input, while continuing to process spatial information through the convolution layers.

All network layers, with the exception of the LSTM, are wrapped by a Time Distributed layer, which ensures that the same operation performed by the layer that it is wrapping is applied to each video frame in the same way, with the same weights.

The architecture of the neural network used in our method is the one proposed by [13] that makes use of Long Short-Term Memory (LSTM) right after some layers of convolutions, as can be seen in Fig. 7. All convolution layers use the Rectified Linear Unit (ReLU) function, padding as same and a 3×3 kernel size.

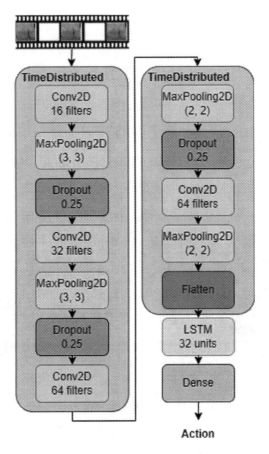

Fig. 7. Neural network architecture used in our method. Source: Prepared by the author.

In the training process, a callback was configured to monitor the validation loss value and restore the best weights of the network at the end of training. The model is compiled using an Adam optimizer and loss being categorical cross-entropy, training takes place in 70 epochs.

The method proposed in this article seeks to explore possible gains in the accuracy of the model represented in Fig. 7 with the features extracted from the feature extraction module, especially with the image of the skeleton joints on a black background.

5   Results

This section presents the results obtained so far by our method on the Weizmann dataset [14], which consists of 10 classes: walking, running, side jumping, ducking, waving with one hand, waving with two hands, jumping in place, jump star, jump with both feet and jump with one foot, performed by 9 different actors, sometimes more than once, resulting in 93 videos. The dataset has a total of 5,701 frames, 228.04 s, captured in 25 frames per second (FPS) and size 180×144 pixels. All actions take place on the same static background as is shown in Fig. 8.

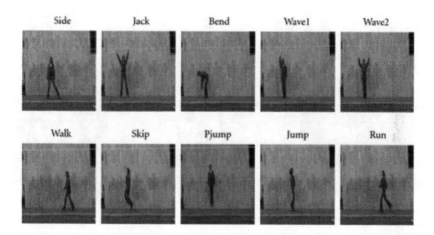

Fig. 8. Images of human actions obtained from videos from the Weizmann dataset. Source: [14]

To carry out the experiments, all the videos in the base were submitted to the PifPaf [5] method in order to estimate the 2D poses in each frame. As already mentioned, the PifPaf method generates an image containing the heat map of the estimated joints, an image containing the skeleton of the individual in the frame under analysis, and the coordinates of each joint in a JSON file. These images are cropped to a predetermined size so that they all have the same dimension and the objects of interest are centered.

Figure 9 illustrates the process of obtaining the image containing the skeleton (pose) of the individual with the application of the PifPaf method, as well as

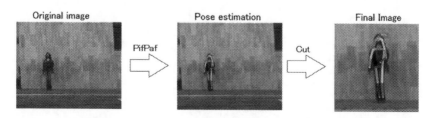

Fig. 9. Steps to obtain an image with a predetermined size containing the 2D pose of a centered individual, from an input video frame. Source: Prepared by the author.

the process of obtaining the cropped image, with the object (in this case the skeleton) centered on the image.

Images generated by plotting the joint points of the human skeleton estimated with the PifPaf method were used, and stored in JSON files, on a black background, as a final image for training the networks. Figure 10 illustrates the process of generating these images. The flow for generating the cropped images with the object of interest centered is similar to the one shown in Fig. 9. This feature is the main contribution of this article, as one can see in the results.

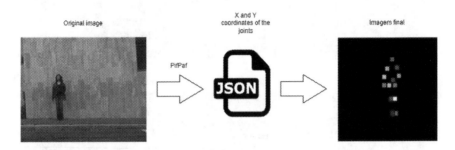

Fig. 10. Flow for generating images containing joint information. Source: Prepared by the author.

To evaluate the effectiveness of the classifiers, accuracy was used as a metric, since most of the correlated works make use of this metric. The classifiers were trained using the leave-one-out technique, where training is performed with all images, leaving only one out to perform the test and repeating this process for all images, always leaving one out of the training.

Table 1 compares the different results using different feature vectors as input to the proposed model. It is interesting to note that the generated images presented in Fig. 10, in which each joint has its own color, obtained better results than using the same images, but considering all joints with the same color.

Table 1. Comparison of the accuracies obtained by different features for the proposed model.

Feature	Accuracy (%)
SJoBB (Skeleton Joints on Black Background)	98.92
Original image	91.39
PifPaf skeleton image	90.32
SJoBB with same color for all joints	95.56

Table 2 shows the result obtained by our SJoBB method on the Weizmann dataset, as well as the results obtained by other methods of literature using the same experimental protocol. One can see that our method obtained the second-best accuracy.

Table 2. Comparison of the accuracy rates obtained by our method as well as by other methods on Weizmann databases, using the same experimental protocol.

Method	Ano	Weizmann (%)
SJoBB (Skeleton Joints on Black Background)	2022	98.92
Guo et al. 2013 [25]	2013	100
Carmona and Climent 2018 [21]	2018	98.80
Ji et al. 2012 [26]	2012	98.00
Moreira et al. 2020 [27]	2020	98.00
Silva 2020 [6]	2020	97.85
Singh and Vishwakarma 2019 [29]	2019	97.66
Chou et al. 2018 [23]	2018	95.56
Zhang and Tao 2012 [24]	2012	93.87
Chaaraoui et al. 2013 [28]	2013	90.32
Junejo and Aghbari 2012 [22]	2012	88.60

6   Conclusion

As the processing capacity and storage of large amounts of data advances with current technologies, image recognition gains space and becomes, more and more, a relevant research field for monitoring public areas, in which the main current motivation is population security, as well as for monitoring private homes in order to detect and respond immediately to possible domestic accidents when they occur.

With the emergence of robust, effective and efficient methods for estimating 2D poses, such as OpenPose [4] and PifPaf [5], a new range of possibilities for the recognition of human actions has opened up, resulting in different approaches to solve this problem, as for example in the study of Silva and Marana [6], which generated new *features* from the results of pose estimation, calculating the angles and joint trajectories to perform the classification.

One of the main benefits of 2D poses is the possibility of preserving the privacy of the people involved in the scene, since, whether in the case of the images generated from the skeletons of the PifPaf poses or even the images of the joint locations, the information that could be used to identify a person are completely occluded, so that market solutions can benefit from this technique and have arguments to include their solutions in people's daily lives without them worrying about having their privacy exposed.

At the same time, deep neural networks and deep learning have been showing great results in different areas that can benefit from this technology, whether for problems involving computer vision or any other type of problem. Particularly in the case of the recognition of human actions, since images are used as input data, the use of convolutional neural networks must be taken into account due to the nature of this architecture to solve this type of situation. In addition, recurrent neural networks are also relevant for solving the problem, since, as it is a sequence of *frames* in which temporal information is important for classification, the RNN can, through the LSTM, capture how the person behaves over time.

Reaching an accuracy of 98.92% for the Weizzman database, our method surpassed other studies that are considered state-of-the-art for the problem of recognizing human actions. In comparison with the work of Guo et al. [25], which obtained 100% accuracy for this database, there are advantages by using SJoBB since the original images are used only at the beginning of the process (in order to obtain the 2D poses) preserving the people's privacy.

Acknowledgements. This study was financed in part by the Coordenação de Aperfeiçoamento de Pessoal de Nível Superior - Brasil (CAPES). The authors also thank Petrobras/Fundunesp (Process 2662/2017) for the financial support.

References

1. Wang, H., Schmid, C.: Action recognition with improved trajectories. In: Proceedings of the IEEE International Conference on Computer Vision, pp. 3551–3558 (2013)
2. Jhuang, H., et al.: Towards understanding action recognition. In: Proceedings of the IEEE International Conference on Computer Vision, pp. 3192–3199 (2013)
3. Wang, H., et al.: Evaluation of local spatio-temporal features for action recognition. In: BMVC 2009-British Machine Vision Conference, p. 124-1. BMVA Press (2009)
4. Cao, Z., et al.: Openpose: realtime multi-person 2d pose estimation using part affinity fields. IEEE Trans. Pattern Anal. Mach. Intell. **43**(1), 172–186 (2019)
5. Kreiss, S., Bertoni, L., Alahi, A.: PifPaf: composite fields for human pose estimation. In: Proceedings of the IEEE/CVF Conference on Computer Vision and Pattern Recognition, pp. 11977–11986 (2019)
6. Silva, M.V.D.: Human action recognition based on spatiotemporal features from videos. Universidade Federal de São Carlos (2020)
7. Toshev, A., Szegedy, C.: DeepPose: human pose estimation via deep neural networks. In: Proceedings of the IEEE Conference on Computer Vision and Pattern Recognition, pp. 1653–1660 (2014)
8. Lin, T.-Y., et al.: Microsoft COCO: common objects in context. In: Fleet, D., Pajdla, T., Schiele, B., Tuytelaars, T. (eds.) ECCV 2014. LNCS, vol. 8693, pp. 740–755. Springer, Cham (2014). https://doi.org/10.1007/978-3-319-10602-1_48
9. Insafutdinov, E., Pishchulin, L., Andres, B., Andriluka, M., Schiele, B.: DeeperCut: a deeper, stronger, and faster multi-person pose estimation model. In: Leibe, B., Matas, J., Sebe, N., Welling, M. (eds.) ECCV 2016. LNCS, vol. 9910, pp. 34–50. Springer, Cham (2016). https://doi.org/10.1007/978-3-319-46466-4_3
10. da Silva, M.V., Marana, A.N.: Human action recognition in videos based on spatiotemporal features and bag-of-poses. Appl. Soft Comput. (Elsevier) **95**, 106513 (2020)

11. Bahdanau, D., Cho, K., Bengio, Y.: Neural machine translation by jointly learning to align and translate. arXiv preprint arXiv:1409.0473 (2014)
12. Vaswani, A., et al.: Attention is All You Need (2017)
13. Donahue, J., et al.: Long-term recurrent convolutional networks for visual recognition and description. In: Proceedings of the IEEE Conference on Computer Vision and Pattern Recognition, pp. 2625–2634 (2015)
14. Gorelick, L., et al.: Actions as space-time shapes. Trans. Pattern Anal. Mach. Intell. **29**(12), 2247–2253 (2007)
15. Cheng, G., et al.: Advances in human action recognition: a survey. arXiv preprint arXiv:1501.05964 (2015)
16. Aggarwal, J.K., Ryoo, M.S.: Human activity analysis: a review. ACM Comput. Surv. (CSUR). ACM, New York **43**(3), 1–43 (2011)
17. Vrigkas, M., Nikou, C., Kakadiaris, I.A.: A review of human activity recognition methods. Front. Robot. AI **2**, 28 (2015)
18. Kong, Y., Fu, Y.: Human action recognition and prediction: a survey. arXiv preprint arXiv:1806.11230 (2018)
19. Antipov, G., et al.: Learned vs. hand-crafted features for pedestrian gender recognition. In: Proceedings of the 23rd ACM International Conference on Multimedia, pp. 1263–1266 (2015)
20. Guo, M.-H., et al.: Attention mechanisms in computer vision: a survey. arXiv preprint arXiv:2111.07624 (2021)
21. Carmona, J.M., Climent, J.: Human action recognition by means of subtensor projections and dense trajectories. Pattern Recogn. (Elsevier) **81**, 443–455 (2018)
22. Junejo, I.N., Aghbari, Z.A.: Using sax representation for human action recognition. J. Vis. Commun. Image Represent. (Elsevier) **23**(6), 853–861 (2012)
23. Chou, K.-P., et al.: Robust feature-based automated multi-view human action recognition system. IEEE Access (IEEE) **6**, 15283–15296 (2018)
24. Zhang, Z., Tao, D.: Slow feature analysis for human action recognition. IEEE Trans. Pattern Anal. Mach. Intell. (IEEE) **34**(3), 436–450 (2012)
25. Guo, K., Ishwar, P., Konrad, J.: Action recognition from video using feature covariance matrices. IEEE Trans. Image Process. (IEEE) **22**(6), 2479–2494 (2013)
26. Ji, S., Xu, W., Yang, M., Yu, K.: 3D convolutional neural networks for human action recognition. IEEE Trans. Pattern Anal. Mach. Intell. (IEEE) **35**(1), 221–231 (2012)
27. Moreira, T.P., Menotti, D., Pedrini, H.: Video action recognition based on visual rhythm representation. J. Vis. Commun. Image Represent. (Elsevier) **71**, 102771 (2020)
28. Chaaraoui, A.A., Climent-Pérez, P., Flórez-Revuelta, F.: Silhouette-based human action recognition using sequences of key poses. Pattern Recogn. Lett. (Elsevier) **34**(15), 1799–1807 (2013)
29. Singh, T., Vishwakarma, D.K.: A hybrid framework for action recognition in low-quality video sequences. arXiv preprint arXiv:1903.04090 (2019)

Self-learning Methodology Based on Degradation Estimation for Underwater Image Enhancement

Claudio Dornelles Mello Jr.$^{(\boxtimes)}$[ID], Bryan Umpierre Moreira[ID],
Paulo Jefferson Dias de Oliveira Evald[ID], Paulo Jorge Lilles Drews Jr.[ID],
and Silvia Silva Costa Botelho[ID]

Center for Computer Science, Federal University of Rio Grande,
Av. Italia - km8, Rio Grande, RS 96203-900, Brazil
claudio.mello@furg.br
http://www.c3.furg.br

Abstract. Underwater images suffer from degradation caused by water turbidity, light attenuation and color casting. An image enhancement procedure improves the perception and the analysis of the objects in the scene. Recent works based on deep learning approaches require synthetically paired datasets to train their models. In this work, it is present a self-learning methodology to enhance images without a paired dataset. The proposed method estimates image degradation from the input image and attenuate it from the image. The output image of an autoencoder is replaced in the loss function by a synthetically degraded version during the training. This procedure drives the network learning to compensate additional degradation. Thereby, the output image is an enhanced version of the input image. It is highlighted that the proposed algorithm requires only one image as input during the training. The results obtained using our method show its effectiveness of color preservation, color cast reduction, and contrast improvement.

Keywords: Self-learning · Enhancement · Underwater

1 Introduction

Modern underwater activities such as monitoring, inspection and environmental research involves the acquisition of images of structures and oceanic fauna and flora [5]. The perception of the underwater objects in the scene depends on the physical properties of water such as turbidity, ambient light and depth [6]. The turbidity is caused by the particles of organic and inorganic materials in suspension in the water [7]. The presence of these elements generates forward

Supported by National Council for Scientific and Technological Development (CNPq), the Coordination for the Improvement of Higher Education Personnel (CAPES) and Agency for Petroleum, Natural Gas, and Biofuels (PRH-ANP).

J. C. Xavier-Junior and R. A. Rios (Eds.): BRACIS 2022, LNAI 13654, pp. 84–95, 2022.
https://doi.org/10.1007/978-3-031-21689-3_7

and backscattering effects, resulting in blurry and dim images [18]. The turbidity, ambient light and distance of the objects from the camera define the intensity of these phenomena [8]. The scene depth affects the color perception and the nature of the material in suspension defines a brownish, greenish or bluish tonality or the *color cast* of the water [19]. Figure 1 illustrates scenarios of underwater images presenting the previously mentioned properties. The diversity in depth, color cast, and turbidity levels defines the challenging task for underwater image enhancement methods.

Fig. 1. Examples of underwater images presenting scenes with distinct color cast, turbidity, and ambient light.

Usually, most of the methods of underwater image restoration use the image description provided by the Image Formation Model (IFM) [1]. This model considers the degradation principle [10] and depends on the estimation of physical parameters.

The IFM-based methods work to find an image without degradation and the results have proven to be a challenging task because the parameters are unknown in most of the real image acquisition situations [2,20].

On the other hand, the methods of image enhancement are usually IFM-free exploring the improvement of the contrast and color of the images focusing on pixel intensity redistribution [21]. Furthermore, methodologies based on deep learning face the additional challenge of the absence of the real reference image (ground-truth). Thus, synthesized reference images are used to train the Neural Networks (NN). A good enough approximation of these synthetic ground-truths to the real non-degraded images impacts on the resulting images of the enhancement method. However, the true intensity and hue of the colors of the objects in the underwater scene are unknown in most cases. Thus, the limit for the improvement action of a method is unknown. The quality of the results is defined mainly from subjective analysis based on visual perception.

In this work, we present a self-learning method, single-image architecture for underwater image enhancement. The basic conception comprises the teaching of a NN to enhance images from a harsher penalty during the training stage. This penalty results from the *trick* of replacement of the output image in the loss function with a synthetically more degraded version. We consider that a degradation method that captures the behavior and intensity degradation tends to generate realistic images more easily than a method using synthesized paired images. The main contributions of the work are:

1. An effective and simple algorithm for underwater image enhancement based on a small-sized neural network trained with a small and no-paired dataset;
2. An alternative approach to enhance underwater images based on degradation content of the image. The algorithm uses the degradation estimation to drive the training of an autoencoder. It learns to compensate the degradation, without pre- or post-processing or synthesized less degraded ground-truths.

The remaining sections of this paper are organized as follows. Section 2 comprises the related works. Section 3 discusses the architecture and methodology. In Sect. 4, the experimental results are presented and the Sect. 5 is dedicated to the conclusion.

2   Related Works

The underwater image enhancement based on deep learning approaches has experimented increasing evolution in the last years [10,21].

In [16], it was proposed the Water Generative Adversarial Network (Water-GAN) to generate realistic underwater images, and the Underwater Image Restoration Network for correcting the color. An improvement to this method is proposed in [9], where the Underwater GAN (UGAN) is trained to generate turbid images from clear ones. A synthetic dataset was produced and used to train another GAN. In [4], it was presented an architecture that concatenates two GANs for unpaired image translation. The method utilizes multiple cyclic consistency losses that capture image features and details of underwater images. The Underwater Denoising Autoencoder (UDAE) was proposed in [11]. The model is based on the Unet architecture. A synthetic dataset was generated via style-transfer between clean and distorted underwater images.

Li *et al.* [14] proposed a model based on underwater scene priors. A synthetic paired dataset was built, combining the underwater image physical model with optical properties of underwater scenes. The resulting dataset is used to train a NN to enhance underwater images. The resulting images required post-processing to restore the dynamic range of the images. Lin *et al.* [17] proposed an approach that combines a convolutional neural network and IFM. The supervised training uses a synthesized dataset that contains clean underwater images, images with vertical distortion, transmission maps, distances and background light. Besides, Li *et al.* [13] proposed a structure based on an encoder-decoder network integrating different color spaces. The algorithm uses attention methodology to aim the features' extraction from the images in the RGB (Red, Green, and Blue), HSV (Hue, Saturation, and Value) and Lab color spaces. A transmission map is estimated and used to drive the encoder-decoder learning to enhance underwater images. The method showed effectiveness in the enhancement task. The paired UIEB (Underwater Image Enhancement Benchmark) dataset ([14]) was used in the training of the neural network.

In this work, we present a single-image architecture and deep learning-based for underwater image enhancement method. The proposed method estimates the image degradation and use it to drive the learning of an autoencoder to remove it from the image. The method uses no paired dataset, requiring low level of supervision during the training of the neural network.

3   Methodology

This section discusses the method and the degradation function. In the images acquired close to the water surface and under sunlight, the color channel-related distortions can be disregarded. But in higher depths the perception of colors changes and the intensities and hues of the real colors are unknown. In addition, the water turbidity generates loss of contrast and blurring. Methodologies for image improvement must address these issues.

The method relies on the assumption that the underwater image presents some level of degradation that can be estimated and used to reference its reduction or removal from the image.

3.1   Proposed Self-learning Method

The architecture of the model is shown in Fig. 2. A degradation step (function) is inserted over the training stage that increases the distortion present in the output image $\hat{I}$ of the autoencoder. The resulting image $\hat{I}^*$ is a synthetically degraded version of $\hat{I}$. Then, the image $\hat{I}^*$ replaces the output image in the loss function. This procedure *cheats* the neural network, which interprets it as that its output is not good enough and learns to correct it. The assumption is that the autoencoder learns to remove the inserted degradation, enhancing the reconstructed image in the output. However, an effective correction occurs if the degradation is feature-coherent in nature and intensity with those present in the input image.

3.2   Degradation Function

The degradation function is presented in Fig. 2. This function produces the degraded image $\hat{I}_k^*$ which is described in (1).

$$\hat{I}_k^*(x,y) = \hat{I}_k(x,y) + I_k^*(x,y) - I_{ck}(x,y),\tag{1}$$

where the index k correspond to the color channel (RGB) and the (x,y) are the pixel coordinates. The I_{ck} image is a stretched histogram version of the input image I_k. The histogram stretching operation improves contrast and intensifies the color perception in the image [3]. The difference between these images in (1) defines the degradation. Thereby, the I_{ck} calculation is given by:

$$I_{ck}(x,y) = \frac{I_k(x,y) - min(I_k(x,y))}{b_{wk}},\tag{2}$$

where $b_{wk} = max(I_k(x,y)) - min(I_k(x,y))$ correspond to the dynamic range of the image. The histogram *stretching* operation allows an apparent improvement

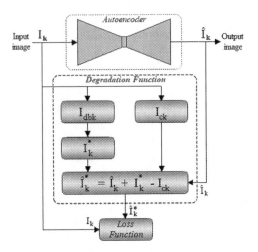

Fig. 2. Diagram of the proposed model. The degradation function described in (1) is represented inside of blue dashed line. (Color figure online)

in the visual perception. However, it produces gaps between adjacent intensity sets in the histogram. In the proposed algorithm, I_{ck} is used as a distortion element of contrast and color.

The I_k^* image is a degraded version of I_k, and it presents additional turbidity and color cast. This image is obtained using the representation described in (3). This representation is defined in the color space, but inspired by the physical model. Similar to IFM, (3) contains terms related to the reflectance of the objects in the scene and another one related to the backscattering effect defined by the interaction between the ambient light and particles in suspension in the water.

$$I_k(x,y) = I_{Jk}(x,y)e^{-gd_k(x,y)} + (1 - e^{-gb_k(x,y)}).\Lambda_k. \tag{3}$$

Moreover, the parameters gd_k and gb_k are defined in (4) and (5), respectively. The pixel coordinates (x,y) were omitted in these expressions for clarity concerns. Both parameters are dependent on dynamic range of the image. Besides, the parameter Λ_k is defined as the Context Luminosity of the image in the color space. It is described by the median of the pixel intensities in each color channel.

$$gd_k = \frac{1 - b_{wk}}{b_{wk}}[max_k(I_k) - I_k].[I_k - min_k(I_k)]. \tag{4}$$

$$gb_k = \frac{1 - b_{wk}}{b_{wk}}[max_k(I_k) - I_k].[\Lambda_k - min_k(I_k)]. \tag{5}$$

The I_k^* is estimated using (3) in two steps as shown in (6) and (7).

$$I_{dbn}(x,y) = I_k(x,y).e^{-gd_k(x,y)} + (1 - e^{-gb_k(x,y)})\Lambda_k. \tag{6}$$

The image I_{dbn} defines a new and increased context of degradation, allowing the calculation of the parameters gd_k^*, gb_k^* and Λ_k^*. These parameters are used in (7).

$$I_k^*(x,y) = I_{dbn}(x,y).e^{-gd_k^*(x,y)} + (1 - e^{-gb_k^*(x,y)})\Lambda_k^*. \tag{7}$$

4   Experimental Results

The autoencoder was implemented in Keras/Tensorflow® and its architecture is shown in Fig. 3. It has 91k trainable parameters and the downscaling steps are performed by *strided* convolutions in the first layer of each dimensional block and the upscale layers use nearest neighbor algorithm. The degradation function was implemented as a non-trainable layer. The optimizer is Adam with learning rate 0.0008 and other parameters at their default values. The training was performed in 300 epochs with batch size equal to 6. The computer configuration is i5-6400 CPU, 32 GB RAM with a Titan X GPU. The image format is RGB $256 \times 256 \times 3$ scaled to the range $[0, 1.0]$.

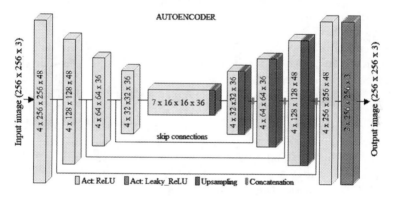

Fig. 3. The implemented autoencoder, where numbers inside each dimensional block indicate number of layers, dimension (*height* $\times$ *width*) and number of feature maps, respectively.

The dataset contains 2200 real underwater images, and it was built with 800 images from UIEBD database [15], 400 images from the SUIM database [12] and 1000 images from the internet. The data were split into train and validation set (70%, 10%) and test set (20%). Images used to compose the dataset were selected to present diversity in degradation levels. However, those presenting mid-to-high degradation levels in terms of turbidity, color cast, and reduced contrast, which were prioritized.

The loss function is composed by terms related to the scene radiance and related to the entire image radiance contexts. The scene radiance term ($\mathcal{L}_{sc}$) is described in (8).

$$\mathcal{L}_{sc} = MSE\{I_k - (1 - e^{-gb_k})\Lambda_k, \quad \hat{I}_k^* - (1 - e^{-gb_k^*})\Lambda_k^*\}, \tag{8}$$

where gb_k^* and Λ_k^* are the attenuation factor for ambient light and ambient light of the degraded image ($\hat{I}_k^*$), respectively. It is a Mean Square Error (MSE) between the radiance terms of the input image (I_k) and degraded image ($\hat{I}_k^*$. The image radiance term ($\mathcal{L}_{im}$) is indicated in (9).

$$\mathcal{L}_{im} = MSE\{I_k, \hat{I}_k^*\}. \tag{9}$$

In addition, the loss function is

$$\mathcal{L} = c_1.\mathcal{L}_{sc} + c_2.\mathcal{L}_{im}, \tag{10}$$

whose coefficients are empirically defined as $c_1 = 0.6$, and $c_2 = 0.4$.

This configuration for c_1 and c_2 presented satisfactory performance, and it is insensible to dataset changes. We obtained these values from empirical tests using a miscellaneous dataset.

Figure 4 shows images obtained from application of proposed method. Degraded and output images are results at end of training phase. As can be noted, input images show different color cast and turbidity levels. However, the method presented a good performance in color and contrast recovery. Output images show a strong reduction in color cast and turbidity perception. Degraded images were calculated using (1) and correspond to the degradation function algorithm output. Retrieved colors correspond to those existent in the input image. This image is the only input information available to the autoencoder during the training stage, since the methodology does not use synthesized ground-truths.

Figure 5 shows the images processed by the method for an example of underwater image, the respective histograms and distributions in color space. These images are related to the degradation function expressed in (1) and they were obtained at the end of the training stage. Essentially, the images in Fig. 5(b) and (c) define the degradation imposed on the output image of the autoencoder. Besides visual perception, degradation can be analyzed from the histograms. The stretched histogram version of the input image in Fig. 5(c) shows the gaps generated by the *stretching* procedure that improves contrast and color. However, the algorithm uses this image as a degradation element. Degraded image in Fig. 5(d) presents reduced intensity range in the color channels. The output image shows a wider intensity range for the three color channels. In addition, Fig. 5 indicates the Number of Discretized Points (NDP) of each image distribution in color space. In the analyzed context, this parameter can be used as indicative of quality improvement. Since each point in the color space indicates a different color, the enhanced image tends to present higher NDP in the respective distribution. The enhanced output image has the highest NDP, indicating the greatest color diversity. The stretched histogram image has an identical NDP as the input image. This fact illustrates the nature of stretching histogram operation that only improves contrast and intensity of the visually perceptible colors in the input image.

(a)   (b)   (c)

Fig. 4. Images resulting from the method at end of training stage of autoencoder. Images are presented for distinct turbidity and color cast contexts. (a) Input image (I), (b) Degraded Image ($\hat{I}^*$) and (c) Output image ($\hat{I}$). (Color figure online)

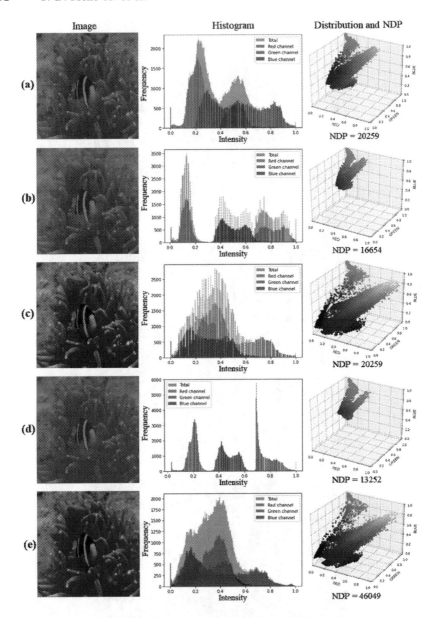

Fig. 5. Example of images resulting from method and respective histogram, distribution, and NDP (Number of Discretized Points) in color space. These images are those generated from (1), (2), and (6). (a) Input image I, (b) Degraded version I^*, (c) Stretched histogram image I_c, (d) Degraded image $\hat{I}^*$ and (e) Output image $\hat{I}$. (Color figure online)

Fig. 6. Images resulting from the method and respective NDP (Number of Discretized Points) in color space.

Figure 6 presents additional examples of input and output images, as well as their respective NDP. The method is based on image degradation estimation. More degraded images demand more intensive enhancement action, and tend to show greater difference between input and output NDP. Although merely quantitative, this parameter suggests an interesting indicative of the enhancement intensity provided by our method.

The architecture allows a generic approach for denoising or restoration-like applications. However, the most important aspect for a successful implementation consists in the correct definition of the degradation function. This element stimulates the autoencoder to learn which features should be removed from the target application. This correct definition can be a challenging task depending on the application nature.

The methodology presents strong dependency with input image parameters. Thus, images showing very similar scenes, but presenting differences in their parameters, may lead to very different results of the enhancement performance. This aspect limit the direct use in applications like underwater video enhancement. In this case, the scene may vary from one frame to another, resulting in different enhancement actions, and requiring the adoption of a time-consistency strategy.

In future work, we intend to perform comparative study involving the proposed method and other consolidated techniques on literature.

5   Conclusion

We presented a deep learning-based methodology for underwater image enhancement. The proposed algorithm requires neither paired datasets nor prior processing of the images. In this method, the output image of an autoencoder is replaced by a synthetically degraded version of the loss function during the training stage. This procedure *cheats* neural network and then, it learns to compensate degradation. At the end of training, the output image is an enhanced version of the input image. Results show the effectiveness of our method in reducing perception of turbidity and color and contrast recovery.

Acknowledgments. The authors would like to thank to National Council for Scientific and Technological Development (CNPq) and the Coordination for the Improvement of Higher Education Personnel (CAPES). In addition, the author thanks Human Resource Program of The Brazilian National Agency for Petroleum, Natural Gas, and Biofuels - PRH-ANP, supported with resources from oil companies considering the contract clause nº 50/2015 of R, D&I of the ANP.

References

1. Akkaynak, D., Treibitz, T.: A revised underwater image formation model. In: 2018 IEEE/CVF Conference on Computer Vision and Pattern Recognition, pp. 6723–6732 (2018). https://doi.org/10.1109/CVPR.2018.00703
2. Berman, D., Levy, D., Avidan, S., Treibitz, T.: Underwater single image color restoration using haze-lines and a new quantitative dataset. IEEE Trans. Pattern Anal. Mach. Intell. **43**(8), 2822–2837 (2021). https://doi.org/10.1109/TPAMI.2020.2977624
3. Burger, W., Burge, M.J.: Digital Image Processing: An Algorithmic Introduction Using Java, 2nd edn. Springer, London (2016). https://doi.org/10.1007/978-1-4471-6684-9
4. Cho, Y., Jang, H., Malav, R., Pandey, G., Kim, A.: Underwater Image Dehazing via Unpaired Image-to-image Translation. Int. J. Control Autom. Syst. **18**(3), 605–614 (2020). https://doi.org/10.1007/s12555-019-0689-x
5. Donaldson, J.A., Drews-Jr, P., Bradley, M., Morgan, D.L., Baker, R., Ebner, B.C.: Countering low visibility in video survey of an estuarine fish assemblage. Pac. Conserv. Biol. **26**(2), 190–200 (2020)
6. Dos Santos, M., De Giacomo, G.G., Drews-Jr, P.L.J., Botelho, S.S.C.: Matching color aerial images and underwater sonar images using deep learning for underwater localization. IEEE Robot. Autom. Lett. **5**(4), 6365–6370 (2020). https://doi.org/10.1109/LRA.2020.3013852
7. Drews-Jr., P., Nascimento, E., Botelho, S., Campos, M.: Underwater depth estimation and image restoration based on single images. IEEE Comput. Graph. Appl. **36**, 24–35 (2016). https://doi.org/10.1109/MCG.2016.26
8. Drews-Jr, P., Nascimento, E., Moraes, F., Botelho, S., Campos, M.: Transmission estimation in underwater single images. In: IEEE ICCV, pp. 825–830 (2013)
9. Fabbri, C., Islam, M.J., Sattar, J.: Enhancing underwater imagery using generative adversarial networks. In: 2018 IEEE International Conference on Robotics and Automation (ICRA), pp. 7159–7165 (2018). https://doi.org/10.1109/ICRA.2018.8460552
10. Fayaz, S., Parah, S., Qureshi, G., Kumar, V.: Underwater image restoration: a state-of-the-art review. IET Image Process. **15**, 269–285 (2020). https://doi.org/10.1049/ipr2.12041

11. Hashisho, Y., Albadawi, M., Krause, T., von Lukas, U.F.: Underwater color restoration using u-net denoising autoencoder. In: 2019 11th International Symposium on Image and Signal Processing and Analysis (ISPA), pp. 117–122 (2019). https://doi.org/10.1109/ISPA.2019.8868679

12. Islam, M.J., Xia, Y., Sattar, J.: Fast underwater image enhancement for improved visual perception. IEEE Robot. Autom. Lett. **5**(2), 3227–3234 (2020). https://doi.org/10.1109/LRA.2020.2974710

13. Li, C., Anwar, S., Hou, J., Cong, R., Guo, C., Ren, W.: Underwater image enhancement via medium transmission-guided multi-color space embedding. IEEE Trans. Image Process. **30**, 4985–5000 (2021). https://doi.org/10.1109/TIP.2021.3076367

14. Li, C., Anwar, S., Porikli, F.: Underwater scene prior inspired deep underwater image and video enhancement. Pattern Recogn. **98**, 107038 (2020). https://doi.org/10.1016/j.patcog.2019.107038, https://www.sciencedirect.com/science/article/pii/S0031320319303401

15. Li, C., et al.: An underwater image enhancement benchmark dataset and beyond. IEEE Trans. Image Process. **29**, 4376–4389 (2020). https://doi.org/10.1109/TIP.2019.2955241

16. Li, J., Skinner, K.A., Eustice, R.M., Johnson-Roberson, M.: WaterGAN: unsupervised generative network to enable real-time color correction of monocular underwater images. IEEE Robot. Autom. Lett. **3**(1), 387–394 (2017)

17. Lin, Y., Shen, L., Wang, Z., Wang, K., Zhang, X.: Attenuation coefficient guided two-stage network for underwater image restoration. IEEE Sig. Process. Lett. **28**, 199–203 (2020). https://doi.org/10.1109/LSP.2020.3048619

18. Ponce-Hinestroza, A.N., Drews-Jr., P.L., Torres-Méndez, L.A.: A probabilistic approach to restore images acquired in underwater scenes. J. Math. Imaging Vision, 1–16 (2022)

19. Ponce-Hinestroza, A.N., Torres-Méndez, L.A., Drews-Jr., P.: Using a MRF-BP model with color adaptive training for underwater color restoration. In: ICPR, pp. 787–792 (2016)

20. Raveendran, S., Patil, M.D., Birajdar, G.K.: Underwater image enhancement: a comprehensive review, recent trends, challenges and applications. Artif. Intell. Rev. **54**(7), 5413–5467 (2021). https://doi.org/10.1007/s10462-021-10025-z

21. Wang, Y., Song, W., Fortino, G., Qi, L.Z., Zhang, W., Liotta, A.: An experimental-based review of image enhancement and image restoration methods for underwater imaging. IEEE Access **7**(07), 140233–140251 (2019). https://doi.org/10.1109/ACCESS.2019.2932130

When Less May Be More: Exploring Similarity to Improve Experience Replay

Daniel Eugênio Neves$^{(\boxtimes)}$ (ID), Lucila Ishitani (ID),
and Zenilton Kleber Gonçalves do Patrocínio Júnior (ID)

Pontifícia Universidade Católica de Minas Gerais, Av. Dom José Gaspar,
500 - Prédio 20, Belo Horizonte, MG 30535-901, Brazil
daniel.eugenio@sga.pucminas.br, {lucila,zenilton}@pucminas.br

Abstract. We propose the *COM Pact Experience Replay* (COMPER)
as a reinforcement learning method that seeks to reduce the required
number of experiences to agent training regarding the total accumulated
rewards in the long run. COMPER uses temporal difference learning
with predicted target values for sets of similar transitions and a new
experience replay approach based on two memories of transitions. We
present an assessment of two possible neural network architectures for
the target network with a complete analysis of the memories' behavior,
along with detailed results for 100,000 frames and about 25,000 iterations
with a small experience memory on eight challenging 2600 Atari games
on the Arcade Learning Environment (ALE). We also present results for
a Deep Q-Network (DQN) agent with the same experimental protocol
on the same set of games as a baseline. We demonstrate that COMPER
can approximate a good policy from a small number of frame observations using a compact memory and learning the similar transitions' sets
dynamics using a recurrent neural network.

Keywords: Deep reinforcement learning · Experience replay · Similar
transition sets · Transitions memories · Recurrence on target value
prediction

1 Introduction

Reinforcement Learning (RL) research dedicates to developing intelligent computational entities called "agents", which try to learn an action policy to interact
with the environment and perform a given task. Each action results in a new
environment state and a reward signal, and the objective is to learn an optimal
policy that maximizes the total expected reward in the long run. If the agent

This study was financed in part by the Coordenação de Aperfeiçoamento de Pessoal
de Nível Superior – Brasil (CAPES) – Finance Code 001. It has also received partial
funding from Brazilian Conselho Nacional de Desenvolvimento Científico e Tecnológico
(CNPq) and from Pontifical Catholic University of Minas Gerais (PUC Minas).

J. C. Xavier-Junior and R. A. Rios (Eds.): BRACIS 2022, LNAI 13654, pp. 96–110, 2022.
https://doi.org/10.1007/978-3-031-21689-3_8

learns an optimal action policy, it will have learned to perform the task. However, one of its main limitations is the required time for agent training, and it is directly related to the agent's ability to converge to a better policy of actions.

After an agent has performed a sequence of actions and received a reward value, knowing how to assign credit or discredit to each state-action pair (to adjust its decision making and improve its effectiveness) consists of a difficult problem, called *temporal credit assignment* [8]. Temporal Difference Learning (TD-learning) represents one of the main techniques to deal with credit attribution, despite being a slow process, especially when it involves credit propagation over a long sequence of actions. Methods such as Adaptive Heuristic Critic (AHC) [13] and Q-Learning [15], which represent the first TD-learning based methods in RL, are characterized by high convergence times. Therefore, a relevant and effective technique named Experience Replay (ER) [8] was proposed to accelerate the credit attribution process and, consequently, reduce the convergence time, by storing the agent experiences in a replay buffer and uniformly sampling past experiences to update the agent model. However, ER has some limitations. An important issue is that ER repeats experiences through uniform sampling and, if those samples define policies that are very different from what is being learned, it can underestimate the evaluation and utility functions. Anyway, the use of ER with random sampling reduces the effect of the correlation between the data (that represents the environment states) and also improves its non-stationary distribution (during the training of the neural network) because it softens the distribution over many previous experiences. However, there are two other limitations: (i) the memory of experiences does not differentiate relevant experiences due to the uniform sampling; and (ii) experiences are often overwritten due to the buffer size limitation.

Thus, using a replay buffer presents two main challenges: (i) the selection of which experiences to store; and (ii) the picking of which ones to repeat. This work addresses the first one and proposes a new method named **COMP**act **E**xperience **R**eplay (COMPER), which improves the model of experience memory to make ER feasible (and more efficient) using smaller amounts of data. The main hypotheses behind this work are two-fold. First, it is possible to produce sets of similar transitions and explore them to build a reduced memory. One can also perform successive updates of their Q-values, learning their dynamics through a deep neural network (DNN) and using this DNN to approximate the target value at the TD-learning. Second, it augments the odds of a rare transition to be observed compared to a sampling performed on the entire set, making updates of the value function more effective. Finally, experimental results demonstrate that our proposal helps reduce the convergence time for agent training. That seems valid, especially for scenarios where agents take a long time to be rewarded and, therefore, need to learn a long-term action policy based on their experiences.

This paper is organized as follows. In Sect. 2, we present some related works, and relevant issues pointed out in the literature. In Sect. 3, we review some concepts related to reinforcement learning and the Deep Q-Network (DQN) method. After that, our new proposed method is described in Sect. 4. Section 5 presents and discuss our experimental methodology, while the results are shown and analyzed in Sect. 6. Finally, we draw some conclusions and possible future works in Sect. 7.

2   Literature Review and Related Work

Deep Q-Network (DQN) [11] and Double Deep Q-Network (DDQN) [5] are two relevant methods that use ER [8] and are based on Q-Learning [15] and Double Q-Learning [4]. The authors carried out experiments and evaluated their agents on a set of Atari 2600 games emulated in the Arcade Learning Environment (ALE) [9], which allows complex challenges for RL agents such as non-determinism, stochasticity, and exploration. To approximate the action-value functions the authors used Convolutional Neural Networks (CNN) on the environment state's representations obtained from the video-game frames without any prior information regarding the games, no manually extracted features, and no knowledge regarding the internal state of the ALE emulator. Thus, agent learning occurred only from video inputs, reward signals, the set of possible actions, and the final state information of each game. In turn, Prioritized Experience Replay (PER) [12] improved DQN performance by ranking the experiences based on the magnitude of the TD-error. Another empirical study about ER demonstrated that a large replay buffer can harm the agent performance and that its length is a very important hyperparameter but neglected in the literature [18]. Thus, the authors proposed a method to minimize the negative influence of a large replay buffer, named Combined Experience Replay (CER).

In an ensemble approach, Rainbow [7] combines DDQN, PER, Dueling Networks [14], Asynchronous Advantage Actor-Critic (A3C) [10], Distributional Q-Learning [1], and Noisy DQN [3] integrating these different but complementary ideas, since each one of them contributes in different aspects. Some research works that uses ER have been seeking to improve the RL agents performances in different ways, including changes in the neural networks architectures [6,14]. So, ER has been a fundamental idea to reinforcement learning and is still being investigated by many researchers to understand its contributions and propose improvements [2,16,17]. In this work, we present a method that addresses the experience memory and how we can model and explore it to make the agents learn smaller amounts of data.

3   Background

Reinforcement Learning is learning what to do (i.e., how to map situations to actions), so as to maximize a numerical reward signal. It uses the formal framework of Markov Decision Process (MDP) to define the interaction between a learning agent and its environment in terms of states, actions, and rewards. A MDP is defined by a tuple $(\mathcal{S}, \mathcal{A}, \mathcal{P}, \mathcal{R}, \gamma)$, so that: $\mathcal{S}$ represents a set of states; $\mathcal{A}$ is a set of actions $\mathcal{A} = \{a_1, a_2, \ldots, a_n\}$; $\mathcal{P}(s' \mid s, a)$ is the probability for transiting from state s to s' $(s, s' \in S)$ by taking action $a \in A$; $\mathcal{R}$ is a reward function mapping each state-action pair to a reward in $\mathbb{R}$; and $\gamma \in [0, 1]$ is a discount factor. The agent behavior is represented by a policy π and the value $\pi(a \mid s)$ represents the probability of taking action a at state s. At each time step t, the agent observes a state $s_t \in \mathcal{S}$, and chooses an action $a_t \in \mathcal{A}$ which determines the reward $r_t = \mathcal{R}(s_t, a_t)$ and next state $s_{t+1} \sim \mathcal{P}(\cdot \mid s_t, a_t)$. A discounted sum of future rewards is called return $R_t = \sum_{t'=t}^{\infty} \gamma^{t'-t} r_{t'}$. The agent goal is to learn (or approximate) an optimal policy π^* that maximizes the long-term expected (discounted) reward value.

Q-Learning [15] is a model-free off-policy algorithm that applies successive steps to update the estimates for the action-value function $Q(s, a)$ (that approximates the long-term expected discounted reward value of executing an action from a given state) using TD-learning and minimizing the TD-error (defined by the difference in Eq. 1). This function is named Q-function and its estimated returns are known as Q-values. A higher Q-value indicates that an action a would yield better long-term results in state s. Q-Learning converges to an π^* even if it is not acting optimally every time as long it keeps updating the Q-value estimates for all state-action pairs, as we can describe in Eq. 1.

$$Q(s_t, a_t) \leftarrow Q(s_t, a_t) + \alpha[r + \gamma \max_a Q(s_{t+1}, a) - Q(s_t, a_t)]. \qquad (1)$$

DQN [11] is based on Q-Learning and uses a CNN to approximate the Q-function, which is parameterized by Θ as $Q(s, a, \Theta)$ and updated through using ER [8]. Specifically, at each time-step t, a transition (or experience) is defined by a tuple $\tau_t = (s_t, a_t, r_t, s_{t+1})$, in which s_t is the current state, a_t is the action taken at that state, r_t is the received reward at t, and s_{t+1} is the resulting state after taking action a_t. Recent experiences are stored to construct a replay buffer $\mathcal{D} = \{\tau_1, \tau_2, \ldots, \tau_{N_\mathcal{D}}\}$, in which $N_\mathcal{D}$ is the buffer size. Therefore, a DNN can be trained on samples $(s_t, a_t, r_t, s_{t+1}) \sim U(\mathcal{D})$, drawn uniformly at random from the pool of experiences by iteratively minimizing the following loss function,

$$\mathcal{L}_{DQN}(\Theta_i) = \mathbb{E}_{(s_t, a_t, r_t, s_{t+1}) \sim U(D)} \left[\left(r_t + \gamma \max_{a'} \widehat{Q}(s_{t+1}, a', \Theta') - Q(s_t, a_t, \Theta_i) \right)^2 \right],$$

$$(2)$$

in which Θ_i are the parameters from the i-th iteration. Instead of using the same network, another one provides the target values $\widehat{Q}(s_{t+1}, a', \Theta')$ used to calculate the TD-error, decoupling any feedback that may result from using the same network to generate its own targets.

4 COMPact Experience Replay (COMPER)

COMPER uses ER and TD-learning to update the Q-value function $Q(s, a)$. However, it does not construct just a replay buffer. Instead, COMPER samples transitions from a much more compact structure named *Reduced Transition Memory* ($\mathcal{RTM}$). The goals behind that are two-fold: (i) allowing rare (and possibly expensive) experiences to be sampled more frequently; and (ii) decreasing the amount of memory needed by a large buffer without hampering the convergence time. To achieve that, COMPER first stores transitions together with estimated Q-values into a structure named *Transition Memory* ($\mathcal{TM}$), which is similar to a traditional replay buffer, except for the presence of the Q-value and the identification and indexing of *Similar Transitions* sets ($\mathcal{ST}$). After that, the similarities between transitions stored in $\mathcal{TM}$ can be explored (as explained

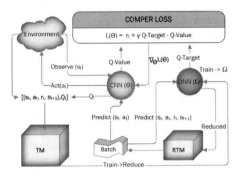

Fig. 1. General COMPER flow and componentes.

in Sect. 4.1) to generate a more compact (but still very helpful) version it – the $\mathcal{RTM}$. Then, transitions $(s_t, a_t, r_t, s_{t+1}) \sim U(\mathcal{RTM})$ are drawn uniformly from $\mathcal{RTM}$ and used to minimize the following loss function,

$$\mathcal{L}_{COMPER}(\Theta_i) = \mathbb{E}_{\tau_t=(s_t,a_t,r_t,s_{t+1})\sim U(\mathcal{RTM})} \left[(r_t + \gamma \, QT(\tau_t, \Omega) - Q(s_t, a_t, \Theta_i))^2 \right], \tag{3}$$

in which $Q(s_t, a_t, \Theta_i)$ is a Q-function approximated by a CNN parameterized by Θ_i at i-th iteration. $QT(\tau_t, \Omega)$ is a Q-target function approximated by another DNN and parameterized by Ω. This function provide the target value and is updated in a supervised way from the $\mathcal{ST}$s stored in $\mathcal{TM}$. Thus, this DNN is also used to build a model to generate the compact structure of $\mathcal{RTM}$ from $\mathcal{TM}$, while seeks to learn the dynamics of $\mathcal{ST}$s to provide better target values at the next agent update step. Figure 1 illustrates how COMPER components interact with each other.

4.1   Modeling the Transition Memory

During training, an agent experiences successive transitions through its interactions with the environment, along with respective rewards. So, these transitions can be stored in a $\mathcal{TM}$ to compose a history of the expected Q-values (analogously to an "*extended*" replay buffer). During agent training runs, each episode starts at an initial state and finishes at a final one. After that, another episode begins. So, transitions with similar state representations may occur and be stored more than once over subsequent episodes. Moreover, we can use sampled transitions (during Q-value function updates steps, when TD-error is computed) and reinsert them in $\mathcal{TM}$ along with its new Q-value estimates. This way, probably several transitions in $\mathcal{TM}$ could be similar in their components (previous state, selected action, immediate reward, and resulting state) but with different Q-value estimates. The criterion (presented ahead) adopted to consider transitions as similar ones is decisive for modeling $\mathcal{TM}$ as a set of $\mathcal{ST}$s. That allows COMPER to predict the Q-values associated with those sets through a DNN and use this estimate as the target value in the next Q-function update step.

Similar Transitions Sets. At each training time-step t, we define a transition by a tuple $\tau_t = (s_t, a_t, r_t, s_{t+1})$, in which s_t is the current state, a_t is the action taken at that state, r_t is the received reward at t, and s_{t+1} is the resulting state after taking action a_t. Consider two transitions $\tau_{t_1} = (s_{t_1}, a_{t_1}, r_{t_1}, s_{t_1+1})$ and $\tau_{t_2} = (s_{t_2}, a_{t_2}, r_{t_2}, s_{t_2+1}), t_1 \neq t_2$. We say that those transitions are similar $(\tau_{t_1} \approx \tau_{t_2})$ when the distance between τ_{t_1} and τ_{t_2} is lesser than a threshold, i.e., $\mathcal{D}(\tau_{t_1}, \tau_{t_2}) \leq \delta$, in which $\mathcal{D}$ could be any distance measure, e.g., Euclidean distance, and δ is a distance (or similarity) threshold value. Let be N the total number of transitions that occurred up to a time instant. Those N transitions are stored in $\mathcal{TM}$ and can be identified as subsets of similar transitions $\mathcal{ST}$ when the similarity condition is satisfied. Moreover, they are stored throughout subsequent agent training episodes and identified by a unique index. Therefore, we can define $\mathcal{TM} = \left\{ [T^i, \mathcal{ST}_i] \,|\, i = 1, 2, 3, \ldots, N_{ST} \right\}$, in which N_{ST} is the total number of distinct subsets of similar transitions, T^i is a unique numbered index and $\mathcal{ST}_i$ represents a set of similar transitions and their Q-values. Thus,

$$\mathcal{ST}_i = \left\{ [\tau_{i(1)}, Q_{i(k)}] \,|\, 1 \leq k \leq N_{ST}^i \right\} \tag{4}$$

in which N_{ST}^i represents the total number of similar transitions in the set $\mathcal{ST}_i$. Thus, $\tau_{i(1)}$ corresponds to some transition $\tau_{t_j}, j \in \{1, \ldots N_{ST}^i\}$ and is the representing transition of similar transitions set $\mathcal{ST}_i$ (e.g., the first one), and $Q_{i(k)}$ is the Q-value corresponding to some transition $\tau_{t_j}, j \in \{1, \ldots N_{ST}^i\}$ such that $\tau_{i(1)} \in \mathcal{ST}_i$ and $\tau_{i(1)} \approx \tau_{i(k)}, 1 \leq k \leq N_{ST}^i$. Therefore, $\mathcal{TM}$ can seem as a set of $\mathcal{ST}$s. A single representative transition for each $\mathcal{ST}$ can be generated together with the prediction of their next Q-value from an explicit model of $\mathcal{ST}$ using a DNN.

Reduced Transition Memory From $\mathcal{TM}$, one can produce a $\mathcal{RTM}$ in which τ_i' is the transition that represents all the similar transitions so far identified in $\mathcal{ST}_i$, so that $\mathcal{RTM} = \{ [\tau_i'] \,|\, i = 1, 2, 3, \ldots, N_{ST} \}$. Unlike $\mathcal{TM}$, $\mathcal{RTM}$ does not take care about sets of similar transitions, since each τ_i' is unique and represents all the transitions in a given $\mathcal{ST}_i$. It gives the transitions stored in $\mathcal{RTM}$ the chance of having their Q-values re-estimated. Besides, sampling from $\mathcal{RTM}$ increases the chances of selecting rare and very informative transitions more frequently, at the same time that helps increasing diversity (because of variability in each sample).

4.2 Identifying and Indexing Similar Transitions

We identify similar transitions by defining a *Transition Memory Index* ($\mathcal{TMI}$) as part of $\mathcal{TM}$. At each training time-step t we insert a transition τ_t together with its estimated Q-value (Q_t) into $\mathcal{TM}$ and check the $\mathcal{TMI}$ for a similar transition given a minimum distance (or similarity) threshold δ. If there is a similar transition, $\mathcal{TMI}$ will return its unique numerical identifier T^i. Otherwise, we insert τ_t together with Q_t into $\mathcal{TMI}$ and get the corresponding T^i. So, a given T^i is used to find the first $\tau_{i(1)}$ similar transition in $\mathcal{TM}$ and update its

---

Algorithm 1: $\mathcal{TM}$-StoreTransition

---

input: transition $[\tau_t, Q_t]$, distance (or similarity) threshold value δ

1 $T^i \leftarrow \mathcal{TMI}.\text{GetIndex}(\tau_t, \delta)$;

2 **if** $T^i == 0$ **then**

3 $\quad\mid\quad$ $T^i \leftarrow \mathcal{TMI}.\text{UpdateIndex}(\tau_t)$;

4 $\quad\mid\quad$ $\mathcal{TM}.\text{Insert}(T^i, [\tau_t, Q_t])$;

5 **else**

6 $\quad\mid\quad$ $\mathcal{TM}.\text{Update}(T^i, Q_t)$;

Q-value, or to insert τ_t as the first similar transition, together with its first Q_t, identified by T^i. The set of subsequent transitions identified as similar under the same identifier T^i are what we call $\mathcal{ST}_i$. But we do not need to store the entire $\mathcal{ST}_i$. We can use its corresponding T^i to locate its representing transition tuple and update its associated Q-value, considering that its previous value contributions were learned by the Q-target network. Algorithm 1 shows details of that procedure.

4.3   COMPER – Detailed Description

COMPER (see Algorithm 2) uses two memories, named Transitions Memory ($\mathcal{TM}$) and Reduced Transitions Memory ($\mathcal{RTM}$). A CNN approximates the action-value function Q to estimates the Q-values (Q_{value}) from a sample of transitions stored in $\mathcal{RTM}$. Another component named QT uses a DNN both to produce the $\mathcal{RTM}$ from $\mathcal{TM}$ and to predict the Q-target value (Q_{target}). The agent observes the current environment state (s_t) at each iteration (t) and selects an action (a_t). Then, it performs a_t on s_t, receives an immediate reward (r_t), observes a new state (s_{t+1}) – that becomes the current state s_t to the next iteration, and an estimate of Q_{value}. These elements make up the transition τ_t which is indexed by the transitions memory index ($\mathcal{TMI}$) and stored in $\mathcal{TM}$. QT is updated and used to produce $\mathcal{RTM}$ from $\mathcal{TM}$ at a frequency defined by the hyper-parameter utf. In turn, Q is updated at a frequency defined by the hyper-parameter tf, and this process consists of: (i) performing a uniform sampling of transitions from $\mathcal{RTM}$; (ii) predicting the Q_{target} using QT; and (iii) estimating the Q_{value} using Q. The TD-error is calculated from these estimates and used to update Q through backpropagation. First, if $\mathcal{RTM}$ is empty or depending on utf, QT is updated, that is, its DNN is trained, and then it is used to update $\mathcal{RTM}$. So, a batch of transitions (with size k) is sampled from $\mathcal{RTM}$ and QT is used to predict the Q_{target} values for each sampled transition. Then, Q is used to estimate the Q_{values} from the state s_t and action a_t for each sampled transition. The TD-error is calculated from Q_{value} and Q_{target}. A gradient vector as a function of TD-error is then obtained and accumulated in a vector Δ. After iterating over all the sampled transitions (which is always done in parallel), the parameters Θ are updated at a learning rate α.

Algorithm 2: COMPER

---

input: batch size k, learning rate α, trainging frequency tf, number of states to be observed sn, ϵ-Greedy probability ϵ, update target frequency utf, discount factor γ, similarity threshold value δ

1 Initialize $TM \leftarrow \emptyset$, $RTM \leftarrow \emptyset$, $t \leftarrow 0$, $\Delta \leftarrow 0$; Initialize Θ, Ω;
2 Initialize $env \leftarrow EnvironmentInstance$, $run \leftarrow True$, $countframes \leftarrow 0$;
3 $s_t \leftarrow env.InitialState()$;
4 $a_t, Q_t \leftarrow \epsilon\text{-Greedy}(s_t, \epsilon, \Theta)$;
5 **while** run **do**
6 $\quad$ $s_{t+1}, r_t \leftarrow step(s_t, a_t)$;
7 $\quad$ $TM.StoreTransition([\tau(s_t, a_t, r_t, s_{t+1}), Q_t], \delta)$;
8 $\quad$ $s_t \leftarrow s_{t+1}$;
9 $\quad$ $t \leftarrow t + 1$;
10 $\quad$ **if** $t \bmod tf == 0$ **then**
11 $\quad\quad$ **if** $RTM == \emptyset$ *or* $t \bmod utf == 0$ **then**
12 $\quad\quad\quad$ $\Omega \leftarrow Train(QT, TM)$;
13 $\quad\quad\quad$ $RTM \leftarrow \text{ProduceRTM}(QT, TM, \Omega)$;
14 $\quad\quad$ **for** $i \leftarrow 1$ **to** k **do**
15 $\quad\quad\quad$ Sample uniformly $\tau' = (s_t, a_t, r_t, s_{t+1})$ from RTM;
16 $\quad\quad\quad$ $Q_{target} \leftarrow Forward(\tau', QT, \Omega)$;
17 $\quad\quad\quad$ $Q_{value} \leftarrow Forward(s_t, Q, \Theta)[a_t]$;
18 $\quad\quad\quad$ $\mathcal{L}(\Theta) \leftarrow r_t + \gamma \times Q_{target} - Q_{value}$;
19 $\quad\quad\quad$ $\Delta \leftarrow \Delta + \mathcal{L}(\Theta) \times \bigtriangledown_\Theta Q_{value}$;
20 $\quad\quad$ $\Theta \leftarrow \Theta + \alpha \times \Delta$;
21 $\quad\quad$ $\Delta \leftarrow 0$;
22 $\quad$ $countframes \leftarrow countframes + env.framesnumber$;
23 $\quad$ **if** $env.ReachedFinalState()$ **then**
24 $\quad\quad$ $run \leftarrow (countframes \leq sn)$;
25 $\quad\quad$ **if** run **then**
26 $\quad\quad\quad$ $env.ResetStates()$;
27 $\quad\quad\quad$ $s_t \leftarrow env.InitialState()$;
28 $\quad$ $a_t, Q_t \leftarrow \epsilon\text{-Greedy}(s_t, \epsilon, \Theta)$;

---

5 Methodology of Experiments

We evaluated COMPER agent on the Arcade Learning Environment (ALE)[1] [9]. Relevant works in the literature have used different methodologies for the development and evaluation of RL agents, making it challenging to analyze and compare their results. Therefore, in [9] the authors proposed a very well-defined methodology for experiments and agent evaluation using ALE, and we follow their propositions with minor adjustments. We define a limit of 100,000 frames for each training run and log the results at every 100 iterations and at the end of each episode. We divided the number of episodes obtained in each run to split the results into 3 checkpoints and calculated the average scores (with standard deviations) for the last 5 episodes preceding each checkpoint. That was necessary because of the smaller number of episodes since we reduced the total number of frames, which is 0.0005% of the total number used in [9]. We have also redefined the decay rate of ϵ, so that it starts at 1.0 and drops to 0.01 in 90,000 frames (instead of 1 million frames used in [9]).

In COMPER, the weights Ω in $QT(\tau_t, \Omega)$ are updated through backpropagation over sets of similar transitions every 100 agent steps, using a similarity threshold $\delta = 10^{-4}$. In turn, the update of $Q(s_t, a_t, \Theta)$ is performed every 4

---

[1] Available at https://github.com/mgbellemare/Arcade-Learning-Environment.

Table 1. Average scores of the last 3* and 10 training episodes. The best results are in bold and the standard deviation in parentheses.

	COMPER (Single)		COMPER(Stacked)		DQN
	LSTM	MLP	LSTM	MLP	CNN
Freeway*	19.53 (9.77)	8.4 (10.9)	**22.33** (0.0)	9.46 (11.59)	0.0 (0.0)
Asteroids	**827.8** (142.93)	781.18 (108.18)	362.4 (52.05)	442.8 (59.52)	237.80 (47.57)
Battle Zone*	**4,733.33** (2,080.6)	3,200.00 (2,049.24)	4,400.0 (2,689.59	1,066.66 (1,289.27)	1,666.66 (1,135.29)
Video Pinball*	**7,353.26** (7,366.18)	3,225.46 (3,828.35)	2,524.73 (84)	6,827.13 (3,605.71)	6,936.13 (2,992.37
Seaquest	**279.6** (24.21)	52.4 (59.21)	73.2 (3.71)	44.4 (16.12)	132.00 (10.2)
Asterix	239.0 (58.3)	248.0 (98.2)	**258.0** (130.64)	207.0 (48.23)	182.00 (22.05)
Beam Rider*	509.06 (89.83)	504.53 (94.87)	416.53 (123.7)	465.33 (73.79)	**563.20** (89.26)
Space Invaders	182.2 (68.27)	131.3 (75.13)	110.7 (53.58)	167.3 (76.92)	**199.80** (49.78)

agent steps, similar to DQN in [9]. Moreover, we start weight updating after the first 100 steps in COMPER and 1,000 steps in DQN (instead of 50,000 as in [9]). Finally, we evaluate COMPER by representing the states of the environment either with a single frame in a matrix with dimensions of $84 \times 84 \times 1$ or with frames stacked in a matrix of $84 \times 84 \times 4$. In both cases, we just used the luminance values for every two frames using the color averaging method of ALE. We implemented our DQN agent as defined in [11] and only adopted new hyperparameters values for the total number of frames, the ϵ value decay, the results log frequency, the learning start, and the target function update frequency to accomplish our experiments. Finally, we evaluated and compared the use of a Long-short Term Memory (LSTM) and a Multi-layer Perceptron (MLP) to model DNN QT, which is used to produce the $\mathcal{RTM}$ and to predict the Q-target value. We adjusted the hyperparameters in just 3 training runs in the game Space Invaders both for COMPER and DQN. We then use the best values to run the experiments on all other games.

6 Evaluation Results

We report results for eight challenging games from ALE in five training runs of COMPER and DQN with 100,000 frames and about 25,000 (single frame) and 6,000 (staked frames) iterations. Moreover, we report the results for COMPER using two different neural network architectures, an LSMT and an MLP, to approximate the Q-target function. We used an 8-core CPU (1 thread per core) and 48 GB of RAM to perform our experiments and spent about 9 to 12 h on each training run using staked frames and 24 to 36 h using single frame.

We evaluated COMPER using single frame and stacked frames and compared the results using an LSTM and an MLP to approximate the Q-target function.

Table 1 presents the average scores (and standard deviation, in parentheses) for five runs of COMPER and DQN, calculated for the last 3 or 10 training episodes with a limit of 100,000 frames from ALE. For the Freeway, Battle Zone, Video Pinball, and Beam Rider, we have computed only the last three episodes because of the fewer total episodes we obtained compared with the other games. We also defined checkpoints at the end of every tertile on the total frames number throughout the training episodes. Tables 2 and 3 present the average scores (and standard deviation) for the last 3 and 5 episodes before each of these checkpoints. COMPER obtains the best results on the games Freeway, Asteroids, Battle Zone, Video Pinball, Seaquest, and Asterix. Whether using single frame or stacked frames, the best results were obtained by approximating the Q-target function through an LSTM. The large standard deviation for the Video Pinball with single frame is due to a training run for which the agent has not scored in the last three episodes. The results for Beam Rider seems to be statistically equivalent, while COMPER results for Space Invaders were not so good. Regarding the evaluation on the checkpoints, we highlight the continuous and stable evolution of COMPER with LSTM on the games Freeway, Asteroids, Seaquest, Asterix, and Beam Rider, while the adoption of MLP decreases the COMPER performance especially for the games Freeway, Battle Zone and Seaquest.

It is worth saying that Freeway, Seaquest, and Asteroids are complex games. The first two present difficulties in agent rewarding related to long-term policy learning needs, while the latter deals with a hard exploration task and complex dynamics [9]. Asterix seems to present a high degree of randomness in the rewarding elements' positions at each time step, making the rewards accumulation strongly related to the number of interactions with the game environment. In turn, there are a lot of simultaneous rewarding elements in Space Invaders

Table 2. COMPER with LSTM - Average scores of the last 3* and 5 last episodes of each tertile. The best results for each tertile are in bold and the standard deviation in parentheses.

	End of First Tertile			End of Second Tertile			End of Third Tertile		
	COMPER (Single)	COMPER (Stacked)	DQN	COMPER (Single)	COMPER (Stacked)	DQN	COMPER (Single)	COMPER (Stacked)	DQN
Freeway*	**4.26** (2.38)	4.0 (0.0)	0.0 (0.0)	12 (6.70)	**16.0** (0.0)	0.0 (0.0)	19.53 (10.92)	**22.33** (0.0)	0.0 (0.0)
Asteroids	**885.20** (124.95)	440.8 (85.75)	376.00 (81.47)	**902.40** (175.34)	334.80 (50.56)	386.00 (51.51)	**846.0** (237.37)	341.20 (78.55)	233.60 (0.0)
Battle Zone*	1,933.33 (862.81)	**3,400.00** (1,673.32)	3,200.00 (2,089.65)	**4,333.33** (2,392.11)	2,333.33 (408.24)	2,066.66 (1,038.16)	**4,733.33** (2,326.17)	4,400.00 (3,003.70)	1,666.66 (1,269.29)
Video Pinball*	10,157.73 (6,695.87)	2,565.73 (1,442.02)	**11,513.86** (7,672.34)	**8,747.33** (8,058.55)	2,665.46 (2,844.67)	4,454.66 (1,127.78)	**8,544.60** (10,671.12)	2,524.73 (2,764.71)	3,936.13 (3,345.57)
Seaquest	**143.2** (17.52)	76.8 (15.59)	78.40 (40.52)	**356.0** (91.82)	80.0 (22.44)	152.00 (23.50)	**222.4** (38.32)	72.0 (4.0)	123.20 (15.88)
Asterix	268.0 (82.28)	258.0 (82.88)	**290.0** (58.99)	228.0 (30.33)	210.0 (24.49)	**234.00** (18.55)	232.0 (52.15)	**256.0.0** (165.92)	166.00 (45.87)
Beam Rider*	**417.33** (119.26)	352.53 (102.05)	381.33 (46.38)	419.46 (49.30)	354.93 (116.59)	**475.20** (56.12)	509.06 (100.43)	416.53 (137.81)	**563.20** (89.26)
Space Invaders	139.8 (42.24)	109.6 (42.84)	**140.80** (59.94)	**201.6** (30.58)	128.4 (31.54)	174.00 (35.57)	193.8 (63.08)	129.2 (75.74)	**213.80** (68.90)

Table 3. COMPER with MLP - Average scores of the last 3* and 5 last episodes of each tertile. The best results for each tertile are in bold and the standard deviation in parentheses.

	End of first tertile			End of second tertile			End of third tertile		
	COMPER (Single)	COMPER (Stacked)	DQN	COMPER (Single)	COMPER (Stacked)	DQN	COMPER (Single)	COMPER (Stacked)	DQN
Freeway*	**2.13** (2.92)	2.0 (2.73)	0.0 (0.0)	6.0 (8.21)	**6.13** (8.39)	0.0 (0.0)	8.4 (11.50)	**9.46** (12.96)	0.0 (0.0)
Asteroids	**883.2** (105.93)	379.6 (96.69)	376.00 (81.47)	**871.2** (288.55)	402.4 (141.02)	386.00 (51.51)	**837.2** (168.31)	420.8 (87.05)	233.60 (0.0)
Battle Zone*	**3,266.66** (2,465.31)	2,200.00 (1,425.94)	3,200.00 (2,089.65)	**3,066.66** (1,876.75)	1,533.33 (1,345.77)	2,066.66 (1,038.16)	**3,200.00** (2,693.61)	1,066.66 (1,441.44)	1,666.66 (1,269.29)
Video Pinball*	9,114.66 (5,096.14)	4,075.40 (2,050.22)	**11,513.86** (7,672.34)	**7,330.33** (9,133.18)	7,303.80 (5,064.68)	4,454.66 (1,127.78)	3,225.46 (4,280.22)	**6,827.13** (4,031.30)	3,936.13 (3,345.57)
Seaquest	67.2 (85.20)	65.6 (36.17)	**78.40** (40.52)	75.2 (101.36)	71.2 (38.71)	**152.00** (23.50)	40.8 (47.19)	39.2 (18.41)	**123.20** (15.88)
Asterix	266.0 (106.91)	212.0 (56.74)	**290.00** (58.99)	**294.0** (45.05)	260.0 (66.33)	234.00 (18.55)	**242.0** (82.88)	204.0 (47.74)	166.00 (45.87)
Beam Rider*	**404.80** (91.35)	390.13 (83.35)	381.13 (46.38)	415.46 (150.63)	437.06 (82.57)	**475.20** (56.12)	504.53 (106.06)	465.33 (82.49)	**563.20** (89.26)
Space Invaders	**188.4** (70.35)	188.2 (88.03)	140.80 (59.94)	132.0 (47.43)	165.4 (63.03)	**174.00** (35.57)	109.4 (77.91)	181.6 (89.83)	**213.80** (68.90)

screen from the first frames until long after the game starts. Thus, the agent has many chances to hit an enemy (and be hit), and the number of frames does not seem to impact the total reward accumulated up to 100,000 frames, contributing more towards reducing the standard deviation.

One should also note that COMPER scores better when using single frame (instead of stacked frames) and that training runs with single frame were the ones that produced more similar transitions. Moreover, memory size from which the agent sampled transitions is considerably lesser than those used in the literature. Therefore, the agent can learn from smaller memories, and similar transition sets help capture the dynamics regarding the expected long-term rewards, which an LSTM seems to better model (compared to an MLP).

To verify the behavior of $\mathcal{TM}$, we evaluated the number of similar transitions throughout the training episodes, and the sizes of these similar sets. Figure 2 illustrates the average sizes of the similar transitions sets for Freeway and Beam Rider. We can verify three main behaviors: (i) new sets were created in different moments; (ii) some of these sets are removed from the memory and do not occur again, while others remain being updated until the last training episode; and (iii) when using single frame, the number of similar transitions is larger than when using staked frames. This behavior is observed in all games. Figures 3a and 3b illustrate the sizes of the similar transition sets for all the games with single and stacked frames, while Figs. 3c and 3d show the occurrence of similarities. This information is relevant because the number of similarities implies the number of times the Q-value for similar transitions was updated instead of reinserting a new tuple in the memory, and that helps to maintain its size small and under control. As the number of observed frames increases throughout the successive episodes, we can see that the size of $\mathcal{TM}$ varies but keeps an upper

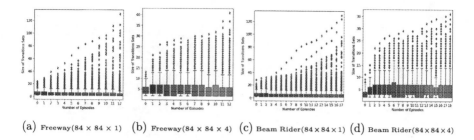

(a) Freeway(84 × 84 × 1)   (b) Freeway(84 × 84 × 4)   (c) Beam Rider(84×84×1)   (d) Beam Rider(84×84×4)

Fig. 2. Sizes of similar transitions sets.

limit because of the reduction step applied when similar transitions are removed to train the Q-target network and update $\mathcal{RTM}$. The small size of $\mathcal{RTM}$ is verified directly by the total number of unique transitions at the end of each run. And, even sampling from such a small number of transitions, COMPER manages to achieve good results. This behaviors are ilustrated on Fig. 4.

A detailed analysis shows the following. For Freeway, COMPER did not score until the end of the second training episode. However, once it received the first point, it began to accumulate rewards continuously (see Figs. 2, 5a and 5b). In turn, DQN was somehow unable to get any score with only 100,000 frames. For Asteroids, agents got high scores in the first episodes and kept values close to the average until the end of the runs when they were only exploiting, and COMPER obtained the best results even at the end of each tertile. For Battle Zone, COMPER did not reduce the average scores at the end of each tertile and maintained the best results compared to DQN. Video Pinball presented a lesser stable behavior for both agents, but COMPER obtained better average scores at the end of the runs and explicit learning progress at the first run with single frame and at the last with stacked frames (Figs. 5c and 5d). For Seaquest, COMPER presented increasing scores from the first to the third tertile at all the runs, both with single and stacked frames and obtained the best result at the last tertile. For Asterix, COMPER scores did not decrease at the end of the tertiles, and

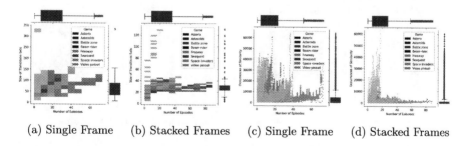

(a) Single Frame   (b) Stacked Frames   (c) Single Frame   (d) Stacked Frames

Fig. 3. Sizes of the similar transitions' sets throughout episodes and occurrences of similarity.

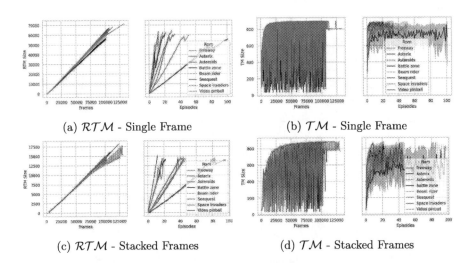

(a) $\mathcal{RTM}$ - Single Frame

(b) $\mathcal{TM}$ - Single Frame

(c) $\mathcal{RTM}$ - Stacked Frames

(d) $\mathcal{TM}$ - Stacked Frames

Fig. 4. Behavior of transition memories.

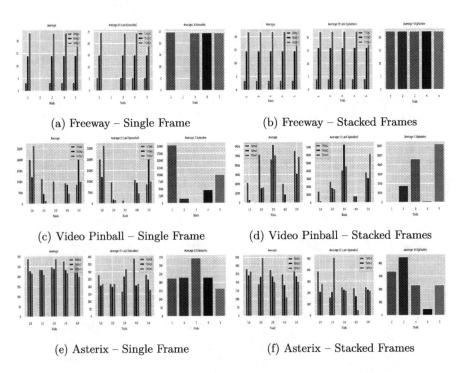

(a) Freeway – Single Frame

(b) Freeway – Stacked Frames

(c) Video Pinball – Single Frame

(d) Video Pinball – Stacked Frames

(e) Asterix – Single Frame

(f) Asterix – Stacked Frames

Fig. 5. Detailed results for Single Frame × Stacked Frames. From left to right: average scores of each tertile per run, averages scores of the last episodes per tertile, and average scores of the last episode per run.

we highlight the third run with single frame and the second with stacked frames (Figs. 5c and 5d). Moreover, COMPER reached the last episodes with better results than DQN. For Beam Rider, COMPER and DQN obtained very close average values and similar behaviors throughout the learning process. Finally, the same did not happen for Space Invaders, COMPER and DQN obtained close average scores throughout the first tertiles, but COMPER got worse results than the DQN for the last tertile. Complete test results are available at the COMPER research repository[2], which contains all the training log files for COMPER and DQN, with Jupyter notebooks used for analysis.

7   Conclusion and Future Work

We propose a new method, named ***COMP**act **E**xperience **R**eplay* (COMPER), to address relevant issues concerning temporal credit assignment and experience replay. We assessed its effectiveness through training and evaluation on ALE. The results demonstrate that it is a promising method in that it achieves excellent performance on difficult games with fewer observations of the environment and a smaller memory than those used in the literature. We highlight that COMPER scores better when using single frame instead of stacked frames and that the training runs with single frame generated the greatest amount of similar transitions. Therefore, using COMPER, agents can learn from smaller memories, and similar transition sets help capture the dynamics regarding the expected long-term rewards, which an LSTM seems to better model (compared to an MLP). However, there are still some aspects to investigate about this method. For instance, COMPER could be evaluated on other games, especially those that depend on learning a long-term action policy. Besides, new experiments can investigate the impact on the results of the similarity threshold value. Also, in future works, would be interesting to investigate the effect of the *Reduced Transitions Memory* (*RT M*) in other methods such as Deep Deterministic Policy Gradient (DDPG). Finally, we believe that the main contribution of this work is to bring a new discussion not only about how to deal with the retrieval of agent experiences but also about how one can store them.

References

1. Bellemare, M.G., Dabney, W., Munos, R.: A distributional perspective on reinforcement learning. In: Precup, D., Teh, Y.W. (eds.) Proceedings of the 34th International Conference on Machine Learning. Proceedings of Machine Learning Research, vol. 70, pp. 449–458 (2017)
2. Fedus, W., et al.: Revisiting fundamentals of experience replay. In: Daumé, H., Singh, A. (eds.) Proceedings of the 37th International Conference on Machine Learning. Proceedings of Machine Learning Research, vol. 119, pp. 3061–3071 (2020)

---

[2] https://github.com/DanielEugenioNeves/COMPER-RELEASE-RESULTS.

3. Fortunato, M., et al.: Noisy networks for exploration. In: Proceedings of the International Conference on Representation Learning (2018)
4. van Hasselt, H.: Double Q-learning. In: Lafferty, J.D., Williams, C.K.I., Shawe-Taylor, J., Zemel, R.S., Culotta, A. (eds.) Advances in Neural Information Processing Systems 23 (NIPS), pp. 2613–2621 (2010)
5. van Hasselt, H., Guez, A., Silver, D.: Deep reinforcement learning with double q-learning. In: Proceedings of the Thirtieth AAAI Conference on Artificial Intelligence, vol. 30 (2016)
6. Hausknecht, M., Stone, P.: Deep recurrent q-learning for partially observable mdps. In: AAAI Fall Symposium on Sequential Decision Making for Intelligent Agents (2015)
7. Hessel, M., et al.: Rainbow: Combining improvements in deep reinforcement learning. In: Proceedings of the AAAI Conference on Artificial Intelligence, vol. 32 (2018)
8. Lin, L.J.: Self-improving reactive agents based on reinforcement learning, planning and teaching. Mach. Learn. 8(3–4), 293–321 (1992)
9. Machado, M.C., Bellemare, M.G., Talvitie, E., Veness, J., Hausknecht, M.J., Bowling, M.: Revisiting the arcade learning environment: Evaluation protocols and open problems for general agents. J. Artifi. Intell. Res. 61, 523–562 (2018)
10. Mnih, V., et al.: Asynchronous methods for deep reinforcement learning. In: Balcan, M.F., Weinberger, K.Q. (eds.) Proceedings of The 33rd International Conference on Machine Learning. Proceedings of Machine Learning Research, vol. 48, pp. 1928–1937 (2016)
11. Mnih, V., et al.: Human-level control through deep reinforcement learning. Nature 518(7540), 529–533 (2015)
12. Schaul, T., Quan, J., Antonoglou, I., Silver, D.: Prioritized experience replay. In: Proceedings of the International Conference on Representation Learning (2016)
13. Sutton, R.S.: Reinforcement learning architectures. In: Proceedings ISKIT 1992 International Symposium on Neural Information Processing (1992)
14. Wang, Z., Schaul, T., Hessel, M., Hasselt, H., Lanctot, M., Freitas, N.: Dueling network architectures for deep reinforcement learning. In: Balcan, M.F., Weinberger, K.Q. (eds.) Proceedings of The 33rd International Conference on Machine Learning. Proceedings of Machine Learning Research, vol. 48, pp. 1995–2003 (2016)
15. Watkins, C.J.C.H., Dayan, P.: Q-learning. Mach. Learn. 8(3), 279–292 (1992)
16. Wei, Q., Ma, H., Chen, C., Dong, D.: Deep reinforcement learning with quantum-inspired experience replay. IEEE Trans. Cybern. 1–13 (2021)
17. Zha, D., Lai, K.H., Zhou, K., Hu, X.: Experience replay optimization. In: Proceedings of the Twenty-Eighth International Joint Conference on Artificial Intelligence (IJCAI), pp. 4243–4249 (2019)
18. Zhang, S., Sutton, R.S.: A deeper look at experience replay. In: Deep Reinforcement Learning Symposium (NIPS) (2017)

Human Identification Based on Gait and Soft Biometrics

Daniel Ricardo dos Santos Jangua$^{(\boxtimes)}$ ⑩ and Aparecido Nilceu Marana ⑩

Faculty of Sciences, UNESP - São Paulo State University, Bauru, SP, Brazil
{daniel.jangua,nilceu.marana}@unesp.br

Abstract. Nowadays, one of the most important and challenging tasks in Biometrics and Computer Vision is the automatic human identification. This problem has been approached in many works over the last decades, that resulted in state-of-art methods based on biometric features such as fingerprint, iris and face. Despite the great development in this area, there are still many challenges to overcome, and this present work aims to present an approach to one of them, which is the automatic person identification in low-resolution videos captured in unconstrained scenarios, at a distance, in a covert and non-invasive way, with little or none subject cooperation. In scenarios like this, the use of classical methods may not perform properly and using features such as gait, can be the only feasible option. Gait can be defined as the act of walking. Early studies showed that humans are able to identify individuals by the way they walk, and this premise is the basis of most recent works on gait recognition. However, even state-of-art methods, still do not present the required robustness to work on a productive environment. The goal of this work is to propose an improvement to state-of-art gait recognition methods based on 2D poses, by merging them using multi-biometrics techniques. The original methods use gait information extracted from 2D poses estimated over video sequences, to identify the individuals. In order to assess the proposed extensions, two public gait datasets were used, CASIA Gait Dataset-A and CASIA Gait Dataset-B. Both datasets have videos of a number of people walking in different directions and conditions. In the original and in the extended method, the classification was carried out by a 1-NN classifier using the chi-square distance function.

Keywords: Gait recognition · Biometrics · Soft biometrics

1 Introduction

In the last decade, the term 'Biometrics' has became increasingly usual. This phenomenon occurred due to the growing need for a fast and reliable way of human identification to avoid frauds and ensure the security of individuals in society, since traditional identification methods such as possession of documents and passwords do not meet today's security and reliability requirements. In this

J. C. Xavier-Junior and R. A. Rios (Eds.): BRACIS 2022, LNAI 13654, pp. 111–122, 2022.
https://doi.org/10.1007/978-3-031-21689-3_9

context, Biometrics consists in the study of physical and behavioral characteristics of human being, in order to identify them [4]. These characteristics that
can be used to identify an individual are called biometric traits or features [1].

It's a fact that there are already a sort of biometrics state-of-art methods that
meet the actual need in most common scenarios of daily life. However, as most
of deployed biometrics systems are based on traits like face and fingerprints, an
important challenge lasts, which is the person identification in scenarios where
the biometric data is captured in low-resolution, at a distance, and the biometric
system must be operated in covert mode [15]. in these cases, the use of gait
features can be the most reliable approach.

Gait can be defined as the behavioral patterns of the human body in the act
of walking, integrating repetitive movements that form a periodic pattern called
'gait cycle' [1]. Many studies conducted in the last decade indicates that gait
features encodes enough discriminating information to perform human identification [10]. There are already a sort of approaches for gait recognition that
presented robust results [3,6,8,16,17].

However, despite the relatively great performance considering all the environments conditions, there is still a need for improvement in these methods in
order to be feasible in a real-world situation. Proposing effective improvements
to state-of-the-art methods tends to be a difficult task, since almost all of their
hyperparameters have already been tuned. In cases like this, the combination
between different methods can be a fast and effective solution to highlight their
strengths and mitigate their flaws.

Multi-biometrics techniques are based on the premise that human beings
identify each others based on multiple biometric characteristics. This process
can be seen as a conciliation of evidence among multiple sources of information.
In this way, the purpose of multi-biometrics is to perform biometric identification based on multiple biometric methods or traits merged at some level of the
biometric system, improving the performance and increasing the robustness of
this system. The merging can occur at the sensor, feature, score, rank or decision
levels [4].

The goal of this work, is to propose improvements to state-of-art model-based
gait recognition methods [6,8]. The improvements were based on multi-biometric
techniques, merging different methods into a single biometric system. The gait
recognition methods were mixed with each other and with a different method,
based on anthropometric measurements [13], and the results were evaluated on
the CASIA Gait Dataset-A and CASIA Gait Dataset-B, comparing each method
individually.

This paper is organized as follows: Section 2 gives an introduction to gait
recognition and human pose estimation. Section 3 discusses multi-biometric techniques. Section 4 presents the methods utilized in the experiments. Section 5
describes the proposed approach. Section 6 shows the carried out experiments in
detail and Sect. 7 draws some conclusions obtained from the results.

Fig. 1. Gait cycle resumed in 4 frames [7].

2   Gait Recognition

Gait has some unique properties that other biometric approaches do not have: (i) it can be captured far away and at low resolution, (ii) it can be done with simple instrumentation, (iii) it does not need the subject cooperation, (iv) it is hard to impersonate; and (v) it works well even with partial occlusion of body parts [15].

According to Nixon et al. [9], since gait is a composition of body parts repetitive movements, it's possible to resume this pattern into a 'gait cycle'. Gait cycle is the time interval between successive instances of initial foot-to-floor contact. Inside each gait cycle the superior and inferior member of the human body realize a movement similar to a pendulum, varying its angulation in relation to the horizontal (or vertical) axis forming a pattern of angle variation and, with this information, it's possible to create a gait signature that can be used to identify the individual. Figure 1 shows a gait cycle presented in four frames, extracted from CASIA Gait Dataset-A.

The most recent gait recognition methods are model-based, which means that they use a pose estimator to extract human poses from each video frame and then extract gait features that are used to identify the subjects. All the methods approached by this work utilize the pose estimator OpenPose [2].

2.1   Pose Estimation

Human pose estimation is an important tool in computer vision for understanding people in images. Pose estimation can be described as the task of detecting joint points in the human body in a given image [14]. In model-based gait recognition methods, pose estimation is an essential step, that provides a 2D model of the human body for each frame of a walking sequence video. With this 2D model, that maps every key point of a pose, it's possible to calculate a variety of features from the subject's limbs movement over time that describe its gait signature.

OpenPose, proposed in [2], is a real-time method for multi-person 2D pose detection on images capable of performing detection with high accuracy and good computational performance. It is the first open-source method for real-time 2D pose detection that includes body, feet, hands and face key-points. Unlike the most common approaches that detects each subject in the input image and estimate their poses individually, OpenPose takes a bottom-up approach that treats the image globally, detecting all body parts in the input image and associating them forming each individual's pose. Figure 2 presents the pipeline of the OpenPose method.

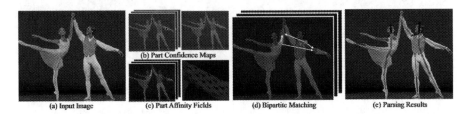

Fig. 2. Pipeline of the OpenPose method presented in [2]. The method uses the Part Confidence Maps (b) to detect the joints of human bodies in the input image and associate them using the Part Affinity Fields (c) by Bipartite Matching (d) forming poses of each individual in the image (e).

3   Multi-biometrics

The term multi-biometrics can be explained as the fusion of different types of information into a single biometric recognition system [11]. Among the main advantages of using this technique, it is possible to mention: (i) the significant improvement in accuracy, depending on the information and methodology of the merger performed, (ii) the treatment of issues such as the non-universality of the biometric method, (iii) greater tolerance to noisy data captured by the sensors, since it has more than one extractor of features and different representations, and (iv) the greater fault tolerance, since there can be more than one algorithm or sensors working simultaneously.

The use of multiple sources of information can be performed in six different scenarios: multi-sensors, multi-algorithms, multi-units (multiple instances of a biometric identifier), multi-samples, multi-modalities (different biometric identifiers) or hybrid, that integrate combinations of the five previous scenarios [11]. For this work, score-level fusion was used. The fusion takes place in the classification phase, and after using a classifier for each method, generating two distinct scores, a combination is made between them to generate a single result.

3.1   Soft-biometrics

According to [5], soft biometric traits are characteristics that encode some information about the individual, but do not have enough distinctiveness and permanence to determine the individual's identity by itself. These traces can be classified into two groups: discrete and continuous. Traits such as gender, ethnicity, eye color, and skin tone are by nature classified as discrete variables, while characteristics such as weight, height, and anthropometry (limb measurements) are continuous variables. Although, they do not perform well in the biometric recognition task individually, soft features can be used to improve the performance of traditional biometric systems [5], such as facial recognition, fingerprints or even gait recognition.

4 Related Works

The method proposed in [6] is based on estimating poses in videos of individuals walking, and the first step of the method consists of using OpenPose [2] to extract the 2D poses of individuals in each frame from the input video. Then, for each frame, the coordinates of the detected joint points are used to calculate the angle of each limb part in relation to the image horizontal axis, such as the distance between the point representing the neck and the line that passes through the two points that delimit a certain member part. This information is used to build, two histograms for each limb part (one for angles and other for distances), that represent the behavior of the limb during the entire gait sequence, and which are used as gait feature vectors. Finally, the two feature vectors are used by a 1-NN (Nearest Neighbour) classifier to identify the individual present in the input video. Figure 3 illustrates the method step-by-step.

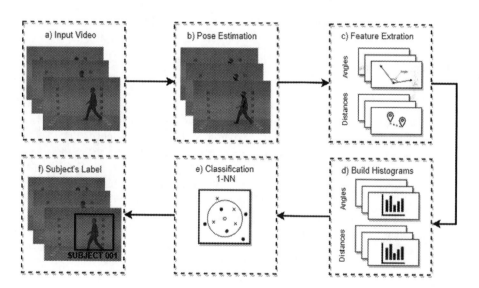

Fig. 3. Block diagram of the method proposed in [6].

In [8], the authors propose a method for gait recognition based on 2D poses extracted by a pose detector. This method utilizes the coordinates of each key point in every video frame to build signals, that represent the behavior of each joint during the gait cycle. Each signal has two components, that are obtained by the calculation of dx and dy, that are the distances to the neck key point in relation to the horizontal and vertical axis, respectively. After obtaining the signals S^i, the next step is the construction of Motion Histograms H^i. The values of S^i are divided into intervals at $(-1,1)$, and each occurrence of a value of S^i increments its corresponding position in the histogram [8]. Each bin of H^i is divided by the number of analyzed frames, making the histograms invariant in relation to the number of frames of each video. Finally, the histograms are concatenated and used as feature vector by a 1-NN classifier.

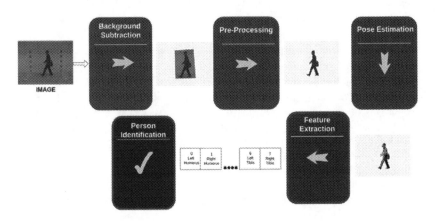

Fig. 4. Block diagram of the method proposed in [13].

The work proposed in [13] is based on soft-biometric features. The method can be divided into five steps: image background subtraction, pre-processing, pose estimation, feature extraction, and finally, individual identification. The first two steps compose the pre-processing stage. First, the foreground is separated from the background using a background subtraction technique, then a high frequency morphological filter is applied to remove noises from the resulting image. Next, a pose estimator is utilized to extract the limbs coordinates and the feature vector is obtained by getting the length of each limb, normalized in relation to the person height. Finally, a 1-NN classifier is used to compare the feature vectors obtained, using two distance functions: Euclidean and Manhattan. Figure 4 illustrates the method's five steps.

5 Proposed Approach

The main goal of this work is to propose and evaluate two different combinations of methods using a multi-biometric fusion on score level. The first combination aimed to join two methods for gait recognition, [6] and [8]. Both methods have characteristics in common that make the fusion feasible without having to modify the structure of none of them: (i) both feature vectors are histograms, (ii) both methods utilizes the 1-NN classifier, and (iii) both extracts gait information directly from the joint points coordinates.

Since both methods present normalized histograms as feature vectors, it was possible to perform classification by first applying the Euclidean distance function separately and then join both distance measures by taking their arithmetic mean. This is possible since the two measures will be represented in the same interval due to histogram normalization. Finally, the resultant measure is utilized to perform nearest neighbour classification.

The second combination aimed to propose an improvement to a gait recognition method [6], by performing a fusion with a method based on a soft biometric feature, anthropometry (limb measurements) [13]. Different from the previous approach, the feature vector used in [13] is not a histogram, due to this, it was necessary to make modifications before performing the fusion. As in the original method, the length of each limb is obtained for every frame video, but for this approach, the values were used to build normalized histograms, with the same number of bins utilized in [6]. Figure 5 shows the final pipeline of the method by [6] after merging it with anthropometric measures [13].

After obtaining the length histograms, the next step taken was similar to the previous approach. The different histograms are compared separately using the chi-square distance, then the similarity measures are merged by using arithmetic mean to perform 1-NN classification. In this case, chi-square function was used since it has presented better results than Euclidean distance.

6 Experimental Results

All the experiments were performed on CASIA Gait Dataset-A and CASIA Gait Dataset-B. The CASIA Gait Dataset-A [7], created in 2001, includes images of 20 individuals walking in an outdoor environment, each one with 12 video sequences, 4 sequences for each camera viewing angle: 0, 45 and 90 °C, which represent the side, oblique and frontal view of the individual walking, respectively. CASIA Gait Database B [12] is a large video database for gait analysis from multiple viewing angles. The base was created in 2005 and has images of 124 individuals walking in three different variations, namely: normal, with a coat and carrying a backpack.

The first experiment aimed to analyze the individual performance of the methods from [8] and [6], and verify the impact caused on this performance by the fusion of these two methods. The fusion between the two methods was performed at the score level, by taking the average between the distances obtained by each one of them. Table 1 shows the rank-1 accuracies obtained by the methods in Dataset-A in each of the three directions. It is possible to notice that although the two methods already present good results individually, the fusion between them provides an even better performance in the biometric identification task.

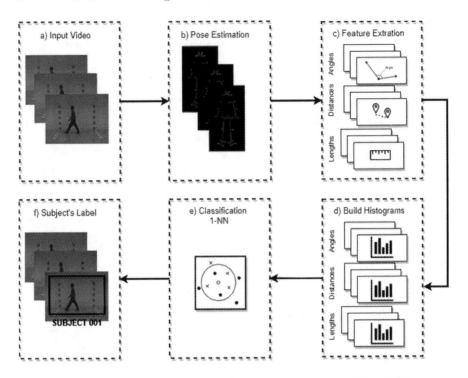

Fig. 5. Block diagram of the proposed approach to merge [6] and [13].

Table 1. Rank-1 accuracies obtained on CASIA Gait Dataset-A.

Method	Lateral	Oblique	Frontal
Jangua and Marana [6]	86.25%	86.25%	96.25%
Lima and Schwartz [8]	85.00%	**97.50%**	97.50%
Fusion	**90.00%**	**97.50%**	**100.00%**

Figure 6 shows the CMC curves obtained individually by the two methods and the CMC curve obtained by merging them. Observing such curves, the performance improvement provided by the application of multi-biometric techniques becomes even more evident. Even using the average recognition rate of the three CASIA Gait Dataset-A camera angles, the fusion between the two methods presents a recognition rate of 95.8% accuracy on rank-1.

The second experiment aimed to analyze the individual performance of the methods of [13] and [6], and to verify the impact caused on this performance by the fusion of these two methods. The fusion was performed at the score level, by taking the average between the scores obtained by each method. Tables 2 and 3 show the accuracies *rank-1* obtained by the methods in the bases Dataset-A, in each of the three directions, and Dataset- B in the lateral direction, using the Chi-square distance function and the 1-NN classifier. It is possible to notice

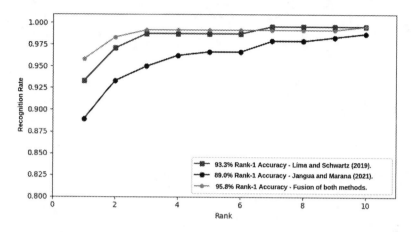

Fig. 6. CMC curves of the gait recognition methods on CASIA Gait Dataset-A.

that the complementary use of soft biometric characteristics, as is the case of anthropometric measurements, provides a significant performance improvement in the biometric identification task.

Table 2. Rank-1 accuracies obtained on CASIA Gait Dataset-A - chi-square.

Method	Lateral	Oblique	Frontal
Jangua and Marana [6] - **chi-square**	87.50%	92.50%	95.00%
Tavares et al. [13] - **chi-square**	85.00%	91.25%	88.75%
Fusion - chi-square	**95.00%**	**97.50%**	**100.00%**

Table 3. Rank-1 accuracies obtained on CASIA Gait Dataset-B - chi-square.

Method	Lateral
Jangua and Marana [6] - **chi-square**	94.22%
Tavares et al. [13] - **chi-square**	86.96%
Fusion - chi-square	**97.18%**

Figure 7 shows the CMC curve obtained individually by the method of [6] and the CMC curve obtained by merging the score level with the method of [13], both using the Chi-square distance function with the 1-NN classifier in the CASIA Gait Dataset-A database.

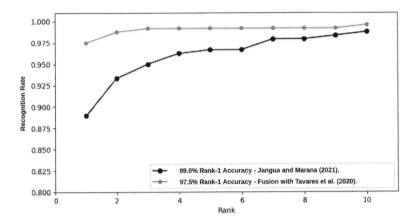

Fig. 7. CMC curves of the gait recognition and soft-biometric methods on CASIA Gait Dataset-A.

In Fig. 8, the CMC curves of the method of [6] and its fusion with that of [13] are shown under the same previous conditions, but using the images from the CASIA Gait Dataset-B database, in side view only.

Observing such curves, the performance improvement provided by the application of multi-biometric techniques using soft features is even more evident. Even using the average recognition rate of the three camera angles of the CASIA Gait Dataset-A, the fusion between the two methods presents a recognition rate of 97.5% accuracy in rank-1, and 97.2% in the Dataset-B. This same behavior could be observed in the results of the first experiment, which evaluated the fusion between the methods of [6] and [8] in the CASIA Gait Dataset-A, using the Euclidean distance function with the 1-NN classifier.

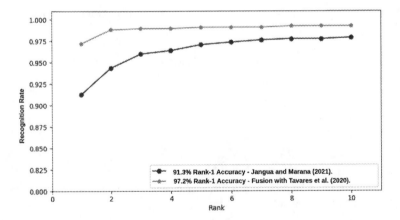

Fig. 8. CMC curves of the gait recognition and soft-biometric methods on CASIA Gait Dataset-B.

7   Conclusions

With the increasing implementation of people recognition techniques in production and increasingly challenging environments, in which classic approaches such as face, fingerprint and iris recognition are insufficient, the search for alternative methods is necessary. In this context, gait recognition shows promise, but even the methods considered state-of-the-art still show deficiencies related to their robustness, generating limitations in applications for real-world environments.

The present work aims to study and evaluate possible solutions to improve the robustness of state-of-the-art gait recognition methods utilizing multi-biometric techniques, performing fusions between different methods based on gait features, as well as methods in the scope soft biometrics.

The first multi-biometrics solution presented was the fusion of two gait recognition methods based on 2D poses. The methods chosen were proposed in [6] and [8]. The results of this experiment corroborated the idea presented in [11], about the possibility of attributing greater robustness to biometric systems by merging different techniques. The results of these experiments showed that the use of the two methods together presents better performance in the biometric identification task than both methods individually, showing that they complement each other, and their individual advantages outweigh their shortcomings.

The second solution also used the concepts of multi-biometrics, but instead of using two methods with the same purpose, the focus was turned to the use of soft biometrics characteristics, such as anthropomorphic measurements, together with gait recognition methods, in order to verify the possible improvements obtained by this technique. The experiments were performed using the method of [6] as a base, and the method presented by [13], based on soft biometrics. Once again, the results were promising, showing significant improvements in the accuracy of the original method, showing that soft biometrics techniques can be strong allies in the search for more robust recognition methods [5].

Acknowledgements. This paper is the result of the research sponsored by the National Council for Scientific and Technological Development (CNPq). This work was also financed by Petrobras/Fundunesp (Process 2662/2017), the São Paulo Research Foundation (FAPESP), and the Coordenação de Aperfeiçoamento de Pessoal de Nível Superior-Brasil (CAPES).

References

1. Arantes, M., Gonzaga, A.: Human gait recognition using extraction and fusion of global motion features. In: Multimedia Tools and Applications, pp. 655–675 (2011). https://doi.org/10.1007/s11042-010-0587-y, https://doi.org/10.1007/s11042-010-0587-y

2. Cao, Z., Hidalgo, G., Simon, T., Wei, S., Sheikh, Y.: Openpose: Realtime multi-person 2d pose estimation using part affinity fields. CoRR abs/ arXiv: 1812.08008 (2018)

3. Chen, C., Liang, J., Zhao, H., Hu, H., Tian, J.: Frame difference energy image for gait recognition with incomplete silhouettes. Pattern Recogn. Lett. **30**, 977–984 (2009)
4. Jain, A.K., Ross, A.A., Nandakumar, K.: Introduction to biometrics. Springer Science & Business Media (2011). https://doi.org/10.1007/978-0-387-77326-1
5. Jain, A.K., Dass, S.C., Nandakumar, K.: Can soft biometric traits assist user recognition? In: Jain, A.K., Ratha, N.K. (eds.) Biometric Technology for Human Identification, vol. 5404, pp. 561–572. International Society for Optics and Photonics, SPIE (2004), https://doi.org/10.1117/12.542890
6. Jangua, D.R.S., Marana, A.N.: Gait recognition using 2d poses. In: Edição Especial REIC: Artigos do 40° Concurso de Trabalhos de Iniciação Científica do CSBC (CTIC/CSBC), vol. 19, Jun 2021
7. Wang, L., Tan, T., Ning, H., Hu, W.: Silhoutte analysis based gait recognition for human identification. IEEE Trans. Pattern Anal. Mach. Intel. (PAMI) **25**(12), 1505–1518 (2003)
8. de Lima, V.C., Schwartz, R.: Gait recognition using pose estimation and signal processing. In: Iberoamerican on Pattern Recognition - CIARP (2019)
9. Nixon, M.S., Tieniu, T.: Human Identification Based on Gait. Springer Science & Business Media, Tan, Rama Chellappa (2006). https://doi.org/10.1007/978-0-387-29488-9
10. Nixon, M.S., Carter, J.N.: Automatic recognition by gait. Proc. IEEE **94**(11), 2013–2024 (2006)
11. Ross, A., Nandakumar, K., Jain, A.K.: Handbook of Multibiometrics. Springer, USA (2006). https://doi.org/10.1007/0-387-33123-9
12. Yu, S., Tan, D., Tan, T.: A framework for evaluating the effect of view angle, clothing and carrying condition on gait recognition. In: 18th International Conference on Pattern Recognition (ICPR 2006), vol. 4, pp. 441–444, Aug 2006. https://doi.org/10.1109/ICPR.2006.67
13. Tavares, H.L., Neto, J.B.C., Papa, J.P., Colombo, D., Marana, A.N.: People identification based on soft biometrics features obtained from 2d poses. In: 9th Brazilizan Conference on Intelligent Systems (BRACIS-2020) (2020)
14. Toshev, A., Szegedy, C.: Deeppose: Human pose estimation via deep neural networks. In: 2014 IEEE Conference on Computer Vision and Pattern Recognition, pp. 1653–1660, Jun 2014. https://doi.org/10.1109/CVPR.2014.214
15. Wan, C., Li, W., Phoha, V.V.: A survey on gait recognition. ACM Digital Library **51**, 1–35 (2018), https://dl.acm.org/doi/10.1145/3230633
16. Wang, L., Tan, T., Hu, W., Ning, H.: Automatic gait recognition based on statistical shape analysis. IEEE Trans. Pattern Anal. Mach. Intell. **12**(9), 1120–1131 (2003)
17. Yu S., Tan D., Huang K., Tan T.: Reducing the effect of noise on human contour in gait recognition. In: International Conference on Biometrics (2007)

Training Aware Sigmoidal Optimization

David Macêdo[iD], Pedro Dreyer, Teresa Ludermir[iD],
and Cleber Zanchettin[✉][iD]

Centro de Informática, Universidade Federal de Pernambuco, PE 50.740-560,
Recife, Brazil
{dlm,phdl,tbl,cz}@cin.ufpe.br
http://www.cin.ufpe.br

Abstract. Proper optimization of deep neural networks is an open
research question since an optimal procedure to change the learning
rate throughout training is still unknown. Manually defining a learning
rate schedule involves troublesome, time-consuming try and error procedures to determine hyperparameters such as learning rate decay epochs
and learning rate decay rates. Although adaptive learning rate optimizers automatize this process, recent studies suggest they may produce
overfitting and reduce performance compared to fine-tuned learning rate
schedules. Considering that deep neural networks loss functions present
landscapes with much more saddle points than local minima, we proposed the Training Aware Sigmoidal Optimizer (TASO), consisting of a
two-phase automated learning rate schedule. The first phase uses a high
learning rate to fast traverse the numerous saddle point, while the second phase uses a low learning rate to approach the center of the local
minimum previously found slowly. We compared the proposed approach
with commonly used adaptive learning rates schedules such as Adam,
RMSProp, and Adagrad. Our experiments showed that TASO outperformed all competing methods in both optimal (i.e., performing hyperparameter validation) and suboptimal (i.e., using default hyperparameters)
scenarios.

Keywords: Deep neural networks · Optimization · Learning rate

1 Introduction

Deep neural networks are being used in many different fields with remarkable
results. Image classification and segmentation [1], speech recognition [2] and
natural language processing [3] are some fields where deep learning is producing state-of-the-art performance [4]. However, while the results are encouraging,
the ideal way to optimize such models is still unclear. The literature presents
many optimizers with no clear dominating method across tasks [5]. One essential hyperparameter common to all optimizers is the learning rate, which dictates
how fast the model parameters are updated at the beginning of the training. The
performance of the optimizer depends on its learning rate change strategy, and
finding the optimal way to achieve this is a fundamental research problem.

© The Author(s), under exclusive license to Springer Nature Switzerland AG 2022
J. C. Xavier-Junior and R. A. Rios (Eds.): BRACIS 2022, LNAI 13654, pp. 123–138, 2022.
https://doi.org/10.1007/978-3-031-21689-3_10

The change of the learning rate throughout training is usually obtained using *learning rate schedule*, or *adaptive learning rate* optimizers [6]. On the one hand, in *learning rate schedule* optimizers, the way the learning rate changes during training is defined before the training begins. On the other hand, *adaptive learning rate* optimizers control the learning rate based on the training history, commonly using gradient information obtained during loss minimization.

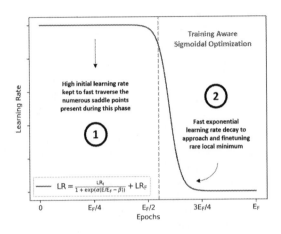

Fig. 1. Inspired by the work of Dauphin et al. [7], the TASO learning rate schedule comprises two distinct phases: during the first phase (1), the learning rate is kept constant for fast pass through the numerous saddle points. In the second phase (2), a rapid decrease in the learning rate allows for an efficient search around the local minimum found in the previous phase. We call TASO an *automated* learning rate schedule because only the initial learning rate needs to be provided, the others are default hyperparameters. In other words, unlike usual learning rate schedules, it is *not* necessary to *manually* define *well-tuned* learning rate decay epochs or learning rate decay rates. Therefore, using TASO is as straightforward as classical methods.

Despite the increasing popularity and the relative success, adaptive learning rate optimizers (e.g., Adam [8], RMSProp [9], and Adagrad [6]), have shown marginal performance gains when compared to a *manually well-tuned* learning rate schedule [10]. Additionally, [10] also showed that adaptive learning rate methods may produce overfitting and, consequently, reduced performance.

Indeed, [10] showed that a *manually well-tuned* learning rate schedule might perform similar to (or even better than) adaptive learning rate methods while avoiding their complexity and propensity to overfitting. However, constructing a manually well-tuned learning rate schedule is a troublesome procedure and demands many trials and errors, as it requires the definition of hyperparameters such as *learning rate decay epochs* and *learning rate decay rates*. Therefore, finding an enhanced optimizer is still an open and relevant research problem.

To combine the best of both approaches (the straightforwardness of the adaptive learning rate methods and the high performance of manually well-tuned learning rate schedules), we propose an *automated* learning rate schedule method called Training Aware Sigmoidal Optimizer (TASO). Our approach is as straightforward as any adaptive learning rate method, as only the initial learning rate needs to be provided. Furthermore, like adaptive learning rate optimizers, we may use the default hyperparameters or perform validation to find optimal.

TASO is a two-phase learning rate schedule based mainly on the work of Dauphin et al. [7]. Based on the mentioned work, we speculate that the training of deep neural networks follows two phases. During the first phase, the optimizer needs to pass through a high amount of saddle points fast. After that, the optimizer finds a local minimum in which it needs to converge to its center slowly. A high learning rate would make traversing the saddle points plateaus faster in the initial stage of the training. Subsequently, once the optimization arrives near the minimum local vicinity, a fast decrease in the learning rate to lower values is more adequate to slowly converge to this critical point. We impose this combined behavior by making the TASO learning rate schedule follow a *Sigmoidal shape* during the network training (Fig. 1).

We compared TASO to the commonly used adaptive learning rate optimizers such as Adam [8], RMSProp [9], and Adagrad [6]. We used the mentioned optimizers to train the LeNet5 [11], VGG19 [12], and ResNet18 [13] models on the MNIST [11], CIFAR10 [14], and CIFAR100 [14] datasets. Our experiments showed that TASO outperformed the compared adaptive learning rate optimizers in all combinations of models and datasets both for optimal (use of specific hyperparameters validate on the same dataset and model) and suboptimal (use of default hyperparameters validate on a different dataset and model) use cases.

2   Background

Duchi et al. [6] proposed the Adagrad optimizer by scaling the global learning rate by the inverse square root of the sum of all squared values of the gradient. Unfortunately, while having some theoretical properties for the convex optimization case, Adagrad does not perform so well for the optimization of deep neural networks. The main issue seems to be the accumulative term, which is a monotonic increasing function that constantly increases. This can lead to an excessive decrease in the learning rate during later parts of the training. The Adagrad optimizer algorithm can be seen in the Algorithm 1.

Tieleman et al. [9] proposed the RMSProp optimizer as a modification of Adagrad by changing the accumulation of gradients into a weighted moving average, similar to the stochastic gradient descent (SGD) using momentum [15]. The RMSProp optimizer algorithm can be seen in the Algorithm 2. A variation of RMSProp was proposed in [16]. In this version, the gradient is normalized by estimating its variance.

Kingma et al. [8] proposed the Adam optimizer by combining the RMSProp with the momentum used in SGD. The two methods are called first-moment terms and second-moment terms in the Adam optimizer. In addition, a bias correction term was included to account for the initialization of the momentum

---

Algorithm 1: Adagrad

Require: Global learning rate ϵ
Require: Initial parameters θ
Require: Small constant δ, normally 10^{-7}, for numerical stability
while *stopping criterion not met* **do**

> Sample a minibatch of n examples from the training set $\{x^{(1)}, \ldots, x^{(n)}\}$ with corresponding targets $y^{(i)}$.
> Compute gradient estimate: $g \leftarrow +\nabla_\theta \sum_i L(f(x^{(i)}; \theta), y^{(i)})$
> Accumulate squared gradient: $r \leftarrow r + g \odot g$
> Compute update: $\Delta\theta \leftarrow -\frac{\epsilon}{\delta + \sqrt{r}} \odot g$
> Apply update: $\theta \leftarrow \theta + \Delta\theta$

Algorithm 2: RMSProp

Require: Global learning rate ϵ, decay rate ρ
Require: Initial parameters θ
Require: Small constant δ, normally 10^{-6}, for numerical stability
while *stopping criterion not met* **do**

> Sample a minibatch of n examples from the training set $\{x^{(1)}, \ldots, x^{(n)}\}$ with corresponding targets $y^{(i)}$.
> Compute gradient estimate: $g \leftarrow +\nabla_\theta \sum_i L(f(x^{(i)}; \theta), y^{(i)})$
> Accumulate squared gradient: $r \leftarrow \rho r + (1 - \rho)g \odot g$
> Compute update: $\Delta\theta \leftarrow -\frac{\epsilon}{\sqrt{\delta r}} \odot g$
> Apply update: $\theta \leftarrow \theta + \Delta\theta$

Algorithm 3: Adam

Require: Learning rate ϵ
Require: Exponential decay rates for moment estimates, ρ_1 and ρ_2 in $[0, 1)$
Require: Small constant δ, normally 10^{-8}, for numerical stability
Require: Initial parameters θ
while *stopping criterion not met* **do**

> Sample a minibatch of n examples from the training set $\{x^{(1)}, \ldots, x^{(n)}\}$ with corresponding targets $y^{(i)}$.
> Compute gradient estimate: $g \leftarrow +\nabla_\theta \sum_i L(f(x^{(i)}; \theta), y^{(i)})$
> $t \leftarrow t + 1$
> Update biased first moment estimate: $s \leftarrow \rho_1 s + (1 - \rho_1)g$
> Update biased second moment estimate: $t \leftarrow \rho_2 r + (1 - \rho_2)g \odot g$
> Correct bias in first moment: $\hat{s} \leftarrow \frac{s}{1 - \rho_1^t}$
> Correct bias in second moment: $\hat{r} \leftarrow \frac{r}{1 - \rho_2^t}$
> Compute update: $\Delta\theta \leftarrow -\epsilon \frac{\hat{s}}{\sqrt{\hat{r}} + \delta}$
> Apply update: $\theta \leftarrow \theta + \Delta\theta$

---

terms at zero. The Adam optimizer algorithm can be seen in the Algorithm 3. However, recent research [17] has found some theoretical shortcomings of the

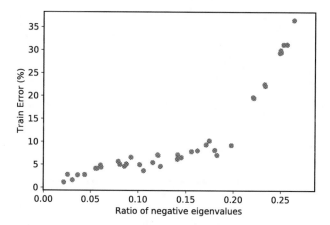

Fig. 2. Critical point training errors relative to its ratio of negative eigenvalues in its Hessian matrix. Adapted from [7]

Adam optimizer, where the usage of exponential moving average caused non-convergence on a convex toy problem. An alternative method, called AmsGrad, was then developed to overcome this deficiency.

3 Training Aware Sigmoidal Optimizer

Training deep neural networks involves optimizing a high-dimensional non-convex space. For decades, this fact has been deemed a shortcoming of gradient descent, as it is a local optimization approach. However, Dauphin et al. [7] showed that the training error of critical points (i.e., a maximum, minimum, or a saddle point) is correlated with the fraction of negative eigenvalues on their hessian matrices (Fig. 2). Consequently, all local minima present similar training errors. Therefore, it does not matter much on which local minimum the optimizer got trapped. The mentioned work also demonstrated that the loss landscape of deep networks presents much more saddle points than local minima.

Based on the previously mentioned observations, we speculate that the optimization of deep neural networks appears to happen in two distinct phases. Initially, the optimizer traverses the numerous saddle points and approaches a rare local minimum. Tishby et al. [18] appear to corroborate the idea that the training of deep networks is composed of two different stages. They argue that during the "fitting" phase, the mutual information between the hidden layers and the input increases, and in the "compression" phase, the same mutual information decreases.

Considering the previously mentioned hypothesis, we argue that the learning rate should behave differently during these two training phases. A high learning rate in the initial training portion allows for fast traversing of the saddle points plateaus. Indeed, Dauphin et al. [7] showed that optimization near saddle points may be challenging, and therefore we propose to keep the initial high learning

---

Algorithm 4: TASO

Require: initial learning rate ϵ_i and final learning rate ϵ_f
Require: hyperparameters α and β
Require: Initial parameters θ
while *stopping criterion not met* **do**

> Sample a minibatch of n examples from the training set $\{x^{(1)}, \ldots, x^{(n)}\}$ with corresponding targets $y^{(i)}$.
> Compute gradient estimate: $g \leftarrow +\frac{1}{n}\nabla_\theta \sum_i L(f(x^{(i)}; \theta), y^{(i)})$
> Compute new learning rate: $\epsilon \leftarrow \frac{\epsilon_i}{1+\exp(\alpha(\frac{k}{k_t}-\beta))} + \epsilon_f$
> Apply update: $\theta \leftarrow \theta - \epsilon g$

---

rate during this phase. However, once the optimization arrives near a rare local minima vicinity, we propose fast decreasing the learning rate to allow fine-tuned local search in the neighborhood of the mentioned critical point.

The main idea to produce a high training rate during the first phase and a fast decreasing learning rates during the second phase is to calculate the learning rate used in each epoch based on the *Sigmoidal shape* curve Eq. (1).

$$LR = \frac{LR_I}{1 + \exp\left(\alpha\left(E/E_F - \beta\right)\right)} + LR_F \tag{1}$$

In the previous equation, ϵ_i and ϵ_f are the initial and final learning rate, k is the current epoch, and k_t is the total number of epochs. Notice that, to know in which epoch the learning rate should start decreasing, we need to inform the number of epochs to the TASO equation. This is the reason we say our solution is *training aware*. To the best of our knowledge, the current learning rate schedule and adaptive learning rate optimizers do not use this information to improve its overall performance.

Additionally, the hyperparameter α control how fast the learning should decay after the first phase. Finally, the hyperparameter β determines when the transition between the first and the second stage should occur. The TASO optimizer algorithm can be seen in the Algorithm 4. Figure 3 present the TASO curve shape for different combinations of hyperparameters. The Eqs. (2–4) demonstrate how TASO produces essentially a constant initial learning rate ϵ_i during the first part of the training, while the Eqs. (5–7) show how TASO approximates the much lower final learning rate through the second part of the optimization process.

$$\epsilon_{(k=1)} = \frac{\epsilon_i}{1 + \exp\left(\alpha\left(\frac{1}{k_t} - \beta\right)\right)} + \epsilon_f \tag{2}$$

$$\approx \frac{\epsilon_i}{1 + \exp(-\alpha\beta)} + \epsilon_f \tag{3}$$

$$\approx \epsilon_i \tag{4}$$

$$\epsilon_{(k=k_f)} = \frac{\epsilon_i}{1 + \exp\left(\alpha\left(\frac{k_t}{k_t} - \beta\right)\right)} + \epsilon_f \tag{5}$$

$$= \frac{\epsilon_i}{1 + \exp(\alpha(1 - \beta))} + \epsilon_f \tag{6}$$

$$\approx \epsilon_f \tag{7}$$

The hyperparameters ϵ_i and ϵ_f do not present exactly the initial and final learning rates effectively used, as we have approximation in the previous equations. However, restricting the choices of α and β can make these differences small enough to be negligible. As a helpful heuristic, both $\alpha\beta$ and $\alpha(1-\beta)$ need to be higher than six to maintain errors below 5%. Figure 3 shows examples of how the choice of non-conforming pairs of α and β can create degenerative cases.

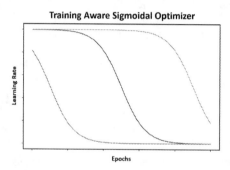

Fig. 3. TASO curves as a function of hyperparameters α and β. The usual sigmoidal shape (blue line). $\alpha\beta < 6$ (orange line) and $\alpha(1 - \beta) < 6$ (green line) represent combinations of α and β values that should be avoided (Collor figure online).

4   Experiments

We compared TASO with the more commonly used optimizers using different models and datasets. In the first set of experiments, we performed validation to find an optimal set of hyperparameters for a predefined pair of dataset and model (Subsect. 5.1). We call the hyperparameters found the *default* hyperparameters for each optimizer. In the second set of experiments, we used the *default* hyperparameters without validation to find suboptimal results for different pairs of datasets and models (Subsect. 5.2).

The study of suboptimal cases using default hyperparameters without performing validation on novel pairs of datasets and models is relevant because it presents a measure of the robustness of the compared approaches. Additionally, it is relevant from a practical use perspective where we desire high-quality results without necessarily performing an exhaustive hyperparameter search for each novel dataset and model used. Indeed, we usually prefer an optimizer that performs well using the default set hyperparameters. We repeated each experiment five times and reported the average and standard deviation. All reported accuracies and loss values were calculated on the test set. If not otherwise mentioned, we used 100 epochs for training. The source code is available[1]

4.1 Optimizers

We used the same adaptive learning rate optimizers evaluated by Wilson et al. [10], which were Adagrad, RMSProp, and Adam. We also searched for the same set of initial learning rates of the mentioned work:

– **Adagrad**: $[0.1, 0.05, 0.01, 0.0075, 0.005]$
– **RMSProp**: $[0.01, 0.005, 0.001, 0.0005, 0.0003, 0.0001]$
– **Adam**: $[0.005, 0.001, 0.0005, 0.0003, 0.0001, 0.00005]$

For the RMSProp optimizer, we opted to use the default value of 0.99 for the exponential decay rate, as it seems to have little influence on the overall result. We tried the alternate version proposed by Graves at al. [16], which we called RMSProp centered. Besides the original Adam, we evaluate its alternative version, AmsGrad. For both Adam and AmsGrad, we left the exponential decay terms ρ_1 and ρ_2 at their default values of 0.9 and 0.99 as, similar to the RMSProp, changes in those values do not seem to impact training meaningfully.

For TASO, we investigated the initial learning rates 2, 1, 0.5, 0.25, 0.05, 0.01, and 0.001. We study the training without moment, with moment equal to 0.9 and Nesterov moment equal to 0.9. Subsequently, we searched for the variants $\alpha = [10, 25, 50]$ and $\beta = [0.3, 0.5, 0.7]$, which seems to encompass an acceptable range of possible configurations. As we initially did not know optimal α and β, we validated those values using the corresponding initial learning rate constant throughout training.

Naturally, in future works, the search for the best initial learning rate for TASO should use *default* values for α and β (which we subsequently found to be 25 and 0.7, respectively) rather than keep the candidate initial learning rates constants throughout training. We recommend using the final learning rate 20 times smaller than the initial learning rate.

4.2 Databases

The experiments were performed using MNIST [11], CIFAR10 [19], and CIFAR100 [19]. All of them are image classification datasets with different degrees of complexity and size. MNIST is a dataset of handwriting digits composed of 70,000 greyscale images. The training set has 60,000 examples, and a test set comprises 10,000 images. The images have a size of 28 pixels by 28 pixels,

---

[1] https://github.com/anonymous.

with the digits being normalized and centralized. CIFAR10 has ten classes, and CIFAR100 has 100 categories. They have 60,000 color images divided between 50,000 training and 10,000 test images. The images have a size of 32 pixels by 32 pixels.

4.3   Models

We used three models in the experiments. LeNet5 [11], VGG19 [12], and ResNet18 [13]. The LeNet was developed in 1998 to identify handwriting digits. The VGG was created in 2014 and was one of the runner-ups of the ILSVRC 2014 competition. ResNet was built in 2015 and won several image tasks competitions, such as the ILSVRC 2015 image detection and localization.

Table 1. Adagrad initial learning rate search for VGG19 on CIFAR10.

Learning Rate	Accuracy	Loss
0.1	89.18 ($\pm$ 0.16)	0.45 ($\pm$ 0.01)
0.05	**89.52** ($\pm$ 0.31)	0.45 ($\pm$ 0.01)
0.01	88.77 ($\pm$ 0.09)	0.46 ($\pm$ 0.01)
0.0075	88.09 ($\pm$ 0.02)	0.47 ($\pm$ 0.01)
0.005	87.80 ($\pm$ 0.09)	0.45 ($\pm$ 0.01)

Table 2. RMSProp initial learning rate and variant search for VGG19 on CIFAR10.

Optimizer	Learning rate	Accuracy	Loss
RMSProp	0.01	89.94 ($\pm$ 0.13)	0.44 ($\pm$ 0.02)
	0.005	90.10 ($\pm$ 0.32)	0.42 ($\pm$ 0.01)
	0.001	90.74 ($\pm$ 0.01)	0.40 ($\pm$ 0.01)
	0.0005	**90.77** ($\pm$ 0.07)	0.39 ($\pm$ 0.02)
	0.0003	90.54 ($\pm$ 0.15)	0.40 ($\pm$ 0.01)
	0.0001	88.75 ($\pm$ 0.39)	0.46 ($\pm$ 0.01)
RMSProp centered	0.01	89.96 ($\pm$ 0.17)	0.43 ($\pm$ 0.01)
	0.005	90.00 ($\pm$ 0.17)	0.42 ($\pm$ 0.01)
	0.001	90.65 ($\pm$ 0.26)	0.39 ($\pm$ 0.03)
	0.0005	**90.76** ($\pm$ 0.21)	0.38 ($\pm$ 0.02)
	0.0003	90.58 ($\pm$ 0.16)	0.38 ($\pm$ 0.03)
	0.0001	88.72 ($\pm$ 0.38)	0.46 ($\pm$ 0.01)

Table 3. Adam initial learning rate and variant search for VGG19 on CIFAR10.

Optimizer	Learning rate	Accuracy	Loss
Adam	0.005	90.17 ($\pm$ 0.05)	0.39 ($\pm$ 0.01)
	0.001	90.93 ($\pm$ 0.34)	0.38 ($\pm$ 0.02)
	0.0005	**91.02** ($\pm$ 0.04)	0.37 ($\pm$ 0.01)
	0.0003	90.77 ($\pm$ 0.18)	0.37 ($\pm$ 0.01)
	0.0001	88.96 ($\pm$ 0.09)	0.44 ($\pm$ 0.01)
	0.00005	86.54 ($\pm$ 0.23)	0.52 ($\pm$ 0.02)
Adam AmsGrad	0.005	90.38 ($\pm$ 0.14)	0.40 ($\pm$ 0.01)
	0.001	91.01 ($\pm$ 0.34)	0.37 ($\pm$ 0.01)
	0.0005	**91.33** ($\pm$ 0.15)	0.36 ($\pm$ 0.01)
	0.0003	91.06 ($\pm$ 0.27)	0.37 ($\pm$ 0.02)
	0.0001	88.66 ($\pm$ 0.11)	0.45 ($\pm$ 0.01)
	0.00005	86.40 ($\pm$ 0.09)	0.53 ($\pm$ 0.01)

5 Results and Discussion

First, we perform a grid search validation to find optimal hyperparameters for VGG19 on CIFAR10 using all optimization methods. Next, we investigate how well the *previously found (default)* hyperparameters generalize to other datasets and models, avoiding validation. Therefore, in this second subsection, we study the robustness of the competing methods using *default (global)* hyperparameters.

5.1 Comparison Using Optimal (Validated) Hyperparameters

For the Adagrad method, an initial learning rate of 0.05 performed best and therefore was used in subsequent experiments (Table 1). For the RMSProp optimizer, Table 2 presents the best results for each hyperparameter set. Figure 4a) compares the best results for centered and non-centered versions. The learning rates from 0.0003 to 0.001 presented similar results across both optimizers, and there is little difference between the centered and non-centered versions. The non-centered version, with a learning rate of 0.00005, was used for further tests since it presented the best results.

For the Adam optimizer, a summary of the results is shown in Table 3. Figure 4b) shows the best result of each version. From the experiments, we noted that the learning rates 0.001, 0.0005, and 0.0003 present very close results. While the AmsGrad version showed a better training accuracy, its test accuracy appears to be very similar to the original Adam optimizer. For further tests, the Adam AmsGrad optimizer was used with a default initial learning rate of 0.0005.

For the TASO optimizer, we concluded that the optimal initial learning rate was 0.05 using a non-Nesterov moment of 0.9 (Table 4). See also Fig. 4c). Subsequently, we searched for optimal α and β. The training results across the

Table 4. TASO initial learning rate search for VGG19 on CIFAR10. Moment = 0.9.

Optimizer	Learning rate*	Accuracy	Loss
SGD	2	35.91 (± 36.64)	1.69 (± 0.87)
	1	88.94 (± 0.18)	0.47 (± 0.01)
	0.5	89.72 (± 0.42)	0.42 (± 0.03)
	0.25	**90.39** (± 0.29)	0.41 (± 0.01)
	0.05	89.66 (± 0.18)	0.44 (± 0.02)
	0.01	86.00 (± 0.14)	0.52 (± 0.01)
	0.001	78.78 (± 0.10)	0.62 (± 0.01)
SGD with Momentum	2	10.05 (± 0.03)	2.48 (± 0.15)
	1	10.04 (± 0.03)	2.33 (± 0.01)
	0.5	25.82 (± 22.38)	1.94 (± 0.53)
	0.25	55.32 (± 33.12)	1.33 (± 0.74)
	0.05	**91.01** (± 0.13)	0.37 (± 0.00)
	0.01	90.55 (± 0.11)	0.40 (± 0.01)
	0.001	86.38 (± 0.13)	0.50 (± 0.01)
SGD with Nesterov	2	10.14 (± 0.10)	2.32 (± 0.00)
	1	10.08 (± 0.09)	2.31 (± 0.00)
	0.5	10.02 (± 0.02)	2.30 (± 0.00)
	0.25	28.70 (± 26.22)	1.93 (± 0.54)
	0.05	90.00 (± 0.71)	0.41 (± 0.01)
	0.01	**90.49** (± 0.28)	0.40 (± 0.01)
	0.001	86.56 (± 0.22)	0.51 (± 0.00)

*The learning rate was kept constant during training.

Table 5. TASO variant search for VGG19 on CIFAR10.

α	β	Acurracy	Loss
10	0.3	90.96 (± 0.12)	0.37 (± 0.01)
10	0.5	91.66 (± 0.31)	0.38 (± 0.01)
10	0.7	91.97 (± 0.19)	0.38 (± 0.02)
25	0.3	90.73 (± 0.17)	0.37 (± 0.01)
25	0.5	91.61 (± 0.27)	0.37 (± 0.01)
25	0.7	**91.98** (± 0.19)	0.35 (± 0.01)
50	0.3	90.85 (± 0.30)	0.36 (± 0.01)
50	0.5	91.94 (± 0.04)	0.37 (± 0.02)
50	0.7	91.95 (± 0.25)	0.37 (± 0.01)

Table 6. Final results using optimal (validated) hyperparameters. VGG19 model on CIFAR10 dataset.

Optimizer	Test acurracy	Loss
Adagrad	89.40 (± 0.31)	0.42 (± 0.01)
RMSProp	90.77 (± 0.01)	0.41 (± 0.01)
Adam	91.33 (± 0.16)	0.37 (± 0.01)
TASO	**91.98** (± 0.19)	0.36 (± 0.02)

Table 7. Final results using optimal (validated) hyperparameters. VGG19 model on CIFAR10 dataset. Training during 25 epochs.

Optimizer	Test Acurracy	Loss
Adagrad	86.10 (± 0.27)	0.44 (± 0.01)
RMSProp	88.20 (± 0.33)	0.41 (± 0.01)
Adam	88.56 (± 0.16)	0.38 (± 0.00)
TASO	**90.02** (± 0.41)	0.34 (± 0.01)

Table 8. Final results using suboptimal (default) hyperparameters. VGG19 model on CIFAR100 dataset.

Optimizer	Test Acurracy	Loss
Adagrad	1.33 (± 0.06)	4.77 (± 0.17)
RMSProp	55.02 (± 0.54)	2.04 (± 0.05)
Adam	61.46 (± 0.13)	1.90 (± 0.04)
TASO	**65.08** (± 0.47)	1.76 (± 0.01)

Table 9. Final results using suboptimal (default) hyperparameters. Resnet18 model on CIFAR10 dataset.

Optimizer	Test Acurracy	Loss
Adagrad	19.03 (± 0.78)	2.19 (± 0.01)
RMSProp	92.13 (± 0.28)	0.37 (± 0.01)
Adam	92.35 (± 0.29)	0.35 (± 0.01)
TASO	**93.15** (± 0.08)	0.35 (± 0.01)

Table 10. Final results using suboptimal (default) hyperparameters. Lenet5 model on MNIST dataset.

Optimizer	Test Acurracy	Loss
Adagrad	75.16 (± 8.01)	1.15 (± 0.36)
RMSProp	**99.09** (± 0.03)	0.03 (± 0.01)
Adam	99.03 (± 0.03)	0.03 (± 0.01)
TASO	**99.09** (± 0.03)	0.03 (± 0.01)

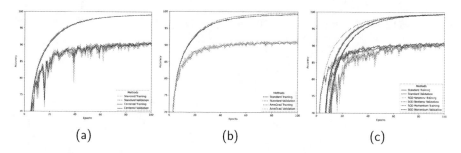

Fig. 4. Validations of hyperparameters for VGG19 on CIFAR10. Solid lines represent the mean behavior of many runs of the same experiment. Shadow areas represent their variation. (a) RMSProp: non-centered worked best. (b) Adam: AmsGrad variant worked best. (c) TASO: non-Nesterov worked best.

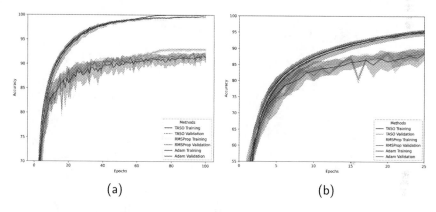

Fig. 5. Final Results for VGG19 on CIFAR10 using optimal (validated) hyperparameters. Solid lines represent the mean behavior of many runs of the same experiment. Shadow areas represent their variation. (a) 100 epochs. (b) 25 epochs.

hyperparameters configurations can be seen in Table 5. According to the results, we see a small difference varying α and β. The results show that TASO is robust for a wide range of α and β values.

The best performance was achieved using α equal to 25 and β equal to 0.7, defined as the default hyperparameters for TASO. In addition, we verified that the new calculations added in the TASO optimizer did not interfere with the training time as backpropagation is much more computationally intensive than calculating the new learning rate for each epoch.

After finding the default hyperparameters for all optimizer, we re-executed all experiments to obtain the final results for VGG19 on CIFAR10 presented in Fig. 5a) and Table 6. There are optimal results, as the default hyperparameters were obtained using the same model and dataset. Experiments were also performed using only 25 epochs. The result can be found in Table 7 and Fig. 5b). The TASO method achieved the best results in both cases. In both experiments, we can easily visualize a bump in the accuracy close to the epochs 20 (25 epochs case) and 70 (100 epochs case), which correspond to the moment the learning rate started to decrease fast.

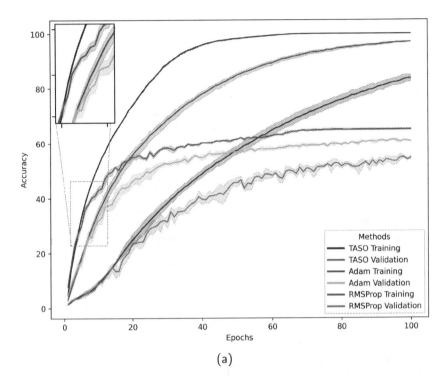

(a)

Fig. 6. Final results for VGG19 on CIFAR100 using suboptimal (default) hyperparameters. Solid lines represent the mean behavior of many runs of the same experiment. Shadow areas represent their variation.

5.2 Comparison Using Suboptimal (Default) Hyperparameters

VGG19 and CIFAR100. We evaluated the same model on the CIFAR100 dataset using the best hyperparameters from the previous experiments. The results can be seen in Table 8 and Fig. 6. We note once again that the TASO has the best overall result. Note that the Adagrad failed to converge, indicating the non-reliability of the optimizer.

ResNet18 on CIFAR10. The results of changing the model but maintaining the CIFAR10 datasets can be seen in Table 9. Those are so far the best results, where the TASO method archives more than 2% from the second-best performing optimizer. This more significant improvement could be because ResNet has a more complex deep model than VGG19, which could have a more complex loss function space, making it harder to optimize without changing the learning rate. Note that Adagrad, while converging this time, presented much lower accuracy than the other methods.

MNIST and LeNet5. The last test, which compares the LeNet5 model trained on the MNIST dataset, is shown in Table 10. The results demonstrated that all the methods except for Adagrad managed to archive near-perfect accuracy and thus could be considered equivalent to the task of best training this particular dataset and model.

6 Conclusion

In this paper, we proposed TASO, a novel deep neural networks optimizer. Based on recent theoretical advances in understanding the deep neural networks loss functions landscape, TASO presents two-phase. The initial learning rate is kept constant in the first training stage, while the learning rate drops abruptly in the second training stage. The transition from the first to the second phase is allowed by knowing the number of epochs used in training.

TASO is what we call an *automated* learning rate schedule. Therefore, similarly to an adaptive learning rate optimizer, it may be used in two ways. In the optimal case, hyperparameter validation is performed to achieve the best possible performance. In the suboptimal scenario, default hyperparameters are used. Differently from *manually well-tuned* learning rate schedules, TASO does no require finding hyperparameters such as *learning rate decay epochs* or the *learning rate decay rates*.

Out experiments showed that TASO outperformed all adaptive learning rate optimizers in both optimal and suboptimal scenarios. We believe this fact may be understood as further evidence that adaptive learning rate optimizers may present a propensity for overfitting. In future works, we plan to use TASO in other computer vision tasks (e.g., objection detection and semantic segmentation) and different research areas such as natural language processing and speech recognition.

References

1. Touvron, H., Vedaldi, A., Douze, M., Jegou, H.: Fixing the train-test resolution discrepancy. In: Neural Information Processing Systems, pp. 8252–8262 (2019)
2. Park, D.S.: "Improved noisy student training for automatic speech recognition. In: Annual Conference of the International Speech Communication Association, pp. 2817–2821 (2020)
3. Devlin, J., Chang, M., Lee, K., Toutanova, K.: BERT: pre-training of deep bidirectional transformers for language understanding. In: Association for Computational Linguistics: Human Language Technologies, pp. 4171–4186 (2019)

4. Alom, M., et al.: A state-of-the-art survey on deep learning theory and architectures. Electronics **8**(3), 292–358 (2019)
5. Schmidt, R.M., Schneider, F., Hennig, P.: Descending through a crowded valley - benchmarking deep learning optimizers, CoRR, vol. abs/ arXiv: 2007.01547 (2020)
6. Duchi, J., Hazan, E., Singer, Y.: Adaptive subgradient methods for online learning and stochastic optimization. J. M. L. Res. **12**, 2121–2159 (2011)
7. Dauphin, Y.N., Pascanu, R., Gülçehre, Ç., Cho, K., Ganguli, S., Bengio, Y.: Identifying and attacking the saddle point problem in high-dimensional non-convex optimization. In: Neural Information Processing Systems, pp. 2933–2941 (2014)
8. Kingma, D.P., Ba, J.: Adam: A method for stochastic optimization. In: International Conference on Learning Representations (2015)
9. Tieleman, T., Hinton, G.: RMSProp: Divide the gradient by a running average of its recent magnitude. In: Neural Networks for Machine Learning (2012)
10. Wilson, A.C., Roelofs, R., Stern, M., Srebro, N., Recht, B.: The marginal value of adaptive gradient methods in machine learning. In: NeurIPS, pp. 4148–4158 (2017)
11. Lecun, Y., Bottou, L., Bengio, Y., Haffner, P.: Gradient-based learning applied to document recognition. Proc. of the IEEE **86**(11), 2278–2324 (1998)
12. Simonyan, K., Zisserman, A.: Very deep convolutional networks for large-scale image recognition. In: International Conference on Learning Representations (2015)
13. He, K., Zhang, X., Ren, S., Sun, J.: Deep residual learning for image recognition. In: IEEE Conference on Computer Vision and Pattern Recognition, pp. 770–778 (2016)
14. Krizhevsky, A.: Learning multiple layers of features from tiny images. Technical Report, University of Toronto (2009)
15. Polyak, B.: Some methods of speeding up the convergence of iteration methods. USSR Comp. Math. and Math. Phys. **4**(5), 1–17 (1964)
16. Graves, A.: Generating sequences with recurrent neural networks, CoRR, vol. abs/ arxiv: 1308.0850 (2013)
17. Reddi, S.J., Kale, S., Kumar, S.: On the convergence of adam and beyond. In: International Conference on Learning Representations (2018)
18. Tishby, N., Zaslavsky, N.: Deep learning and the information bottleneck principle. In: IEEE Information Theory Workshop, pp. 1–5 (2015)
19. Krizhevsky, A.: Learning multiple layers of features from tiny images. Learning multiple layers of features from tiny images, Science Department, University of Toronto (2009)

Combining Neural Networks and a Color Classifier for Fire Detection

Davi Magalhães Pereira(ID), Marcelo Bernardes Vieira(ID),
and Saulo Moraes Villela$^{(\boxtimes)}$(ID)

Department of Computer Science, Federal University of Juiz de Fora, Juiz de Fora,
Minas Gerais, Brazil
davi.magalhaes@estudante.ufjf.br,
{marcelo.bernardes,saulo.moraes}@ufjf.br

Abstract. Deep learning methods have solved several problems in the computer vision area, mainly for image classification. The use of these methods for fire detection can bring great improvements to security systems and prevent many losses. Effective fire detection systems help fire situations to have lesser consequences than they could have by signaling as quickly as possible the experts. This paper proposes a combination of modern image classification models and a color classifier to detect and localize the fire. The CoAtNet-4 architecture is used to detect and localize fire in still images, while the color classifier refines the mask obtained. State-of-the-art works show a high number of parameters, imbalanced results and lower true positive rates (TPR), while our results show high TPR, great accuracy and a balanced classification.

Keywords: Fire detection · Fire localization · Fire segmentation · Pixel-color classification · Image classification · Neural networks · Deep learning

1 Introduction

Natural disasters, accidents and emergencies happen all the time and have severe impacts. In order to prevent or alleviate these problems, all kinds of sensors, alarms and security systems are implemented. Fires are incidents that can spread quickly and pose a great danger to lives and property, so it is important to deal with them in the early stages. According to a natural disaster report [15], there were 19 wildfire events in 2021, causing the loss of 128 human lives and 9.2 billion dollars. In addition, the U.S. Fire Administration (USFA) states that there were 1 291 500 fires, 3 704 deaths, 16 600 injuries and $14.8 billion loss in the year 2019 in the United States [21]. Festag [9] investigates in his work the false alarm rate of sensitive sensors in Germany, which reaches 86.07% on average per year, it is clear how inaccurate these systems can be. This demonstrates the need for autonomous systems to detect fires more efficiently so firefighters can be dispatched to the location quickly.

J. C. Xavier-Junior and R. A. Rios (Eds.): BRACIS 2022, LNAI 13654, pp. 139–153, 2022.
https://doi.org/10.1007/978-3-031-21689-3_11

Traditional fire alarms are broadly used to prevent great losses. But these solutions are based on optical and infrared sensors, thus needing to be set near the fire, which is difficult in open areas. Also, not all fires happen when someone is around, so human monitoring is recommended to confirm the fire and assess its severity. In addition, these systems are expensive to install and maintain, and have a high false alarm rate.

Alternatively, vision-based sensors can provide more information, such as fire location and severity. For instance, fire segmentation can provide an accurate report of the fire size and location, and it also makes it possible to assess the growth rate by analyzing a series of images. Researchers have been exploring the use of vision to address these fire detection obstacles and showed considerable progress toward an efficient vision-based sensor. Some of them extracted images, motion and temporal features to detect fire in videos [10]. Others investigated the use of different color spaces to build a color-based detector for still images [3,5]. But they still struggle with images with too much lighting, sun, brightness, etc.

More recent works have implemented Convolutional Neural Networks (CNNs) in their approaches, using them for image classification and fire localization. These showed promising good results by combining the power of CNNs and superpixel clustering [20] or extracting feature maps from the models to produce a mask [13].

We propose an approach with three steps to produce a fire segmentation mask, the first being the classification of still images as containing fire or not. Then the fire images go through a process in which 50×50 pixels patches are extracted from the image and given to a neural network. Afterward, we use a color classifier to produce a mask based on a fire-like color range. Finally, the images are merged to generate our final segmented image. To evaluate our method, we conducted experiments on the dataset proposed by Chino *et al.* [6], which contains 226 images, divided into two categories: 119 images containing fire and 107 images without fire. Other datasets collected from previous works to train the models are detailed in Sect. 4.1.

The main contribution of this paper is a novel method for fire detection that presents balanced results and a better true positive rate (TPR) result by combining neural networks and a color classifier to detect and localize fire in still images. Moreover, by using a classifier prior to the segmentation phase the method is able to discard a large number of false positive pixels in the resulting mask and make the process faster. Our method achieves the best classification of fire, achieving a TPR of 0.91 while maintaining a good false positive rate (FPR). This approach can be used in security systems and frameworks to detect and assess fire situations.

The remaining of this paper is organized as follows: Sect. 2 summarizes how related works addressed the problem. Section 3 provides the details of our method. Next, Sect. 4 presents a description of the datasets used, the experiment setting and the results of the experiments. Finally, Sect. 5 gives conclusions and future works.

2   Related Work

Chen *et al.* [5] investigated the color of fire using RGB and HSI color spaces and proposed a fire detection method based on three rules. Celik *et al.* [3] conducted experiments to define a fire-like color range and proposed a set of five mathematical rules to examine the behavior of fire in the YCbCr color space. This color space is used to separate the luminance from the chrominance more effectively.

Rossi *et al.* [16] presented a process to extract geometric fire features from videos. A clustering method is used to locate the fire, in which the image is split into two clusters based on the channel V of the YUV color space. The cluster with the highest value of V is classified as fire. Subsequently, a 3D Gaussian model is used for pixel classification. This method was made for supervised environment fires and has limitations. For instance, it does not perform well in outdoor fire emergencies, as discussed in [6].

Rudz *et al.* [17] proposed another method based on clustering. They compute four clusters using the channel Cb of the YCbCr color space. The one with the lowest value of Cb is classified as a fire region. Afterward, false positive pixels are discarded by using a dataset as a reference. The method handles small and large regions differently, small regions are compared with the mean of a reference region and large ones are compared with the reference histogram. They perform this process for each color channel.

The BoWFire method [6] proposed three steps to detect fire pixels in still images, a color classifier that uses Naïve Bayes and k-NN algorithms, a texture classifier that uses superpixels and the merge of what was generated in the previous stages.

A similar approach was explored by Muhammad *et al.* [13]. They proposed a CNN based on SqueezeNet and AlexNet and used it for fire detection and localization. For fire localization, their method performs a feature map selection to find fire-sensitive feature maps. Once the segmentation is done, they examine the segmented image to assess the impact of the fire. Their method outperformed the state of the art at the time, showing better accuracy and recall results while keeping computational cost to a minimum.

Thomson *et al.* [20] explored the use of more compact versions of NasNet-A-Mobile and ShuffleNetV2 to detect and localize fire in video frames. They use these CNNs to find fire frames and then perform iterative clustering to extract superpixels of the image, using the SLIC (Simple Linear Iterative Clustering) algorithm [1], and classify them with another CNN. They achieved good results on their dataset using these simplified CNNs.

Mlích *et al.* [12] compiled a dataset with polygon annotations and investigated the use of the DeepLabV3 semantic segmentation architecture to tackle the given problem. Their method showed impressive improvements in the false positive rate compared to others.

In contrast with previous methods, our method takes advantage of a low-complexity color classifier to refine the network predictions. The combination of a neural network to find regions of fire in the image and a color classifier to refine the segmentation brings novelty to the current literature.

3   Proposed Approach

Our method consists of three steps, an image classifier prior to the segmentation process, an in-image fire localization step that generates two masks and the final step outputs an intersection of both masks from the previous step. Each of these is described as follows:

1. In order to help with the segmentation step we filter input images using an image classification model to perform segmentation only on fire-containing images, this will be referred to as the prior classifier throughout this paper.
2. Images classified as containing fire by the previous step go to the second phase where we perform in-image fire localization.
   (a) The first mask is obtained by giving another model 50×50 pixels patches to detect fire.
   (b) Another mask is generated by our color classifier. We define a fire-like color range in the HSV (Hue, Saturation, Value) color space, and then pixels in the range are classified as fire.
3. A mask produced by classifying image patches will only detect fire regions and will not be very accurate. To refine these regions into fire-like shapes we merge them with the color classifier one and attain our final result.

For the neural networks, we use the CoAtNet-4 model [7], which achieved a top 1 accuracy of 89.11% on ImageNet combining convolution and self-Attention mechanisms. Transformers networks have stood out in Natural Language Processing (NLP) works and aroused great interest in the area of computer vision. However, visual data require specific network architecture and training methods. Thus, different authors have implemented their version of a Transformer model for vision tasks. Recently, Vision Transformer (ViT) [8] has experimented with the use of a standard Transformer with very few modifications. To do that, they use as input small patches of the image that are treated as tokens, these patches are flattened and a learnable positional embedding is added to it. Although ViT achieves notable results on recognition benchmarks when pre-trained on the JFT-300M dataset [19], it still struggles with a low number of data, being inferior to CNNs in this case. To overcome this problem, CoAtNet proposes a combination of depthwise **Co**nvolution and self-**At**tention in an attempt to bring together the CNN generalization and Transformer's model capacity, since Transformers showed a higher ceiling. To do so, their architecture is divided into 5 stages, 1 Conv block, 2 MBConv blocks and 2 Transformer blocks, as displayed in Fig. 1.

This architecture is implemented in the first step classification and the second step patch classification. The input image is given to the first model, if classified as non-fire it is discarded and an empty mask is generated. Otherwise, the image goes to step two where fire localization is performed. Step two will produce two masks, one of them is obtained by classifying regions of the image with

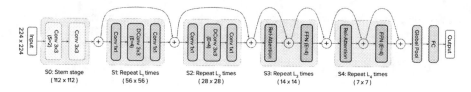

Fig. 1. CoAtNet architecture. Source: [7].

the network, this network will be called patch classifier throughout this paper. Moreover, we iterate through the image extracting small 50×50 pixels (patch size) patches every 25 pixels (step size), so that pixels of fire are not lost, and passing them to the patch classifier. Since it is a patch-based classification, this mask will not be very accurate therefore having a high FPR. To overcome this issue we perform an intersection with the color classifier mask. Algorithm 1 shows how the mask is produced by the patch classifier. The function *colorRegion* will update the mask filling patches predicted as fire with white, that is when the prediction is equal to one.

Algorithm 1: Patch classifier

---

1 **input** I *(image)*, SS *(step size)*, PS *(patch size)*;
2 **output** *black-and-white mask;*
3 **begin**
4      $Mask \leftarrow zeros(I.width, I.height)$;
5      $i \leftarrow 0$;
6      $j \leftarrow 0$;
7   **while** $i < I.width$ **do**
8   **while** $j < I.height$ **do**
9              $patch \leftarrow newImage(I, i, j, PS)$;
10             $prediction \leftarrow model(patch)$;
11   **if** $prediction = 1$ **then**
12                $colorRegion(Mask, i, j, PS)$;
13   **end if**
14             $j \leftarrow j + SS$;
15   **end while**
16         $i \leftarrow i + SS$;
17   **end while**
18   **return** $Mask$;
19 **end**

The other mask produced in step two is obtained by a color classifier. The color classifier is based on a fire-like color range that will classify as fire all bright, fire-colored, or lightened pixels whose color is in the range. Thus, presenting a high TPR but also a high FPR. But when this mask is merged with our patch-based fire localization, the color classification will be limited to patches classified as fire, lowering the FPR. Our method converts the image from the RGB color space to the HSV color space before performing pixel-color classification. The HSV color space allows us to define a specific range for hue and value channels to obtain a fire-like subspace. The saturation channel did not present relevance for the classification and was discarded. Therefore, by using the HSV space we are able to detect fire-like colored pixels using only the hue and value channels. This will lower the complexity by removing one dimension from the color space. Further details of the color classifier step are given in Algorithm 2. The function *discardChannel* removes a given dimension from a matrix, in this case, the saturation channel, or dimension one. Next, the algorithm will iterate through each pixel in the matrix, and if the pixel color is located in our fire color range, the function *colorPixel* will update the mask coloring this pixel white.

Algorithm 2: Color classifier

---

1 **input** I *(image)*, LB *(color range lower bound)*, UB *(color range upper bound)*;
2 **output** *black-and-white mask*;
3 **begin**
4     $I \leftarrow RGBtoHSV(I)$;
5     $I \leftarrow discardChannel(I, 1)$;
6     $Mask \leftarrow zeros(I.width, I.height)$;
7     $i \leftarrow 0$;
8     $j \leftarrow 0$;
9   **while** $i < I.width$ **do**
10   **while** $j < I.height$ **do**
11   **if** $LB \leq I[i, j] \leq UB$ **then**
12              $colorPixel(Mask, i, j)$;
13   **end if**
14           $j \leftarrow j + 1$;
15   **end while**
16        $i \leftarrow i + 1$;
17   **end while**
18   **return** $Mask$;
19 **end**

The final step is where both masks are merged to obtain the fire segmentation result. This is accomplished by an intersection operation between the images, so pixels will only be considered fire if classified as such in both masks. Figure 2 illustrates the entire method. A sample image with its respective segmentation mask for each step of our method is given in Fig. 3.

Therefore, by combining powerful image classification networks with a color classifier that helps to refine the segmentation, it is possible to generate fire segmentation masks with results comparable to the state of the art. In addition, these masks can be useful not only for detecting fire but also for localizing and assessing fire severity. Which is of great importance in providing information to the competent authorities in situations of danger.

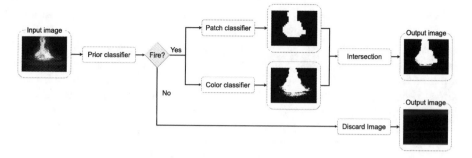

Fig. 2. Architecture of the proposed method.

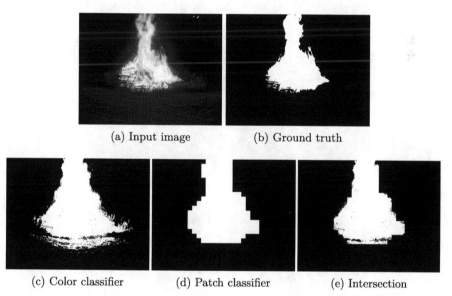

(a) Input image   (b) Ground truth

(c) Color classifier   (d) Patch classifier   (e) Intersection

Fig. 3. Result of each step of the method for a fire image from the test set.

4   Experiments and Results

In this section, we specify details of the experiments, datasets used and the results obtained. We also present comparisons of our results with other approaches and the impact of a few parameters in the results.

4.1   Datasets

For the training of the prior classifier, we assembled a dataset of 6321 images, where 5416 images are a subset taken from the dataset created in [11] and 905 new images collected from [4,18] are added. We split this dataset into a training and a validation set, 85% are used for training and the remaining 15%

for validation. Regarding the number of images per class, the dataset contains 2605 fire images and 3716 non-fire images.

The patch classifier was trained on the training dataset used in [6]. This dataset consists of 50×50 pixels images, where 80 of them are fire regions and 160 are non-fire regions. To have a more balanced dataset 240 images from [2] were added resulting in 240 fire images and 240 non-fire images, 75% of these images were used for training and 25% for validation. Finally, for testing, we used 226 images, 119 images containing fire and 107 images without fire obtained from [6]. Their respective ground truth images were used to test the performance of our method. Although the dataset is small, it contains many challenging images such as sunrises and lightened places.

Figure 4 presents sample images used to train the patch classifier, where Figs. 4a, 4b, 4e and 4f are from the training dataset used in [6], and Figs. 4c, 4d, 4g and 4h are from [2]. A set of sample images used to train the prior classifier is shown in Fig. 5. Lastly, Fig. 6 shows a few images from the test set assembled by [6].

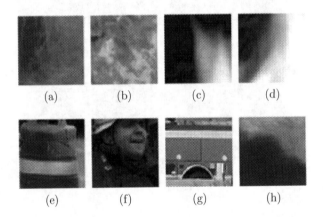

Fig. 4. Sample images from the training set of the patch classifier.

4.2 Experiment Setting

Regarding the networks, the entire architecture was implemented in the PyTorch framework [14] and the weights were randomly initialized. The patch classifier network was trained with the following configuration: Adaptive Moment Estimation (Adam) optimizer, cross entropy loss function, learning rate of 0.001, batch size of 8. Similarly, the prior classifier training also used the Adam optimizer, the cross entropy loss function, but with a learning rate of 0.0001 and a batch size of 12. Both networks were trained for 40 epochs. The learning rate in the prior classifier training decays by a factor of 0.1 in the 12th, 24th and 36th epochs. We also modified a class threshold to improve the performance of the

Fig. 5. Sample images from the training set of the prior classifier.

Fig. 6. Sample images from the test set.

first step model and have a more balanced classification. Instead of classifying images with an output probability of 0.5 or greater as non-fire, they will only be classified as non-fire if the probability is greater than 0.7. In such a way that a given image will only be discarded if the model is sure it is not a fire image. And even though some non-fire images go to the next step, the patch classifier can still correct this error by not detecting fire regions in the image.

4.3   Evaluation Metrics

This section introduces the main metrics used to evaluate fire detection methods. The most common are recall, precision, accuracy, F-measure and F_β-score. With C being the confusion matrix of a binary problem, $C_{i,j}$ refers to the number of samples known to be in class i and predicted to be in class j, with $i, j = 1, 2$. Hence, the overall accuracy is defined as the number of correctly predicted pixels divided by the total number of pixels:

$$A = \frac{\sum_{i=1}^{2} C_{i,i}}{\sum_{i=1}^{2} \sum_{j=1}^{2} C_{i,j}}. \tag{1}$$

The F-measure or balanced F-score (F_1-score) is the harmonic mean of the precision (P) and recall (R) and is defined as follows:

$$P = \frac{TP}{TP + FP}, \quad R = TPR = \frac{TP}{TP + FN}, \quad F\text{-measure} = 2 \times \frac{P \times R}{P + R}, \tag{2}$$

where TP is the number of true positive pixels correctly predicted as positive (fire), FP is the number of true negative pixels predicted as positive and FN is is the number of true positive pixels predicted as negative (non-fire).

Finally, the F_β-score is a generalization of the F-measure where the balance of precision and recall is controlled by the β coefficient. The β parameter determines how much weight will be put on precision, a $\beta < 1$ raises the importance of precision and might be used for problems where it is interesting to minimize false positive predictions. On the other hand, a $\beta > 1$ lowers the importance of precision and gives more attention to minimizing false negative predictions:

$$F_\beta\text{-score} = (1 + \beta^2) \times \frac{P \times R}{\beta^2 \times P + R} \tag{3}$$

4.4   Results

To evaluate the performance of our method, we tested it on the dataset obtained from [6] and compared the results with other approaches. In order to detect fire regions properly, the parameters of patch size and step size are very important. The patch size will dictate how big each region is going to be and step size defines the spacing between the start of each region and helps the method not miss small areas of fire that appear in a region by not skipping that area completely. The values shown in Table 1 are a sample of patch sizes and step sizes, these were empirically defined as the ones that best fit our experimental setup. To evaluate how these parameters affect performance, we used only the patch classifier segmentation. Except for a step size of 50 pixels, which will skip some pixels, patches of 25×25 pixels result in a better FPR. This indicates that small patch sizes are better for the non-fire class. Although the 50×50 pixels patches do not achieve such small FPR values, they are more balanced and have the best TPR value using a step size of 12 pixels.

The results of the experiments with each step of the method and their combinations are showcased in Table 2. It can be seen that the color classifier alone achieves a high TPR value but also misses a lot of true negative pixels. Although the patch classifier misses more true positive pixels, it makes the resulting intersection more balanced and with better FPR. It is also important to highlight the

Table 1. Results of tests with various patch sizes and step sizes

Patch size	Step size	TPR	FPR
25 × 25	12	0.81	0.05
	25	0.69	**0.03**
	50	0.17	0.99
50 × 50	12	**0.92**	0.10
	25	0.91	0.08
	50	0.82	0.05

impact of adding the prior classifier to the method, e.g., the color classifier has a drastic 66.10% decrease in its FPR. In all cases, the prior classifier improves the FPR and brings more balanced results. This proves that it is able to efficiently discard non-fire images and, consequently, false positive pixels.

Table 2. Results of each step and their combinations

Algorithm	TPR	FPR
Color classifier	**0.99**	0.59
Color classifier with prior classifier	0.91	0.20
Patch classifier	0.94	0.11
Patch classifier with prior classifier	0.87	0.06
Intersection	0.94	0.12
Intersection with prior classifier	0.91	**0.04**

Table 3 presents the values of TPR and FPR obtained in the experiments comparing with state-of-the-art methods. Although our method has a lower FPR, it also has the best TPR and a more balanced result.

Table 3. Comparison of TPR and FPR with various approaches

Method	TPR	FPR
Color Classification [6]	0.77	0.13
BoWFire [6]	0.65	0.03
CNNFire T = 0.40 [13]	0.82	0.02
CNNFire T = 0.45 [13]	0.85	0.04
CNNFire T = 0.50 [13]	0.89	0.07
Mlích et al. [12]	0.87	**0.01**
Our method	**0.91**	0.04

Although Table 4 shows that our method is inferior to other approaches using these metrics, it is important to emphasize how imbalanced the dataset is. Despite having a similar number of fire and non-fire images, the dataset has approximately 21 times more non-fire pixels than fire pixels. For this reason, we also calculated the F_β-score for our results, using $\beta = 2$, the method achieved an F_2-score of 0.78. For the fire detection problem, it is more important not to miss fire cases, in other words, false alarms are less harmful than undetected fires. And our method has the best classification of fire (TPR) among the methods cited. Additionally, the proposed method achieves an accuracy of 0.95 which is comparable to the accuracy of 0.97 obtained in [12].

Table 4. Comparison of Precision and F-measure with different methods

Method	Precision	F-measure
BoWFire [6]	0.50	0.57
Rudz *et al.* [17]	0.63	0.52
Rossi *et al.* [16]	0.39	0.28
Celik *et al.* [3]	0.55	0.54
Chen *et al.* [5]	**0.75**	0.25
Mlích *et al.* [12]	0.73	**0.79**
Our method	0.50	0.65

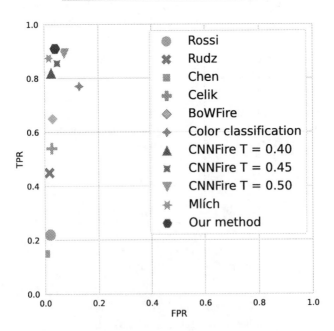

Fig. 7. Comparison of our approach with other methods.

Furthermore, using the Receiver Operating Characteristic (ROC) space we are able to compare the performance of various works in terms of TPR and FPR. It is noticeable in Fig. 7 that our method presents the best TPR while having a comparable FPR.

It is illustrated in Fig. 8 the resulting masks of several different approaches, our method once again shows comparable results. It is evident in this image that Chen's method has a great FPR but at the cost of missing a lot of true positive pixels. Still, Rossi holds the worst result in this image, where his method misses the fire almost completely. Celik and Rudz have similar results. To illustrate how

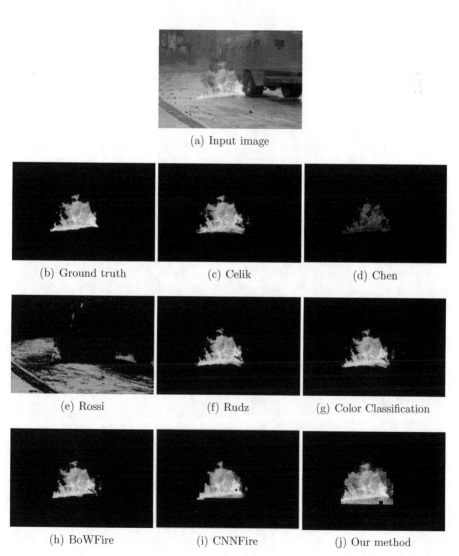

(a) Input image

(b) Ground truth   (c) Celik   (d) Chen

(e) Rossi   (f) Rudz   (g) Color Classification

(h) BoWFire   (i) CNNFire   (j) Our method

Fig. 8. Result of various approaches for a fire image.

the mask evolves from each step, Fig. 3 shows the result obtained by the color classifier, the patch classification and the final intersection.

5   Conclusion

In this paper, we propose a method that combines the use of a modern deep learning model, which merges the generalization of CNNs and the model capacity of Transformers, and a color classifier for fire detection and localization in still images. The main objective of this paper is to overcome the limitations of conventional fire detection sensors and the lower TPR present in previous methods. Such a high TPR had not yet been reported for this dataset, so the goal is to fulfill this gap.

To evaluate the performance of our method we tested it on the dataset presented in [6] and compared the results with state-of-the-art approaches. The results showed that our method has a competitive accuracy and outperforms others on TPR. It is important to emphasize that the proposed method is also comparable to the most recently proposed method presented in [12], which uses a semantic segmentation architecture. These architectures usually show a greater number of parameters than CoAtNet-4 and require specific dataset annotations, which can be difficult as datasets grow. And overall, we still achieve better TPR.

Despite the capabilities of our approach, we have noticed issues in Sect. 4 for segmentation of fire in daylight images, when the patch classification is not able to completely limit the color classification to fire and the method fails to obtain more accurate fire shapes in the masks. Hence a higher number of false positive predictions is obtained, which lowers the precision. The inaccuracy of using square patches shows the necessity of further improvements. Thus, in future works, we intend to conduct a deeper analysis to address this problem and experiment with pixel clustering, using color and texture information. Another possible future research direction refers to investigating the use of a refining algorithm or a better color classifier to improve the final mask and lower the FPR. We also aim to use pretrained models and bigger datasets for training the networks. This work focuses only on images from the visible light spectrum. However, it can be easily extended to datasets composed of multispectral images with RGB and Near Infrared bands.

References

1. Achanta, R., Shaji, A., Smith, K., Lucchi, A., Fua, P., Süsstrunk, S.: SLIC Superpixels Compared to State-of-the-Art Superpixel Methods. IEEE Trans. Pattern Anal. Mach. Intell. **34**(11), 2274–2282 (2012)
2. Cazzolato, M.T., et al.: FiSmo: a compilation of datasets from emergency situations for fire and smoke analysis. In: Brazilian Symposium on Databases. SBC (2017)
3. Celik, T., Demirel, H.: Fire detection in video sequences using a generic color model. Fire Saf. J. **44**(2), 147–158 (2009)
4. Centre for Artificial Intelligence Research: Fire-Detection-Image-Dataset. https:// github.com/cair/Fire-Detection-Image-Dataset, (Accessed 11 Jun 2022)

5. Chen, T.H., Wu, P.H., Chiou, Y.C.: An early fire-detection method based on image processing. In: 2004 International Conference on Image Processing, ICIP 2004, vol. 3, pp. 1707–1710. IEEE (2004)
6. Chino, D.Y., Avalhais, L.P., Rodrigues, J.F., Traina, A.J.: Bowfire: detection of fire in still images by integrating pixel color and texture analysis. In: 2015 28th SIBGRAPI Conference on Graphics, Patterns and Images, pp. 95–102. IEEE (2015)
7. Dai, Z., Liu, H., Le, Q.V., Tan, M.: CoAtNet: Marrying Convolution and Attention for All Data Sizes (2021)
8. Dosovitskiy, A., et al.: An Image is Worth 16×16 Words: Transformers for Image Recognition at Scale. CoRR abs/ arXiv: 2010.11929 (2020)
9. Festag, S.: False alarm ratio of fire detection and fire alarm systems in Germany - A meta analysis. Fire Saf. J. **79**, 119–126 (2016)
10. Kim, Y.H., Kim, A., Jeong, H.Y.: RGB color model based the fire detection algorithm in video sequences on wireless sensor network. Int. J. Dis. Sensor Netw. **10**(4), 923609 (2014)
11. Li, S., Yan, Q., Liu, P.: An efficient fire detection method based on multiscale feature extraction, implicit deep supervision and channel attention mechanism. IEEE Trans. Image Process. **29**, 8467–8475 (2020). https://doi.org/10.1109/TIP. 2020.3016431
12. Mlích, J., Koplík, K., Hradiš, M., Zemčík, P.: Fire segmentation in still images. In: Blanc-Talon, J., Delmas, P., Philips, W., Popescu, D., Scheunders, P. (eds.) ACIVS 2020. LNCS, vol. 12002, pp. 27–37. Springer, Cham (2020). https://doi. org/10.1007/978-3-030-40605-9_3
13. Muhammad, K., Ahmad, J., Lv, Z., Bellavista, P., Yang, P., Baik, S.W.: Efficient deep CNN-based fire detection and localization in video surveillance applications. IEEE Trans. Syst. Man Cybern. Syst. **49**(7), 1419–1434 (2019). https://doi.org/ 10.1109/TSMC.2018.2830099
14. Paszke, A., et al.: PyTorch: an imperative style, high-performance deep learning library. In: Wallach, H., Larochelle, H., Beygelzimer, A., d' Alché-Buc, F., Fox, E., Garnett, R. (eds.) Advances in Neural Information Processing Systems, vol. 32. Curran Associates, Inc. (2019)
15. ReliefWeb: 2021 Disasters in numbers. https://reliefweb.int/report/world/2021-disasters-numbers, (Accessed 06 Nov 2022)
16. Rossi, L., Akhloufi, M., Tison, Y.: On the use of stereovision to develop a novel instrumentation system to extract geometric fire fronts characteristics. Fire Saf. J. **46**(1–2), 9–20 (2011)
17. Rudz, S., Chetehouna, K., Hafiane, A., Laurent, H., Séro-Guillaume, O.: Investigation of a novel image segmentation method dedicated to forest fire applications. Meas. Sci. Technol. **24**(7), 075403 (2013)
18. Saied, A.: FIRE Dataset. https://www.kaggle.com/phylake1337/fire-dataset, (Accessed 06 Nov 2022)
19. Sun, C., Shrivastava, A., Singh, S., Gupta, A.: Revisiting Unreasonable Effectiveness of Data in Deep Learning Era. CoRR abs/ arXiv: 1707.02968 (2017)
20. Thomson, W., Bhowmik, N., Breckon, T.P.: Efficient and Compact Convolutional Neural Network Architectures for Non-temporal Real-time Fire Detection. CoRR abs/ arXiv: 2010.08833 (2020)
21. U.S. Fire Administration: U.S. Fire Statistics. https://www.usfa.fema.gov/data/ statistics/, (Accessed 06 Jun 2022)

A Study of Emergency Siren Recognition on Resource-Constrained Devices

Davi Francisco Caetano dos Santos$^{(\boxtimes)}$ and Levy Boccato

University of Campinas, Av. Albert Einstein, 400, Campinas, SP 13083-852, Brazil
d228971@dac.unicamp.br, lboccato@dca.fee.unicamp.br

Abstract. The Emergency Siren Recognition (ESR) constitutes a relevant task in audio processing, which can be useful to the development of driver assistance systems or wearable devices to generate alternative alerts that make the user aware of emergency signals in the vicinity. In this context, an effective ESR solution involves deploying the model on a resource-constrained device, in which aspects such as energy consumption and memory size are critical. In this work, we studied and applied two state-of-the-art deep learning architectures to ESR: a modified version of the well-known GhostNet model, and an end-to-end 1D convolutional neural network (CNN). The performance in classification as well as computational metrics considering a low-power device (STM32F407VGT6) implementation were assessed. Distinct sampling rates, signal lengths and representations of sound were tested, considering three publicly available datasets: ESC-50, US8K and AudioSet. The best performing model on ESC-50 was GhostNet, achieving an F-Score of 0.96 ± 0.01, with a Multiply-and-Accumulate Complexity (MACC) of $0.517M$, whereas the 1D CNN obtained the best F-Score on US8K (0.93 ± 0.05), with an MACC of $27.125M$. Additionally, we verified that 32 filters log-Mel spectrograms on 1.5-s long signals sampled at 16000 Hz led to the best performances. Interestingly, the most efficient model was GhostNet, trained using 32 filters MFCCs, 1-s long signals with a sampling rate of 8820 Hz, which achieved an F-Score of 0.92 ± 0.07 on ESC-50, just 0.04 below the best overall performance, but with a 33% lower MACC (0.347M) and 40% less running time.

Keywords: Emergency siren recognition · Sound classification · Neural networks · Embedded system · IoT · Edge-AI

1 Introduction

A siren is a distinct audible alert commonly emitted in emergency situations, such as when, for example, an emergency vehicle is performing its task and needs to warn pedestrians or drivers nearby. It may be possible for a driver not to perceive an audible alert due to high soundproofing in vehicle compartments or a pedestrian due to the use of headphones. Additionally, there is the risk that a hearing-impaired person may be the driver or pedestrian in the situation

© The Author(s), under exclusive license to Springer Nature Switzerland AG 2022
J. C. Xavier-Junior and R. A. Rios (Eds.): BRACIS 2022, LNAI 13654, pp. 154–168, 2022.
https://doi.org/10.1007/978-3-031-21689-3_12

described. Not realizing such an alert not only may cause delays in the service intended by the emergency vehicle, but also traffic accidents.

An automatic siren detector system could be useful in mitigating risky events in traffic. It can provide some kind of visual assistance to the driver with regard to a nearby siren, as an Advanced Driver-Assistance System (ADAS), or it can be embedded in smart bracelets to generate a tactile warning signal to a hearing-impaired person. Moreover, in the field of smart cities, such a system could be explored to optimize the activation of traffic lights when the presence of an emergency vehicle is detected. The aforementioned use cases possibly require the implementation of algorithms in low-power devices (microcontrollers), because of either the demand for more optimized system battery life or the low acquisition cost.

The Emergency Siren Recognition (ESR) task represents an important sub-problem of Environmental Sound Classification (ESC), and it amounts to the challenge of automatically detecting the occurrence of emergency sirens given audio recordings of the environment. In the past decade, deep learning techniques have had a significant impact on the ESC task. In particular, Convolutional Neural Networks (CNNs) originally developed for image recognition have been evaluated in [4], and 1D CNN architectures were proposed in [1]. Eventually, these deep learning techniques have also been used in the ESR task [21,32].

Most of the state-of-the-art methods for ESC based on deep learning have high computational requirements. Still, with the increasing interest in Internet of Things (IoT) devices and Edge-AI, many works have investigated the development of smaller and more efficient models for mobile devices with high computing power (smartphones) [9,11,30]. However, only a few works have explored the deployment on low-power microcontrollers [7,18]. Thus, there is a lack of works that explore the implementation of ESR algorithms inspired by modern techniques, like CNNs, in devices with limited computational resources.

This paper brings a study of two state-of-the-art deep learning architectures applied to the ESR task, providing an evaluation both in terms of accuracy and computational performance considering a low-power device (STM32F407VGT6) implementation. The first architecture is a modified version of the image recognition model GhostNet [9], while the second architecture is an end-to-end 1D CNN [4]. Different sampling rates, signal lengths, and pre-processing techniques were tested and an assessment of the F-Score, the number of trainable parameters, computation cycles, and runtime was performed.

The rest of this paper is organized as follows: Sect. 2 presents an overview of the related literature; Sect. 3 outlines the architectures studied along with the data processing and augmentation techniques; Sect. 4 details the experiments including datasets description, implementation and embedded system; Sect. 5 presents the evaluation metrics; in Sect. 6, the experimental results are presented and discussed, while Sect. 7 brings the final considerations and perspectives for future works.

2   Related Work

Several techniques have already been explored on ESR. For instance, in [16] a method was proposed to detect periodic patterns in acoustical signal frequency components, or, as presented in [13], signal frames can be classified by their main frequencies by comparison with a real siren based on the Longest Common Subsequence (LCS). The use of neural networks in conjunction with signal processing schemes, such as Mel-Frequency Cepstral Coefficients (MFCCs), has also been tested [3].

More recent strategies for ESC rely on deep learning techniques originally tailored for image classification. In this case, the audio signal is converted to an image that represents the sound, such as a spectrogram [4]. In terms of specifically detection of warning signals, the use of multiple Convolutional Neural Networks (CNNs) combined with data augmentation techniques was tested and showed promising results in [22]. In [21] the authors proposed a Multi-Channel CNN in which a log-Mel spectrogram is passed through four parallel CNN channels that are later connected by a fully-connected layer.

Another possible approach is to evaluate the sound wave without any pre-processing by using one-dimensional (1D) CNNs. The authors in [1] presented a framework on CNN using this concept, where the feature extraction process is performed by the neural network itself and not by a signal pre-processing analysis. This technique can be advantageous for the extraction of signal features in the time domain.

The combination of the two aforementioned strategies, that is, using pre-processed signal and raw waveform together as inputs for neural networks was tested in [32] and presented results that surpassed the state-of-the-art until then. Three CNN-based models were created, the first combining MFCCs and log-Mel spectrogram in a 2D-CNN, the second, a 1D-CNN that learns the features for classification from raw waveform, and finally, a CNN-based model ensembles both networks. Nonetheless, the implementation lacks necessary details about how the samples of the dataset were split, which might have introduced a bias towards higher accuracy.

Regarding the implementation of neural networks in microcontrollers, two major challenges prevail: (i) the entire neural network including inputs, outputs, weights, and activations must be compact enough to fit in the limited available memory (of the order of KB); (ii) the need for fast enough inference imposes a low complexity on the network due to the low device processing power [34].

Most modern CNNs for image recognition require a large number of parameters and Float Point Operations (FLOPs) to achieve high accuracy. For instance, in [10] the proposed ResNet-50 requires over 25.6M parameters and 4.1B FLOPs. With the increasing demand of compact models for embedded systems, several architectures were proposed in recent years. MobileNetV3 [11] employs depthwise separable convolutions and AutoML techniques. EfficientNet-B0 [30] uses a method that uniformly scales all dimensions of depth, width, and resolution. In GhostNet [9] a series of cheap linear transformations are applied to generate many of the so-called ghost feature maps.

There are some works that address the challenges related to using microcontrollers. The authors in [17] developed an algorithm for analysing the signal by taking the fast Fourier transform twice and implemented it in a dsPIC microcontroller. Although it was possible to detect a siren even under the Doppler effect, the inference time was, in some cases, 8 s long. Additionally, the authors in [23] presented a recursive algorithm which compared the mean and variance of the coefficients of reflection in different frames and implemented it in a Texas Instrument's microcontroller. However, as pointed out in [32], algorithms such as those described presented unsatisfactory performance in prediction quality, in addition to not having an evaluation in a dataset varied enough to be generic, such as Environmental Sound (ESC-50) [25] and UrbanSound8K (US8K) [26].

3   Materials and Methods

3.1   Network Architectures

Two distinct approaches were tested, although both used neural networks with convolutional layers. The first one explored a modified version of a well-recognized neural network for image recognition in mobile devices, the GhostNet [9]. The second one followed with minor adaptations the proposed end-to-end 1D CNN architecture for environmental sound classification presented in [1].

Image Recognition Approach with 2D CNN. In GhostNet the standard convolution layer is replaced by the Ghost Module, which is a serialization of two operations: first, a fixed portion of the final output stack is generated by a primary block comprised of a standard convolution layer followed by batch normalization and a Rectified Linear Unit (ReLU) activation function; then, this output passes through a secondary block consisting of a deepthwise convolution layer, batch normalization and ReLU. Finally, the outputs of the primary and secondary blocks are stacked together, creating the final output.

Although the default GhostNet architecture already offers a compact model, we introduced a few modifications in order to further reduce the complexity. The width multiplier parameter was adjusted to 0.2, which works as a multiplier factor for the width of the entire network. Moreover, the number of neurons in the last fully-connected layer was reduced from 1280 to 512.

End-to-End Approach with 1D CNN. Some of the models proposed in [1] are compact enough to fit embedded systems and presented good results. For instance, the chosen architecture for this work achieved on US8K an accuracy of $83\% \pm 1.3\%$ with $256k$ parameters.

The output size of each layer may vary depending on the input length of the signal. Table 1 shows the architecture used throughout our experiments for sampling rates of 22050 Hz, 16000 Hz, and 8820 Hz. The table entries marked with an asterisk (*) are not present in the implementation for sampling rate of 8820 Hz, while the entry marked with two asterisks (**) is present only in this implementation.

Table 1. End-to-end CNN 1D architecture for sampling rates of 22050 Hz, 16000 Hz, and 8820 Hz. Signal length l and sampling rate sr. The table entries marked with an asterisk (*) are not present in the implementation for sampling rate of 8820 Hz, while the entry marked with two asterisks (**) is present only in this implementation.

Layers	Kernel size	Stride	Filters	Output shape
Input				$(1, w = sr \cdot l)$
Conv. 1	(1, 64)	(1, 2)	16	$(16, w = (\frac{w-64}{2} + 1))$
Max Pool. 1	(1, 8)	(1, 8)	16	$(16, w = (\frac{w}{8}))$
Conv. 2	(1, 32)	(1, 2)	32	$(32, w = (\frac{w-32}{2} + 1))$
Max Pool. 2	(1, 8)	(1, 8)	32	$(32, w = (\frac{w}{8}))$
Conv. 3	(1, 16)	(1, 2)	64	$(64, w = (\frac{w-16}{2} + 1))$
*Conv. 4	(1, 16)	(1, 2)	128	$(128, w = (\frac{w-16}{2} + 1)$
Flatten				
Fully Connected 1	*(1, 128 $\cdot$ w) **(1, 64 $\cdot$ w)			(64)
Fully Connected 2	(1, 64)			(2)

3.2 Signal Processing

For both 1D and 2D CNN architectures, the following pre-processing methods were applied: Re-Sampling, Resize and Data Augmentation. For the 2D CNN architectures, different representations for the input audio signals were considered: Spectrogram with log-Mel scale, and MFCCs.

Re-sampling. Three distinct sampling rates were tested, so that some of the audio samples were either downsampled or upsampled. The adopted values for the sampling rates were: 22050 Hz, 16000 Hz, and 8820 Hz.

Resize. All datasets described in Sect. 4.1 have audio files that are much longer than one second. Therefore, for training and testing shorter segments were cropped from these audio files, thus reducing the size of input signal and, ultimately, the response time of the ESR system. The evaluated signal lengths were 1 and 1.5 s.

It is worth mentioning that the cropped signal may be silent. This poses a challenge, especially when the cropped segment comes from an audio signal originally related to the positive target class (i.e. it represents an emergency alarm). Therefore, to avoid muted clippings from being used as positive samples, a RMS (Eq. (1)) pre-assessment was used. During the training phase, if the random cropped section had a RMS value lower or equal to a threshold of 0.001, a new random crop was extracted until the observed RMS value was higher than the threshold.

$$RMS\{x(n)\} = \sqrt{\frac{1}{N} \sum_n x^2(n)} \tag{1}$$

Data Augmentation. In a certain sense, the resize method already plays the role of a data augmentation mechanism. However, an additional procedure was applied randomly to further expand the training dataset.

As presented in [31], two cropped samples are mixed using a random ratio r from a standard uniform distribution $U(0, 1)$. The original labels, denoted by t_1 and t_2, are mixed as described by Eq. (2)

$$l = rt_1 + (1 - r)t_2, \tag{2}$$

while the samples are mixed according to Eq. (3), which takes into account the measured gains g_1 and g_2 for samples 1 and 2, respectively

$$S_{mix} = \frac{p \cdot signal_1 + (1 - p) \cdot signal_2}{\sqrt{p^2 + (1 - p)^2}}, \tag{3}$$

and the mix ratio is given by

$$p = \frac{1}{1 + 10^{\frac{g_1 - g_2}{20}} \frac{1-r}{r}}. \tag{4}$$

Spectrogram. The spectrogram is an intensity plot on a log-scale of the Short-Time Fourier Transform (STFT) magnitude. The STFT works by dividing the input vector into segments and computing the Discrete Fourier Transform (DFT) on each of them, generating a chronological sequence of frequency spectra [27]. The mathematical definition for the STFT is (5) [2]:

$$\text{STFT}\{x[n]\}(m, \omega) \equiv X_m(m, \omega) = \sum_{n=-\infty}^{\infty} x[n]\text{w}[n - mR]e^{-j\omega n}, \tag{5}$$

where $x[n]$ is the input signal, $\text{w}[n - mR]$ the window function with length m, and R is the hop size in samples between.

Therefore, the spectrogram on a log-scale can be defined as in Eq. (6)

$$\text{spectrogram}_{db} \equiv 10 \log_{10}(|\text{STFT}\{x[n]\}(m, \omega)|^2). \tag{6}$$

The chosen window length (m) and hop size (R) were 1024 and 512 samples, respectively.

Log-Mel. The Mel scale is based on the human ear's ability to perceive changes in the frequency of a sound. As the goal of the work is related to the detection of sirens, which are signals that are intended to be perceived by humans, it is reasonable to use such a scale.

The mathematical relationship between the Mel scale and the real frequency scale is given by Eq. (7) [20]

$$m = 2595 \log_{10} \left(1 + \frac{f}{700}\right). \tag{7}$$

To obtain a log-Mel scale spectrogram, a bank of triangular filters must be applied to a power spectrum obtained from the STFT [20]. In this work, the number of filters assessed were 32 and 64.

Mel Frequency Cepstral Coefficients. The MFCCs were originally developed for speech recognition tasks, but due to their capability of describing the tone of a sound, they were also explored in the classification of musical genres [19].

The MFCCs are the coefficients that compose an MFC, which is a representation of the power spectrum of a signal on a logarithmic scale based on a cosine transformation of a power spectrum on the Mel scale [5]. Commonly, MFCCs are calculated from a log-Mel spectrogram with the additional step of the discrete cosine transform. In this work, the number of filters used for calculating the MFCCs were 32 and 64.

4   Experiments

4.1   Datasets

The experiments were carried out by combining three different datasets: Environmental Sound (ESC-50), UrbanSound8K (US8K) and AudioSet. The ESC-50 dataset contains 2000 samples of 5 s long audio recordings sampled at 44.1 kHz, which are equally distributed over 50 classes [25]. On the other hand, the US8K contains 8732 audio samples of urban sounds up to 4 s long and with a sampling rate ranging from 4 to 192 kHz, which are equally distributed in 10 classes [26]. Finally, the AudioSet dataset, which was used solely for mitigating the class imbalance during training, is a collection of $2,084,320$ 10-s sound clips from YouTube videos arranged over 527 classes. However, in this work only the balanced training section of the siren class was used, which sums up to 169 samples, since not all of them were available for download [8]. Table 2 shows in detail the data distribution among all the considered datasets.

4.2   Implementation

The neural networks and the workflow processing steps were implemented using mainly the following Python libraries: (*i*) PyTorch version 1.10.2 [24]; (*ii*) Pytorch-Lightning version 1.5.9; (*iii*) Torchaudio version 0.10.2 for audio processing [33]; (*iv*) ONNX version 1.10.0. The full code is available in [6].

Table 2. Summary of the experimental data.

	ESC-50	US8K	AudioSet (balanced train)	Total
Siren class samples	40	929	169	1138
Total samples	2000	8732	169	9101
Total length (hours)	2.8	9.7	0.47	12.97
Sample length (seconds)	5	≤ 4	10	
Sampling rate (kHz)	44.1	$4 \leq 192$	44.1	

Loss Function. Since there is a strong imbalance among the positive (emergency sirens) and negative samples available in the datasets, the loss function chosen for the task was the focal loss [14].

The focal loss gives less importance to the classification of simple negative samples, which are predominant in the dataset, and focuses training on the hard negatives. The mathematical definition for the focal loss associated with the i-training sample is:

$$FL(p_t) = -(1 - p_t)^\gamma \log(p_t), \tag{8}$$

where

$$p_t = \begin{cases} p, & \text{if } y = 1 \\ 1 - p, & \text{otherwise} \end{cases}, \tag{9}$$

γ is an adjustable focusing parameter, y denotes the true label of the sample and p is the estimated probability.

Optimizer. The algorithm chosen for gradient optimization was Adam [12], mainly due to its computational efficiency and low memory requirements. Experiments in [12] have shown that the Adam algorithm is well-suited for optimizing convolutional neural network parameters.

Training. The AudioSet dataset was combined either with the ESC-50 or US8K. The motivation was to increase the number of positive samples. Both CNNs were trained for 200 epochs, with a starting learning rate of $1 \cdot 10^{-2}$ for the 2D CNN network and $1 \cdot 10^{-3}$ for the 1D CNN network. A learning rate scheduler was used for reducing the learning rate by 10 times when the loss has stopped improving for more than 20 epochs. On top of that, 20% of the samples from the training dataset were randomly selected for validation and not used for training, the loss function performance on the validation set was monitored and the model from the best performing epoch was selected for testing.

Testing. The signals longer than the input size of the network were sliced into multiple segments, but considering the RMS criterion stated in Sect. 4.1. Then, the average of the output predictions was used to classify the entire test sound. Furthermore, a division of the ESC-50 dataset into 5 folds was explored. The best performing model on ESC-50 according to the metric further detailed in Sect. 5 was also trained and tested on US8K using a 10 folds scheme. It is worth mentioning that both fold divisions were carried out considering the original divisions stated by the authors in [25] and in [26].

4.3   Embedded System Performance

Typically, a microcontroller consists of a processor core, a Static Random Access Memory (SRAM) module, and a flash memory module. The specifications may vary among manufactures and versions. Usually the program application stored in the flash memory is loaded into the SRAM during startup so that the core processor can run it. Consequently, the size of the SRAM limits the size of the program application, which includes the weights of the neural network.

The ARM Cortex-M family offers microcontrollers optimized for low-cost and energy-efficiency. Some microcontrollers have integrated Digital Signal Processing (DSP) instructions that can be useful for running neural network applications. For instance, Cortex-M4 and Cortex-M7 have integrated features of Single Instruction Multiple Data (SIMD) and Single Precision (SP) Floating Point Instructions that are useful for the computation required for neural networks.

STM32F407VGT6. The microcontroller chosen to implement the neural network and run the system performance test is based on the ARM Cortex-M4 architecture, and has a DSP with a Floating Point Unit (FPU) and a core frequency of up to 168 MHz [28]. In addition, the microcontroller has 1 MByte of flash memory and 192 kByte of RAM, resources that delimited the size of the neural network to be used.

STM32Cube and X-Cube AI. The STM32Cube Integrated Development Environment (IDE) was used to generate the base code for system performance inference. It has several extension packages, one of which is the X-Cube AI. The package is capable of converting neural networks developed in high-level architectures to C language codes optimized in memory usage (SRAM and flash memory) [29].

STM32F4DISCOVERY. The development kit board connected to the microcontroller offers a series of useful peripherals for the purpose of the project, such as the ST-LINK/V2-A debug module used for the system performance evaluation.

System Performance Evaluation. The selected PyTorch trained model was converted to the Open Neural Network Exchange (ONNX) format, which provides a computational graph neural network model and the definitions of built-in operators and standard types [15]. The neural network model in ONNX format was later loaded by the STM32 X-Cube AI package so that the Multiply-and-Accumulate Complexity (MACC) could be obtained. Hence, a default application was generated and flashed into the microcontroller allowing for the measurement of critical aspects of the system. The application workflow is as follows: Random inputs are generated and fed into the network sixteen times while the number of CPU cycles is measured; then; the results are averaged among the multiple runs and from that the runtime in milliseconds is obtained. Additionally, the pre-processing runtime was estimated using a firmware developed for calculating a log-Mel spectrogram with 30 Mel filters of a 1-s long signal sampled at 16000 Hz.

5   Evaluation Metrics

In order to evaluate the classification results, the F-Score (Eq. (10)) metric was used:

$$F = \frac{\text{True Positive}}{\text{True Positive} + \frac{1}{2}(\text{False Positive} + \text{False Negative})}. \tag{10}$$

An F-Score value for each class was calculated, considering one class (Siren and Non-siren) as positive at a time. The results were then combined by macro-averaging:

$$F_{macro} = \frac{F_{siren} + F_{non-siren}}{2}. \tag{11}$$

Finally, the resulting F-Score values were averaged among the folds used for the testing and the standard deviation was calculated.

The metrics for evaluating the embedded system performance are related to the neural network complexity. Memory footprint and execution time are the two main factors and they can be evaluated by: number of parameters, number of arithmetic operations, given by Multiply-and-Accumulate Complexity (MACC) [29], and runtime in milliseconds [34].

6   Results and Discussion

The classification results on ESC-50 5-fold scheme obtained by GhostNet and End-to-end 1D CNN for macro averaged F-Score is presented in Table 3. First, it is possible to perceive that 16000 Hz is the best sampling rate for all cases, except for MFCCs obtained using 64 and 32 filters; in these cases the best F-Score is achieved for sampling rates of 8820 Hz and 22050 Hz, respectively. Furthermore, the best signal length for all cases is 1.5 s, except for MFCCs obtained using 64 filters, which presented a better F-Score with a signal length of 1 s.

With respect to the classification networks, the approach using GhostNet reached the best F-Score for the ESC-50 dataset (0.96 ± 0.01), while the End-to-end 1D CNN achieved a maximum F-Score of 0.91 ± 0.07.

Table 3. Average F-Score and standard deviation for ESC-50 dataset from 5-fold cross validation.

Sampling Rate (Hz)	Signal Length (s)	GhostNet				End-to-End 1D CNN
		Log-Mel Spectrogram		MFCC		
		64 filters	32 filters	64 filters	32 filters	
22050	1.5	0.83 ± 0.15	0.86 ± 0.07	0.78 ± 0.11	0.94 ± 0.06	0.88 ± 0.04
	1	0.88 ± 0.05	0.87 ± 0.05	0.86 ± 0.08	0.83 ± 0.07	0.83 ± 0.07
16000	1.5	0.96 ± 0.05	**0.96 ± 0.01**	0.91 ± 0.05	0.92 ± 0.07	**0.91 ± 0.07**
	1	0.91 ± 0.05	0.89 ± 0.07	0.88 ± 0.05	0.85 ± 0.06	0.85 ± 0.06
8820	1.5	0.88 ± 0.09	0.83 ± 0.07	0.84 ± 0.15	0.90 ± 0.09	0.83 ± 0.15
	1	0.88 ± 0.04	0.87 ± 0.05	0.93 ± 0.09	0.92 ± 0.07	0.85 ± 0.05

The best performing models on ESC-50 (GhostNet and End-to-end 1D CNN) were also trained and tested on US8K and the results are presented in Table 4. The table shows a decrease of 0.05 for F-Score of GhostNet on the US8K when compared to ESC-50. On the other hand, the opposite happens to the End-to-end 1D CNN, which presented an increase of 0.02 for F-Score. The reason might be that more samples in a less diverse dataset (8732 samples and 10 classes on US8K, compared to 2000 samples and 50 classes on ESC-50) offer a better chance of learning the representation directly from the audio signal.

Table 4. Average F-Score and standard deviation for the ESC-50 and US8K dataset from 5-fold and 10-fold cross validation, respectively.

Model	Sampling Rate (Hz)	Signal Length (s)	ESC-50	US8K
GhostNet	16000	1.5	0.96 ± 0.01	0.91 ± 0.03
End-to-end 1D CNN	16000	1.5	0.91 ± 0.07	0.93 ± 0.05

Table 5 shows the number of parameters, MACC and runtime for each architecture, sampling rate, and signal length tested. Although the number of parameters does not vary in GhostNet according to the input size, the network complexity increases three times from the lowest to the highest value. On the other hand, for the End-to-end 1D CNN not only the complexity increases four times as the input size increases, but also the number of parameters increases more than three times as the input size increases. This poses a clear challenge in scaling the End-to-End 1D CNN architecture for longer signal lengths.

It is important to note that not all neural networks were deployed to the microcontroller due to limitations in the available SRAM and flash memories. Moreover, the calculated runtime concerns only the neural network, not including the required signal pre-processing for GhostNet. The experiments conducted for this work showed that the runtime needed for calculating a log-Mel spectrogram with 30 Mel filters of a 1-s long signal sampled at 16000 Hz is approximately 160 ms.

The final best performing models for each sampling rate along with their number of parameters, operations and runtime are summarized in Table 6. From the table we can see that the image recognition approach using GhostNet achieved the best results for both prediction and performance assessments, even if 160 ms are added to the runtime considering the needed pre-processing.

Interestingly, when comparing GhostNet models with an input height of 32 of which have signals sampled at 8820 Hz and 16000 Hz, we can see that a reduction of 33% on MACC and 40% in runtime comes at the cost of approximately only 4 percentage points in F-Score, which can be seen as a pertinent trade-off when working with IoT or edge devices.

Table 5. Parameters, MACC and runtime in milliseconds for each architecture tested. GhostNet models are presented according to the input height (number of Mel filters). The entries marked with hyphens (−) indicate that the corresponding models exceeded the microcontroller memory.

Model	Sampling Rate (Hz)	Signal Length (s)	Parameters (k)	MACC (M)	Runtime (ms)
GhostNet Input Height 64	22050	1.5	221	1.047	−
		1		0.850	−
	16000	1.5		0.867	−
		1		0.610	−
	8820	1.5		0.581	61.7
		1		0.521	60.0
GhostNet Input Height 32	22050	1.5	221	0.609	−
		1		0.511	51.4
	16000	1.5		0.517	52.6
		1		0.391	38.2
	8820	1.5		0.377	35.6
		1		0.347	30.8
End-to-end 1D CNN	22050	1.5	320	37.827	−
		1	231	24.846	−
	16000	1.5	247	27.125	−
		1	182	17.706	−
	8820	1.5	120	14.094	−
		1	87	9.200	1283.0

Table 6. Summary of the best performing models and the needed computation requirements.

Model	Sampling Rate (Hz)	Signal Size (s)	Pre Process.	ESC-50	US8K	Params (k)	MACC (M)	Runtime (ms)
GhostNet	22050	1.5	MFCC 64 filters	0.94 ± 0.06	–	221	1.047	–
	16000	1.5	Log-Mel Spec. 32 filters	0.96 ± 0.01	0.91 ± 0.03		0.867	52.6
	8820	1	MFCC 64 filters	0.93 ± 0.09	–		0.521	35.6
End-to-End 1D CNN	22050	1.5		0.88 ± 0.04	–	320	37.827	–
	16000	1.5		0.91 ± 0.07	0.93 ± 0.05	247	27.125	–
	8820	1		0.85 ± 0.05	–	87	9.200	1283.0

7 Conclusion

In this paper, a modified version of the GhostNet model and an End-to-end 1D CNN architecture were evaluated on the task of Emergency Siren Recognition (ESR) regarding their accuracy and computational performance. The GhostNet model was modified to fit a commonly used microncontoller, the STM32F407VGT6.

In our experiments we also evaluated different sampling rates, signal lengths, and two representations of sound – log-Mel spectrograms and Mel-Frequency Cepstral Coefficients (MFCCs) – using three publicly available datasets – ESC-50, US8K, and Audioset.

The best classification F-Score achieved on the ESC-50 and US8K datasets were 0.96±0.01 and 0.93±0.05, respectively. GhostNet had a higher classification F-Score on ESC-50 than the End-to-end 1D CNN architecture, while the opposite happened on US8K. We believe that the main reason for this is the less diverse number of classes in US8K compared to ESC-50. In most cases, we obtained the highest classification F-Score when using log-Mel spectrograms of 32 filters on 1.5-s long signals sampled at 16000 Hz.

The most efficient model was GhostNet when trained with MFCCs obtained using 32 filters from 1-s long signals sampled at 8820 Hz. It achieved a classification F-Score of 0.92 ± 0.07 on ESC-50, with an MACC of 0.347M and a runtime of 30.8 ms, which corresponds to a reduction of approximately 33% in the model complexity and 40% in runtime when compared to the model with the best overall classification F-Score.

As future works, some sort of knowledge distillation and quantization can be explored for compacting even further the tested models. Additionally, a complete microcontroller application can be developed, including signal acquisition and processing, as well as the neural network inference.

References

1. Abdoli, S., Cardinal, P., Lameiras Koerich, A.: End-to-end environmental sound classification using a 1D convolutional neural network. Expert Syst. Appl. **136**, 252–263 (2019). https://doi.org/10.1016/j.eswa.2019.06.040,https://www.sciencedirect.com/science/article/pii/S0957417419304403
2. Allen, J.B., Rabiner, L.R.: A unified approach to short-time Fourier analysis and synthesis. Proc. IEEE **65**(11), 1558–1564 (1977)
3. Beritelli, F., Casale, S., Russo, A., Serrano, S.: An automatic emergency signal recognition system for the hearing impaired. In: 2006 IEEE 12th Digital Signal Processing Workshop 4th IEEE Signal Processing Education Workshop, pp. 179–182 (2006). https://doi.org/10.1109/DSPWS.2006.265438
4. Boddapati, V., Petef, A., Rasmusson, J., Lundberg, L.: Classifying environmental sounds using image recognition networks. Procedia Comput. Sci. **112**, 2048–2056 (2017). https://doi.org/10.1016/j.procs.2017.08.250,https://www.sciencedirect.com/science/article/pii/S1877050917316599, knowledge-Based and Intelligent Information & Engineering Systems: Proceedings of the 21st International Conference, KES-20176-8 September 2017, Marseille, France
5. Davis, S., Mermelstein, P.: Comparison of parametric representations for monosyllabic word recognition in continuously spoken sentences. IEEE Trans. Acoust. Speech Signal Process. **28**(4), 357–366 (1980). https://doi.org/10.1109/TASSP.1980.1163420
6. Caetano dos Santos, D.F.: Emergency siren recognition (2022). https://github.com/davifcs/acoustic_alert_detector.git
7. Fedorov, I., Adams, R.P., Mattina, M., Whatmough, P.: Sparse: sparse architecture search for CNNs on resource-constrained microcontrollers. Adv. Neural Inf. Process. Syst. **32** (2019)
8. Gemmeke, J.F., et al.: Audio set: an ontology and human-labeled dataset for audio events. In: 2017 IEEE International Conference on Acoustics, Speech and Signal Processing (ICASSP), pp. 776–780. IEEE (2017)
9. Han, K., Wang, Y., Tian, Q., Guo, J., Xu, C., Xu, C.: Ghostnet: more features from cheap operations. In: Proceedings of the IEEE/CVF Conference on Computer Vision and Pattern Recognition (CVPR) (2020)
10. He, K., Zhang, X., Ren, S., Sun, J.: Deep residual learning for image recognition. In: Proceedings of the IEEE Conference on Computer Vision and Pattern Recognition, pp. 770–778 (2016)
11. Howard, A., et al.: Searching for mobilenetv3. In: Proceedings of the IEEE/CVF International Conference on Computer Vision (ICCV) (2019)
12. Kingma, D.P., Ba, J.: Adam: a method for stochastic optimization. arXiv preprint arXiv:1412.6980 (2014)
13. Liaw, J.J., Wang, W.S., Chu, H.C., Huang, M.S., Lu, C.P.: Recognition of the ambulance siren sound in Taiwan by the longest common subsequence. In: 2013 IEEE International Conference on Systems, Man, and Cybernetics, pp. 3825–3828 (2013). https://doi.org/10.1109/SMC.2013.653
14. Lin, T.Y., Goyal, P., Girshick, R., He, K., Dollár, P.: Focal loss for dense object detection. In: Proceedings of the IEEE International Conference on Computer Vision, pp. 2980–2988 (2017)
15. Linux Foundation: Open neural network exchange (2022). https://onnx.ai/
16. Meucci, F., Pierucci, L., Del Re, E., Lastrucci, L., Desii, P.: A real-time siren detector to improve safety of guide in traffic environment. In: 2008 16th European Signal Processing Conference, pp. 1–5 (2008)

17. Miyazakia, T., Kitazonoa, Y., Shimakawab, M.: Ambulance siren detector using FFT on DSPIC. In: Proceedings of the 1st IEEE/IIAE International Conference on Intelligent Systems and Image Processing, pp. 266–269 (2013)
18. Mohaimenuzzaman, M., Bergmeir, C., West, I.T., Meyer, B.: Environmental sound classification on the edge: a pipeline for deep acoustic networks on extremely resource-constrained devices. arXiv preprint arXiv:2103.03483 (2021)
19. Müller, M.: Information Retrieval for Music and Motion. Springer, Berlin Heidelberg (2007). https://doi.org/10.1007/978-3-540-74048-3, https://books.google.com.br/books?id=kSzeZWR2yDsC
20. O'Shaughnessy, D.: Speech Communication: Human and Machine. Addison-Wesley series in electrical engineering, Addison-Wesley Publishing Company (1987). https://books.google.com.br/books?id=mHFQAAAAMAAJ
21. Padhy, S., Tiwari, J., Rathore, S., Kumar, N.: Emergency signal classification for the hearing impaired using multi-channel convolutional neural network architecture. In: 2019 IEEE Conference on Information and Communication Technology, pp. 1–6. IEEE (2019)
22. Padhy, S., Tiwari, J., Rathore, S., Kumar, N.: Emergency signal classification for the hearing impaired using multi-channel convolutional neural network architecture. In: 2019 IEEE Conference on Information and Communication Technology, pp. 1–6 (2019). https://doi.org/10.1109/CICT48419.2019.9066252
23. Park, S.W., Trevino, J.: Automatic detection of emergency vehicles for hearing impaired drivers. Texas A&M Univ.-Kingsville EE/CS Dept. MSC **192**, 637–665 (2013)
24. Paszke, A., et al.: Pytorch: an imperative style, high-performance deep learning library. Adv. Neural Inf. Process. Syst. **32** (2019)
25. Piczak, K.J.: ESC: dataset for environmental sound classification. In: Proceedings of the 23rd ACM international conference on Multimedia, pp. 1015–1018 (2015)
26. Salamon, J., Jacoby, C., Bello, J.P.: A dataset and taxonomy for urban sound research. In: Proceedings of the 22nd ACM International Conference on Multimedia, pp. 1041–1044. MM 2014, Association for Computing Machinery, New York, NY, USA (2014). https://doi.org/10.1145/2647868.2655045
27. Smith, J.O.: Spectral audio signal processing (2022). http://ccrma.stanford.edu/~jos/sasp/. 2011 edition
28. STMicroeletronics: STM32F405xx STM32F407xx - Datasheet - production data (2020)
29. STMicroeletronics: Getting started with X-CUBE-AI Expansion Package for Artificial Intelligence (AI) (2022)
30. Tan, M., Le, Q.: Efficientnet: rethinking model scaling for convolutional neural networks. In: International Conference on Machine Learning, pp. 6105–6114. PMLR (2019)
31. Tokozume, Y., Ushiku, Y., Harada, T.: Learning from between-class examples for deep sound recognition. arXiv preprint arXiv:1711.10282 (2017)
32. Tran, V.T., Tsai, W.H.: Acoustic-based emergency vehicle detection using convolutional neural networks. IEEE Access **8**, 75702–75713 (2020). https://doi.org/10.1109/ACCESS.2020.2988986
33. Yang, Y.Y., et al.: Torchaudio: building blocks for audio and speech processing. arXiv preprint arXiv:2110.15018 (2021)
34. Zhang, Y., Suda, N., Lai, L., Chandra, V.: Hello edge: keyword spotting on microcontrollers (2017). https://doi.org/10.48550/ARXIV.1711.07128, https://arxiv.org/abs/1711.07128

A Probabilistically-Oriented Analysis of the Performance of ASR Systems for Brazilian Radios and TVs

Diego Marques de Azevedo[✉], Guilherme Souza Rodrigues, and Marcelo Ladeira

Programa de Pós-Graduação em Computacão Aplicada, University of Brasília, Brasília, Brazil
diegomarques.azevedo@gmail.com, {guilhermerodrigues,mladeira}@unb.br

Abstract. With the use of neural network-based technologies, Automatic Speech Recognition (ASR) systems for Brazilian Portuguese (BP) have shown great progress in the last few years. Several state-of-art results were achieved by open-source end-to-end models, such as the Kaldi toolkit and the Wav2vec 2.0. Alternative commercial tools are also available, including the Google and Microsoft speech to text APIs and the Audimus System of VoiceInteraction. We analyse the relative performance of such tools – in terms of the so-called Word Error Rate (WER) – when transcribing audio recordings from Brazilian radio and TV channels. A generalized linear model (GLM) is designed to stochastically describe the relationship between some of the audio's properties (e.g. file format and audio duration) and the resulting WER, for each method under consideration. Among other uses, such strategy enables the analysis of local performances, indicating not only which tool performs better, but when exactly it is expected to do so. This, in turn, could be used to design an optimized system composed of several transcribers. The data generated for conducting this experiment and the scripts used to produce the stochastic model are public available.

Keywords: Speech recognition · Wav2vec 2.0 · Kaldi · Google Speech-to-Text · Microsoft Azure Speech · Audimus.Media · Text corpus · GLM · Brazilian Portuguese

1 Introduction

The importance of the Automatic Speech Recognition (ASR) systems is clearly seen by its widespread adoption in human-computer interaction area, like personal assistants, automated calls, healthcare tools and others [12–14,28]. Essentially, ASR systems map an acoustic signal containing speech to a sequence of words intended by the speaker [11].

In previous approaches, ASR systems were based on Gaussian mixture models and hidden Markov models [23]. Their accuracy are known to severely deteriorate in the presence of background noise and far speech. The ASR systems based

© The Author(s), under exclusive license to Springer Nature Switzerland AG 2022
J. C. Xavier-Junior and R. A. Rios (Eds.): BRACIS 2022, LNAI 13654, pp. 169–180, 2022.
https://doi.org/10.1007/978-3-031-21689-3_13

on deep learning techniques made progress by training their models with different levels of noise and microphone distances [31], which mitigate the problem of performance degradation. However, the deep learning approach requires considerable amounts of training data, imposing an operational obstacle for Brazilian Portuguese (BP) language models.

In 2020, an open dataset of 376 h was publicly available. It was mostly formed by non-conversational speech and included: Common Voice Corpus version 6.1[1], Sid dataset[2], VoxForge[3], LapsBM1.5[4], Multilingual LibriSpeech (MLS) [21] and CETUC dataset [1]. In 2021, the Multilingual TEDx Corpus [24] and the Common Voice Corpus 7.0[5] incremented the amount of avaliable data, for a total of 574 h. The CORAA dataset [10] was also released in 2021, contributing with 290.77 additional hours of predominantly spontaneous and noise speech; It is composed by five other corpora: ALIP, C-ORAL Brasil I, NURC-Recife, SP2010 and TEDx Portuguese talks.

Several works contributed to the advancement of BP Automatic Speech Recognition. Batista et al. [5] trained a hidden Markov with deep neural network model (HMM-DNN) using the Kaldi tools [20], achieving a WER of 4.75% in the LapsBM1.4 corpora. Quintanilha et al. [22] proposed an end-to-end model based on the DeepSpeech 2 [2] topology. This work achieved a WER of 25.45% using the following: Sid dataset, Voxforge, LapsBM1.4, CSLU Spoltech [26] and CETUC. Junior et al. [10] and Stefanel Gris et al. [27] presented a fine-tuned Wav2vec model based on the Wav2Vec-XLSR-53 [8]. While Stefanel Gris et al. [27] obtained a WER of 10.5% using an assembled dataset (Sid dataset, Voxforge, LapsBM1.4, CSLU Spoltech, MLS and Common Voice Corpus), Junior et al. [10] achieved a WER of 24.18% over the CORAA dataset. Commercial tools, including the following, are competitive alternatives; Google Cloud Speech-to-Text[6], Microsoft Azure Speech[7] and the Audimus system of VoiceInteraction[8].

Junior et al. [10] showed that, even though a model presents a good result, it is still limited for the audio types over which the model was trained. In their work, their model – trained over spontaneous and noise speech – generalizes better for audios with this properties than the model that achieved the best performance over audios recorded in a controlled environment. In a real scenario, an ASR system can be applied in audio files with high degree of variability, recorded in both environments. In this context, it would be ideal to choose the best ASR system for each type of audio.

Our work presents a structured and detailed statistical comparison of the relative performance of speech recognition systems for data with a high degree

---

[1] https://commonvoice.mozilla.org/pt/datasets.

[2] https://doi.org/10.17771/PUCRio.acad.8372.

[3] http://www.voxforge.org/pt/downloads.

[4] https://laps.ufpa.brfalabrasil/.

[5] https://commonvoice.mozilla.org/pt/datasets.

[6] https://cloud.google.com/speech-to-text?hl=pt-br.

[7] https://azure.microsoft.com/en-us/services/cognitive-services/speech-to-text/.

[8] https://www.voice-interaction.com/br/audimus-media-legendagem-automatica-em-tempo-real/.

of variability. For this, it is introduced a dataset composed of 9 h of manually transcribed audios recorded from Brazilian radios and TVs. This dataset is used in a detailed study (Sect. 5) that estimates, given some characteristics of the audio, the Word Error Rate of models developed by Kaldi, Wav2vec 2.0 and the commercial systems listed above. Such approach can be used to create a composite transcriber, in which the original systems are selected to transcribe a given audio according their predicted performances.

In our analysis, the Word Error Rate (WER) was calculated using as reference the formula described in Eq. 1, where H, S, D and I denote the total number of word hits, substitutions, deletions and insertions, respectively. The *local* WER was estimated for each recognized sentence transcribed from an audio file. The observed *global* WER was calculated using the sum of the edit operations (H, D, I, C) for each recognized sentence. To do so, we used the jiwer library[9].

$$WER = \frac{S + D + I}{S + D + H}. \tag{1}$$

This paper is organized as follows. Section 2 presents a related work which focuses on evaluating some commercial ASR tools using BP datasets. In Sect. 3, we discuss in detail the ASR models used in our evaluation. Section 4 presents our approach to create our train and test datasets, to train our Kaldi-based model and to use the others models under consideration. The results are presented in Sect. 5 and the conclusions in Sect. 6.

2   Related Work

Sampaio et al. [25] compared commercial ASR systems like Facebook Wit.ai, Microsoft Azure Speech and Google Cloud Speech-to-Text. In their experiments, they tested the performance using the Common Voice Mozilla and the VoxForge datasets. In addiction, they *measured* the empirical *global* accuracy using several metrics (WER, BLEU, METEOR and Cosine Similarity). They concluded that the speech recognition systems had, in general, similar performances, with an advantage to Microsoft Azure Speech.

Our work differs in two meaningful ways. They considered different ASR models and the dataset used to evaluate the systems was composed by audios recorded in a controlled, artificial environment. Also, their work did not endeavour to estimate the *expected, local* performance.

3   Models

In this section we describe the models and toolkits under examination. This work focuses on the Kaldi toolkit and the Wav2Vec 2.0 approaches, both of which provide a flexible code that is easy to modify and extend [3,20,27]. Additionally, FalaBrasil Research Group at Federal University of Pará (UFPA) made available

---

[9] https://github.com/jitsi/jiwer.

a public repository[10] which shares scripts to train Kaldi-based models, as well as free resources for BP under open licenses [4]. Junior et al. [10] and Stefanel Gris et al. [27], in turn, provided a set of models trained with Wav2Vec using an assembled dataset.

In our analysis, the model based on Kaldi was custom-trained using the CORAA dataset. For the Wav2vec model, we used the speech recognition tool published in [10].

3.1 Kaldi

The Kaldi toolkit treats ASR systems as a set of independent components, called modules, that work jointly as a pipeline. These modules are responsible for tasks like feature extraction, acoustic and phonetical modeling and language modeling. The first one extracts speech features from acoustic signals. During this process, the acoustic waveform is windowed at every 25 ms with 10 ms of overlap. Then, it is encoded as low or high-resolution features, depending of the type of the acoustic model that will be trained [9]. The acoustic and phonetical modeling provides the probabilities for each speech feature given a corresponding sequence of words. To do so, Kaldi generates a set of HMM-GMM models using as input the speech features extracted from the audio files and a phonetic dictionary created with a grapheme-to-phoneme tool. The best HMM-GMM acoustic model produces high-level alignments, which are used as reference for the final acoustic DNN-based model.

Succinctly, a language model (LM) estimates the probability of a certain word in a context given by several preceding or succeeding words. In Kaldi, LM is used as part of the decoding process. The n-gram model defines the dependency probabilities of the words estimated by a weighted finite state transducer (WFST), called HCLG. This process is described in details in [9,20]. As a result, it gives the most probable sequence of words based on the speech signals passed as input.

3.2 Wav2vec

The Wav2Vec 2.0 can be divided in two stages. Firstly, it applies self supervising to learn good representations from a large amount of unlabeled speech. This is done by a multi-layer convolutional neural network and a Transformer. The convolutional neural network (CNN) is responsible for the feature encoder. It generates latent speech representations of the raw audio that it is used as input. Then, they are fed to a Transformer used to build contextualized representations. In this step, a finite set of latent representation is discretized by the quantized module to be used as target during the learning process. This is done by a contrastive task to differentiate true quantized latent representations from a set of false examples in a masked time-step context. In the next stage, the model is fine-tuned for speech recognition by learning representations on labeled data.

---

[10] https://gitlab.com/fb-asr/.

To do so, a randomly initialized output layer is added on top of the context network to predict characters or phonemes by using Connectionist Temporal Classification (CTC) [3].

Although Wav2Vec 2.0 does not require an external LM or a dictionary to generate coherent transcriptions, their combination can yield a significant improvement in model performance [3]. At each time-step, during the decoding process, a beam search is applied to the probabilities of all possible output characters defined by the fine-tuned model while the probability of the next letters, given by the n-gram LM, is taken into account. It prevents the transcriber to generate sequences of letters that do not form valid words (according to the LM).

3.3   Google Speech-to-Text

The commercial ASR methodologies are not fully disclosed for business reasons. However, Google AI team proposed an end-to-end model based on Encoder-Decoder with Recurrent Neural Network (RNN) architecture, called Listen, Attend, and Spell (LAS) [6]. Then, it was improved by using a Multi-headed Attention Layer, a new training metric based on minimum rate of word errors and an external language model [7]. Both works were trained and evaluated over the Google Voice Search dataset.

3.4   Microsoft Azure Speech

The Microsoft AI team described a version of the Microsoft's conversational speech recognition system for Switchboard and CallHome datasets [30]. This version is formed by a set of model architectures, detailed in [29], added to a CNN model with a Bidirectional Long Short Term Memory (BI-LSTM) and a LSTM-based language model.

3.5   Audimus.Media

Audimus.Media is an ASR system developed by VoiceInteraction company that focuses on closed captioning service. It was first built for European Portuguese language [16]. It is currently available for more than 30 languages, including BP. In Brazil, it is used by one of the principals media companies[11]. This system resulted from the works published by [15,17,18]. It is a hybrid speech recognizer that combines HMM with Multi-Layer Perceptrons (MLPs). The HMM-MLP architecture is used by the acoustic model to generate the posterior phone probabilities given the observed audio segments. During the decoding process, a WFST integrates the acoustic model output to a lexicon transducer and a language model. The decoder generates a series of features as output, which are used to measure the word confidence. Additionally, a maximum entropy classifier estimates the certainty associated to each word.

---

[11] https://voiceinteraction.ai/platforms/audimus_media.html.

4   Methodology

In this section, we present the approach used for comparing the ASR systems and generating the stochastic model, in order to estimate the *expected* WER, given the audio properties.

4.1   Test Dataset

The *expected local* and *global* WER were calculated over a test dataset of (frequent speaker and acoustically diverse) audios and their respective human-made transcriptions. The audio files were collected along the year 2020 from Brazilian radio and TV channels. They have spontaneous speech from interviews, conversational speech recorded in natural contexts, noisy environments, musical background and news recorded in a controlled environment. They were recorded from 91 channels (43 radios and 48 TVs) from the north, southeast and northeast Brazilian regions. There are a total of 418 audio files, which combined account for 9 h and 1,225,785 words, with their individual duration ranging from 3 to 892 s. They represent a stratified sample of a database that belongs to a company that offers clipping service. Each audio was transcribed and revised by pair-annotators of a specialized company. The dataset is publicly available[12] and represents a useful by-product of this work.

During a pre-processing stage, we removed from the transcriptions characters such as punctuation and non-language symbols, like parenthesis and hyphen; the percentage sign (%) was expanded for its transcribed form (percentage); the cardinal and ordinal numbers were expanded to their literal form using num2words library[13]; the texts were normalized to lower case.

We analyse the performance of the ASR models in two separate settings: (1) with the recordings in their original form and (2) after the application of a basic noise reduction process, called in our experiments as *nr pre-processing technique*. The latter was obtained by filtering the audio frequencies, only allowing the ones 200 Hz and 1500 HzHz. For each setting, we applied a loudness normalization technique (FFMPEG loudnorm method[14]) and extracted the audio's maximum volume, average volume, bitrate and signal-to-noise ratio (SNR). The obtained values are showed in Table 1.

4.2   Training Dataset

The CORAA dataset was used for training our Kaldi-based model and the Wav2vec-based model presented in [10]. It totals 290.77 h and is composed by five other corpora: ALIP, C-ORAL Brasil I, NURC-Recife, SP2020 and TEDx Portuguese talks. This dataset focuses on spontaneous and noise speech, but also contains prepared speech (in controlled environment). The audio recordings are

---

[12] https://github.com/diegomarq/BRTVRAD.

[13] https://github.com/savoirfairelinux/num2words.

[14] http://ffmpeg.org/ffmpeg-all.html#loudnorm.

Table 1. Audios' properties values in their original form and with *nr pre-processing technique.*

Audio Properties	Min	Avg	Max
Max volume	−41.4	−18.8	−7.1
Avg volume	−22.6	−3.1	0.0
Bitrate (Kbs)	8.0	40.7	134.0
Snr	−0.369	−0.012	0.381
Max volume nr	−84.3	−25.6	−22.3
Avg volume nr	−60.8	−8.3	−2.4
Bitrate nr (Kbs)	64.0	64.0	68.0
Snr nr	−0.007	−0.000	0.005

formed by interviews, dialogues, monologues, conference and class talks, reading and stage talks. The audios' durations range for 2.4 to 7.6 s. The transcriptions were revised by pair-annotators and the texts were normalized to lower case; characters such as punctuation and non-language symbols were removed and the percentage sign (%) was expanded for its transcribed form; cardinal and ordinal numbers were expanded to their literal form using num2words library.

4.3 Model Processing

Kaldi. For the kaldi-based model, we used 273 h to the training process and 5 h to the validations process. We adopted as model language the Audimus.Media LM. The phonetic dictionary was created via FalaBrasil's grapheme-to-phoneme (G2P) tool which mapped approximately 23k words presented in Audimus.Media LM vocabulary to phonemes. By default, Kaldi uses mono channel audio with 16 kHz in a WAVE format. In this step, the data was prepared using FFMPEG. Then, it was encoded as MFCC-based vector to be fed as input to acoustic model. During the HMM-GMM training step, the lowest WER was obtained with 4200 leaves and 40000 gaussians. After that, a DNN-based acoustic model was trained on the best HMM-GMM model over 10 epochs. On this step, the same parameters defined in Kaldi Common Voice recipe[15] were used. The model was trained in a Google Cloud Computer Engine with 96 CPUs and 210GB RAM during aproximately 90 h. It was created a docker in order to make setup easier. The scripts are public available in github repository[16]

Wav2vec. We adopted the wav2vec2-large-xlsr-coraa-portuguese model which is publicly available in HuggingFace repository[17]. The authors used the CORAA dataset to fine-tune a Wav2Vec 2.0 XLSR-53 model with the same training and testing configuration of our Kaldi based model. In our analysis, their model was combined with the Audimus.Media LM.

---

[15] https://github.com/kaldi-asr/kaldi/blob/master/egs/commonvoice.
[16] https://github.com/diegomarq/docker-kaldi-coraa-pt.
[17] https://huggingface.co/Edresson/wav2vec2-large-xlsr-coraa-portuguese.

In our analysis, this model did not support audio files with more then $30\,s$ when using a Google Cloud Computer Engine with GPU NVIDIA K80. For long audio files, the application crashes for lack of memory. So, we adopted a solution proposed by the HuggingFace team. They proposed a kind of chunking with stride in the audio frames mapped to a single letter predicion, called logit. It starts doing inference on overlapping chunks (frame applied to the CTC algorithm). Then, it drops the inferenced logits on the side and chains the logits without their dropped sides. This process is explained in details in [19].

Commercial. A license is required to use Audimus.Media. The system was installed in a Windows Server 2019 with Intel Core i7 CPU and 8GB RAM. The audio files used in our evaluation were placed in an input directory defined by the system. For each file, it is created a transcribed text saved in an output directory.

The audio transcriptions made by Microsoft Azure Speech and Google Speech-to-Text were required via API using Google Colab. For Google Speech-to-Text, we used the default model, `pt-BR` as language and `LINEAR16` as encoding. These parameters were used in a `SteamingRecognitionConfig` structure. For Microsoft Azure Speech, we defined `pt-BR` as the language parameter. To the audio configuration, a `PushAudioInputStream` instance was created. The speech configuration (key and service region) was generated by Azure plataform.

5   Results and Discussion

We now investigate the relative merits of the ASR systems described above. For a comprehensive comparison, two crucial aspects need to be observed. First, some audio recordings are easier to transcribe than others, and the performance of any given method vary as a function of the audios' features. The WER defined in Eq. 1 defines a global measure of accuracy, but does not provide a detailed description of when exactly the system excels or underperforms. Second, interest lies on the expected (as estimated by a probabilistic model), rather than the observed, performance – that is, instead of simply verifying how did a system fared on a particular audio, it is more informative to estimate how it is expected to perform when transcribing audios with that particular profile (i.e., with the same characteristics).

For each audio in the test set, we computed the WER for each system and recorded a number of readily available features (covariates), namely, *state of recording* (São Paulo, Goiás or others), *source* (TV or radio), *bitrate, length, average volume, maximum volume* and *signal-to-noise ratio*. We then fitted a binomial regression[18], with the numerator of Eq. 1 acting as the number of failures and the denominator as the number of trials. In principle, the former can be greater than the later, but as the probability of such is negligible in our context,

---

[18] https://github.com/diegomarq/glm-asr-brtvrad.

that decision does not impose any practical concern. This construction is associated with an interpretation that the WER approximately corresponds to the probability of correctly transcribing a single word. The regression features were selected by a BIC (Bayesian Information Criteria) stepwise procedure searching backwards from an initial set formed by all the main effects (covariates and methods), pairwise linear interactions and second order polynomial terms (for the quantitative variables). Even though this is a low-capacity model, with only 75 degrees of freedom, parameter interpretation and inference is not straightforward.

The first panel in Fig. 1 graphically illustrates the quality of the binomial regression fit. The model seems generally well calibrated, although not particularly precise. Notice that short audio files, with few words to be identified, are more volatile – i.e. varies more widely around the fitted line. The plot on the right clearly indicates that the expected accuracy is heavily dependent on the audios' properties. Also, for 13.9% of the recordings in the test set, the Audimus is expected to outperform the Wav2Vec system, even though the later has a lower global WER. When it comes to the comparison between Kaldi and Google, each outperforms the other in roughly half of test instances. The implications are appreciable. A company which uses Google Speech-to-Text API, for instance, could decide in advance which audio should be transcribed by it and which should be directed to the Kaldi. Such an implementation could be interpreted as an ensemble transcriber, with a performance superior than the individual systems by which it is composed. In such scenario, the expected global WER achieved 44.6%, an advance of 1%. But, the economic impact is greater than the WER obtained. Kaldi was chosen in 52.2% of the audios. It could lead the company, in a hypothetical case, using less the Google Speech-to-Text API. If we consider all analysed ASR systems, Azure is uniformly more accurate across the covariate space, according to the fitted probabilistic model (Table 2).

Table 2. The values in the table correspond to the average (over the test set) of the Expected and Observed WER. For the reader's convenience, they are visually indicated in the right-hand side of Fig. 1 by the blueish line. The "nr" suffix means that the *nr pre-processing technique* was applied to the audio files used in ASR system.

ASR system	Average Expected WER	Observed WER
Azure nr	19.4%	17.9%
W2v	29.5%	27.2%
Audimus	32.4%	33.2%
Google nr	45.6%	45.8%
Kaldi nr	48.0%	45.6%

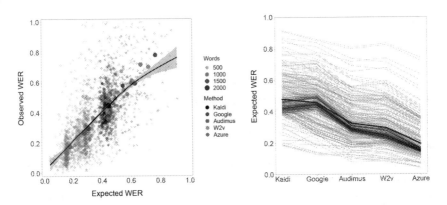

Fig. 1. The left-hand side panel compares the expected and the observed WERs. Each point depicts an audio file. The point size is proportional to the number of words in the reference transcription, and the color is determined by the ASR system. The panel in the right-hand side shows the expected WER for each method under consideration. Here, each line corresponds to an single audio file, and the coloured line represents the overall averages. (Color figure online)

6   Conclusions

This work analysed some commercial and open-source ASR tools in terms of the *expected, local* performance. Such comparison is not common in speech recognition literature, which emphasizes the *global* accuracy measured using WER. As a test set, our experiments used a new dataset composed by audio recordings with high degree of variability in terms of audios' features.

Although it was observed that the Azure expected performance was superior for all recordings of our test set, this system cannot accurately transcribe all of them. In some profiles, the Audimus and Wav2vec shown to be competitive, as well as the Kaldi and Google based systems. In this context, it is possible to build an ensemble transcriber capable of performing better then the individual systems by which it is composed.

Our analyses should not be viewed as a definitive comparison between the ASR tools, as the open-source frameworks (Kaldi and Wav2vec) can be implemented in an infinite number of ways (in terms of the training dataset, the hyperparameter tuning procedure and so forth).

For future work, more sophisticated stochastic models can be constructed. Also other practical dimensions can be considered when comparing the systems, including the license price, the maintenance and operational costs and the transcription speed.

The authors thank to the Graduate Program in Applied Computing, called (Programa de Pós-Graduação em Computação Aplicada - PPCA, in Portuguese) from the University of Brasilia, which financed in part the research, making possible the usage of Google Cloud Computer Engine and the manual transcribing service of a specialized company. The Sergio Machado Reis Epp company supported this research by offering the audio files collected along the year 2020 from brazilian radio and tv channels. This company also provided computers for using in this research and access to its transcribing database. These made possible the creation of the BRTVRAD domain.

References

1. Alencar, V., Alcaim, A.: LSF and LPC-derived features for large vocabulary distributed continuous speech recognition in Brazilian Portuguese. In: 2008 42nd Asilomar Conference on Signals, Systems and Computers, pp. 1237–1241. IEEE (2008)
2. Amodei, D., et al.: Deep speech 2: end-to-end speech recognition in English and mandarin. In: International Conference on Machine Learning, pp. 173–182. PMLR (2016)
3. Baevski, A., Zhou, Y., Mohamed, A., Auli, M.: wav2vec 2.0: a framework for self-supervised learning of speech representations. Adv. Neural. Inf. Process. Syst. **33**, 12449–12460 (2020)
4. Batista, C., Dias, A.L., Neto, N.: Free resources for forced phonetic alignment in Brazilian Portuguese based on Kaldi toolkit. EURASIP J. Adv. Signal Process. **2022**(1), 1–32 (2022)
5. Batista, C.T., Dias, A.L., Neto, N.C.S.: Baseline acoustic models for Brazilian Portuguese using Kaldi tools. In: IberSPEECH, pp. 77–81 (2018)
6. Chan, W., Jaitly, N., Le, Q., Vinyals, O.: Listen, attend and spell: a neural network for large vocabulary conversational speech recognition. In: 2016 IEEE International Conference on Acoustics, Speech and Signal Processing (ICASSP), pp. 4960–4964. IEEE (2016)
7. Chiu, C.C., et al.: State-of-the-art speech recognition with sequence-to-sequence models. In: 2018 IEEE International Conference on Acoustics, Speech and Signal Processing (ICASSP), pp. 4774–4778. IEEE (2018)
8. Conneau, A., et al.: Unsupervised cross-lingual representation learning at scale. In: Proceedings of the 58th Annual Meeting of the Association for Computational Linguistics, pp. 8440–8451. Association for Computational Linguistics (2020). https://doi.org/10.18653/v1/2020.acl-main.747, https://aclanthology.org/2020.acl-main.747
9. Georgescu, A.L., Cucu, H., Burileanu, C.: Kaldi-based DNN architectures for speech recognition in Romanian. In: 2019 International Conference on Speech Technology and Human-Computer Dialogue (SpeD), pp. 1–6. IEEE (2019)
10. Junior, A.C., et al.: CORAA: a large corpus of spontaneous and prepared speech manually validated for speech recognition in Brazilian Portuguese (2021)
11. Jurafsky, D., Martin, J.H.: Speech and Language Processing: An Introduction to Speech Recognition, Computational Linguistics and Natural Language Processing. Prentice Hall, Upper Saddle River, NJ (2008)
12. Karpagavalli, S., Chandra, E.: A review on automatic speech recognition architecture and approaches. Int. J. Signal Process. Image Process. Pattern Recogn. **9**(4), 393–404 (2016)
13. Leviathan, Y., Matias, Y.: Google duplex: an AI system for accomplishing real-world tasks over the phone (2018)
14. de Lima, T.A., Da Costa-Abreu, M.: A survey on automatic speech recognition systems for Portuguese language and its variations. Comput. Speech Lang. **62**, 101055 (2020)

15. Meinedo, H., Abad, A., Pellegrini, T., Trancoso, I., Neto, J.: The l2f broadcast news speech recognition system. Proc. Fala, 93–96 (2010)
16. Meinedo, H., Caseiro, D., Neto, J., Trancoso, I.: AUDIMUS.MEDIA: a broadcast news speech recognition system for the European Portuguese language. In: Mamede, N.J., Trancoso, I., Baptista, J., das Graças Volpe Nunes, M. (eds.) PROPOR 2003. LNCS (LNAI), vol. 2721, pp. 9–17. Springer, Heidelberg (2003). https://doi.org/10.1007/3-540-45011-4_2
17. Meinedo, H., Souto, N., Neto, J.P.: Speech recognition of broadcast news for the European Portuguese language. In: IEEE Workshop on Automatic Speech Recognition and Understanding, 2001. ASRU 2001, pp. 319–322. IEEE (2001)
18. Neto, J., Meinedo, H., Viveiros, M.: A media monitoring solution. In: 2011 IEEE International Conference on Acoustics, Speech and Signal Processing (ICASSP), pp. 1813–1816. IEEE (2011)
19. Patry, N.: Making automatic speech recognition work on large files with wav2vec2 in transformers (2022). https://huggingface.co/blog/asr-chunking
20. Povey, D., et al.: The Kaldi speech recognition toolkit. In: IEEE 2011 Workshop on Automatic Speech Recognition and Understanding. No. CONF, IEEE Signal Processing Society (2011)
21. Pratap, V., Xu, Q., Sriram, A., Synnaeve, G., Collobert, R.: MLS: a large-scale multilingual dataset for speech research. In: Interspeech 2020, 21st Annual Conference of the International Speech Communication Association, Virtual Event, Shanghai, China, 25–29 October 2020, pp. 2757–2761. ISCA (2020). https://doi.org/10.21437/Interspeech. 2020–2826
22. Quintanilha, I.M., Netto, S.L., Biscainho, L.W.P.: An open-source end-to-end ASR system for Brazilian Portuguese using DNNs built from newly assembled corpora. J. Commun. Inf. Syst. **35**(1), 230–242 (2020)
23. Rabiner, L.R.: A tutorial on hidden Markov models and selected applications in speech recognition. Readings Speech Recogn. 267–296 (1990)
24. Salesky, E., et al.: The multilingual TEDX corpus for speech recognition and translation. In: Interspeech 2021, 22nd Annual Conference of the International Speech Communication Association, Brno, Czechia, 30 August - 3 September 2021, pp. 3655–3659. ISCA (2021). https://doi.org/10.21437/Interspeech. 2021–11
25. Sampaio, M.X., et al.: Evaluation of automatic speech recognition systems. In: Anais do XXXVI Simpósio Brasileiro de Bancos de Dados, pp. 301–306. SBC (2021)
26. Schramm, M., Freitas, L., Zanuz, A., Barone, D.: CSLU: spoltech Brazilian Portuguese version 1.0 ldc2006s16 (2006)
27. Stefanel Gris, L.R., Casanova, E., de Oliveira, F.S., da Silva Soares, A., Candido Junior, A.: Brazilian Portuguese speech recognition using Wav2vec 2.0. In: Pinheiro, V., et al. (eds.) PROPOR 2022. LNCS (LNAI), vol. 13208, pp. 333–343. Springer, Cham (2022). https://doi.org/10.1007/978-3-030-98305-5_31
28. Vase, S.: The maturing of automatic speech recognition in healthcare practices. Proceedings (2021). http://ceur-ws.org. ISSN 1613, 0073
29. Xiong, W., et al.: Toward human parity in conversational speech recognition. IEEE/ACM Trans. Audio Speech Lang. Process. **25**(12), 2410–2423 (2017)
30. Xiong, W., Wu, L., Alleva, F., Droppo, J., Huang, X., Stolcke, A.: The Microsoft 2017 conversational speech recognition system. In: 2018 IEEE International Conference on Acoustics, Speech and Signal Processing (ICASSP), pp. 5934–5938. IEEE (2018)
31. Yu, D., Deng, L.: Automatic Speech Recognition. SCT, Springer, London (2015). https://doi.org/10.1007/978-1-4471-5779-3

A Reward Function Using Image Processing for a Deep Reinforcement Learning Approach Applied to the Sonic the Hedgehog Game

Felipe Rafael de Souza$^{(\boxtimes)}$ ⓘ, Thiago Silva Miranda ⓘ,
and Heder Soares Bernardino ⓘ

Federal University of Juiz de Fora, Minas Gerais, Brazil
{feliperafael,heder}@ice.ufjf.br

Abstract. Research in the Deep Reinforcement Learning (DRL) field has made great use of video game environments for benchmarking performance over the last few years. Most researches advocate for learning through high-dimensional sensory inputs (i.e. images) as observations in order to simulate scenarios that more closely approach reality. Though, when using these video game environments, the common practice is to provide the agent a reward signal calculated through accessing the environment's internal state. However, this type of resource is hardly available when applying DRL to real-world problems. Thus, we propose a reward function that uses only the images received as observations. The proposal is evaluated in the Sonic the Hedgehog game. We analyzed the agent's learning capabilities of the proposed reward function and, in most cases, its performance is similar to that obtained when accessing the environment's internal state.

Keywords: Deep reinforcement learning · Reward modeling · Image processing · Sonic the hedgehog

1 Introduction

In Reinforcement Learning, an agent interacts with an environment by receiving observations and performing actions. At each step of the interaction, the agent receives a new observation and a reward signal. The agent's goal is to develop a policy that maps states into actions in order to maximize the expected value of the cumulative rewards.

Deep Reinforcement Learning (DRL) agents have been widely tested in video games over the last few years. Common benchmarks include the Arcade Learning Environment (ALE) [3], Sonic the Hedgehog [20], Mario Bros [22], etc. These environments provide complex tasks designed to be solved by human agents [28]. The Sonic games, especially, offer a vast set of different challenges. For example, the player must learn to accelerate and maintain momentum to pass through

J. C. Xavier-Junior and R. A. Rios (Eds.): BRACIS 2022, LNAI 13654, pp. 181–195, 2022.
https://doi.org/10.1007/978-3-031-21689-3_14

loops, wait for the correct time to jump over moving platforms, use springs to jump higher, and press buttons to release the passage.

Although most of the recent advances in DRL concentrate on creating agents able to perform well in these environments using only high dimensional sensory inputs as observations [17], generally, the reward signal is still obtained by accessing the environment's internal dynamics, i.e. an emulator internal state. In more realistic and complex scenarios, it is likely for the reward signal not to be easily accessible or even easily calculated [8]. In these conditions, the reward may suffer from noise coming from the environment and end up presenting high variance.

This is concerning in terms of the agent's learning, as the concept of reward is central to Reinforcement Learning theory [10]. When defining a reward function, one can guide the agent towards the desirable behavior [30]. Furthermore, the definition of the reward function significantly impacts the agent's performance. Reward functions that provide more constant and specific feedback tend to lead to faster learning and better policy development [11] [19].The behavior of a DRL agent, then, can be severely different depending if it has access to a perfect or imperfect reward signal.

Thus, we develop a method to calculate the reward signal based only on the observations received by the agent using image processing methods. We believe that calculating rewards through observations in virtual environments leads to scenarios that more closely approach reality. We call this method Image-Based Reward Calculation Module (IBRCM). IBRCM is able to reward the agent by finding common points between two sequential observations and, then, using this common points to calculate the offset between these two images. As a result, this approach generates a value that is analogous to the agent's displacement.

We evaluate the effectiveness of the method and the impacts of this limitation on our agent performance. To do so, we compare it with an agent that receives the standard reward used in this environment, i.e. that one with information from the emulator internal state. To that, we chose to use The Sonic the Hedgehog game due to the amount of challenges present in this game. Ultimately, the IBRCM agent achieves similar results to the one that uses the emulator's reward for most test levels. We are also able to draw important insights when analyzing the cases in which the performance of the two agents diverged.

2   Sonic the Hedgehog

The Sonic the Hedgehog^{TM} is the first game in the franchise of the same name. Released on June 23, 1991, by the Japanese company Sega, the game quickly became a hit, belonging to a broader category of games called side-scrolling. In a side-scroller game, the camera is placed at a side-view angle and follows the player as he moves around the scenario. Generally, in this type of game, the player starts at the left-most point in the level and is tasked to get to the end of the level, which is usually placed at the right-most point.

In Sonic, the player has to traverse this distance while facing multiple different enemies and interacting with different obstacles, he can also collect rings that are lost on contact with enemies, but prevent the player from dying. The Sonic games are particularly challenging for artificial agents, as the textures, objects and enemies for each level often vary greatly. As such, it has been used in research to benchmark DRL agents' performance [7]. More well known, OpenAI assembled multiple levels from all three original Sonic games to serve as a benchmark for generalization of RL agents [20].

2.1   Retro Gym

Gym Retro [20] is the base behind the Sonic benchmark. It is a project whose goal is to create RL environments from several traditional video games. The project was developed in python and was released by OpenAI.

The library uses an interface with game emulators, making it easy to add a new game to evaluate in a reinforcement learning model. The Gym Retro python package includes a dataset of games. Each of these games is composed by: a ROM (The codes and data that constitute a game), and at least one save state (a picture of the console's state at some point in the game. It also includes all variables of a game, such as those that contain a score, the number of lives, and items of the player), at least one scenario (the level of the game), and a data file (metadata of the game, such as the score of each attempt).

2.2   Sonic - Game and Levels

The Sonic the Hedgehog game is divided into seven different zones, and each zone is subdivided into acts. Generally speaking, each zone has a different set of textures, objects, and enemies. Acts within the same zone tend to share the same textures, objects, and enemies but offer a different arrangement of them. The triple of (Game, Zone, and Act) is called level. The game Sonic provides an excellent challenge for the player due to the amount of different tasks present in this game. All game levels are listed in Table 4.

2.3   Controls

The Sega Genesis controller (also known as Megadrive, the console for which the sonic game was originally released) has 12 buttons. To represent each button, the library uses a 12-position Boolean vector that indicates the pressed buttons at the current instant of time. In the present work, we removed equivalent combinations and combinations that do not make sense in *Sonic The HedgeHog*, leaving only the 8 combinations of buttons present in Table 1, reducing the space of actions that the agent needs to learn.

2.4   Observation

The Gym [5] library was used as an interface between the game and the algorithm. It provides a 320×224 matrix of RGB pixels, which represents the image of the game at a given instant of time, as shown in Fig. 1.

Table 1. Table with corresponding actions and buttons.

Action	Buttons
Idle	
Walk left	Left
Walk right	Right
Roll right	Right, Down
Roll left	Left, Down
Look down	Down
Roll	Down, B
Jump	B

Fig. 1. Example of the current state provided by the emulator at a given moment of time, represented by an RGB image with a resolution of 320×224 pixels.

To train the policy of the proposed model, we resize the output image from the emulator to a resolution of 96×96 pixels and convert it to grayscale. This strategy is important due to the reduction of the input space.

2.5   Evaluation

The interaction with the game is divided into episodes, which correspond to the player's life. At the end of each episode, the level is set to its initial state. An episode is concluded when:

– The agent completes the level, i.e., when a certain horizontal offset is reached;

– The agent dies; or
– Over 4500 timesteps, which is equivalent to 5 min of gameplay.

During an episode, the agent's accumulated reward is proportional to the horizontal offset concerning the starting position, as the objective is always to the right of the starting point. In this way, going to the right always yields positive rewards. However, on some levels, it is necessary to go to the left at certain moments to be able to advance in the level. The final reward is split into two components: a horizontal offset and a completion bonus. The horizontal reward is normalized by level, so the maximum amount the agent receives for finishing it is 9000. The completion bonus is 1000 for instant level completion and decays linearly to zero in 4500 timesteps. Thus, the maximum theoretical score that the agent can obtain is 10000.

3   Deep Reinforcement Learning

Reinforcement Learning (RL) is a sub-area of machine learning that uses multidisciplinary concepts from psychology, neuroscience, statistics and computing. RL studies how intelligent agents can perform tasks in an environment without being properly programmed to do so, but to maximize an accumulated reward signal [10]. In RL, one has an agent in an environment E. This agent interacts with E through observations and actions, as described in Fig. 2. The agent chooses an action a at time t based on its internal policy π. This action, in turn, changes the state of the environment, generating a measure that is communicated to the agent through a value, called reward (r). The agent's policy (π) is a function that maps the states of the environment into actions. The learning process takes place to optimize the policy so that it maximizes the sum of the reinforcement received.

Deep Reinforcement Learning is any Reinforcement Learning that uses Deep Neural Networks (DNNs) to approximate the value, policy, or model function (state transition function and reward function) [12].

DNNs made possible to apply reinforcement learning (RL) to problems that were previously intractable, due to the massive number of states, partial observability, among other factors. Some of the formerly impossible feats achieved through DRL are being able play video games directly from pixels [17], driving autonomous cars [9] and achieving super human performance in games such as Go [29], which has a gigantic number of possible states.

3.1   Proximal Policy Optimization

The Proximal Policy Optimization (PPO) algorithm was proposed in [27] by the OpenAI team. It follows the core idea of Trust Region Policy Optimization (TRPO) [26]. PPO proposes to take the most significant step toward the optimal policy without straying too far from the current policy. For this, PPO uses a clipping function so that the policy update can have a maximum variation (defined by the value of the clipping function) during sequential training updates.

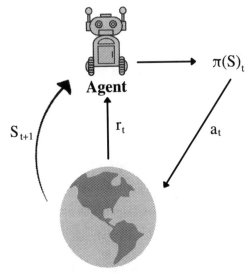

Fig. 2. The agent (represented by the robot) performs actions in the environment (planet) through a π policy. In turn, the environment returns a reward r_t for the action performed at time t and a new state S_{t+1}.

4   Related Work

In this section, we present some of the work that has been done in DRL with focus on the calculation of the reward signal for side-scrolling video game environments. Both of the works presented use privileged information that comes from the emulator in order to guide their respective agents.

Chiang et al. [7] explored an efficient way to train the agent in side-scrolling games in order to guide the search process by creating a trajectory replay module (TOM) in combination with a penalty module that penalizes deviations from the best route. These modules work together to replace the reward provided by the environment. For the agent policy modeling, a Convolutional Neural Network (CNN) and the Proximal Policy Optimization (PPO) algorithm were used. In that work, additional information from the environment was used, such as the agent's position (x, y) at each instant of time. This strategy obtained superior or equivalent results (depending on the level) than when compared to using the reward coming directly from the environment.

Pathak et al. [22] investigated the use of curiosity aspects for sparse-reward reinforcement learning models. The model generates a reward intrinsic to the agent, which is combined with the reward coming from the environment. In that work, curiosity was formulated as the error in the agent's ability to predict the consequences of its actions in the environment (Forward Model). In turn, the environment is represented by an "inverse model", that tries to predict which action was taken using the previous state and the state after the action. It was observed in the experiments, a better exploration of the search space in addition to a better agent performance in environments with sparse and very sparse rewards.

Furthermore, there are also methods within reinforcement learning that dismiss the use of privileged information. In inverse reinforcement learning (IRL) [1], for instance, the agent's reward function is inferred by observing its behavior or policy. In that manner, IRL reduces the manual design of task specification and, therefore, can be used to generate a reward signal independent of the environment's internal dynamics. However, the IRL techniques can only be applied when a policy is given or one has a demonstration of the desired behavior.

5   The Proposed Approach

We propose here a strategy for calculating the reward of the RL approach when applied to the Sonic the Hedgehog game using only visual information of the state of the environment. This proposal is called Image-Based Reward Calculation Module (IBRCM) and is detailed in the following.

5.1   Image-Based Reward Calculation Module (IBRCM)

The proposed approach measures the offset of two consecutive observations of the environment. The observation in timestep t is compared with the observation in timestep $t - 1$, generating a value corresponding to the number of pixels that the destination image (t) moved with respect to the source image ($t - 1$). We call this offset d_t.

The d_t values are then summed in $x_{current}$. One can see that $x_{current}$ is analogous to how far away the agent is from the start of the level. We also keep track of the maximum value achieved in $x_{current}$ and store it in x_{max}. When $x_{current}$ is greater than x_{max} (i.e. the agent has reached a new distance that is farthest away from the start of the level), we give d_t as reward to the agent and x_{max} is updated. Otherwise, the agent receives 0 reward when $x_{current}$ is smaller than or equal to x_{max} (i.e. the agent has moved towards the start of the level or stayed still).

5.2   The Offset Between Images

The calculation of the offset between the images consists of initially extracting features from the source (in $t-1$) and destination (t) images using scale-invariant feature transform (SIFT) [15]. SIFT can extract features based on the image so that these features are invariant to translation, resizing, rotation, and variation of image lighting [13].

Once we found the features of the source and destination images, we applied the Fast Approximate Nearest Neighbors (FLANN) [18] to map feature points

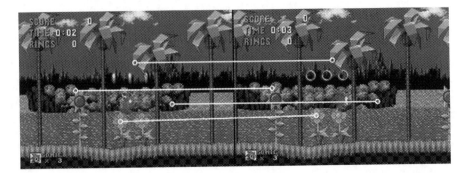

Fig. 3. An illustrative example of a match of features between the source image $(t-1)$, on the left, and the destination image (t), on the right side. Based on the difference in the positioning of the features between the images, it is possible to calculate the offset.

Algorithm 1: An algorithm to calculate an offset between two images.

$obs_{t-1} \leftarrow$ observation on time $t-1$;
$obs_t \leftarrow$ observation on time t;
$obsFeatures_{t-1} \leftarrow sift.Features(obs_{t-1})$;
$obsFeatures_t \leftarrow sift.Features(obs_t)$;
$matches = flannKnnMatch(obsFeatures_{t-1}, obsFeatures_t, k = 2)$;
$goodMatches = applyRatioTest(matches, 0.7)$;
Result: $Mean(EuclidianDistance(goodMatches))$

---

from the source image to two feature points of the destination image. Assuming that a feature in the source image cannot have more than one equivalent in the destination image, we know that at least one of them is wrong. Based on Lowe's work [14], the match with the smallest distance is called "good match", and the match with the second smallest distance is the equivalent of random noise, a base rate of sorts[1]. If this "good match" can not be distinguished from noise, then it does not bring any new information, and this feature should be rejected.

The resulting distance is multiplied by -1 when the shift/movement occurs to the left side. Finally, the average of the offset values is returned. A pseudo-code for the calculation of the offset between images is presented in Algorithm 1(Fig. 3) .

6   Computational Experiments

In this section, we describe the computational experiments that were made in order to comparatively evaluate the performance of an agent that uses IBRCM in contrast to one that uses the default reward that comes from the emulator. Furthermore, we clarify some implementation details and discuss the results obtained.

---

[1] In this work, we adopted Lowe's ratio test 0.7.

Table 2. Parameters used for model training.

Parameter	Value
Timesteps	1000000
λ	0.95
γ	0.99
Epochs	4
Entropy coefficient	0.001
Learning rate	2e−4
Clip rate	0.2
Test ratio	0.7
n_steps	512

IBRCM is built on top of the Stable-Baselines3 library [23], a python based library that implements several DRL algorithms with PyTorch [21], including PPO. Our method also makes use of the OpenCV library [4], which implements the SIFT and FLANN algorithms mentioned in Sect. 5.2. The source code is publicly available[2].

We conducted our experiments at the same six levels presented in the work of [7]. For each level we compare the performance of a PPO agent that receives the default reward described in Sect. 2.5 and one that receives the reward calculated through the IBRCM. We evaluate both agents using the learning curves based in the reward in Sect. 2.5 In both cases, we train our agent up to one million timesteps with four CPU workers. The PPO hyperparameters used for training the models can be found in Table 2.

We used the Mann-Whitney test [16] to analyze if the performance of the model that uses IBRCM is statistically better than that of PPO. To that, we assume as a null hypothesis that the distributions of the results obtained by PPO and IBRCM are equal. If the p-value obtained with the test is smaller than or equal to 0.05 (i.e. probability less than or equal to 5%), one can assume that there is a small probability that the difference observed between the groups is random.

Ten independent runs were performed for each agent in each level. Figure 4 shows the learning curves, and Table 3 shows the final scores, each with the respective mean, standard deviation and p-value of Mann-Whitney test.

Based on the results obtained, we can see that PPO using an IBRCM reward presented results competitive to those reached by PPO with an internal emulator reward and can be a good alternative when there is no internal emulator reward function available. We emphasize that the proposed model achieves the best results or results statistically similar to those of the PPO in 5 of the 6 cases tested. We can also see that IBRCM presented results statistically better (p-value ≤ 0.05) than those obtained by PPO in three of the six levels evaluated. PPO obtained results statistically better than the proposal only when solving the StarLightZone.Act2 level.

---

[2] https://github.com/feliperafael/IBRCM.

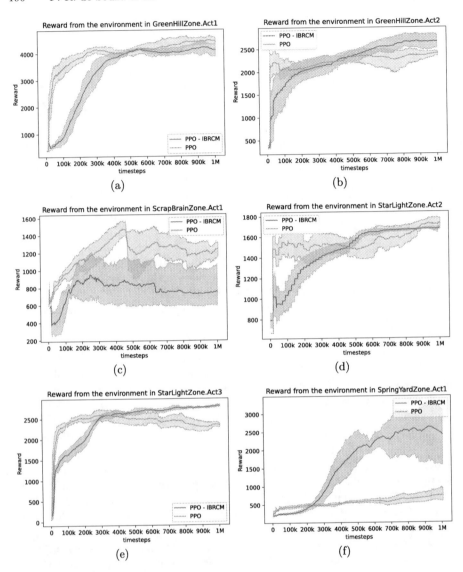

Fig. 4. Curves of the mean scores (lines) and standard deviations (shaded area around the lines) obtained when PPO and PPO + IBRCM is applied to each level. These values were generated with 10 runs of each technique in each level.

Table 3. Final mean score, standard deviation, and p-value for each level. The best values reached when solving each level and the p-values smaller than 0.05 are highlighted in boldface.

Level	PPO	PPO + IBRCM	p-value
GreenHillZone.Act1	**4359.68 ± 290.04**	4130.06 ± 260.23	1.2×10^{-1}
GreenHillZone.Act2	2413.61 ± 67.36	**2636.46 ± 158.93**	1.0×10^{-3}
ScrapBrainZone.Act1	**1188.47 ± 163.41**	882.21 ± 337.32	1.4×10^{-1}
StarLightZone.Act2	**1704.40 ± 105.69**	1671.62 ± 21.10	2.6×10^{-2}
StarLightZone.Act3	2358.36 ± 84.04	**2766.43 ± 66.83**	2.0×10^{-4}
SpringYardZone.Act1	807.12 ± 265.05	**2086.5 ± 1050.41**	5.8×10^{-3}

There are large differences between the average results when the levels Scrap Brain Zone Act 1 and Spring Yard Zone Act 1 are analyzed. In the first case, the performance of IBRCM agent is worst than that of the default PPO agent. On the other hand, in Spring Yard Zone Act 1, the IBRCM agent found a policy that can progress much further into the level. We analyze the agents' behavior at both levels in order to obtain better insight and understand these discrepancies.

In Spring Yard Zone, the default PPO agent gets stuck after reaching a point where it needs to do a bit of backtracking in order to progress. Since it receives reward proportional to it's displacement on the X-axis - meaning that every positive displacement (i.e. moving to the right) yields positive reward and every negative displacement (i.e. moving to the left) yields negative reward - the agent learns to move to the right almost all the time, thus, being unable to backtrack. The IBRCM agent, in contrast, receives reward only when reaching a new maximum distance traveled in the level. On all other time steps the IBRCM agent receives zero reward. This allows the agent to explore more to the left when it can't get a new maximum distance. It is, then, able to backtrack where the default PPO agent cannot and, so, achieve better performance in this level.

For Scrap Brain Zone, we discover that, in some runs, IBRCM can achieve comparable results to the default reward PPO agent. The problem lies at the beginning of the level. Right when the IBRCM agent starts to move it is faced with a cliff. When the agent falls off the cliff - something that is bound to happen in pretty much all the runs, due to the agent being trained from scratch - it travels a considerable distance on the Y-axis before eventually dying and terminating the episode. When this happens, the IBRCM sets a new maximum distance traveled that has a large value, due to all the displacement that occurred on the Y-axis. To be able to set a new max distance and start earning more reward, the agent has to cover a lot of ground moving to the right of the level without receiving any positive reward. Furthermore, there are several hard obstacles on the way, like enemies and fire coming through the floor, all of which terminate the episode if the agent takes a hit without having any rings.

This makes progressing through the level significantly harder for the IBRCM agent in this case, as it does not have a sufficiently informative reward signal

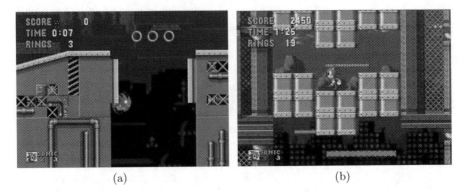

(a)   (b)

Fig. 5. This figure illustrates the main aspects of the environment that cause the divergence in results between the IBRCM agent and the default PPO agent. In (a), one can find the moment when the agent falls off the cliff at the ScrapBrainZone.Act1 level. In (b), one can observe the backtrack behavior, which makes the agent perform better at the SpringYardZone.Act1 level.

for a big amount of time after falling off the cliff. The default PPO agent does not suffer from this conditions, as it's reward is calculated based, only, on X-axis displacement, which means that just falling has no impact on it's reward function.

In some cases, the IBRCM agent is able to cover this ground through exploration alone, and start earning rewards again; eventually reaching the same point as the default PPO agent is able to reach this level. In most cases, however, the agent is not able to find its way through the obstacles and became trapped in local optima. In this scenario, the agent develops a policy that, generally, walks right into the cliff, resulting in the poor performance presented in the plot (Fig. 5).

7   Concluding Remarks and Future Work

The computation of the reward function is a central factor in reinforcement learning. The use of methods that can provide a good approximation for the reward function using the least amount of information is desired since, often, this function cannot be easily obtained or cannot be calculated. In this line, methods that use only the observations of the environment to extract the reward are highlighted. The IBRCM uses the observations of the environment to calculate the agent's offset in the environment, thus generating a proportional reward.

Based on the results of the experiments, it is possible to notice that the IBRCM presented superior performance to the use of the reward from the emulator in three of the six test levels, in addition to presenting equivalent performance in two of the levels and presenting an inferior performance in only one of the test levels. These results show that IBRCM can be competitive with methods that take advantage of privileged information, being able to guide the search process to a similar level. The proposed model can be used in occasions where the reward cannot be easily accessed or cannot be calculated. Another facet of the IBRCM is that it matches the access information level of the computational model with the human player information access level, thus creating an agent that is more closely aligned with human behavior.

In future works, we intend to investigate the performance of IBRCM in other side-scrolling games. We would also like to explore the impact of using different image feature extraction methods instead of SIFT, such as SURF (Speeded-Up Robust Features) [2], FAST [24], BRIEF (Binary Robust Independent Elementary Features) [6], and ORB [25].

Acknowledgements. The authors thank the financial support provided by CNPq (316801/2021-6), Capes, FAPEMIG (APQ-01832-22), and UFJF.

A   Appendix

Table 4 presents the number of acts of each level of The Sonic the hedgehog game, as described in Sect. 2.2.

Table 4. Number of acts in each level of The Sonic the Hedgehog game.

Level	Number of acts
Green hill zone	3
Marble zone	3
Spring yard zone	3
Labyrinth zone	3
Star light zone	3
Scrap brain zone	3
Final zone	1

References

1. Arora, S., Doshi, P.: A survey of inverse reinforcement learning: challenges, methods and progress. Artif. Intell. **297**, 103500 (2021)
2. Bay, H., Tuytelaars, T., Van Gool, L.: SURF: speeded up robust features. In: Leonardis, A., Bischof, H., Pinz, A. (eds.) ECCV 2006. LNCS, vol. 3951, pp. 404–417. Springer, Heidelberg (2006). https://doi.org/10.1007/11744023_32
3. Bellemare, M.G., Naddaf, Y., Veness, J., Bowling, M.: The arcade learning environment: an evaluation platform for general agents. J. Artif. Intell. Res. **47**, 253–279 (2013)
4. Bradski, G., Kaehler, A.: Learning OpenCV: Computer vision with the OpenCV library. O'Reilly Media, Inc. (2008)
5. Brockman, G., et al.: OpenAI gym. arXiv preprint arXiv:1606.01540 (2016)

6. Calonder, M., Lepetit, V., Strecha, C., Fua, P.: BRIEF: binary robust independent elementary features. In: Daniilidis, K., Maragos, P., Paragios, N. (eds.) ECCV 2010. LNCS, vol. 6314, pp. 778–792. Springer, Heidelberg (2010). https://doi.org/10.1007/978-3-642-15561-1_56

7. Chiang, I., Huang, C.M., Cheng, N.H., Liu, H.Y., Tsai, S.C., et al.: Efficient exploration in side-scrolling video games with trajectory replay. Comput. Games J. **9**(3), 263–280 (2020)

8. Dewey, D.: Reinforcement learning and the reward engineering principle. In: 2014 AAAI Spring Symposium Series (2014)

9. Fayjie, A.R., Hossain, S., Oualid, D., Lee, D.J.: Driverless car: autonomous driving using deep reinforcement learning in urban environment. In: 2018 15th International Conference on Ubiquitous Robots (UR), pp. 896–901. IEEE (2018)

10. Kaelbling, L.P., Littman, M.L., Moore, A.W.: Reinforcement learning: a survey. J. Artif. Intell. Res. **4**, 237–285 (1996)

11. Laud, A.D.: Theory and Application of Reward Shaping in Reinforcement Learning. University of Illinois at Urbana-Champaign (2004)

12. Li, Y.: Deep reinforcement learning: an overview. arXiv preprint arXiv:1701.07274 (2017)

13. Lowe, D.G.: Object recognition from local scale-invariant features. In: Proceedings of the Seventh IEEE International Conference on Computer Vision, vol. 2, pp. 1150–1157. IEEE (1999)

14. Lowe, D.G.: Distinctive image features from scale-invariant keypoints. Int. J. Comput. Vis. **60**(2), 91–110 (2004)

15. Lowe, G.: Sift-the scale invariant feature transform. Int. J. **2**(91–110), 2 (2004)

16. McKnight, P.E., Najab, J.: Mann-Whitney U test. Corsini Encycl. Psychol. pp. 1–1 (2010)

17. Mnih, V., et al.: Human-level control through deep reinforcement learning. Nature **518**(7540), 529–533 (2015)

18. Muja, M., Lowe, D.G.: Fast approximate nearest neighbors with automatic algorithm configuration. VISAPP (1) **2**(331–340), 2 (2009)

19. Ng, A.Y., Harada, D., Russell, S.: Policy invariance under reward transformations: theory and application to reward shaping. In: ICML, vol. 99, pp. 278–287 (1999)

20. Nichol, A., Pfau, V., Hesse, C., Klimov, O., Schulman, J.: Gotta learn fast: a new benchmark for generalization in RL. arXiv preprint arXiv:1804.03720 (2018)

21. Paszke, A., et al.: Automatic differentiation in pytorch. In: Proceedings of the Conference on Neural Information Processing Systems (NIPS) (2017)

22. Pathak, D., Agrawal, P., Efros, A.A., Darrell, T.: Curiosity-driven exploration by self-supervised prediction. In: International Conference on Machine Learning, pp. 2778–2787. PMLR (2017)

23. Raffin, A., Hill, A., Gleave, A., Kanervisto, A., Ernestus, M., Dormann, N.: Stable-baselines3: reliable reinforcement learning implementations. J. Mach. Learn. Res. **22**(268), 1–8 (2021)

24. Rosten, E., Drummond, T.: Machine learning for high-speed corner detection. In: Leonardis, A., Bischof, H., Pinz, A. (eds.) ECCV 2006. LNCS, vol. 3951, pp. 430–443. Springer, Heidelberg (2006). https://doi.org/10.1007/11744023_34

25. Rublee, E., Rabaud, V., Konolige, K., Bradski, G.: ORB: an efficient alternative to sift or surf. In: 2011 International Conference on Computer Vision, pp. 2564–2571. IEEE (2011)

26. Schulman, J., Levine, S., Abbeel, P., Jordan, M., Moritz, P.: Trust region policy optimization. In: International Conference on Machine Learning, pp. 1889–1897. PMLR (2015)

27. Schulman, J., Wolski, F., Dhariwal, P., Radford, A., Klimov, O.: Proximal policy optimization algorithms. arXiv preprint arXiv:1707.06347 (2017)
28. Shao, K., Tang, Z., Zhu, Y., Li, N., Zhao, D.: A survey of deep reinforcement learning in video games. arXiv preprint arXiv:1912.10944 (2019)
29. Silver, D., et al.: Mastering the game of go with deep neural networks and tree search. Nature **529**(7587), 484–489 (2016)
30. Sutton, R.S., Barto, A.G.: Reinforcement Learning: An Introduction. MIT press, Cambridge (2018)

Predicting Failures in HDDs with Deep NN and Irregularly-Sampled Data

Francisco Lucas F. Pereira[✉], Raif C. B. Bucar, Felipe T. Brito,
João Paulo P. Gomes, and Javam C. Machado

LSBD - Federal University of Ceará, Fortaleza, Brazil
`lucas.falcao@lsbd.ufc.br`

Abstract. As information systems became basic requirements for essential human services, safeguarding stored data became a requirement to maintaining these services. Predicting Hard Disk Drive (HDD) failure can bring efficiency gains in HDD maintenance and reduce the risk for data loss. Recurrent Neural Networks (RNN) are powerful tools for predicting HDD failure but require complete data entries sampled at regular intervals for efficient model training, testing, and deployment. Data imputation is a baseline method to preprocess data for RNN models. However, typical data imputation methods introduce noise into datasets and erase missing data patterns that would otherwise improve model predictions. This article surveys existing RNN models robust to the presence of substantial amounts of missing data and benchmarks the predictive capabilities of these methods on HDD failure prediction using Self-Monitoring, Analysis, and Reporting Technology (SMART) data. To evaluate different missing data conditions, we simulate binomial and exponential sampling schema with varying levels of missing data. The successful implementation and comparison of these methods demonstrated that the GRU-D, phased-LSTM, and CT-LSTM methods are well-rounded methods for multiple missing data conditions, having achieved better performance than basic LSTM networks.

Keywords: Hard disk drives · Reccurent neural networks · Missing data · Irregular sampling

1 Introduction

As information systems became basic requirements for essential human services, safeguarding stored data became a requirement to maintaining these services. Hard Disk Drives (HDD) are the prevalent storage technology in big data environments, and their unexpected failure may lead to data loss, and hindrances to business operations and essential services [26].

Numerous works have investigated the task of preventing sudden failures by classifying the degradation state of an HDD based on the Self-Monitoring Analysis and Reporting Technologies (SMART) system. SMART is a computational

ⓒ The Author(s), under exclusive license to Springer Nature Switzerland AG 2022
J. C. Xavier-Junior and R. A. Rios (Eds.): BRACIS 2022, LNAI 13654, pp. 196–209, 2022.
https://doi.org/10.1007/978-3-031-21689-3_15

system that collects and monitors HDD data, and it detects anomalies using a predefined threshold-based approach [19].

Although useful, the SMART system alone has a low detection rate, typically ranging from 3% to 10% [16]. On the other hand, this condition-based maintenance is generally more efficient than performing preventive maintenance based on average HDD life.

Machine learning synergizes with SMART to achieve superior detection rates [18]. Our study emphasizes estimating the Remaining Useful Life (RUL) - the remaining lifetime of equipment until failure - of HDDs using SMART data. Deep neural networks are among the most successful approaches for RUL prediction. Xu *et al.* [25] introduced RNN formulations to verify HDD health degree. The authors report being able to provide early warnings between 200 and 500 h before failure. Lima *et al.* [13] benchmarked RNN, Long-Short Term Memory (LSTM), and Convolutional Neural Networks (CNN) methods for useful life estimation of HDDs, achieving prognostic horizons between 150 (CNN) and 200 (LSTM) days before failure. Zhang *et al.* [27] propose the ASTGCNN, a modified CNN approach that captures spatial and temporal dependencies of sensor inputs, achieving better prediction performance on turbofan RUL prediction when compared to other powerful methods such as deep LSTMs and bi-directional LSTMs.

However, traditional RNN models assume data is sampled continuously at regular intervals, which is not always feasible. While organizations might have the resources for rigorous SMART monitoring, individual users are unlikely to run these tests frequently. Furthermore, collecting all SMART features in an HDD can be costly, forcing checkups to be either less frequent or with a partial collection of SMART features, which results in datasets with irregular sample frequency and missing data.

Although preliminary approaches to missing data rely on data imputation, many researchers argue that simple data imputation methods can destroy important missing data patterns, which could otherwise boost model performance. [2,5,6,10,14,17,21,24].

Motivated by these results, this paper expands on RNN techniques robust to irregular sampling and benchmarks these methods for HDD failure prediction. In particular, we summarize our contributions as follows:

- We evaluate the effects of missing data rate and distribution on the predictive performance of RNN models. We simulate missing data using binomial and exponential missing data schema with 20% and 80% missing data.
- We benchmark RNN model performance on HDD RUL prediction in computational cost and test accuracy for varying missing data conditions. We have also provided insights on best-performing models and potential trade-offs between cost and accuracy.

The remainder of this paper is structured as follows: Sect. 2 briefly reviews the related work and existing state-of-the-art methods for HDD failure prediction and missing data. We present the background information for both RNN and Irregular Time Series in Sect. 3. In Sect. 4 we give details about the experimental procedure. Additionally, Sect. 5 presents the results of our survey. Finally, Sect. 6 concludes the paper and gives future research directions.

2   Related Work

Many papers address the task of failure prediction in hard drives. Several authors proposed different approaches based on mixture models [20], ensemble algorithms [23] and decision trees [11] among others. In such approaches, the failure time estimation is usually performed using the time series comprised of SMART attributes.

The use of Deep Recurrent Neural Networks (DRNN) recently gained popularity mainly due it its remarkable performances. Gated Recurrent Units (GRU) and Long Short-Term Memory RNN (LSTM) networks have been evaluated for hard disk drive failure prediction in various setups, and datasets [7,9,12]. Although such methods achieved good results, it is well known that, in many scenarios, SMART time series may be irregularly sampled. The absence of some features - often referred to as the missing data problem - is common in many real-world machine learning applications.

The design of DRNN for time series with missing data (irregularly sampled time series) was the subject of many recent works such as [5,6,10,15,17]. Neil et al. [17] proposed an LSTM variant, named phased-LSTM, that incorporates a new time gate that controls the update frequency of the LSTM cell. Such a variant is useful for missing data situations and time series with different sampling frequencies. Che et al. proposes two simple strategies to deal with missing data in GRUs. The strategies are named masking and time interval. Masking informs the model of which inputs are observed, and time interval incorporates the input observation patterns.

Mei and Eisner [15] address the problem by designing a continuous-time LSTM. The proposed model combines LSTM with continuous-time neural Hawkes processes. Lechner and de Brouwer [6,10] explore the idea of continuous modeling of time series. The authors propose LSTM and GRU variants trained by backpropagation through time through Ordinary Differential Equation (ODE) solvers. These models encode a continuous-time dynamical flow within the RNN to respond to inputs arriving at arbitrary time-lags. Furthermore, none of the mentioned works have been tested for hard disk drive failure prediction, which is the main objective of this work.

3   Background

This section describes some background concepts about recurrent neural networks and irregular time series techniques.

3.1   Recurrent Neural Networks

Recurrent neural networks (RNNs) are a general class of neural architecture that captures and models sequential data information. The recurrent model overcomes (in sequential problems) the standard one because of the persistence of the previous information into the recurrent loop. However, RNNs settle in short-term dependencies but not long-term dependencies [3]. Such fact encouraged the design of the LSTM [8], which works by adding a gating mechanism that controls the entrance and exit of information in the cell state.

Figure 1 represents a LSTM cell unit. The gates control the flow of information from the input and the previous states. The LSTM unit has the forget, input, and output gates to control its information flow. The output gate controls how much information the unit accepts from the input and the last state. On the other hand, the input state regulates how much information persists in the current state cell. The output gate controls the output, determining how much information can be output from the current cell state. The following equations define how to calculate all these gates, cell states, and hidden states for the forward pass of an LSTM layer.

$$\tilde{c}_t = tanh(W_c h_{t-1} + U_c x_t + b_c) \qquad \text{candidate state} \qquad (1)$$

$$i_t = \sigma(W_i h_{t-1} + U_i x_t + b_i) \qquad \text{input gate} \qquad (2)$$

$$f_t = \sigma(W_f h_{t-1} + U_f x_t + b_f) \qquad \text{forget gate} \qquad (3)$$

$$c_t = i^t \odot \tilde{c}^t + f^t \odot c^{t-1} \qquad \text{cell state} \qquad (4)$$

$$o_t = \sigma(W_o h_{t-1} + U_o x_t + b_o) \qquad \text{output gate} \qquad (5)$$

$$h_t = o_t \odot tanh(c_t) \qquad \text{output} \qquad (6)$$

In the above equations, t denotes the processed index within a sequence x. The symbol $\odot$ represents the Hadamard product. W and U are the recurrent and input matrices, respectively, with a subscript indicating the associated gate. The parameter b is the bias term.

3.2   Irregular Time Series Techniques

Lipton et al. [14] argues that data imputation destroys information about missing data patterns which could otherwise boost model performance. The researchers demonstrated in their study that extracting missing data patterns and using them as additional inputs to LSTM models can lead to better predictive performance.

Although much research exists in creating RNN methods robust to irregular sample frequency and missing data, there are not many studies benchmarking the predictive capabilities of these methods. The researchers who proposed the phased-LSTM [17], T-LSTM [2], and GRU-D [5] methods only benchmarked their methods with traditional machine learning models (e.g., logistic regression, support vector machines) and other RNN methods. Neil [17] tested surveyed methods in the N-MNIST dataset and reported accuracy improvements of 1% as compared to batch-normalized LSTM networks. Baytas [2] tested surveyed methods in healthcare data and reported T-LSTM generated AUC improvements of 6% compared to regular LSTM networks. Che [5] tested surveyed methods

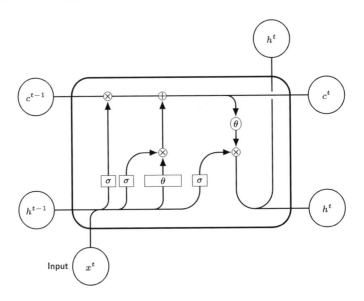

Fig. 1. Details of a LSTM cell.

in healthcare data and reported AUC improvements between 1% and 3% when using GRU-D instead of GRU or LSTM networks.

Rubanova [21], de Brouwer [6], and Lechner [10] benchmarked their methods against other robust RNN methods. Rubanova [21] reported ODE-RNN AUC and accuracies 2% higher than GRU-D on the PhysioNet dataset (healthcare). De Brouwer [6] indicated their model outperformed both GRU-D and T-LSTM in climate forecast and healthcare datasets. Lechner [10] conducted the most comprehensive benchmark, testing many models in the literature: ODE-RNN, GRU-OD, GRU-D, phased-LSTM, and ODE-LSTM. The authors tested all models on person activity and sequential MNIST data. They concluded that ODE-LSTM had the best overall accuracy across all models and datasets. Contrary to results from Rubanova and de Brouwer, Lechner reported better accuracy results for regular LSTM (with missing data features), GRU-D, and phased-LSTM on all datasets.

The research gap this study covers is threefold: i) shed additional light on the predictive performance of RNN-based models with missing data, ii) verify the effects of different missing data conditions, and iii) evaluate the effectiveness of these methods for RUL prediction with missing data.

4   Experimental Procedure

This section presents details about the utilized dataset provided by Backblaze company. We also show the proposed missing data generation methods and the evaluated models.

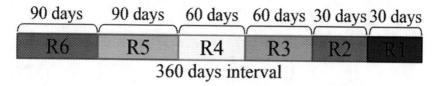

Fig. 2. Health Levels defined by the RUL intervals. The RUL decreases from left to right.

4.1 Dataset

We used the Backblaze dataset [1] in all experiments in this study. This dataset contains 60M daily reports of SMART attributes of several HDDs ranging from April/2013 until June/2021. These observations contain the serial number, model, SMART attributes, and a label indicating if the HDD has failed. A disk is labeled as faulty if i) it stops working (it does not turn on, or it does not receive commands) or ii) if the SMART self-test fails. In this work, we have selected the SMART attributes, which are presented in Table 1, according to [4].

Among all daily reports, we selected only serials labeled as faulty that belonged to the model with most data entries (i.e., ST4000DM000). We limited our analysis to the last 360 days of HDD life. We performed additional cleaning by removing HDD serials where daily observations were interrupted without a faulty label or data measurements after being labeled faulty. The final dataset contained 204,762 daily observations divided into 3921 serials. Since we can see each serial's last days of life, we can obtain their RUL. We defined health levels (classes) based on how close the HDD is to fail and transformed the task of predicting HDD failure into a classification problem. The health levels were defined as in [22] and shown in Fig. 2.

4.2 Missing Data Generation

We followed missing data formulations provided by previous authors, which is detailed by Weerakody [24]. First, we extracted a binary missing data vector indicating which SMART samples were missing. Second, we used the missing data vector to calculate the Time Between Samples (TBS). These vectors are necessary to correctly apply the RNN-based methods we employed in this research. Figure 3 shows a visual depiction of the missing data generation task.

We assumed missing data occurs across all features simultaneously. We believe this is a reasonable assumption for modeling SMART data missing due to system checkups not being conducted frequently. From such a perspective, it is also reasonable to assume data is sampled at intervals following an exponential distribution (e.g., the user does not follow a system checkup schedule) or binomial distribution (e.g., the user follows a checkup schedule but skips some checkups). Equation 7 describes the Time Between Samples (TBS) for the binomial model, and Eq. 8 describes TBS for the exponential model.

Table 1. SMART attributes used as features to the models.

Attribute ID	Attribute name
SMART 1	Read error rate
SMART 5	Reallocated sectors count
SMART 7	Seek error rate
SMART 184	End-to-end error
SMART 187	Reported uncorrectable errors
SMART 188	Command timeout
SMART 189	High fly writes
SMART 190	Temperature difference
SMART 193	Load cycle count
SMART 194	Temperature
SMART 197	Current pending sector count
SMART 198	Uncorrectable sector count
SMART 240	Head flying hours
SMART 241	Total LBAs written
SMART 242	Total LBAs read

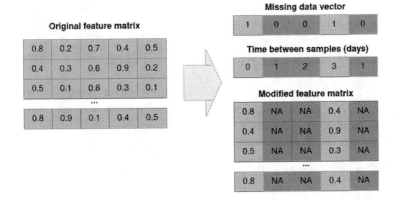

Fig. 3. Missing data generation procedure

$$TBS \sim Bin(n = TBS, p, x = TBS) \tag{7}$$

$$TBS \sim exp(\lambda) \tag{8}$$

We tested binomial and exponential missing data models with parameters that resulted in similar missing data rates. For example, the binomial model with $p = 20\%$ produces - on average - a missing data rate of 20%, similarly to the exponential distribution model with $\lambda = 0.6$. This study verified the impacts of 20% and 80% missing data on model performance. Table 2 shows the set of tested parameters.

Table 2. Set of tested missing data parameters.

TBS distribution	Parameter values
Binomial	$p = 20\%$, $p = 80\%$
Exponential	$\lambda = 0.6$, $\lambda = 4.0$

4.3   Evaluated Models and Parameters

In this study, we built upon the benchmarking methods employed by Lechner [10], and tested seven models: LSTM, Bidirect LSTM, phased-LSTM [17], GRU-D [5], CT-LSTM [15], GRU-ODE [6], and ODE-LSTM [10]. We built our models on top of code published by the authors on their GitHub page [10]. Some of these models have additional hyperparameters that must be set prior to training. We decided to use the default values of these hyperparameters as suggested by each of the original authors. The other hyperparameters can be seen in Table 3.

Table 3. Common RNN-based model hyperparameters.

Hyperparameter	Value
RNN cell dimension	64
Minibatch size	256
Epochs	3,000
Early stopping patience	300
Learning rate	5E-4

5   Results

This section reports results from applying the seven proposed models (Bidirect LSTM, GRU-D, GRU-ODE, CT-LSTM, LSTM, ODE-LSTM, and Phased-LSTM) under the Backblaze dataset. Table 4 presents the test accuracy results for all methods across all missing data conditions. Bold values indicate each missing data condition's top 3 test accuracy performance.

Table 4. Model accuracy results for different missing data conditions.

Model	Missing data conditions			
	Bin (20%)	Bin (80%)	Exp (0.6)	Exp (4.0)
Bidirect LSTM	**0.6917**	0.5510	**0.6950**	0.5586
GRU-D	**0.6919**	**0.5590**	**0.6950**	**0.5604**
GRU-ODE	0.6899	0.5539	0.6947	**0.5653**
CT-LSTM	0.6887	**0.5545**	0.6945	**0.5628**
LSTM	**0.6938**	0.5497	0.6935	0.5582
ODE-LSTM	0.6856	0.5466	0.6766	0.5518
Phased-LSTM	0.6896	**0.5566**	**0.6961**	0.5591

Baseline LSTM accuracy with no missing data: 0.7065

The preliminary results in Table 5 show sharp decreases in model accuracy with increasing levels of missing data, which indicates that a higher missing data rate leads to poorer model performance across all models. No model achieved similar performance to the LSTM under no missing data conditions, indicating loss of all model's predictive capabilities compared to baseline conditions. On the other hand, reductions in model performance were minimal for 20% missing data rates, whereas sharp drops could be observed for 80% missing data. This pattern is consistent across both binomial and exponential missing data distributions.

While the basic LSTM model showed good performance at lower missing data rates, it was outperformed by every other model we tested for higher missing data rates. Among higher missing data rates, the models that performed better were the GRU-D, GRU-ODE, and CT-LSTM. Each model's performance was consistent across the binomial and exponential missing data distributions.

Our results show no model had a comparatively inferior performance on any experimented missing data conditions, with less than 2% test accuracy differences across different models. Our results also demonstrated that the GRU-D model scored among the top 3 test accuracy across all missing data conditions, indicating an overall well-round model. The Phased-LSTM, CT-LSTM, and GRU-ODE scored among the top 3 in at least one of the tested scenarios, and the ODE-LSTM did not score among the top 3 for any of the test missing data conditions.

Figure 4 shows the confusion matrix for each surveyed model under each missing data condition. The grid values were normalized for the total data points in each actual health degree class. Correctly predicted data points appear on the main diagonal of each confusion matrix. There are two types of error in this problem: overestimation of health degree classes (i.e., upper right quadrant of confusion matrix) and underestimation of health degree classes (i.e., lower left quadrant of confusion matrix). Overestimation of health degree classes can potentially lead to sudden failure, data loss, and system outages. These are more severe consequences than underestimation errors, generally resulting in maintenance efficiency losses.

Figure 4 shows consistently increasing overestimation errors for higher degrees of missing data across all surveyed models, indicating that higher degrees of missing data introduce the necessity to control and reduce overestimation errors, such as using class weights with higher weights for classes closer to failure. Figure 4 also shows a better depiction of model performance than the accuracy shown in Table 4 because we can visualize over and underestimation errors. The LSTM network shows an accuracy only 1% lower than the GRU-D for the binomial case with $p = 80\%$, but the confusion matrix shows 10% more HDDs with imminent failure (i.e., class 1) being overestimated.

Table 5 shows the average training time for each surveyed model in seconds. Bold values indicate the lowest three average training times.

Table 5. Model average training time for different missing data conditions.

Model	Training time (s)
Bidirect LSTM	10,611
GRU-D	**5,833**
GRU-ODE	14,286
CT-LSTM	6,741
LSTM	**3,658**
ODE-LSTM	9,335
Phased-LSTM	**6,595**

Bold values indicate the lowest three average training times.

The results in Table 5 indicate the computational toll introduced by using more sophisticated models. The simplest model tested - the basic LSTM model - had an average training time of 1 h, a value at least 35% lower than any other model we tested. The GRU-D, phased-LSTM, and CT-LSTM models had similar training times, ranging between 1.5 and 2 h. All other models had significantly longer training times.

Our results indicate that using the GRU-D, phased-LSTM, and CT-LSTM models are viable options for trading off computational cost for additional predictive capabilities across virtually all missing data conditions. All other models could not consistently achieve higher accuracy than the basic LSTM model.

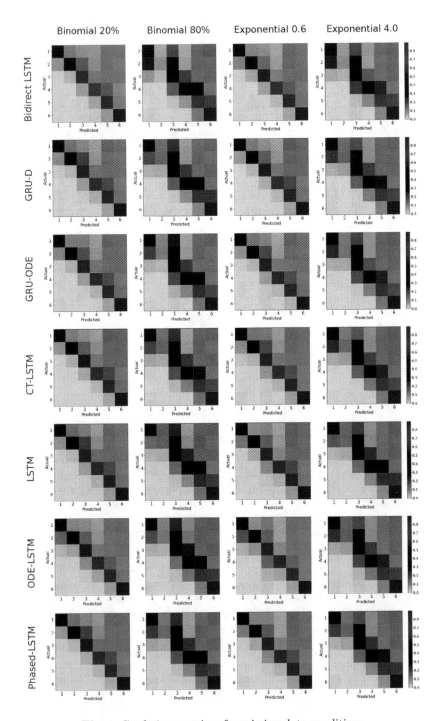

Fig. 4. Confusion matrices for missing data conditions

6 Conclusion

This paper provided a comprehensive benchmark analysis for RNN-based models robust to missing data and irregular time series. We tested surveyed methods across many missing data conditions and observed consistencies and inconsistencies in their accuracy for measuring HDD RUL.

We hope our results shed light on the comparability of existing models across a wide range of missing data conditions and help guide each models' application in a practical setting. Namely, the GRU-D, phased-LSTM, and CT-LSTM models introduced accuracy gains across all tested missing data conditions but took 35% longer to train than basic LSTM networks. All other tested models showed no consistent accuracy gains compared to the basic LSTM model.

Future work includes testing a wider variety of missing data conditions and testing model accuracy's replicability through k-fold cross-validation.

Acknowledgements. This research was partially funded by Lenovo, as part of its R&D investment under Brazilian Informatics Law, and by CAPES under the grant #88887.609134/2021-00.

References

1. Backblaze: Hard drive data and stats. www.backblaze.com/b2/hard-drive-test-data.html (2021). Accessed 10 Feb 2022
2. Baytas, I.M., Xiao, C., Zhang, X., Wang, F., Jain, A.K., Zhou, J.: Patient subtyping via time-aware LSTM networks. In: Proceedings of the 23rd ACM SIGKDD International Conference On Knowledge Discovery and Data Mining, pp. 65–74 (2017)
3. Bengio, Y., De Mori, R., Flammia, G., Kompe, R.: Global optimization of a neural network-hidden Markov model hybrid. IEEE Trans. Neural Netw. **3**(2), 252–259 (1992)
4. Botezatu, M.M., Giurgiu, I., Bogojeska, J., Wiesmann, D.: Predicting disk replacement towards reliable data centers. In: Krishnapuram, B., Shah, M., Smola, A.J., Aggarwal, C.C., Shen, D., Rastogi, R. (eds.) Proceedings of the 22nd ACM SIGKDD International Conference on Knowledge Discovery and Data Mining, San Francisco, CA, USA, 13–17 August 2016, pp. 39–48. ACM (2016)
5. Che, Z., Purushotham, S., Cho, K., Sontag, D., Liu, Y.: Recurrent neural networks for multivariate time series with missing values. Sci. Rep. **8**(1), 1–12 (2018)
6. De Brouwer, E., Simm, J., Arany, A., Moreau, Y.: GRU-ODE-Bayes: continuous modeling of sporadically-observed time series. Adv. Neural Inf. Proces. Syst. **32**, 1–12 (2019)
7. Demidova, L., Fursov, I.: Software implementation of neural recurrent model to predict remaining useful life of data storage devices. In: Jordan, V., Tarasov, I., Faerman, V. (eds.) High-Performance Computing Systems and Technologies in Scientific Research, Automation of Control and Production, pp. 391–400. Springer International Publishing, Cham (2022). https://doi.org/10.1007/978-3-030-94141-3_31

8. Graves, A., Schmidhuber, J.: Framewise phoneme classification with bidirectional LSTM and other neural network architectures. Neural Netw. **18**(5–6), 602–610 (2005)
9. Hu, L., Han, L., Xu, Z., Jiang, T., Qi, H.: A disk failure prediction method based on LSTM network due to its individual specificity. Proc. Comput. Sci. **176**, 791–799 (2020). https://doi.org/10.1016/j.procs.2020.09.074
10. Lechner, M., Hasani, R.: Learning long-term dependencies in irregularly-sampled time series. arXiv preprint arXiv:2006.04418 (2020)
11. Li, J., Stones, R., Wang, G., Liu, X., Li, Z., Xu, M.: Hard drive failure prediction using decision trees. Reliab. Eng. Syst. Saf. **164**, 55–65 (2017). https://doi.org/10.1016/j.ress.2017.03.004
12. Lima, F.D.S., Pereira, F.L.F., Chaves, I.C., Machado, J.C., Gomes, J.P.P.: Predicting the health degree of hard disk drives with asymmetric and ordinal deep neural models. IEEE Trans. Comput. **70**(2), 188–198 (2021). https://doi.org/10.1109/TC.2020.2987018
13. Lima, F.D.S., Pereira, F.L.F., Leite, L.G., Gomes, J.P.P., Machado, J.C.: Remaining useful life estimation of hard disk drives based on deep neural networks. In: 2018 International Joint Conference on Neural Networks (IJCNN), pp. 1–7. IEEE (2018)
14. Lipton, Z.C., et al.: Modeling missing data in clinical time series with RNNs. Mach. Learn. Healthcare **56**, 253–270 (2016)
15. Mei, H., Eisner, J.M.: The neural Hawkes process: a neurally self-modulating multivariate point process. Adv. Neural Inf. Process. Syst. **30**, 1–10 (2017)
16. Murray, J.F., Hughes, G.F., Kreutz-Delgado, K., Schuurmans, D.: Machine learning methods for predicting failures in hard drives: a multiple-instance application. J. Mach. Learn. Res. **6**(5), 1–34 (2005)
17. Neil, D., Pfeiffer, M., Liu, S.C.: Phased LSTM: accelerating recurrent network training for long or event-based sequences. Adv. Neural Inf. Process. Syst. **29**, 1–9 (2016)
18. Pereira, F.L.F., Chaves, I.C., Gomes, J.P.P., Machado, J.C.: Using autoencoders for anomaly detection in hard disk drives. In: 2020 International Joint Conference on Neural Networks (IJCNN), pp. 1–7. IEEE (2020)
19. Pinheiro, E., Weber, W.D., Barroso, L.A.: Failure trends in a large disk drive population (2007)
20. Queiroz, L.P., et al.: A fault detection method for hard disk drives based on mixture of gaussians and nonparametric statistics. IEEE Trans. Industr. Inf. **13**(2), 542–550 (2016)
21. Rubanova, Y., Chen, R.T., Duvenaud, D.K.: Latent ordinary differential equations for irregularly-sampled time series. Adv. Neural Inf. Process. Syst. **32**, 1–9 (2019)
22. dos Santos Lima, F.D., Amaral, G.M.R., de Moura Leite, L.G., Gomes, J.P.P., de Castro Machado, J.: Predicting failures in hard drives with LSTM networks. In: 2017 Brazilian Conference on Intelligent Systems (BRACIS), pp. 222–227. IEEE (2017)
23. Shen, J., Wan, J., Lim, S.J., Yu, L.: Random-forest-based failure prediction for hard disk drives. Int. J. Distrib. Sens. Netw. **14**(11), 1550147718806480 (2018). https://doi.org/10.1177/1550147718806480
24. Weerakody, P.B., Wong, K.W., Wang, G., Ela, W.: A review of irregular time series data handling with gated recurrent neural networks. Neurocomputing **441**, 161–178 (2021)

25. Xu, C., Wang, G., Liu, X., Guo, D., Liu, T.Y.: Health status assessment and failure prediction for hard drives with recurrent neural networks. IEEE Trans. Comput. **65**(11), 3502–3508 (2016)
26. Ye, Z.S., Xie, M., Tang, L.C.: Reliability evaluation of hard disk drive failures based on counting processes. Reliab. Eng. Syst. Saf. **109**, 110–118 (2013)
27. Zhang, Y., Li, Y., Wei, X., Jia, L.: Adaptive spatio-temporal graph convolutional neural network for remaining useful life estimation. In: 2020 International Joint Conference on Neural Networks (IJCNN), pp. 1–7. IEEE (2020)

Protein Molecular Function Annotation Based on Transformer Embeddings

Gabriel Bianchin de Oliveira$^{(\boxtimes)}$, Helio Pedrini, and Zanoni Dias

Institute of Computing, University of Campinas, Campinas, SP, Brazil
{gabriel.oliveira,helio,zanoni}@ic.unicamp.br

Abstract. The next-generation sequencing technologies decreased the cost of protein sequence identification. However, the cost of determining protein functions is still high, due to the laboratory methods needed. With that, computational models have been used to annotate protein functions. In this work, we present and discuss a new approach for protein Molecular Function prediction based on Transformers embeddings. Our method surpassed state-of-the-art classifiers when it used only the amino acid sequence as input and when it employed amino acid sequence and homology search in $F_{\max}$ and AuPRC metrics.

Keywords: Protein function prediction · Transformers · Natural language processing

1 Introduction

Protein plays paramount activities in the body of living beings. It is responsible for different biological processes, ranging from biochemical reactions up to immunity [23], as well as the development of diseases because of its misfolding, such as Alzheimer's and Parkinson's diseases [9].

With the next-generation sequencing technologies, the number of sequenced proteins has grown in the recent decades, yet the number of proteins with annotation about their functions has not followed this growth. This difference occurs due to the expensive and time-consuming laboratory methods needed to annotate the function [28], exemplified by 230 million proteins deposited in UniProt, and only 0.25% have functional evaluation [21], making prediction methods crucial to decrease this gap.

In the literature, the most common method applied to organize the functions is the Gene Ontology (GO) [3]. GO is divided into three ontologies: (i) Molecular Function, which is responsible of describe the molecular activities, (ii) Cellular Component, used to describe the location in the cell where the specific protein performs a function, and (iii) Biological Process, related to complex processes that each protein is involved. In the three ontologies, the terms are structured as a directed acyclic graph, considering that deeper terms are more specific than the shallow ones, and, during the annotation, it is necessary to follow the true

J. C. Xavier-Junior and R. A. Rios (Eds.): BRACIS 2022, LNAI 13654, pp. 210–220, 2022.
https://doi.org/10.1007/978-3-031-21689-3_16

path rule, that is, if a protein is classified as a specific term, it is also classified as the term's ancestors until the root term. Proteins can play many roles at the same time, consequently, the annotation task can be considered a multi-label classification.

Natural Language Processing (NLP) techniques have been applied to different biological tasks, including biomedical text mining [17] and DNA enhancer prediction [16]. In the case of proteins, the methods considered that the sequences are paragraphs or sentences, and the amino acids are words, applying techniques ranging from traditional approaches, such as tf-idf [20], up to state-of-the-art approaches, such as Transformers and deep learning methods [10].

Among the ontologies, Molecular Function is the most dependent on amino acid sequence [4]. Due to this fact, the application of NLP techniques has become an option with good results in this ontology.

In this work, we present and discuss a new approach to annotate protein functions considering Molecular Function ontology using Transformers embeddings and homology search. Our main contributions are (i) to present a method based on Transformers that uses only the amino acid sequence and our model surpassed state-of-the-art approaches, including deep learning and Transformers-based classifiers, and (ii) the ensemble of a homology-based classifier to our method achieved the state-of-the-art results.

The remaining of the paper is organized as follows. In Sect. 2, we describe some relevant approaches in the literature for protein function annotation. In Sect. 3, we present our model, the comparison methods, the dataset and the evaluation metrics used in the experiments. In Sect. 4, we report and discuss the results of our method compared to the literature. In Sect. 5, we highlight the principal points of our work and draw possible research lines for future work.

2   Related Work

The methods applied to protein function prediction task can be divided into five groups: prediction based on homology search, networks, sequence, sequence information, and text mining.

Homology search-based classifiers use the alignment and matching between sequences to transfer the functions, according to the premise that proteins with similar sequences have similar functions. Methods from this group apply tools, such as BLAST [2] and DIAMOND [5], to find homologies, such as OntoBlast [27] and GOFDR [12]. Nonetheless, this type of methodology is not able to correctly classify remote homologies, which can occur due to diversity in the evolution and differences in the length of the sequences [20]. We can also highlight that this approach depends on proteins on the reference set, that is, proteins used as benchmark, with high similarity and with annotated function.

Network-based classifiers apply techniques of network analysis to extract features from the complex relationship of proteins, as presented by Wang et al. [25] and Peng et al. [19]. Even achieving good results, this approach needs the laboratorial annotation of networks, which is expensive, time-consuming, and can have noise and incomplete data [6].

The methods that employ biological features from the amino acid sequence, such as family and domains [14], signal peptide and secondary structures [24], are classified as sequence information models. The main problem of this approach is the possible lack of information of some proteins, which have only the sequence determined by laboratorial methods.

Text mining can also be applied to annotate protein functions, as described by Fodeh et al. [11]. In this approach, the methods use natural language processing techniques to transfer functions cited in the paper to close proteins. However, text mining classifiers depend on scientific papers reporting protein functions, which represent a small number of available proteins.

The main source of data available on proteins is the amino acid sequence. Due to this fact, classifiers that can annotate the functions only from the sequence and without additional sources have been studied in recent years, mainly using deep learning techniques [23], such as convolutional neural networks [13,15] and natural language processing techniques [6,20].

3   Material and Methods

In this section, we explain the state-of-the-art methods applied to our database, our model, the dataset, and the evaluation metrics employed in the experiments.

3.1   State-of-the-Art Methods

To compare our results with the state-of-the-art methods that use the amino acid sequence as input, we evaluate DeepGO [15], DeepGOPlus [13] and TALE+ [6] in our dataset. We also compared our model with the naive and DIAMOND Score (DS) [5] models.

DeepGO. This classifier is a method based on amino acid sequences and protein-protein interaction networks. In our experiments, we applied only the amino acid part of the architecture. This model employs trigrams technique to generate the input of the network. After that, the features go through the embedding layer, followed by convolutional and pooling layers. Before the output, there are neurons arranged considering the hierarchy of GO.

DeepGOPlus. This model uses only the amino acid sequence as input. This method has two parts. In the first one, the model transforms the amino acid sequence into one-hot encoding and passes the features into the Convolutional Neural Network (CNN) architecture. In the second part, the model utilizes DIAMOND to search and find homologies with the training set, putting the score of each label as a weighted average based on bitscore. In the end, they apply an ensemble between these two parts. In our experiments, we employed the first part, which we called DeepGOPlusCNN, and the ensemble of the two parts, which we called DeepGOPlus.

TALE+. This method uses Transformers [22] and DIAMOND to make protein functions predictions. The Transformers part takes the amino acid sequence and the hierarchy of GO as input and generates embeddings to perform the classification. In addition, TALE+ makes an ensemble between different configurations of the Transformer architecture. After the deep learning prediction, they gathered the predictions from Transformer and DIAMOND parts. In our experiments, we used the three best configurations of Transformers architectures in the CAFA3 dataset [29], as reported in the original paper, to make the ensemble of Transformers, which we call TALE+Transformers, and the entire model, with Transformers and DIAMOND Score, which we call TALE+.

Naive. As proposed in the CAFA competition [29], we applied a naive model that predicts that each term in the test set has the score equal to the mean of each term in the training set. Equation 1 presents the method of this classifier, where $S(p, f)$ represents the score of a protein p in the test set with a function f, N_f is the number of proteins in the training set with a function f, and N_T is the number of proteins in the training set.

$$S(p, f) = \frac{N_f}{N_T} \tag{1}$$

DIAMOND Score. The DIAMOND Score (DS) prediction method uses DIAMOND [5] to transfer the labels of homolog proteins to the query.

DIAMOND is a tool that generates sequence alignment faster than BLAST. This sequence aligner uses e-value parameter, which represents a threshold of the number of expected good alignments that can be found by chance with a specific score, and generates alignments with a bitscore, which measures the normalized score of each alignment.

As used in DeepGOPlus and TALE+, we set the e-value equal to 0.001 and used the bitscores to predict the functions. This model is presented in Eq. 2, where $S(p, f)$ is the score of a protein p and function f, s is a protein in the set E of homologies of p, and T_s is the ground truth of a protein s.

$$S(p, f) = \frac{\sum_{s \in E} I(f \in T_s) \times \text{bitscore}(p, s)}{\sum_{s \in E} \text{bitscore}(p, s)} \tag{2}$$

3.2   TEMPO and DS-TEMPO

In this subsection, we present our method, Transformer Embeddings for Molecular function PredictiOn (TEMPO) and DIAMOND Score Transformer Embeddings for Molecular function PredictiOn (DS-TEMPO). The codes of our work are available in our GitHub repository[1].

---

[1] https://github.com/gabrielbianchin/TEMPO-and-DSTEMPO-MF.

```
      Position: 0        2  5   7   1   1
                          5  0   5   0   2
                          0  0   0   0   5
                                          0
Sequence #1:  MF...VF...LF...LL...PL...VS...SQ

Sequence #2:  FN...GI...PL...TQ...NP.LY
```

Fig. 1. Representation of slices from sequence #1 and #2. The blue boxes are the standard slices and the red boxes are the overlap slices. (Color figure online)

TEMPO. Based on the recent success of BERT [8], we fine-tuned ProtBERT-BFD [10], a BERT-based Transformer pre-trained on BFD database, which is a database with 2.5 billion protein sequences, on our dataset.

As this architecture has restrictions on the size of the input, we split the proteins into slices of the size of 500 amino acids using the sliding window technique, and, if two consecutive slices have at least 250 amino acids (note that this restriction occurs only to the second slice), we create an extra slice, using the last 250 amino acids of the first slice and the first 250 amino acids of the second slice, making overlap and allowing the model to generalize better the characteristics of the sequence. Figure 1 illustrates this process, where sequence #1 has 1300 amino acids, and, because of that, we created 5 slices (3 standard slices, that is, 0 up to 499, 500 up to 999, and 1000 up to 1299, and 2 overlap slices, that is, 250 up to 749, and 750 up to 1249), and sequence # 2 has 1200 amino acids with 4 slices (3 standard slices, 0 up to 499, 500 up to 999, and 1000 up to 1199, and 1 overlap slice, 250 up to 749). All of the slices had the same labels as the original protein.

To improve the generalization of the model, we created a data augmentation technique to generate new proteins in our dataset. For each protein in the training set, we duplicated and applied substitutions in the amino acid sequence, considering the PAM1 matrix [7] probabilities. We used Eq. 3 to select the number of changes in the amino acid sequence, considering L the length of the protein and k one constant. We assessed different values of k, including 0, that is, without any augmentation, and the best results were achieved with a value equal to 2, that is, for a sequence with 500 amino acids, there will be 1,000 substitutions. In the end, for the new samples in our augmented data, we employed the same approach to divide the protein into slices and gathered it with the original training set.

$$\text{Subs}(p) = L \times k \qquad (3)$$

During the fine-tuning process, we used `ktrain` [18] and `huggingface` [26] libraries, training our model during 10 epochs with early stopping technique, batch size equal to 4, and learning rate equal to 10^{-5}.

After the fine-tuning processes, we extracted the embeddings of each slice from the CLS token. CLS is a special token in BERT-based models that can understand the general context of the sentence. It is used as input to the classifier layer for text classification task, and, in our case, the CLS token is accountable

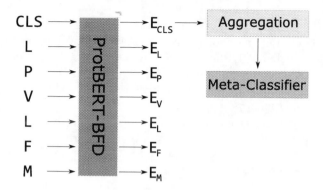

Fig. 2. Pipeline of our method. First, we fine-tuned ProtBERT-BFD for our dataset using the protein sequences broke into tokens, plus CLS token. Then, we extracted the embeddings from CLS token (represented by E_{CLS}) and combined the embeddings from different slices of the same protein in order to have a unique representation. In the end, we used the features as input to the meta-classifier.

for understanding the general context of the protein sequence, which can be seen as text classification problem, that is, given a protein, the model needs to predict which functions the input belongs to.

Then, with the features from all the slices, we aggregated the embeddings of the same protein with mean operation on each position of the feature vectors, achieving a unique representation of each protein. In the end, we trained a meta-classifier to predict the protein functions. All this process is shown in Fig. 2.

As a meta-classifier, we used Multi-Layer Perceptron (MLP). We made a grid search ranging from 1 up to 5 layers with 1,000 neurons per layer, and the best result was obtained with 1 layer. To train the MLP classifier, we employed TensorFlow [1] library, with a training of 100 epochs with early stopping and reduced learning rate on plateau, batch size equal to 32 and learning rate equal to 10^{-3}.

DS-TEMPO. Similarly to TALE+ and DeepGOPlus models, we made an ensemble using TEMPO and DS prediction based on homology search.

For prediction of DS, we applied DIAMOND [5] to search homologies between test and training set. We set the e-value equal to 0.001 and we used the bitscore to make the predictions.

After that, we made the ensemble between TEMPO and DS annotations. To do so, we applied the linear combination between them, following Eq. 4, where $S(p, f)$ represents the score of a protein p with a function f, y_t are the predictions of TEMPO, and y_d are the predictions of DS. We ran a grid search to find the best value of α on the validation set, and the optimal parameter was 0.24.

$$S(p, f) = \alpha \times y_t + (1 - \alpha) \times y_d \tag{4}$$

3.3   Dataset

To train and test our method and compare with the literature, we used the data presented in DeepGOPlus, which is derived from CAFA3 challenge [29]. However, we removed the duplicated proteins in the training and validation set, that is, proteins that are on test and training sets, test and validation sets, and training and validation sets.

In our experiments, we considered only the Molecular Function ontology. In addition, we used only functions that are present in at least 50 proteins, as employed on DeepGOPlus paper, which represent 677 terms. Table 1 present the number of proteins on each set.

Table 1. Number of proteins on the dataset.

Training	Validation	Test	Total
32,421	3,587	1,137	37,145

3.4   Evaluation Metrics

To score our model, we applied two evaluation metrics. The first is F_{max}, presented in Eq. 5. In this metric, for each threshold τ in the range 0.01 to 1.00, with steps of 0.01, is computed the precision $pr(\tau)$ and recall $rc(\tau)$, and the maximum harmonic mean is stored.

$$F_{max} = \max_{\tau} \left\{ \frac{2 \times pr(\tau) \times rc(\tau)}{pr(\tau) + rc(\tau)} \right\} \tag{5}$$

Equations 6 and 7 show the computation of $pr(\tau)$ and $rc(\tau)$. In the equations, $m(\tau)$ is the number of proteins with at least one prediction equal to or greater than the threshold τ, n_e is the number of proteins in the evaluation, f is a function of the ontology, $P_i(\tau)$ is the set of functions predicted in a threshold τ for a protein i, T_i is the ground-truth of a protein i, $I(\cdot)$ is a identity function that returns 1 if the condition inside is true or 0 if it is false.

$$pr(\tau) = \frac{1}{m(\tau)} \sum_{i=1}^{m(\tau)} \frac{\sum_f I(f \in P_i(\tau) \wedge f \in T_i)}{\sum_f I(f \in P_i(\tau))} \tag{6}$$

$$rc(\tau) = \frac{1}{n_e} \sum_{i=1}^{n} \frac{\sum_f I(f \in P_i(\tau) \wedge f \in T_i)}{\sum_f I(f \in T_i)} \tag{7}$$

The second metric used to assess our model is the area under precision and recall curve (AuPRC), which uses the $pr(\tau)$ and $rc(\tau)$ values in all thresholds τ. To generate the precision and recall curves, we applied the interpolated precision technique, considering all the 100 points of τ. To do so, we employed Eq. 8, where the value of precision in a specific recall $P(R)$ is equal to the maximum value of the precision results taking into account all recall thresholds R', where R' is equal or greater than R.

$$P(R) = \max P(R') \tag{8}$$

4   Results and Discussion

In our first experiment, we compared the methods that use only the amino acid sequence. Consequently, we evaluated TEMPO with DeepGO, DeepGOPlusCNN, TALE+Transformers and naive models. Table 2 presents the results obtained by each classifier. The outcomes show that TEMPO achieved the best performance on both F_{max} and AuPRC metrics, surpassing TALE+Transformers, the second best score, by 16.9% on F_{max} and by 20.9% on AuPRC.

Table 2. Comparison using the amino acid sequence as input.

Method	F_{max}	AuPRC
TEMPO	0.643	0.664
TALE+Transformers	0.550	0.549
DeepGOPlusCNN	0.531	0.528
DeepGO	0.489	0.465
Naive	0.446	0.370

We highlight some implementation improvements of TEMPO compared to the other classifiers. DeepGO and DeepGOPlus can only use sequences with lengths up to 1,000 and 2,000, respectively, which represents a loss of 10% and 2% of proteins in the training set. TALE+Transformers cuts chains longer than 1,000 amino acids and generates a subsequence of size 1,000, losing the rest of the protein. Differently of these methods, TEMPO uses the entire sequence, regardless of its length.

Figure 3 shows the precision-recall curve of each classifier. The curve of TEMPO is higher than the other curves in most thresholds, achieving reliable precision values in the same threshold of recall compared to the other methods.

In the second experiment, we evaluated DS-TEMPO with methods that use amino acid sequence and homology search as input, that is, TALE+ and Deep-GOPlus, and a baseline based on DS. The results of DS-TEMPO achieved the best F_{max} value, surpassing TALE+ by 4.3%, and the best outcomes in AuPRC metric, surpassing TALE+ by 6.2%, as shown in Table 3.

According to Fig. 4, our method has, in most threshold values, the highest values of the precision-recall curve. Thus, DS-TEMPO, as shown in the experiments using only the amino acid sequence, has better precision values considering the same recall thresholds, especially in higher recall parameters.

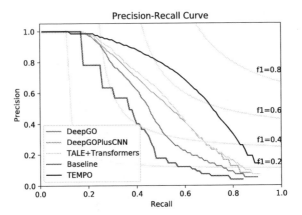

Fig. 3. Precision-Recall curve using the amino acid sequence as input.

Table 3. Comparison using the amino acid sequence and homology search as input.

Method	F_{max}	AuPRC
DS-TEMPO	0.658	0.683
TALE+	0.631	0.643
DeepGOPlus	0.619	0.635
DS	0.572	0.462

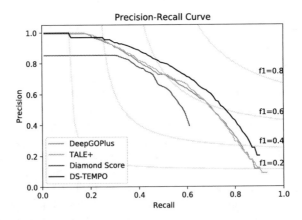

Fig. 4. Precision-Recall curve using the amino acid sequence and homology search as input.

5   Conclusions

The difference between the number of sequenced proteins and proteins with annotated functions, which occurs due to expensive and time-consuming laboratory methods, requires computational methods to help to decrease this gap.

In this work, we present our method based on Transformer embeddings for protein Molecular Function annotation. As the most common information available about proteins is their sequence, we compared our model with the literature classifiers, which showed the best performance using F_{max} and AuPRC metrics. We also evaluated the models considering the amino acid sequence and homology search, and our method also obtained the best values in F_{max} and AuPRC. With that, we conclude that our classifier can help in the annotation of Molecular Function in real scenarios, that is, when only the sequence is available, and DS-TEMPO can achieve the state-of-the-art outcomes when annotated proteins that have the same degree are available with similarity as the query ones.

As directions for future work, we intend to investigate other types of data augmentation, such as insertions and deletions, as well as increase new samples in the augmented dataset. We also noticed the importance of experiments on biological processes and cellular component ontologies.

Acknowledgements. This research was supported by São Paulo Research Foundation (FAPESP) [grant numbers 2015/11937-9, 2017/12646-3, 2017/16246-0, 2017/12646-3 and 2019/20875-8], the National Council for Scientific and Technological Development (CNPq) [grant numbers 161015/2021-2, 304380/2018-0 and 309330/2018-1], and Coordination for the Improvement of Higher Education Personnel (CAPES).

References

1. Abadi, M., et al.: TensorFlow: Large-Scale Machine Learning on Heterogeneous Systems (2015). https://www.tensorflow.org
2. Altschul, S.F., et al.: Gapped BLAST and PSI-BLAST: a new generation of protein database search programs. Nucleic Acids Res. **25**(17), 3389–3402 (1997)
3. Ashburner, M., et al.: Gene ontology: tool for the unification of biology. Nat. Genet. **25**(1), 25–29 (2000)
4. Bonetta, R., Valentino, G.: Machine learning techniques for protein function prediction. Proteins Struct. Fun. Bioinform. **88**(3), 397–413 (2020)
5. Buchfink, B., Reuter, K., Drost, H.G.: Sensitive protein alignments at tree-of-life scale using DIAMOND. Nat. Methods **18**(4), 366–368 (2021)
6. Cao, Y., Shen, Y.: TALE: transformer-based protein function annotation with joint sequence-label embedding. Bioinformatics **37**(18), 2825–2833 (2021)
7. Dayhoff, M.O.: Atlas of Protein Sequence and Structure. National Biomedical Research Foundation (1972)
8. Devlin, J., Chang, M.W., Lee, K., Toutanova, K.: BERT: Pre-training of Deep Bidirectional Transformers for Language Understanding. arXiv:1810.04805, May 2019
9. Dobson, C.M.: Protein misfolding, evolution and disease. Trends Biochem. Sci. **24**(9), 329–332 (1999)
10. Elnaggar, A., et al.: Towards Cracking the Language of Life's Code Through Self-Supervised Deep Learning and High Performance Computing. arXiv:2007.06225 (2021)
11. Fodeh, S., Tiwari, A., Yu, H.: Exploiting Pubmed for protein molecular function prediction via NMF based multi-label classification. In: IEEE International Conference on Data Mining Workshops (ICDMW), pp. 446–451 (2017)

12. Gong, Q., Ning, W., Tian, W.: GoFDR: a sequence alignment based method for predicting protein functions. Methods **93**, 3–14 (2016)
13. Kulmanov, M., Hoehndorf, R.: DeepGOPlus: improved protein function prediction from sequence. Bioinformatics **36**(2), 422–429 (2019)
14. Kulmanov, M., Hoehndorf, R.: DeepGOZero: improving protein function prediction from sequence and zero-shot learning based on ontology axioms. bioRxiv, pp. 1–9 (2022)
15. Kulmanov, M., Khan, M.A., Hoehndorf, R.: DeepGO: predicting protein functions from sequence and interactions using a deep ontology-aware classifier. Bioinformatics **34**(4), 660–668 (2018)
16. Le, N.Q.K., Ho, Q.T., Nguyen, T.T.D., Ou, Y.Y.: A Transformer architecture based on BERT and 2D convolutional neural network to identify DNA enhancers from sequence information. Brief. Bioinform. **22**(5), bbab005 (2021)
17. Lee, J., et al.: BioBERT: a pre-trained biomedical language representation model for biomedical text mining. Bioinformatics **36**(4), 1234–1240 (2020)
18. Maiya, A.S.: KTrain: A Low-Code Library for Augmented Machine Learning. arXiv:2004.10703 (2020)
19. Peng, J., Xue, H., Wei, Z., Tuncali, I., Hao, J., Shang, X.: Integrating multi-network topology for gene function prediction using deep neural networks. Brief. Bioinform. **22**(2), 2096–2105 (2021)
20. Ranjan, A., Fernandez-Baca, D., Tripathi, S., Deepak, A.: An ensemble TF-IDAF based approach to protein function prediction via sequence segmentation. IEEE/ACM Trans. Comput. Biol. Bioinf. **14**(8), 1–12 (2021)
21. UniProt: UniProt Database (2022). https://www.uniprot.org
22. Vaswani, A., et al.: Attention is all you need. In: Advances in Neural Information Processing Systems (NIPS), pp. 5998–6008 (2017)
23. Vu, T.T.D., Jung, J.: Protein function prediction with gene ontology: from traditional to deep learning models. Peer J. **9**, e12019 (2021)
24. Wan, C., Jones, D.T.: Protein function prediction is improved by creating synthetic feature samples with generative adversarial networks. Nat. Mach. Intell. **2**(9), 540–550 (2020)
25. Wang, S., Cho, H., Zhai, C., Berger, B., Peng, J.: Exploiting ontology graph for predicting sparsely annotated gene function. Bioinformatics **31**(12), i357–i364 (2015)
26. Wolf, T., et al.: Huggingface's transformers: state-of-the-art natural language processing. arXiv:1910.03771 (2019)
27. Zehetner, G.: OntoBlast function: from sequence similarities directly to potential functional annotations by ontology terms. Nucleic Acids Res. **31**(13), 3799–3803 (2003)
28. Zhang, F., Song, H., Zeng, M., Li, Y., Kurgan, L., Li, M.: DeepFunc: a deep learning framework for accurate prediction of protein functions from protein sequences and interactions. Proteomics **19**(12), 1900019 (2019)
29. Zhou, N., et al.: The CAFA challenge reports improved protein function prediction and new functional annotations for hundreds of genes through experimental screens. Genome Biol. **20**(1), 244 (2019)

Event Detection in Therapy Sessions for Children with Autism

Guilherme Ocker Ribeiro$^{(\boxtimes)}$, Alexandre Soli Soares, Jônata Tyska Carvalho, and Mateus Grellert

Universidade Federal de Santa Catarina, Florianópolis, Brazil
guilhermeocker@gmail.com

Abstract. Autism spectrum disorder (ASD) affects the cognitive development and communication skills of children and adults, limiting the functional capacity of these individuals. ASD has a worldwide prevalence of 1% on children and it affects not only the people with this disorder, but also their family and the surrounding community. In the family circle, individuals on the spectrum require greater support and attention relative to its cognitive capacity, impacting the mental and emotional health and even the financial life of families. The lack of infrastructure, trained professionals, and public health policies to deal with ASD is a known problem, specially in low income countries. To mitigate this issue, computer-aided ASD diagnosis and treatment represent a powerful ally, reducing the workload of professionals and allowing a better overall therapeutic experience. This paper intends to investigate how machine learning techniques can help specialists by providing an automated analysis of ASD recorded therapy sessions. The proposed solution is capable of handling large amounts of video data, filtering out irrelevant frames and keeping only relevant scenes for posterior analysis. Our results show that the proposed solution is capable of reducing manual checks by up to 51.4%, which represents a significant workload reduction for health experts. This solution will hopefully provide researchers, therapists and specialists with a tool that assists the automated identification of features and events of interest in video-recorded therapy sessions, reducing the amount of time spent in this task.

Keywords: Autism spectrum disorder · Machine learning · Therapy

1 Introduction

Autism spectrum disorder (ASD) is considered a complex developmental disorder that influences the ability to communicate and learn. The number of children diagnosed within the autism spectrum worldwide is rising and posing challenges to clinical, familiar and social contexts [12]. Data from the USA's Centers for Disease Control and Prevention (CDC)[1] shows that around 1 in 44 children are diagnosed

---

[1] https://www.cdc.gov/ncbddd/autism/data.html.

J. C. Xavier-Junior and R. A. Rios (Eds.): BRACIS 2022, LNAI 13654, pp. 221–235, 2022.
https://doi.org/10.1007/978-3-031-21689-3_17

within the autism spectrum disorder, occurring in all racial, ethnic and socioeconomic groups. It also shows that ASD is 4 times more prevalent among boys than among girls. Another recent study points out that ASD affects approximately 1/100 children worldwide [31]. While still alarming, this reduced prevalence compared to the USA study suggests the lack of proper diagnosis in some countries.

The rising number of cases, combined with the life-long need for care and support that most individuals with ASD require in several aspects of their life (healthcare, education and social services), turns this disorder into a major societal concern. It can be associated with significant costs for the diagnosed individual, his/her family, private and/or public health systems, state financial aid programs, and more generally the whole society [12].

According to Ramirez-Duque et al. [20], early diagnosis is very important to improve social and cognitive functioning. Despite of it, traditional ways of obtaining behavioral evidence of social and communication deficits through direct behavioral observation and comprehensive screening result is a delay in ASD diagnosis. Clinicians need numerous sessions as well as manual coding behavior to validate the diagnosis. Computer vision can help assessing the child's actions and provide automated or semi-automated video analysis for the recorded video interventions. These interventions can aid mental health professionals in reducing the time it takes to diagnose ASD, and also noticing changes and evolution between therapy sessions, providing children with ASD early therapeutic interventions and better treatment.

With this urgency in mind, several approaches of machine learning techniques have been proposed for helping the diagnosis, and therapies in the past few years [12,16,18,19,27]. Interest on researches like these are mainly boosted by the ASD increasing prevalence rate, its heterogeneous nature and the rising amount of data that is being generated by diagnosis and therapeutics methods for dealing with ASD. Therefore, in order to benefit from the digital technologies and the highly-availability of data to improve ASD diagnosis and therapies, techniques that could automate, at least part of, the data analysis are required.

This study aims to provide an automated event detection mechanism that is capable of filtering out irrelevant scenes of recorded therapy sessions to assist professionals in their analysis. The designed system is capable of processing a large amount of video data, and automatically detect interactions between actors of the scenes. This is done by using state-of-the-art machine learning techniques for object detection combined with an ad hoc heuristic. The detected events are then used to build a user-friendly timeline of interactions for each therapy session footage. The proposed system is capable of recognizing different pairs of interactions among the actors that includes: child-toy, child-therapist and therapist-toy. Our results indicate a reduction that goes up to 51.4% of the length of the videos requiring manual analysis when considering a single pair of interactions, and a reduction of 9% on average for all three pairs of interactions.

This paper is organized as follows: Sect. 2 presents the related works on this field; Sect. 3 incorporates the methods applied and the data-set used in this research; Sect. 4 shows the analysis of the experimental results and discussion, ending in Sect. 5 with the conclusion and future work.

2   Background and Related Work

This section describes the background and related work regarding tools to assist professionals in their analysis on ASD video recorded therapy sessions. First, ASD, its characteristics and the observational techniques that are used on these analysis are described, then computer vision and its application on this specific field is discussed. Finally, we present the background on the YOLO model, a state-of-the-art real-time object detection system [8,11,28].

2.1   Autism Spectrum Disorder - ASD

Autism spectrum disorder (ASD) is defined as persistent deficits in social communication and social interaction across multiple contexts, according to the Diagnostic and Statistical Manual of Mental Disorders, 5th Edition (DSM-5) [7]. ASD encompass a range of neurodevelopmental disorders characterized by impairments in social interaction, communication, and restricted, repetitive behaviours [14].

ASD presents a range of symptoms that can vary from mild to severe in particular cases, also from skill to skill and child to child. These characteristics make diagnosis and therapy progress evaluation difficult and at the same time crucial for the effectiveness of the therapy [12]. According to Rogge(2019) [22], ASD is also related to many potential comorbidities such as epilepsy, attention problems, gastrointestinal problems, oppositional behaviour, anxiety and depression, sleeping disorder and feeding disorders. Other studies estimate that between 30 and 50% of individuals with ASD also have some kind of intellectual disability [22].

2.2   Observation Techniques

Bertamini(2021) [5] points out that studying the early interactions of children is a core issue for research in infant typical and atypical development. Therefore, observational research is considered one of the main approaches in this area. Inside the clinical context, where ethical issues often put restrictions on the feasibility of controlled experiments, observational techniques are a keystone in developmental research in those individuals. These techniques are further emboldened by studies that showed similar results between behavioral observation and randomized controlled trials (RCTs) along with a set of quality criteria to strengthen observational results [3]. With that in mind, observational studies and RCTs can be used as complementary approaches to balance discovery and explanation, increasing generalizability to the wider population and generating data-driven hypotheses for subsequent confirmative designs.

Observational studies were leveraged by many techniques that were developed over the years across several large projects that aim to detect and classify human behavior [15]. These studies mainly include cross-sectional, longitudinal and case-control designs, and have often been mistakenly considered as merely qualitative [5]. On the other hand, recent techniques on observational analysis enable researchers to collect quantitative data and to employ more sophisticated computational approaches for the systematic observation of behavior, notably Hidden Markov Models (HMM), Artifial Neural Networks (ANN), Spatio-Temporal approaches among others [15]. These techniques present a great opportunity that is highly relevant in the context of developmental and clinical research, where observational techniques have the great advantage of being almost completely non-invasive, or minimally invasive in many cases [5].

2.3   Computer Vision

Computer vision has been helping those observational studies to achieve it's results in the past decade via a multitude of ways [25]. Some of them include classification and segmentation of images [29], object detection [32], video analysis [17], facial expression analysis [1] and behavioral patterns detection [13] to cite a few. Shabaz (2021) [23], Abirami (2020) [2] and Ramirez-Duque(2018) [20] use deep learning techniques of Computer vision to analyse and extract relevant information from videos of daily routines or tests of individuals with ASD and then use that information to support diagnosis and therapy studies.

According to observational therapies [5], the success of the therapy is directly connected to the feedback that the patient delivers. Feedback from an unrecorded session is limited to the therapist's local perception and memory, which is prone to misinterpretation and forgetfulness. A video-recorded session, on the other hand, allows the therapist to revisit events of interest noticed during the live session and also the perception of new events not detected before, thus generating a kind of record [10].

In this record, each therapist is free to annotate the events of interest that make the most sense as an ASD professional, qualitatively and/or quantitatively, such as whether the child has had a good evolution concerning past sessions, how many times the child interacted with the therapist and the environment, how long the session lasted, among many others.

However, two interesting problems arise in this scenario, the first being the time spent on this manual analysis. Reviewing and taking notes of a therapy session could take more time than the session itself, which ends up being unfeasible for a large amount of data and/or when the responsible therapist treats other patients. And if the recording is not done by the same therapist who performed the session, the problem is the recording pattern. For one professional, certain events of interest are more important and descriptive than for others, so the type, format, and metrics of each record quickly disperse and become inconsistent from professional to professional.

2.4   YOLO Algorithm

Regarding object detection and classification, YOLO (You Only Look Once) is a state-of-the-art real-time object detection system [8,21,28]. YOLO's goal is to recognize items faster than traditional convolutional neural networks without sacrificing accuracy by glancing at the image only once and treating object detection as a single problem. The pipeline resizes the input before running it through a single convolutional neural network and thresholding the results based on the model's confidence level. To execute the detection, YOLO divides the image into many sub-regions and assigns five anchor boxes to each one. The likelihood of a certain object is calculated, and the zone with the highest probability is chosen. Since it's original release, several iterations have been developed looking to improve its performance, access and easy to use, currently on the 5th major iteration(YOLOv5)[2].

The network internal structure of YOLOv5 involves three distinct parts: backbone, neck, and output. The backbone is based on a incorporation of CSP-Net which not only decreases the parameters and FLOPS (floating-point operations per second) but also the whole model size, increasing efficiency [26]. As its neck, path aggregation network (PANet) which improves the propagation of low-level features together with adaptive feature pooling which links feature grid and all feature levels. Finally, the head (Yolo layer) generates 3 different sizes $(18 \times 18, 36 \times 36, 72 \times 72)$ of feature maps to achieve multi-scale prediction, enabling the model to handle small, medium, and big objects [26,30] (Fig. 1).

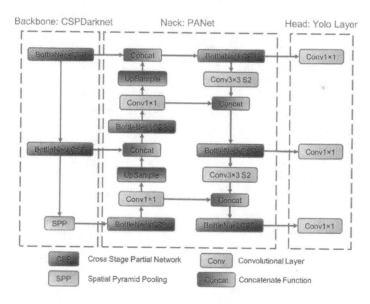

Fig. 1. YOLOv5 network architecture. Composed of three parts: (1) Backbone: CSP-Darknet, (2) Neck: PANet, and (3) Head: Yolo Layer. The data are first input to CSPDarknet for feature extraction, and then fed to PANet for feature fusion. Finally, Yolo Layer outputs detection results (class, score, location, size). [30].

---

[2] https://docs.ultralytics.com/.

3   Proposed Solution

Considering the length and the quantity of therapy sessions that an individual with ASD demands, and the need for review of such recordings for documenting relevant interactions for the therapy assessment, we propose an end-to-end tool capable of providing an automated analysis of actors' interactions in ASD therapy sessions as shown in Fig. 2.

3.1   Dataset

The data used for training and testing the proposed solution are videos of therapy sessions for children with ASD. It was provided by the european project PlusMe[3] as supplementary material published in [24].

Typically, in these therapy sessions there is a toddler, a caretaker and a teddy bear interactive cushion, which is named after the aforementioned project, PlusMe(+me). PlusMe is an experimental interactive soft toy developed in collaboration with neurodevelopmental therapists. The shape, material and functionality are designed with the concept of Transitional Wearable Companion (TWC) which is a "smart" companion toy, neither too complex as a standard robot nor too simple as a teddy bear [9].

During a session, the toddler interacts with the +me, the caretaker and the environment around (see Fig. 2 [9]). According to the observation techniques mentioned earlier these interactions and its characteristics are important factors that could serve as evidence of cognitive and social development of the toddler.

The dataset consisted in a total of 8 videos of different sessions with different toddlers. These videos were divided in 4 for the training phase, 2 for the validation phase and finally 2 for the test phase. For each video in the training and validation phases, 600 frames were manually labeled by identifying the bounding boxes of each actor in each frame. For the test phase, 200 frames were labelled with the interactions among actors.

3.2   Proposed Solution

The first step is to process the video recorded session through a computer vision tool that aims to detect, classify and retrieve the bounding boxes delimiting the existing actors in each frame. The actors in this context are specifically the toddler, the caretaker and the PlusMe device. These bounding boxes alone do not indicate any sort of interaction between actors, nor any notion of interaction length or type, only their position in each frame. Therefore, the second step is a bounding box event detection mechanism that process information from the boxes coordinates, and identify the overlap among them. Finally, based on the overlaps, an interaction timeline is built showing in which frames of the videos there are potential interactions. This functionality helps the therapists team to rapidly identify the highlighted video snippets where interactions between the

---

[3] https://www.plusme-h2020.eu/.

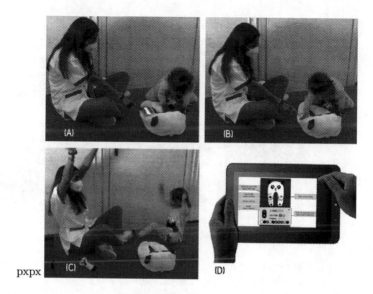

Fig. 2. An example of the experimental setting. A) the therapist points to the red blinking panda's paw, during the whack a mole activity; B) the child touches the paw, which reacts changing colour to green and emitting a brief song; C) child and therapist rejoice for the reward; D) the control tablet in the hand of the experimenter (in the same room) [9]. (Color figure online)

actors potentially occurs, streamlining the process of video assessment, saving time and reducing the overall costs of ASD research, diagnosis and therapy, as shown in Fig. 3.

Actors Detection Tool - YOLOv5 - For the task of actors detection, we employed YOLOv5 model available from the Ultralytics repository[4] under the GNU General Public License v3.0, and implemented with the open-source machine learning framework PyTorch 2[5]. The only modifications with respect to the default hyper-parameters were changing the batch-size to 1 and image size to 256×256 pixels. Such modifications had to be done due to memory limitations of the training environment (GPU) detailed later. The network was trained using transfer learning with the default YOLO network (trained on COCO dataset[6]), and the training dataset.

The result of this step is a model capable of processing any video within the trained characteristics and detect the actors, correctly classifying them and generating a correspondent bounding box for each frame. The bounding boxes output, adjusted to a pixel-coordinate format is then used as an input for our next step.

---

[4] https://github.com/ultralytics/yolov5.

[5] https://pytorch.org.

[6] https://cocodataset.org/.

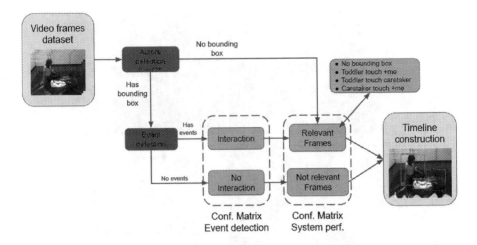

Fig. 3. Proposed solution outline. First, the content of a recorded therapy session is loaded into a Computer vision tool, generating bounding box of each actor. Next, a heuristic-based event detection mechanism outputs relevant information about interactions.

Bounding Box Event Detection - Based on the actors bounding boxes detected on the previous step, we use an event detection algorithm built upon the IoU (intersection over union) operation between each bounding box coordinates, generating information of the "perceived interaction" between the actors. The IoU operation is largely used to evaluate how two bounding boxes interact, and is also used inside the YOLOv5 algorithm to evaluate and further improve its own prediction [11,21]. The proposed event detection tool compute whether two bounding boxes intersect for each frame. Since a simple overlap, be it big or small, not always mean an interaction, we treated this as a "possible interaction event". Such predictions are then evaluated against the "ground truth" to evaluate the accuracy of the event detection tool. For sake of simplicity, at the current state of our system, interaction between the actors are defined by any overlap between their bounding boxes. Once again, the results of this step are adjusted accordingly, and then used as input for the next and final step of the proposed solution.

Event Detection Timeline Construction- Finally, we use the detected bounding box interactions information from the previous step, group them accordingly and merge this information as an overlay on the original video, highlighting the actors interaction frames and enabling a faster evaluation of the interaction between them in the recorded video therapy.

4   Results and Discussions

4.1   Actors Detection Tool - YOLOv5

The actors detection tool used was the extra large model YOLOv5x, that produce better results in nearly all cases, but have more parameters[7]. This model was trained for 189 epochs, in a batch size of 1 and image size of 256×256 due to GPU limitations. We used a NVIDIA GeForce GTX 1650 GPU with 4 Gb VRAM for training model. Other hyperparameters like SGD optimizer and initial learning rate of 0.01 were used as they were provided by default. The training took a around 16 h. The best results were found around 100 epochs (specifically 89th epoch) achieving a precision of 0.94, recall of 0.82 and mAP@0.5 of 0.90.

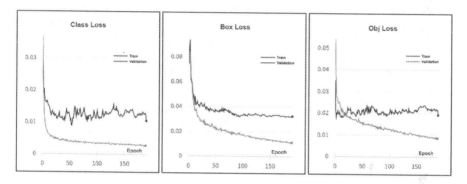

Fig. 4. YOLOv5 model losses through the training epochs timeline

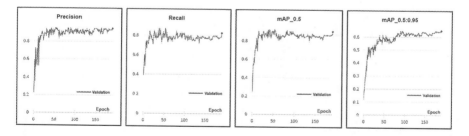

Fig. 5. YOLOv5 model main metrics, precision, recall and mAP through the training epochs timeline

The training evolution of the YOLO model can be seen on Fig. 4. YOLO loss function is applied to both the training set (4 videos) and validation set (2 videos), totalizing 600 frames fed into the neural network, and is composed of three parts:

---

[7] https://github.com/ultralytics/yolov5/wiki/Tips-for-Best-Training-Results.

1. box_loss - bounding box regression loss (Mean Squared Error) - Represents how well the algorithm can locate the centre of an object and how well the predicted bounding box covers an object.
2. obj_loss - objectness loss (Binary Cross Entropy) - A measure of the probability that an object exists in a proposed region of interest. If the objectivity is high, this means that the image window is likely to contain an object.
3. cls_loss - the classification loss (Cross Entropy) - How well the model could predict the class of the object correctly.

Also, on Fig. 5, we have precision/recall of the model and finally the mean average precision (mAP). The main component of mAP is the average precision metric (AP), which in turn, is composed by both precision and recall that are calculated for each class (caretaker, toddler and plusme). The average precision (AP)(1) is the mean of the precisions after each relevant image is retrieved, where P_r is precision at r'th element for each image. After calculated each element in each image, the summation is divided by recall (R). Average precision is a measure that combines recall and precision for ranked retrieval results. The Mean Average Precision (2) is the arithmetic mean of the average precision values for an information retrieval system over a set of n query topics [4].

$$AveragePrecision = \frac{\sum_n P_r}{R} \qquad (1)$$

$$mAP = \frac{1}{n} \sum_n AP_n \qquad (2)$$

4.2   Events Detector

Since the events detection tool predicts the existence of interactions of the bounding boxes, we can evaluate these predictions by manually asserting if there is in fact an interaction at the given frame (ground truth). Then we can assert the accuracy of the events detection tool in detecting the real events and pointing out metrics like false positives and false negatives (Fig. 6) and perceive improvements in these metrics by fine-tuning the event detection algorithm.

By prior knowledge of this particular dataset and to properly evaluate the events detector algorithm, we applied a filter beforehand and sent all the frames where the actors detection tool failed to provide a bounding box for any of the actors directly to the end of the system. These filtered frames are annotated as relevant for the final analysis and bypass the event detector algorithm entirely.

4.3   System Prediction Performance

In the final step of the system, where we join both actor's and event's detection streams, its possible to assess the prediction of each frame to compose the highlighted snippets that the system propose. Like a binary prediction, again, we can evaluate the results in a confusion matrix view (Fig. 6).

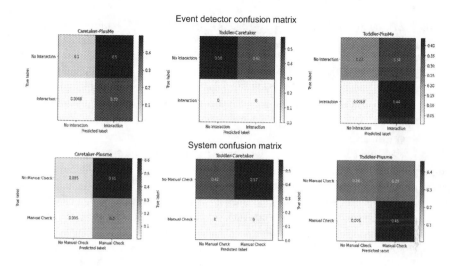

Fig. 6. Confusion matrix for event detector and for the system as a whole

4.4 Video Length Reduction

We extracted a sample of 100 frames from the 2 videos reserved for test purposes (not used in training or validation of the model). For these videos, the reduction of the frames were computed for each interaction detected between the classes and finally we can evaluate the reduction of the videos when considering only the relevant frames. The interactions assessed were Ct&+me (Caretaker and +me), Ct&Td (Caretaker and Toddler) and Td&+me (Toddler and +me) (Table 1).

Table 1. Reduction of analysed video data considering different types of interaction

Video	Frames	Ct&Td	Ct&+me	Td&+me	All interactions
Video 1	100	34.0%	0.00%	35.0	0.0%
Video 2	100	51.4%	17.8%	18.8	17.8%

5 Future Work

The actors detection tool used a very basic configuration for detection of the bounding box of the actors. As mentioned in Sect. 4, the configuration used was downgraded from the recommended setup due to time and resources constraints. Changes on both the initial parameters and the training environment can provide a significant boost for the overall accuracy and reliability of YOLO's result for this project (namely bigger image input size, bigger batches, CV and hyper-parameter fine-tuning for the model).

Since YOLO's relies on labeled inputs to provide better results on particular usages like the one that is proposed in this project, a bigger and more diverse amount of data used to train and test the model can boost the model performance as well.

We noticed that in some interactions between the toddler and the +me, the actor detection tool had issues in correctly identifying the +me in a few particular angles like those shown in Fig. 7. Data augmentation techniques can be applied on the +me by generating a specific library of images changing angles, shape and characteristics of the toy, improving the capacity of the model to recognize it in such different circumstances.

Also, a few studies [4,30] suggest improvements in the results by using data augmentation techniques on the original images by altering its exposure, saturation and noise, increasing the training set and enabling the tool to perform properly in unseen scenarios. This step also can be improved by generating a bigger training set with labeled interactions that can identify directly the interaction between the actors, more specifically hands interacting with the +me. Also there are tools for detecting hand poses [6] that can be implemented to help the actors detection tool to directly detect hands and complex interactions between then.

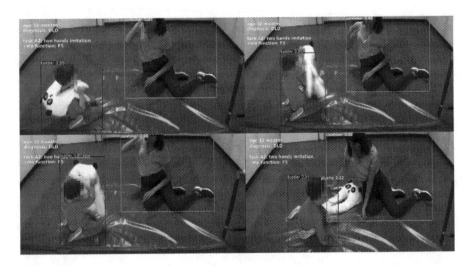

Fig. 7. Actors detection tool can't detect properly the +me while being interacted with the toddler and changing its regular shape/form. Data augmentation techniques can be applied on the +me toy to help the detection tool perceive these changes.

At this moment, the event detector tool only detects the intersection in a binary form of a given frame (there are interactions or not between the actors), but improvements can be made by properly quantifying the IoU result and extrapolating those results between frames, enabling "perceived interaction qualifications" where a larger and longer intersections between the bounding boxes are detected. As an additional layer of automation, observational coding systems could be implemented in the event detector tool for it to be able to directly quantify and qualify recognizable coded events [5].

The event detection timeline construction interface can be redesigned into a proper video tool or use some kind of annotation interface within major video service providers, allowing a better overall experience.

A new depth of automatic interaction detection can be achieved by adding tools to help estimate the gaze/sight of the toddler in relation of the +me and the caretaker [20].

References

1. Abdullah, S.M.S., Abdulazeez, A.M.: Facial expression recognition based on deep learning convolution neural network: a review. J. Soft Comput. Data Mining **2**(1), 53–65 (2021)
2. Abirami, S., Kousalya, G., Balakrishnan, P.: Activity recognition system through deep learning analysis as an early biomarker of ASD characteristics. In: Interdisciplinary Approaches to Altering Neurodevelopmental Disorders, pp. 228–249. IGI Global (2020)
3. Anglemyer, A., Horvath, H., Bero, L.: Healthcare outcomes assessed with observational study designs compared with those assessed in randomized trials. Cochrane Database Syst. Rev. (2014)
4. Ataş, K., Vural, R.A.: Detection of driver distraction using yolov5 network. In: 2021 2nd Global Conference for Advancement in Technology (GCAT), pp. 1–6 (2021). https://doi.org/10.1109/GCAT52182.2021.9587626
5. Bertamini, G., Bentenuto, A., Perzolli, S., Paolizzi, E., Furlanello, C., Venuti, P.: Quantifying the child–therapist interaction in ASD intervention: an observational coding system. Brain Sci. **11**(3), 366 (2021)
6. Dima, T.F., Ahmed, M.E.: Using yolov5 algorithm to detect and recognize American sign language. In: 2021 International Conference on Information Technology (ICIT), pp. 603–607. IEEE (2021)
7. Edition, F., et al.: Diagnostic and statistical manual of mental disorders. Am. Psychiatric Assoc. **21**, 591–643 (2013)
8. Fang, Y., Guo, X., Chen, K., Zhou, Z., Ye, Q.: Accurate and automated detection of surface knots on sawn timbers using yolo-v5 model. BioResources **16**(3) (2021)
9. Giocondo, F., et al.: Leveraging curiosity to encourage social interactions in children with autism spectrum disorder: preliminary results using the interactive toy plusme. In: CHI Conference on Human Factors in Computing Systems Extended Abstracts. CHI EA '22, Association for Computing Machinery, New York (2022). https://doi.org/10.1145/3491101.3519716
10. Hailpern, J., Karahalios, K., Halle, J., Dethorne, L., Coletto, M.K.: A3: Hci coding guideline for research using video annotation to assess behavior of nonverbal subjects with computer-based intervention. ACM Trans. Access. Comput. **2**(2), 1–29 (2009). https://doi.org/10.1145/1530064.1530066
11. Jocher, G., et al.: ultralytics/yolov5: v6.1 - tensorrt, tensorflow edge TPU and openvino export and inference (2022). https://doi.org/10.5281/ZENODO.6222936
12. Kołakowska, A., Landowska, A., Anzulewicz, A., Sobota, K.: Automatic recognition of therapy progress among children with autism. Sci. Rep. **7**(1) (2017). https://doi.org/10.1038/s41598-017-14209-y

13. Lu, J., Nguyen, M., Yan, W.Q.: Deep learning methods for human behavior recognition. In: 2020 35th International Conference on Image and Vision Computing New Zealand (IVCNZ), pp. 1–6. IEEE (2020)

14. Maenner, M.J., et al.: Prevalence and characteristics of autism spectrum disorder among children aged 8 years — autism and developmental disabilities monitoring network, 11 sites, united states, 2018. MMWR. Surveill. Summ. **70**(11), 1–16 (2021). https://doi.org/10.15585/mmwr.ss7011a1

15. Nigam, S., Singh, R., Misra, A.K.: A review of computational approaches for human behavior detection. Arch. Comput. Meth. Eng. (2018)

16. Nogay, H.S., Adeli, H.: Machine learning (ml) for the diagnosis of autism spectrum disorder (ASD) using brain imaging. Rev. Neurosci. **31**(8), 825–841 (2020)

17. Oprea, S., et al.: A review on deep learning techniques for video prediction. IEEE Trans. Pattern Anal. Mach. Intell. (2020)

18. Parikh, M.N., Li, H., He, L.: Enhancing diagnosis of autism with optimized machine learning models and personal characteristic data. Front. Comput. Neurosci. **13**, 9 (2019)

19. Rahman, M., Usman, O.L., Muniyandi, R.C., Sahran, S., Mohamed, S., Razak, R.A., et al.: A review of machine learning methods of feature selection and classification for autism spectrum disorder. Brain Sci. **10**(12), 949 (2020)

20. Ramirez-Duque, A.A., Frizera-Neto, A., Bastos, T.F.: Robot-assisted diagnosis for children with autism spectrum disorder based on automated analysis of nonverbal cues. In: 2018 7th IEEE International Conference on Biomedical Robotics and Biomechatronics (Biorob), pp. 456–461 (2018). https://doi.org/10.1109/BIOROB.2018.8487909

21. Redmon, J., Divvala, S., Girshick, R., Farhadi, A.: You only look once: unified, real-time object detection. In: 2016 IEEE Conference on Computer Vision and Pattern Recognition (CVPR), pp. 779–788. IEEE Computer Society, Los Alamitos, CA, USA (2016). https://doi.org/10.1109/CVPR.2016.91

22. Rogge, N., Janssen, J.: The economic costs of autism spectrum disorder: a literature review. J. Autism Dev.Disorders **49**(7), 2873–2900 (2019)

23. Shabaz, M., Singla, P., Jawarneh, M.M.M., Qureshi, H.M.: A novel automated approach for deep learning on stereotypical autistic motor movements. In: Advances in Medical Diagnosis, Treatment, and Care, pp. 54–68. IGI Global (2021). https://doi.org/10.4018/978-1-7998-7460-7.ch004

24. Sperati, V., et al.: Acceptability of the transitional wearable companion + me in children with autism spectrum disorder: a comparative pilot study. Front. Psychol. **11**, 951 (2020)

25. Thevenot, J., López, M.B., Hadid, A.: A survey on computer vision for assistive medical diagnosis from faces. IEEE J. Biom. Health Inform. **22**(5), 1497–1511 (2018). https://doi.org/10.1109/JBHI.2017.2754861

26. Wang, C.Y., Liao, H.Y.M., Wu, Y.H., Chen, P.Y., Hsieh, J.W., Yeh, I.H.: CSPNet: a new backbone that can enhance learning capability of cnn. In: Proceedings of the IEEE/CVF Conference on Computer Vision and Pattern Recognition Workshops, pp. 390–391 (2020)

27. Wang, M., Yang, N.: Ota-nn: Observational therapy-assistance neural network for enhancing autism intervention quality. In: 2022 IEEE 19th Annual Consumer Communications and Networking Conference (CCNC), pp. 1–7 (2022). https://doi.org/10.1109/CCNC49033.2022.9700714

28. Wang, Y., et al.: Remote sensing image super-resolution and object detection: benchmark and state of the art. Expert Syst. Appl. **197**, 116793 (2022)

29. Wu, H., Liu, Q., Liu, X.: A review on deep learning approaches to image classification and object segmentation. Comput. Mater. Continua **60**(2), 575–597 (2019)
30. Xu, R., Lin, H., Lu, K., Cao, L., Liu, Y.: A forest fire detection system based on ensemble learning. Forests **12**, 217 (2021). https://doi.org/10.3390/f12020217
31. Zeidan, J., et al.: Global prevalence of autism: a systematic review update. Autism Res. **15**(5), 778–790 (2022)
32. Zhao, Z.Q., Zheng, P., Xu, S.T., Wu, X.: Object detection with deep learning: a review. IEEE Trans. Neural Netw. Learn. Syst. **30**(11), 3212–3232 (2019)

On Social Consensus Mechanisms for Federated Learning Aggregation

Igor Felipe de Camargo$^{(\boxtimes)}$, Rodolfo Stoffel Antunes, and Gabriel de O. Ramos

Graduate Program in Applied Computing, Universidade do Vale do Rio dos Sinos,
São Leopoldo, Brazil
`igorfelcam@edu.unisisnos.br`

Abstract. The possibility of training Machine Learning models in a decentralized way has always been a challenge when maintaining data privacy and accuracy. Federated Learning stands out for allowing accurate inference by combining multiple models trained on their data locally. It uses the strategy of local learning, where each node learns from its individual data, and then groups the learned models into a single, unified one, thus preserving data privacy. However, this raises some points of attention, such as ensuring security, the accuracy of the aggregate model, and communication optimization between federated nodes. This article analyzes aggregation techniques based on Game Theory in the aggregation stage in federated learning networks, aiming to validate the exploration of new concepts and contribute to the evolution of future research. We implemented three mechanisms of the decision by consensus in the aggregation of the models, including the well-known majority voting, as well as two other mechanisms never previously used in the context of FL, namely weighted majority voting and Borda count. To properly validate, we proposed a reference pipeline based on the CIFAR-10 dataset. The proposed benchmark partitions and allocates the dataset into a number of clients, and sets up a common pipeline for them. Such a pipeline allows one to train multiple clients and then test different aggregations in a fairly, reproducible way. Moreover, the proposal increased the precision of individual inference by more than 50%, showing efficiency in using non-trivial consensus mechanisms, such as weighted majority voting.

Keywords: Federated learning · Model aggregation · Social choice · Consensus mechanisms

1 Introduction

Federated learning (FL) is a machine learning (ML) approach that uses data and computing power present in a distributed and decentralized network of devices to train predictive models [1]. The general concept is that each member in FL trains a local model using its local dataset, and a central entity receives the local models and uses an aggregation strategy to build a global model. In general, a distributed ML framework has the storage, operation of tasks, and organization

© The Author(s), under exclusive license to Springer Nature Switzerland AG 2022
J. C. Xavier-Junior and R. A. Rios (Eds.): BRACIS 2022, LNAI 13654, pp. 236–250, 2022.
https://doi.org/10.1007/978-3-031-21689-3_18

of model results fully allocated [2]. Still, it needs to manage the dataset used by a central entity responsible for spreading training tasks. In contrast, FL keeps datasets local and private, meaning that data is never shared with the central server, given that only the learned models are. In this way, it gives autonomy on when and how the client with its local data will participate in the federated training round, simplifying the learning task on the one hand but resulting in a more complex learning environment.

Nonetheless, distributed computing presents more security and privacy challenges in the learning task due to communication between multiple potentially untrusted hosts, even when the data is anonymous [3]. What makes FL more attractive is that the original datasets used for training will never be shared between nodes, preventing exposure of entities conducting studies and allowing data subjects to use their data for broader purposes [4]. For example, the FL approach is attractive in solving some limitations of ML in healthcare, such as difficulties in centralizing data in a single location for training and restrictions on the sharing itself [5]. Besides that, it allows for the evolution of the traditional FL use itself, combining strategies to improve the performance of ML models, such as evaluating and selecting the best local models for aggregation ("best subset"), resulting in a more accurate global model [6]. Therefore, FL makes it easy to use ML on sensitive data, which would be impossible if the data had to be shared.

FL is not an approach that fits all problems equally well, as in some cases are, there are more factors favorable for their use than others. For example, when the data access of data lake are approximations, and the performance gain using real data is significant, or when the training data is too sensitive or too big to be collected completely and economically viable. In addition, if there is control over the trained model of the task it is possible to infer the label from the user's behavior. From this interaction, it is possible to know if the model is working well or not [1,3].

Several works seek to solve the challenges of applying the FL. Approaches such as selecting only the best clients to generate the global model [6–8], or even changing the architecture of the network itself [9,10], among other examples [1,11,12], are the most common formats found in the literature. However, finding an approach that simultaneously solves most of the challenges in FL is difficult, as it requires a high complexity. The environment, privacy and availability of data and customers are some of the main factors that must be considered in FL [3]. The issue is that the works related to the area leave some gaps among the challenges already mentioned. Focusing on a specific point within the FL pipeline can be more interesting, as it allows its incorporation into other works, such as using new approaches in the FL model aggregation step. The aggregation step is responsible for combining the parameters received from each local model and generating a unified global model. Some studies propose solutions to improve the aggregation process and obtain more optimized models, which seek to improve the accuracy of global models by learning transfer [13]. The methodology applied in the aggregation step influences the system architecture's accuracy, privacy and optimization. This paper seeks to present a new approach to the aggregation step of FL models using robust consensus mechanisms based on Game Theory that guarantees greater accuracy and that can be extended to learning tasks in other fields, regardless of how the data is distributed.

This article presents an empirical study on using social consensus methods in the FL's model aggregation stage. Implementation of aggregation client models in order to create an FL network was analyzed. Based on the Gibbard-Satterthwaite Theorem [14], which stipulates parameters for consensus decisions, the inferences resulting from the models used were submitted to social consensus mechanisms, obtaining a single answer to each inference individually related. In order to assess our approach, we also devise an FL benchmark based on the CIFAR-10 dataset [15]. This way, we have a controlled environment to analyse each scenario carefully, controlling variations and adjusting for better performance.

We seek to expand the discussions and approaches around the methods of aggregating models in FL. In particular, the main contributions of this work can be enumerated as follows.

- Building an FL pipeline for image classification, containing C classes and N clients, focused on each dataset and precisely tuned to have an environment conducive to the validation of different social consensus mechanisms;
- A study of different social choice techniques to be applied in the model aggregation stage, using the majority voting, weighted majority voting, and Borda count consensus mechanisms;
- Conducting an in-depth experimental evaluation to understand the behavior of social consensus mechanisms in each circumstance;
- A benchmark based on CIFAR-10 to run and analyze the experiments.

The remainder organization of this paper is as follows. Section 2 presents an analysis of some theorems about social choice in Game Theory, used as a basis for this paper. Section 3 discusses the most relevant methods of aggregating models in state-of-the-art. Section 4 describes the steps for building and applying the pipeline proposed. Section 5 presents the results of each used social consensus method. Finally, Sect. 6 concludes the paper by discussing the methods applied and results obtained, limitations, and future research directions on the proposed approach.

2   Background

In the following sections, which make up the background, aspects of social consensus mechanisms in the context of federated learning are detailed, discussing factors that favor the aggregation of models with consensus decisions.

2.1   Federated Learning

Before starting the analysis, it is necessary to clarify the general concept of federated learning. FL is an approach to Machine Learning that uses data and computational power in a distributed, decentralized network of devices and can be employed to train the model [1]. In this case, instead of aggregating the data in the central training server, the models are sent to be trained in the client servers (federates units), being an ideal application when you have sensitive data.

The aggregation step in an FL structure occurs when the nodes have already trained the model with their local data and reported it to the global server. This structure allows the use of social consensus mechanisms, where each node can be seen as a voter, sending the prediction vector to the global server and, by consensus decision, obtaining the prediction together.

2.2 Social Consensus Mechanisms

Consensus mechanisms have always been part of the social life in the animal world, mainly humans, from international agreements to decisions between a small group [16]. Still, it also has importance in computing as the application of average consensus algorithms to calculate network metrics [17]. In this way, sharing choices in a group optimizes their differences, resulting in a joint decision.

Applying this technique in artificial intelligence is attractive, as it makes it possible to use the concept in the results obtained through the models. Moreover, several works have shown gains in this application, such as classifying proteins efficiently, overcoming individual classifiers, increasing precision, and decreasing error rate [18].

In this paper, the proposed study began by approaching social consensus decisions concerning most voters (nodes in FL) on global preference. Then, in Game Theory, Condorcet's Paradox shows that an election by choices can result in a Condorcet Cycle [19].

For example, assuming a finite set of alternatives how x_1, x_2, and x_3, in which three players are labeled $i = 1$, 2, 3, the result of the election can be $x_1 \succ^{1,3} x_2 \succ^{1,2} x_3 \succ^{2,3} x_1$, where all alternatives are better and worse among themselves, thus characterizing the Condorcet Cycle.

Starting from Condorcet's premise, Arrow's Impossibility Theorem explains that preference voting systems must have principles, such as: not having a dictator, there being consensus on the global preference for the local majority and respecting the principle IIA (independence of irrelevant alternatives) [20].

Moving forward in the analysis, the Gibbard-Satterthwaite Theorem [14], based on the work of Arrow, proves that every preference election that has greater than or equal to three candidates is either a dictatorship or encourages tactical voting, where the voter stops voting for its preference and vote for the least bad alternative. In summary, these studies show that rational agents can make irrational collective decisions, which is crucial to consider when exploring solutions using social consensus decisions.

Observing the proposed application, implementing a consensus system among the agents of a federated network implies challenges, such as defining a social choice function (SCF) that satisfies the accuracy condition for a global model. Clients of an FL can be seen as voters in this scenario, where each node will receive one or more initial models to weight the parameters according to its private local data. That way, trained voters nodes will be capable of voting according to their prediction. At this point comes a social consensus decision, establishing a method capable of aggregating the client's parameters fairly and accurately. State of the art contains several different approaches to model aggregation in FL, and they all share the goal of seeking accurate, compact, and secure solutions. Thus, social consensus methods become attractive because they allow a less complex approach, ensuring the model's accuracy.

3   Related Work

Several studies seek solutions to improve the aggregation process in FL, with the primary objective of obtaining more accurate global models. For example, evaluating the local models and selecting only the best ones to be sent to the aggregation server, based on the local models' cross-entropy loss concerning the global model's median cross-entropy loss, presented excellent results about the traditional model FedAvg [7]. However, severely skewed non-IID data results in a loss of performance. That makes it possible to evaluate the performance of consensual decisions in this scenario, as they present exciting results in environments with more outstanding varieties [18].

Similarly, it is also possible to discard models from clients that take a long time to train the local model, which helps to optimize the communication between client and server nodes, in addition to not abruptly impacting the loss of performance [8]. On the other hand, discarding local models generates unnecessary computational costs for the client, not making it clear whether there are gains over the transmission cost.

Some works analyze how each client influences the global model. For example, an individual influence function applied to each client allows comparing the influence of the federated node in the global model [11]. Another approach that the studies use is to change the aggregation algorithm itself, selecting the parameters that will be aggregated from a classification step, proving to be even more efficient than the Gradient Descent generally used by other works [12]. It is also possible to add a local translation step to stabilize the high data variation in the clients, using a modified Generative Adversarial Network (GAN) applied to the data before training the local model [9]. However, making direct modifications to the local data of the federated node generates distortions that directly impact the performance of the trained ML models.

Other studies focus on proposing methods to increase the protection of model aggregation against users who try to degrade the global model. In turn, strategies such as modifying the Gradient Descent at the time of aggregation of the models to the point of tolerating the entry of corrupted data by malicious clients sound promising [10]. But it is essential to consider that there is an external interference that can compromise the performance of the global model.

Finally, model aggregation is the step that results in a single, global model for FL from the models trained on each federated node [1]. The high production of works explicitly related to this theme shows its literary relevance. Hence, it is a fertile environment for developing and experimenting with new techniques for aggregating models in FL. This paper explores social consensus mechanisms for model aggregation, which is unprecedented in the literature. Furthermore, the objective is to analyze a new approach to model aggregation in an FL network, using different consensus mechanisms executed from the point of view of each federated node, to obtain an experimental evaluation and understand how these voting methods behave in this scenario.

4   Proposed Method

The consensus decision strategy is one of the most important ways to resolve social impasses. Applying consensus decisions in weak models and with different levels of accuracy allows combining them to obtain better and more accurate predictions [21]. In addition to possible performance gains, it would enable exploring and even evolving other means of joint decision-making already existing in the literature. Treating each local model in FL as a voter allows us to abstract the model's speciality since the result of your choice will be independent of the type of data used in your training. Furthermore, we can observe the consensus mechanism's behaviour in different datasets. In this paper, CIFAR-10 was used as a dataset for the tests because, despite not having a high complexity, it is ideal for analyzing the initial results of the proposed new aggregation approach. The majority decision consensus mechanism, the most objective method, was chosen as a baseline for comparing the results obtained. In addition, we can perform an in-depth experimental evaluation to understand the behaviour where each type of consensus mechanism might serve better.

4.1   FL Environment

Before all, it is necessary to simulate a federated environment and for that, some assumptions were adopted to focus on the model aggregation step, adapting the environment for division and training in the proper way:

– The communication step between the global server and the client servers will not be taken into account;
– The dataset used was fragmented, and each part separately linked to each client node of the FL network;
– The CIFAR-10 dataset has 50000 images in 10 classes for training. As shown in Table 1, the data distribution sought to simulate a non-IID environment that maintained a reasonable accuracy in at least one of the models in the federated node;
– To achieve greater diversity in individual results, each client received four different, non-complex models, something inspired by ensemble learning, seeking to use multiple learning algorithms to extract better predictive performance together than individually.

Table 1. For CIFAR-10 training, images were organized and divided into batches of proportional labels non-IID at 38%, 12%, 12%, 9%, 9%, 5%, 5%, 4%, 3%, and 3% of 50,000 available, according to the number of client nodes in the FL network, totaling 5,000 images for training on each client node.

Node-ID	Airpl.	Auto.	Bird	Cat	Deer	Dog	Frog	Horse	Ship	Truck
1	1900	150	150	200	250	250	450	450	600	600
2	600	1900	150	150	200	250	250	450	450	600
3	600	600	1900	150	150	200	250	250	450	450
4	450	600	600	1900	150	150	200	250	250	450
5	450	450	600	600	1900	150	150	200	250	250
6	250	450	450	600	600	1900	150	150	200	250
7	250	250	450	450	600	600	1900	150	150	200
8	200	250	250	450	450	600	600	1900	150	150
9	150	200	250	250	450	450	600	600	1900	150
10	150	150	200	250	250	450	450	600	600	1900
Total	5000	5000	5000	5000	5000	5000	5000	5000	5000	5000

4.2 Models Architecture

It is important to note that the focus of this paper is not to implement a new model for CIFAR-10, but we must have at least one good model for the tests to be relevant. It is a fact that there are models available in the literature with excellent performance. Still, we propose to evaluate the social consensus decision mechanisms in the aggregation stage in an FL environment, so it is unnecessary to use the model with the best performance ever developed. Including an approach with less accurate models will serve to analyze whether the use of consensus decision methods is more effective than the individual forecast of each client.

Based on this premise, we built four different models: a Convolutional Neural Network with 21 layers, a Random Forest with a maximum depth of 10, a Logistic Regression, and a K-Nearest Neighbors with Manhattan distance. Details about the architecture of the models will be explained in Sect. 5.2.

4.3 Proposed Pipeline

The method proposed in this article defines a pipeline for image classification containing C classes evaluated by N clients. Each customer was individually trained with their local data and thus had a different level of knowledge about the entire dataset used. Figure 1 presents the proposed pipeline, where the base models are initially built and introduced equally in each client node of the FL network.

As detailed in Fig. 2, once each client has trained the models using local data, it can perform the inferences. For each model used in the FL node client, a prediction matrix is reported in each inference performed. They will often have

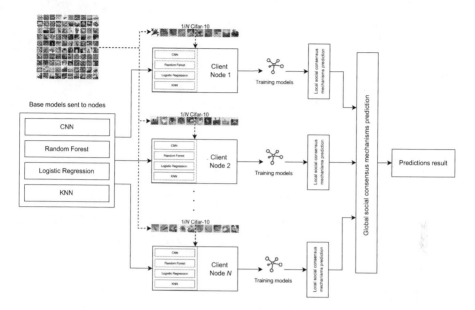

Fig. 1. The proposed pipeline is composed of the initial global model distribution stage, individual training of each client, and that, through social voting methods, results in a Social Consensus Decision Model used for inference on the dataset.

different structures, making it impossible to apply the consensus mechanism. As a solution, each inference goes through a normalization step, standardizing the structure of the predictions and enabling the application of the social consensus mechanism.

Finally, all predictions go through a new global consensus step again, thus obtaining the final prediction in a Consensus Decision Model.

4.4 Consensus Mechanisms

To analyze each clients prediction matrix, some consensus decision method was applied, thus obtaining a Consensus Decision Model. Model aggregation used three different forms of social consensus decision to analyze and compare the results obtained: majority voting, weighted majority voting, and Borda count.

Majority Voting (MV). Majority voting is the simplest method and will be used as a baseline compared to other voting methods. Within the proposed pipeline, each FL client node performs the prediction for each CIFAR-10 image requested, having as output a vector of predictions with the activation values corresponding to the possible classes of the dataset.

An algorithm is applied to compute the vote on the outcome of each prediction. The algorithm analyzes the class with the highest activation value and assigns it the client's vote, according to Algorithm 1.

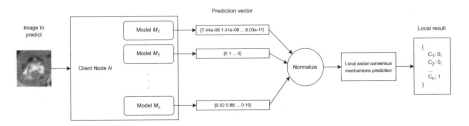

Fig. 2. Local image inference, where each local model M results in a distinct prediction vector normalized to execute the local consensus step.

Algorithm 1: Pseudo-code to majority voting, where FL clients nodes are C, test dataset image is I, and V is a dictionary of class predictions by consensus decisions

---

Input: $C=C_1, C_2, \ldots, C_n, I$
Output: $V=V_1, V_2, \ldots, V_n$

1 **for** $c \in C$ **do**
2      $P \leftarrow c.predict(I)$;
3      $v \leftarrow argmax(P)$;
4      $V[v] \leftarrow V[v] + 1$;
5 **end**
6 **return** V

Some studies show effectiveness when MV is used correctly, despite not being a complex method. For example, to optimized the communication between servers in a decentralized ML framework by applying the MV over the parameters, reducing the volume of information on the network, and maintaining accuracy [22].

Weighted Majority Voting. The weighted MV method is a variation of majority voting. What differs is the inclusion of a certainty coefficient, used to weigh the client's vote on the highest activation value of the output of the chosen class.

For example, suppose that result of a prediction by an FL client node on an image is in class 4, with an activation value of 1.5865423. Using majority voting will be computed for this client the 1 vote for class 4. Using the weighted MV, before computing the vote, the weight will be assigned considering the activation value of the class. Then, the weight is calculated by adding the activation value by 1 and multiplying the result of this sum by the activation value. Thus, the example results in $(1.5865423 + 1) * 1.5865423 = 4.10365877$, where the resulting value will be used to compute vote instead of value 1, according to Algorithm 2.

This strategy ensures that the vote of the most expert client will have greater importance in the common choice. If all clients have the same level of competence, the probability of correct voting is more significant, so majority voting is best applied for this scenario. However, suppose that the clients have different

---

Algorithm 2: Pseudo-code to weighted MV, where FL clients nodes are C, test dataset image is I, and V is a dictionary of class predictions by consensus decisions

---

Input: $C=C_1, C_2, \ldots, C_n, I$
Output: $V=V_1, V_2, \ldots, V_n$

1 **for** $c \in C$ **do**
2     $P \leftarrow c.predict(I)$;
3     $v \leftarrow argmax(P)$;
4     $w \leftarrow (P[v] + 1) \times P[v]$;
5     $V[v] \leftarrow V[v] + w$;
6 **end**
7 return V

---

levels of precision (precisely what happens with the clients of the FL network), the weighted MV ends up becoming more suitable [23], besides being able to observe the characteristics of Gibbard's Theorem -Satterthwaite, like those voters with more significant influence who turn out to be partial dictators.

Borda Count Voting. Borda Count is a voting method that aims to make the consensus decision fairer, as it allows voters to rank candidates according to the order of preference considered in the vote count [24].

In the proposal presented in this article, the candidates are the numbers from 0 to 9 that make up the C classes in CIFAR-10, and the voters are the N clients that make up the FL network. Each prediction that results from the FL client node already provides a vector with the level of certainty (activation value) about each dataset class, allowing for the application of the Borda count.

In the voting phase, prediction is analyzed for each client and ranked by the resulting values, stored as a voting ballot along with the preference value (from 1 to C_j) assigned to each C. Soon after, all the values of the client's ballots are added, and only the highest resulting value is considered, thus obtaining the candidate C chosen by preference, as shown in Algorithm 3.

5   Experimental Evaluation

The social consensus decision methods (majority voting, weighted majority voting, and Borda count) were chosen to perform a behavior analysis of each of them when applied to the federated environment. However, the weighting strategy methods are expected to have greater precision about the majority vote, as an applied bias may or may not be directed to the correct value. We want to assess this point using the social choice strategy in an FL network.

5.1   Methodology

In the federated environment, we define an amount of $N = 10$ clients to compose the nodes in the network. This amount is enough to validate the implementation,

---

Algorithm 3: Pseudo-code to Borda count voting, where FL clients nodes are C, client predictions is P, ballot to votation is B, test dataset image is I, and V is a dictionary of class predictions by consensus decisions

---

    Input: $C=C_1, C_2, \ldots, C_n, I$
    Output: $V=V_1, V_2, \ldots, V_n$
1 **for** $c \in C$ **do**
2   **for** $P_i \in c.P$ **do**
3   **for** $j \leftarrow 0$ **to** $length(P_i)$ **do**
4           $\mathbf{B}[j]['option'] \leftarrow j$;
5           $\mathbf{B}[j]['confidence'] \leftarrow \mathbf{P}_i[j]$;
6           $\mathbf{B}[j]['weight'] \leftarrow 0$;
7   **end**
8        $b.sort(reverse = True)$;
9   **for** $k \leftarrow 0$ **to** $length(\mathbf{B})$ **do**
10          $\mathbf{B}[k]['weight'] \leftarrow length(\mathbf{B}) - k$;
11   **end**
12   **end**
13 **end**
14 **for** $i \in I$ **do**
15   **for** $c \in C$ **do**
16        $v \leftarrow c.\mathbf{B}[i]['option']$;
17        $\mathbf{V}[v] \leftarrow \mathbf{V}[v] + c.\mathbf{B}[i]['weight']$;
18   **end**
19 **end**
20 return V

---

in addition to keeping the dataset fragmentation robust enough for training to be viable since CIFAR-10 is composed of 50000 training images, so $50000/N$ results in 5000 training images local in each N client node, simulating individual servers allocated remotely.

5.2 Hyper-parameter Optimization

Four different and non-complex models were implemented to compose the pipeline, used individually in each client of the FL structure. Initially, a Convolutional Neural Network was built, trained in 100 epochs to maintain more excellent stability, with 23 layers merged and divided into:

- Six Conv2D layers with 32, 64 and 128 neurons with activation relu;
- Three layers MaxPooling2D;
- Four layers of Dropout;
- Seven layers of Batch Normalization;
- A Flatten layer;
- Two dense layers, with 128 relu activation neurons and the last layer with 10 softmax activation neurons (corresponding to the output of the 10 classes of CIFAR-10).

To tune the parameters of the Random Forest, a grid search was performed from the available options:

- To criterion: ['gini', 'entropy'];
- To max depth: [5, 10, 100, 200, 500];
- To min samples leaf: [1, 2, 5, 10];
- To max features: ['auto', 'sqrt', 'log2'].

The best combination of the parameters resulting from the analysis, and used in the pipeline, were:

- To criterion: 'gini';
- To max depth: 10;
- To min samples leaf: 10;
- To max features: 'sqrt'.

For the Logistic Regression model, only 2 parameters were specified: *random_state* as 0 and *max_iter* as 200. Finally, the parameters for the K-Nearest Neighbors model were:

- To n neighbors: 3;
- To weights: 'distance' (Manhattan distance);
- To algorithm: 'brute'.

With these configurations, models obtained sufficient precision to meet the proposal implemented in the pipeline.

5.3   Numerical Results

Table 2 shows in detail the accuracy achieved by each model and in each local FL client node, trained with the local data allocated, as explained in Sect. 4. Therefore, it can be assessed from the table that FL client nodes increase accuracy by using consensus mechanisms. It is also evident how close the percentages are between the nodes, with an average variation of 5.89%. This happens because of the proportion of the CIFAR-10 aeroplane class that client node N_n received, which is the same proportion that client node N_{n+1} received of automobile, for example, and so on among all. This distribution was detailed in Table 1. It is expected to have a lower level of precision, and this is because the dataset in the node is 1/10 smaller than the complete dataset. Despite this, even being lower, the percentage value reached is still interesting for the proposal to implement the mechanisms of social consensus in the federated environment.

The last step in the pipeline was to run each social consensus method in the federated built environment. Upon completion of training for CIFAR-10, client nodes N were subjected to social consensus predictions and decisions locally and globally in that sequence. The result was positive and interesting because, in all consensus methods, there was an increase in the precision of individual predictions, e.g. the maximum accuracy obtained individually on the local client node

Table 2. Table of post-training local models accuracy for each FL client node

Node-ID	CNN	Random forest	Logistic regression	KNN
1	65.90%	25.22%	29.11%	25.63%
2	66.62%	22.81%	30.22%	30.02%
3	61.36%	24.34%	27.48%	22.74%
4	62.53%	23.14%	28.17%	26.44%
5	66.87%	24.29%	27.87%	22.19%
6	63.66%	23.18%	25.45%	25.59%
7	64.29%	23.27%	28.36%	25.07%
8	66.25%	20.60%	29.00%	25.99%
9	62.80%	24.97%	29.59%	25.70%
10	65.53%	26.03%	28.44%	27.48%
Min-max	*61.36%–66.87%*	*20.60%–26.03%*	*25.45%–30.22%*	*22.19%–30.02%*

Table 3. Table of global precision after carrying out the social consensus mechanisms

By model	Majority	Weighted majority	Borda counting
CNN	77.74%	78.06%	77.30%
Random forest	35.71%	40.49%	37.11%
Logistic regression	37.93%	39.30%	38.80%
KNN	32.22%	33.16%	24.45%
Global	*62.89%*	*63.16%*	*62.04%*

for Random Forest was 26.03%. Still, when applying the global context social consensus mechanism to this model, the accuracy was 40.49%, about 55.55% higher than the individual one in a local context, as detailed in Table 3.

An increase in precision in context global also occurs for the other models but to a lesser extent. It is also important to note that the global accuracy obtained when applying the social consensus mechanism ended up being close to the value of the average precision of the model with the highest local performance, the CNN. This lower global accuracy is a consequence of the other models with a much lower accuracy rate, but even so, the global accuracy approaches the best local result. Finally, if you use other models with greater precision, the global value tends to be higher than that obtained locally.

Finally, the proposed method proves that the decision taken by the N customers together was more effective than the individual precision of each FL node, resulting in a better percentage of accuracy in the analyzes performed. These results open possibilities to expand the analysis of social consensus mechanisms for aggregation in federated learning. Furthermore, even with the fragmented dataset, the social choice among the client nodes N managed to be more accurate about the individual N.

6 Conclusions

The implementation of consensus decisions is part of the natural process of social processes. Implementing this concept in federated learning shows how this architecture is easy to adapt to new techniques, opening possibilities for several other applications. Voting methods are also widely seen in game theory and have diverse applicability. Putting the two concepts together allowed us to explore diversified gains from our Social Consensus Decision Model.

In this study, it was evident the significant increase in performance of the inference of a set of less experienced clients on the individual deduction of federated units. In the test scenarios, gains of more than 50% in overall accuracy were obtained in relation to the maximum accuracy achieved locally. Therefore, this shows potential in the use of social consensus mechanisms for the aggregation step in FL.

Furthermore, a benchmark with CIFAR-10 on a non-IID distribution was built, which contributed to more positive results. The objective was to explore the concepts presented, relaxing the complexities to evaluate the proposed premise. There is still evolving in FL, mainly in the aggregation stage discussed in this paper. We will be able to address in the future other methods involved in Game Theory, such as the social consensus decision one worked here, in addition to expanding to more complex datasets, and evaluating the performance of the aggregation when compared to state-of-the-art, as traditional FedAvg [25].

Acknowledgements. We thank the anonymous reviewers for their valuable feedback. This research was partially supported by Coordenação de Aperfeiçoamento de Pessoal de Nível Superior - Brasil (CAPES) - Finance Code 001, and Conselho Nacional de Desenvolvimento Científico e Tecnológico - CNPq (grant 303763/2021-3).

References

1. Hard, A., et al.: Federated learning for mobile keyboard prediction. CoRR, novembro de 2018. arxiv.org/abs/1811.03604
2. Yang, Q., Liu, Y., Chen, T., Tong, Y.: Federated machine learning: concept and applications. ACM Trans. Intell. Syst. Technol. **10**(2), 19 (2019). Article 12. https://doi.org/10.1145/3298981
3. Li, T., Sahu, A.K., Talwalkar, A., Smith, V.: Federated learning: challenges, methods, and future directions. IEEE Signal Process. Mag. **37**(3), 50–60 (2020)
4. Gu, R., et al.: From server-based to client-based machine learning: a comprehensive survey. ACM Comput. Surv. (CSUR) **54**(1), 1–36 (2021)
5. Horvitz, E., Mulligan, D.: Data, privacy, and the greater good. Science **349**(6245), 253–255 (2015)
6. Liu, Z., et al.: Contribution-aware federated learning for smart healthcare. In: Proceedings of the 34th Annual Conference on Innovative Applications of Artificial Intelligence (IAAI-22) (2022)
7. Huang, L., Yin, Y., Fu, Z., Zhang, S., Deng, H., Liu, D.: Loadaboost: loss-based adaboost federated machine learning on medical data (2018). arXiv:1811.12629

8. Zhang, W., et al.: Dynamic fusion-based federated learning for Covid-19 detection. IEEE Internet Things J., 1–8 (2021)
9. Yan, Z., Wicaksana, J., Wang, Z., Yang, X., Cheng, K.-T.: Variation-aware federated learning with multi-source decentralized medical image data. IEEE J. Biomed. Health Inf., 1–14 (2020)
10. Su, L., Xu, J.: Securing distributed gradient descent in high dimensional statistical learning. IN: ACM SIGMETRICS Performance Evaluation Review, vol. 47, pp. 83–84 (2019)
11. Xue, Y., et al.: Toward understanding the influence of individual clients in federated learning. In: Proceedings of the AAAI Conference on Artificial Intelligence, vol. 35, no. 12, pp. 10560–10567 (2021)
12. Jiang, J., Ji, S., Long, G.: Decentralized knowledge acquisition for mobile internet applications World Wide Web 23, 2653–2669 (2020)
13. Chen, Y., Qin, X., Wang, J., Yu, C., Gao, W.: FedHealth: a federated transfer learning framework for wearable healthcare. IEEE Intell. Syst. 35, 83–93 (2020)
14. Benoıt, J.P.: The Gibbard-Satterthwaite theorem: a simple proof. Econ. Lett. 69(3), 319–322 (2000)
15. Krizhevsky, A., Hinton, G.: Learning multiple layers of features from tiny images. Technical report, University of Toronto (2009)
16. Conradt, L., Roper, T.: Consensus decision making in animals. Trends Ecol. Evol. 20(8), 449–456 (2005). ISSN 0169-5347. https://doi.org/10.1016/j.tree.2005.05.008
17. Chen, Z., Larsson, E.G.: Consensus-based distributed computation of link-based network metrics. IEEE Signal Process. Lett. 28, 249–253 (2021)
18. Can, T., Camoglu, O., Singh, A.K., Wang, Y.-F.: Automated protein classification using consensus decision. In: Proceedings.: IEEE Computational Systems Bioinformatics Conference, CSB 2004. Outubro 2004, pp. 224–235 (2004)
19. Herings, P.J.-J., Houba, H.: The Condorcet paradox revisited. Soc. Choice Welfare 47(1), 141–186 (2016). https://doi.org/10.1007/s00355-016-0950-7
20. Sandroni, A., Sandroni, A.: A comment on Arrow's impossibility theorem. BE J. Theor. Econ. 21(1), 347–354 (2021)
21. Raheja, H., Goel, A., Pal, M.: Prediction of groundwater quality indices using machine learning algorithms. Water Pract. Technol. 17(1), 336–351 (2022)
22. Bernstein, J., Zhao, J., Azizzadenesheli, K., Anandkumar, A.: signSGD with majority vote is communication efficient and fault tolerant (2018). arXiv preprint arXiv:1810.05291
23. Tao, D., Cheng, J., Yu, Z., Yue, K., Wang, L.: Domain-weighted majority voting for crowdsourcing. IEEE Trans. Neural Netw. Learn. Syst. 30(1), 163–174 (2018)
24. Panja, S., Bag, S., Hao, F., Roy, B.: A smart contract system for decentralized Borda count voting. IEEE Trans. Eng. Manage. 67(4), 1323–1339 (2020)
25. Sun, T., Li, D., Wang, B.: Decentralized federated averaging (2021). arXiv preprint arXiv:2104.11375

MEGALITE^PT: A Corpus of Literature in Portuguese for NLP

Igor Morgado[1(✉)] ⓘ, Luis-Gil Moreno-Jiménez[2] ⓘ, Juan-Manuel Torres-Moreno[2] ⓘ, and Roseli Wedemann[1] ⓘ

[1] PPG-Ciências Computacionais, Universidade do Estado do Rio de Janeiro,
Rua São Francisco Xavier, 524, 20550-900 Rio de Janeiro, Brazil
{igor.morgado,roseli}@ime.uerj.br
[2] Laboratoire Informatique d'Avignon, Université d'Avignon, (Avignon) France,
339 Chemin des Meinajariès, 84911 Avignon, cédex 9, France
{luis-gil.moreno-jimenez,juan-manuel.torres}@univ-avignon.fr
https://ccomp.ime.uerj.br, https://lia.univ-avignon.fr

Abstract. We present the section of the MEGALITE corpus based on literary texts in Portuguese. This new section has been developed and adapted to be used for Computational Creativity tasks, such as Natural Language Processing, Automatic Text Generation (ATG), and other similar purposes. We highlight characteristics of the Portuguese section, such as the numbers of documents, authors, sentences and tokens and also how it is structured and formatted. We show how the ATG algorithms, which we have previously developed, behave when trained on this corpus, by using a human evaluation protocol where a mixture of automatically generated and *natural* texts is classified, using four criteria: grammaticality, coherence, identification of context, and an adapted Turing test.

Keywords: Portuguese literary corpus · Corpus for emotion detection · Learning algorithms · Linguistic resources

1 Introduction

Linguistic corpora have been widely used in Natural Language Processing (NLP) tasks in recent years. Experiment has shown that a well constructed and analyzed corpus can be exploited to improve the quality of the linguistic objects produced by NLP algorithms in general, and also in the specific case of Automatic Text Generation (ATG) procedures. However, the construction of consistent literary corpora is often unattainable [17] due to the complexity of the process, which requires much time for analysis.

Moreno-Jiménez and collaborators [10, 14] have recently presented a corpus for use in NLP formed only by literary texts in Spanish. This corpus was applied in tasks such as sentiment analysis [9] and automatic generation of literary sentences [12, 14]. The corpus reached the mark of approximately 200 million (M) tokens from literature in Spanish and for this reason was named MEGALITE. The last available version of the Spanish section contains approximately 5 000 documents, 1 300 different authors, approximately 15 M sentences, 200 M tokens, and 1 000 M characters. In [11], the corpus was extended to encompass a section composed of literature in French. This

J. C. Xavier-Junior and R. A. Rios (Eds.): BRACIS 2022, LNAI 13654, pp. 251–265, 2022.
https://doi.org/10.1007/978-3-031-21689-3_19

addition contains 2 690 documents, 1 336 different authors, approximately 10 M sentences, close to 182 M tokens, and approximately 1 082 M characters. To contemplate the addition of a new language, the sections of the corpus acquired two new names, MEGALITE^{ES} for the Spanish section and MEGALITE^{FR} for French the part.

In this work, we present an extension of MEGALITE [20], formed by adding to it a new section based on literature produced in Portuguese, from different lusophone countries, such as Brazil, Portugal, and Mozambique, to name a few. It also contains literature translated to Portuguese taken from sources from different countries around the globe. We describe how the corpus was produced and formatted, its main properties, some ATG experiments carried out on the corpus and their results. We use two different representations of the corpus to better understand its structure and possible applications.

In Sect. 2, we present some work related to the development and analysis of corpora. In Sect. 3, we describe the new corpus MEGALITE^{PT}. Section 4 briefly describes the algorithm for ATG and, in Sect. 5, we present some experiments and evaluate the performance of the ATG algorithms trained with MEGALITE^{PT}. Finally, in Sect. 6, we propose some ideas for future work before concluding.

2   Related Work

In this section, we discuss some work related to the topic of the construction of literary corpora. We note that most of these corpora are composed of documents written in English. For this reason, we have concentrated our efforts on collecting literary documents written in Portuguese, in order to extend the MEGALITE [11] corpus, which already contains a section of literary documents in Spanish and another in French. We hypothesize that the richness and variability of styles found in literature can improve the quality of texts obtained with ATG algorithms, overcoming the limitations of the overly rigid styles of technical documents, or the stereotypes of the journalistic style.

In [17], the authors introduced the RiQua[1] corpus composed of literary quotation structures in 19th century English. The RiQua corpus provides a rich view of dialogue structures, focusing on the importance of the relation between the content of a quotation and the context in which it is inserted in a text. Another interesting approach presented in [19] describes the SLäNDa corpus that consists of 44 chapters of Swedish narratives, with over 220 K manually annotated tokens. The annotation process identified 4733 occurrences of quoted material (quotes and signs) that are separate from the main narrative, and 1143 named speaker-to-speech correspondences. This corpus has been useful for the development of computer tools for analyzing literary narratives and discourse.

A Spanish corpus called LiSSS has been proposed in [9]. It is constituted by literary sentences collected manually from many literary works. The LiSSS corpus has been annotated according to five emotions: love, anger, happiness, hope and fear. It is available in two versions: the first one has 500 sentences manually multi-annotated (by 13 persons), and the second one has 2 000 manually mono-annotated sentences.

---

[1] This corpus is available on the official website of the University of Stuttgart https://www.ims.uni-stuttgart.de/en/research/resources/corpora/riqua/.

Concerning corpora with emotional content, we have the SAB corpus introduced in [15]. This corpus is composed of tweets in Spanish, representing reviews about seven types of commercial products. The tweets are classified into eight categories: *Confidence, Satisfaction, Happiness, Love, Fear, Disaffection, Sadness and Anger*. In [2], another very complete work with three resources is described. The first of these is an emotional lexicon composed of words from 136 of the most spoken languages in the world. The second resource is a knowledge graph that includes 7 M words from the same 136 languages, with about 131 M inter-language semantic links. Finally, the authors detected the emotional coherence expressed in Wikipedia texts about historical figures in 30 languages.

3 Megalite Corpus

This section describes MEGALITE^PT, a literary corpus for the Portuguese language. It consists of thousands of literary documents, spanning more than a thousand different authors from different countries, writing styles, and literary genres. The documents in this corpus come from a personal collection and hence, for copyright reasons, we are not allowed to share them in their original form. Nevertheless, following the same formatting standards used in the Sections MEGALITE^ES and MEGALITE^FR, the corpus is available as files indexed by author surname and title, in the form of embeddings, represented in a Parts Of Speech (POS) tags version and a lemma version, and also in files displaying the lists and frequencies of unigrams, bigrams, and SU4-bigrams.

3.1 Structure of the Corpus

The original corpus was built from literary documents in the Portuguese language, written by lusophone authors and also by text translated from other languages to Portuguese. The corpus contains 4311 documents, from 1418 authors, in different literary genres, such as plays, poems, novels, essays, chronicles, etc. The original documents, obtained in heterogeneous formats (ordinary text, epub, pdf, HTML, ODT, doc, etc.), were processed and stored as plain text, UTF-8 document files. Textual metadata such as indexes, titles, remarks, author notes and page numbering were filtered out using techniques that detect regular expressions and pattern matching, and by manual removal. Afterwards, we performed a textual segmentation using a tool developed in PERL 5.0 to detect regular expressions [5]. Some of the properties of the corpus, after pre-processing, are detailed in Table 1.

Table 1. Properties of MEGALITE^PT, with 4311 literary texts ($K = 10^3$ and $M = 10^6$).

	Sentences	Tokens	Characters
Total in corpus	19.9 M	253.3 M	1 488.1 M
Average per document	4.6 K	58.7 K	345.2 K

In its current state, the MEGALITE corpus is very extensive, containing literary documents in French and Spanish, so that it is suitable for use in automatic learning and translation. It has, however, a small amount of noise formed by a few textual objects not detected in the pre-processing stages, leading to some mistakes in the segmentation process. This is not unusual in a corpus of the size of MEGALITE, and these same kind of objects may also be found in most corpora containing unstructured text, and they also occur in the Portuguese corpus MEGALITE^{PT}.

The names of all files in MEGALITE^{PT} follow the same naming patterns used in the other sections of MEGALITE, that is `authorLastName, authorName-title`. We also group all authors with the same last name initials in directories. In Table 2, we display the properties of the corpus, for each one of the directories identified by the initial of the last names of the authors.

Table 2. Properties of MEGALITE^{PT}. Numbers of documents, authors, sentences, tokens, and characters in each directory, which is identified by the initials of the last name of the authors.

Directory ID	Docs	Authors	Sentences	Tokens	Characters
Anonymous	6	1	1525	31498	179396
A	757	94	1549969	21288326	124192498
B	355	124	1501439	19679748	116339567
C	459	135	2099142	25127600	147580607
D	271	53	1018850	13018034	76255904
E	36	27	180806	2311665	13598473
F	115	53	679664	8554513	50880932
G	197	86	1020259	13010596	76451978
H	151	62	1184486	14943679	87933493
I	19	8	163198	2151577	12734549
J	69	35	414045	4965709	29099689
K	83	32	908103	10261876	59643611
L	142	79	812392	10526168	61949313
M	314	150	2076862	25689661	150826348
N	62	33	241849	3288980	19089347
O	31	14	108397	1687042	10060641
P	188	95	804049	11936237	70067586
Q	58	9	373289	4645910	27354438
R	278	80	1708858	20295900	118948880
S	431	126	1633717	19842890	116187506
T	70	34	513741	7219323	42511885
U	3	2	25263	357202	2111702
V	120	36	309611	4373096	25933238
W	68	35	501221	6146484	36197624
Y	2	2	12637	172111	1022010
Z	26	14	148242	1861954	11019596
Total	4,311	1,419	19,991,614	253,387,779	1,488,170,811

3.2 Word2vec Embeddings

Word embeddings are representations of words that quantify semantic similarities between linguistic terms. These embeddings can be determined from the analysis of relations among words in a large corpus. Embeddings for the MEGALITE^PT corpus were generated using the Word2vec model [7] with the Gensim [18] library, which resulted in a set of $389,340$ embeddings. Each embedding is an s-dimensional vector whose elements were obtained from semantic relationships among words in the MEGALITE^PT corpus. The training process performed to generate our embeddings used the parameters shown in Table 3. Iterations, i, represents the number of training epochs. Minimal count, m, indicates the minimal frequency of occurrence of a word in the corpus needed for it to be added to the vocabulary. For any word x, its embedding has vector size, s (s specifies the dimension of the vector representation of x), and window size, ws, represents the number of words adjacent to x in a sentence (that are related to it within the sentence) that will be considered to form the embedding. In this model, we used the skip-gram approach [6], with a negative sampling of five words and a downsampling threshold of 0.001.

Table 3. Word2Vec configuration parameters.

Parameter	Values
Iterations, i	5
Minimal count, m	3
Vector size, s	60
Window size, ws	5

Table 4 displays the 10 nearest tokens found in MEGALITE^PT for the word queries **Azul** (*blue*), **Mulher** (*woman*) and **Amor** (*love*). The distance between the query and a token is determined by the cosine similarity given by Eq. (2) (see the model description in Sect. 4). For each query word, Q, in Table 4, the left column shows a word, x, associated to Q chosen from the corpus by Word2vec, and the right column shows the cosine similarity between Q and x. We chose to not translate the words associated to the queries within the table, since many of these are synonymous to each other or do not have an English translation to a single word. This is an interesting feature of MEGALITE, that it captures some literary/artistic meanings of words which normally do not emerge from non-literary corpora.

3.3 POS Tag and Lemma Representations

In this section, we present two representations of MEGALITE^PT. The first one is a corpus built by using only POS tags and the second one uses only lemmas. This is a solution found that enables sharing the corpus without breaking copyright laws, although still preserving semantic meaning. Table 5 contains a very small subset of these representations, it shows a few sentences from Machado de Assis's "Memórias Póstumas de Brás Cubas". The first column displays the line number, which corresponds to the order of

256   I. Morgado et al.

Table 4. List of 10 nearest tokens found in MEGALITE^{PT} for queries Azul, Mulher and Amor.

Keyword	Azul (blue)	Cosine Similarity	Mulher (woman)	Cosine Similarity	Amor (love)	Cosine Similarity
	verde	0.922	moça	0.951	ternura	0.848
	violeta	0.902	menina	0.934	eterno	0.819
	lilás	0.898	mocinha	0.904	amante	0.818
	turquesa	0.895	meninazinha	0.903	ideal	0.788
	cinza	0.895	garota	0.894	deidade	0.787
	alaranjado	0.884	garotinha	0.883	ente	0.781
	cobalto	0.882	mulherzinha	0.883	crença	0.774
	azulado	0.882	menininha	0.880	senhôr	0.771
	centáurea	0.876	velhota	0.879	encanto	0.770
	amarelo	0.876	rapariga	0.873	tema	0.765

the sentence in the original text document (its line number in the file). The second column shows the original sentence as it appears in the original text. The third column displays the version of the original sentence in the POS tag representation, and the fourth column shows the sentence in its lemma representation. These two representations of MEGALITE^{PT} are formed as we describe in what follows.

POS Tag Corpus. This representation is constructed by making a morpho-syntactic analysis of each document, and replacing each word of the document with its corresponding POS tag. The analysis was performed using Freeling version 4.0 [16]. The POS tag[2] shows grammatical information for each word within a given sentence.

Lemma Corpus. The second representation is a lemmatized version of the original documents. This was achieved by using Freeling POS tags as references to first extract only meaningful lexical words, in this case only verbs, nouns, and adjectives. Every extracted word was then substituted by the corresponding lemma, which is a basic form of a given word, without conjugation, in its singular form and neutral or male genre. Words corresponding to all other types of POS tags, i.e. not verbs, nouns, and adjectives, were removed from this corpus.

3.4 n-Gram Statistics

MEGALITE also provides the frequencies of occurrences of unigrams, bigrams, and skip-grams of the type SU4-bigrams [1]. SU4-bigrams are obtained by taking a pair of words from a sentence such that from the first word in the pair one takes n steps to find the second word, i.e., using n-sized skip-grams, for $n = 1, 2, 3, 4$. For example, for the sentence "Não tive filhos, não transmiti a nenhuma criatura o legado da nossa miséria.",

---

[2] A detailed description of Freeling POS tags can be found at https://freeling-user-manual.readthedocs.io/en/latest/tagsets/tagset-pt/.

Table 5. Samples of sentences recovered from Machado de Assis's novel "Memórias Póstumas de Brás Cubas", in different versions of MEGALITE^{PT}.

Line	Original	MEGALITE POS	MEGALITE lemmas
2967	Não alcancei a celebridade do emplasto, não fui ministro, não fui califa, não conheci o casamento.	RN VMIS1S0 DA0FS0 NCCS000 SP DA0MS0 NCMS000 Fc RN VMIS1S0 NCMS000 Fc RN VMIS1S0 NCMS000 Fc RN VMIS1S0 DA0MS0 NCMS000 Fp	ALCANÇAR CELEBRIDADE EMPLASTO IR MINISTRO IR CALIFA CONHECER CASAMENTO
2968	Verdade é que, ao lado dessas faltas, coube - me a boa fortuna de não comprar o pão com o suor do meu rosto.	NP00000 RG Fc SP DA0MS0 NCMS000 SP DD0FP0 NCFP000 Fc VMIS3S0 Fg PP1CS00 DA0FS0 AQ0FS00 NCFS000 SP RN VMN0000 DA0MS0 NCMS000 SP DA0MS0 NCMS000 SP DA0MS0 DP1MSS NCMS000 Fp	VERDADE LADO FALTA CABER BOM FORTUNA COMPRAR PÃO SUOR ROSTO
2969	Mais; não padeci a morte de Dona Plácida, nem a semidemência do Quincas Borba.	RG Fx RN VMIS1S0 DA0FS0 NCFS000 SP NP00000 Fc CC DA0FS0 NCFS000 SP DA0MS0 NP00000 Fp	PADECER MORTE DONA_PLÁCIDA SEMIDEMêNCIA QUINCAS_BORBA
2970	Somadas umas coisas e outras, qualquer pessoa imaginará que não houve míngua nem sobra, e, conseguintemente que saí quite com a vida.	VMP00PF DI0FP0 NCFP000 CC DI0FP0 Fc DI0CS0 NCFS000 VMIF3S0 CS RN VMIS3S0 NCFS000 CC NCFS000 Fc CC Fc RG CS NCMS000 AQ0CS00 SP DA0FS0 NCFS000 Fp	SOMAR COISA PESSOA IMAGINAR HAVER MÍNGUA SOBRA SAÍ QUITE VIDA

given the word *filhos*, the SU4 bigrams are: *filhos/não, filhos/transmiti, filhos/a* and, *filhos/nenhuma*. The same procedure is applied to every token in every sentence in the text. Then all the occurrences of the same pair are summed up to compute the total frequency of occurrence of each pair of tokens and they are sorted in decreasing order of frequency. In Table 6, we display the top 5 most frequent bigrams and SU-4 bigrams for 4 texts of different authors.

4   Model for Generating Artificial Literary Sentences

In this section, we present a brief description of an adaptation of our previously developed model for literary sentence generation [8,12,13]. We have used this model to generate sentences in Spanish and French, using MEGALITE^{ES} and MEGALITE^{FR} and we will show results of its use in experiments of ATG with MEGALITE^{PT}, in the next section. The model consists of the two following stages.

First Stage - *Canned Text*. This step consists of using the canned text method, commonly used for ATG [3]. The process begins by selecting a sentence f from the original version of MEGALITE^{PT}, which will be used to generate a new phrase. Sentence f is then parsed with FreeLing [16] to replace the lexical words[3] by their morpho-syntactic labels (POS tags) and thus generate a Partially Empty Grammatical Structure (PGS). Functional words such as prepositions, pronouns, auxiliary verbs, or conjunctions are

---
[3] Verbs, adjectives, and nouns.

Table 6. Bigrams and SU4-Bigrams with the 5 highest frequencies from 4 literary works in MegaLite[PT].

Bigrams	Frequency	SU4-Bigrams	Frequency
Fernando Pessoa, Livro do Desassossego			
rua douradores	28	vida vida	57
patrão vasques	25	sonho sonho	32
guarda livros	18	mim mim	30
vida real	18	sonho vida	30
vida vida	17	mim vida	30
Eça de Queirós, Os Maias			
maria eduarda	119	maria eduarda	120
affonso maia	94	affonso maia	94
castro gomes	85	castro gomes	85
santa olavia	78	disse carlos	81
á porta	72	santa olavia	78
Érico Veríssimo, O Continente			
santa fé	127	santa fé	127
ana terra	91	ana terra	92
rio pardo	81	pedro terra	83
pedro terra	77	rio pardo	82
maria valéria	58	maria valéria	58
Clarice Lispector, A Descoberta do Mundo			
san tiago	19	ovo ovo	60
dona casa	15	amor amor	53
homem mulher	14	vida vida	43
caneta ouro	14	ovo galinha	28
vou contar	13	homem homem	27

kept in the sentence. To maintain semantic accuracy in our algorithm, the generated sentences must have at least 3 lexical words, but no more than 10. Once the PGS has been generated, it will be analyzed by the semantic module in the second stage.

Second Stage - Semantic Module (Word2vec) Training. We next replace the POS tags of the PGS by lexical words using the Word2vec model. This model has been implemented for our experiments under the *Skip-gram* architecture [6] using MegaLite[PT] for training. We have used the hyper-parameter values specified in Table 3 during the Word2vec training phase, to obtain $389,340$ embeddings.

In order to select the vocabulary that will replace the POS tags in the PGS formed from f to construct the new sentence, we have implemented a procedure based on an arithmetic analogy proposed by [4]. We consider the three embeddings corresponding to the words Q, O and A defined as

$\vec{Q}$: the embedding associated with the context word Q, the query, given by the user,

$\vec{O}$: the embedding associated with the original word O in f which has been replaced by the POS tag,

$\vec{A}$: the embedding associated with the word adjacent to O on the left in the sentence f.

With these embeddings, we calculated a fourth embedding $\vec{y}$ with the expression

$$\vec{y} = \vec{A} - \vec{O} + \vec{Q}. \tag{1}$$

This embedding $\vec{y}$ has the features of $\vec{A}$ and $\vec{Q}$ enhanced and the features of $\vec{O}$ decreased, so that it is more distant to $\vec{O}$.

We then obtain the embeddings of the best word associations related to $\vec{y}$ with Word2vec, and store the first $M = 4\,000$ of the these in a list $\mathcal{L}$, i.e. we take the 4000 first outputs of Word2vec, when $\vec{y}$ is given as input. $\mathcal{L}$ is thus an ordered list of 4000 vectors, a matrix, where each row, j, corresponds to an embedding of a word, w_j associated to $\vec{y}$. The value of M has been established as a compromise between the execution time and the quality of the embeddings for the procedure we are describing. The next step consisted of ranking the M embeddings in $\mathcal{L}$, by calculating the cosine similarities between the jth embedding in $\mathcal{L}$, $\vec{L}_j$, and $\vec{y}$ as

$$\theta_j = \cos(\vec{L}_j, \vec{y}) = \frac{\vec{L}_j \cdot \vec{y}}{||\vec{L}_j|| \cdot ||\vec{y}||} \quad 1 \leq j \leq M. \tag{2}$$

$\mathcal{L}$ is ranked in decreasing order of θ_j.

Another important characteristic to consider when choosing the substitute word is *grammatical coherence*. We have therefore implemented a **bigram analysis**, by estimating the conditional probability of the presence of the nth word, w_n, in a sentence, given that a previous, adjacent word, w_{n-1}, on the left is present,

$$P(w_n|w_{n-1}) = \frac{P(w_n \wedge w_{n-1})}{P(w_{n-1})}. \tag{3}$$

The conditional probability of Eq. (3) corresponds to the frequencies of occurrence of each bigram in MEGALITE^{PT}, which was obtained from the n-gram detection procedure used when constructing this corpus, as described in Subsect. 3.4. Among the bigrams in MEGALITE^{PT}, we considered only the bigrams formed by lexical and functional words (punctuation, numbers, and symbols are ignored) to form a list, LB, used to calculate the frequencies.

For each $\vec{L}_j$ in $\mathcal{L}$, we compute two bigrams, $b1_j$ and $b2_j$, where $b1_j$ is formed by the left word adjacent to O in f (corresponding to embedding $\vec{A}$) concatenated with the word w_j (corresponding to embedding $\vec{L}_j$). Then, $b2_j$ is formed by w_j concatenated with the word adjacent to O to the right in f. We then calculate the arithmetic mean, bm_j, of the frequencies of occurrence of $b1_j$ and $b2_j$ in LB. If O is the last word in f, bm_j is simply the frequency of $b1_j$. The value bm_j for each $\vec{L}_j$ is then combined with the cosine similarity θ_j, obtained with Eq. (2), and the list $\mathcal{L}$ is re-ranked in decreasing order of the new value

$$\theta_j := \frac{\theta_j + bm_j}{2}, \quad 1 \le j \le M.\tag{4}$$

Next, we take the word corresponding to the first embedding in $\mathcal{L}$ as the candidate chosen to replace O. The idea is to select the word semantically closest to $\vec{y}$, based on the analysis performed by Word2vec, while keeping the coherence of the text obtained with the linguistic analysis done by the language model and the structure of MEGALITE^{PT}. The definition of $\vec{y}$ given by Eq. (1) should allow a substituion of O by a word more distant in meaning, so that potentially more creative phrases may arise. Finally, to respect the syntactic information given by the POS tag, we use Freeling to convert the selected word to the correct gender and number inflection of the word O, which is specified by its respective POS tag. This process is repeated for each replaceable word in f (each POS tag). The result is a new sentence that does not exist in the corpus MEGALITE^{PT}. The model is illustrated in Fig. 1, where the sentence f converted to PGS can be appreciated on the top of the illustration. The PGS sends inputs to the Word2vec module that receives Q, A, and O to generate the list $\mathcal{L}$. This list is then filtered with the language model, to obtain the best choice with the correct grammatical struture returned by Freeling.

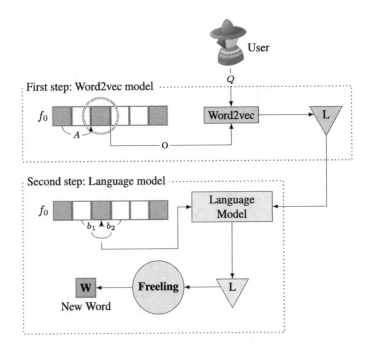

Fig. 1. Second step: vocabulary selection

5   Experiments of Automatic Sentence Generation in Portuguese

In this section, we describe a group of experiments implemented to evaluate the influence of corpus MEGALITE^PT in the task of automatic sentence generation. We describe
the evaluation protocol, show some examples of generated sentences and present our
results. We have chosen 45 sentences, with different grammatical structures and lengths
varying from 3 to 10 lexical words, to be used as input to the canned text method. In
Table 7, we display some of the queries and the corresponding generated sentences
obtained with the model explained in Sect. 4.

Table 7. Generated sentences based on user input queries

Query	Generated sentence
lua	A primeira não deixava nada, olhava sentada, no argumento, indignada contra aquela tempestade de uma confusão nos problemas pelo seu trabalho
tristeza	A mulher me sentiu, me segurou, me levou, é bem verdade
amor	Sim, egoísmo, não tenho outra lei
guerra	Em uma ínfima fração de minuto, João também partiu
sol	Nevava nas casas, e nas cores, e nos palácios, e em galpões

5.1   Evaluation Protocol and Results

Using the method described in Sect. 4, we have automatically generated a set of fifteen
sentences for each of the queries *amor*, *guerra*, and *sol*, with a total 45 sentences. We
grouped according to query and submitted these sentences for human evaluation to 18
persons, each of whom completed the evaluation survey. Each sentence was evaluated
for the three following qualitative categories.

Grammaticality. This category is used to measure the grammatical quality of the generated text. The main characteristics that should be evaluated are orthography, verb
conjugations, gender, number agreement and punctuation. Other grammatical rules
can also be evaluated but to a lesser degree of importance.

Coherence. In this case, we require the evaluation of how harmonic and well placed the
words are within the sentence. The principal points of analysis are the correct use of
words and word sequences, the sentence should have a clear meaning and should be
read without difficulty.

Context. represents how the sentence is related to the topic of the query. Naturally, in a
literary sentence, the relation with the topic can be subtle or even antagonistic.

Each one of these criteria should be evaluated by attributing a numerical, discrete value
of 0, 1 or 2, where 0 represents that the sentence does not match that category at all. A
value of 1 means that the sentence satisfies some of the conditions in that category, but
not all. And finally, a value of 2 is given, if the sentence seems correct in relation to that
category.

In the instructions for the evaluators, we stated that some sentences were generated using a computational algorithm, and others were extracted from multiple literary

works. We didn't inform the evaluator of the correct ratio between these two categories. We also performed an adapted Turing test where, for each sentence, we asked the evaluator to predict if the sentence is artificial, that is generated by a computer or if it is natural, that is written by some human author.

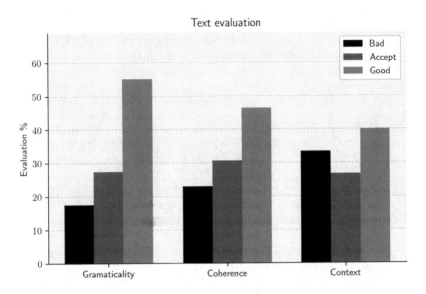

Fig. 2. Evaluation of coherence, grammaticality and context of 45 automatically generated sentences.

The results of our evaluation procedure can be seen in Fig. 2, where we can notice that 55% of the sentences are evaluated as grammatically correct, while 28% as acceptable, and only 17% are considered bad. The coherence values also display positive results with 47%, 30% and 23% evaluated as good, acceptable and bad, respectively. Finally, in the context category we have 40%, 27%, and 33% evaluated as good, acceptable and bad, respectively. All these values were rounded to integer values and the sum is 100% in each category, as expected.

Figure 3 shows the ratio of the evaluation for the Turing test for each one of the 45 sentences. Each bar sums up to 100, and represents in blue the percentage of evaluators that consider the text as written by a human (a natural sentence), while the other part, in yellow, represents the percentage of evaluators who consider the sentence as generated by a computer (an artificial sentence). The fact is that all sentences were generated by the model. The dashed line indicates the mean ratio between sentences evaluated as natural and artificial. This line shows that, on average, 56% of the evaluators consider that sentences were written by humans. Table 8 shows some sentences evaluated by human evaluators and how they were categorized by the majority (more than 80%) of the evaluators.

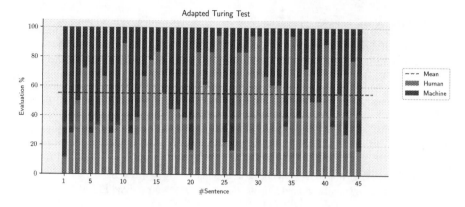

Fig. 3. Evaluations for the adapted Turing test.

Table 8. Example of sentences and results for the adapted turing test.

Evaluation	Query	Generated sentence
Human	amor	O cérebro é inocente; ninguém sabe escravizá-lo, nem o próprio dono
Human	guerra	Embora não seja o que você e eu chamássemos de dança
Machine	guerra	João está atualmente deixando a uma luta incrivelmente rápida pelo fio do caderno
Machine	sol	Não havia lugar onde fosse vermelho, e não havia como mudar dele
Machine	amor	Torturava pelo apelo dele como um beduíno morrendo de sede que entra uma fonte

6 Conclusions and Perspectives

We have introduced MEGALITE^{PT}, an extension of the MEGALITE literary corpus consisting of literary documents in Portuguese. We have provided versions of MEGALITE^{PT} in the POS tag format and in a lemmatized form. We also made available the lists and distributions of unigrams, bigrams, and SU4-bigrams for statistical analysis. The embeddings of 60-dimensional vectors, were obtained using the Word2vec model. In our experiments, we have shown that MEGALITE^{PT} is useful for NLP tasks such as automatic sentence generation. Our embeddings display a high degree of literary information and are very well suited for creative tasks.

In a human evaluation, 56% of the sentences produced using our model were considered to be generated by real human authors. These sentences were evaluated with good degrees of grammaticality, only 17% being considered bad in this category. Also very good coherence and context were perceived, with only 23% and 33% of the sentences being considered bad in each respective category. Hence, we strongly recommend MEGALITE^{PT} for NLP tasks such as Deep Learning Algorithms, textual assessment, text generation and text classification.

6.1 Future Work

We can extend this corpus to build a subset of MEGALITE^{PT} using only native writers. We believe that this corpus will be able to better model the nuances, details, and characteristics of Portuguese literature. We intend to build deep statistical analysis based on our corpus to find possible patterns and metrics that could help us to investigate structural properties of literature, artistic texts, and of ATG.

References

1. Cabrera-Diego, L.A., Torres-Moreno, J.M.: SummTriver: a new trivergent model to evaluate summaries automatically without human references. Data Knowl. Eng. **113**, 184–197 (2018). https://doi.org/10.1016/j.datak.2017.09.001
2. Chen, Y., Skiena, S.: Building sentiment lexicons for all major languages. In: Proceedings of the 52nd Annual Meeting of the Association for Computational Linguistics (Short Papers), vol. 2, pp. 383–389. Association for Computational Linguistics, Baltimore (2014). https://doi.org/10.3115/v1/P14-2063
3. Deemter, K.V., Theune, M., Krahmer, E.: Real versus template-based natural language generation: a false opposition? Comput. Linguist. **31**(1), 15–24 (2005). https://doi.org/10.1162/0891201053630291
4. Drozd, A., Gladkova, A., Matsuoka, S.: Word embeddings, analogies, and machine learning: beyond King - Man + Woman = Queen. In: Proceedings of COLING 2016, the 26th International Conference on Computational Linguistics: Technical Papers, pp. 3519–3530. The COLING 2016 Organizing Committee, Osaka (2016). aclanthology.org/C16-1332
5. Manning, C., Schutze, H.: Foundations of Statistical Natural Language Processing. MIT Press (1999)
6. Mikolov, T., Chen, K., Corrado, G., Dean, J.: Efficient estimation of word representations in vector space. arXiv:1301.3781 [cs], September 2013. arXiv: 1301.3781
7. Mikolov, T., Sutskever, I., Chen, K., Corrado, G., Dean, J.: Distributed representations of words and phrases and their compositionality. In: Burges, C.J.C., Buttou, L., Welling, M., Ghahrramani, Z., Weinberger, K.Q. (eds.) Advances in Neural Information Processing Systems, vol. 26, pp. 3111–3119. Curran Associates Inc., Lake Tahoe, October 2013. proceedings.neurips.cc/paper/2013/hash/9aa42b31882ec039965f3c4923ce901b-Abstract.html. arXiv: 1310.4546
8. Moreno-Jiménez, L.-G., Torres-Moreno, J.-M., Wedemann, R.S.: Literary natural language generation with psychological traits. In: Métais, E., Meziane, F., Horacek, H., Cimiano, P. (eds.) NLDB 2020. LNCS, vol. 12089, pp. 193–204. Springer, Cham (2020). https://doi.org/10.1007/978-3-030-51310-8_18
9. Moreno Jiménez, L.G., Torres Moreno, J.M.: LiSSS: a new corpus of literary Spanish sentences for emotions detection. Computación y Sistemas **24**(3), 1139–1147 (Sep 2020). https://doi.org/10.13053/cys-24-3-3474
10. Moreno-Jiménez, L.G., Torres-Moreno, J.M.: Megalite: a new Spanish literature corpus for NLP tasks. In: Computer Science & Information Technology (CS & IT), pp. 131–147. AIRCC Publishing Corporation, January 2021. https://doi.org/10.5121/csit.2021.110109
11. Moreno-Jiménez, L.-G., Torres-Moreno, J.-M.: **MegaLite-2**: an extended bilingual comparative literary corpus. In: Arai, K. (ed.) Intelligent Computing. LNNS, vol. 283, pp. 1014–1029. Springer, Cham (2022). https://doi.org/10.1007/978-3-030-80119-9_67
12. Moreno-Jiménez, L.G., Torres-Moreno, J.M.S., Wedemann, R., SanJuan, E.: Generación automática de frases literarias. Linguamática **12**(1), 15–30 (2020). https://doi.org/10.21814/lm.12.1.308

13. Moreno-Jiménez, L.G., Torres-Moreno, J.M., Wedemann, R.: A preliminary study for literary rhyme generation based on neuronal representation, semantics and shallow parsing. In: Anais do XIII Simpósio Brasileiro de Tecnologia da Informação e da Linguagem Humana, pp. 190–198. SBC, Porto Alegre (2021). https://doi.org/10.5753/stil.2021.17798. sol.sbc.org.br/index.php/stil/article/view/17798

14. Moreno-Jiménez, L.G., Torres-Moreno, J.M., Wedemann, R.S.: Generación de frases literarias: un experimento preliminar. Procesamiento del Lenguaje Natural **65**, 29–36 (2020). https://doi.org/10.26342/2020-65-3

15. Navas-Loro, M., Rodríguez-Doncel, V., Santana-Perez, I., Sánchez, A.: Spanish corpus for sentiment analysis towards brands. In: Karpov, A., Potapova, R., Mporas, I. (eds.) SPECOM 2017. LNCS (LNAI), vol. 10458, pp. 680–689. Springer, Cham (2017). https://doi.org/10.1007/978-3-319-66429-3_68

16. Padró, L., Stanilovsky, E.: FreeLing 3.0: towards wider multilinguality. In: FreeLing 3.0: Towards Wider Multilinguality (2012). upcommons.upc.edu/handle/2117/15986. Accepted 8 June 2012

17. Papay, S., Padó, S.: RiQuA: a corpus of rich quotation annotation for English literary text. In: Proceedings of the 12th Language Resources and Evaluation Conference, pp. 835–841. European Language Resources Association, Marseille, May 2020

18. Řehůřek, R., Sojka, P.: Software framework for topic modelling with large corpora. In: Proceedings of the LREC 2010 Workshop on New Challenges for NLP Frameworks, pp. 45–50. ELRA, Valletta, May 2010. https://doi.org/10.13140/2.1.2393.1847

19. Stymne, S., Östman, C.: SLäNDa: an annotated corpus of narrative and dialogue in Swedish literary fiction. In: Proceedings of the 12th Language Resources and Evaluation Conference, pp. 826–834. European Language Resources Association, Marseille, May 2020

20. Torres-Moreno, J.M.: Megalite (2022). hdl.handle.net/11403/megalite. ORTOLANG (Open Resources and TOols for LANGuage). www.ortolang.fr

A Survey of Recent Advances on Two-Step 3D Human Pose Estimation

João Renato Ribeiro Manesco[(⊠)] [iD] and Aparecido Nilceu Marana[iD]

Faculty of Sciences, UNESP - São Paulo State University, Bauru, SP, Brazil
{joao.r.manesco,nilceu.marana}@unesp.br

Abstract. Human pose estimation in images is an important and challenging problem in Computer Vision. Currently, methods that employ deep learning techniques excel in the task of 2D human pose estimation. 2D human poses can be used in a diverse and broad set of applications, of great relevance to society. However, the use of 3D poses can lead to even more accurate and robust results. Since joint coordinates for 3D poses are difficult to estimate, fully convolutional methods tend to perform poorly. One possible solution is to estimate 3D poses based on 2D poses, which offer improved performance by delegating the exploration of image features to more mature 2D pose estimation techniques. The goal of this paper is to present a survey of recent advances on two-step techniques for 3D human pose estimation based on 2D human poses.

Keywords: 3D human pose estimation · 2D human poses · Two-step 3D human pose estimation

1 Introduction

Human pose estimation is an important and challenging computer vision problem. Its objective is to estimate the human body shape (pose) based on a single image, usually monocular. This shape can be inferred by detecting the joints of the skeleton, which are connected in such a way that each connection represents a part of the human body.

Currently, methods that use deep learning techniques in the 2D pose estimation task already present good accuracy in real-time scenarios. Among these methods, we can cite OpenPose [3], PifPaf [22], Stacked Hourglass [32] and Cascaded Pyramid Networks [6].

Although 2D poses already can be employed in a diverse and vast set of applications, of major relevance to society, the usage of 3D poses can help to solve problems related to accuracy and dependency of camera angles in specific applications, as seen, for instance, in action recognition 2D pose-based methods that, despite showing good results, rely on the proper camera positioning to achieve success [37].

There are a few ways to obtain 3D human poses, for example by using depth sensors, infrared sensors, radio sensors, or even multiple camera perspectives by pose triangulation. However, these solutions end up being costly to implement or

J. C. Xavier-Junior and R. A. Rios (Eds.): BRACIS 2022, LNAI 13654, pp. 266–281, 2022.
https://doi.org/10.1007/978-3-031-21689-3_20

work in highly controlled environments [7]. Besides those restrictions, with the growing increase of digital cameras shipped in mobile devices, like smartphones and webcams, a necessity to approach the 3D human pose estimation problem by using monocular RGB images emerges.

The usage of a singular RGB camera introduces several challenges in the task, like the appearance of occlusion and self-occlusion, variations in clothing, body type, and camera angle. All of those scenarios can have a negative impact on the performance of the methods [2]. The referred challenges are further aggravated when the objective of the analysis is 3D poses since the majority of datasets used for the training of this task is obtained in controlled environments, through the usage of motion capture systems [12], which decreases the amount of relevant data present, making it very difficult to apply the methods in real environments.

As such, due to the lack of real-life data found in the common 3D pose datasets, current end-to-end convolutional pose estimation techniques tend to work only on very specific scenarios. A solution to this problem involves taking advantage of the maturity of 2D pose estimation methods to obtain the 3D pose in two steps: a first step where the 2D pose is obtained using traditional already-established methods, followed by a second step where from a 2D pose input the 3D pose is estimated [29].

This work presents a review of recent advances in this two-step solution, covering a wide range of approaches and discussing the state-of-the-art on this task. The contributions of this review involve the proposition of a proper taxonomy of the two-step 3D human pose estimation found in literature as well as a detailed compilation of this specific type of approach.

This paper is organized as follows: Sect. 2 discusses the methodology followed by this review; Sect. 3 discusses the proposed taxonomy used during this review for the proper comparison of techniques; Sect. 4 presents a brief introduction on the 3D human pose estimation problem, as well as the techniques discussed; Sect. 6 presents a comparison and discussion on the performance of the analyzed techniques and, finally, Sect. 7 ends the review with some conclusions.

2   Review Methodology

This review was conducted aiming to identify the state-of-the-art on two-step monocular 3D human pose estimation, in which 42 peer-reviewed papers were chosen for the analysis. The review was carried out by using StArt [14], a tool created to simplify and organize the different elements of the review in a single environment.

During the identification phase, 405 papers were obtained from 5 commonly used databases: IEEE Digital Library, ACM Digital Library, ISI Web of Knowledge, SCOPUS and Science Direct. A selection step was employed by reading the title and abstract of every paper, rejecting the ones that were not related to the topic, resulting in 79 papers selected for being fully read.

The relevance of the reviewed papers to this study was evaluated through inclusion and exclusion criteria aimed at selecting only 3D pose estimation techniques that use 2D poses as input in a monocular single-person environment, with a proper detailed experimental protocol.

An extraction phase was conducted aiming at extracting relevant information from those papers through data extraction forms. In this extraction phase, 38 papers were rejected because they were not related to the topic, leaving 41 articles in the final review.

3   Proposed Taxonomy

After carrying out the review, a set of information relevant to the selected papers was extracted from their bodies. That information was used to propose a taxonomy that aims to classify the different 3D pose estimation methods based on the main characteristics shared between them. The proposed taxonomy, presented in Fig. 1, has a supporting role in the analysis of the results, by clustering similar techniques, resulting in a fairer analysis step.

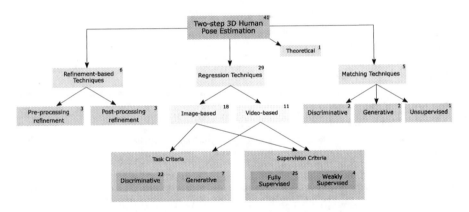

Fig. 1. Proposed taxonomy used to categorize the different two-step 3D pose estimation approaches. The numbers in the top right corner specify the number of papers in each category.

In general, three major types of 3D pose estimation techniques based on 2D poses have been proposed: refinement-based, regression, and matching techniques.

Refinement techniques are defined by a pre-processing or post-processing step in the pose dataset, in order to find a common space or perspective for the poses, or, through a refining step applied on the 3D poses already predicted, based on joint error, a frame sequence, or bone consistency, improving the accuracy of an already established 3D pose estimator.

Matching techniques are characterized by the creation of a dictionary with poses from the training set, in such a way that the 2D pose input is matched with the most similar pose that can be found in the dictionary and the corresponding 3D pose is chosen as a pose candidate. Matching techniques can operate in a partial context, that divides the poses dictionaries by kinematic groups, or in a complete context, where the whole body is used as input. In addition, they can work in a discriminative context whose objective is to only obtain the desired pose, or in a generative context, which aims to create an artificially generated dictionary to help.

Lastly, regression-based techniques consist of using mechanisms such as neural networks to recover a 3D pose from the input 2D pose, in a regression learning context. Regression techniques can operate in an image-based analysis, i.e. a single frame is considered for the evaluation, or in video-based analysis, where a sequence of frames is observed. Finally, regression-based techniques are divided between both task and supervision criteria.

Regarding the task criteria, regression-based techniques resemble matching techniques, in which there is a discriminative context, whose goal is to regress the 3D pose, and a generative context, which can operate through data augmentation mechanisms or in adversarial generative scenarios aimed to generate new poses and increase the generalization capacity of the system. As for the supervision criterion, we can classify the techniques into fully supervised, whose 3D ground truth data is used during the regression step, or weakly supervised, where only the 2D pose information is considered, making use of other types of information as the label, such as the projections of the predicted 3D poses into a 2D camera.

4   3D Pose Estimation

A human pose can be described as an articulated body, that is, an object composed of a set of rigid parts connected through joints, which allow the execution of translational and rotational movement in six degrees of freedom [38].

Therefore, human pose estimation is a problem that aims to find a particular pose P in a space Π that contains all possible articulated poses. In the context of RGB images, the objective is to extract a set of features from the image that represent each joint of the human body, when talking about 3D poses, this set of features represents the tridimensional coordinates of the pose in the space.

Although there are commercial solutions that address the 3D pose estimation problem, those solutions work mostly in restricted environments, as is the case of those based on Kinect, which has a depth sensor, or uses markers for body detection, however, these approaches are often costly or work only in very restricted scenarios [7].

In a monocular environment, 3D pose estimation is particularly challenging, since RGB images do not carry depth information. Early approaches to the problem sought to use traditional image processing techniques for 3D pose estimation, such as gradient-oriented histograms to create a set of features that identifies joints on the body [52]. This type of approach, however, was not able to properly obtain accurate predictions of 3D poses, especially in real life situations.

With the emergence of deep learning and convolutional neural networks, the performance of the methods began to improve. An initial solution involving end-to-end networks for 3D pose regression was proposed [24], however, this type of solution is difficult to be employed in scenarios different from those used on training, as the databases for 3D pose estimation need to be captured in controlled environments, decreasing the diversity of the data and impacting the generalization ability of the networks.

Nevertheless, with current state-of-the-art 2D pose estimation techniques achieving surprising results, approaches that aim to take advantage of the maturity of 2D pose estimators are gaining popularity. This is done through a two-step pose estimation process: (i) a first step responsible for obtaining valid 2D poses; and (ii) a final step in which a 3D pose is retrieved from the 2D pose.

The idea is that 2D pose estimation techniques, whose labels are easier to retrieve in a diverse range of situations, can help to ease the labor of obtaining 3D data, and can provide accurate enough information for the 3D pose lifting [29]. This is, however, a difficult problem, since depth information, which is already scarce in images, is lost with the 2D pose, and the problem itself is non-invertible, as a single 3D pose may have more than one 2D pose projection representing itself.

Despite dealing with a difficult problem, 3D pose estimation has been properly achieved in the recent literature. One of the first proposed techniques to solve the problem in two steps used Euclidean distance matrices to represent the relationship between different joints in a spatial context and achieved results comparable to end-to-end networks [31]. More recent techniques show that, through proper pre-processing of the poses, a simple residual architecture is able to estimate 3D poses with greater accuracy than end-to-end networks using only a 2D pose as input [29], the proposed architecture can be observed in Fig. 2.

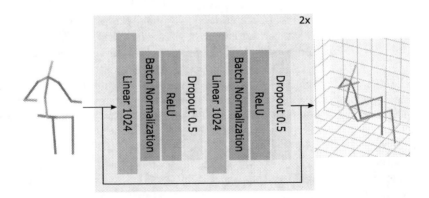

Fig. 2. Residual architecture used to solve the 3D pose estimation problem in two-steps proposed by Martinez et al. [29].

4.1 Matching Techniques

Matching techniques work on top of a dictionary created from the training dataset. One of the pioneers in this approach were Chen and Ramanan [4], proposing a discriminative method that consists of creating a dictionary of 2D projections from the training set. The method operates by searching for the 2D projection with the highest probability of representing the input 2D pose and relating it to the target 3D pose.

An alternative approach works in a generic generative schema that can accommodate various types of matching techniques, their method consists of augmenting the dataset based on a set of anatomical constraints [18], upon which, traditional matching techniques can be employed.

Localized approaches, such as the one proposed by Yang et al. [50] work by dividing the pose matching into upper and lower kinematic groups, which are then used to populate the 2D pose dictionary through several camera perspectives, by combining different groups. Other locality-based methods further spread the local kinematic groups, aiming to divide the task into different local-matching problems [57]. A different approach works on an unsupervised scenario, where a sparse representation in a linear combination of pose basis is learned before the matching occurs [19].

4.2 Regression Techniques

Regression techniques aim to estimate 3D pose values through neural networks. Moreno-Noguer [31] was one of the pioneers in this area through Euclidean-distance matrices. Another relevant work is the one proposed by Martinez et al. [29] where the authors create a baseline for pose estimation through proper pose processing and a simple residual neural network. Other works have been inspired by the baseline, such as one approach that uses siamese networks to find a rotation equivariant representation in the pose space [40].

Pavlakos, Zhou and Daniilidis [33] treat the lack of depth information through an ordinal relationship, modelled through a neural network. Another method aims to diversify the set of predicted poses, through the usage of a Gaussian mixture model, used to predict more than one valid pose. Xu et al. [49] utilizes pose grammars and data augmentation to deal with the problem. Another fresh perspective to the problem, deals with a bone representation, instead of 2D joints to estimate the 3D poses [43].

Graph-based approaches have been gaining popularity in recent years, due to their success in the action recognition task. Early uses of this approach involved employing SemGCNs to solve the problem [56]. This concept was further expanded by other authors, such as solutions that employ Locally Connected Networks to solve the problem [8] by incorporating useful mechanisms of fully connected networks into GCNs, or techniques that enhance the baseline network by changing linear layers to convolutional graph layers [1].

Expanding the concept of graphs, Zou et al. [58] combine SemGCNs with density mixture models to generate multiple valid poses. Generative-based approaches that employ a SemGCN in a discriminative adversarial setting were also discussed in the literature [45], going as far as transforming the monocular pose estimation problem into a multi-view problem through artificially generated poses.

4.3   Video-Based Approaches

Early video-based approaches commonly used an LSTM to predict the 3D pose based on a sequence of frames, such as the work of Hossain and Little [17] that aimed to predict the current pose based only on the previous frames. This approach was further explored by the usage of BiLSTMs after dividing the pose into relevant kinematic groups [16]. The idea of dividing the pose was also used by Zeng et al. [53], through a group of recurrent neural networks called SRNet.

Other approaches are aimed at using temporal convolutional methods, either through the creation of memory banks [11] or through the usage of bone consistency, like the approach proposed by Chen et al. [5] which explores anatomical constraints by using a bone length network that analyses randomly sampled frames, in conjunction with a bone direction network used to evaluate consecutive poses. Zhang et al. [54] propose a graph-based temporal convolutional technique that updates the graph vertices according to the euclidean distance of all the other vertices in the frame. A more recent approach employs the usage of attention mechanisms on diluted temporal convolutional networks for 3D pose estimation [26].

Some different perspective for the video-based scenario is concerned more with the physical consistency of the 3D pose with the environment and ends up creating a complete MockUp system, whose objective is to define force vectors temporally consistent to facilitate real-life interaction at the cost of accuracy [35].

4.4   Refinement-Based Techniques

Refinement-based techniques work on improving the pose representation, so that other pose estimation techniques can achieve better results. Wang et al. [41], for example, realize the post-processing of the poses by learning a distance matrix, upon which k pose-basis will be retrieved and used to reposition the 3D pose in a new space. Another post-processing technique involves grouping the poses into different categories, according to how big is their error, and further refining the poses afterward [15].

Regarding the pre-processing of the poses, one approach aims to fix the poses by maintaining the consistency of the gravity center along the frames [47]. Liang et al. [25] employs a neural network on the 2D poses, such as all of the 2D poses are represented in the same perspective, dealing with camera angles overfitting. Lastly, following a similar idea, Wei et al. [44] employs a hierarchical correction network in a generative adversarial context, to find a new perspective for the 2D poses.

Xu et al. [48] create a video processing technique through a cinematic analysis based on the bone's length and angle that projects 2D poses to a common perspective, and at the end of the prediction, refine the predicted poses with a low 2D confidence score based on their trajectory.

4.5   Weakly Supervised and Transfer Learning

Weakly supervised methods usually use the information present in the extracted 3D pose itself as a label, without the need for direct information from the 3D ground truths. Early techniques worked by making sure that the estimated 3D pose satisfies a set of anatomical constraints [10]. Following a similar line, another work employs geometric symmetry-based constraints, in the context of graph networks, to perform method supervision [46]. Another approach involves the usage of pose generating mechanisms through adversarial networks and pose refining [42].

Klug et al. [21] defines a theoretical limit for weakly supervised techniques that employ weak projections. The limit is based on the error propagated by the distortions caused by the projection, so even if a technique can estimate almost perfectly a 3D pose, the distortion will be taken into account and a lower bound can be set for each of the databases analyzed.

There are a few methods that employ transfer learning techniques, such as the one proposed by Zhang et al. [55] in which a synthetic depth-based dataset is used for domain adaptation during the learning step. Another approach employs the usage of synthetic pose datasets artificially generated to enhance the amount of data available during the training [10]. The same idea is followed by Yang et al. [51], proposing a generative adversarial framework that encompasses 2D poses from different datasets.

This idea of using distinct datasets is further explored in the literature, by a work that employs semi-supervised learning in a domain adaptation scenario, based on temporal convolutions [34], or by another project, that employs a CVAE to synthetically generate poses from another dataset distribution and decrease the overfitting problem [20].

5   3D Pose Datasets and Experimental Protocols

In general, the vast majority of work utilizes the Human3.6M dataset [27], composed of images captured from real people using a marker-based MoCap (Motion Capture) system, containing scenes of 11 professional actors performing 15 common everyday tasks. The dataset contains about 3.6 million annotations of 3D poses, considering four different angles for single-person pose estimation. Methods for 3D pose estimation are assessed on this database through three different protocols:

Protocol 1: Utilizes five subjects for training (S1, S5, S6, S7, and S8) and two for evaluation (S9, S11). The methods are evaluated according to the MPJPE (Mean Per Joint Position Error) metric, after the root joint alignment;

Protocol 2: Same training/testing methodology as Protocol 1, but evaluation with the PA-MPJPE metric, obtained by performing the Procrustes Alignment (PA) before calculating the MPJPE;

Protocol 3: Employed to evaluate the generalization capability of the methods according to the camera angle. Same training/testing methodology as Protocol 1, but removing all the frontal camera images during training and utilizing them only during evaluation.

Other commonly used datasets are the HumanEva [36] and the MPI-INF-3DHP datasets. The HumanEva database contains videos of three individuals performing light activity obtained using a MoCap system. The dataset is composed of 7 video sequences synchronized with the 3D poses. The evaluation is done according to the PA-MPJPE metric. The MPI-INF-3DHP [30] dataset is a database obtained on a multi-camera MoCap system, without the use of body markers, consisting of 1.3 M frames from 14 different perspectives, with 8 recorded individuals performing 8 activities. When using this dataset, the methods are customarily evaluated with respect to 3DPCK (3D Percentage of Correct Keypoints) and AUC (Area Under the Curve of the 3DPCK graph) metrics.

Other datasets commonly mentioned, but not very often used for assessment of 3D human pose estimation methods, are: Joint Track Auto (JTA) [13], 3DPW [28] and Total Capture [39]. Figure 3 depicts images of the datasets most commonly used for 3D pose estimation.

6   Comparison and Discussion

Table 1 shows the performance of the 3D pose estimation methods on different 3D human pose databases followed by a 2D pose extractor. As one can observe, the matching-based methods have considerably worse results than regression-based methods. This is expected since the poses in the dictionary do not necessarily represent exactly the action of the person.

Among the matching techniques, the method of Yang et al. [50] stood out the most, achieving results close to some regression techniques, thus proving that, localized kinematic analysis is indeed able to provide more diversity for the set of techniques by matching parts.

Regarding video and image-based techniques, in general, video-based techniques outperform their image-based counterparts, highlighting the importance of using temporal information during prediction. However, the image-based technique proposed by Ci et al. [8] produced the second best overall result through the use of locally connected networks.

A few refinement techniques with competitive results were proposed, such as one that makes use of the center of gravity information [47]. The best result in this category was achieved by Xu et al. [48], by the usage of temporal information and bone consistency for the refinement. The best overall technique is a video-based network that utilizes a novel approach encompassing bone length and direction for 3D pose estimation [5]. Wei et al. [43] achieved similar performance

Fig. 3. Datasets most commonly used for assessment of 3D pose estimation methods: Human3.6 M (first row), HumanEva (second row) and MPI-INF-3DHP (third row).

on the MPII-INF-3DHP dataset, by integrating the MPII data in a portion of the training set.

Even with the impressive performance of current 3D pose estimation techniques, recent papers still discuss certain problems with the current methodology employed on the pose estimation task, that end up resulting in the overfitting of poses and camera angles [5,40,44,48,49]. This problem can be further emphasized by the lack of methods that are evaluated on the third protocol of the Human3.6M database. The use of data augmentation techniques is often treated as a normal solution to the overfitting problem, but recent weakly supervised techniques and the applicability of transfer learning ideas may be essential to increase the generalization capabilities of the methods.

Although observing, in most papers of this survey, the lack of discussion on the computational cost of the proposed methods, some of them indicates that the task can be executed in real time [4,17,26,43].

Table 1. Performance and categorization of two-step 3D pose estimation methods selected in this review applied to the most used 3D pose databases. Results in bold indicate the best performances in the category, while underlined results indicate the best overall performances.

Author	Approach	Human3.6M MPJPE (mm)	P-MPJPE (mm)	HumanEva P-MPJPE (mm)	MPI-INF-3DHP 3DPCK (%)	AUC (%)
Regression (Video)						
[35]	Discriminative; Weakly supervised	76.5	58.2	–	69.80%	30.20%
[42]	Generative; Supervised	63.7	63.7	19.9	–	
[16]	Discriminative; Supervised	58.9	–	–	–	–
[17]	Discriminative; Supervised	51.9	42.0	22.0	–	–
[34]	Generative; Semi-supervised	46.8	36.5	19.75		
[54]	Discriminative; Supervised	45.3	35.4	19.5	87.50%	53.80%
[26]	Discriminative; Supervised	44.8	35.6	**15.4**		
[53]	Discriminative; Supervised	44.8	39.4	–	77.60%	43.80%
[5]	Discriminative; Supervised	**44.1**	**35.0**		87.90%	**54.00%**
Regression (Image)						
[55]	Generative; Unsupervised	78.5	68.9		–	–
[43]	Discriminative; Supervised	63.1	42.7	–	**88.70%**	53.10%
[29]	Discriminative; Supervised	62.9	52.1	24.6	–	–
[46]	Discriminative; Weakly supervised	62.4	–	–	–	
[40]	Discriminative; Supervised	61.1	49.4			
[51]	Generative; Supervised	58.6	37.7	–	69.00%	32.00%
[49]	Discriminative; Supervised	58.1	43.8	21.9	–	–
[56]	Discriminative; Supervised	57.6	–		–	
[45]	Generative; Supervised	56.7	45.1	**13.7**	–	
[44]	Generative; Supervised	56.6	42.8	–	76.10%	40.20%
[33]	Discriminative; Supervised	56.2	41.8	18.3	71.90%	35.30%
[23]	Discriminative; Supervised	52.7	42.6		67.90%	
[9]	Discriminative; Supervised	52.7	42.2	–	74.00%	36.70%
[10]	Discriminative; Weakly supervised	52.1	**36.3**	–	76.70%	39.10%
[20]	Discriminative; Supervised	51.1	38.9	15.4	–	–
[58]	Discriminative; Supervised	46.8	38.9	–	–	
[8]	Discriminative; Supervised	**44.2**	37.3	–	74.00%	36.70%
Matching (Image)						
[18]	Generative	–	**68.0**	–	–	–
[19]	Unsupervised	87.7	83.0	**21.1**	–	–
[4]	Discriminative	82.7	114.2	–	–	–
[57]	Discriminative	76.1	89.5	53.2	–	–
[50]	Generative	**69.2**	–	–	–	–
Refinement (Video)						
[48]	Pre-Processing; Discriminative	**45.6**	**36.2**	**15.2**	–	–
Refinement (Image)						
[31]	Pre-Processing; Discriminative	85.6	81.5	**22.56**	–	–
[15]	Post-Processing; Regressive	60.6	**46.5**	–	–	–
[25]	Pre-Processing; Generative	60.4	46.9	–	–	–
[47]	Post-Processing; Supervised	**59.0**	–	–	–	–

7 Conclusion

Although 3D pose estimation is a constantly developing area, there are still several scenarios to be explored. The evaluation of techniques in real life scenarios is practically null for this type of technique, and the usage of transfer learning and synthetic domains can still be more widespread since few methods make direct mention of this type of approach.

A trend can be observed in the use of graph networks in the image-based scenario, however, techniques with non-traditional approaches have been gaining prominence in terms of performance, since the best technique currently proposed involves the use of a novel representation of the datasets, using bone consistency.

Even with novel research being produced in 3D pose estimation, current computer vision trends could be explored, such as techniques using neural architectural search, transformers, and attention mechanisms. Discussions related to the explainability or interpretability of the models would be welcomed.

Finally, it can be stated that despite the presence of great developments in the area and the considerable progress in the state-of-the-art methods, there is still much room for growth and development from diverse perspectives.

Acknowledgements. The authors thank FAPESP (Process: 2021/02028-6) and Petrobras/Fundunesp (Process 2662/2017) for the financial support. This study was financed in part by the Coordenação de Aperfeiçoamento de Pessoal de Nível Superior-Brasil (CAPES).

References

1. Banik, S., García, A.M., Knoll, A.: 3D human pose regression using graph convolutional network. In: 2021 IEEE International Conference on Image Processing (ICIP) pp. 924–928 (2021). https://doi.org/10.1109/ICIP42928.2021.9506736
2. Bartol, K., Bojanic, D., Petkovic, T., D'Apuzzo, N., Pribanic, T.: A review of 3D human pose estimation from 2D images. In: Proceedings of 3DBODY.TECH 2020–11th International Conference and Exhibition on 3D Body Scanning and Processing Technologies, Online/Virtual, 17–18 November 2020. Hometrica Consulting - Dr. Nicola D'Apuzzo (2020). https://doi.org/10.15221/20.29
3. Cao, Z., Hidalgo, G., Simon, T., Wei, S.E., Sheikh, Y.: OpenPose: realtime multi-person 2D pose estimation using part affinity fields. IEEE Trans. Pattern Anal. Mach. Intell. **43**(1), 172–186 (2019)
4. Chen, C., Ramanan, D.: 3D human pose estimation = 2D pose estimation + matching. In: 2017 IEEE Conference on Computer Vision and Pattern Recognition (CVPR), pp. 5759–5767. IEEE Computer Society, Los Alamitos, CA, USA (2017). https://doi.org/10.1109/CVPR.2017.610
5. Chen, T., Fang, C., Shen, X., Zhu, Y., Chen, Z., Luo, J.: Anatomy-aware 3D human pose estimation with bone-based pose decomposition. IEEE Trans. Circ. Syst. Video Technol. **32**, 198–209 (2021)
6. Chen, Y., Wang, Z., Peng, Y., Zhang, Z., Yu, G., Sun, J.: Cascaded pyramid network for multi-person pose estimation. In: Proceedings of the IEEE Conference on Computer Vision and Pattern Recognition (CVPR) (2018)

7. Chen, Y., Tian, Y., He, M.: Monocular human pose estimation: a survey of deep learning-based methods. Comput. Vis. Image Underst. **192**, 102897 (2020). https://doi.org/10.1016/j.cviu.2019.102897

8. Ci, H., Ma, X., Wang, C., Wang, Y.: Locally connected network for monocular 3D human pose estimation. IEEE Trans. Pattern Anal. Mach. Intell. **44**, 1429–1442 (2020)

9. Ci, H., Wang, C., Ma, X., Wang, Y.: Optimizing network structure for 3D human pose estimation. In: Proceedings of the IEEE/CVF International Conference on Computer Vision, pp. 2262–2271 (2019)

10. Dabral, R., Mundhada, A., Kusupati, U., Afaque, S., Sharma, A., Jain, A.: Learning 3D human pose from structure and motion. In: Proceedings of the European Conference on Computer Vision (ECCV), pp. 668–683 (2018)

11. Deng, W., Zheng, Y., Li, H., Wang, X., Wu, Z., Zeng, M.: VH3D-LSFM: video-based human 3D pose estimation with long-term and short-term pose fusion mechanism. In: Peng, Y., et al. (eds.) PRCV 2020. LNCS, vol. 12305, pp. 589–601. Springer, Cham (2020). https://doi.org/10.1007/978-3-030-60633-6_49

12. Doersch, C., Zisserman, A.: Sim2real transfer learning for 3D human pose estimation: Motion to the rescue. CoRR abs/1907.02499 (2019)

13. Fabbri, M., Lanzi, F., Calderara, S., Palazzi, A., Vezzani, R., Cucchiara, R.: Learning to detect and track visible and occluded body joints in a virtual world. In: Ferrari, V., Hebert, M., Sminchisescu, C., Weiss, Y. (eds.) ECCV 2018. LNCS, vol. 11208, pp. 450–466. Springer, Cham (2018). https://doi.org/10.1007/978-3-030-01225-0_27

14. Fabbri, S., Silva, C., Hernandes, E., Octaviano, F., Di Thommazo, A., Belgamo, A.: Improvements in the start tool to better support the systematic review process. In: Proceedings of the 20th International Conference on Evaluation and Assessment in Software Engineering, EASE 2016. Association for Computing Machinery, New York (2016). https://doi.org/10.1145/2915970.2916013

15. Guo, Yu., Zhao, L., Zhang, S., Yang, J.: Coarse-to-fine 3D human pose estimation. In: Zhao, Y., Barnes, N., Chen, B., Westermann, R., Kong, X., Lin, C. (eds.) ICIG 2019. LNCS, vol. 11903, pp. 579–592. Springer, Cham (2019). https://doi.org/10.1007/978-3-030-34113-8_48

16. He, X., Wang, H., Qin, Y., Tao, L.: 3D human pose estimation with grouping regression. In: Wang, Y., Huang, Q., Peng, Y. (eds.) IGTA 2019. CCIS, vol. 1043, pp. 138–149. Springer, Singapore (2019). https://doi.org/10.1007/978-981-13-9917-6_14

17. Hossain, M.R.I., Little, J.J.: Exploiting temporal information for 3D human pose estimation. In: Ferrari, V., Hebert, M., Sminchisescu, C., Weiss, Y. (eds.) ECCV 2018. LNCS, vol. 11214, pp. 69–86. Springer, Cham (2018). https://doi.org/10.1007/978-3-030-01249-6_5

18. Jahangiri, E., Yuille, A.L.: Generating multiple diverse hypotheses for human 3D pose consistent with 2D joint detections. In: Proceedings of the IEEE International Conference on Computer Vision Workshops, pp. 805–814 (2017)

19. Jiang, M., Yu, Z., Zhang, Y., Wang, Q., Li, C., Lei, Y.: Reweighted sparse representation with residual compensation for 3D human pose estimation from a single RGB image. Neurocomputing **358**, 332–343 (2019)

20. Jiang, Y., Liu, X., Wu, D., Zhao, P.: Residual deep monocular 3D human pose estimation using CVAE synthetic data. In: Journal of Physics: Conference Series, vol. 1873, p. 012003. IOP Publishing (2021)

21. Klug, N., Einfalt, M., Brehm, S., Lienhart, R.: Error bounds of projection models in weakly supervised 3D human pose estimation. In: 2020 International Conference on 3D Vision (3DV), pp. 898–907. IEEE (2020)

22. Kreiss, S., Bertoni, L., Alahi, A.: PifPaf: composite fields for human pose estimation. In: Proceedings of the IEEE/CVF Conference on Computer Vision and Pattern Recognition, pp. 11977–11986 (2019)

23. Li, C., Lee, G.H.: Generating multiple hypotheses for 3D human pose estimation with mixture density network. In: 2019 IEEE/CVF Conference on Computer Vision and Pattern Recognition (CVPR), pp. 9879–9887 (2019). https://doi.org/10.1109/CVPR.2019.01012

24. Li, S., Chan, A.B.: 3D human pose estimation from monocular images with deep convolutional neural network. In: Cremers, D., Reid, I., Saito, H., Yang, M.-H. (eds.) ACCV 2014. LNCS, vol. 9004, pp. 332–347. Springer, Cham (2015). https://doi.org/10.1007/978-3-319-16808-1_23

25. Liang, G., Zhong, X., Ran, L., Zhang, Y.: An adaptive viewpoint transformation network for 3D human pose estimation. IEEE Access **8**, 143076–143084 (2020)

26. Liu, R., Shen, J., Wang, H., Chen, C., Cheung, S., Asari, V.K.: Enhanced 3D human pose estimation from videos by using attention-based neural network with dilated convolutions. Int. J. Comput. Vis. **129**(5), 1596–1615 (2021). https://doi.org/10.1007/s11263-021-01436-0

27. von Marcard, T., Henschel, R., Black, M.J., Rosenhahn, B., Pons-Moll, G.: Recovering accurate 3D human pose in the wild using IMUs and a moving camera. In: Proceedings of the European Conference on Computer Vision (ECCV), pp. 601–617 (2018)

28. von Marcard, T., Henschel, R., Black, M.J., Rosenhahn, B., Pons-Moll, G.: Recovering accurate 3D human pose in the wild using IMUs and a moving camera. In: Ferrari, V., Hebert, M., Sminchisescu, C., Weiss, Y. (eds.) ECCV 2018. LNCS, vol. 11214, pp. 614–631. Springer, Cham (2018). https://doi.org/10.1007/978-3-030-01249-6_37

29. Martinez, J., Hossain, R., Romero, J., Little, J.J.: A simple yet effective baseline for 3D human pose estimation. In: 2017 IEEE International Conference on Computer Vision (ICCV), pp. 2659–2668 (2017). https://doi.org/10.1109/ICCV.2017.288

30. Mehta, D., et al.: Monocular 3D human pose estimation in the wild using improved CNN supervision. In: 2017 International Conference on 3D Vision (3DV), pp. 506–516. IEEE (2017)

31. Moreno-Noguer, F.: 3D human pose estimation from a single image via distance matrix regression. In: Proceedings of the IEEE Conference on Computer Vision and Pattern Recognition, pp. 2823–2832 (2017)

32. Newell, A., Yang, K., Deng, J.: Stacked hourglass networks for human pose estimation. In: Leibe, B., Matas, J., Sebe, N., Welling, M. (eds.) ECCV 2016. LNCS, vol. 9912, pp. 483–499. Springer, Cham (2016). https://doi.org/10.1007/978-3-319-46484-8_29

33. Pavlakos, G., Zhou, X., Daniilidis, K.: Ordinal depth supervision for 3D human pose estimation. In: Proceedings of the IEEE Conference on Computer Vision and Pattern Recognition, pp. 7307–7316 (2018)

34. Pavllo, D., Feichtenhofer, C., Grangier, D., Auli, M.: 3D human pose estimation in video with temporal convolutions and semi-supervised training. In: Proceedings of the IEEE/CVF Conference on Computer Vision and Pattern Recognition, pp. 7753–7762 (2019)

35. Shimada, S., Golyanik, V., Xu, W., Pérez, P., Theobalt, C.: Neural monocular 3D human motion capture with physical awareness. ACM Trans. Graph. **40**(4), 1–15 (2021). https://doi.org/10.1145/3450626.3459825

36. Sigal, L., Balan, A.O., Black, M.J.: Humaneva: synchronized video and motion capture dataset and baseline algorithm for evaluation of articulated human motion. Int. J. Comput. Vision **87**(1–2), 4 (2010). https://doi.org/10.1007/s11263-009-0273-6

37. da Silva, M.V., Marana, A.N.: Human action recognition in videos based on spatiotemporal features and bag-of-poses. Appl. Soft Comput. **95**, 106513 (2020)

38. Stamou, G., Krinidis, M., Loutas, E., Nikolaidis, N., Pitas, I.: 2D and 3D motion tracking in digital video. In: Handbook of Image and Video Processing, pp. 491–XVIII. Elsevier (2005). https://doi.org/10.1016/B978-012119792-6/50093-0

39. Trumble, M., Gilbert, A., Malleson, C., Hilton, A., Collomosse, J.: Total capture: 3D human pose estimation fusing video and inertial sensors. In: 2017 British Machine Vision Conference (BMVC) (2017)

40. Véges, M., Varga, V., Lőrincz, A.: 3D human pose estimation with siamese equivariant embedding. Neurocomputing **339**, 194–201 (2019)

41. Wang, C., Qiu, H., Yuille, A.L., Zeng, W.: Learning basis representation to refine 3D human pose estimations. In: Proceedings of the AAAI Conference on Artificial Intelligence, vol. 33, pp. 8925–8932 (2019)

42. Wang, K., Lin, L., Jiang, C., Qian, C., Wei, P.: 3D human pose machines with self-supervised learning. IEEE Trans. Pattern Anal. Mach. Intell. **42**(5), 1069–1082 (2019)

43. Wei, G., Wu, S., Tang, K., Li, G.: BoneNet: real-time 3D human pose estimation by generating multiple hypotheses with bone-map representation. Comput. Aided Design Appl. **18**(6), 1448–1465 (2021). https://doi.org/10.14733/cadaps.2021.1448-1465 https://doi.org/10.14733/cadaps.2021.1448-1465 https://doi.org/10.14733/cadaps.2021.1448-1465

44. Wei, G., Lan, C., Zeng, W., Chen, Z.: View invariant 3D human pose estimation. IEEE Trans. Circuits Syst. Video Technol. **30**(12), 4601–4610 (2019)

45. Xia, H., Xiao, M.: 3D human pose estimation with generative adversarial networks. IEEE Access **8**, 206198–206206 (2020)

46. Xie, Z., Xia, H., Feng, C.: A multi-scale recalibrated approach for 3D human pose estimation. In: Yang, Q., Zhou, Z.-H., Gong, Z., Zhang, M.-L., Huang, S.-J. (eds.) PAKDD 2019. LNCS (LNAI), vol. 11441, pp. 400–411. Springer, Cham (2019). https://doi.org/10.1007/978-3-030-16142-2_31

47. Xu, H., Wu, S.: 3D human pose estimation based on center of gravity. In: 2020 International Joint Conference on Neural Networks (IJCNN), pp. 1–7. IEEE (2020)

48. Xu, J., Yu, Z., Ni, B., Yang, J., Yang, X., Zhang, W.: Deep kinematics analysis for monocular 3D human pose estimation. In: Proceedings of the IEEE/CVF Conference on Computer Vision and Pattern Recognition, pp. 899–908 (2020)

49. Xu, Y., Wang, W., Liu, T., Liu, X., Xie, J., Zhu, S.C.: Monocular 3D pose estimation via pose grammar and data augmentation. IEEE Trans. Pattern Anal. Mach. Intell. **44**, 6327–6344 (2021)

50. Yang, J., Wan, L., Xu, W., Wang, S.: 3D human pose estimation from a single image via exemplar augmentation. J. Vis. Commun. Image Represent. **59**, 371–379 (2019)

51. Yang, W., Ouyang, W., Wang, X., Ren, J., Li, H., Wang, X.: 3D human pose estimation in the wild by adversarial learning. In: Proceedings of the IEEE Conference on Computer Vision and Pattern Recognition, pp. 5255–5264 (2018)

52. Yang, Y., Ramanan, D.: Articulated human detection with flexible mixtures of parts. IEEE Trans. Pattern Anal. Mach. Intell. **35**(12), 2878–2890 (2013). https://doi.org/10.1109/TPAMI.2012.261

53. Zeng, A., Sun, X., Huang, F., Liu, M., Xu, Q., Lin, S.: SRNet: improving generalization in 3D human pose estimation with a split-and-recombine approach. In: Vedaldi, A., Bischof, H., Brox, T., Frahm, J.-M. (eds.) ECCV 2020. LNCS, vol. 12359, pp. 507–523. Springer, Cham (2020). https://doi.org/10.1007/978-3-030-58568-6_30

54. Zhang, J., Wang, Y., Zhou, Z., Luan, T., Wang, Z., Qiao, Y.: Learning dynamical human-joint affinity for 3D pose estimation in videos. IEEE Trans. Image Process. **30**, 7914–7925 (2021)

55. Zhang, X., Wong, Y., Kankanhalli, M.S., Geng, W.: Unsupervised domain adaptation for 3D human pose estimation. In: Proceedings of the 27th ACM International Conference on Multimedia, pp. 926–934 (2019)

56. Zhao, L., Peng, X., Tian, Y., Kapadia, M., Metaxas, D.N.: Semantic graph convolutional networks for 3D human pose regression. In: Proceedings of the IEEE/CVF Conference on Computer Vision and Pattern Recognition, pp. 3425–3435 (2019)

57. Zhou, S., Jiang, M., Wang, Q., Lei, Y.: Towards locality similarity preserving to 3D human pose estimation. In: ACCV Workshops, pp. 136–153 (2020)

58. Zou, L., Huang, Z., Gu, N., Wang, F., Yang, Z., Wang, G.: GMDN: a lightweight graph-based mixture density network for 3D human pose regression. Comput. Graph. **95**, 115–122 (2021)

Exploring Advances in Transformers and CNN for Skin Lesion Diagnosis on Small Datasets

Leandro M. de Lima[1,2(✉)] [iD] and Renato A. Krohling[1,2] [iD]

[1] Graduate Program in Computer Science, Federal University of Espirito Santo, Vitória, Brazil
leandro.m.lima@ufes.br, rkrohling@inf.ufes.br
[2] Labcin – Nature-inspired Computing Lab, DEPR, Federal University of Espirito Santo, Vitória, Brazil

Abstract. Skin cancer is one of the most common types of cancer in the world. Different computer-aided diagnosis systems have been proposed to tackle skin lesion diagnosis, most of them based on deep convolutional neural networks. However, recent advances in computer vision achieved state-of-the-art results in many tasks, notably transformer-based networks. We explore and evaluate advances in computer vision architectures, training methods and multimodal feature fusion for skin lesion diagnosis task. Experiments show that PiT (0.800 ± 0.006), CoaT (0.780 ± 0.024) and ViT (0.771 ± 0.018) transformer-based backbone models with MetaBlock fusion achieved state-of-the-art results for balanced accuracy on PAD-UFES-20 dataset.

Keywords: Transformer · Convolutional neural network · Skin lesion · Multimodal fusion · Classification

1 Introduction

A third of cancer diagnoses in the world are skin cancer diagnoses according to the World Health Organization (WHO). In order to diagnose skin cancer, dermatologists screen the skin lesion, assess the patient clinical information, and use their experience to classify the lesion [33]. The high incidence rate and the lack of experts and medical devices, specifically in rural areas [14] and in emerging countries [36], have increased the demand for computer-aided diagnosis (CAD) systems for skin cancer.

Over the past decades, different CAD systems have been proposed to tackle skin cancer recognition [11,40]. In general, these systems are based on clinical information from the patient and information extracted from lesion images [57]. Image features and features extracted from clinical information need to be merged. This task is known as multimodal data fusion.

The use of neural network has become the de-facto standard as a backbone for extracting visual features in various tasks. Deep convolutional neural network (CNN) based architectures are widely used for this. However, recently,

J. C. Xavier-Junior and R. A. Rios (Eds.): BRACIS 2022, LNAI 13654, pp. 282–296, 2022.
https://doi.org/10.1007/978-3-031-21689-3_21

transformer-based networks stand out for achieving comparable performance in various tasks. Other recent advances, such as new training methods [37] and the proposal of new architectures [24], may also contribute to an improvement in the performance of the skin lesion diagnosis.

This work aims to investigate the performance of the most recent architectures for skin lesion classification. Additionally, we investigate how these new architectures and the fusion methods can be integrated.

The key research contributions of the proposed work are listed as follows:

- we conduct extensive experiments on the open dataset PAD-UFES-20 [34] and achieved performance comparable to state-of-the-art (SOTA) methods.
- we show that transformer-based image feature extractors achieve competitive performance against CNN-based backbones to skin lesion diagnosis task.
- we show that transformer-based image extracted features can be fused with clinical information using already existent fusion methods.
- we show that recent training methods (distillation) and recent architectures (ViT [13], PiT [22] and CoaT [52]) effectively can improve performance in skin lesion diagnosis.

2 Literature Review

2.1 CNN Backbones for Image Classification

A deep convolutional neural network (CNN) model consists of several convolution layers followed by activation functions and pooling layers. Additionally, it has several fully connected layers before classification. It comes into deep structure to facilitate filtering mechanisms by performing convolutions in multi-scale feature maps, leading to highly abstract and discriminative features [15].

Several architectures have been developed since the AlexNet, considered as the foundation work of modern deep CNN, with great emphasis on architectures such as ResNet, DenseNet and EfficientNet [5]. More recently, improvements in these networks have been proposed as in ResNet V2 [21], ResNexT [51] and EfficientNet V2 [42]. In addition to the development of architectures, there are proposals for new mechanisms (e.g. Efficient Channel Attention [47]) and new training methods (e.g. Semi-weakly Supervised Learning [54], Distillation [23]).

2.2 Transformers Backbones for Image Classification

With the great success of transformer-based architectures for NLP tasks, there has recently been a great research interest in researching transformer-based architectures for computer vision [18,25,28,53]. Vision Transformer (ViT) [13] was one of the pioneers to present comparable results with the CNN architectures. Its architecture is heavily based on the original Transformer model [46] and it process the input image as a sequence of patches, as shown in Fig. 1.

Inspired by the advances achieved by the ViT model, various models and modifications (e.g. TNT [19], Swin [30], SwinV2 [29], CrossViT [9], XCiT [1],

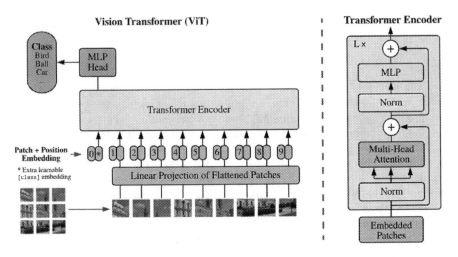

Fig. 1. ViT architecture overview (left) and details of Transformer Encoder (right) [13].

PiT [22], CaiT [44]) were proposed and presented promising results. In addition, several improvements in training methods (e.g. BeiT [2], DeiT [43], iBOT [56], DINO [8]) have also contributed to an improvement in the performance of transformer-based models.

An interesting ability of transformer-based models is that ViTs trained on ImageNet exhibit higher shape-bias in comparison to similar capacity of CNN models [31]. Transformer-based models can reach human-level shape-bias performance when trained on a stylized version of ImageNet (SIN [16]) and they can even model contradictory cues (as in shape/texture-bias) with distinct tokens [31].

2.3   Multimodal Fusion

There are some aggregation-based multimodal fusion approaches. The most common method of multimodal fusion is aggregation via concatenation of features [33]. This fusion method consists of concatenating the features into a single tensor with all features.

Channel-Exchanging-Network (CEN) [48], a parameter-free multimodal fusion framework, is another approach that proposes an exchanging in CNN channels of sub-networks. There is an intrinsic limitation in it as the framework assumes that all sub-networks are made up of a CNN architecture.

An interesting alternative is the Metadata Processing Block (MetaBlock) [32], that is an attention-based method that uses a LSTM-like gates to enhance the metadata into the feature maps extracted from an image for skin cancer classification. This method main limitation is that it is proposed for only one feature map and one metadata source and there is no clear information how to scale it for multiple sources.

Also, there is MetaNet [27], a multiplication-based data fusion to make the metadata directly interact with the visual features. It uses the metadata to control the importance of each feature channel at the last convolutional layer.

Mutual Attention Transformer (MAT) [57] uses an attention-based multi-modal fusion method (Transformer and Fusion unit) that is inspired by transformer architecture. Being proposed for only two features sources is a limitation in it. MAT presents a guided-attention module which has some similarities with the cross-attention module in the Cross-Attention Fusion [9] proposed for multi-scale feature fusion in CrossViT architecture.

3 Proposed Evaluation Methodology

Focused on investigating performance, techniques and recent architectures that bring advantage to skin lesion classification, we selected 20 models with 30M parameters or less and that needed less than 12 GB GPU memory (due to hardware limitation). In case of identical architectures and techniques, we use only the best model of them. We took the 20 best top-1 validation scores in TIMM pre-trained models collection [49] evaluated in ImageNet "Reassessed Labels" (ImageNet-ReaL) [3], the usual ImageNet-1k validation set with a fresh new set of labels intended to improve on mistakes in the original annotation process. All selected models are listed in Table 1 with their number of parameters and the kind of architecture they are based on.

For the evaluation of the models, we follow the fusion architecture as shown in Fig. 2 [33]. The input data is composed of a clinical image of the lesion and clinical information. The clinical image features are extracted by a backbone model pre-trained for general image tasks. Since we test a large range of different architectures, we need a image feature adapter to reformat it to a standard shape. That adapter consists of a 2D adaptive average pooling layer for hybrid or CNN-based image features. For transformers-based image features, the adapter only selects the class token and discard other image information, except for CrossViT that big and small class tokens are concatenated and selected. The adapter also has a flatten layer after it to properly reformat the image features to a standard shape. Next, a fusion block add clinical information to reformatted image features. In this paper we analyze four alternatives to the fusion block, i.e., Concatenation, MetaBlock, MetaNet and MAT. For a fair comparison, before the classifier, we apply a feature reducer to keep the classifier input the same size to all models, as most of those image feature extractor models have different image features size.

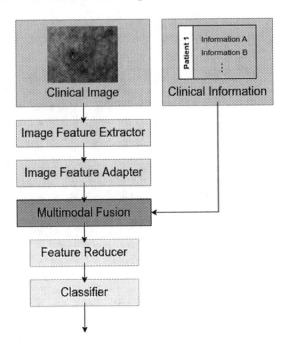

Fig. 2. Fusion architecture [32]. Multimodal Fusion layer input data composed of clinical image (after feature extractor and adapter layer) and clinical information. Feature Reducer layer keep the classifier input the same size to all models.

The selected pre-trained models are fine-tuned with supervised learning on PAD-UFES-20 dataset [34]. The dataset contains 2298 samples of 6 types of skin lesions, consisting of a clinical image collected from smartphone devices and a set of patient clinical data containing 21 features. The skin lesions are Melanoma, Basal Cell Carcinoma, Squamous Cell Carcinoma, Actinic Keratosis, Seborrheic Keratosis and Nevus. The clinical features include patient's age, skin lesion location, Fitzpatrick skin type, skin lesion diameter, family background, cancer history, among others. That dataset was chosen because it deals with multimodal data and is one of the few containing this type of information for skin lesion diagnosis. Most deal only with dermoscopic images without clinical information of the lesion.

Table 1. Number of parameters and base architecture of the top-20 selected models.

Model	Based	# of parameters	Ref.
cait_xxs24_384	Transformer	12.03 M	[44]
coat_lite_small		19.84 M	[52]
vit_small_patch16_384		22.20 M	[13,39]
tnt_s_patch16_224		23.76 M	[19]
pit_s_distilled_224		24.04 M	[22]
twins_svt_small		24.06 M	[10]
xcit_small_12_p16_384_dist		26.25 M	[1]
crossvit_15_dagger_408		28.50 M	[9]
gc_efficientnetv2_rw_t	CNN	13.68 M	[7,42]
rexnet_200		16.37 M	[17]
tf_efficientnet_b4_ns		19.34 M	[41,50]
regnety_032		19.44 M	[35]
tf_efficientnetv2_s_in21ft1k		21.46 M	[42]
eca_nfnet_l0		24.14 M	[6,47]
swsl_resnext50_32x4d		25.03 M	[51,54]
resnetv2_50x1_bit_distilled		25.55 M	[4,21,26]
ecaresnet50t		25.57 M	[20]
regnetz_d8		27.58 M	[12]
halo2botnet50ts_256	Hybrid	22.64 M	[38,45]
halonet50ts		22.73 M	[20,45]

4   Experiments

Our experiments follow the setup used in [32]. Training runs for 150 epochs using batch size 30 and reducer block size of 90. An early stop strategy is set if training for 15 epochs without improvement. We use the SGD optimizer (initial learning rate is 0.001, momentum is 0.9 and weight decay is 0.001) with reduce learning rate on plateau strategy (patience is 10, reduce factor is 0.1 and lower bound on the learning rate is 10^{-6}). For evaluation, we adopted holdout validation, using 5/6 of data for training and the remaining 1/6 of the data for testing. Next, we adopted 5-fold cross-validation on training set to generate 5 trained models. The results in Table 2 and Table 3 are average and standard deviation values of those 5 models evaluated on testing set. Source code is publicly available[1].

4.1   General Analysis

Table 2 lists the balanced accuracy (BAC) and the area under the ROC curve (AUC) of each pre-trained backbone model using Concatenation fusion. The

---

[1] https://github.com/lmlima/BRACIS2022-Exploring-Advances-for-SLD.

model "resnetv2_50x1_bit_distilled" achieved the best balanced accuracy and area under the ROC curve with 0.765 ± 0.013 and 0.934 ± 0.002, respectively. The "tf_efficientnetv2_s_in21ft1k" backbone model achieved the same best area under the ROC curve 0.934 ± 0.004.

Table 2. Top-20 selected models concatenation fusion performance ordered by balanced accuracy (BAC). Mean and standard deviation of BAC and area under the ROC curve (AUC) metrics.

Model	BAC (mean ± std dev)	AUC (mean ± std dev)
resnetv2_50x1_bit_distilled	**0.765** ± 0.013	**0.934** ± 0.002
pit_s_distilled_224	0.763 ± 0.025	0.928 ± 0.009
coat_lite_small	0.759 ± 0.024	0.929 ± 0.002
vit_small_patch16_384	0.751 ± 0.017	0.926 ± 0.011
regnety_032	0.748 ± 0.018	0.927 ± 0.010
twins_svt_small	0.747 ± 0.027	0.927 ± 0.005
ecaresnet50t	0.742 ± 0.039	0.924 ± 0.008
tf_efficientnetv2_s_in21ft1k	0.741 ± 0.027	**0.934** ± 0.004
regnetz_d8	0.739 ± 0.021	0.930 ± 0.007
gc_efficientnetv2_rw_t	0.739 ± 0.026	0.926 ± 0.010
eca_nfnet_l0	0.736 ± 0.037	0.926 ± 0.007
swsl_resnext50_32x4d	0.731 ± 0.028	0.925 ± 0.004
rexnet_200	0.728 ± 0.028	0.928 ± 0.007
xcit_small_12_p16_384_dist	0.727 ± 0.032	0.921 ± 0.010
tf_efficientnet_b4_ns	0.726 ± 0.017	0.923 ± 0.016
tnt_s_patch16_224	0.725 ± 0.025	0.925 ± 0.007
crossvit_15_dagger_408	0.718 ± 0.033	0.919 ± 0.008
halo2botnet50ts_256	0.701 ± 0.023	0.916 ± 0.011
cait_xxs24_384	0.660 ± 0.027	0.910 ± 0.006
halonet50ts	0.644 ± 0.054	0.903 ± 0.015

From the results listed in Table 2 we conclude that the use of transformer-based backbone improves skin lesion diagnosis, since in the top 5 balanced accuracy three of them are transformer-based architectures – "pit_s_distilled_224" (PiT), "coat_lite_small" (CoaT) and "vit_small_patch16_384" (ViT) – and two of them are CNN-based architectures – "resnetv2_50x1_bit_distilled" (ResNet V2) and "regnety_032" (RegNetY). It can also be noted the presence of two architectures that used the model distillation [23] technique for training.

Next, we will detail the main architectures and present the main characteristics that may have contributed to the good results in the top-5 pre-trained models.

Model Distillation. Also known as Knowledge Distillation [23], refers to the training paradigm in which a student model leverages "soft" labels coming from a strong teacher network. The output vector of the teacher's softmax function is used rather than just the maximum of scores, which gives a "hard" label. This process can be seen as a way of compressing the teacher model into a reduced student model. In transformer-based models, a distillation token can be added to the model, along class and patch tokens, and used to improve learning [43]. In the top-5 selected backbones models, "resnetv2_50x1_bit_distilled" and "pit_s_distilled_224" are pre-trained with knowledge distillation.

ResNet V2. The Residual Neural Network (ResNet) V2 [21] mainly focuses on making the second non-linearity as an identity mapping by removing the last ReLU activation function, after the addition layer, in the residual block, i.e., using the pre-activation of weight layers instead of post-activation.

The arrangement of the layers in the residual block moves the batch normalization and ReLU activation to before 2D convolution, as shown in Fig. 3.

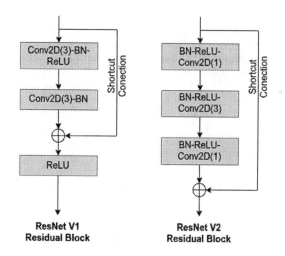

Fig. 3. Differences in residual block of ResNet versions [21].

PiT. Pooling-based Vision Transformer (PiT) architecture [22] is inspired by ResNet-style dimensions settings to improve the model performance, as shown in Fig. 4. PiT uses a newly designed pooling layer based on depth-wise convolution to achieve channel multiplication and spatial reduction.

CoaT. Co-scale conv-attentional image Transformers (CoaT) [52] is a transformer-based model equipped with co-scale and conv-attentional mecha-

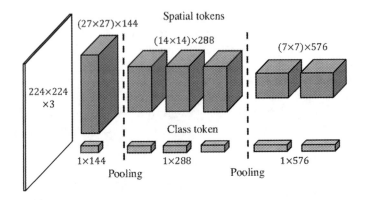

Fig. 4. Pooling-based Vision Transformer (PiT) architecture [22].

nisms. It empowers image Transformers with enriched multi-scale and contextual modeling capabilities. The conv-attentional module realize relative position embeddings with convolutions in the factorized attention module, which improves computational efficiency. CoaT designs a series of serial and parallel blocks to realize the co-scale mechanism as shown in Fig. 5. The serial block models image representations in a reduced resolution. Next, CoaT realizes the co-scale mechanism between parallel blocks in each parallel group.

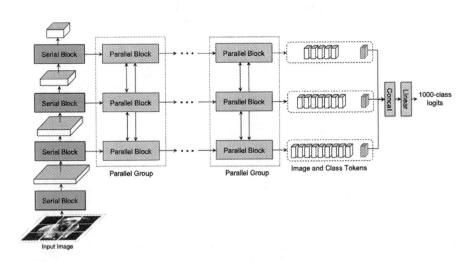

Fig. 5. Co-scale conv-attentional image Transformers (CoaT) architecture [52].

ViT. Due to the success of transformer-based architectures for NLP tasks, there has recently been a great research interest in transformer-based architectures for computer vision [18,25,28,53]. Vision Transformer (ViT) [13] was one of the pioneers to present comparable results with the CNN architectures, so far dominant. Its architecture is heavily based on the original Transformer model [46] and it process the input image as a sequence of patches, as shown in Fig. 1.

RegNetY. RegNetY [35] is one of a family of models proposed by a methodology to design network in a parametrized set of possible model architectures. Each RegNet network consists of a stem, followed by the network body that performs the bulk of the computation, and then a head (average pooling followed by a fully connected layer) that predicts n output classes. The network body is composed of a sequence of stages that operate at progressively reduced resolution. Each stage consists of a sequence of identical blocks, except the first block which uses stride-two convolution. While the general structure is simple, the total number of possible network configurations is vast. For RegNetY models, the blocks in each stage are based on the standard residual bottleneck block with group convolution and with the addition of a Squeeze and Excite Block after the group convolution, as shown in Fig. 6.

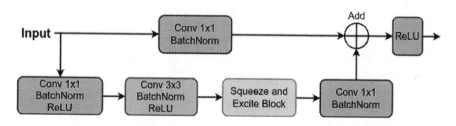

Fig. 6. Y block diagram for RegNet Y (when *stride* > 1).

4.2   Feature Fusion Analysis

Aiming to analyze alternatives to feature extraction models and their impact for the fusion of clinical image and clinical information features, the top-5 models with the best balanced accuracy in Table 2 are compared using multiple fusion methods. Each selected model is evaluated using the fusion methods: Concatenation (already presented in Table 2), MetaBlock, MetaNet and MAT. As baseline we use the best performance result in [32], which is a balanced accuracy of 0.770 ± 0.016 (EfficientNet-B4 with MetaBlock fusion) and area under the ROC curve (AUC) of 0.945 ± 0.005 (EfficientNet-B4 with Concatenation fusion). Currently, those are the best results published for PAD-UFES-20 dataset.

Results listed in Table 3 show that most of CNN-based models evaluated present a better BAC and AUC with concatenation Fusion and most of transformer-based models evaluated present a better BAC and AUC with MataBlock fusion. Analysing the balanced accuracy, "pit_s_distilled_224" (0.800 ±

0.006), "coat_lite_small" (0.780 ± 0.024) and "vit_small_patch16_384" (0.771 ± 0.018) models with MetaBlock fusion achieved SOTA results. For area under the ROC curve, "pit_s_distilled_224" (0.941±0.006) model with MetaBlock fusion provided the best mean result among the proposed models, but EfficientNet-B4 with concatenation fusion baseline obtained the best AUC among all of them. All models with highest average AUC (in bold in Table 3) did not achieve SOTA results.

Table 3. Top-5 selected models with performance comparison for the 4 fusion methods investigated. In bold is highlighted the highest average for each backbone model.

Model	BAC (mean ± std dev)	AUC (mean ± std dev)
Baseline [32]		
EfficientNet-B4 w/MetaBlock	**0.770** ± 0.016	0.944 ± 0.004
EfficientNet-B4 w/Concatenation	0.758 ± 0.012	**0.945** ± 0.005
Concatenation Fusion		
coat_lite_small	0.759 ± 0.024	0.929 ± 0.002
pit_s_distilled_224	0.763 ± 0.025	0.928 ± 0.009
regnety_032	**0.748** ± 0.018	**0.927** ± 0.010
resnetv2_50x1_bit_distilled	**0.765** ± 0.013	0.934 ± 0.002
vit_small_patch16_384	0.751 ± 0.017	0.926 ± 0.011
MAT Fusion		
coat_lite_small	0.685 ± 0.015	0.909 ± 0.009
pit_s_distilled_224	0.704 ± 0.027	0.913 ± 0.013
regnety_032	0.678 ± 0.012	0.913 ± 0.006
resnetv2_50x1_bit_distilled	0.716 ± 0.022	0.917 ± 0.007
vit_small_patch16_384	0.729 ± 0.032	0.920 ± 0.015
MetaBlock Fusion		
coat_lite_small	**0.780** ± 0.024	**0.940** ± 0.002
pit_s_distilled_224	**0.800** ± 0.006	**0.941** ± 0.006
regnety_032	0.705 ± 0.015	0.920 ± 0.005
resnetv2_50x1_bit_distilled	0.702 ± 0.015	0.918 ± 0.004
vit_small_patch16_384	**0.771** ± 0.018	0.936 ± 0.008
MetaNet Fusion		
coat_lite_small	0.732 ± 0.038	0.927 ± 0.011
pit_s_distilled_224	0.754 ± 0.028	0.932 ± 0.008
regnety_032	0.717 ± 0.013	0.923 ± 0.010
resnetv2_50x1_bit_distilled	0.752 ± 0.020	**0.936** ± 0.006
vit_small_patch16_384	0.767 ± 0.021	**0.938** ± 0.011

Our findings are not in accordance with that provided by Zhao [55], since they conclude that CNN-based models obtained better results in small datasets (840 images and 21 labels, smaller dataset than PAD-UFES-20) and here experiments indicate that transformer-based backbones achieved promising SOTA results.

5 Conclusion

Computer-aided diagnosis (CAD) has been developed aiming to provide effective models for automated skin lesions recognition. Recent advances in computer vision, as newly architectures and training methods have provided performance improvements in many tasks. This work seeks to clarify and guide researchers about which architectures and other advances present an effective improvement in skin lesion diagnosis. It also attempts to elucidate which are the most suitable pre-trained models available for the task.

The average AUC of PiT (0.941 ± 0.006) and CoaT (0.940 ± 0.002) models with MetaBlock fusion achieved competitive results. Experiments also show that PiT (0.800 ± 0.006), CoaT (0.780 ± 0.024) and ViT (0.771 ± 0.018) models with MetaBlock fusion achieved competitive results in terms of balanced accuracy. In addition, the results indicate that distillation and transformer architectures (PiT, CoaT and ViT) can improve performance in skin lesion diagnosis.

For future work, one can investigate a fusion method that takes advantage of the format of the features extracted by transformer-based backbones. Novel architectures or training methods can be further investigated.

References

1. Ali, A., et al.: XCiT: cross-covariance image transformers. In: Advances in Neural Information Processing Systems, vol. 34, pp. 20014–20027 (2021)
2. Bao, H., Dong, L., Piao, S., Wei, F.: BEiT: BERT pre-training of image transformers. In: International Conference on Learning Representations (2022)
3. Beyer, L., Hénaff, O.J., Kolesnikov, A., Zhai, X., Oord, A.V.D.: Are we done with ImageNet? arXiv preprint arXiv:2006.07159 (2020)
4. Beyer, L., Zhai, X., Royer, A., Markeeva, L., Anil, R., Kolesnikov, A.: Knowledge distillation: a good teacher is patient and consistent. In: Computer Vision and Pattern Recognition, pp. 10925–10934 (2022)
5. Bhatt, D., et al.: CNN variants for computer vision: history, architecture, application, challenges and future scope. Electronics **10**(20), 2470 (2021)
6. Brock, A., De, S., Smith, S.L., Simonyan, K.: High-performance large-scale image recognition without normalization. In: International Conference on Machine Learning, pp. 1059–1071 (2021)
7. Cao, Y., Xu, J., Lin, S., Wei, F., Hu, H.: GCNet: non-local networks meet squeeze-excitation networks and beyond. In: International Conference on Computer Vision Workshops, pp. 1971–1980 (2019)
8. Caron, M., Touvron, H., Misra, I., Jégou, H., Mairal, J., Bojanowski, P., Joulin, A.: Emerging properties in self-supervised vision transformers. In: International Conference on Computer Vision, pp. 9650–9660 (2021)

9. Chen, C.F.R., Fan, Q., Panda, R.: CrossViT: cross-attention multi-scale vision transformer for image classification. In: International Conference on Computer Vision, pp. 357–366 (2021)

10. Chu, X., et al.: Twins: revisiting the design of spatial attention in vision transformers. In: Advances in Neural Information Processing Systems, vol. 34, pp. 9355–9366 (2021)

11. Das, T., Kumar, V., Prakash, A., Lynn, A.M.: Artificial intelligence in skin cancer: diagnosis and therapy. In: Dwivedi, A., Tripathi, A., Ray, R.S., Singh, A.K. (eds.) Skin Cancer: Pathogenesis and Diagnosis, pp. 143–171. Springer, Singapore (2021). https://doi.org/10.1007/978-981-16-0364-8_9

12. Dollár, P., Singh, M., Girshick, R.: Fast and accurate model scaling. In: Computer Vision and Pattern Recognition, pp. 924–932 (2021)

13. Dosovitskiy, A., et al.: An image is worth 16×16 words: transformers for image recognition at scale. In: International Conference on Learning Representations (2020)

14. Feng, H., Berk-Krauss, J., Feng, P.W., Stein, J.A.: Comparison of dermatologist density between urban and rural counties in the united states. JAMA Dermatol. **154**(11), 1265–1271 (2018)

15. Feng, X., Jiang, Y., Yang, X., Du, M., Li, X.: Computer vision algorithms and hardware implementations: a survey. Integration **69**, 309–320 (2019)

16. Geirhos, R., Rubisch, P., Michaelis, C., Bethge, M., Wichmann, F.A., Brendel, W.: ImageNet-trained CNNs are biased towards texture; increasing shape bias improves accuracy and robustness. In: International Conference on Learning Representations (2019)

17. Han, D., Yun, S., Heo, B., Yoo, Y.: Rethinking channel dimensions for efficient model design. In: Computer Vision and Pattern Recognition, pp. 732–741 (2021)

18. Han, K., et al.: A survey on vision transformer. Pattern Anal. Mach. Intell. (2022)

19. Han, K., Xiao, A., Wu, E., Guo, J., Xu, C., Wang, Y.: Transformer in transformer. In: Advances in Neural Information Processing Systems, vol. 34, pp. 15908–15919 (2021)

20. He, K., Zhang, X., Ren, S., Sun, J.: Deep residual learning for image recognition. In: Computer Vision and Pattern Recognition, pp. 770–778 (2016)

21. He, K., Zhang, X., Ren, S., Sun, J.: Identity mappings in deep residual networks. In: Leibe, B., Matas, J., Sebe, N., Welling, M. (eds.) ECCV 2016. LNCS, vol. 9908, pp. 630–645. Springer, Cham (2016). https://doi.org/10.1007/978-3-319-46493-0_38

22. Heo, B., Yun, S., Han, D., Chun, S., Choe, J., Oh, S.J.: Rethinking spatial dimensions of vision transformers. In: International Conference on Computer Vision, pp. 11936–11945 (2021)

23. Hinton, G., Vinyals, O., Dean, J.: Distilling the knowledge in a neural network. arXiv preprint arXiv:1503.02531 (2015)

24. Karthik, R., Vaichole, T.S., Kulkarni, S.K., Yadav, O., Khan, F.: Eff2Net: an efficient channel attention-based convolutional neural network for skin disease classification. Biomed. Signal Process. Control **73**, 103406 (2022)

25. Khan, S., Naseer, M., Hayat, M., Zamir, S.W., Khan, F.S., Shah, M.: Transformers in vision: a survey. ACM Comput. Surv. **54**, 1–41 (2021)

26. Kolesnikov, A., et al.: Big transfer (BiT): general visual representation learning. In: Vedaldi, A., Bischof, H., Brox, T., Frahm, J.-M. (eds.) ECCV 2020. LNCS, vol. 12350, pp. 491–507. Springer, Cham (2020). https://doi.org/10.1007/978-3-030-58558-7_29

27. Li, W., Zhuang, J., Wang, R., Zhang, J., Zheng, W.S.: Fusing metadata and dermoscopy images for skin disease diagnosis. In: International Symposium on Biomedical Imaging, pp. 1996–2000. IEEE (2020)
28. Liu, Y., et al.: A survey of visual transformers. arXiv preprint arXiv:2111.06091 (2021)
29. Liu, Z., et al.: Swin transformer V2: scaling up capacity and resolution. In: Computer Vision and Pattern Recognition, pp. 12009–12019 (2022)
30. Liu, Z., et al.: Swin transformer: hierarchical vision transformer using shifted windows. In: International Conference on Computer Vision, pp. 10012–10022 (2021)
31. Naseer, M., Ranasinghe, K., Khan, S., Hayat, M., Khan, F., Yang, M.H.: Intriguing properties of vision transformers. In: Advances in Neural Information Processing Systems, vol. 34, pp. 23296–23308 (2021)
32. Pacheco, A.G., Krohling, R.A.: An attention-based mechanism to combine images and metadata in deep learning models applied to skin cancer classification. IEEE J. Biomed. Health Inform. **25**(9), 3554–3563 (2021)
33. Pacheco, A.G., Krohling, R.A.: The impact of patient clinical information on automated skin cancer detection. Comput. Biol. Med. **116**, 103545 (2020)
34. Pacheco, A.G., et al.: PAD-UFES-20: a skin lesion dataset composed of patient data and clinical images collected from smartphones. Data Brief **32**, 106221 (2020)
35. Radosavovic, I., Kosaraju, R.P., Girshick, R., He, K., Dollár, P.: Designing network design spaces. In: Computer Vision and Pattern Recognition, pp. 10428–10436 (2020)
36. Scheffler, R.M., Liu, J.X., Kinfu, Y., Dal Poz, M.R.: Forecasting the global shortage of physicians: an economic-and needs-based approach. Bull. World Health Organ. **86**, 516-523B (2008)
37. Sirotkin, K., Viñolo, M.E., Carballeira, P., SanMiguel, J.C.: Improved skin lesion recognition by a self-supervised curricular deep learning approach. arXiv preprint arXiv:2112.12086 (2021)
38. Srinivas, A., Lin, T.Y., Parmar, N., Shlens, J., Abbeel, P., Vaswani, A.: Bottleneck transformers for visual recognition. In: Computer Vision and Pattern Recognition, pp. 16519–16529 (2021)
39. Steiner, A., Kolesnikov, A., Zhai, X., Wightman, R., Uszkoreit, J., Beyer, L.: How to train your ViT? Data, augmentation, and regularization in vision transformers. arXiv preprint arXiv:2106.10270 (2021)
40. Takiddin, A., Schneider, J., Yang, Y., Abd-Alrazaq, A., Househ, M., et al.: Artificial intelligence for skin cancer detection: scoping review. J. Med. Internet Res. **23**(11), e22934 (2021)
41. Tan, M., Le, Q.: EfficientNet: rethinking model scaling for convolutional neural networks. In: International Conference on Machine Learning, pp. 6105–6114 (2019)
42. Tan, M., Le, Q.: EfficientNetV2: smaller models and faster training. In: International Conference on Machine Learning, vol. 139, pp. 10096–10106 (2021)
43. Touvron, H., Cord, M., Douze, M., Massa, F., Sablayrolles, A., Jégou, H.: Training data-efficient image transformers & distillation through attention. In: International Conference on Machine Learning, pp. 10347–10357 (2021)
44. Touvron, H., Cord, M., Sablayrolles, A., Synnaeve, G., Jégou, H.: Going deeper with image transformers. In: International Conference on Computer Vision, pp. 32–42 (2021)
45. Vaswani, A., Ramachandran, P., Srinivas, A., Parmar, N., Hechtman, B., Shlens, J.: Scaling local self-attention for parameter efficient visual backbones. In: Computer Vision and Pattern Recognition, pp. 12894–12904 (2021)

46. Vaswani, A., et al.: Attention is all you need. In: Advances in Neural Information Processing Systems, vol. 30, pp. 5998–6008 (2017)
47. Wang, Q., Wu, B., Zhu, P., Li, P., Zuo, W., Hu, Q.: ECA-Net: efficient channel attention for deep convolutional neural networks. In: Computer Vision and Pattern Recognition, pp. 13–19 (2020)
48. Wang, Y., Huang, W., Sun, F., Xu, T., Rong, Y., Huang, J.: Deep multimodal fusion by channel exchanging. In: Advances in Neural Information Processing Systems, vol. 33, pp. 4835–4845 (2020)
49. Wightman, R.: PyTorch image models. https://github.com/rwightman/pytorch-image-models (2019). https://doi.org/10.5281/zenodo.4414861
50. Xie, Q., Luong, M.T., Hovy, E., Le, Q.V.: Self-training with noisy student improves ImageNet classification. In: Computer Vision and Pattern Recognition, pp. 10687–10698 (2020)
51. Xie, S., Girshick, R., Dollár, P., Tu, Z., He, K.: Aggregated residual transformations for deep neural networks. In: Computer Vision and Pattern Recognition, pp. 1492–1500 (2017)
52. Xu, W., Xu, Y., Chang, T., Tu, Z.: Co-scale conv-attentional image transformers. In: International Conference on Computer Vision, pp. 9981–9990 (2021)
53. Xu, Y., et al.: Transformers in computational visual media: a survey. Comput. Vis. Media 8(I), 33–62 (2022)
54. Yalniz, I.Z., Jégou, H., Chen, K., Paluri, M., Mahajan, D.: Billion-scale semi-supervised learning for image classification. arXiv preprint arXiv:1905.00546 (2019)
55. Zhao, P., Li, C., Rahaman, M.M., Yang, H., Jiang, T., Grzegorzek, M.: A comparison of deep learning classification methods on small-scale image data set: from convolutional neural networks to visual transformers. arXiv preprint arXiv:2107.07699 (2021)
56. Zhou, J., Wei, C., Wang, H., Shen, W., Xie, C., Yuille, A., Kong, T.: iBOT: image BERT pre-training with online tokenizer. In: International Conference on Learning Representations (2022)
57. Zhou, L., Luo, Y.: Deep features fusion with mutual attention transformer for skin lesion diagnosis. In: International Conference on Image Processing (ICIP), pp. 3797–3801 (2021)

A Comparative Study of Federated Versus Centralized Learning for Time Series Prediction in IoT

Lia Sucupira Furtado[2], Leonardo Ferreira da Costa[1(✉)],
Paulo Henrique Gonçalves Rocha[1], and Paulo Antonio Leal Rego[1]

[1] Federal University of Ceara, Fortaleza, Brazil
leonardo.costa@alu.ufc.br, paulorocha@great.ufc.br, pauloalr@ufc.br
[2] Université de Lyon 2, Lyon, France
lia.furtado@univ-lyon2.fr

Abstract. IoT devices have become increasingly popular in the last few years due to the potential of their sensors to feed data and provide insights into various applications in many fields. Today, such sensors are used in health care, environmental forecasting, and finance systems, to name a few. Predictive algorithms can leverage the temporal data provided by IoT sensors to enrich real-time applications to, for example, predict CO2 and temperature levels in a given region and provide public alerts. In this context, to find out the best solution for predicting time series generated from data collected by IoT devices, this work evaluates two machine learning approaches: federated learning and centralized learning. Federated learning implies training the algorithms in a distributed way across devices, while centralized learning takes data from devices into a server and focuses training on it. We performed experiments using Long Short Term Memory (LSTM) to predict the time series with federated and centralized strategies. The results show that the Federated Learning model predicts five time-steps of a time series with, on average, 78% less mean squared error and intakes 86% less communication load in the network than a Centralized solution.

Keywords: Centralized learning · Federated learning · LSTM · Time series

1 Introduction

Traditional Machine Learning (ML) schemes in Internet of Things (IoT) use Centralized Learning (CL), an approach to training a ML model in a central data center with data collected from heterogeneous participating devices. This requires transferring distributed data from a large number of IoT devices to this central third-party location. In addition, the cost of device communication can be expensive due to the large size of data over the network and the lack of data privacy (especially for sensitive data). To circumvent these problems, the

J. C. Xavier-Junior and R. A. Rios (Eds.): BRACIS 2022, LNAI 13654, pp. 297–311, 2022.
https://doi.org/10.1007/978-3-031-21689-3_22

Federated Learning (FL) alternative was created, which allows calculations to be performed within the data source devices with distributed ML algorithms.

FL is an approach to train the ML models directly in the user's devices with their own data, so there is no need to send the data to a centralized server. Thus, the computational power of the training process is distributed spatially. IoT has become one of the most important data sources in our connected environment because of the ability to monitor buildings, nature, transportation, and more [18]. That said, these large volumes of data collected are useful for ML applications, especially, more distributed implementations.

FL also exploits the massive amount of user-generated data samples on IoT devices to train a globally shared model on-device [17]. However, this can be a challenge because IoT devices have extremely limited capabilities, and model training might require a much larger computational and memory capacity than these simple equipment can provide [3]. This is why it is important to analyze the viability and performance of training a predictive model locally in this scenario. Moreover, depending on the application load, it is worthy to use a centralized approach that requires less computational power from devices. Since both these approaches have different constraints, it is important to analyze which one is more suited for our problem.

The study of air quality in indoor facilities is important due to the potential effects that high concentrations of some gases can cause to human health and performance when exposed for a long period of time. Especially the CO2 gas, which, in high indoor concentrations, can increase headache intensity, sleepiness, fatigue, and concentration difficulty [19]. Thus, being able to forecast an air pollutant in educational facilities is primordial due to the fact that students spend a substantial amount of their time (6–7 h per day) in schools. In this context, pollution data can be collected by IoT sensors that can feed ML models for prediction.

The main objective of this work is to compare the performance of two different ML approaches (CL and FL) to create a model for predicting time-series data. In addition, another objective is to assess the device requirements needed to apply each solution in an IoT environment. To validate the solutions in a real-world scenario, we used indoor air quality data from a school in Barcelona, Spain to predict five-hour emission of carbon dioxide (CO2) levels.

The contributions of this work are summarized as follows:

- We compare FL and CL frameworks using real systems (virtual instances) to develop a deep learning model;
- We implemented a Long Short Term Memory (LSTM) capable of predicting five time steps from time series data;
- We present experimental results to show device resource requirements to train a deep learning model;
- We make code and data available to the community in a publicly accessible repository. Available in https://github.com/liasucf/federated_centralized_improved.

This work is organized as follows: In Sect. 2, the related works were presented. In Sect. 3, we have the preparations for the performance evaluation tests. In Sect. 4, the results were presented. Finally, in Sect. 5, we have the conclusion.

2   Related Work

Liu et al. [8] introduce a new communication-efficient on-device FL-based deep anomaly detection framework for sensing time-series data in IoT. The FL framework runs in a simulation of 10 edge devices running in a single Ubuntu machine.

In the work of [2], the FL approach is evaluated by verifying the impact of different parameters of computer networks on the performance of convolutional neural networks (CNNs) that use this methodology. The results showed the potential of federated learning to maintain users' privacy and still achieve accuracy rates close to the centralized case.

In the work of [14], they present a novel privacy-by-design federated stacked long short-time memory model for anomaly detection in smart buildings using IoT sensor data. Moreover, they too compare the Federated and Centralized approach using a Deep Learning model to detect anomalies and build a FL framework with simulated devices. Their results show that the federated LSTM model can reduce the loss function significantly and reach a stable performance two times faster than the centralized counterpart.

Kourtellis et al. propose a FL as a Service (FLaaS) system, enabling different scenarios of a 3rd-party application collaborative model addressing permission, privacy management, and usability challenges. They deploy their solution in mobile Android phones to assess the practical overheads of running such a service on mobiles. One of the contributions of this work was the realization of an experimental investigation of on-device training costs of FL modeling on actual real-systems mobile devices. They evaluated the implementation for ML Performance, Execution Time, Memory Consumption, and CPU Utilization to measure these costs [6].

In [18], the authors presented the FL framework in healthcare IoT devices. Considering a large amount of health care-sensitive data in these devices, they decided to implement a more data-private and secure approach compared to Traditional Centralized Machine Learning. The authors show that the federated learning framework for healthcare IoT devices reduced the computational load and communication overhead between the IoT devices and the server.

In the work of [11], they use LSTM models to predict the air quality in the region of Madrid. They build alternative setups of the LSTM network by changing the layer's size, neurons, and architectural structure. During the experiments, they train with data of different pollutant types and locations to analyze the performance of the LSTM model in as disparate as possible time-series data.

This work combines all the main features of the cited related works. We perform a Federated and Centralized learning comparison using an experimental environment with real devices as our participant clients. We also analyze the device's resources required to execute each learning approach. And finally, we apply an ML model (LSTM) to solve our time-series prediction problem. Table 1 summarizes each related work's similarities and differences compared to this work.

Table 1. Comparison of the related works with this works key features

Work	FL and CL comparison	Device resources requirement analysis	FL with IoT devices	LSTM for prediction
Liu et al. 2020	Yes	No	No	Yes
Bochie et al. 2021	Yes	Yes	Yes	No
Sater and Hamza 2021	Yes	No	No	Yes
Kourtellis et al. 2020	No	Yes	No	No
Yuan et al. 2020	Yes	No	Yes	No
Navares and Aznarte 2020	No	No	No	Yes
This work	Yes	Yes	Yes	Yes

3   Methodology

The steps described in Fig. 1 were followed to compare the FL and CL approaches for a time series forecasting problem.

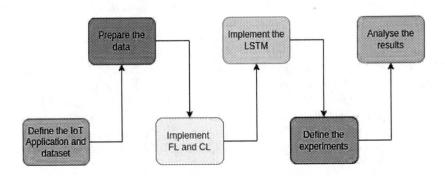

Fig. 1. Flow diagram that represents the steps performed to achieve the objective.

First, we defined the data to be used in this work, which was then collected and prepared for the experiments. In the third step, we implemented the FL and CL structures. Next, we defined the environment where the experiments were conducted. And finally, we analyzed the results obtained in the experiments. The following subsections present details of the steps performed.

3.1   Dataset

A dataset was collected that contained information on the building's indoor climate and air quality. Data were collected by sensors on IoT devices from the internal monitoring systems of schools in Barcelona, Spain. In these data, carbon dioxide was used as a metric to measure the quality of the air level in these environments. The choice of the dataset is due to the fact that the data collected by these sensors are multivariate, in addition to being quite voluminous due to the number of captures, which is a very interesting case study for experimentation.

The data collected in this study were obtained through a real-time online platform that collects environmental information such as air quality and climate called SmartCitizen[1]. This platform is a crowdsourced project in a collaborative effort between the Fab Lab of Barcelona and the Institute of Advanced Architecture of Catalonia. A SmartCitizen kit can be deployed by ordinary citizens to monitor the status of the environment. It is equipped with low-cost Arduino-based sensors to monitor temperature, light intensity, sound levels, CO2 and eTVOC.

The features collected by the sensors include: Light (Lux), Noise (dBA), Air Temperature (ºC), Humidity (%), Barometric Pressure (kPa), PM 2.5 (ug/m3), PM 10 (ug/m3), PM 1 (ug/m3), eCO2 (ppm) and TVOC (ppb). The example chosen for this work consists of the collections carried out at the Vila Olímpica School, Barcelona, Spain. The dataset consists of 4963 captures and is 436 KB in size. The data was collected every hour from the study period of 2020-03-15 to 2020-07-07.

CO2 levels are also considered for classification, they can be categorized as shown in Table 2 [4].

Table 2. Summary of the consequences to the human health the exposure of each of the three levels of CO2 concentration and their class accordingly.

Levels in the air (ppm)	Potential health consequences	Class
<1000	Typical concentration of indoor spaces with good air exchange so no harm to the human health	**Good**
1000–1500	Complaints of drowsiness and poor air	**Minor Problems**
1000–1500	Headaches, sleepiness and stagnant, stale, stuffy air. Poor concentration, loss of attention, increased heart rate and slight nausea may also be present	**Hazardous**

3.2 LSTM

The LSTM deep neural network was chosen for time series prediction as it can provide better results than parametric models or other recurrent neural networks when dealing with complex autocorrelation sequences, large data sets and the probability distribution of the underlying process is unknown using standard parametric methods [5].

The LSTM was implemented using the Python language [16] with the help of PyTorch [12], Skorch [15], and Scikit-learn [13] libraries.

---

[1] https://smartcitizen.me/.

The LSTM has one LSTM Layer with 50 hidden cells, one Dropout layer of $p = 0.5$ to prevent overfitting, and one Dense Layer to flatten the output. We used an epoch of 300 and a batch size of 8 samples. As the gradient-based optimizer that minimizes the loss function, we use the Stochastic Gradient Descent (SGD) algorithm. The learning rate parameter is set to 0.01.

For training and testing, the features used were the internal temperature in Celsius (ºC), humidity in (%), and eTVOC (ppb) for the prediction of CO2 (ppm).

The data set was prepared to be used in a multivariate time series forecasting problem. This problem uses more than one variable (resources) and their n_{input_time} time-steps as the model input to predict the n_{output_time} time-steps of the target variable.

In order for these time steps to be considered, a sliding window method is implemented. In this method, given an observation x at time t, a spatial vector is constructed with n previous values $x_t, x_{t-1}, ..., x_{t-n+1}$ with n denoting the length of the sliding window. Thus, in a multivariate time series, the input features of the dataset are arranged in the input matrix of size $f * n$, where f is the total number of features and n is the length of the sliding window. The predicted value y has the same vector structure as $y_t, y_{t+1}, ..., y_{t+k}$, where t is the time interval of the target value and k is the number of output samples, which correspond to the k-sample prediction.

The input vector is an array in the form of $[n_{samples}, n_{features} * n_{input\_time}]$. The size of n_{input_time} is the length of the sliding window. The output vector takes the form of $[n_{samples}, n_{output\_time}]$, where n_{output_time} number of output time is the value of the time steps we want to predict.

In addition, the outliers identified by the sklearn LocalOutliers algorithm were removed. Resource time series are standardized by removing the mean and scaling to the unity range. Sequentially, the data is split in a time series cross-validation. In this technique, is chosen k number of divisions and in the kth division, it first returns k folds as a train set and the $(k+1)th$ fold as a test set. In our work, we split the data into five folds with $k = 5$.

Each of the models was trained syncrementally in each round of communication with additional data. This method is often used in real-time applications where the model needs to learn from new data all the time. As IoT devices typically produce a large amount of data on the device, we decided to apply this method to prepare our model to be fed new data on each iteration. The training and testing splits are updated according to the iteration.

3.3   FL and CL Structures

Based on the state-of-the-art FedAvg approach [9], FL algorithm execution starts initially on the server machine. A socket with an IP address is created on the server and waits for clients to connect via that IP address. In our solution, the customers were four instances of AWS Linux ARMV8 running the docker container to run the Python algorithm. Each of these clients connects to the server marking the opening point of the communication flow. Then the server randomly chooses a portion (C) of the clients to whom it sends the initial values of the prediction model.

At the beginning, each client contains a dataset. Then, each of the chosen clients receives the initial model and the dataset is divided in a cross-validation method into training and test data. Training is done on each training batch separately, several times according to the defined epoch. Then the parameters are updated to reduce the loss error value obtained during data prediction. When the training finally ends, the client sends the updated model to the server. In each round, the data is incremented because in IoT devices, data is constantly produced on the device.

Communication between devices occurs synchronously, so the server communicates separately with each client and waits until each client has sent its locally trained model parameters, then performs the Federated Average of the model parameter, and as result, you get the world model. This decision was made by comparing it to asynchronous FL, a solution where the server updates the global model whenever it receives a local update from the client.

If the maximum number of communication rounds is not reached, the generalized model becomes the new initial model, and a fraction (C) of the clients are randomly sent for training (four clients in our experiments). This process can be repeated several times until the desired precision or the maximum number of iterations is reached.

At the end, when the number of communication rounds is reached, the global model is sent to all the participants' machines so that they can use it as their learning model.

Within these devices, the predictive model is trained in an FL approach. When the models finish training, the devices send the model parameters to the aggregator. Finally, the aggregator sends the global model to be used in each device for the prediction of carbon dioxide levels in schools. Depending on the threshold of these levels, precautionary measures need to be taken by the building administrators.

When running the FedAVG algorithm, settings are important. As explained, only a fraction of customers equal to $C*K$ are chosen in each round to participate in the global weight update model, where K is the total number of customers.

Implementing CL is the standard ML operation. Clients are connected to the server through a socket. Each client sends its current local data to the server. The training takes place inside the central device (server) and when finished, the global model is sent to the clients. This process is repeated when the server receives more data from the clients. The server only starts training when it has all the client data. The output is a single universal forecasting model made by collecting data from all customers.

The data on each client is incremented over time, as it would in a real-time application, so with each round of communication, more data is sent to the server.

To use a predictive model as a model for the five-hour forecast of carbon dioxide in the Centralized solution, we reorganized our data at the input. Considering that each client sends data with three characteristics (temperature, humidity and eTOV) to the server and there are four clients with data from the school, the input vector is represented by $[n\_samples, n\_input\_time\ n\_features]$ and the output vector has the form of $[\ n\_samples, n\_output\_time]$. In our case $n\_samples = 4963$, $n\_features = 3$, $n\_output\_time = 5$ and $n\_input\_time = 5$. The training settings were the same used for the Federated Learning System.

3.4   Metrics

The performance of predictive models was evaluated by mean absolute error (MAE) and mean square error (MSE) criteria, as shown in the Eqs. 1 and 2, respectively.

$$MAE = \frac{1}{n}\sum_{i=1}^{n}|\alpha_i - \dot{\alpha}_i| \tag{1}$$

$$MSE = \frac{1}{n}\sum_{i=1}^{n}(\alpha_i - \dot{\alpha}_i)^2 \tag{2}$$

The classification for the level of CO2 in the air will have the performance measured by accuracy.

Accuracy is a metric used for evaluating classification problems, as shown in the Eq. 3.

$$Accuracy = \frac{Number\_of\_correct\_predictions}{Total\_of\_Predictions} \tag{3}$$

Since the dataset has a significant disparity in the number of samples in each class of CO2 (Table 2), we use the precision and recall classification metrics.

Precision metrics focus on the positive identifications of your classification, and recall in the proportion of current positive identifications. The Eqs. 4 and 5 define, respectively, these two metrics.

$$Precision = \frac{True\_Positive}{True\_Positive + False\_Positive} \tag{4}$$

$$Recall = \frac{True\_Positive}{True\_Positive + False\_Negative} \tag{5}$$

In an effort to analyze the device's resource expenses, we collected the information on memory, CPU, and network traffic requirements. We used the percentage of CPU rate utilization (%), the RAM usage (MB), and the training time as measures for analyzing the computational load of each device. Furthermore, we collect the total time taken to receive bytes by the server by summing each communication round to estimate communication expenses.

3.5 Experiment Setup

The experiments were performed using five Amazon Web Services [1] (AWS) ARMV8 instances, which consisted of four instances that acted as clients and one that acted as a server. Each client is connected to the server through a socket bound by an IP and port. The server in had the Linux OS system, two CPU cores, 4 GB of RAM and is located in São Paulo. In order to evaluate the behavior of the devices in each approach, we decided to configure two scenarios for the clients. In the first scenario, described in Table 3, the clients vary among themselves in terms of ram, in order to verify the influence of this hardware resource in the experiments and identify the minimum acceptable. And in the second scenario, described in Table 4, the clients vary among themselves in terms of location with the objective of verifying the influence of the distance in the communication between the devices.

Usually, in IoT devices, the data is produced locally. This generation can be by a user or sensor information gathering. This way, in our environment, each client contains the data of the Spanish school.

The algorithms are packaged in a lightweight Docker [10] image that occupies only 1.32 GB with all the packages installed, dependencies, and files necessary to run in ARM architecture. This way, our AWS instances to run the algorithms need a maximum of 3.5 GB of HD (with all the extra O.S and libraries space).

Table 3. Summary of the Instances with different memories settings.

Client	Architecture	OS	HD	CPU cores	RAM	Location
1	ARM64	Linux	8 GB	2	1 GB	São Paulo
2	ARM64	Linux	8 GB	2	2 GB	São Paulo
3	ARM64	Linux	8 GB	2	4 GB	São Paulo
4	ARM64	Linux	8 GB	2	8 GB	São Paulo

Table 4. Summary of the Instances with different location settings.

Client	Architecture	OS	HD	CPU cores	RAM	Location
1	ARM64	Linux	8 GB	2	1 GB	Frankfurt
2	ARM64	Linux	8 GB	2	1 GB	London
3	ARM64	Linux	8 GB	2	1 GB	Ohio
4	ARM64	Linux	8 GB	2	1 GB	California

4 Results

Firstly, we introduced a scenario to measure the effect of devices with different memory configurations in the federated and centralized approach.

In the experimentation using the FL framework, we obtained the effort of each device measured by their memory, CPU utilization, and time to communicate with the server. Because in the FL framework, only a fraction of the clients participates in a communication round, some clients train less data locally than others. For example, we had a client that trained over 4000 samples in the last iteration and another that trained 1846 samples. These specifications and results are shown in Table 5. This experiment with 5 communication rounds lasted 33 min and the final model parameters that were sent by the server had 59KB.

Table 5. Specifications and Results of Training the LSTM model using the FL.

Client	Train	Test	Training time	CPU (%)
1	2848	773	08 min31 s	14.6
2	2805	783	07 min27 s	18.7
3	1846	775	04 min47 s	25.6
4	4267	762	12 min05 s	49.3

Given this result, we can see that the client 4 used a big percentage of its CPU capacity available. We noticed that this is directly affected by the amount of data used for training. Additionally, training a model with over 4000 samples requires around 50% of an instance with 2 CPU cores. In the case of 1 CPU core, this training process would overload the equipment.

On other hand, we did the experiments in the same configured environment with the CL solution. The clients in this process didn't have relevant CPU utilization because in this approach, the training process happened internally in the server. The total execution time was 24 min, and the number of bytes was 436 KB, which corresponds to the size of the 4963 samples transferred from a client to the server. The training time in the last round was 10 min. In order to build a universal model in a centralized way, we needed to use the same size of train and test data for all the clients. This way, the train data was 3971 samples, and the test size was 992 samples. We notice that the CL framework takes less time to complete the execution than the corresponding FL. This usually happens because it is not susceptible to different heterogeneous clients' computational abilities and depends only on the central server.

The main goal of our Deep Learning model was to predict five hours of carbon dioxide in each of your instances with their test samples. Therefore, we used some evaluation metrics usual for time-prediction problems, the Mean-Squared Error (MSE) and the Mean Absolute Error (MAE). The results of the prediction evaluation in both learning frameworks are in Table 6. Moreover, we also have communication time and memory utilization.

Table 6. Evaluation of prediction error (MSE and MAE) and requirements (Communication time and RAM utilization) for both FL and CL.

Client	MSE	MAE	Communication time (s)	RAM utilization (MB)
FL				
1	0.1745	0.2651	1.0241	312
2	0.0369	0.1264	1.0819	315
3	0.0077	0.0591	0.9705	278
4	0.0382	0.1221	1.1745	373
CL				
1	0.2877	0.3736	0.0263	104
2	0.2877	0.3736	0.0263	104
3	0.2877	0.3736	0.0263	104
4	0.2877	0.3736	0.0263	104

The communication time is measured given how many seconds it took for the server to receive the information sent by the client. In CL, this information is the raw data, and in FL, it is the model parameters used in the model aggregation.

From the comparison of the two approaches in Table 6, we can see that FL has the lowest error rates among the clients. Therefore, this approach using our LSTM configured model is capable of predicting with an average of 0.0643 MSE. On the other hand, the CL prediction gives a 0.2877 MSE by averaging the errors of all four clients. Considering this, the FL builds a model that predicts five hours of CO2 with close to 78% less error than the CL.

Depending on the client, we had an increase of 145% of the mean absolute error in predicting five-hours of gas. Even though this error tends to be higher in time-series with inconstant patterns, the MAE didn't decrease in any client compared to the FL framework. Thus, our Deep Learning model loses performance when trained using the CL approach.

Considering the communication costs, the work of [9] states that these costs of sending the updates to the server are often higher than computational expenses. Nowadays, computing complex models with big dimensionality of data are less expensive because the devices have a higher computational power. However, the communication costs to send high dimensions of data are still costly.

We had that for the CL approach 436KB was sent to the server by each client, putting a load of approximately 1.8 MB in the network with the data transfer of the four clients. On the other hand, the FL only transferred 59 KB (approximately 86% less) related to the updated model parameters. This happened because the model parameters dimension was smaller than the sample data.

In Table 7, we have the results of the classification of each client's prediction. We show the predicted label obtained from the test set. Also, we have the accuracy, the mean of the precision, and the recall in each label.

Table 7. Results of the Classification of predicted values in Good, Minor Problems and Hazardous evaluated by the accuracy, mean recall and mean precision.

Client	Accuracy (%)	Mean precision (%)	Mean Recall (%)
FL			
1	87.19	77.78%	76.06%
2	89.63	78.93%	75.45%
3	86.04	80.74%	71.47%
4	89.05	81.30%	72.64%
CL			
1	85.63	76.61%	49.85%
2	85.63	76.61%	49.85%
3	85.63	76.61%	49.85%
4	85.63	76.61%	49.85%

The FL framework manages to build a LSTM model which is capable of classifying with an average accuracy of approximately 88%. And CL got a slightly lower average accuracy of approximately 86%.

Due to precision and recall metrics, the centralized model proved to be inferior to all the possibilities generated by each client of the federated model in the classification of air quality by the amount of CO_2.

According to [7], the FL framework makes more efficient use of network bandwidth and provides lower latency, especially in close to real-time applications, because there is no need to send large data volumes to the server.

Lastly, we have a scenario where the instances are in different locations of the world. Our learning approaches are dependent on the communication between the instances for the transfer of model parameters or sample data and this communication is affected by the distance between devices. This way it is important to analyze the degree of this influence. Therefore we configured the clients with the same OS, CPU cores, and RAM so the only difference was their location.

Since the LSTM model, data and parameters are the same, the model performance was equal to that shown in the first scenario. However, in other instances resource metrics were relevant to be monitored. In Table 8 we can see the communication time and memory usage of this environment setup.

We compare the results of memory usage in both scenarios and noticed that it barely changed even with the configuration of the instance being different. Moreover, the memory usage of CL instances is around 3 times less than the FL, notably because they don't train the LSTM locally. Although the AWS network infrastructure doesn't have the same congestion as a wireless network, the location of the instances highly affected the communication costs.

We provide in Fig. 2 a comparison of the communication time in the First and Second Scenario in the FL Framework. From the table, we can easily see that the AWS instances location actively affects the communication time. In this

Table 8. Results of the communication time and memory utilization of each client in FL and CL during the second scenario experiments.

Client	Communication time (s)	RAM utilization (MB)
FL		
1	1.6909	314
2	2.7482	314
3	1.9654	280
4	2.2310	370
CL		
1	1.0555	103
2	1.2371	103
3	0.7625	104
4	0.7537	103

experiment, the data transferred size was the same in both scenarios, but some clients took twice as much time to send the model parameters in the second scenario.

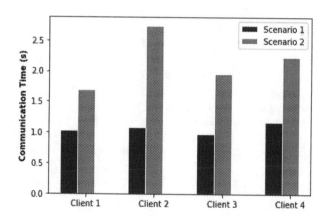

Fig. 2. Comparison of the communication time in the First and Second Scenario in the FL.

Considering that the communication over an unstable wireless network with limited bandwidth is costly, the communication time between devices very far apart in this network would be much longer than what we obtained by testing in the AWS infrastructure.

5 Conclusion

In this work, we have performed the comparison of two ML approaches: FL and CL. This is important because either a distributed or centralized solution can be more suited depending on the scenario. Additionally, we assessed the necessary device requirements to participate in each framework, especially, to train a DL model on device.

In CL, the instances need only 100 MB to send the data to the server and can train 5 communication rounds in half the time than in FL. However, the size of the information sent in each communication round is really high achieving close to 1 GB for 4000 samples. Moreover, the CL model has a much higher MAE compared to the FL.

That said, a CL approach is more suited when the instance's resources are very limited and a small execution time is required at the expense of losing in performance and communication load.

We also show that training a deep learning model on a device with limited resources is possible in an FL framework. An IoT ARM device needs 50% of 2 CPU cores powers and close to 400 MB of RAM memory reserved to train a Deep Learning model with 4000 samples.

This way, this solution can be deployed for an IoT system with connected devices such as mobile telephones, Raspberry Pi, and development boards.

In conclusion, we found that the FL approach loads the network with 84% less KB and can build models that predict five time-steps of the time series with 40% less error than the corresponding CL approach on ARM instances in 5 communication rounds, in less than 1 h and across 4 devices. As such, FL proves to be the best approach for an IoT application to predict time-series data using a DL model. In the FL framework, we built a LSTM model capable of predicting with 10% of mean squared error (MSE).

There are still some drawbacks to this research, which can be addressed in future works. First, deploying real devices such as Raspberry Pi instead of virtual instances in the ML frameworks will be useful to explore if the device requirements are the same or if the processing power of cloud instances is higher. Second, running the experiments in a wireless network will enable an additional analysis of the system communication functionally, especially, the relation of communication time with the size of information sent between the devices.

Acknowledgment. This study was financed in part by the Coordenação de Aperfeiçoamento de Pessoal de Nível Superior - Brasil (CAPES) - Finance Code 001.

The authors would like to thank The Ceará State Foundation for the Support of Scientific and Technological Development (FUNCAP) for the financial support (6945087/2019).

References

1. Amazon, E.: Amazon web services. http://aws.amazon.com/es/ec2/(November 2012), p. 39 (2015)
2. Bochie, K., Sammarco, M., Detyniecki, M., Campista, M.E.M.: Análise do aprendizado federado em redes móveis. In: Anais do XXXIX Simpósio Brasileiro de Redes de Computadores e Sistemas Distribuídos, pp. 71–84. SBC (2021)
3. Imteaj, A., Thakker, U., Wang, S., Li, J., Amini, M.H.: Federated learning for resource-constrained IoT devices: panoramas and state-of-the-art. arXiv preprint arXiv:2002.10610 (2020)
4. Janssen, J.: Ventilation for acceptable indoor air quality. ASHRAE J. **31**(10), 40–48 (1989)
5. Korstanje, J.: LSTM RNNs. In: Advanced Forecasting with Python, pp. 243–251. Springer (2021). https://doi.org/10.1007/978-1-4842-7150-6_18
6. Kourtellis, N., Katevas, K., Perino, D.: FLaaS: federated learning as a service. In: Proceedings of the 1st Workshop on Distributed Machine Learning, pp. 7–13 (2020)
7. Lim, W.Y.B., et al.: Federated learning in mobile edge networks: a comprehensive survey. IEEE Commun. Surv. Tutorials **22**(3), 2031–2063 (2020)
8. Liu, Y., et al.: Deep anomaly detection for time-series data in industrial IoT: a communication-efficient on-device federated learning approach. IEEE Internet Things J. **8**(8), 6348–6358 (2020)
9. McMahan, B., Moore, E., Ramage, D., Hampson, S., y Arcas, B.A.: Communication-efficient learning of deep networks from decentralized data. In: Artificial Intelligence and Statistics, pp. 1273–1282. PMLR (2017)
10. Merkel, D.: Docker: lightweight Linux containers for consistent development and deployment. Linux J. **2014**(239), 2 (2014)
11. Navares, R., Aznarte, J.L.: Predicting air quality with deep learning LSTM: towards comprehensive models. Eco. Inform. **55**, 101019 (2020)
12. Paszke, A., et al.: Pytorch: an imperative style, high-performance deep learning library. In: Wallach, H., Larochelle, H., Beygelzimer, A., d'Alché-Buc, F., Fox, E., Garnett, R. (eds.) Advances in Neural Information Processing Systems 32, pp. 8024–8035. Curran Associates, Inc. (2019). http://papers.neurips.cc/paper/9015-pytorch-an-imperative-style-high-performance-deep-learning-library.pdf
13. Pedregosa, F., et al.: Scikit-learn: machine learning in Python. J. Mach. Learn. Res. **12**, 2825–2830 (2011)
14. Sater, R.A., Hamza, A.B.: A federated learning approach to anomaly detection in smart buildings. ACM Trans. Internet Things **2**(4), 1–23 (2021)
15. Tietz, M., Fan, T.J., Nouri, D., Bossan, B.: SKORCH: a scikit-learn compatible neural network library that wraps PyTorch, July 2017
16. Van Rossum, G., Drake, F.L.: Python 3 Reference Manual. CreateSpace, Scotts Valley, CA (2009)
17. Wu, Q., He, K., Chen, X.: Personalized federated learning for intelligent IoT applications: a cloud-edge based framework. IEEE Open J. Comput. Soc. **1**, 35–44 (2020)
18. Yuan, B., Ge, S., Xing, W.: A federated learning framework for healthcare IoT devices. arXiv preprint arXiv:2005.05083 (2020)
19. Zhang, X., Wargocki, P., Lian, Z., Thyregod, C.: Effects of exposure to carbon dioxide and bioeffluents on perceived air quality, self-assessed acute health symptoms, and cognitive performance. Indoor Air **27**(1), 47–64 (2017)

A Hybrid System with Nonlinear Combination for Wind Speed Forecasting

Leonardo de Leon Dias[(✉)] [iD], Emerson Alexandre de Oliveira Lima[iD], and João Fausto Lorenzato de Oliveira[iD]

University of Pernambuco, Recife, Brazil
lld@ecomp.poli.br, eal@poli.br, fausto.lorenzato@upe.br

Abstract. The contribution of wind energy to the world energy consumption has been growing substantially and represents a large share in the production of clean energy. However, wind power generation capacity is directly related to wind speed, which is an intermittent clean energy source and dependent on exogenous meteorological variables such as temperature, pressure and precipitation. Thus, the ability to forecast wind speed is essential for the wind energy generation processes. Several models and different approaches for wind speed forecasting have been proposed in the literature. Among them, hybrid systems combining different models are good options for performing this task, since they aim to overcome the limitations of single models by combining the forecasts achieved by different models. In this sense, the combination of linear models for time series and nonlinear models for the residual series forecasting is a promising approach in the literature. This article proposes a hybrid system for forecasting wind speed series with hourly and monthly intervals and uses different statistical models to generate a nonlinear combination function between linear and nonlinear models. The proposed approach selects which models are more suitable to provide better performance in the prediction task. Evaluations were made in different scenarios using data from three meteorological stations in the northeast region of Brazil. The results obtained showed that the proposed hybrid system in general outperformed other methods found in the literature.

Keywords: Hybrid systems · Wind speed forecast · Artificial neural networks

1 Introduction

The planet is at an accelerated rate of warming and studies point to the growing need to reduce greenhouse gas emissions [1]. The employment of renewable

This work was supported by the Foundation for Science and Technology Support from Pernambuco (FACEPE) - Process No. APQ-1252-1.03/21, and the Coordination for the Improvement of Higher Education Personnel - Brazil (CAPES) - Financing Code 001 for the financial support.

J. C. Xavier-Junior and R. A. Rios (Eds.): BRACIS 2022, LNAI 13654, pp. 312–327, 2022.
https://doi.org/10.1007/978-3-031-21688-3_23

energy sources represents an effective way to achieve this goal [2]. Several studies have indicated a significant evolution in the energy contribution from the renewable energy generation systems, and present wind generation as an important representation in this scenario [2,3]. In data analyzed until the end of 2020, Brazil was among the 5 countries with the highest installed renewable energy generation capacity, surpassed only by China and the United States. Annually, electricity generated from renewable energy is breaking records. In terms of global numbers, wind energy reached 26% of renewable energy production in 2020 [4].

Between 2008 and 2021, wind energy went from an installed capacity of 121 GW to 837 GW, with an increase of 12.45% just in the last year [5]. Regarding the Brazilian exploration potential, the northeast region is identified as strategic for the generation of wind energy, where 80% of Brazilian wind farms are located in this region and annually exceed its historical production maximums [6].

Wind speed can be influenced by weather conditions, such as pressure and temperature, and is often variable and intermittent over different time intervals. These intervals are usually classified as very short term (30 min), short-term (30 min to 6 h), medium-term (6 h to 1 day) and long-term (more than 1 day) [7]. Observation of shorter timescales allows planning operational tasks such as electricity market compensation and load planning, while observations at longer timescales are employed in planning problems such as allocation and economic feasibility [8].

In the literature, there are a variety of models for forecasting wind speed series [9]. In general, these models can be classified into physical, statistical and artificial intelligence (AI). Physical models are generally used for forecast of long time intervals, 48–72 h or more, and employ data from weather conditions such as pressure, temperature, terrain information, wind farm layout, among others [10]. However, the accuracy of physical models can be affected by the parametrization process, which often requires that instruments of observation are well calibrated.

Statistical models are often used in short-term forecasting and cover a variety of approaches and methods, such as the autoregressive integrated moving average (ARIMA), Kalman filtering and exponential smoothing methods [11]. However, these models assume a linear correlation structure between patterns [12] and may present reduced performance in real world time series where both linear and nonlinear patterns can be present [12,13].

Artificial intelligence models are nonlinear methods robust to noise, usually used for both short-term and long-term prediction and perform nonlinear mappings in data [7]. It's possible to cite such as example, Long Short-Term Memory networks (LSTM) [14], Convolution Neural Networks (CNN) [15,16], Support Vector Machine (SVM) [17,18], among others [11]. However, nonlinear models may present problems due to misspecification of parameters, such as overfitting and under fitting [19].

Taking into consideration the disadvantages of the employment of statistical and artificial intelligence based models individually, several hybrid models have been employed in order to overcome their limitations. The combination of forecasting models have been employed as a strategy to reduce the chances of selecting an inaccurate model, and improving the overall accuracy of the system [17,20]. In order to improve the accuracy over the base forecasters, the diversity of the models must be ensured. A good strategy is to use a model to perform time series forecasting, another model in the residual forecasting, and lastly performed the combination of forecasts. In this approach, in each stage, different tasks are performed using different data sets (time series and residual series) [12,13,17,21]. The residual represents the calculation of the difference between the values predicted by the first prediction model, and the values of the original series. Approaches that use the prediction of residual series, explore this set of data in the search to identify possible patterns that have not been modeled by the prediction method applied to the initial series.

Hybrid systems based on residual modelling can be grouped by means of its combination strategies. Some hybrid systems assume a linear relation between time series and residual forecasts, in which a sum operator is used to perform combinations [12,13,22]. Other hybrid models, assume that the true relation between forecasts is unknown, and could be better represented by nonlinear models [17,23,24]. However, regardless of the combination strategy adopted, one major issue in hybrid systems based on residual modelling is the model selection process, where to the best of the author knowledge, was not addressed appropriately. The selection of suitable models for each stage can have an important impact on the accuracy of the system. Moreover, this task can be hard since it involves several forecasting models, and trial and error approaches could be infeasible. In this sense, a hybrid system based on residual forecast is proposed where an automatic model selection is performed in the time series, residual modelling and forecast combination stages. In addition, the proposed hybrid system takes into consideration the possibility of using exogenous variables, through the employment of ARIMAX models and seasonal models SARIMA and SARIMAX. Thus, the proposed hybrid system has the following advantages:

- Selects most suitable models in hybrid systems for time series forecasting, residual series forecasting, and forecasts combination.
- Evaluates the possibility of using exogenous variables by means of ARIMAX and seasonal models SARIMA and SARIMAX.
- The proposed model is versatile since different models could be used in the selection process.
- It improves the accuracy of wind speed forecasting data.

This article is organized as follows: Sect. 2 briefly summarizes related works regarding hybrid systems and wind speed forecasting; Sect. 3 presents the proposed hybrid system; Sect. 4 shows the observed experimental results comparing our proposal with hybrid systems in the literature; Sect. 5 discusses the results; Sect. 6 presents the conclusions and avenues for future research.

2   Related Works

In general, hybrid systems based on residual modelling often consists of three major stages: i) time series forecasting, ii) residual series forecasting, iii) forecasts combination. Such hybrid systems have been explored in the wind speed forecasting literature [17, 22, 25–27].

Zhang [12] assumed that a time series (Z_t) could be considered as a decomposition of its linear (L_t) and nonlinear (N_t) counterparts, as presented in Eq. 1.

$$Z_t = L_t + N_t \tag{1}$$

In this sense, an ARIMA model was employed to perform linear forecasts $\hat{L}_t$, which were employed to determine the residual series (E_t) as presented in Eq. 2.

$$E_t = Z_t - \hat{L}_t. \tag{2}$$

The residual modelling stage was performed by a multilayer perceptron (MLP) neural network, which was used as a nonlinear function of past information from the residual to perform forecasts as presented in Eq. 3, where k is the number of lags in the time series.

$$\hat{N}_t = f(e_{t-1}, e_{t-2}, ..., e_{t-k}). \tag{3}$$

In this way, a linear relation between $\hat{L}_t$ and $\hat{N}_t$, and the combination of forecasts produced the final forecast as presented in Eq. 4.

$$\hat{Z}_t = \hat{L}_t + \hat{N}_t. \tag{4}$$

For the sake of simplicity, this architecture will be henceforward referred to as ARIMA+MLP, representing the ARIMA model used in the first stage, the MLP model used in the second stage, and the combination through the sum operator.

Several other works follow the same architecture. Camelo et al. [22], proposed an ARIMAX+MLP hybrid system to wind speed forecasting in the northeast region of Brazil, and used temperature, pressure and precipitation as exogenous variables. Alencar et al. [25] proposed a SARIMA+MLP in wind speed forecasting considering a multi-step ahead scenario. Liu et al. [26] used an empirical mode decomposition method to decompose the data, and then an ARIMA+LSTM hybrid system was employed. Duan et al. [27] proposed an improved complete ensemble empirical mode decomposition with adaptive noise (ICEEMDAN) with the ARIMA to perform wind speed forecasts, neural networks such as MLP and LSTM were employed in the residual step.

The above mentioned works assume a linear relation between forecasts, however the true relation is unknown. In this sense, De Mattos Neto et al. [24] proposed a hybrid system with a nonlinear combination stage, where an ARIMA model is used in the time series forecasting stage, an MLP model in the residual forecasting stage, and an SVR in the combination stage. In order to better represent this formulation, this architecture will be referred to as SVR(ARIMA,

MLP) in order to represent the forecasts achieved by the ARIMA and MLP models, combined by the SVR. Santos Júnior [23] employed a similar strategy, using past information of forecasts in the combination process. De Mattos Neto [17] proposed an SVR(ARIMAX, MLP) method to perform wind speed forecasting in the northeast region of Brazil, using temperature, pressure and precipitation as exogenous variables.

The proposed model differs significantly from previous works since it performs the selection of the most appropriate models in each stage of the hybrid system. In addition, it chooses from four ARIMA variations (ARIMA, SARIMA, ARIMAX, SARIMAX) to perform time series forecasts, five nonlinear models in the residual forecasting stage (SVR, MLP, radial basis function networks (RBF), LSTM and CNN), and three nonlinear models for the combination stage (MLP, RBF and SVR).

3   Proposed Method

In a similar way regarding previous methods, the proposed method is composed of three major stages. Time series forecasting, residual series forecasting, and forecasts combination, presented in Fig. 1 by colors green, yellow and blue, respectively. It performs the selection of the most suitable models from a pool of linear and nonlinear models to time series and residual forecasting, respectively. Then, selects nonlinear models, from another pool, to perform the forecast combination from the previous models.

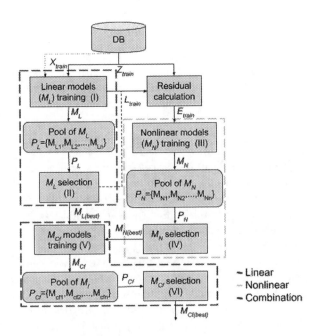

Fig. 1. Training phase of the proposed hybrid system. (Color figure online)

Equation 5 represents the function of the system, where Z_{t+1} is the final forecast obtained from the combination process at time $t + 1$ (one-step ahead). $L_{best(t+1)}$ and $N_{best(t+1)}$ represent the forecasts obtained from the best linear model $M_{L(best)}$ and the best nonlinear model $M_{N(best)}$, respectively. Cf_{best} is the selected combination function.

$$Z_{t+1} = Cf_{best}(L_{best(t+1)}, N_{best(t+1)}) \tag{5}$$

The training phase of the proposed method is presented on Fig. 1, where it has six main steps: (I) training of the linear models M_L (ARIMA, SARIMA, ARIMAX, SARIMAX), (II) selection of the most suitable linear model for the data set under observation $M_{L(best)}$, (III) training of nonlinear models M_N (SVR, MLP, RBF, LSTM, CNN), (IV) selection of the most suitable nonlinear model for the observation data set $M_{N(best)}$, (V) training of nonlinear models M_{Cf} (SVR, MLP, RBF) to obtain the combination function Cf, (VI) selection of the most suitable model M_{Cf} for the combination of models $M_{L(best)}$ and $M_{N(best)}$. Steps (I, III and V) use a part of the database intended for training the models. Steps (II, IV and VI) use a data set intended for validation. The evaluation metric adopted in all steps of the system was the Mean-Squared Error (MSE), which penalizes greater differences between the real value and the predicted values.

Step (I) receives as input the training set Z_{train} for training models without exogenous variables and X_{train} used for models that consider exogenous variables. This step feeds a pool with trained linear models to prediction L_{train}. The estimation of the parameters of the linear models M_L aims to model the linear patterns of the Z_{train}, which will be used to obtain a series of errors or residues E_{train} that represents the difference between Z_{train} and L_{train}. At the end of this step, it is expected to obtain a purely nonlinear series.

Step (II) receives as input data a pool of linear models P_L and offers as output the indication of the model that presents the best performance in the prediction of Z_{train}. It is expected that this step can provide guidance on the best linear method $M_{L(best)}$ to be used to predict the data set under observation.

Step (III) receives as input data the error series E_{train} associated with $M_{L(best)}$ and provides as result the prediction of these series. This step feeds a pool with trained nonlinear models and aims to model the nonlinear pattern of the error series through the application of 5 different machine learning algorithms.

Step (IV) receives as input a pool of nonlinear models P_N, offers as an output, the indication of the model that presents the best performance for the residual prediction. It is expected, in this step, to obtain a direction of the best nonlinear method $M_{N(best)}$ to be associated with the linear method $M_{L(best)}$ for prediction of the set of observation data. Step (V) receives as input $M_{L(best)}$ and $M_{N(best)}$, and feeds a pool with trained nonlinear models M_{Cf} to obtain a function to combining the inputs.

Step (VI) receives, as input data, the pool of nonlinear models P_f and offers as output the indication of the model that presents the best combination function of the models $M_{L(best)}$ and $M_{N(best)}$. It is expected to obtain in this step the

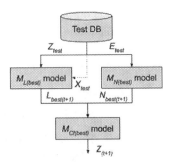

Fig. 2. Testing phase of the proposed hybrid system.

direction of which the nonlinear model is able to offer the most adequate function for the combination of the models proposed by the previous steps.

The testing phase of the proposed system presented in Fig. 2 is divided in two steps: I) receives the best linear model, the best nonlinear model and the test series Z_{test}, X_{test} and E_{test} as input data; offers as output the linear and nonlinear predictions $L_{best(t+1)}$ and $N_{best(t+1)}$; II) combines the outputs of step I through a combination function M_{Cf}, and gives as output the final forecast of the hybrid system, Z_{t+1}.

The proposed hybrid system points out which linear and nonlinear models can present better accuracy in the forecast task of the observed wind speed series. It indicates the most suitable nonlinear model to generate a function to combine the predictions of linear and nonlinear models. Secondarily, it allows observing whether the use of linear models that consider exogenous data and/or the seasonality of the data can contribute to the improvement of the hybrid system generated.

4   Experiments and Analysis

This section is divided into three subsections. Subsection 4.1 presents the data sets used in the experiments, Subsect. 4.2 describes the parameter configuration of all linear and nonlinear models and the experimental setup, and Subsect. 4.3 presents the results.

4.1   Data Set

The databases used in this work are divided into 2 groups according to their sampling intervals, which can be hourly or monthly. Data from different geographic positions were collected from three meteorological stations located in different cities in northeastern Brazil: Recife (8.05° S and 34.95° W, altitude: 10.00 m), Fortaleza (3.75° S and 38.54° W, altitude: 26.45 m) and Natal (5.91° S and 35.2° W, altitude: 48.60 m). The collection period was from January 2003 to December 2014, in order to compare with the results obtained by [17] and [22].

In addition, each of these sets has four observed variables: temperature in (C°), pressure in (hPa), precipitation in (mm) and wind speed in (m/s). The first three will be treated as exogenous variables and the last one, the series that will be the objective of the prediction model.

The data series for the cities of Recife and Fortaleza, with an hourly sampling interval, have a total of 744 samples, while the Natal series, with the same interval, has a total of 722 samples. For experiments with hourly sampling intervals, a time window of only 1 month was used. Datasets with monthly sampling intervals have a total of 144 samples, and their values represent the monthly averages of the collection period. All data were obtained through the National Institute of Meteorology (INMET).

Table 1 present the results of a correlation analysis between the series of the different variables that make up the set of hourly and monthly data. Pearson's coefficient was used to observe the correlation between the wind speed series and exogenous data (temperature, pressure and precipitation).

Table 1. Correlation between the wind speed series and exogenous data with monthly interval

Interval	Database	Temperature		Pressure		Precipitation	
		Pearson	P-value	Pearson	P-value	Pearson	P-value
Monthly	Recife	0.36	6.45e−6	−0.06	4.17e−1	−0.76	8.61e−29
	Fortaleza	0.65	1.14e−18	0.26	1.41e−3	−0.83	2.17e−38
	Natal	−0.14	7.5e−2	0.31	9.92e−5	−0.58	2.37e−14
Hourly	Recife	0.77	9.1e−149	0.02	6.11e−1	−0.14	1.27e−4
	Fortaleza	0.81	1.2e−177	−0.07	4.72e−2	−0.06	1.30e−1
	Natal	0.83	7.4e−187	−0.09	1.17e−2	−0.01	7.37e−1

Observing the data set with monthly intervals, the precipitation variable of Recife and Fortaleza series presents a strong negative correlation with the wind speed series. From the correlation analysis with hourly intervals, it is important to highlight that the temperature variable presents a strong positive correlation with the series of the three observed regions, Recife, Fortaleza and Natal. It can also be observed that the low P-value referring to the analysis of this variable supports the information indicated by the Pearson coefficient.

4.2 Experimental Setup

The experiments were carried out by using linear and nonlinear models to obtain a hybrid system. The linear models ARIMA, SARIMA, ARIMAX and SARI-MAX had their orders (p, d, q)(P, D, Q)s and their respective coefficients determined using the methodology proposed by Hyndman [28]. The input data for the ARIMA and SARIMA models were purely the wind speed series, while the

ARIMAX and SARIMAX models also had exogenous variables (temperature, pressure and precipitation) as input data, same configuration adopted in [17] and [22].

The nonlinear models used to predict the residual were MLP, SVR, RBF, LSTM and CNN, some of these models were used to ensure a good basis for comparison with [17], as well as all of them showed good performance in works related to wind speed series prediction [14,17]. The configuration of the parameters of these nonlinear models was determined through a grid search methodology, where the search space of possible configurations is presented in Table 2.

The combination of linear and nonlinear models was performed by 3 nonlinear models, SVR, MLP and RBF. The use of these models was justified by the good results presented in previous works with proposals for the prediction of wind speed series [17,23]. The training phase of these models had as input data the series resulting from the prediction of linear models and the series of prediction of residuals. The parameter configuration of these models is also based on grid search.

Table 2. GridSearch Values

Model	Parameters	Value
ARIMA(X)	p, d, q	Hyndman Method [28]
MLP	Algorithm	Adam
	Activation Function	Sigmoid
	Number of Hidden Layer Nodes	2, 5, 10, 15, 20
SVR	Kernel	RBF
	Gamma	1, 0.1, 0.01, 0.001
	C	0.1, 1, 100, 1000, 10000
	Epsilon	0.1, 0.01, 0.001
RBF	Algorithm	Adam
	Activation Function	Radial Basis Function
	Number of Hidden Layer Nodes	2, 5, 10, 15, 20
LSTM	Algorithm	Adam
	Activation Function	ReLu
	Recurrent Activation Function	Sigmoid
	Number of Hidden Layer Nodes	2, 5, 10, 15, 20
CNN	Algorithm	Adam
	Activation Function	ReLu
	Number of filters in Convolutional Layer	2, 5, 10, 15, 20

The performance metric adopted to system evaluate was the MSE and MAPE. The latter, allows observing the percentage error in relation to the performance of the models [17]. The data set was divided into training, validation and testing. For the train and validation sets, Cross-Validation method was used. The test set was composed of the last samples of the time series and was intended only for the evaluation of results and comparisons with other models. The number of lags used for all data sets was 12 sampling periods.

The simulations were carried out separately in the databases with hourly and monthly intervals. In the monthly database, the time series of the 3 cities, Recife, Fortaleza and Natal, were divided into 91 points for training, 23 samples for validation and 30 points for testing. Some hybrid models of the literature using the sum operator as combination were used as a basis for comparison, as well as the model proposed by [17], that will be referred to in this work as Hybrid SVR. The model proposed by the current work will be called Proposed M_{Cf}, resulting from the evaluation of a combination of the best models evaluated in each of the steps described in Sect. 3. Furthermore, it is important to mention that all forecasts are performed as one-step ahead.

The simulations performed in the database with hourly intervals had the Recife and Fortaleza series divided again into training, validation and testing, with dimensions of 475, 119, 150, respectively. The Natal series was divided into dimensions of 432, 144, 144. The entire training and validation procedure was equivalent to that used in the database with monthly intervals. For the training and testing of all the models used, a previous normalization of the data was performed, later these data were placed in their original scales.

The linear models ARIMA, ARIMAX, SARIMA and SARIMAX were generated using the programming language R, The nonlinear models, MLP, LSTM, CNN and RBF were developed using Python 3.7 with the aid of Tensorflow and Keras, the SVR model was implemented using the Sklearn library.

4.3   Results

Table 3 presents the selected models from the proposed method for each analyzed database. It is important to highlight that most of the models presented use linear methods that consider exogenous variables and techniques for mapping seasonality. Another interesting factor to be exposed is the indication of the SVR as the best combiner in most of the analyzed bases.

Table 3. Selected models for each database

Database	Time interval	Proposed model
Recife	Monthly	SVR(SARIMA, LSTM)
	Hourly	SVR(ARIMAX, CNN)
Fortaleza	Monthly	MLP(SARIMAX, CNN)
	Hourly	RBF(SARIMAX, SVR)
Natal	Monthly	SVR(SARIMAX, MLP)
	Hourly	SVR(SARIMA, SVR)

Table 4 presents the comparison of the results obtained by 5 different prediction approaches observing the data sets with monthly and hourly sampling intervals for the cities of Recife, Fortaleza and Natal. The linear models M_L ARIMA and SARIMA do not consider exogenous variables, unlike the ARIMAX and SARIMAX models. The SARIMA and SARIMAX models have elements to represent the seasonality present in the data, the ARIMA and ARIMAX models do not have these elements. In almost all linear models, it can be seen that the use of the element to represent seasonality guaranteed greater assertiveness in the predictions, save the exceptions from the MAPE in natal database. The use of exogenous variables showed good applicability in the bases of Natal hourly, Recife and Fortaleza.

The nonlinear models M_N presented in Table 4 represent the application of the CNN, LSTM, RBF, MLP and SVR algorithms as predictors of the wind speed series applied directly to the initial data series. According to the MSE, in all series, these models surpass the results obtained purely by the linear models. In the Fortaleza and Natal bases, the results are similar for the combination of linear and nonlinear methods with sum operators.

In the results obtained by combining linear and nonlinear models by nonlinear methods, a considerable improvement is achieved when compared to single models. When evaluating the MSE performance of the proposed model, it performs better than all other methods when applied to the Recife and Fortaleza series. In the Natal monthly basis, the proposed model was not able to point out the best method, however, the result had a slightly lower MSE, which could justify the use of the proposed system due to its ability to reduce the training time and choice between several models.

The results obtained by the proposed model for the wind series data for the cities of Recife, Fortaleza and Natal, with hourly sampling intervals, surpasses all other techniques in the 3 series observed, according to MSE. The linear models ARIMAX and SARIMAX had a similar behavior in the bases of Recife and Fortaleza hourly, it can be inferred that the variable for seasonality mapping did not contribute to the model for these two series. It is also possible to observe that the consideration of exogenous variables is relevant and significant for the prediction of all series with hourly intervals. Again, the vast majority of nonlinear models M_N outperformed, with a good margin, the results obtained by the linear models in the 3 hourly series. The same occurred in the comparison of these models with the combination of linear and nonlinear methods using sum operators.

In regard to the MAPE metric, the best results were achieved by the proposed method in the Fortaleza data set, in both monthly and hourly intervals. In Recife and Natal data, the SARIMAX+MLP and Hybrid SVR methods obtained the best values.

Figure 3 presents the forecasts of the proposed method, against the SARIMA and LSTM individual models in the Recife monthly dataset (a), ARIMAX and CNN in the Recife hourly (b), SARIMAX and CNN in the Fortaleza monthly (c), SARIMAX and SVR in the Fortaleza hourly (d), SARIMAX and MLP in

Table 4. Comparison of results

Data	Approach	Model	Monthly		Hourly	
			MSE	MAPE	MSE	MAPE
RECIFE	M_L	ARIMA	8,11e−02	13,16	4,14e−01	22,87
		SARIMA	5,77e−02	11,22	4,03e−01	23,04
		ARIMAX	5,79e−02	11,15	3,28e−01	18,29
		SARIMAX	4,30e−02	8,87	3,28e−01	18,29
	M_N	CNN	3,91e−02	16,51	1,69e−02	23,49
		LSTM	2,81e−02	13,94	1,36e−02	22,88
		MLP	4,53e−02	18,02	1,41e−02	21,01
		RBFN	2,42e−02	12,77	1,39e−02	22,28
		SVR	2,14e−02	11,92	1,30e−02	22,20
	$M_L + M_N$	ARIMA+MLP [12]	5,92e−02	10,40	4,19e−01	23,89
		ARIMA+SVR	6,67e−02	11,65	4,22e−01	23,19
		ARIMAX+MLP [22]	1,33e−01	17,93	3,39e−01	18,58
		SARIMAX+MLP	3,55e−02	**7,57**	4,23e−01	23,33
	Hibrid SVR [17]	SVR(ARIMAX, MLP)	1,75e−02	10,80	1,04e−02	**17,59**
	Proposed M_{Cf}		**1,70e−02**	10,49	**1,03e−02**	17,71
FORTALEZA	M_L	ARIMA	1,31e−01	10,10	4,56e−01	15,10
		SARIMA	1,49e−01	10,57	4,42e−01	14,68
		ARIMAX	1,10e−01	9,74	3,45e−01	13,01
		SARIMAX	8,09e−02	8,37	3,45e−01	13,01
	M_N	CNN	1,82e−02	11,14	1,21e−02	15,01
		LSTM	2,04e−02	13,14	1,59e−02	18,46
		MLP	3,20e−02	13,05	1,90e−02	17,45
		RBFN	2,85e−02	13,62	1,27e−2	14,81
		SVR	1,66e−02	10,88	1,11e−02	14,81
	$M_L + M_N$	ARIMA+MLP [12]	1,35e−01	10,59	5,32e−01	15,03
		ARIMA+SVR	1,32e−01	10,32	5,26e−01	15,69
		ARIMAX+MLP [22]	1,13e−01	9,68	3,48e−01	13,34
		SARIMAX+MLP	8,32e−02	7,68	3,57e−01	14,07
	Hibrid SVR [17]	SVR(ARIMAX, MLP)	1,19e−02	8,98	8,58e−03	13,25
	Proposed M_{Cf}		**1,09e−02**	**7,59**	**8,27e−03**	**13,14**
NATAL	M_L	ARIMA	2,29e−01	9,57	7,05e−01	13,10
		SARIMA	2,21e−01	9,65	6,61e−01	12,75
		ARIMAX	2,71e−01	10,80	4,52e−01	10,79
		SARIMAX	2,74e−01	10,70	4,50e−01	10,91
	M_N	CNN	1,96e−02	11,21	1,18e−02	14,39
		LSTM	1,74e−02	10,21	1,64e−02	17,43
		MLP	1,38e−02	9,34	1,01e−02	13,01
		RBFN	3,31e−02	14,25	9,80e−3	12,26
		SVR	1,43e−02	9,02	1,01e−02	12,87
	$M_L + M_N$	ARIMA+MLP [12]	2,25e−01	9,36	6,94e−01	13,43
		ARIMA+SVR	2,50e−01	9,80	6,75e−01	12,56
		ARIMAX+MLP [22]	2,51e−01	10,17	5,20e−01	11,84
		SARIMAX+MLP	2,86e−01	11,01	4,34e−01	**10,56**
	Hibrid SVR [17]	SVR(ARIMA, RBF)	**1,32e−02**	**8,43**	9,41e−03	12,20
	Proposed M_{Cf}		1,86E−02	11,09	**8,91E−03**	12,08

the Natal monthly (e), and SARIMA and SVR in the Natal hourly dataset (f). It is important to point out that the graphs presented in Figures (b), (d) and (f), referring to the series with hourly intervals, had only 72 h represented visually, which corresponds to approximately 50% of the test values of each database. This decision was purely for a more user-friendly visual representation.

5   Discussion

The use of hybrid systems for forecasting tasks aims to obtain better results through the joint use of different mathematical models, whether physical or statistical. The modeling of the system and the way of combining the models used can significantly impact the final result [7]. The comparison of the results obtained in this work with other hybrid systems proposed in the literature, which have similar approaches, allowed us to observe that, for the analyzed wind series, the nonlinear combination between the methods of the prediction steps of the real series and the residual series proved to be more suitable. What was observed corroborated with previous works that point out the choice of the combination function as an important issue to be observed.

It is important to highlight that the use of models capable of identifying the seasonality present in the time series was more relevant for the series with monthly intervals, while the use of models that took into account the exogenous

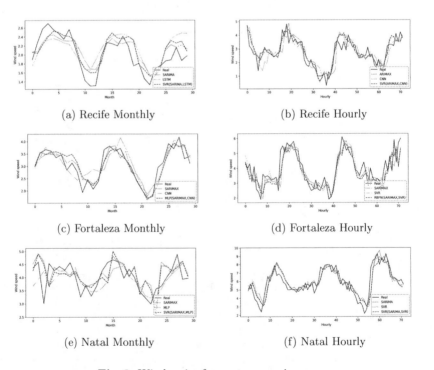

(a) Recife Monthly

(b) Recife Hourly

(c) Fortaleza Monthly

(d) Fortaleza Hourly

(e) Natal Monthly

(f) Natal Hourly

Fig. 3. Wind series forecast comparisons

data was more relevant for the series with hourly intervals. Relating this last observation with the Table 1 seems there is a possibility that the exogenous variable temperature had a greater influence in the final result due to its higher correlation values.

Moreover, when analysing both MSE and MAPE results in Table 4, the best MSE values do not necessarily correspond to the best MAPE. This is due to the asymmetry of the MAPE metric [29] which evaluates differently positive and negative errors. Therefore, since the MSE perform symmetric evaluations, their values may not always be the same.

6 Conclusion

The analysis of the results showed that the hybrid system proposed for prediction of wind series surpassed all other methods used for comparison in 5 of the 6 series analyzed, in addition to significantly reducing the time to obtain an optimal combination between different techniques. The use of different methods to obtain a nonlinear combination function allowed to obtain results superior to previous works that search for this function by a single method. The use of exogenous variables showed a good potential to increase performance in prediction models of the wind series with hourly intervals. The use of linear models that allow a mapping of the seasonality present in the data can contribute favorably to the reduction of the error in the prediction of the wind series with monthly intervals.

Future research may explore multistep forward prediction scenarios, or different methods of model selection, as well as explore the prediction of exogenous variable series separately and add them to the system at later times. Another possible approach is the combination of multiple linear and nonlinear models in an ensemble fashion.

References

1. Allen, M., et al.: Special report: global warming of 1.5°C. Intergovernmental Panel on Climate Change (IPCC) (2018)
2. Jansen, M., et al.: Offshore wind competitiveness in mature markets without subsidy. Nat. Energy **5**, 614–622 (2020)
3. Heptonstall, P.J., Gross, R.J.: A systematic review of the costs and impacts of integrating variable renewables into power grids. Nat. Energy **6**, 72–83 (2021)
4. IRENA: Renewable energy statistics. International Renewable Energy Agency (IRENA) (2021)
5. Junginger, M., Hittinger, E., Williams, E., Wiser, R.: Chapter 6 - Onshore wind energy, pp. 87–102 (2020)
6. Neoenergia Group: Infographic: operational map of Neoenergia
7. Soundarapandian, V., Srie, E., Janani, V.: A review on the hybrid approaches for wind speed forecasting. Int. J. Sci. Technol. Res. **8**, 1584–1590 (2020)
8. Soman, S.S., Zareipour, H., Malik, O., Mandal, P.: A review of wind power and wind speed forecasting methods with different time horizons. In: Proceedings of the 2010 North American Power Symposium, Arlington (2010)

9. Jalli, R.K., Mishra, S.P., Naik, J., Sharma, P., Senapati, R.: Prediction of wind speed with optimized EMD based RVFLN. In: Proceedings of 2020 IEEE-HYDCON International Conference on Engineering in the 4th Industrial Revolution, HYDCON 2020 (2020)

10. Tascikaraoglu, A., Uzunoglu, M.: A review of combined approaches for prediction of short-term wind speed and power. Renew. Sustain. Energy Rev. **34**, 243–254 (2014)

11. Wang, L., Tao, R., Hu, H., Zeng, Y.-R.: Effective wind power prediction using novel deep learning network: stacked independently recurrent autoencoder. Renew. Energy **164**, 642–655 (2021)

12. Zhang, G.P.: Time series forecasting using a hybrid ARIMA and neural network model. Neurocomputing **50**, 159–175 (2003)

13. Panigrahi, S., Behera, H.S.: A hybrid ETS-ANN model for time series forecasting. Eng. Appl. Artif. Intell. **66**, 49–59 (2017)

14. Shahid, F., Zameer, A., Muneeb, M.: A novel genetic LSTM model for wind power forecast. Energy **223**, 120069 (2021)

15. Harbola, S., Coors, V.: One dimensional convolutional neural network architectures for wind prediction. Energy Convers. Manag. **195**, 70–75 (2019)

16. Wan, T., Li, H., Wang, C., Kou, P.: Turbine location wind speed forecast using convolutional neural network, pp. 1417–1421 (2019)

17. de Mattos Neto, P.S., et al.: A hybrid nonlinear combination system for monthly wind speed forecasting. IEEE Access **8**, 191365–191377 (2020)

18. Zhang, S., Liu, C., Wang, W., Chang, B.: Twin least square support vector regression model based on gauss-laplace mixed noise feature with its application in wind speed prediction. Entropy **22**, 1102 (2020)

19. Taskaya-Temizel, T., Ahmad, K.: Are ARIMA neural network hybrids better than single models?, vol. 5, pp. 3192–31975 (2005)

20. Zhang, Y., Gao, S., Han, J., Ban, M.: Wind speed prediction research considering wind speed ramp and residual distribution. IEEE Access **7**, 131873–131887 (2019)

21. Ferreira, M., Santos, A., Lucio, P.: Short-term forecast of wind speed through mathematical models. Energy Rep. **5**, 1172–1184 (2019)

22. do Nascimento Camelo, H., Lucio, P.S., Leal Junior, J.B.V., de Carvalho, P.C.M., von Glehn dos Santos, D.: Innovative hybrid models for forecasting time series applied in wind generation based on the combination of time series models with artificial neural networks. Energy **151**, 347–357 (2018)

23. de O. Santos Júnior, D.S., de Oliveira, J.F.L., de Mattos Neto, P.S.G.: An intelligent hybridization of ARIMA with machine learning models for time series forecasting. Knowl.-Based Syst. **175**, 72–86 (2019)

24. de Mattos Neto, P.S.G., Cavalcanti, G.D.C., Madeiro, F.: Nonlinear combination method of forecasters applied to pm time series. Pattern Recogn. Lett. **95**, 65–72 (2017)

25. Alencar, D.B., Affonso, C.M., Oliveira, R.C.L., Filho, J.C.R.: Hybrid approach combining SARIMA and neural networks for multi-step ahead wind speed forecasting in brazil. IEEE Access **6**, 55986–55994 (2018)

26. Liu, M.-D., Ding, L., Bai, Y.-L.: Application of hybrid model based on empirical mode decomposition, novel recurrent neural networks and the ARIMA to wind speed prediction. Energy Convers. Manag. **233**, 113917 (2021)

27. Duan, J., Zuo, H., Bai, Y., Duan, J., Chang, M., Chen, B.: Short-term wind speed forecasting using recurrent neural networks with error correction. Energy **217**, 119397 (2021)

28. Hyndman, R.J., Khandakar, Y.: Automatic time series forecasting: the forecast package for R. J. Stat. Softw. **27**(3), 1–22 (2008)
29. Hyndman, R.J., Koehler, A.B.: Another look at measures of forecast accuracy. Int. J. Forecast. **22**(4), 679–688 (2006)

Detecting Malicious HTTP Requests Without Log Parser Using RequestBERT-BiLSTM

Levi S. Ramos Júnior[(✉)] [ID], David Macêdo [ID], Adriano L. I. Oliveira [ID], and Cleber Zanchettin [ID]

Centro de Informática, Universidade Federal de Pernambuco,
Recife, PE 50.740-560, Brazil
{lsrj,dlm,alio,cz}@cin.ufpe.br
http://www.cin.ufpe.br

Abstract. Web servers provide most internet services, such as information sharing, financial, health, entertainment, and education. In this context, the web has become the principal place for attackers. Unfortunately, most defensive techniques for web servers cannot deal with the complexity and evolution of cyber attacks on HTTP requests. However, machine learning approaches can help detect some attacks. This work presents the RequestBERT-BiLSTM, a new model to detect possible HTTP request attacks without using Log Parser. We evaluated the model on public datasets such as CSIC 2010, ECML/PKDD 2007, and BGL. We also developed a new dataset from a real environment to evaluate the method. In addition, we illustrate that the traditional log analysis step can degrade the model's performance due to parser errors. Furthermore, we compared the performance of the proposed approach with literature models, and we obtained a detection rate above 95%.

Keywords: HTTP requests · Attack detection · Log parser

1 Introduction

Web servers are widely used and essential for many organizations, regardless of business area, and are constant targets of numerous attacks that cause enormous damage. Thus, developers and security experts must build secure systems to prevent these attacks. Among all network communication protocols among servers, the HTTP (Hypertext Transfer Protocol) is used by most web applications to communicate between web browsers and web servers. There are usually two types of HTTP messages: requests (*requests*) sent by the client to trigger an action on the server and the responses (*responses*), the replica of the server's requests. Among the numerous web security solutions, the web application firewall (WAF) is a component that explicitly applies to web services. Inspection of HTTP traffic can prevent attacks originating from the Internet using security vulnerabilities. However, current WAFs typically work on a rules-based model

© The Author(s), under exclusive license to Springer Nature Switzerland AG 2022
J. C. Xavier-Junior and R. A. Rios (Eds.): BRACIS 2022, LNAI 13654, pp. 328–342, 2022.
https://doi.org/10.1007/978-3-031-21689-3_24

and rely heavily on attack signatures to detect and prevent intrusions. In addition, they must have sufficient characterization and generalization capability to analyze normal or malicious behavior, which in practice is a time-consuming and laborious task [12]. In contrast to this approach, some anomaly detection approaches study the user's behavior, whether client or server, and detect if the behavior is normal or anomalous using machine learning techniques.

Therefore, some intrusion detection techniques use machine learning for web servers based on HTTP requests. In [25] and [12] both use the request line. The request line comprises the HTTP method, the HTTP-URL, and the HTTP version. They assume that the vast majority of attacks on the web are implemented by manipulating the HTTP-URL, as the experiments considered only the CSIC 2010 dataset [22], which contains only HTTP-URL attacks. However, other attacks can also use other parts of the HTTP header, such as *Session Hijacking and Cross-Site Request Forgery (CSRF)* that utilize the user's session cookie on the page. Another approach is to extract resources from URLs as in [2,24], and [18], which consists of selecting the most relevant attributes extracted from the URLs contained in the requests. These approaches tend to have difficulty detecting attacks, as the complete request has more information than the URL alone can provide. Thus, most works in the literature use only the URL to extract information and try to predict possible attacks on HTTP requests.

Still, there are some efficient approaches based on deep learning, especially recurrent neural networks (RNNs), which are already used in the literature [4,13], and [5] to deal with this problem. Unfortunately, these models rely on log analysis to preprocess unstructured log data and, therefore, suffer from losing important information during interpretation. Log parsers remove the jagged part of the log messages and retain the constant part to get the meaning of the log. In this process, existing Log Parsers produce various parsing errors, which reduce detection performance [13]. Finally, it is worth mentioning that these models still impose some specific adjustments to the set of data used, and none of these deal with HTTP requests.

This paper proposes using the BERT model to learn sequential patterns of HTTP requests and represent the information. We use a BiLSTM layer from this representation to add bidirectional information in this context and allow the hidden state vector to capture past and future information in each connection. Therefore, the proposed RequestBERT-BiLSTM approach removes the parser log phase of the process and uses all the requests' information to detect possible attacks. We evaluate the proposed approach on four datasets, three public datasets, ECML/PKDD 2007, CSIC 2010, BGL, and finally, one dataset generated in this paper from a security asset *F5 Big-IP*.

2   Background

Log analysis automatically converts each log message into a specific event model by removing parameters and keeping keywords. Log preprocessing converts raw log entries into structured data such as vectors. This process consists of log parsing and log string extraction.

In [17] the authors summarized 13 parsers based on their existing characteristics and categorized them into six categories based on parsing strategies: clustering, frequent pattern mining, evolutionary, heuristics, and longest common subsequence. For more details, refer to [17].

We will focus on the Log Parsers *Drain, AEL, LogSig, and LFA*, each one with different approaches [17]. These log analyzers are widely used in existing studies [6,26] and [8]. The main characteristics of these methods are:

1. **Drain** [7] - It is a tree-based online log analysis method. When a new log arrives, Drain preprocesses it based on expressions according to domain knowledge.
2. **AEL** [10] - is one of the state-of-the-art log analysis approaches, comprising four steps: anonymize, tokenize, categorize, and reorganize. However, abstracting log lines for events is a challenging and time-consuming task.
3. **LogSig** [21] - LogSig works on generating system events from raw log data, and its purpose is to group log messages.
4. **LFA** [16] - In LFA, token frequencies are compared in each log message rather than all log messages, so it identifies parameters by distinguishing token frequencies in a log message.

To evaluate the proposed method, we used literature approaches as a baseline. Each chosen model has a different approach and is summarized below:

1. **Word2Vec** - is a statistical method for efficiently learning a *Word Embedding* independent of a text corpus. In addition, we used Word2Vec to show the performance of a traditional word embedding approach.
2. **NeuralLog** [13] -The method detects anomalies in the logs without performing the Log Parser. However, it has a function that performs the treatment of logs removing all numbers and special characters, leaving only letters.
3. **CNN** [14] - The authors built a parser that structures the log lines and creates a unique key for each log. In these keys, the less used information is excluded. After that, the embedding is inserted into a CNN network.
4. **BERT** -The model used is the simple BERT with the transformer *BertForSequenceClassification* library.
5. **BERT-CNN** - It uses BERT with a CNN network following the same parameters as [14], with 3 CNN layers: 3×128, 4×128 and 5×128.

3   Related Works

HTTP requests are widely used in communication between clients and web servers. Given this scenario, several attempts were created to detect or prevent attacks based on HTTP requests. This section will show some works that have tried these goals with different architectures.

Yu et al. [25] its scope was only on HTTP requests from the CSIC 2010 [22] dataset. His project consisted of 3 steps: application of TextCNN [11] for feature extraction; creating URL-based statistical resource transfer; and building an SVM model on the last layer of TextCNN to perform classification based on the concatenated features. Its preprocessing consisted of removing duplicate requests, converting each character of the requests to lowercase, and decoding characters encoded by browsers or attackers. In the data processing step, they use TextCNN to extract features automatically, and later this information is fed into a CNN network with 2×64, 3×64, 4×64, and 5×64.

Lu et al. [14] built a log parser that structures the log lines and creates a unique key for each input. The less-used information is excluded from these keys [14]. This log parser applies a window-based partitioning, where padding or truncation is used to get consistent string lengths. Mainly, they first created a trainable matrix whose shape equals a single log x embedding size [3]. After that, the embedding is inserted into a CNN network: 3 CNN layers in parallel with sizes 3×128, 4×128, and 5×128.

Xiaohui et al. [12] created DeepWAF to detect malicious HTTP requests and, similar to Yu et al. [25] only worked with CSIC. First, the request to the web server is parsed from the HTTP headers and the message body. After preprocessing, a URL is generated to feed the detector. Next, this same URL is decoded as in [25], lowercase and finally, the URL is divided following the sequence of special characters. And in the classification step, several RNNs are combined with CNN, LSTM, CNN+LSTM, and LSTM+CNN.

Le et al. [13] proposed NeuralLog that consists of three steps: preprocessing, neural representation, and transformer-based classification. The first step is log preprocessing. After that, each log message is encoded into a semantic vector using BERT. Finally, it leverages the model used in [23] to detect anomalies [13].

The above works presented significant advances, but few have explored machine learning approaches in this context. Nevertheless, deep learning techniques are a promising approach to learning from legitimate or malicious sample data without the requirement for classical log parsing tasks and detecting web attacks.

4   RequestBERT-BiLSTM

The proposed approach aims to detect anomalies in HTTP requests by combining Bidirectional Encoder Representations from Transformer and Bidirectional Long Short Term Memory (BERT-BiLSTM). The main purpose of RequestBERT-BiLSTM is to learn contextual information from HTTP requests.

RequestBERT-BiLSTM is an improved supervised algorithm based on *BERT* and *BiLSTM*. It adopts BERT as part of data entry and BiLSTM as part of the classification. With the BiLSTM network, it is possible to efficiently use past resources (through advanced states) and future resources (through previous states) for a specific period, learning the sequences of information in both directions of the LSTM. The purpose is to build a model combining these two approaches, and the result is the possibility of predicting possible attacks on HTTP requests.

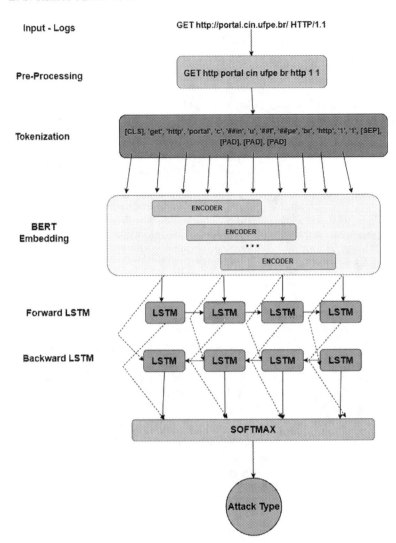

Fig. 1. Architecture of the RequestBERT-BiLSTM proposal. The input in the model is the HTTP requests and then a treatment of the input data by making it lowercase and removing special characters. The *BertTokenizer* realizes the tokenization process by dividing the words into subwords. In this step, we add tokens as *[CLS], [PAD] and [SEP]*, more details in the Sect. 4.2. In the BERT Embedding step, after receiving a sequence of 512 tokens, we generate the representation of the sequence. The next step adds a BiLSTM network consisting of two LSTMs: one receiving input in a forward direction and the other in reverse. Finally, after processing the information and extracting the context, the model labels whether the HTTP request is an attack or not.

```
GET   /sell-media-search/?keyword=%22%3E%3Cscript%3Ealert
    %281337%29%3C%2Fscript%3E HTTP/1.1\r\n
Host: sismil.7rm.eb.mil.br\r\n
User-Agent: Mozilla/5.0 (Windows NT 10.0; Win64; x64)
...
```

Fig. 2. HTTP request for an XSS attack attempt on a provider's web server.

```
get sell media search keyword 22 3e 3cscript 3ealert 281337
    29 3c 2fscript 3e http 1 1 r n
host sismil 7rm eb mil br r n
user agent mozilla 5 0 windows nt 10 0 win64 x64 r n
...
```

Fig. 3. Request HTTP after initial handling of stripping special characters and making it lowercase.

```
['get', 'sell', 'media', 'search', 'key','##word', '22', '3',
    '##e', '3', '##cs', '##cript','3','##e', 'http', '1',
    '1', ...]
```

Fig. 4. BERT to avoid the cases of the unknown token [UNK], uses the algorithm *WordPiece* that splits a word into several subwords to maintain the context.

```
[101, 1243, 4582, 2394, 3403, 2501, 12565, 1659, 124, 1162,
    124, 6063, 13590, 124, 13003, 7340, 25567, 23493,
    102,...]
```

Fig. 5. The unique IDs of the words or subwords corresponding to the request in Fig. 2. Where IDs 101 and 102 indicate [CLS] and [SEP], which serve, respectively, to indicate the beginning of the sentence and to indicate the end of the sentence.

```
[101,1243, 4582, 2394, 3403, 2501, 12565, 1659, 124, 1162,
    124, 6063, 13590, 124, 102, ...,0, 0, 0, 0, 0, 0, 0, 0,
    0, 0, 0]
```

Fig. 6. For the case of log entries smaller than the maximum size provided, it is necessary to add padding [PAD] to the sentences to compose the maximum length, and normally the value 0 is used.

```
[1, 1, 1, 1, 1, 1, 1, 1, 1, 1, 1, 1, 1, 1, 1, 1, 1, 1, 1, 1,
    1, 1, 1, 1, 1, 1, 1, 0, 0, 0, 0, 0, 0, 0, 0, 0..., 0]
```

Fig. 7. *Attention Mask* is a binary tensor that indicates the position of filled indices. For *BertTokenizer*, 1 indicates a value that must be met, while 0 indicates a populated value.

RequestBERT-BiLSTM was developed and enhanced for HTTP requests and uses all content to extract the semantics of HTTP requests. In addition, it implements transfer learning using BERT. With this, we were able to recycle the knowledge of the previously trained model, so it was possible to train only the new BiLSTM layer.

Another point to highlight in RequestBERT-BiLSTM is that it is not restricted to HTTP requests. It can also detect anomalies in other log categories.

Figure 1 shows the architecture of RequestBERT-BiLSTM.

4.1   Pre-processing

Initially, the logs are extracted in text format, and we create a Python script to convert them to CSV with the separation of data in columns from a Regex[1]. It is possible to search, validate, and change any character pattern in any text with regex. The next step with CSV was to make the data lowercase and remove all special characters. These removed special characters contain accents, punctuation, and math signs. Figure 2 shows a request and Fig. 3 shows how it looks after preprocessing.

4.2   Tokenization and Transformer-Based Classification

Tokenization aims to divide strings into subword token strings, convert token strings into ids, and reverse processes. In addition, in this step, token insertions such as [CLS], [PAD], and [SEP] serve, respectively, to indicate the beginning of the sentence, padding for sentences to reach the defined token size, and to indicate the end of the sentence. The tokenization process is shown in the sequence from Figs. 4, 5, 6 and 7.

BERT works with fixed-length strings. Therefore, we will use a simple strategy to choose the maximum length. Let us store the token length of each request and then perform the average and choose the best value to avoid making the embedding array sparse and not risk losing much information from larger requests.

5   Experiments

RequestBERT-BiLSTM was evaluated on four datasets, using the AdamW optimizer with the learning rate at $2e-5$ and the batch size at 16 with a maximum of 5 epochs. The model adopted in this work was developed in Pytorch at GoogleColab, using a Tesla T4 GPU with 16 GB.

We used literature models with approaches to explore the advantages of the RequestBERT-BiLSTM in detecting anomalies in HTTP requests.

Based on the choices of log parser methods (*Drain, AEL, LogSig, and LFA*), it is possible to confirm that the option of using log parsing should be careful and not simply rely on ready-made tools.

---

[1] Regex is the abbreviation of the English *Regular Expressions*, for regular expressions.

```
GET  /?server=db&username=root&db=mysql&table=event%3C%2
     Fscript%3E%3Cscript%3Ealert%28document.domain%29%3C%2
     Fscript%3E HTTP/1.1\r\nHost: sismil.7rm.eb.mil.br\r\nUser
     -Agent: Mozilla/5.0 (Windows NT 6.3; WOW64) AppleWebKit
     /537.36 (KHTML, like Gecko) Chrome/41.0.2226.0 Safari
     /537.36\r\nConnection: close\r\nAccept: */*\r\nAccept-
     Language: en\r\nAccept-Encoding: gzip\r\nX-Forwarded-For:
     45.155.205.137\r\n\r\n
```

Fig. 8. HTTP request extracted from the original log of a possible attack.

```
GET <*> HTTP/1.1\r\nHost: <*> Mozilla/5.0 <*> <*> <*> <*>
    AppleWebKit/537.36 <*> like Gecko) <*> <*> close\r\
    nAccept: */*\r\nAccept-Language: en\r\nAccept-Encoding:
    gzip\r\nX-Forwarded-For: <*>
```

Fig. 9. Template created by parser - DRAIN.

```
<*> <*> HTTP/1.1\r\nHost: <*> Mozilla/5.0 <*> <*> <*> <*>
    AppleWebKit/537.36 <*> like Gecko) <*> <*> <*> <*> <*> <*
    > <*>
```

Fig. 10. Template created by parser - AEL.

```
GET HTTP/1.1\r\nHost: Mozilla/5.0 (Windows NT AppleWebKit
    /537.36 (KHTML, like Gecko) Safari/537.36\r\nConnection:
    close\r\nAccept: */*\r\nAccept-Language: en\r\nAccept-
    Encoding: gzip\r\nX-Forwarded-For: 45.155.205.137\r\n\r\n
```

Fig. 11. Template created by parser - LogSig.

```
GET <*> HTTP/1.1\r\nHost: <*> Mozilla/5.0 <*> <*> <*> <*> <*>
    <*> <*> <*> <*> <*> <*> <*> <*> <*> <*>
```

Fig. 12. Template created by parser - LFA.

For each log analyzer, the experimental methodology was the same. Taking as input the request of the Fig. 8 that is part of the Log-Security dataset, we can visualize the results of each log analyzer ranging from Figs. 9, 10, 11 and 12, where it is easily noticeable the different understandings that each log analyzer had for the same entry.

As the objective of this work is to handle the entire HTTP request, we have not used regex to extract any specific information. Each method requires two Python scripts to run. The first is receiving the text file with the requests without the classifications and pre-treatment. The second script is responsible for producing the CSV files, where these files are divided into generated templates that the parser reproduced, and the other is the requests handled based on the parser templates.

5.1   Datasets

Four datasets were used for the project, three public datasets, ECML/PKDD 2007 [20], CSIC 2010 [22], BGL [19] and one dataset generated in this work from one asset of security *F5 Big-IP* (Table 1).

Table 1. Dataset characteristics

Dataset	Category	Size	Classes	Anomalies
BGL [19]	Supercomputer	4.7M	Binary	348.460
Log-Security	Request HTTP	98K	Multi	67.265
CSIC 2010 [22]	Request HTTP	97K	Binary	25.000
ECML/PKDD [20]	Request HTTP	50K	Multi	15.110

The objective of ECML/PKDD 2007 was to build an algorithm based on machine learning techniques to perform multiclass classification and isolation of attack patterns.

The HTTP CSIC 2010 dataset contains the generated traffic directed to an e-commerce web application. This web application allows users to purchase items using a shopping cart and register by providing personal information.

The BGL dataset is an open dataset of logs collected from a BlueGene/L supercomputer system at Lawrence Livermore National Labs (LLNL) in Livermore, California, with 131,072 processors and 32,768 GB of memory. The log contains alert and non-alert messages identified by alert category tags [19].

The dataset we created was extracted from a security asset initially configured to filter only requests considered offensive. That is, these requests would already be labeled based on the knowledge of the equipment's signatures. As a result, all Dataset requests are destined for sites hosted on a provider's infrastructure.

The asset used to collect the logs was the *F5-Big-Ip* whose main function is to direct different types of protocol and application traffic to an appropriate destination server. Figure 13b and Fig. 13a show characteristics of the Log-Security dataset. To evaluate RequestBERT-BiLSTM in detecting anomalies in HTTP requests, we used the following metrics: Precision, Recall, F1-Score, and Accuracy.

6   Discussion and Results

After executing the log analyzers, it was possible to extract information such as execution time and the number of templates created by each method. The Table 2 shows this information.

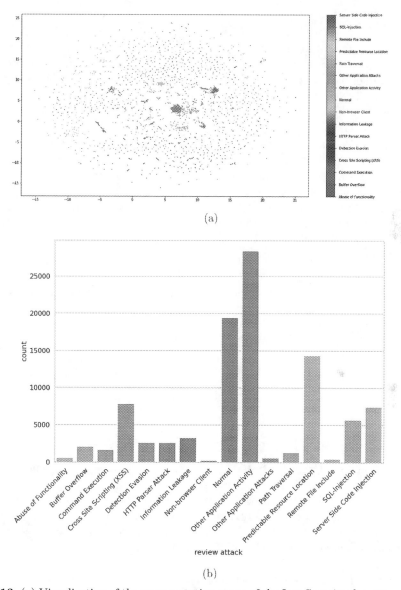

(a)

(b)

Fig. 13. (a) Visualization of the representation space of the Log-Security dataset using *UMAP*. It is possible to verify some clusters in the center, such as *SQL_Injection, Command Execution, and Buffer Overflow* attacks. For the three types of attacks, some characteristics can be highlighted: for SQL_Injection, there is a need for some keyword like *DDL/DML* in SQL request; for Command Execution, with specific commands like - *cat, run* etc. Finally, in cases of Buffer Overflow, the highlight is the size of its requests, so these types of attacks have well-defined patterns. It is also possible to notice small groups of Normal and *Other Application Attacks* classes, reflecting several requests with similar characteristics. However, it is normal that these two classes do not have any standardization. (b)Distribution of classes in the Log-Security Dataset. In terms of attack type, the *Other Application Attacks* represents attacks that do not fall into the more explicit attack classifications. [1]

6.1   Comparisons Between Log Parser Methods

Figure 14b shows the behavior of the models based on the resulting data from each log analyzer. Again, it is possible to notice a behavior for most models: that the heuristic-based log analyzer was superior to the others. Thus, despite the difficulty encountered with the data generated by the log analyzers. And Fig. 14a shows a compilation of models tested with and without Log Parser.

Another point is that the models that adopt the traditional embedding obtained an advance. The improvement is due to the "cleaning" of the log requests. As both methods incorporate words from the requests in a smaller number of words, the model tends to reduce the number of occurrences of Out-of-vocabulary (OOV), that is, words that do not have representation, thus improving the complete requests. The performance degradation of models that use BERT is caused due to the absence of essential words for certain attacks and behaviors, and how BERT uses context dramatically affects the model's performance.

Table 2. Comparison table of log parsers methods in the log-security dataset

Log parser	Category	Qty of templates	Time
DRAIN	Heuristic	1781	1 m 3 s
AEL	Heuristic	1471	18 m
LogSig	Clustering	16	3 h 37 m
LFA	Frequent Patterns	428	15 s

6.2   Comparisons Between the Analyzed Models

Table 3 shows all models tested and results from other models in different datasets.

In this scenario, the superiority of RequestBERT-BiLSTM over Word2Vec and CNN in Table 3 can be explained by several factors. The first is how word embeddings work. Because the traditional method deals with word-based context forms, whereas RequestBERT-BiLSTM uses BERT for the context of each request.

For NeuralLog, both use BERT and do not have the Log Parser step. However, two factors affect its performance for the HTTP request scenario. The first is the action of excluding the numerical data from the requests. The other is that in its implementation, there is the creation of a window composed of 20 log messages to build log sequences, similar to [15], with this for datasets whose numeric characters are relevant and log turnover is high NeuralLog performs poorly. Another point that can be highlighted is the difficulty that NeuralLog had in the CSIC and ECML datasets due to the dataset imbalance.

For RequestBERT-BiLSTM, it considers each log line as input. It does not discard the numbers, as they are relevant in the anomaly detection scenario and should not be disregarded.

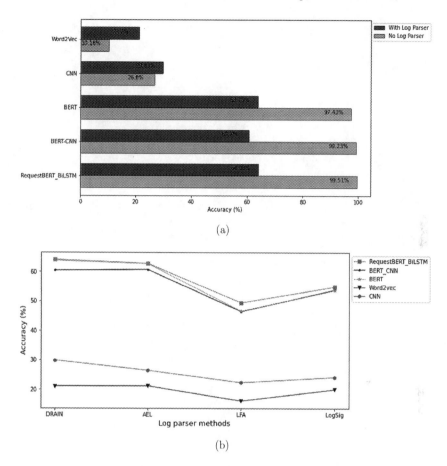

Fig. 14. (a)The figure shows a compilation of models tested with and without Log Parser. As a result, the image makes clear the difference in performance between the models that use BERT using Log Parser and without. In addition, it shows the slight evolution of the models that use word embedding. This improvement is due to the treatment that occurs in requests with the use of Log Parser because as the models perform the word embedding of the requests with their pre-trained corpus in a smaller amount of words, the model tends to reduce the number of occurrences of Out-of-vocabulary (OOV). And the difficulty for models with BERT is caused by the absence of essential words for certain attacks and behaviors, and how BERT uses context dramatically affects the model's performance. (b) The figure shows the performance of the models taking as input the data resulting from each log analyzer. And there is a notable behavior for most models: the method DRAIN outperforms most tested models, except for BERT-CNN and Word2Vec. For these two models, the AEL was the best. On the other hand, the LFA was the worst of all. Another point that can be highlighted is how close the models that use BERT were and, simultaneously, much superior to others. Thus, despite the difficulty encountered with the data generated by the log analyzer methods, RequestBERT-BiLSTM was superior to the other models. The Figs. 9, 10, 11 and 12 show the difference in the understanding that a Log Parser category can have for the same request. In this way, the adopted method can affect the results for the same model.

Table 3. Performance comparison between models and datasets

Dataset	Model	Recall (%)	Precision (%)	F1-Score (%)	Accuracy (%)
CSIC 2010 [22]	Word2Vec	63	62	62	62.66
	BERT	98	97	98	98.4
	BERT-CNN	95	95	95	95.06
	Le et al. [13]	–	–	–	–
	Lu et al. [14]	58	58	58	58.34
	Ito et al. [9]	n/a	n/a	n/a	98.8
	Kuang et al. [12]	n/a	96.92	95.57	96.44
	RequestBERT-BiLSTM(Ours)	**100**	**100**	**100**	**99.50**
ECML/PKDD 2007 [20]	Word2Vec	63	50	56	63.48
	BERT	96	96	96	96.83
	BERT-CNN	94	94	94	94.23
	Le et al. [13]	–	–	–	–
	Lu et al. [14]	52	52	52	51.64
	RequestBERT-BiLSTM(Ours)	**96**	**97**	**97**	**97.26**
BGL [19]	Word2Vec	–	–	–	–
	BERT	100	99	99	99.61
	BERT-CNN	100	99	99	99.58
	Le et al. [13]	98	98	98	98.7
	Lu et al. [14]	–	–	–	–
	Meng et al. [15]	94	97	96	n/a
	Guo et al. [5]	92.32	89.40	90.83	n/a
	RequestBERT-BiLSTM(Ours)	**100**	**100**	**100**	**99.98**
Log-Security	Word2Vec	10	18	10	10.18
	BERT	98	97	97	97.43
	BERT-CNN	99	99	99	99.23
	Le et al. [13]	76	76	76	76.24
	Lu et al. [14]	27	27	27	26.80
	RequestBERT-BiLSTM(Ours)	**99**	**100**	**99**	**99.51**

"–" The model failed to reproduce results with the original project settings.
"n/a" There was no result in the original article.

BERT and BERT-CNN models use the same settings and hyperparameter values as RequestBERT-BiLSTM. The difference is that BERT uses the standard BertForSequenceClassification class, which has only one dense layer with dropout in the output, and BERT-CNN uses a convolutional network configuration used in [14].

7   Conclusion and Future Work

Log anomaly detection is essential to protect computer systems from malicious attacks. We presented RequestBert-BiLSTM, a new supervised model for detecting attacks on HTTP requests based on BERT and BiLSTM to detect log anomalies. For training, RequestBERT-BiLSTM considers all information from HTTP requests as input without the need for *Parser Log* and with the elimination of only special characters.

Based on experimental results on four log datasets and compared to literature models, RequestBERT-BiLSTM outperformed traditional and state-of-the-art approaches to detect HTTP request attacks and log anomalies. In addition, based on the results, Log Parser does not improve the model performance. It may prejudice the method due to important information lost in the log analysis process.

Future work should consider evaluating the proposed method on other datasets and applying unsupervised machine learning techniques. Finally, there is the possibility to predict zero-day attacks based on suspicious requests, combining the proposed approach, the number of requests in a short time, the IP geographic location, and other contextual information.

References

1. Assigning attack signatures to security policies (2022). https://techdocs.f5. com/kb/en-us/products/big-ip_asm/manuals/product/asm-bot-and-attack-signatures-13-0-0/1.html
2. Althubiti, S., Yuan, X., Esterline, A.: Analyzing http requests for web intrusion detection (2017)
3. Chen, Z., Liu, J., Gu, W., Su, Y., Lyu, M.R.: Experience report: deep learning-based system log analysis for anomaly detection. CoRR abs/2107.05908 (2021). https://arxiv.org/abs/2107.05908
4. Du, M., Li, F., Zheng, G., Srikumar, V.: DeepLog: anomaly detection and diagnosis from system logs through deep learning, pp. 1285–1298 (2017). https://doi.org/10.1145/3133956.3134015
5. Guo, H., Yuan, S., Wu, X.: LogBERT: log anomaly detection via BERT, pp. 1–8 (2021). https://doi.org/10.1109/IJCNN52387.2021.9534113
6. He, P., Zhu, J., He, S., Li, J., Lyu, M.R.: An evaluation study on log parsing and its use in log mining, pp. 654–661 (2016). https://doi.org/10.1109/DSN.2016.66
7. He, P., Zhu, J., Zheng, Z., Lyu, M.R.: Drain: an online log parsing approach with fixed depth tree, pp. 33–40 (2017). https://doi.org/10.1109/ICWS.2017.13
8. He, S., Zhu, J., He, P., Lyu, M.R.: Experience report: system log analysis for anomaly detection, pp. 207–218 (2016). https://doi.org/10.1109/ISSRE.2016.21
9. Ito, M., Iyatomi, H.: Web application firewall using character-level convolutional neural network, pp. 103–106 (2018). https://doi.org/10.1109/CSPA.2018.8368694
10. Jiang, Z., Hassan, A.E., Hamann, G., Flora, P.: An automated approach for abstracting execution logs to execution events, pp. 249–267 (2008). https://doi.org/10.1002/smr.374
11. Kim, Y.: Convolutional neural networks for sentence classification. CoRR abs/1408.5882 (2014). http://arxiv.org/abs/1408.5882
12. Kuang, X., et al.: DeepWAF: detecting web attacks based on CNN and LSTM models. In: Vaidya, J., Zhang, X., Li, J. (eds.) CSS 2019. LNCS, vol. 11983, pp. 121–136. Springer, Cham (2019). https://doi.org/10.1007/978-3-030-37352-8_11
13. Le, V., Zhang, H.: Log-based anomaly detection without log parsing. CoRR abs/2108.01955 (2021). https://arxiv.org/abs/2108.01955
14. Lu, S., Wei, X., Li, Y., Wang, L.: Detecting anomaly in big data system logs using convolutional neural network, pp. 151–158 (2018). https://doi.org/10.1109/DASC/PiCom/DataCom/CyberSciTec.2018.00037
15. Meng, W., et al.: LogAnomaly: unsupervised detection of sequential and quantitative anomalies in unstructured logs. In: IJCAI (2019)
16. Nagappan, M., Vouk, M.A.: Abstracting log lines to log event types for mining software system logs, pp. 114–117 (2010). https://doi.org/10.1109/MSR.2010.5463281

17. Nedelkoski, S., Bogatinovski, J., Acker, A., Cardoso, J., Kao, O.: Self-supervised log parsing. In: Dong, Y., Mladenić, D., Saunders, C. (eds.) ECML PKDD 2020. LNCS (LNAI), vol. 12460, pp. 122–138. Springer, Cham (2021). https://doi.org/10.1007/978-3-030-67667-4_8

18. Odumuyiwa, V., Chibueze, A.: Automatic detection of http injection attacks using convolutional neural network and deep neural network (2020)

19. Oliner, A., Stearley, J.: What supercomputers say: a study of five system logs, pp. 575–584 (2007). https://doi.org/10.1109/DSN.2007.103

20. Raïssi, C., Brissaud, J., Dray, G., Poncelet, P., Roche, M., Teisseire, M.: Web analyzing traffic challenge: description and results (2007)

21. Tang, L., Li, T., Perng, C.S.: LogSig: Generating System Events from Raw Textual Logs. Association for Computing Machinery, New York (2011). https://doi.org/10.1145/2063576.2063690

22. Torrano-Gimenez, C., Perez-Villegas, A., Alvarez, G.: A self-learning anomaly-based web application firewall. In: Herrero, Á., Gastaldo, P., Zunino, R., Corchado, E. (eds.) Computational Intelligence in Security for Information Systems. AISC, pp. 85–92. Springer, Heidelberg (2009). https://doi.org/10.1007/978-3-642-04091-7_11

23. Vaswani, A., et al.: Attention is all you need. CoRR abs/1706.03762 (2017). http://arxiv.org/abs/1706.03762

24. Xuan, C., Dinh, H., Victor, T.: Malicious URL detection based on machine learning. 11 (2020). https://doi.org/10.14569/IJACSA.2020.0110119

25. Yu, L., et al.: Detecting malicious web requests using an enhanced TextCNN, pp. 768–777 (2020). https://doi.org/10.1109/COMPSAC48688.2020.0-167

26. Zhu, J., et al.: Tools and benchmarks for automated log parsing. CoRR abs/1811.03509 (2018). http://arxiv.org/abs/1811.03509

Aiding Glaucoma Diagnosis from the Automated Classification and Segmentation of Fundus Images

Lucas M. Ceschini[✉], Lucas M. Policarpo, Rodrigo da R. Righi, and Gabriel de O. Ramos

Graduate Program in Applied Computing, Universidade do Vale do Rio dos Sinos, São Leopoldo, Brazil
{lceschini,lmpolicarpo,rrrighi,gdoramos}@unisinos.br

Abstract. Glaucoma is the most significant cause of irreversible vision loss and the second biggest cause of blindness globally. The first signs of the disease will only appear in an advanced stage when there is no more recovery. Early diagnosis is of the utmost importance and is currently performed primarily through fundoscopy. This fundus image exam is a tedious and manual process, prone to human errors that can result in false negatives, which could promote vision loss. Deep learning approaches are being used to detect glaucoma directly from eyes fundus images, achieving promising results. However, there is no apparent interest in deploying these systems in medical clinics, which would require lightweight models with minimal false negatives and comprehensive outputs. The present study explores these gaps and proposes an architecture composed of one segmentation network for disc and cup and one classification network for direct glaucoma classification. Our main contribution is optimizing a glaucoma-aiding system by increasing model sensitivity by 3% and simplifying the architecture. Unlike related works, we present a lighter model that shows valuable information to the physician, building their trust in the system.

Keywords: Deep learning · Computer vision · Glaucoma · Fundoscopy

1 Introduction

Glaucoma is an ocular disease responsible for most global irreversible vision loss and the second biggest cause of blindness [8]. Early diagnosis is of utmost importance to prevent vision loss. The degeneration of the optic nerve is the primary pathology of glaucoma, usually preceded by an increase in intraocular pressure [9]. This increase causes a common enlargement on the angle of the optic disc cup, erosion of the rim tissue, and, as a result, visual field damage. Evaluation of the optic nerve head through digital fundoscopy is one of the most feasible exams because of its less invasive approach and capability of generating high-resolution images of the back of the eye [4].

J. C. Xavier-Junior and R. A. Rios (Eds.): BRACIS 2022, LNAI 13654, pp. 343–356, 2022.
https://doi.org/10.1007/978-3-031-21689-3_25

However, fundoscopy exam is manual, tedious, complex, and prone to human errors. As a result, this can lead to irreversible vision loss, a consequence of false-negative prognosis done by tired or inexperienced physicians [1]. To address these issues, deep learning models are being explored to classify glaucoma from fundus images, achieving promising results [2,6,15]. However, only a few studies discuss the possibility of deploying their systems in the medical clinic. In these cases, expert trust in the system is required and can be increased by showing more than just the final prediction, such as the segmentation of the eye structures and the system's confidence level on the prognostic. Also, lighter models must be adopted to make this possible while aiming to increase sensitivity more than just accuracy.

The main goal of this study is to optimize the state-of-the-art models used on the diagnosis aiding tool created by Civit-Masot et al. [4]. Their system is an ophthalmic aid tool that uses deep learning and fundus images to classify and segment the image directly. It provides robust information to support the final diagnosis, in addition to using modules light enough to be installed in embedded systems of low storage and processing power. We choose this study as the basis for this research.

The base model architecture consists of a direct classification network based on MobileNetV2 [13], and two modified U-net [11] segmentation networks, for the disc and cup segmentation. This study adds an ensemble of MobileNetV2 and EfficientNet for the direct classification network and a unified segmentation network for the disc and cup features. By adding a second classification network, we increased sensitivity by 3% compared to the base model. We achieved comparable results with the unified segmentation network while simplifying the architecture and reducing processing time by 36.35%. Therefore, our contribution is made by exploring the gaps in the literature left in evidence by the authors, namely:

- Increasing the sensitivity of the model, further reducing the number of false negatives and thus ensuring even more value for its use in the clinic;
- Architecture simplification, taking up less storage space and using less processing resources, without losing accuracy, having as an only consequence the need for more initial training time.

The remainder of the paper is organized as follows. In Sect. 2 we give a review of related works. Section 3 introduces the proposed model and the implementation process. Then, Sect. 4 report the experiments made and the results obtained. Lastly, Sect. 5 concludes this work.

2   Related Work

The evaluation of related works was done to understand the state-of-art of glaucoma detection using machine learning. Our study followed the systematic review pipeline proposed by Kitchenham et al. [7] and can be addressed in four main steps: **1)** Define research questions; **2)** Elaborate a research protocol; **3)**

List inclusion and exclusion criteria; **4)** Review selected papers and answer the research questions. This questions include describing the techniques and technologies commonly used in automated glaucoma classification, the metrics used to measure the efficacy and accuracy of glaucoma classification models, the private and public datasets and, finally, the state-of-the art models.

Research process started by creating a search string and applying it in different journals, followed by inclusion and exclusion filtering and finishing with the acquisition and review of selected papers.

Civit-Masot el al. [4] used a U-shaped network for the segmentation and RANSAC to calculate and improve the expected elliptic shape. Xu et al. [17] also made use of the U-shaped network. However, it has segmented not only the optic disc and cup, but also defects in the retinal nerve fiber layer. Yu et al. [18] used a modified U-net with ResNet-34 as the encoder, achieving top performance in dice values for the cup and the disk.

Sreng et al. [15] used the DeepLabV3+ network, which had not been explored for segmentation yet, testing its performance with five different convolutional neural networks (CNNs), the best combination being DeepLabV3+ with MobileNet. Sallam et al. [12] used several pre-trained CNN architectures and trained them all using transfer learning from the same dataset, thus comparing their performances. Chai et al. [2] used heterogeneous data such as retinal images, medical indicators, and patient complaint texts, integrate them using representation integration, and predict using a Bayesian's model.

Ahn et al. [1] elaborated on three models to classify glaucoma. The first uses logistic regression, the second InceptionV3 with transfer learning, and the last was an CNN manually architected by the authors. The authors elaborated the one with the better performance among the three. Phasuk et al. [10] combined the results of several integrated networks with the DenseNet-121 for feature extraction and a neural network for the final classification.

Chai et al. [2] created a heterogeneous dataset using retina images, medical charts and text-based pacient complaints, training a bayesian neural network model using representation integration.

Sallam et al. [12] gathered 9 of the most successful models in image classification challenges and, with their pre-trained weights, compared their performance against a single glaucoma classification dataset, the Large-scale Attention based Glaucoma (LAG) dataset. Selected models were AlexNet, VGG16, VGG19, GoogleNet (Inception V1), ResNET-18, ResNET-50, ResNet-101 and ResNet-152. Best results were achieved by ResNet-152, with an accuracy, precision and recall of 86,9.

The work of Serte et al. [14] compared four popular image classification networks using five public glaucoma classification datasets. While a single dataset was used as the testing set, the other four were used to train the models, comparing model performance for each dataset. Selected networks included Xception, ResNet-50, GoogLeNet and ResNET-152. Datasets used in this work were HRF, Drishti-GS1, RIM-ONE, sjchoi86-HRF and ACRIMA. According to author's results, each network performed better on specific datasets.

As seen, deep learning has shown promising results on classifying fundus images as normal or glaucomatous in an automated way. However, more studies are needed to be focused on the clinic, where issues in addition to accuracy are of paramount importance, such as the explainability and transparency of the results obtained by the models. Moreover, the best-performing models need a large volume of data to extract relevant features and patterns. In the medical field, such information is difficult to obtain, with considerable effort from researchers to model systems capable of working with small amounts of data without losing performance.

Our research focuses on recreating the methodology of Civit-Masot et al. [4] and tackling the open issues of architecture simplification and sensitivity increase, leading to better clinical usage of the model. Section 3 describes the proposed model.

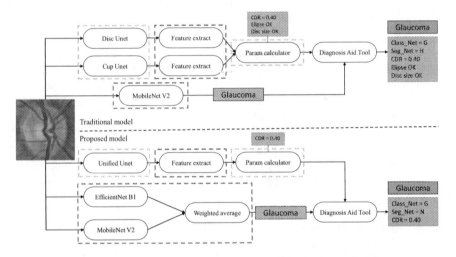

Fig. 1. Base model and proposed model architectures. Each color highlights a subsystem. The proposed model segments both disc and cup using a single U-net model and improve the classification subsystem with the ensemble of two lightweight models.

3   Proposed Method

In this paper, we extend the work of Civit-Masot et al. [4] by adding a second classification network and unifying the two segmentation networks. In that way, we aim to increase model sensitivity and simplify its architecture to enable its deployment in medical clinics. Initially, the pipeline of the base model was replicated, followed by the implementation of the ensemble of the classification networks, and lastly, the unification of the segmentation networks. Both architectures and execution flow are presented in Fig. 1. Highlighted colors represent the correlated areas between models.

The network proposed by Civit-Masot et al. [4] employed distinct networks for disc and cup segmentation. Such an improvement simplified development and helped adopting datasets with separated label masks for each structure. On the other hand, this approach leads to an increase in processing and storage loads. In order to enhance user's trust in the system while keeping it light enough to deploy it in embedded systems, our proposed method joins both disc and cup segmentation networks into a single one, reducing processing time and cost.

The application pipeline is as follows: first, the back of the patient's eye is captured by a digital fundus camera. Then, the image is loaded into the system and preprocessed, fed afterward to both prediction subsystems, classification, and segmentation. The classification system outputs its prediction, while the segmentation system will extract disc and cup features and compute the cup-to-disc ratio (CDR) as its output prediction.

The diagnosis system then evaluates both outputs, and if one is true for glaucoma, this is the final prognostic printed into the medic screen. In addition to the prognostic, a processed image with disc and cup highlighted by the segmentation network is presented, followed by the CDR value. Even though the system's internal parts are not self fully explainable, these features aim to increase the medical trust in the final prediction. Since the system can output a processed image and its computed values, it is more evident how the machine came to a conclusion.

3.1 Dataset

RIM-ONE DL [5] was used as the dataset for this study. It consists of 485 fundus images, with its matching binary masks for cup and disc. Of the 485 samples, 313 (65%) were labeled as healthy cases, and 172 (35%) as glaucomatous cases. This dataset is part of a research project, developed as a joint work of three Spanish's hospitals. The main purpose of the work was to offer a dataset of reference ophthalmology images, specifically developed for glaucoma diagnosis. Labels were made by five experts in the field, with a final segmentation unifying the singular results. An example of images and labels can be seen in Fig. 2 and Fig. 3.

3.2 Preprocessing

Following the details presented in the baseline work, the data were preprocessed as follows. First, the images and their masks were concatenated in a list, followed by the transformation of this list in a tf.dataset object. Thereby, Tensorflow preprocessing functions became available and were applied to the dataset.

Images were of different dimensions and had to be resized to specific input dimensions, this is 224×224 px in the classification system and 128×128 px in the segmentation system.

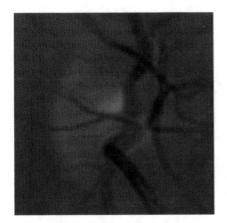 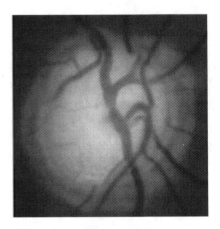

Fig. 2. RIM-ONE dataset input image sample.

Image quality was also variable, and to help enhance those poor-quality samples, contrast limited adaptive histogram equalization (CLAHE) was applied. By doing so, the morphological structures present in the images were highlighted.

The dataset's number of samples was insufficient to train robust deep learning models. Data augmentation techniques were utilized to solve that issue, increasing samples from 485 to 9215 images. The process consisted of applying random brightness or random contrast filters, followed by small rotations of less than 15°. It is crucial to notice that glaucoma diagnosis is related to the orientation of the segmented image, so it is crucial to keep rotations to a minimum [4].

To implement the unified segmentation network, it was also necessary to unify the cup and disc masks. In this new mask, each of the structure masks corresponds to a color channel from the RGB system. The disc mask was set to the red channel and the cup mask to green.

Difference between original and preprocessed image samples can be seen at Fig. 4.

3.3   Neural Network Architecture

The baseline system [4] consists of three neural networks, two modified U-nets for disc and cup segmentation, and one direct classification network based on MobileNetV2. On the other hand, in this work, we propose two neural networks, one modified U-net for both disc and cup segmentation, and one direct classification network composed of the ensemble of MobileNetV2 and EfficientNetB1. These networks are detailed below.

Segmentation Using U-Net. For disc and cup segmentation, the baseline work used a generalized U-net architecture [3]. This network has six levels of coding and decoding, with 64 channels in the first coding stage, and a channel growth rate of 1.1. Even though it has one level extra compared to the original

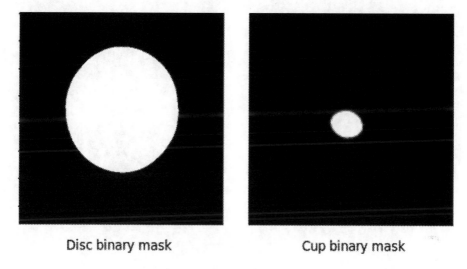

Fig. 3. RIM-ONE dataset label mask sample.

U-net, the reduction in the growth rate from 2 to 1.1 reduced the number of parameters from 138M to 2.5M [4].

The unified segmentation network proposed by this study follows the same architecture previously described but changes the optimizer from Adam to RMSprop. Also, due to the increased complexity, the number of training epochs was increased from 100 to 300.

Classification Using MobileNetV2 and EfficientNetB1. For the direct classification subsystem, a MobileNetV2 network was chosen by the baseline authors. The top layers were removed, and an average pooling layer was added. Its output was fed to a 64-node dense layer, followed by a dropout stage and a two-node final layer to distinguish between normal and glaucoma [4].

The proposed classification subsystem consists of an ensemble of the baseline MobileNetV2 model and an EfficientNetB1 model that follows the same structure in its top layers. Each model will output its prediction, passing it to an average layer responsible for the final subsystem output.

3.4 Hyperparameters Optimization

To train the neural networks, some hyperparameters were defined. Those described in the baseline work were chosen. In the case of a lack of details, the selection of hyperparameters was made by the author of this study.

Segmentation Using U-Net. Adam optimizer was used for the segmentation networks, with an adaptive learning rate between 1e−3 (0.001) and 2e−4 (0.0002). The cost function was DICE, and it was trained through 100 epochs,

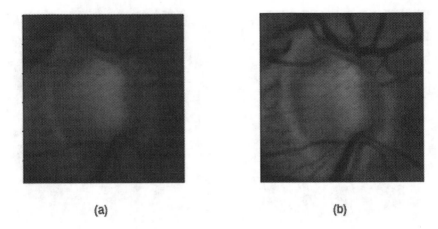

(a)   (b)

Fig. 4. Original (a) and Preprocessed (b) image samples

with a batch size of 120. The last layer has a sigmoid activation function, and the metrics for evaluation were IoU and DICE.

The unified segmentation network proposed used the same hyperparameters of the baseline described above, only changing the optimizer from Adam to RMSprop, and increasing training epochs from 100 to 300.

Classification Network: MobileNetV2 and EfficientNetB1. Pre-trained weights from the ImageNet challenge were used for the classification network, with the initial layers frozen. The optimizer was RMSprop with a learning rate of 1e−03. The cost function was Binary Cross-Entropy, and the batch size was 64.

First, the network was trained for 50 epochs, as described in Civit-Masot et al. [4], however it did not achieve the expected metrics. Because of that, the number of epochs was increased to 100. Evaluated metrics were AUC, accuracy, specificity, and sensitivity. The EfficientNetB1 proposed by this study adopted the same hyperparameters.

3.5   Final Output

After passing through both subsystems, the final step in the pipeline is to join their predictions and display them graphically to the physician. If one of the subsystem's outputs is glaucoma, this is the final prediction. Doing this increases the sensitivity of the model. Not just the prediction but also the semantic segmentation of both disc and cup features are graphically displayed, followed by what each subsystem predicted and the cup-to-disc ratio found. Figure 5 shows the final result of the base model, replicated by the authors of this paper.

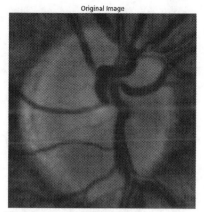

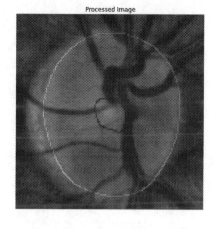

```
Classification subsystem:  Normal
Segmentation subsystem:  Normal
Cup-to-disc ratio:  0.1956521739130435
Final diagnosis:  Normal
```

Fig. 5. Base model final output. Together with the input image, the system displays the identified cup and disc, what was predicted by the two subsystems, the CDR and the final prediction.

4   Experimental Evaluation

This section aims to describe and evaluate the results obtained in each step of the development process. Moreover, validate our hypothesis and contributions based on the results. We start this section from the evaluation of the base model replication, followed by adding the second classification network and its ensemble with the original, then the union of the segmentation networks. Lastly, we present an execution time benchmark for each analog part of the architecture.

Replicating the Base Model. To implement our contributions, the base model was first replicated by following the paper implementation details [4]. The classification system was replicated after collecting the dataset and applying the preprocessing pipeline.

Table 1 compares the original metrics from Civit-Masot et al. [4] classification system to our version. Results are almost identical, which means that the replication was a success. However, specificity went down by two points, mainly because the authors didn't sufficiently specify the last layers of the base model.

Next, we replicated the segmentation networks, for both disc and cup features. DICE values for the original networks and ours can be seen in Table 2. Our results were far better than the baseline primarily due to the increase in available image samples from the datasets, compared to those obtainable by the time of the baseline paper.

Table 1. Comparison of the classification metrics as reported in [4] and as replicated by us.

Metric	Base model	Replicated model
AUC	0.93	**0.95**
Accuracy	0.88	0.88
Specificity	**0.86**	0.84
Sensitivity	0.91	0.91

Table 2. Comparison of the segmentation metrics as reported in [4] and as replicated by us.

Metric	Base model	Replicated model
Disc DICE	0.92	**0.99**
Cup DICE	0.84	**0.94**

4.1   Contribution 1: Modifying the Classification Network

Aiming to improve the classification network predictions, a second lightweight network was proposed. With that in mind, the chosen network was Efficient-NetB1 [16], composed of less than eight million parameters. It is considered a light model capable of providing results as efficient as those of the more robust architectures, like VGG or Inception.

It was trained with the same hyperparameters of the original MobileNetV2, and it resulted in an increase in sensitivity, from 0.9140 to 0.9462. While it did not increase AUC and reduced specificity, it is still an improvement, primarily because of how critical false negatives are to the medical clinic compared to false positives. Table 3 compares the results obtained for the original MobileNetV2, the new network added by this study, EfficientNetB1, and the ensemble of both MobileNetV2 and EfficientNetB1 as the final output of the proposed classification subsystem.

4.2   Contribution 2: Unifying the Segmentation Networks

To simplify the architecture and make it lighter for possible deployment on embedded systems, we developed a single segmentation network capable of identifying both disc and cup features. Due to the increased complexity, training epochs were increased from 100 to 300 to achieve similar results to those of the individual networks. However, it became clear that a single segmentation network can achieve state-of-the-art results with a more straightforward and lighter architecture, increasing the feasibility of an embedded system for the medical

Table 3. Evaluation metrics for MobileNetV2, EfficientNetB1 and their ensemble

Metric	MobileNetV2	EfficientNetB1	Ensemble
AUC	**0.9567**	0.9394	0.9512
Accuracy	**0.8897**	0.8345	**0.8897**
Specificity	**0.8461**	0.6538	0.7884
Sensitivity	0.9140	0.9355	**0.9462**

clinic. Table 4 compares these results. Comparable results were obtained using only one U-net model. By doing so, we reduced the storage and processing cost of the segmentation subsystem in half. This can prove valuable to those interested in deploying the system in standard desktop hardware.

Table 4. Segmentation done by disc, cup, and unified networks

Metric	Disc net	Cup net	Unified net
IoU	**0.9872**	0.8892	0.9455
DICE	**0.9936**	0.9406	0.9502

4.3   Benchmark

To better visualize the impact on the simplification of the system, a benchmark evaluation of the baseline model and the proposed one was made. Both networks were executed from end to end with the same inputs and on the same hardware. Each model ran 50 times, providing high fidelity results. Table 5 shows the obtained results. Each color represents a highlighted region from Fig. 1. As seen in Table 5, the proposed model has a lower average response time for the diagnosis outcome, mostly because of the simplification of the U-net networks. In this manner, the architecture also reduced the times for generating the diagnosis, reducing the patients' waiting time for the generation of the report.

Unifying the segmentation networks reduced the segmentation subsystem processing time by 24.24%. On the other hand, the ensemble of the two classification systems increased classification subsystem processing time by 33.25%. This is not critical, though, because the pipeline's bottleneck is the segmentation networks, and by reducing its time, the overall processing time gets reduced. Also, the training process is much slower on the segmentation networks than on the classification networks, increasing the value of this reduction.

Table 5. Comparison Between architectures execution time

	Unet (s)	Feature extract (s)	Param calculator (ns)	Mobile Net (s)	Total time (s)
Base model	68.796	0.078	3200	4.437	73.311
Proposed model	35.225	0.078	2300	11.357	46.661

5   Conclusion

Glaucoma is a silent disease that only shows signs in the advanced and irreversible stages of the disease. Fundoscopy is the primary diagnostic test, a manual process requiring years of expertise and specialization. It is possible to solve this problem by employing computer vision techniques to generate the diagnosis. However, these techniques often lack transparency and justification, not presenting more than the classification or the why of that result and the algorithm's reliability.

Our contribution is increasing the model sensitivity, further reducing the number of false negatives and thus ensuring even more value for its use in the clinic. Also, the architecture simplifies, taking up less storage space and using less processing resources without losing accuracy, resulting in the need for more initial training time.

Even though we obtained better results in processing time and sensitivity, our system does not address those situations where the segmented disc or cup does not form a fully connected ellipse. Without this shape enhancement, feature extraction of disc and cup diameter can not be computed, resulting in crashes. Even though CLAHE reduced crash rates by improving image quality, this can only be addressed by changing the logic behind the segmentation feature extraction or optimizing the ellipse fitting function. Because of these issues, our system performed better than the baseline on high-resolution images, and its use is recommended on such occasions. However, this is not the reality in most medical clinics, and fixing it is a priority in future works.

Lastly, we perceive that explainability is crucial for the future implementation of the system in a clinic. Our approach does not entirely address this type of issue. For this, it is necessary to evolve the system into an independent application in a production environment. Learning cycles and direct application are inserted in the process flow from an embedded system that receives the image directly from the capture system. This requires an advance and a future collaboration between researchers and medical institutions, being one of the main future works. Since the study's main objective is to assist the clinical diagnosis, it is essential to consider the reality of patients. This includes conditions other than glaucoma, varied ethnicities with specific eye characteristics, and images with different resolutions and specifications.

Acknowledgements. We thank the anonymous reviewers for their valuable feedback. This research was partially supported by Coordenação de Aperfeiçoamento de Pessoal de Nível Superior - Brasil (CAPES) - Finance Code 001, and Fundação de Amparo à Pesquisa do Estado do Rio Grande do Sul (FAPERGS).

References

1. Ahn, J.M., Kim, S., Ahn, K.S., Cho, S.H., Lee, K.B., Kim, U.S.: A deep learning model for the detection of both advanced and early glaucoma using fundus photography. PLoS ONE **13** (2018)
2. Chai, Y., Bian, Y., Liu, H., Li, J., Xu, J.: Glaucoma diagnosis in the Chinese context: an uncertainty information-centric Bayesian deep learning model. Inf. Process. Manag. **58** (2021)
3. Civit-Masot, J., Billis, A., Dominguez-Morales, M.J., Vicente-Diaz, S., Civit, A.: Multidataset incremental training for optic disc segmentation. In: Iliadis, L., Angelov, P.P., Jayne, C., Pimenidis, E. (eds.) EANN 2020. PINNS, vol. 2, pp. 365–376. Springer, Cham (2020). https://doi.org/10.1007/978-3-030-48791-1_28
4. Civit-Masot, J., Domínguez-Morales, M.J., Vicente-Díaz, S., Civit, A.: Dual machine-learning system to aid glaucoma diagnosis using disc and cup feature extraction. IEEE Access **8**, 127519–127529 (2020)
5. Fumero, F., Alayón, S., Sanchez, J.L., Sigut, J., Gonzalez-Hernandez, M.: RIM-ONE: an open retinal image database for optic nerve evaluation. In: Proceedings of the IEEE Symposium on Computer-Based Medical Systems (2011)
6. Hemelings, R., et al.: Accurate prediction of glaucoma from colour fundus images with a convolutional neural network that relies on active and transfer learning. Acta Ophthalmologica **98** (2020)
7. Kitchenham, B., Charters, S.: Guidelines for performing systematic literature reviews in software engineering (2007)
8. Mantravadi, A., Vadhar, N.: Glaucoma. Primary Care - Clinics Office Pract. **42**(3) (2015)
9. NICE: Glaucoma: diagnosis and management. NICE Guideline **81**(3) (2017)
10. Phasuk, S., et al.: Automated glaucoma screening from retinal fundus image using deep learning. In: Proceedings of the Annual International Conference of the IEEE Engineering in Medicine and Biology Society, EMBS (2019)
11. Ronneberger, O., Fischer, P., Brox, T.: U-Net: convolutional networks for biomedical image segmentation. In: Navab, N., Hornegger, J., Wells, W.M., Frangi, A.F. (eds.) MICCAI 2015. LNCS, vol. 9351, pp. 234–241. Springer, Cham (2015). https://doi.org/10.1007/978-3-319-24574-4_28
12. Sallam, A., et al.: Early detection of glaucoma using transfer learning from pretrained CNN models. In: 2021 International Conference of Technology, Science and Administration (ICTSA) (2021)
13. Sandler, M., Howard, A., Zhu, M., Zhmoginov, A., Chen, L.C.: MobileNetv2: inverted residuals and linear bottlenecks. In: Proceedings of the IEEE Conference on Computer Vision and Pattern Recognition, pp. 4510–4520 (2018)
14. Serte, S., Serener, A.: A generalized deep learning model for glaucoma detection. In: Proceedings of the 3rd International Symposium on Multidisciplinary Studies and Innovative Technologies, ISMSIT 2019 (2019)
15. Sreng, S., Maneerat, N., Hamamoto, K., Win, K.Y.: Deep learning for optic disc segmentation and glaucoma diagnosis on retinal images. Appl. Sci. (Switzerland) **10**, 4916 (2020)

16. Tan, M., Le, Q.: EfficientNet: rethinking model scaling for convolutional neural networks. In: 36th International Conference on Machine Learning, ICML 2019 (2019)
17. Xu, Y., et al.: A hierarchical deep learning approach with transparency and interpretability based on small samples for glaucoma diagnosis. NPJ Digit. Med. **4**, 1–11 (2021)
18. Yu, S., Xiao, D., Frost, S., Kanagasingam, Y.: Robust optic disc and cup segmentation with deep learning for glaucoma detection. Comput. Med. Imaging Graph. **74**, 61–71 (2019)

Offline and Online Neural Network Learning in the Context of Smart Homes and Fog Computing

Lucas V. S. De Mamann[1]([⊠]) [ID], Daniel Fernando Pigatto[2] [ID],
and Myriam Regattieri Delgado[1] [ID]

[1] CPGEI - Universidade Tecnológica Federal do Paraná, Curitiba, Brazil
lucasmamann@alunos.utfpr.edu.br, myriamdelg@utfpr.edu.br
[2] PPGCA - Universidade Tecnológica Federal do Paraná, Curitiba, Brazil
pigatto@utfpr.edu.br

Abstract. As Artificial Neural Network (ANN) smart applications become highly popular, some drawbacks of traditional cloud-based deployment emerge. Issues like high monetary cost, for storing and running applications, low privacy on data and models, and high latency experienced by cloud-based neural networks, might difficult their use, leading to poor user experiences. This paper explores, in the context of smart homes, ANN-based models running offline and a fog topology as an alternative to online learning methods. The work proposes four different approaches and compares their performance when solving eight distinct classification problems. Each problem regards activities performed in one out of eight rooms in the addressed smart home. Results show that hybridization of an autoencoder model with MLP-based classifiers can detect rare activities and provide good results for almost all rooms particularly when encompassing suitable pipelines. In the online context, although the performance of the hybrid approach decreases, as expected, some interesting insights result from experiments, particularly the fact that fog computing provides results not too far from cloud systems, yet demanding less resources. The online fog-based proposal appears therefore as an alternative for restricted computing on streaming data.

Keywords: Multilayer perceptron · Autoencoder · Classification problems · User activities

1 Introduction

Artificial neural networks (ANN) have been widely used in mobile devices and smart applications such as smart homes and cities, achieving promising results on various tasks. Current examples include object recognition [2,12], computer vision, speech recognition, smart city [1] and smart home [14] applications. ANN structures are composed of connected layers, in which input data is processed by each layer until the last one outputs the calculated result [8]. As more layers are

J. C. Xavier-Junior and R. A. Rios (Eds.): BRACIS 2022, LNAI 13654, pp. 357–372, 2022.
https://doi.org/10.1007/978-3-031-21689-3_26

used, more computational resources are demanded as well. A common solution for that is to use such networks in cloud computing services with nearly unlimited computing resources. Although highly available and scalable, cloud servers may experience issues such as high latency, high costs, and low privacy [15], which can negatively impact task requirements. In this context, fog computing presents itself as an alternative to cloud solutions. It is a paradigm that extends cloud to the edge of the network, aimed at achieving reduced latency, better privacy and improved location-based applications [4]. This opens space for a new profile of online applications that can take advantage of geographically closer processing and more secure response.

In the present paper, we explore offline and online ANN learning methods. An offline learning method receives the whole problem data from the beginning and is expected to output an answer which entirely solves the problem at hand. In contrast, an online learning method is one capable of processing streaming data, piece-by-piece in a serial fashion, without having the entire input available from the start. Online and offline neural models have their own advantages and disadvantages. Models running in an offline way can handle large data as computation time is usually not critical in this context. They are robust for small variations but fail to adapt to larger changes in the system. Online models can be less accurate because of small sets of training data given as batches [13]. Moreover, due to their usual low memory capability, forgetting large amounts of past data is frequent in online models functioning. Nevertheless, online models can adapt quickly to variations in the non-linear behaviour of inputs. This characteristic can be useful in a smart home scenario, where the inhabitants of a house are likely to change their routines over time and the system needs to detect and adapt to such changes.

There are several studies on ANN using either online or offline learning; discussing each of them is out of scope of this paper. Although less frequent, works exploring both methods are likewise not new [9]. In [13], the authors compare the methods when training two networks models used to calculate lateral and longitudinal dynamics of an Unmanned Aerial Vehicle (UAV). [3] adopts entropy concepts to the training of neural networks, aiming to predict wind power based on speed and direction characteristics for wind parks connected to a power grid. Even though the authors do not compare both methods, they use them to evaluate the benefits of introducing the entropy concepts. More recently, [17] proposes new benchmarks for both online and offline handwritten Chinese character recognition, as well as a deep model to solve them. Less related to ANN learning, but also in the deep context, [11] proposes a method that balances online and offline information aimed at improving sample-efficiency and final performance of fine tuned robotic agents on various locomotion and manipulation tasks.

Although other works have already explored the subject [14], the investigation of modular ANN online and offline learning in the context of smart homes and fog/cloud computing is, to the best of our knowledge, an unexplored field. The paper proposes a comparison between four (deep) ANN based models in this context.

The research questions are: i) can a shallow model running standalone, solve the addressed problems? ii) can two classification levels improve the solution provided by a unique classification level? iii) can hybridization of shallow models outperform the non-hybrid ones? iv) what is a component dimension suitable to provide improvements in the deepest model? v) what is a good trade-off between transmission rate and memory/processing capacity to run the deepest/largest model in online mode? Aiming to answer these questions, the present paper contributes first by providing different models trained offline to solve the smart home addressed problems (classify activities in each room); and then by exploring different configurations of one particular model in a specific room using online learning and fog/cloud computing resources.

2   The Addressed Problem: Cloud *versus* Fog Solutions

A classification problem can be formally defined as the task of estimating the label $y \in Y = \{c_1, c_2, ...\}$ of an n-dimensional input vector $\mathbf{x} \in \mathbb{R}^n$. Most of the time, particularly on the ANN context, input variables have to be real-valued. In the present paper, we address eight different classification problems each one described as the problem of classifying the activities that occur in a particular room of a smart home, based on the information provided by sensors distributed in the room. Therefore, we have $n = \#S$, where $\#S$ is the number of sensors in the room, and $\#C$ is the total of classes ie., the total of possible activities in each room performed by the smart home user. Inspired by [5], in the present paper we have the following setup for each room classification problem:

1. **Entrance** with $\#S = 55$ and $\#C = 2$: $\mathbf{x} \in \mathbb{R}^{55}$, $Y = \{c_1, c_2\}$, where c_1 is *entering the house* and c_2 is *leaving the house*;
2. **Staircase** with $\#S = 51$ and $\#C = 2$: $\mathbf{x} \in \mathbb{R}^{51}$, $Y = \{c_1, c_2\}$; c_1 is *going up stairs* and c_2 is *going down stairs*;
3. **Bathroom** with $\#S = 68$ and $\#C = 4$: $\mathbf{x} \in \mathbb{R}^{68}$, $Y = \{c_1, c_2, c_3, c_4\}$; c_1 is *showering*, c_2 is *using the sink*, c_3 is *using the toilet* and c_4 is *cleaning*;
4. **Livingroom** with $\#S = 80$ and $\#C = 4$: $\mathbf{x} \in \mathbb{R}^{80}$, $Y = \{c_1, c_2, c_3, c_4\}$; c_1 is *watching TV*, c_2 is *computing*, c_3 is *eating* and c_4 is *cleaning*;
5. **Toilet** with $\#S = 47$ and $\#C = 1$: $\mathbf{x} \in \mathbb{R}^{47}$, $Y = \{c_1\}$; c_1 is *using the toilet*;
6. **Office** with $\#S = 62$ and $\#C = 3$: $\mathbf{x} \in \mathbb{R}^{62}$, $Y = \{c_1, c_2, c_3\}$ where c_1 is *watching TV*, c_2 is *computing* and c_3 is *cleaning*;
7. **Kitchen** with $\#S = 94$ and $\#C = 4$: $\mathbf{x} \in \mathbb{R}^{94}$, $Y = \{c_1, c_2, c_3, c_4\}$; c_1 is *preparing food*, c_2 is *cooking*, c_3 is *washing the dishes* and c_4 is *cleaning*;
8. **Bedroom** with $\#S = 76$ and $\#C = 4$: $\mathbf{x} \in \mathbb{R}^{94}$, $Y = \{c_1, c_2, c_3, c_4\}$; c_1 is *cleaning*, c_2 is *dressing*, c_3 is *reading* and c_4 is *napping*.

As more smart home applications become cloud-based and the number of constrained connected devices increases, the volume of data generated and the need for solutions with reduced cost and improved privacy increase as well. Cloud architectures are known for the large geographic distance between end devices and servers in the cloud, which is often criticized regarding privacy issues. Cloud services usually charge for processing time and data traffic, which may lead to higher costs. In many cases, this scenario makes applications that handle large amounts of data unfeasible.

Fog Computing, as proposed by Cisco [4], is a way to minimize latency, centralized processing and cloud privacy problems. According to [4], the main characteristics of Fog are: a) Low latency and location knowledge; b) Widespread geographic distribution; c) Mobility; d) Large number of nodes; e) Predominant role of wireless access; f) Strong presence of streaming and real-time applications; and g) Heterogeneity.

3   Proposed Approaches

In the present paper, ANN-based components are proposed to compose MLP-based models and pipelines of hybrid models, aimed at solving the classification problem described in the previous section. In summary, it has at most 5 classes: up to 4 classes indicating activities in a particular room at the smart home being addressed and NA indicating no-activity in the room.

3.1   From Shallow to Deep Models

The proposed approaches aim to answer the questions raised at the introduction. For this, we build four different approaches: a) MLP1 (see Fig. 1(a)) - pure multilayer perceptron model; b) MLP2 (see Fig. 1(b)) - hierarchical model composed of two MLP-based classifiers used in the pipeline; c) HybSmall and d) HybLarge (see Fig. 1(c)) - hybrid and hierarchical models encompassing an autoenconder and two MLP classifiers in their pipelines.

The models presented here are built up from a combination of shallow models, except for model MLP1. Therefore, they could be considered deep models, since they involve learning a 'deep-enough' sequence of representations via composite functions.

The four shallow components addressed here are: C1) an autoencoder with one single hidden layer, to detect outliers (e.g., sparse room activities) [6,7,16]; C2) an MLP binary classifier conceived to separate activities from non-activities; C3) an MLP classifier designed with a softmax final layer to separate among the different possible activities in a particular room; C4) an MLP-based classifier designed with a softmax final layer to perform the entire classification task (ie. to separate among all possible classes: up to 4 different possible activities in the room plus non-activity NA). Besides the shallow ANN-based components, the two Hybrid approaches also encompass a component $\mathcal{L}$mod that compares the autoencoder input and the reconstructed output. First it uses the reconstruction error to evaluate the addressed loss function $\mathcal{L}$ used in weights update, and further it provides $\mathcal{L}$ as a single input for the next component in the pipeline.

1. Pure MLP depicted in Fig. 1 (a) - it is composed of a unique component: C4, responsible for the whole classification process. C4 has an input layer

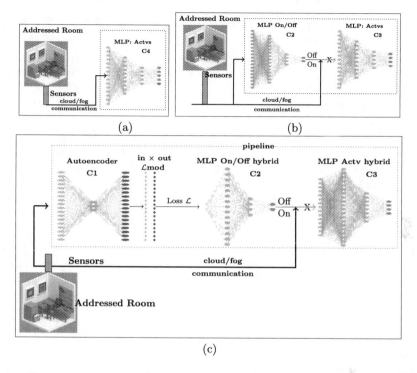

Fig. 1. Proposed approaches: (a) **MLP1**; (b) **MLP2**; (c) hybrid models prototype - **HybSmall** will encompass small MLP components and **HybLarge** with large ones.

with n neurons (n is #S), 2 hidden layers with $H_1 > H_2$ neurons, $f = \tanh$ activation function, and an output layer with $\#C + 1$ neurons using $f = \tanh$ + softmax, each neuron associated with a particular class or activity and the last one indicating a non-activity output.

2. Hierarchical MLPs depicted in Fig. 1(b) - it encompasses two components: C2 and C3.

   (a) C2 (an MLP on/off) - input layer with $n = \#S$ neurons, 2 hidden layers with $H1 > H_2$ neurons, $f = \tanh$, and an output layer with 2 neurons, $f = \tanh$ + softmax, indicating if there is (On) or there is not (Off) an activity occurring in the addressed room.

   (b) C3 (an MLP actv) - input layer with $n = \#S$ neurons, 2 hidden layers with $H_1 > H_2$ neurons, $f = \tanh$, and an output layer with $\#C$ neurons, $f = \tanh$ + softmax, each neuron associated with a particular activity.

3. Hybrid with Small components depicted in Fig. 1(c). It encompasses four modules (three ANN shallow components and a Loss module) in its pipeline C1 $\rightarrow$ $\mathcal{L}$mod $\rightarrow$ C2 $\rightarrow$ C3:

   (a) C1 (Autoencoder) - input layer with $n\#S$ neurons, 1 hidden layer with 3 neurons, an output layer also with n neurons.

   (b) $\mathcal{L}$mod (loss module) - it calculates the difference between the autoencoder input $\mathbf{x}$ and its output $\hat{\mathbf{x}}$; then it uses it to update the autoencoder weights and also to feed the next component. It might update the ith input importance ξ_i to the target output to provide the loss function whenever the weighted version is adopted.

(c) C2 (small MLP on/off) - input layer with 1 neuron (ie. the output received from $\mathcal{L}$mod), 2 hidden layers with $H_1 > H_2$ neurons, f=tanh, and an output layer with 2 neurons, indicating if there is (On) or there is not (Off) an activity occurring in the addressed room.

(d) C3 (small MLP actv) - an input layer with n = #S neurons, f=tanh, 2 hidden layers with $H_1 > H2$ neurons, and an output layer with #C neurons, f=tanh+softmax, each one associated with a particular class or activity.

4. Hybrid with Large components depicted in Fig. 1(c) - its pipeline also encompasses four modules C1 $\rightarrow$ $\mathcal{L}$mod $\rightarrow$ C2 $\rightarrow$ C3 of the previous model. The main difference between the two hybrid models is the number of neurons in each hidden layer of components C2 and C3. The hidden layers in the large model have 5 to 20 times more neurons compared to small one, leading to a more complex network (more weights to adjust).

The dataset used to train these models is imbalanced, as presented in the following sections. A naive approach to this kind of data, would result in a solution that always outputs the class with the majority of samples as its prediction. Therefore, the models need to consider strategies to tackle this issue. Models MLP1 and MLP2 use class weights during training, to reduce the influence of the major class over the loss function. On the other hand, for the two hybrid models, activity labels are regarded as outliers, as they represent a small percentage of the dataset. In this case, an autoencoder component is used to detect/filter these "outliers", which will later be classified as one of the possible activities. This allows extracting characteristics of activities in an unsupervised way, which would be impossible for MLPs.

All the components assume the classic neuron modeled as a node with n inputs $x_1, x_2, \ldots, x_n$, associated with weights $w_1, w_2, \ldots, w_n$, a bias b; a dot product $\mathbf{w} \cdot \mathbf{x} = \sum_{i=1}^{n} w_i x_i$ that is computed in order to generate an *activation potential*; and finally an *activation function* $f(\mathbf{w} \cdot \mathbf{x} + \mathbf{b})$ which, except for specific choices, always poses nonlinear characteristics in the neuron's behavior.

As detailed in the next section, we adopt three different loss functions ($\mathcal{L}$) depending on the type of component being considered and the learning mode taking place, which can be conducted in an offline or online way.

3.2   Training the Shallow Components

In both modes of learning (offline and online), independently of which type of components, weights and biases are randomly initialized, and then iteratively updated through the chosen optimizer. In the training of shallow components, the target output depends on which component is being trained. Considering the whole set of training data, we then have the inputs and target outputs given by: $\{(\mathbf{x}, \hat{\mathbf{x}})\}$ for C1 with $\hat{x}_i = x_i$, $i = 1, .., n$; and for the remaining components we have $\{(\mathbf{x}, y)\}$, with $y = \{\text{on,off}\}$ for C2, $y \in \{c_1, c_2, ...c_{\#C}, \text{off}\}$ for C3.

All shallow components use an optimizer whose basis is the backpropagation algorithm. One training parameter of a paramount importance is the *loss function* $\mathcal{L}$, which can be based on:

- cross entropy: $\mathcal{L}(\mathbf{y}, \hat{\mathbf{y}}) = -\sum_{k=1}^{S} y_k \cdot \log \hat{y}_k$
- squared error: $\mathcal{L}(\mathbf{y}, \hat{\mathbf{y}}) = \|\mathbf{y} - \hat{\mathbf{y}}\|_2^2 = \sum_{k=1}^{S}((y_k - \hat{y}_k))^2$
- weighted squared error: $\mathcal{L}_\xi(\mathbf{y}, \hat{\mathbf{y}}) = \|\mathbf{y} - \hat{\mathbf{y}}\|_{2\xi}^2 = \sum_{k=1}^{S}(\xi_k(y_k - \hat{y}_k))^2$.

where $\mathbf{y}$ and $\hat{\mathbf{y}}$ are, respectively, the vectors of target and component estimated outputs, for all data in the addressed set whose cardinality is S; and ξ_k is estimated before training based on the correlation input $\times$ output.

As depicted in Fig. 1, in the present paper *loss function* rule can extrapolate the training phase, as it can also support the inference process. In our hybrid models, it is used as an input of C2 component in addition to setting the weights/bias updates. In this case, S relies on testing or validation sets.

In the offline learning mode, the whole set of training data is available and the validation and testing phases occur only when the model finishes its training. Then, for each pattern presented at each iteration t, the output produced by the neural network is compared with the desired outcome through the *loss function* $\mathcal{L}^1$. For each layer, the adjustments $\Delta(\mathbf{w}(t)) = -\eta\nabla\mathcal{L}$ in the weights $\mathbf{w}$ can be calculated to minimize the error in the output according to the gradient descent with momentum, where η is the learning rate. For a batch size $\mathcal{B} = 1$, i.e. the weights are updated at every iteration t, we have $\mathbf{w}(t+1) = \mathbf{w}(t) + \Delta(\mathbf{w}(t)) + \zeta\Delta(\mathbf{w}(t-1))$ where ζ is the momentum parameter. For higher batch size values, $\Delta(\mathbf{w}(t))$ for each pattern is only accumulated and the weight updates occur only when the batch is complete.

For the autoencoder components, the updates are performed just like other feedforward neural networks. In other words, they aim to minimize the reconstruction error measured by a "loss" function $\mathcal{L}$ like, for example, the squared error: $\mathcal{L}(\mathbf{x}, \hat{\mathbf{x}}) = \|\mathbf{x} - f'(\mathbf{W}'(f(\mathbf{W}\mathbf{x} + \mathbf{b})) + \mathbf{b}')\|_2^2$, where $\|.\|_2^2$ is the squared error dependent on the euclidean norm; f and f' are the activation functions of encoder and decoder neurons; $\mathbf{b} = (b_1, ..., b_m)$, $\mathbf{b}' = (b'_1, ..., b'_n)$, are the vectors encompassing all the biases of encoder and decoder neurons respectively, $\mathbf{W} = [\mathbf{w}_1, \mathbf{w}_2, ..., \mathbf{w}_m]^T$ is the matrix of encoder weights, $\mathbf{W}' = [\mathbf{w}'_1, \mathbf{w}'_2, ..., \mathbf{w}'_n]^T$ is the matrix of decoder weights.

Concerning the online learning performed in the present paper, the main differences for offline mode rely on i) the role played by each pattern - it can be used for both, first testing and then training, since all data matter; ii) the concept of iteration that completely changes in online learning and iii) the two novel control parameters: a) the rate τ in which data is sent from sensors to cloud/fog systems, where the shallow components are built in; b) the budget of memory M considered for each component, that might be less restrictive in cloud compared to the

---

[1] For hidden layers such an outcome is estimated based on the backpropagated error.

fog computing. Besides these two control parameters there are two additional factors that impact the system performance, nevertheless they are not under control. First, there is a delay that naturally occurs in communication systems, particularly for cloud system, where the communication occurs mainly through the internet. Second, there is the actual processor capacity of systems that operate with multiple users in cloud computing. Although not directly controlled, it is usually assumed superior than the one available for fog computing.

In the case of online learning, training time is an important criterion as the system runs on small values of sample time. Thus, differently from the offline learning, when adapting weights/bias in the online way, the proposals use each sample as soon as it arrives and past experience can be completely lost since data streaming can provide new data when there is not enough memory to store all patterns. As in the offline case, some components could be trained separately - e.g. the coupled block (C1+$\mathcal{L}$mod$\rightarrow$C2) independently from the C3 component - but it is necessary to synchronize them in a way that whenever the output of coupled block is 'on' it enables the direct communication between the inputs (ie. sensors information) and the C3 component. Due to their longer pipelines, synchronization is more critical in deeper models (HybSmall and HybLarge).

4   Experiments

In this section, we describe the setup for the experiments. First we separate data of each room of the addressed smart home. Table 1 shows data distribution according to the rooms: number of sensors #S, number of activities or classes #C (excluding NA class), total of samples, and the percentage of samples that represent an output class other than NA (non-activity), of each room separately.

Table 1. A summary of Dataset used in the experiments

Room	#S	#C	Total of samples	Activity
Entrance	55	2	30216	2.34%
Staircase	51	2	33629	2.83%
Bathroom	68	4	36860	18.82%
Livingroom	80	4	120598	18.83%
Toilet	47	1	28947	0.33%
Office	62	3	104290	84.24%
Kitchen	94	4	69417	10.46%
Bedroom	76	4	45405	19.46%

The experiments conducted in the present paper compare the four proposed approaches described in Sect. 3 (MLP1, MLP2, HybSmall and HybLarge), whose parameters are shown in Table 2. We have also performed some experiments with

Table 2. Model parameters

Model	Component	Parameter	Value
MLP1	C4	Number of inputs	#S
		Number of outputs	#C + 1
		Hidden layers	2 [10, 5]
MLP2	C2	Number of inputs	#S
		Number of outputs	2
		Hidden layers	2 [10, 5]
	C3	Number of inputs	#S
		Number of outputs	#C
		Hidden layers	2 [10, 5]
HybSmall	C1	Number of inputs	#S
		Number of outputs	#S
		Hidden layer	1 [3]
	C2	Number of inputs	1
		Number of outputs	2
		Hidden layers	2 [10, 5]
	C3	Number of inputs	#S
		Number of outputs	#C
		Hidden layers	2 [10, 5]
HybLarge	C1	Number of inputs	#S
		Number of outputs C	#S
		Hidden layer	1 [3]
	C2	Number of inputs	1
		Number of outputs	2
		Hidden layers	2 [100, 25]
	C3	Number of inputs	#S
		Number of outputs	#C
		Hidden layers	2 [200, 50]

a Long Short Term Memory (LSTM) model, but as it achieved a quite poor performance, we decided to exclude it from the comparison.

The learning process can occur in two different modes: offline and online. In the online mode, neural network models can be built in two computing systems: cloud and fog. First we use each model to learn, in an offline way, the behavior of the smart home user in the eight different rooms described in Sect. 2. Then we evaluate, in a particular room (kitchen), the performance of HybLarge model when receiving streaming data in an online learning scheme.

In the offline learning mode, we divide the total of samples in each room, i.e. sensors measures and the respective target output (one activity among the

#C possible ones), into three different groups. Therefore in the offline learning we have $\{(\mathbf{x}, y)\}$ for a particular room divided into training $\{(\mathbf{x}, y)\}_{tr} = 64\%$, validation $\{(\mathbf{x}, y)\}_{vl} = 16\%$ and testing $\{(\mathbf{x}, y)\}_{ts} = 20\%$ groups of data. The set $\{(\mathbf{x}, y)\}_{ts}$ changes according to each fold of a 5-fold cross validation process performed in the room. In online learning there is no such distinction and the whole dataset for each room encompasses individual samples $(\mathbf{x}, y)_{\tau t}$ that are sent to the fog/cloud system in a rate τ and received and processed at time t by the addressed model. Such a sample plays the role of a test sample first and then it is (re)trained as many times as the memory buffer size M allows it to.

Besides initialization of internal model parameters (weights and bias of every layer in the neural models), it is also necessary to set up the parameters that control the learning process. Table 3 describes the main *learning parameters* as well as their values considered in the experiments. The table separates parameters whose values are common to both learning modes (Opt, η, β_1, β_1), from others that are exclusive for each mode E - exclusive of offline learning - and M - exclusive of online mode) or those that are common but have different values depending on the learning mode, i.e. parameters $\mathcal{L}$, $\mathcal{B}$ and Stp.

Table 3. Offline and Online Learning Parameters

Name/symbol	Description
Adam Opt	Adaptive Moment Estimation (Adam) is an optimizer that combines two other approaches i) AdaGrad and ii) RMSProp, using moving averages of the first and second moments of the gradient [10];
Learning rate η	Controls how the weights are updated during the training;
Decay rates β_1, β_2	Decay rates for the first and second moment estimates;
Loss function $\mathcal{L}$	Measures how high is the (reconstruction) error
Epochs E	The number of times the learning algorithm will work through The entire training dataset;
Batch size $\mathcal{B}$	Refers to the number of training samples propagated through The network before each weights update takes place;
stop condition Stp	the rule established to finish the learning process;
Transmission rate τ	Samples per second transmitted by sensors in the smart home;
Memory buffer M	Size of the buffer of each component in the proposed models.

Symbol (learning mode)	Autoencoder	MLP
Opt (online & offline)	Adam	Adam
η (online & offline)	0.01	0.01
β_1, β_2 (online & offline)	$\beta_1 = 0.9$, $\beta_1 = 0.999$	$\beta_1 = 0.9$, $\beta_1 = 0.999$
$\mathcal{L}$ (offline)	$\mathcal{L}_\xi$: weighted Squared Error	$\mathcal{L}$: Cross Entropy
$\mathcal{L}$ (online)	$\mathcal{L}$: Squared Error	
$\mathcal{B}$ (offline)	10	25
$\mathcal{B}$ (online)	1	1
Stp (offline)	achieve $E = 1000$ epochs	achieve $E = 200$ epochs
Stp (online)	Number of tested samples (4000)	Number tested of samples (4000)
τ (online)	{high,med,low}	{high,med,low}
M (online)	cloud = {low,high} fog = {low,high}	cloud = {low,high} fog = {low,high}

For online learning experiments, two environments are setup: one with higher processing capacity, to simulate a cloud platform; and another with less computing power, to simulate a fog system. The first environment run on a computer with Intel(R) Core(TM) i7-8565U processor, having 8 CPUs @ 1.80 GHz, to receive the streaming data and train the NNs. A Raspberry Pi 4 Model B, with Cortex-A72 processor, 4 CPUs @ 1.5 GHz, is used as the fog platform. To also take into account traffic of data in the experiments, the cloud scenario has data being sent from US East (N. Virginia) region to a local computer in Brazil whilst in the fog scenario, data is exchanged between two computers within a local network.

5   Results

In the first phase of the experiments, we assume that all the proposed approaches have been trained offline considering each room individually. Having the best results highlighted, Table 4 shows the performance (F-score average and standard deviation) from a 5-fold cross validation process, where each non-overlapping set $\{(\mathbf{x}, y)\}_{ts}$ is fixed as a fold test once in the five repetitions.

Table 4. Offline: models' average F-score for each room

Room/Model	Fscore from 5-fold	Room/Model	Fscore from 5-fold
Entrance	Avg ± stdv	**Toilet**	Avg ± stdv
MLP1	0.906 ± 0.006	MLP1	0.800 ± 0.171
MLP2	0.924 ± 0.031	MLP2	0.817 ± 0.073
HybSmall	0.915 ± 0.011	HybSmall	0.889 ± 0.025
HybLarge	0.908 ± 0.015	HybLarge	0.865 ± 0.014
Staircase	Avg ± stdv	**Office**	Avg ± stdv
MLP1	0.831 ± 0.009	MLP1	0.768 ± 0.318
MLP2	0.858 ± 0.016	MLP2	0.591 ± 0.216
HybSmall	0.821 ± 0.021	HybSmall	0.857 ± 0.204
HybLarge	0.854 ± 0.028	HybLarge	0.963 ± 0.021
Bathroom	Avg ± stdv	**Kitchen**	Avg ± stdv
MLP1	0.858 ± 0.018	MLP1	0.626 ± 0.258
MLP2	0.695 ± 0.129	MLP2	0.791 ± 0.040
HybSmall	0.682 ± 0.228	HybSmall	0.715 ± 0.245
HybLarge	0.911 ± 0.021	HybLarge	0.884 ± 0.017
Livingroom	Avg ± stdv	**Bedroom**	Avg ± stdv
MLP1	0.910 ± 0.012	MLP1	0.795 ± 0.345
MLP2	0.719 ± 0.286	MLP2	0.921 ± 0.050
HybSmall	0.551 ± 0.151	HybSmall	–
HybLarge	0.614 ± 0.101	HybLarge	–

From Table 4, we notice that hybrid models perform quite differently depending on the size of their components. Considering the rooms' characteristics shown in Table 1, we see that HybSmall performs well on rooms with low number of sensors/classes and samples/activities, i.e. Entrance, Staircase, and Toilet, highlighting the outlier (rare activity) detection capability of its autoencoder. HybLarge in contrast is best for most difficult problems: the rooms with the highest number of sensors/classes (kitchen) and activities (office). Finally, MLP model is better for the room with highest number of samples (Livingroom). In the case of HybLarge, it is important to point out that, except for Bedroom and Livingroom, where it does not perform well, HybLarge is among the best ones for the remaining rooms. Therefore, it is chosen to run on fog/cloud systems while learning online the behavior of the smart home user through streaming data received from the sensors in the Kitchen, i.e. the room with highest number of sensors and classes. LSTM F-Score was $\cong 0.45$ for all cases and thus, has been disregarded.

In the online mode we consider the HybLarge proposed model running either on cloud or fog computing. Aiming to compare both systems under different conditions of sensors and NN components, we consider six combinations of memory buffer sizes $M \in \{1000, 100, 10\}$ and transmission rates $\tau \in \{2.5, 1.25, 0.83\}$ (samples per second).

Table 5 shows average times (in seconds) spent by different topology setups of HybLarge to process each test sample. As expected, the average time to process each sample in the fog system is higher (almost twice) than that in the cloud. The time seems mainly affected by processing capacity, which is quite lower in the fog system. However, fog system seems to be more robust to changes in M and τ than cloud. Whereas in cloud, when memory increases 10 times, time relative gains are $\{\cong 20\%, \cong 10\%, \cong -6\%\}$ for the three τ rates, in fog the corresponding relative gains are smaller and almost constant $\{\cong 4\%, \cong 4\%, \cong 1\%\}$ for all τ.

Table 5. Online: results for the different combinations of setups

Setup combinations	τ (smp/s)	Cloud M	Cloud time (s)	Fog M	Fog time (s)
High τ with Low M	2.5	100	1.43	10	2.43
High τ with High M	2.5	1000	1.14	100	2.34
Med τ with Low M	1.25	100	1.22	10	2.36
Med τ with High M	1.25	1000	1.10	100	2.27
Low τ with Low M	0.83	100	1.20	10	2.31
Low τ with High M	0.83	1000	1.31	100	2.28

Figure 2 presents the curves for the average F-Score *versus* total of samples presented so far. They result from three runs, each one with $Stp{=}4000$ testing samples, as well as different weight/bias initialization and order of samples presentation. From Fig. 2, we notice that in general fog performs quite similarly

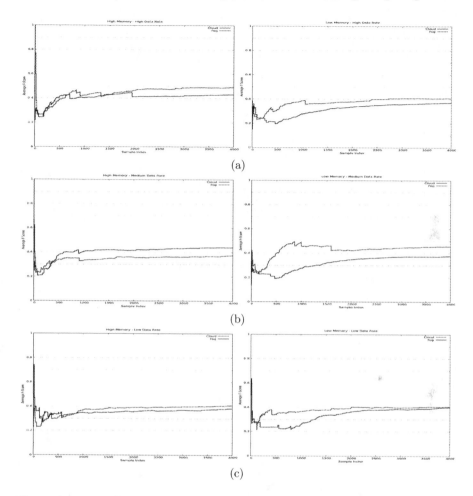

Fig. 2. Average F-Score vs. Tested Samples for Online learning with High and Low Memory sizes *versus* a) High, b) Medium and c) Low Data Rate.

to cloud. The exceptions occur for Medium τ, where High M provides the best fog's performance and Low M, the worst one.

Figure 3 shows, in a log-scale to enable cloud $\times$ fog comparison, the average number of times each sample is retrained. It is important to highlight that every streaming sample is first tested and then (re)trained as many times as possible, until the memory buffer M becomes full and the oldest samples start getting discarded. The gap (most visible for larger M sizes) in the average retraining curves is due to the time taken to fill the memory buffer, after which discarding process starts and the number of retraining per sample can be computed. The initial peak on the graphs, indicating a higher number of repetitions, occur because first training rounds take less time to complete, since they have fewer examples to go through. Subsequently to this 'warm-up' period, the curves tend

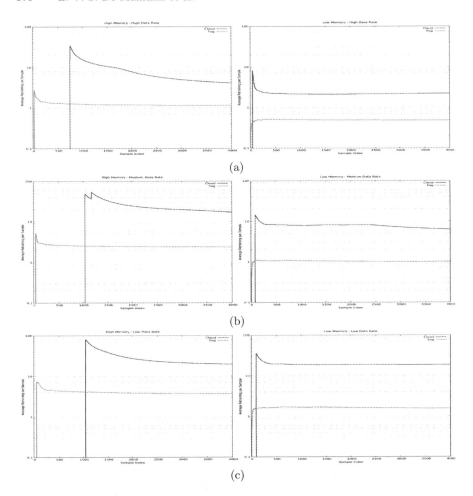

Fig. 3. Average Retraining per Sample vs. Tested Samples for Online learning with High and Low Memory sizes *versus* a) High, b) Medium and c) Low Data Rate.

to become stable, and the stabilization F-score value represents the bottleneck of processor capacity for that hardware. As expected, in all scenarios the cloud environment is capable of training each sample many more times (4 to 10 times), because of its more powerful processor and larger memory.

Taking all results into account, we can notice that, even though the NNs executing in the fog take a larger time to process samples and to converge, they stabilize in a similar performance level. That means the amount of retraining has low impact on the final result over time, i.e. a less expensive fog hardware could be used as replacement or as a support to a cloud solution and could still achieve comparable performance.

6   Conclusions

This paper has investigated ANN-models under offline and online learning in the context of smart homes and fog/cloud computing. First it has evaluated four different models trained offline to solve the addressed problems of classifying activities in each room of a smart home. Then it has explored different configurations of streaming data in online learning and one particular model - the one with a good performance in offline mode - running in a specific room using fog/cloud computing resources.

Based on achieved results, we note that in offline learning, adding an extra classification level to the NN architecture to split samples into activity/non-activity, before actually performing the activity classification, improves the results mainly when it is coupled with an autoencoder. Otherwise, a simple multilayer perceptron is capable of performing the whole task. We noticed that autoencoder is capable of learning, in an unsupervised way, the characteristics of activities that are addressed as "outliers" in the model. In online learning, the fog proposed topology was capable of performing comparably with one using cloud computing even if it uses much less retrained samples.

In future works we intend to consider the online learning for all models and rooms and include other online learning algorithms. Another topic for future studies is the modification of the NN models to solve time series prediction problems instead of classification ones, as already addressed in the current work. This, besides opening room for solving predictive control problems, could help eliminate the dependency on human feedback when determining the ground truth activity class during training phase. Such task can be quite challenging, particularly for online learning.

References

1. Alsamhi, S.H., Almalki, F., Ma, O., Ansari, M.S., Lee, B.: Predictive estimation of optimal signal strength from drones over IoT frameworks in smart cities. IEEE Trans. Mob. Comput. 1 (2021)
2. Bangaru, S.S., Wang, C., Busam, S.A., Aghazadeh, F.: Ann-based automated scaffold builder activity recognition through wearable EMG and IMU sensors. Autom. Constr. **126**, 103653 (2021)
3. Bessa, R.J., Miranda, V., Gama, J.: Entropy and correntropy against minimum square error in offline and online three-day ahead wind power forecasting. IEEE Trans. Power Syst. **24**(4), 1657–1666 (2009)
4. Bonomi, F., Milito, R., Zhu, J., Addepalli, S.: Fog computing and its role in the internet of things. In: Proceedings of the First Edition of the MCC Workshop on Mobile Cloud Computing - MCC 2012, p. 13 (2012)
5. Cumin, J.: Recognizing and predicting activities in smart homes. Ph.D. thesis, Université Grenoble Alpes (2018)
6. Dong, G., Liao, G., Liu, H., Kuang, G.: A review of the autoencoder and its variants: a comparative perspective from target recognition in synthetic-aperture radar images. IEEE Geosci. Remote Sens. Mag. **6**(3), 44–68 (2018)

7. Hawkins, S., He, H., Williams, G., Baxter, R.: Outlier detection using replicator neural networks. In: Kambayashi, Y., Winiwarter, W., Arikawa, M. (eds.) DaWaK 2002. LNCS, vol. 2454, pp. 170–180. Springer, Heidelberg (2002). https://doi.org/10.1007/3-540-46145-0_17

8. Haykin, S., Network, N.: A comprehensive foundation. Neural Netw. **2**(2004), 41 (2004)

9. Keskinocak, P.: On-line algorithms: how much is it worth to know the future. IBM Thomas J, Watson Research Division (1998)

10. Kingma, D.P., Ba, J.: Adam: a method for stochastic optimization. arXiv preprint arXiv:1412.6980 (2014)

11. Lee, S., Seo, Y., Lee, K., Abbeel, P., Shin, J.: Offline-to-online reinforcement learning via balanced replay and pessimistic q-ensemble. In: Conference on Robot Learning, pp. 1702–1712 (2022)

12. Lian, C., et al.: ANN-enhanced IoT wristband for recognition of player identity and shot types based on basketball shooting motion analysis. IEEE Sens. J. **22**(2), 1404–1413 (2022)

13. Puttige, V.R., Anavatti, S.G.: Comparison of real-time online and offline neural network models for a UAV. In: 2007 International Joint Conference on Neural Networks, pp. 412–417 (2007)

14. Skocir, P., Krivic, P., Tomeljak, M., Kusek, M., Jezic, G.: Activity detection in smart home environment. In: KES (2016)

15. Yi, S., Hao, Z., Qin, Z., Li, Q.: Fog computing: platform and applications. In: 2015 Third IEEE Workshop on Hot Topics in Web Systems and Technologies (HotWeb), pp. 73–78 (2015)

16. Zhai, J., Zhang, S., Chen, J., He, Q.: Autoencoder and its various variants. In: 2018 IEEE International Conference on Systems, Man, and Cybernetics (SMC), pp. 415–419 (2018)

17. Zhang, X.Y., Bengio, Y., Liu, C.L.: Online and offline handwritten Chinese character recognition: a comprehensive study and new benchmark. Pattern Recogn. **61**, 348–360 (2017)

Improved Alternative Average Support Value for Automatic Ingredient Substitute Recommendation in Cooking Recipes

Luciano D. S. Pacifico[1]([✉])[iD], Larissa F. S. Britto[2,3][iD],
and Teresa B. Ludermir[2][iD]

[1] Departamento de Computação, Universidade Federal Rural de Pernambuco, Recife,
PE, Brazil
luciano.pacifico@ufrpe.br
[2] Centro de Informática, Universidade Federal de Pernambuco, Recife, PE, Brazil
{lfsb,tbl}@cin.ufpe.br
[3] Centro de Pesquisa e Desenvolvimento em Telecomunicações, Campinas, SP, Brazil

Abstract. Nowadays, any individual interested in learning how to prepare a new dish or complete meal can consult specialized cooking recipe websites and video sharing platforms. Such online repositories are able to keep hundreds of thousands of entries in their databases, being rich sources of information for users with the most vast degrees of expertise. But sometimes it is hard for a user to find an adequate recipe that fits, simultaneously, his nutritional needs, tastes, dietary restrictions and the set of ingredients at hand, and, for non-expert users, it may be too much complicated, or even impossible, to adapt the recipes returned by such systems into his current state of needs. In this work, we propose a new cooking recipe recommendation and generation system, based on improved alternative Average Support Value (ASV) filters and a data-driven text mining approach, for single ingredient substitution. Three new ASV variants are proposed as mechanisms to aggregate recipe context and ingredient relevance into standard ASV, in an attempt to promote better ingredient substitute recommendations to adapt recipes into new culinary domains. The proposed ASV-based recipe generation systems are tested and evaluated by means of qualitative analysis, and the proposed filters performances are compared with standard ASV, when adapting recipes with no restrictions into different dietary restriction domains, showing promising results.

Keywords: Ingredient substitution · Recommendation systems · Text mining · Natural language processing · Machine learning

1 Introduction

In the last few decades, cooking recipe sharing has changed from physical media (like books, notebooks, magazines, etc.), to virtual recipe sharing (websites, video

J. C. Xavier-Junior and R. A. Rios (Eds.): BRACIS 2022, LNAI 13654, pp. 373–387, 2022.
https://doi.org/10.1007/978-3-031-21689-3_27

sharing repositories, blogs, social networks, etc.). Today, users can publish their recipes in specialized websites instantly, reaching other people from almost anywhere worldwide, building a global community and increasing the popularity of recipe sharing habit. Recipe websites are developed with the participation of their community of users, making the amount of data available in such repositories enormous.

In this context of Big Data repositories, Recommendation Systems [5] have been proposed as computational tools to help users in finding useful and personalized information in their application fields. In cooking recipes, recommendation systems perform tasks like assisting users in finding personalized and balanced diets [4,17,22], adapting recipes to the user's needs and dietary restrictions (such as allergies and intolerances) [1,12,14], as well as in helping reducing food waste, once such systems would guide their users towards the right use of leftover food and ingredients.

One relevant application of recommendation systems in food recipes is the automatic recipe generation by ingredient substitution. In such applications, ingredients are selected to be replaced by other ingredients that are not present in the original recipe, through automatic processes based on Data Mining and Machine Learning techniques. The most common approach for recipe generation is the substitution of single ingredients [10,12,14,18], where techniques like filtering [15], semantic models [8,18], machine and deep learning [1,16] and hybrid models [10] are employed to find adequate ingredient substitutes.

This work proposes three new alternative versions of Average Support Value filter [10], named ASV_w, ASV_s and ASV_{ws}, using Natural Language Processing and Text Mining-based data driven approaches, to aggregate recipe context and ingredient relevance into decision mechanisms of standard ASV. Complete recipe ingredient substitute recommendations systems are proposed to illustrate the effectivity of proposed ASV variants, in comparison to standard ASV, through recipe generation by single ingredient replacement.

The remainder of the work is organized as follows. A brief discussion on related works is presented in Sect. 1.1. The proposed methodology is discussed in Sect. 2, followed by the experimental evaluation (Sect. 3) and conclusions (Sect. 4).

1.1   Related Works

One of the first attempts towards the development of computational systems to help in recipe planning was proposed by Hammond [3]. The proposed system (CHEF) simulated human cognitive process in culinary decision making in Szechwan cooking.

Currently, there are three main approaches for cooking recipe recommendation: traditional Information Retrieval techniques, like filtering [2,14], Social Navigation [20] and Sentiment Analysis [21]; Recipe recommendation based on Ontological/Semantic Analysis [11–13,18], such as food context, food ingredient, and food equipment; Contextual analysis of ingredient correlations and nutritional information [10,23].

Some works on recipe generation by single ingredient substitution from the literature are briefly described as follows.

Ooi *et al.* [12] developed an ingredient substitution method to generate allergy-safe cooking recipes based on the analysis of food context, obtained by examining recipe similarity. The recipe similarity analysis has been employed by examining three groups of recipe meta-data: meta-data of food ingredient, meta-data of food equipment (all equipment listed on the recipe method of preparation), and meta-data of food context (employed to extract food information like the role of the allergy ingredient, food color and food texture).

Shino *et al.* [18] proposed a recommendation system for alternative ingredients based on co-occurrence frequency of ingredients on the recipe database. The authors also employed an ingredient categorization method by the use of a cooking ontology.

In Nirmal *et al.* [10], a ingredient substitution has been employed based on the optimization of both flavor and nutritional value of the ingredients. The proposed system has used a three phase filtering process to optimize the similarity between target ingredient and candidate ingredients flavor characteristics. Also, a recipe categorization (classification) is employed, in such a way that the flavor optimization and substitute ingredient recommendation are performed on the input recipe cuisine category.

Pan *et al.* [16] examined how to use Natural Language Processing techniques, such as word embeddings, to find alternative components in a data-driven, similarity-based manner. The proposed system seeks to replace one ingredient with similar ingredients, or one recipe with similar recipes.

Pacifico *et al.* [14] proposes an ingredient substitute recommendation system based on a filtering process that takes into consideration the original recipe context, the relationship among sets of ingredients and the user preferences. The authors aimed to convert recipes containing ingredients that would disrespect user dietary restrictions into restriction-safe recipes.

Shirai *et al.* [19] coupled explicit semantic information about ingredients, encapsulated in a knowledge graph of food, and implicit semantics, captured through word embeddings, to create the DIISH heuristic to rank plausible ingredient substitute options automatically, which provides recommendations depending on user context linked to health.

2   Proposed Approach

Current approach aims to convert a given *source recipe* $r_s \in R_s$ (where R_s is the *source recipe set*) into a new recipe r_t by replacing a given *source ingredient* $i_s \in r_s$ by a *target ingredient* $i_t \in I_t$, where I_t is the *set of ingredients* in all recipes in *target recipe set* R_t. The proposed system is presented in Fig. 1.

In this section, the proposed alternative Average Support Value mechanisms are explained, as well as the automatic model for ingredient substitute recommendation. In that sense, considering the adopted data-driven approach, the

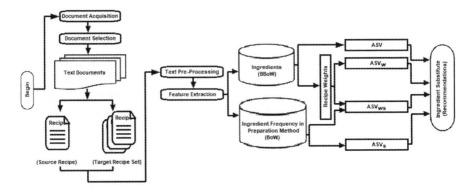

Fig. 1. The proposed automatic ingredient substitute recommendation system.

dataset acquisition process (Sect. 2.1) and the proposed ASV variants (Sect. 2.2) are discussed as follows.

2.1 Dataset

Once the proposed approach is data-driven, the quality of the adopted recipe dataset is essential. In this work, the recipe dataset proposed in [9] is selected for experimental purposes. This data set has been extracted from Food.com[1] website, and is available online[2]. The original dataset contains more than 230,000 recipes in English, and more than 1,000,000 user interactions with the website, between the years 2000 and 2018. Each recipe is described by some of its features, such as **recipe name, ingredient list, recipe description, steps of the method of preparation, nutritional information by category, user tags,** etc.

Although we implement our proposed system as a general-purpose automatic ingredient substitute recommender, in this work, we are interested in *allergy-free recipe generation* by the substitution of a single ingredient that would represent a dietary restriction in the selected *target recipe set*. In that sense, three recipe categories are selected as the target sets: **diabetic-friendly** recipes (from now on, **Diabetic**), **gluten-free** recipes (from now on, **Gluten**) and **lactose-free** recipes (from now on, **Lactose**).

In this work, only the recipe **ingredient list, set of user labels,** and **preparation steps** features from the raw dataset are considered, once our aim is to perform ingredient substitution in recipes. The selected feature sets are represented as **text data** in the original dataset, so Natural Language Processing tools are used as data pre-processing and feature extraction steps. Although the original dataset presents some degree of text pre-processing provided by the authors in [9], we opt to execute a whole set of text pre-processing methods, to

---

[1] https://www.food.com/.

[2] https://www.kaggle.com/shuyangli94/food-com-recipes-and-user-interactions.

promote a better data cleaning by eliminating redundant and irrelevant information from original raw dataset. The following text pre-processing steps have been executed:

1. **Lowercase Conversion:** The conversion of all document uppercase letters into lowercase letters. This conversion removes the problem of terms that, despite being the same, are considered different by algorithms, such as 'Egg' and 'egg'.

2. **Special Character Conversion:** The special characters, such as accented characters (i.e., 'é'), and other special characters (i.e., 'ç') are converted and standardized into ASCII characters (i.e., 'e' and 'c').

3. **URLs and Punctuation Removal:** Punctuation and URLs are not relevant for the purposes of current proposed approach, once we are mainly interested in data concerning the ingredient occurrences in text features (like method of preparation and ingredient lists) from each recipe.

4. **Stop Word Removal:** Stop words are the words considered non-informative, that occur with high frequencies in a document, which contain information that may not be required [6], like conjunctions, determiners and prepositions. The elimination of this words may reduce the execution time and storage memory requirements for the recommendation system.

5. **Lemmatization:** Lemmatization is the process of grouping together different inflected forms of a term, so they can be analyzed as a single item. The original raw dataset considers equivalent words, such as 'egg' and 'eggs' as different concepts, but for the purpose of our proposed recommender system, they are equivalent and should represent the same concept/ingredient.

As feature extraction methods, we opt to use **Bag-of-Words** and **Binary Bag-of-Words** models, briefly described as follows:

1. **Bag-of-Words (BoW):** A textual document (i.e., *cooking recipe*) is represented by its set of words. The text is converted into a matrix, where every column represents a word (in our case, *ingredient*), each row represents a document, and each position contains the number of occurrences of a word in a document. The structure of the original document or the order of the words in that document are not taken into consideration by this representation [7]. The dataset is also converted into a *Document-Term Matrix* (DTM).

2. **Binary Bag-of-Words (BBoW):** Similar to standard BoW, but this time the DTM is a **binary matrix**, where each position indicates whether a given word belongs in or does not belong in the corresponding document.

Table 1 summarizes the main information for the selected dataset. The total number of ingredients is shown in Table 1 before (*raw* value) and after (*final* value) the text pre-processing step.

Figure 2 shows the most frequent ingredients in each one of the selected *target recipe sets*.

Table 1. Dataset stats.

Recipe category	Diabetic	Gluten	Lactose
Original tag(s)	'diabetic'	'gluten-free'	'lactose', 'dairy-free', 'vegan'
Number of recipes	6458	5743	13129
'Raw' number of ingredients	4487	3793	5205
Final number of ingredients	4155	3492	4766
Average number of recipe ingredients	8.8587	8.5195	8.89793
Maximum number of recipe ingredients	31	28	30
Maximum number of recipe ingredients	1	1	1
Average ingredient frequency in method of preparation	13.4667	13.3889	13.6464
Maximum ingredient frequency in method of preparation	63	52	60
Maximum ingredient frequency in method of preparation	1	1	1

(a) Diabetic   (b) Gluten   (c) Lactose

Fig. 2. Most frequent ingredients for each selected target recipe set.

2.2 Average Support Value (ASV)

Average Support Value was introduced by Nirmal *et al.* [10]) as a filter to evaluate the pairwise co-occurrence relation between each *candidate target ingredient* i_t and all ingredients from *source recipe* r_s. The main idea behind ASV is that when two ingredients co-occurs with high frequency in a dataset, it means that their combination is more likely to be tasty or nutritionally balanced, so if a given *target ingredient* i_t presents a high ASV when replacing a *source ingredient* i_s, it most likely will represent a good substitute for i_s in *source recipe* r_s.

To obtain the ASV value for each *target ingredient*, we first compute the pairwise co-occurrence value $C(i_j, i_t)$ between each ingredient $\{i_t \in I_t | i_t \notin r_s\}$ in *target ingredient set* I_t and all ingredients $i_j \in r_s (j \neq s)$ considering the complete *target recipe set* R_t. The Average Support Value for each *target ingredient* is computed as (Eq. (1)):

$$ASV(i_t) = \sum_{i_j \in r_s (j \neq s)} C(i_j, i_t)/(|r_s| - 1) \tag{1}$$

where $|r_s|$ represents the number of ingredients in *source recipe* r_s.

For standard ASV, we compute the pairwise co-occurrence between each pair of ingredients considering the DTM obtained by BBoW for each selected *target recipe set* R_t, individually.

2.3 Average Support Value Based on Ingredient Frequency in Recipe Method of Preparation (ASV_s)

The standard ASV presents a limitation concerning the relevance of each ingredient in a given recipe: from an ASV point-of-view, each ingredient is as much relevant as the other ingredients in a recipe. Also, since only ingredient pairwise co-occurrences are taken into consideration (whether two ingredients occur in the same recipe or not), there is no distinction among recipe contexts when ASV is computed. It is known that the same ingredient may perform different functions according to the recipe context, and also, the relevance of a given ingredient may vary according to that context.

As an alternative way to compute the ASV, we evaluate the frequency of each recipe ingredient in the method of preparation. Our hypothesis is that ingredients with high occurrences in method of preparation may be more relevant in that recipe context, so they should have a higher influence in the computation of ASV for that recipe. We perform the following modifications on pairwise co-occurrence (Eq. (2)) computation:

$$C_s(i_x, i_y) = \sum\nolimits_{\forall r_j \in R_t | i_x \in r_j, i_y \in r_j} (f(i_x) + f(i_y))/2 \qquad (2)$$

where $f(\cdot)$ denotes the frequency of a given ingredient in a recipe method of preparation, represented by the DTM obtained with BoW. The new ASV is, then, computed as follows (Eq. (3)).

$$ASV_s(i_t) = \sum\nolimits_{i_j \in r_s (j \neq s)} C_s(i_j, i_t)/(|r_s| - 1) \qquad (3)$$

2.4 Weighted ASV (ASV_w) and Weighted ASV$_s$ (ASV_{ws})

The final modification to ASV proposed in this work consists of a weighting system for each recipe in R_t. This weighting system seeks out to evaluate how close related are the source recipe r_s and the recipes in *target recipe set*, according to their ingredient lists. The main hypothesis here is that recipes that are close related belong in the same recipe context (i.e., culinary category, cultural domain, meal type, etc.), so ingredients in such recipes should represent better choices as replacements between each other. To evaluate recipe relationships, we calculate the similarity between *source recipe* r_s and all other recipes $r_j \in R_t$ using **cosine measure** (Eq. (4)) [12]:

$$w(r_s, r_j) = \frac{r_s \cdot r_j}{|r_s||r_j|} \qquad (4)$$

The new pairwise co-occurrence for ASV and ASV$_s$ (Eq. (5) and Eq. (6), respectively) and the new weighted ASV and ASV$_s$ (Eq. (7) and Eq. (8), respectively) values are given as follows:

$$C_w(i_j, i_t) = \sum_{\forall r_j \in R_t | i_x \in r_j, i_y \in r_j} w(r_s, r_j) \tag{5}$$

$$C_{ws}(i_x, i_y) = \sum_{\forall r_j \in R_t | i_x \in r_j, i_y \in r_j} w(r_s, r_j)(f(i_x) + f(i_y))/2 \tag{6}$$

$$ASV_w(i_t) = \sum_{i_j \in r_s (j \neq s)} C_w(i_j, i_t)/(|r_s| - 1) \tag{7}$$

$$ASV_{ws}(i_t) = \sum_{i_j \in r_s (j \neq s)} C_{ws}(i_j, i_t)/(|r_s| - 1) \tag{8}$$

3   Experimental Evaluation

In this section, the proposed recipe generation systems are evaluated by means of a **qualitative analysis**. Two main research questions are elaborated:

1. Is the proposed system capable of recommend good substitute ingredients automatically, considering the context of the selected source recipe? (Research Question 1 - RQ1)
2. Are the recommended substitute ingredients adequate to the new recipe domain and its restrictions? (Research Question 2 - RQ2)

The proposed analysis takes into consideration four *source recipes* (shown in Table 2), which contains at least one ingredient that would be forbidden or restricted into the selected *target recipe sets* (**Diabetic, Gluten and Lactose** - se Sect. 2.1). The selected evaluation metric is the number of adequate substitute ingredients recommended in a **top-10 analysis** for each *source recipe* [10,12, 18], considering the substitute recommendations obtained through specialized websites on food and health[3,4,5,6].

Table 2. Selected source recipes (with no dietary restrictions).

Recipe name	Ingredients	Number of ingredients
Quick pound cake	Flour, egg, sugar, butter, almond extract	5
Simple fudge brownies	All-purpose flour, butter, cocoa, egg, sugar, vanilla	6
Wheat germ and Banana muffins	All-purpose flour, baking powder, banana, egg, milk, salt, sugar, toasted wheat germ, vanilla extract, vegetable oil	10
Whole wheat Corn bread	Baking powder, cornmeal, egg, milk, salt, sugar, vegetable oil, whole wheat flour	8

---

[3] www.healthline.com.
[4] www.medicalnewstoday.com.
[5] https://www.eatingwell.com/.
[6] www.bhg.com.

Table 3. Experimental results for Diabetic recipes.

Quick Pound Cake

Ingredient	ASV Candidate	Score	ASV$_w$ Candidate	Score	ASV$_s$ Candidate	Score	ASV$_{ws}$ Candidate	Score
sugar	baking powder	0.1190	baking powder	0.0336	baking powder	0.0140	baking powder	0.0039
	salt	0.1018	baking soda	0.0257	salt	0.0128	salt	0.0031
	baking soda	0.0949	salt	0.0249	milk	0.0102	milk	0.0029
	milk	0.0759	milk	0.0215	baking soda	0.0100	baking soda	0.0027
	vanilla	0.0673	vanilla	0.0189	vanilla	0.0081	vanilla	0.0022
	cinnamon	0.0594	cinnamon	0.0146	cinnamon	0.0067	cinnamon	0.0016
	all-purpose flour	0.0559	splenda granular	0.0135	water	0.0063	vanilla extract	0.0015
	vanilla extract	0.0514	vanilla extract	0.0134	vanilla extract	0.0062	splenda granular	0.0014
	onion	0.0499	all-purpose flour	0.0124	onion	0.0061	water	0.0013
	splenda granular	0.0496	water	0.0110	all-purpose flour	0.0056	all-purpose flour	0.0012
Adequate Substitutes	4		4		3		4	

Simple Fudge Brownie

Ingredient	ASV Candidate	Score	ASV$_w$ Candidate	Score	ASV$_s$ Candidate	Score	ASV$_{ws}$ Candidate	Score
sugar	baking powder	0.1423	baking powder	0.0416	baking powder	0.0151	baking powder	0.0044
	baking soda	0.1297	baking soda	0.0368	baking soda	0.0126	baking soda	0.0036
	salt	0.0919	salt	0.0223	salt	0.0107	salt	0.0025
	splenda granular	0.0750	splenda granular	0.0217	milk	0.0088	milk	0.0023
	cinnamon	0.0699	cinnamon	0.0173	flour	0.0085	splenda granular	0.0021
	flour	0.0675	milk	0.0172	splenda granular	0.0076	flour	0.0020
	milk	0.0659	flour	0.0168	cinnamon	0.0075	cinnamon	0.0018
	splenda sugar substitute	0.0573	splenda sugar substitute	0.0149	splenda sugar substitute	0.0063	splenda sugar substitute	0.0016
	whole wheat flour	0.0551	whole wheat flour	0.0135	vanilla extract	0.0054	pecan	0.0014
	vanilla extract	0.0513	vanilla extract	0.0129	water	0.0053	vanilla extract	0.0013
Adequate Substitutes	4		4		4		5	

Wheat Germ Banana Muffin

Ingredient	ASV Candidate	Score	ASV$_w$ Candidate	Score	ASV$_s$ Candidate	Score	ASV$_{ws}$ Candidate	Score
sugar	baking soda	0.1287	baking soda	0.0435	baking soda	0.0123	baking soda	0.0041
	whole wheat flour	0.0668	whole wheat flour	0.0217	butter	0.0086	butter	0.0022
	butter	0.0665	cinnamon	0.0182	flour	0.0077	flour	0.0021
	cinnamon	0.0640	splenda granular	0.0179	vanilla	0.0070	vanilla	0.0020
	flour	0.0617	vanilla	0.0178	cinnamon	0.0068	whole wheat flour	0.0019
	vanilla	0.0606	butter	0.0174	whole wheat flour	0.0059	cinnamon	0.0018
	splenda granular	0.0583	flour	0.0173	splenda granular	0.0054	splenda granular	0.0015
	splenda sugar substitute	0.0496	splenda sugar substitute	0.0138	water	0.0053	splenda sugar substitute	0.0013
	egg white	0.0469	unsweetened applesauce	0.0136	egg white	0.0050	skim milk	0.0012
	water	0.0439	skim milk	0.0126	splenda sugar substitute	0.0049	egg white	0.0011
Adequate Substitutes	4		5		4		4	

Whole Wheat Corn Bread

Ingredient	ASV Candidate	Score	ASV$_w$ Candidate	Score	ASV$_s$ Candidate	Score	ASV$_{ws}$ Candidate	Score
sugar	baking soda	0.1407	baking soda	0.0468	baking soda	0.0134	baking soda	0.0044
	all-purpose flour	0.0982	all-purpose flour	0.0320	butter	0.0097	flour	0.0029
	flour	0.0759	flour	0.0232	flour	0.0095	all-purpose flour	0.0027
	butter	0.0744	vanilla	0.0210	all-purpose flour	0.0086	butter	0.0026
	vanilla	0.0692	cinnamon	0.0204	vanilla	0.0079	vanilla	0.0023
	cinnamon	0.0689	butter	0.0201	cinnamon	0.0066	cinnamon	0.0019
	vanilla extract	0.0607	vanilla extract	0.0184	vanilla extract	0.0061	vanilla extract	0.0018
	onion	0.0527	splenda granular	0.0152	water	0.0060	water	0.0014
	splenda granular	0.0502	splenda sugar substitute	0.0126	onion	0.0058	splenda granular	0.0013
	water	0.0496	unsweetened applesauce	0.0123	pepper	0.0051	buttermilk	0.0012
Adequate Substitutes	4		6		3		4	

The experimental results obtained considering **Diabetic** *target recipe set* are shown in Table 3. For all four *source recipes*, **sugar** is selected as the *source ingredient* to be replaced. Some adequate substitutes for sugar in *baking* recipes are *vanilla extract, cinnamon, stevia-based sweeteners, sucralose-based sweeteners, some fresh fruits*, etc[7]. For **Diabetic**, all the ASV variants are able to find at least three good recommendations at the *top*-10, which could be considered a good result. The Weighted ASV (ASV$_w$) presented better results then standard ASV in two out of four recipes, and the same results as ASV in the remaining two recipes. The best number of adequate *target ingredients* has been found by ASV$_w$ in **Whole Wheat Corn Bread** recipe, where 6 adequate **sugar** substitutes were found.

---

[7] https://www.diabetesselfmanagement.com/nutrition-exercise/meal-planning/baking-and-cooking-with-sugar-substitutes/.

Table 4. Experimental results for Gluten recipes.

Quick Pound Cake	ASV		ASV_w		ASV_s		ASV_{ws}	
Ingredient	Candidate	Score	Candidate	Score	Candidate	Score	Candidate	Score
flour	salt	0.1323	salt	0.0315	salt	0.0165	milk	0.0041
	baking powder	0.1106	baking powder	0.0296	milk	0.0139	salt	0.0040
	milk	0.0965	milk	0.0277	baking powder	0.0119	baking powder	0.0033
	baking soda	0.0937	baking soda	0.0235	water	0.0112	vanilla	0.0028
	xanthan gum	**0.0834**	vanilla	0.0215	vanilla	0.0098	baking soda	0.0025
	vanilla	0.0768	**xanthan gum**	**0.0212**	baking soda	0.0097	water	0.0024
	water	0.0722	**rice flour**	**0.0175**	**xanthan gum**	**0.0078**	**xanthan gum**	**0.0020**
	rice flour	**0.0682**	vanilla extract	0.0174	**rice flour**	**0.0073**	vanilla extract	0.0019
	vanilla extract	0.0644	**gluten-free flour**	**0.0168**	vanilla extract	0.0071	**rice flour**	**0.0018**
	cinnamon	0.0622	water	0.0154	cinnamon	0.0069	**gluten-free flour**	**0.0016**
Adequate Substitutes	2		3		2		3	
Simple Fudge Brownie	ASV		ASV_w		ASV_s		ASV_{ws}	
Ingredient	Candidate	Score	Candidate	Score	Candidate	Score	Candidate	Score
all-purpose flour	baking powder	0.1256	baking powder	0.0372	salt	0.0144	milk	0.0041
	salt	0.1173	baking soda	0.0303	milk	0.0134	baking powder	0.0039
	baking soda	0.1096	milk	0.0289	baking powder	0.0130	salt	0.0034
	milk	0.0940	salt	0.0282	baking soda	0.0108	baking soda	0.0029
	xanthan gum	**0.0904**	**xanthan gum**	**0.0243**	water	0.0098	**rice flour**	**0.0022**
	rice flour	**0.0777**	**rice flour**	**0.0218**	**xanthan gum**	**0.0081**	water	0.0021
	brown sugar	0.0702	brown sugar	0.0182	**rice flour**	**0.0078**	**xanthan gum**	**0.0020**
	cinnamon	0.0671	**gluten-free flour**	**0.0181**	brown sugar	0.0077	brown sugar	0.0019
	water	0.0648	cinnamon	0.0167	cinnamon	0.0072	cinnamon	0.0018
	gluten-free flour	**0.0586**	tapioca flour	0.0143	**gluten-free flour**	**0.0056**	**gluten-free flour**	**0.0017**
Adequate Substitutes	3		4		3		3	
Wheat Germ Banana Muffin	ASV		ASV_w		ASV_s		ASV_{ws}	
Ingredient	Candidate	Score	Candidate	Score	Candidate	Score	Candidate	Score
all-purpose flour	baking powder	0.1192	baking soda	0.0387	butter	0.0125	butter	0.0034
	xanthan gum	**0.0985**	**xanthan gum**	**0.0319**	baking soda	0.0104	baking soda	0.0033
	butter	0.0897	butter	0.0254	water	0.0091	**xanthan gum**	**0.0026**
	vanilla	0.0760	**gluten-free flour**	**0.0249**	vanilla	0.0085	vanilla	0.0025
	cinnamon	0.0724	vanilla	0.0226	**xanthan gum**	**0.0080**	**gluten-free flour**	**0.0023**
	rice flour	**0.0686**	**rice flour**	**0.0225**	cinnamon	0.0069	**rice flour**	**0.0020**
	water	0.0670	cinnamon	0.0206	**rice flour**	**0.0062**	water	0.0019
	gluten-free flour	**0.0648**	potato starch	0.0201	**gluten-free flour**	**0.0059**	cinnamon	0.0018
	brown sugar	0.0601	brown rice flour	0.0166	brown sugar	0.0056	potato starch	0.0016
	potato starch	**0.0593**	cornstarch	0.0163	onion	0.0054	cornstarch	0.0015
Adequate Substitutes	4		6		3		5	
Whole Wheat Corn Bread	ASV		ASV_w		ASV_s		ASV_{ws}	
Ingredient	Candidate	Score	Candidate	Score	Candidate	Score	Candidate	Score
whole wheat flour	baking soda	0.1084	baking soda	0.0341	butter	0.0132	butter	0.0038
	xanthan gum	**0.1000**	**xanthan gum**	**0.0322**	water	0.0098	baking soda	0.0028
	butter	0.0951	butter	0.0275	baking soda	0.0094	**xanthan gum**	**0.0027**
	vanilla	0.0772	**gluten-free flour**	**0.0245**	vanilla	0.0087	vanilla	0.0026
	rice flour	**0.0726**	**rice flour**	**0.0242**	**xanthan gum**	**0.0083**	**gluten-free flour**	**0.0024**
	water	0.0724	vanilla	0.0236	**rice flour**	**0.0068**	water	0.0023
	cinnamon	0.0666	potato starch	0.0196	cinnamon	0.0064	**rice flour**	**0.0022**
	gluten-free flour	**0.0641**	cinnamon	0.0189	onion	0.0063	cinnamon	0.0018
	cornstarch	0.0590	cornstarch	0.0180	**gluten-free flour**	**0.0060**	cornstarch	0.0017
	potato starch	0.0580	water	0.0171	cornstarch	0.0057	oil	0.0016
Adequate Substitutes	5		5		4		4	

In Table 4, the *top*-10 ingredient substitutes for the selected *source recipes* are presented for **Gluten** *target recipe set*. In this context, **flour (Quick Pound Cake)**, **all-purpose flour (Simple Fudge Brownie** and **Wheat Germ Banana Muffin)** and **whole wheat flour (Whole Wheat Corn Bread)** are selected as the *source ingredients* to be replaced. For all cases, examples of adequate ingredient substitutes are *xathan gum, rice, coconut, tapioca and potato flours, corn and potato starches*, and so on[8]. Once more, at least two

---

[8] https://www.thekitchn.com/16-gluten-free-flour-alternatives-22943791.

Table 5. Experimental results for Lactose recipes.

Quick Pound Cake	ASV		ASV_w		ASV_s		ASV_{ws}	
Ingredient	Candidate	Score	Candidate	Score	Candidate	Score	Candidate	Score
butter	baking powder	0.1153	baking powder	0.0299	baking powder	0.0128	baking powder	0.0033
	baking soda	0.1070	baking soda	0.0263	baking soda	0.0113	baking soda	0.0028
	salt	0.0711	vanilla	0.0171	water	0.0087	vanilla	0.0019
	vanilla	0.0656	salt	0.0152	salt	0.0085	salt	0.0018
	vanilla extract	0.0580	vanilla extract	0.0141	vanilla	0.0075	water	0.0017
	cinnamon	0.0576	cinnamon	0.0129	**oil**	**0.0066**	**oil**	**0.0016**
	water	0.0564	water	0.0115	cinnamon	0.0061	vanilla extract	0.0015
	oil	**0.0498**	**oil**	**0.0114**	vanilla extract	0.0060	cinnamon	0.0014
	soymilk	**0.0482**	**soymilk**	**0.0106**	**margarine**	**0.0054**	**margarine**	**0.0013**
	brown sugar	0.0411	**margarine**	**0.0098**	**soymilk**	**0.0050**	**soymilk**	**0.0011**
Adequate Substitutes	2		3		3		3	
Simple Fudge Brownie	ASV		ASV_w		ASV_s		ASV_{ws}	
Ingredient	Candidate	Score	Candidate	Score	Candidate	Score	Candidate	Score
butter	baking soda	0.1209	baking soda	0.0301	baking soda	0.0116	baking soda	0.0029
	baking powder	0.1131	baking powder	0.0270	baking powder	0.0113	baking powder	0.0027
	salt	0.0611	flour	0.0155	flour	0.0073	flour	0.0018
	flour	0.0600	**soymilk**	**0.0131**	water	0.0072	salt	0.0015
	cinnamon	0.0565	salt	0.0127	salt	0.0069	water	0.0014
	soymilk	**0.0541**	cinnamon	0.0116	cinnamon	0.0058	**soymilk**	**0.0013**
	whole wheat flour	0.0522	whole wheat flour	0.0114	**soymilk**	**0.0053**	**margarine**	**0.0012**
	water	0.0481	**margarine**	**0.0101**	**margarine**	**0.0051**	cinnamon	0.0011
	vanilla extract	0.0473	vanilla extract	0.0100	vanilla extract	0.0046	chocolate chip	0.0010
	brown sugar	0.0428	**canola oil**	**0.0096**	**oil**	**0.0045**	**oil**	**0.0009**
Adequate Substitutes	1		3		3		3	
Wheat Germ Banana Muffin	ASV		ASV_w		ASV_s		ASV_{ws}	
Ingredient	Candidate	Score	Candidate	Score	Candidate	Score	Candidate	Score
milk	baking soda	0.1141	baking soda	0.0351	baking soda	0.0107	baking soda	0.0033
	water	**0.0650**	**soymilk**	**0.0194**	**water**	**0.0089**	flour	0.0021
	cinnamon	0.0643	flour	0.0177	flour	0.0073	**soymilk**	**0.0019**
	soymilk	**0.0642**	cinnamon	0.0174	**soymilk**	**0.0065**	**water**	**0.0018**
	flour	0.0603	whole wheat flour	0.0171	cinnamon	0.0064	cinnamon	0.0017
	whole wheat flour	0.0571	vanilla	0.0144	vanilla	0.0057	vanilla	0.0015
	vanilla	0.0535	canola oil	0.0135	whole wheat flour	0.0050	whole wheat flour	0.0014
	canola oil	0.0453	**water**	**0.0131**	onion	0.0046	canola oil	0.0011
	brown sugar	0.0427	ground cinnamon	0.0110	oil	0.0045	oil	0.0010
	onion	0.0423	brown sugar	0.0108	olive oil	0.0040	brown sugar	0.0009
Adequate Substitutes	2		2		2		2	
Whole Wheat Corn Bread	ASV		ASV_w		ASV_s		ASV_{ws}	
Ingredient	Candidate	Score	Candidate	Score	Candidate	Score	Candidate	Score
milk	baking soda	0.1164	baking soda	0.0347	**water**	**0.0110**	baking soda	0.0032
	water	**0.0790**	flour	0.0221	baking soda	0.0109	flour	0.0027
	flour	0.0725	all-purpose flour	0.0219	flour	0.0089	**water**	**0.0023**
	all-purpose flour	0.0685	**soymilk**	**0.0190**	all-purpose flour	0.0065	all-purpose flour	0.0021
	cinnamon	0.0673	cinnamon	0.0189	cinnamon	0.0063	**soymilk**	**0.0018**
	vanilla	0.0602	vanilla	0.0177	vanilla	0.0061	vanilla	0.0017
	soymilk	**0.0601**	vanilla extract	0.0172	onion	0.0060	cinnamon	0.0016
	vanilla extract	0.0591	**water**	**0.0170**	**soymilk**	**0.0057**	vanilla extract	0.0015
	onion	0.0542	canola oil	0.0130	vanilla extract	0.0055	oil	0.0013
	canola oil	0.0473	**applesauce**	**0.0111**	oil	0.0054	canola oil	0.0011
Adequate Substitutes	2		3		2		2	

adequate substitutes have been found for each *source recipe*, and, also, weighted approaches are able to outperform their corresponding non-weighted filters, in most of the cases. The best overall result for **Gluten** was found by ASV_w in **Wheat Germ Banana Muffin** recipe, where 6 adequate *target ingredients* were found for **all-purpose flour**.

Table 5 presents the obtained results for **Lactose** *target recipe set*. Two *source ingredients* are selected to be replaced: **butter** (**Quick Pound Cake** and **Simple Fudge Brownie**) and **milk** (**Wheat Germ Banana Muffin**

Table 6. Experimental results: overall evaluation.

Diabetic	ASV	ASV_w	ASV_s	ASV_{ws}
Quick pound cake	4	4	3	4
Simple fudge brownies	4	4	4	5
Wheat germ and banana muffins	4	5	4	4
Whole wheat corn bread	4	6	3	4
Average	4	**4.75**	3.5	4.25
Gluten	ASV	ASV_w	ASV_s	ASV_{ws}
Quick pound cake	2	3	2	3
Simple fudge brownies	3	4	3	3
Wheat germ and banana muffins	4	6	3	5
Whole wheat corn bread	5	5	4	4
Average	3.5	**4.5**	3.25	3.75
Lactose	ASV	ASV_w	ASV_s	ASV_{ws}
Quick pound cake	2	3	3	3
Simple fudge brownies	1	3	3	3
Wheat germ and banana muffins	2	2	2	2
Whole wheat corn bread	2	3	2	2
Average	1.75	**2.75**	2.5	2.5
Overall Average Value	3.0833	**4.0**	3.0	3.5

and **Whole Wheat Corn Bread**). Good butter substitutes in *baking* recipes are *oils, applesauce, margarine, buttermilk, some fruit and vegetable purees*, and so on[9]. Although **soymilk** is not considered a straight substitute for butter, we opt to consider it a good replacement for that ingredient, once soymilk is the main ingredient in **Vegan Buttermilk** recipe, which take only two ingredients (*soymilk* and *lemon juice*)[10]. For butter substitute recommendation, all alternative ASV filters have been able to outperform standard ASV for the two selected *source recipes*. In the context of **milk** substitutes in *baking* recipes (such as **Wheat Germ Banana Muffin** and **Whole Wheat Corn Bread**), *soymilk* and other nut milks, as much as *applesauce* and, with some restrictions, *water*, are considered good substitutes, according to specialized websites[11,12]. Most ASV-based filter are able to find at least two adequate substitutes in the *top*-10. In **Whole Wheat Corn Bread** recipe, ASV$_w$ was able to find 3 good substitute ingredients for **milk**.

In an overall evaluation (Table 6), all ASV-based filters have been able to find at least one good substitute ingredient for the *source ingredient* in a *top*-10 anal-

---

[9] https://delishably.com/dairy/Substitutes-for-Butter-in-Baking.

[10] https://lovingitvegan.com/how-to-make-vegan-buttermilk/.

[11] https://blogchef.net/substitute-for-milk-in-cornbread/.

[12] https://www.sheknows.com/food-and-recipes/articles/1116425/milk-substitutions/.

ysis, which indicates the good capabilities of ASV, once only data-driven text mining approaches have been adopted to generate the final substitute recommendations, properly answering RQ1. The same way, none of the *top*-10 *candidate target ingredients* returned by the ASV-based mechanisms, for all evaluated *source recipes*, disrespected the dietary restrictions imposed by each one of the *target recipe sets*, providing a positive answer to RQ2. For almost all evaluated scenario, the weighted ASV-based models have been able to obtain performances at least as good as standard ASV, and in most of the evaluated cases (8 out of 12), ASV_w outperformed standard ASV. The best average overall results have been reached by ASV_w, ASV_{ws}, and standard ASV, respectively.

4   Conclusions

In this work, three alternative Average Support Value mechanisms are proposed to improve ingredient substitute recommendation for cooking recipes. The proposed models are based on data-driven approaches and text mining techniques. To illustrate the effectivity of the proposed alternative ASV filters, a complete recipe generation system is proposed based on single ingredient substitution.

We evaluate the proposed recipe generation systems considering the conversion of source recipes which present no associated dietary restrictions into restricted target food domains (diabetic-friendly, gluten-free and lactose-free). Four recipes have been selected and converted into restriction-safe recipes, and the adopted evaluation metric was the number of adequate substitutes recommended in a *top*-10 analysis. The experimental results showed that weighted ASV approaches are able to present better performances than ASV variants that do not take the context of each recipe into consideration when computing the ingredient pairwise co-occurrences. The proposed recommendation systems have been able to recommend at least one adequate ingredient substitute, and none of the returned recommendations have been considered inadequate according to the dietary restrictions of the selected target recipe domains.

As future works, we will evaluate alternative weighting mechanism for ASV, and also, perform deeper analysis on the influence and relevance of each ingredient in recipes and recipe categories, as a manner to promote a better individual ingredient weighting for each recipe, avoiding dataset biases towards some ingredients (such as 'water' and 'salt') [10]. We intend to expand our analysis by including new recipes in the future, as much as other recipe features, such as nutritional information.

Acknowledgements. The authors would like to thank CAPES, CNPq and FACEPE.

References

1. Britto, L.F.S., Pacifico, L.D.S., Ludermir, T.B.: Geração automática de receitas culinárias para pessoas com restrições alimentares. Rev. Eletrônica de Iniciação Científica em Computação **18**(3) (2020). https://doi.org/10.5753/reic.2020.1749, https://sol.sbc.org.br/journals/index.php/reic/article/view/1749

2. Freyne, J., Berkovsky, S.: Intelligent food planning: personalized recipe recommendation. In: Proceedings of the 15th International Conference on Intelligent User Interfaces, pp. 321–324. ACM (2010). https://doi.org/10.1145/1719970.1720021, https://dl.acm.org/doi/abs/10.1145/1719970.1720021

3. Hammond, K.J.: Chef: a model of case-based planning. In: AAAI, pp. 267–271 (1986). https://www.aaai.org/Papers/AAAI/1986/AAAI86-044.pdf

4. Haussmann, S., et al.: FoodKG: a semantics-driven knowledge graph for food recommendation. In: Ghidini, C., et al. (eds.) ISWC 2019. LNCS, vol. 11779, pp. 146–162. Springer, Cham (2019). https://doi.org/10.1007/978-3-030-30796-7_10

5. Isinkaye, F., Folajimi, Y., Ojokoh, B.: Recommendation systems: principles, methods and evaluation. Egypt. Inf. J. **16**(3), 261–273 (2015). https://doi.org/10.1016/j.eij.2015.06.005, https://www.sciencedirect.com/science/article/pii/S1110866515000341

6. Kaur, J., Buttar, P.K.: A systematic review on stopword removal algorithms. Int. J. Futur. Revolut. Comput. Sci. Commun. Eng. 4(4), 207–210 (2018). http://www.ijfrcsce.org/index.php/ijfrcsce/article/view/1499

7. Kowsari, K., Meimandi, K.J., Heidarysafa, M., Mendu, S., Barnes, L.E., Brown, D.E.: Text classification algorithms: a survey. CoRR abs/1904.08067 (2019). http://arxiv.org/abs/1904.08067

8. Ławrynowicz, A., Wróblewska, A., Adrian, W.T., Kulczyński, B., Gramza-Michałowska, A.: Food recipe ingredient substitution ontology design pattern. Sensors **22**(3), 1095 (2022). https://doi.org/10.3390/s22031095, https://pubmed.ncbi.nlm.nih.gov/35161841/

9. Majumder, B.P., Li, S., Ni, J., McAuley, J.: Generating personalized recipes from historical user preferences. arXiv preprint arXiv:1909.00105 (2019). https://doi.org/10.48550/arXiv.1909.00105, https://arxiv.org/abs/1909.00105

10. Nirmal, I., Caldera, A., Bandara, R.D.: Optimization framework for flavour and nutrition balanced recipe: a data driven approach. In: 2018 5th IEEE Uttar Pradesh Section International Conference on Electrical, Electronics and Computer Engineering (UPCON), pp. 1–9. IEEE (2018). https://doi.org/10.1109/UPCON.2018.8596886, https://ieeexplore.ieee.org/document/8596886

11. Oliveira, E.G., Britto, L.F.S., Pacifico, L.D.S., Ludermir, T.B.: Recipe recommendation and generation based on ingredient substitution. In: Anais do XVI Encontro Nacional de Inteligência Artificial e Computacional, pp. 238–249. ENIAC 2019, SBC, Sociedade Brasileira de Computação, Porto Alegre, RS, BRA (2019). https://doi.org/10.5753/eniac.2019.9287, https://sol.sbc.org.br/index.php/eniac/article/view/9287

12. Ooi, A., Iiba, T., Takano, K.: Ingredient substitute recommendation for allergy-safe cooking based on food context. In: 2015 IEEE Pacific Rim Conference on Communications, Computers and Signal Processing (PACRIM), pp. 444–449. IEEE (2015). https://doi.org/10.1109/PACRIM.2015.7334878, https://ieeexplore.ieee.org/document/7334878

13. Pacifico, L.D.S., Oliveira, E.G., Britto, L.F.S., Ludermir, T.B.: Sistemas de recomendaçao e geraçao de receitas através da categorizaçao ontológica dos ingredientes. In: Proceedings of the Symposium in Information and Human Language Technology. STIL 2019, vol. 1, pp. 81–85. SBC, Sociedade Brasileira de Computação, Porto Alegre, RS, BRA (2019). http://comissoes.sbc.org.br/ce-pln/stil2019/proceedings.html

14. Pacifico, L.D.S., Britto, L.F.S., Ludermir, T.B.: Ingredient substitute recommendation based on collaborative filtering and recipe context for automatic allergy-safe

recipe generation. In: Proceedings of the Brazilian Symposium on Multimedia and the Web, pp. 97–104. Association for Computing Machinery (2021). https://doi. org/10.1145/3470482.3479622, https://dl.acm.org/doi/10.1145/3470482.3479622

15. Pacifico, L.D., Britto, L.F., Ludermir, T.B.: Geração de receitas culinárias para usuários com restrições alimentares pela substituição automática de ingredientes. In: Anais do XLVIII Seminário Integrado de Software e Hardware, pp. 183– 190. SBC (2021). https://doi.org/10.5753/semish.2021.15821, https://sol.sbc.org. br/index.php/semish/article/view/15821

16. Pan, Y., Xu, Q., Li, Y.: Food recipe alternation and generation with natural language processing techniques. In: 2020 IEEE 36th International Conference on Data Engineering Workshops (ICDEW), pp. 94–97 (2020). https://doi.org/10. 1109/ICDEW49219.2020.000-1, https://ieeexplore.ieee.org/document/9094119

17. Pecune, F., Callebert, L., Marsella, S.: A socially-aware conversational recommender system for personalized recipe recommendations. In: Proceedings of the 8th International Conference on Human-Agent Interaction, pp. 78–86 (2020). https://doi.org/10.1145/3406499.3415079, https://dl.acm.org/doi/abs/10.1145/3406499.3415079

18. Shino, N., Yamanishi, R., Fukumoto, J.: Recommendation system for alternative-ingredients based on co-occurrence relation on recipe database and the ingredient category. In: 2016 5th IIAI International Congress on Advanced Applied Informatics (IIAI-AAI), pp. 173–178. IEEE (2016). https://doi.org/10.1109/IIAI-AAI. 2016.187, https://ieeexplore.ieee.org/document/7557598

19. Shirai, S.S., Seneviratne, O., Gordon, M.E., Chen, C.H., McGuinness, D.L.: Identifying ingredient substitutions using a knowledge graph of food. Front. Artif. Intell. 3, 621766 (2021). https://doi.org/10.3389/frai.2020.621766, https://www. frontiersin.org/articles/10.3389/frai.2020.621766/full

20. Svensson, M., Höök, K., Cöster, R.: Designing and evaluating kalas: a social navigation system for food recipes. ACM Trans. Comput. Hum. Interact. (TOCHI) 12(3), 374–400 (2005). https://doi.org/10.1145/1096737.1096739, https://dl.acm.org/doi/10.1145/1096737.1096739

21. Trattner, C., Elsweiler, D.: Investigating the healthiness of internet-sourced recipes: implications for meal planning and recommender systems. In: Proceedings of the 26th International Conference on World Wide Web, pp. 489–498. International World Wide Web Conferences Steering Committee (2017). https://doi.org/10. 1145/3038912.3052573, https://dl.acm.org/doi/10.1145/3038912.3052573

22. Twomey, N., Fain, M., Ponikar, A., Sarraf, N.: Towards multi-language recipe personalisation and recommendation. In: Fourteenth ACM Conference on Recommender Systems, pp. 708–713 (2020). https://doi.org/10.1145/3383313.3418478, https://dl.acm.org/doi/fullHtml/10.1145/3383313.3418478

23. Toledo, Y.R., Alzahrani, A.A., Martínez, L.: A food recommender system considering nutritional information and user preferences. IEEE Access 7, 96695–96711 (2019). https://doi.org/10.1109/ACCESS.2019.2929413, https://ieeexplore. ieee.org/abstract/document/8765311

Augmenting a Physics-Informed Neural Network for the 2D Burgers Equation by Addition of Solution Data Points

Marlon S. Mathias[1,2]([✉]) [iD], Wesley P. de Almeida[1,3] [iD],
Jefferson F. Coelho[1,3] [iD], Lucas P. de Freitas[1,3] [iD], Felipe M. Moreno[1,3] [iD],
Caio F. D. Netto[1,3] [iD], Fabio G. Cozman[1,3] [iD], Anna Helena Reali Costa[1,3] [iD],
Eduardo A. Tannuri[1,3] [iD], Edson S. Gomi[1,3] [iD], and Marcelo Dottori[1,4] [iD]

[1] Center for Artificial Intelligence (C4AI) – University of Sao Paulo, Av. Prof. Lúcio
Martins Rodrigues, 370, Butantã, São Paulo 05508-020, Brazil
{marlon.mathias,wesleyalmeida,jfialho,lfreitasp2001,
felipe.marino.moreno,caio.netto,fgcozman,anna.reali,eduat,gomi,
mdottori}@usp.br
[2] Instituto de Estudos Avançados – University of São Paulo, São Paulo, Brazil
[3] Escola Politécnica – University of Sao Paulo, São Paulo, Brazil
[4] Instituto Oceanográfico – University of Sao Paulo, São Paulo, Brazil
https://c4ai.inova.usp.br/

Abstract. We implement a Physics-Informed Neural Network (PINN)
for solving the two-dimensional Burgers equations. This type of model
can be trained with no previous knowledge of the solution; instead, it
relies on evaluating the governing equations of the system in points of the
physical domain. It is also possible to use points with a known solution
during training. In this paper, we compare PINNs trained with different
amounts of governing equation evaluation points and known solution
points Comparing models that were trained purely with known solution
points to those that have also used the governing equations, we observe
an improvement in the overall observance of the underlying physics in
the latter. We also investigate how changing the number of each type
of point affects the resulting models differently. Finally, we argue that
the addition of the governing equations during training may provide a
way to improve the overall performance of the model without relying on
additional data, which is especially important for situations where the
number of known solution points is limited.

Keywords: Physics-informed neural networks · Burgers equation

1 Introduction

The rapid development of Machine Learning (ML) models has led to significant
progress in various areas and allowed a new approach to problems involving
time-series forecasts. By training these models with large datasets, the models

© The Author(s), under exclusive license to Springer Nature Switzerland AG 2022
J. C. Xavier-Junior and R. A. Rios (Eds.): BRACIS 2022, LNAI 13654, pp. 388–401, 2022.
https://doi.org/10.1007/978-3-031-21689-3_28

can recognize complex patterns and address the prediction of physical systems. However, a purely data-driven approach may also not be entirely desirable, as such models require substantial amounts of data to train, which might not always be available, and they may lead to non-physical solutions when presented to previously unseen scenarios [4].

Physics-Informed Machine Learning models present a compromise between purely data-driven and purely physics-based approaches in an attempt to combine their advantages and minimize their shortcomings. The literature presents several ways of combining both models [5,9,12]. These approaches include, but are not limited to: using ML to estimate the error in the physics-based models [14]; using ML to increase the resolution of known flow fields [2,8]; substituting the governing equations by trained neural networks [13]; adding physical constraints to the ML model [1,10].

In this work, we implement a Physics-Informed Neural Network (PINN) that uses the governing equations of the physical system in its fitness evaluation. [7] calls this approach a neural-FEM, comparing it to the Finite Elements Method (FEM) of solving partial differential equations. In this analogy, the neural network works as one large and complex finite element, which spans the whole domain and solves the equation within its solution space, similarly to the classical FEM, in which several elements, each with a relatively simple solution space, are spread along with the domain in a mesh.

In this paper, we will find solutions for the Burgers equation in a two-dimensional space. Computational Fluid Dynamics researchers widely use this equation as a toy problem intended to test novel ideas that may be used to improve fluid dynamics solvers.

One advantage of PINN models over regular physics-based models is that the neural network may be trained using the governing equations and a set of points where the solution is known beforehand, comprising a hybrid solution between physics-driven and data-driven models. This paper compares neural networks that were trained solely by the governing equations, data points, or an array of combinations between both scenarios.

In real-world uses of machine learning models, there are situations where a limited amount of data is available for training. By adding physical knowledge to the model, it might be possible to reduce the amount of data needed without impacting its quality. Furthermore, it may aid the model in making accurate predictions even for previously unseen situations.

The remainder of this paper is structured as follows: In Sect. 2, we present the governing equations of our physical system and its boundary conditions and describe the PINN implementation and training procedure. Section 3 shows the results obtained after training was complete. Finally, Sect. 4 finishes with some conclusions and suggestions for future works.

2   Methods

We begin this section by describing the governing equations of the physical system and its initial and boundary conditions. Then, we proceed to define the neural network and the loss function that is minimized during training.

2.1   Governing Equations

The Burgers equation with two spatial dimensions is given by the system:

$$\frac{\partial U}{\partial t} + U\frac{\partial U}{\partial x} + V\frac{\partial U}{\partial y} = \nu\left(\frac{\partial^2 U}{\partial x^2} + \frac{\partial^2 U}{\partial y^2}\right), \tag{1}$$

$$\frac{\partial V}{\partial t} + U\frac{\partial V}{\partial x} + V\frac{\partial V}{\partial y} = \nu\left(\frac{\partial^2 V}{\partial x^2} + \frac{\partial^2 V}{\partial y^2}\right), \tag{2}$$

where x and y are the spatial coordinates, and U and V are the velocities in each direction, respectively. t is the solution time, and ν is the viscosity. If ν is set to zero, the solution would eventually lead to extremely high gradients, akin to shock waves in compressible fluids, by setting a positive value to ν, the right-hand side of both equations allows some dissipation, which leads to a smoother solution field.

The solution will be evaluated in the domain $0 \le t \le 1, 0 \le x \le 1, 0 \le y \le 1$, with Dirichlet boundary conditions setting both velocities to zero at the domain boundaries. The initial condition is given by:

$$U(t = 0, x, y) = \sin(2\pi x)\sin(2\pi y), \tag{3}$$

$$V(t = 0, x, y) = \sin(\pi x)\sin(\pi y). \tag{4}$$

Figure 1 shows U and V at this condition.

2.2   Physics-Informed Neural Network

The neural network in our implementation is a Multilayer Perceptron (MLP) and receives coordinates t, x, and y and outputs the variables U and V for any point of the domain. The MLP network is fully connected and has 4 hidden layers of 20 neurons each, with a hyperbolic tangent activation function. Larger amounts of layers and neurons were tested with little impact on the results. Residual connections are added every two layers, which allows for better computations of the gradients and aids the convergence during training [3]. There are two outputs: $\tilde{U}$ and $\tilde{V}$, one for each variable in the problem. The tilde denotes that these variables are the direct output of the MLP and may not observe the boundary conditions of the problem.

After the MLP, there is a Boundary-encoded output layer, as described by [11]. This layer makes sure that the Dirichlet boundary conditions are always

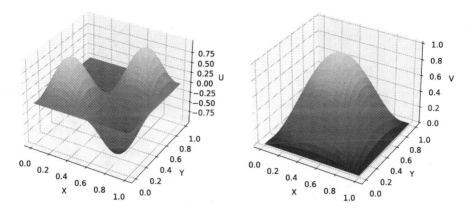

Fig. 1. Initial condition for U and V.

observed. The layer works by combining the output of the MLP to a known function that perfectly observes the Dirichlet boundary condition in the following manner:

$$U = d(t, x, y)\tilde{U} + (1 - d(t, x, y)) U_p, \tag{5}$$

where U_p is the particular solution for the velocity in the x direction and d is a distance function, which is continuous and differentiable and is equal to zero, where the value of U is set by either a Dirichlet boundary condition or by the initial condition and non-zero everywhere else. The concept behind this definition is that the value of U is fixed to U_p at the boundary and initial conditions but remains under the control of the neural network everywhere else in the domain. This operation is analogous to V. We have defined the following equations for d:

$$d = 16x(1 - x)y(1 - y)\tanh(\alpha t). \tag{6}$$

The hyperbolic tangent function is used so that the value of d is constant and close to one when away from the initial condition. α is set to 26.4, which causes d to reach 0.99 at $t = 0.1$. The constant 16 is used, so d becomes close to 1 at the center of the domain. In case other types of boundary conditions, such as Neumann, were present, they would have to be implemented via an additional loss function during training, as they cannot be set by using this method, similarly to the implementation of all boundary conditions by [9].

We have set the particular solution of this case as U and V being constant in time and equal to the initial condition values. Therefore:

$$U_p(t, x, y) = \sin(2\pi x)\sin(2\pi y). \tag{7}$$

$$V_p(t, x, y) = \sin(\pi x)\sin(\pi y). \tag{8}$$

In summary, Fig. 2 shows the final configuration of the network.

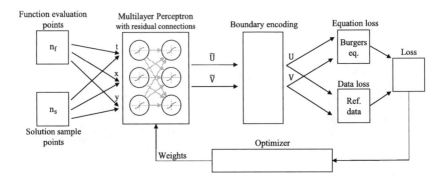

Fig. 2. Summary of the PINN network.

2.3   Loss Function

In this work, there are two distinct loss functions whose values are added to obtain the overall loss. First, we will define the loss function relative to the observance of the governing equations, and its value is defined as the sum of the mean absolute value of the residual of each governing equation.

Therefore, given that U_i and V_i are the PINN's output at coordinate (t_i, x_i, y_i), as given by Eq. 5 and its analogous for V, the residuals relative to the governing equations are computed as:

$$R_{f,1,i} = \left| \frac{\partial U_i}{\partial t} + U_i \frac{\partial U_i}{\partial x} + V_i \frac{\partial U_i}{\partial y} - \nu \left(\frac{\partial^2 U_i}{\partial x^2} + \frac{\partial^2 U_i}{\partial y^2} \right) \right| \tag{9}$$

and

$$R_{f,2,i} = \left| \frac{\partial V_i}{\partial t} + U_i \frac{\partial V_i}{\partial x} + V_i \frac{\partial V_i}{\partial y} - \nu \left(\frac{\partial^2 V_i}{\partial x^2} + \frac{\partial^2 V_i}{\partial y^2} \right) \right|. \tag{10}$$

The second type of loss is relative to the data-driven part of the training and is given by the mean absolute distance between the predicted values and known solution values. Naturally, this loss depends on previous knowledge of the solution at given domain points.

The loss function of the model is given by:

$$\mathcal{L} = \frac{1}{n_f} \sum_{i=1}^{n_f} (R_{f,1,i} + R_{f,2,i}) + \frac{1}{2n_s} \sum_{i=1}^{n_s} \left(|U_i - U_i^{gt}| + |V_i - V_i^{gt}| \right). \tag{11}$$

where U_i^{gt} and V_i^{gt} are the ground truth values of U and V at point i. n_s is the number of points with known solutions. The governing equations are evaluated at n_f random points uniformly distributed along with the domain. One characteristic of PINNs is that there is an infinite pool of points for the loss to be evaluated. Consequently, there is no limit for the value of n_f, while n_s is limited to the set of points where the solution is known beforehand.

2.4 Implementation

Our code is written in Python and uses the PyTorch module for machine learning tasks. The governing equations' partial derivatives are obtained using PyTorch's autograd feature. The optimization is performed with the Adam algorithm. All tests were executed on a Nvidia® GeForce™ RTX3080 graphics card, with 10 GB of available memory. The code is available on GitHub[1].

2.5 Generation of Reference Data

The data-driven part of the models requires previous knowledge of the solution at some points in the domain. Therefore, we have used numerical differentiation and integration techniques to approximate a solution for the 2D Burgers equation. For this, a mesh of 401 nodes in each direction was uniformly distributed in x and y. A sixth-order compact finite differences scheme [6] was used to approximate the spatial derivatives of the governing equations, while a fourth-order Runge-Kutta scheme was used to integrate the solution through time, with a time step of 10^{-5}. For training, n_s points are randomly chosen from this solution. This model was implemented in Matlab™ and will also be available on Github at the time of publication.

3 Results

In this section, we compare the solutions obtained by models trained with an array of values for the number of function evaluation points (n_f) and the number of solution sample points (n_s). We have chosen five values for each variable: 0, 100, 1000, 10000, and 100000. All combinations of values were run with the obvious exception of $n_f = n_s = 0$. When $n_f = 0$, no knowledge of the governing equation is used, and training is performed solely from the reference data. Similarly, when $n_s = 0$, no reference data is used, and the training is purely physics-based.

These cases will also be compared against our reference data, which was generated by more conventional techniques, as described in Sect. 2.5. For all cases, the value to ν is set to $0.01/\pi$.

3.1 Sample Results

Figure 3 shows contours of both velocity components as modeled by a PINN trained with 10^5 samples of each type. As the field evolves in time, large gradients form in the middle of the x domain for the U component and at the end of the y domain for the V component. This behavior is expected for the Burgers equation and is representative of shock waves in compressible gasses. The dissipative part, corresponding to the right-hand side of Eqs. 1 and 2, causes these large gradients to dissipate as time passes, as can be seen in the images to the right-hand side

---

[1] https://github.com/C4AI/PINN_for_Burgers.

of the figure. If ν were set to zero, we would be solving the inviscid Burgers equation, which leads to larger and larger gradients, which are notoriously hard to solve with the techniques presented in this paper.

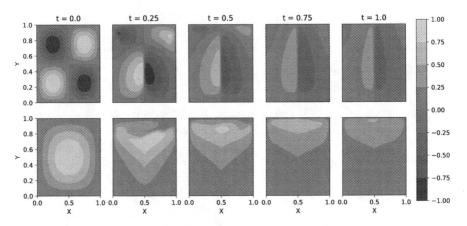

Fig. 3. Contours of U (top) and V (bottom) for five equally spaced instants from $t = 0$ to $t = 1$ (left to right), as modeled by a PINN trained with $n_f = n_s = 10^5$.

3.2   Comparison to Reference Data

The numerical solution described in Sect. 2.5 was evaluated in a mesh of 401 by 401 equally spaced nodes, with a time step of 10^{-5}. Figure 4 shows the velocity contours for the reference data.

The solution by the PINN and by the finite differences solver – Figs. 3 and 4, respectively – are visually similar for most of the domain. Nonetheless, both solutions have a clear difference near the $Y = 1$ boundary, especially for the V velocity. This variable presents large gradients in this region, physically equivalent to a shock wave in a compressible gas. Interestingly, a similar region of large gradients for U near $X = 0$ has reached a much better agreement between the PINN and the reference data. Figure 5 overlaps contours of both cases at $t = 0.25$. This result leads us to believe that there might be some influence on the implementation of the boundary conditions; perhaps the function chosen for $d(t, x, y)$ in Eq. 6 is too smooth near the boundaries and makes it difficult for the MLP to model large gradients in this region. Further investigation on the optimal choice of $d(t, x, y)$ is needed.

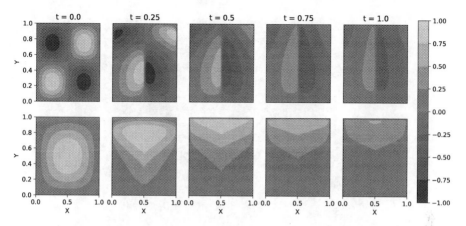

Fig. 4. Contours of U (top) and V (bottom) for five equally spaced instants from $t = 0$ to $t = 1$ (left to right), as modeled by the finite differences numerical solver.

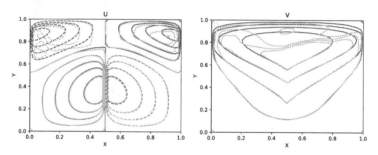

Fig. 5. Contours of U (left) and V (right) at $t = 0.25$ for the reference data, in blue, and for the PINN with $n_f = n_s = 10000$, in red. (Color figure online)

3.3 Governing Equations Residuals

The PINN was trained for all combinations of n_f and n_s in the range 0, 100, 1000, 10000 and 100000, with the natural exception of $n_f = n_s = 0$. After training, the governing equation residuals were measured on a uniformly spaced grid of points across the domain in its three dimensions, one temporal and two spatial. Figure 6 shows the root mean square of the residuals for each combination. It is possible to reduce the residual and thus improve the model by increasing either n_f or n_s. One significant result we can observe in this figure is when we increase n_f from 0 to 100 at the lower values of n_s, such as 100 and 1000. This result illustrates that adding physical knowledge ($n_f > 0$) to cases where few data points are known may be a key to increasing the overall model's accuracy without additional data.

For further understanding the effect of adding physical knowledge to a data-based approach, we have plotted the value of U along the x axis (with $y = 0.25$ and $t = 0.5$) for various values of n_f, and n_s fixed at 1000. This plot can be seen

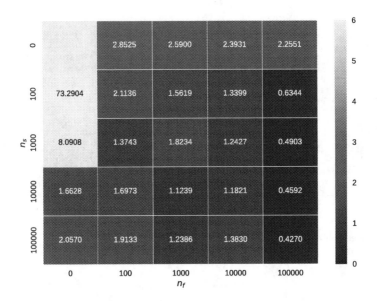

Fig. 6. Root mean square of the governing equations' residuals for different combinations of function evaluation points (n_f) and solution sample points (n_s).

on the left-hand side of Fig. 7. Interestingly, the case with no physical knowledge $(n_f = 0)$ follows the reference data more closely than some cases with physical knowledge, despite the higher residual. Nonetheless, the higher residual can be easily explained by noting that the values of U for the $n_f = 0$ case are not as smooth as those with $n_f > 0$. Therefore, despite coming close to the absolute value of the reference data, the derivatives are considerably off, which directly influences the residuals of the governing equations. For $n_f = 100$, the curve is much smoother than for the $n_f = 0$ case, and, despite being considerably further from the reference data in absolute values, the residuals are lower. For $n_f = 1000$ or higher, the curves are much closer to the reference data both in terms of absolute values and in terms of its derivative. The right-hand side of Fig. 7 shows a similar plot, but of V with respect to y at $x = 0.25$ and $t = 0.5$. This time, only the $n_f = 100000$ case can approach the reference data in terms of absolute values, but the overall conclusion remains.

For completeness, a similar behaviour can be seen when the same plots are made for both $n_s = 0$ and varying n_f and for $n_f = 0$ and varying n_s, shown in Figs. 8 and 9, respectively. For the cases with no sample data $(n_s = 0)$, as the number of function evaluation points increases, the values of U and V move away from null values and approximate the reference solution. On the other hand, when the model has no physical reference $(n_f = 0)$, the predictions quickly approximate the reference data, even for low values of n_s; however, only models trained with larger values of n_s can reach a smooth prediction, which more closely observes the governing equations.

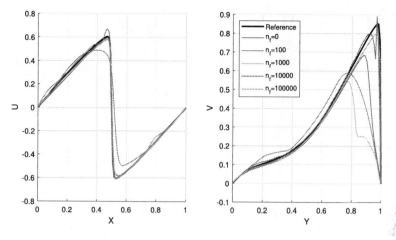

Fig. 7. (Left) Plot of U with respect to x at $y = 0.25$ and $t = 0.5$ for $n_s = 1000$ and various values of n_f. (Right) Plot of V with respect to y at $x = 0.25$ and $t = 0.5$ for $n_s = 1000$ and various values of n_f.

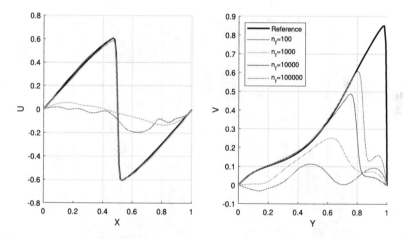

Fig. 8. (Left) Plot of U with respect to x at $y = 0.25$ and $t = 0.5$ for $n_s = 0$ and various values of n_f. (Right) Plot of V with respect to y at $x = 0.25$ and $t = 0.5$ for $n_s = 0$ and various values of n_f.

The errors of each model concerning the reference data were estimated by computing the model at a grid of uniformly spaced points and comparing it to the reference. Figure 10 summarizes the root mean square of the errors of each case. It is possible to note that the physics-less case often produces lower errors when compared to the physics-informed model, especially at the larger values of n_s. Nonetheless, by further increasing n_f, the errors decrease considerably. This phenomenon can be explained by looking back at Fig. 7, where we have argued that, despite reaching values that are closer to the reference data in an

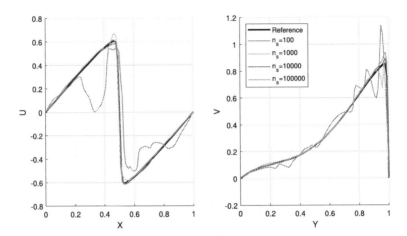

Fig. 9. (Left) Plot of U with respect to x at $y = 0.25$ and $t = 0.5$ for $n_f = 0$ and various values of n_s. (Right) Plot of V with respect to y at $x = 0.25$ and $t = 0.5$ for $n_f = 0$ and various values of n_s.

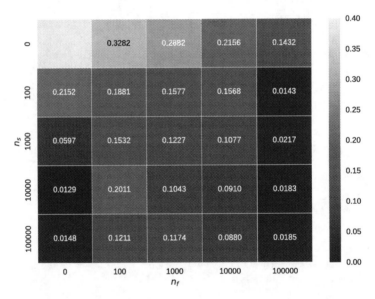

Fig. 10. Root mean square of the error for different combinations of function evaluation points (n_f) and solution sample points (n_s).

absolute sense, the solution produced by the physics-less model is not smooth, which incurs a larger non-observance of the governing equations.

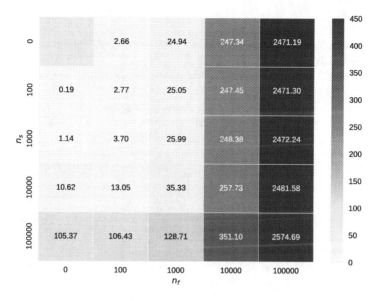

Fig. 11. Maximum allocated GPU memory, in megabytes, for different combinations of function evaluation points (n_f) and solution sample points (n_s).

3.4   Computational Cost

Each case's memory footprint was measured using PyTorch's native method `cuda.max_memory_allocated`, which returns the largest amount of GPU memory allocated during execution. Naturally, increasing either n_f or n_s has caused more memory to be allocated. Both values presented a roughly linear relation to the allocation size. Nonetheless, the number of function evaluations had a much larger impact than the number of sample points. This result is caused by the much larger complexity in computing the residuals of the governing equations as opposed to simply comparing the model's output to the reference data. The case with $n_f = 0$ and $n_s = 100000$ has allocated just over 100 MB of memory, while the $n_f = 100000$ and $n_s = 0$ has needed over 2.5 GB. Figure 11 shows the values for each combination of n_f and

4   Discussion

In this paper, we implemented a Physics-Informed Neural Network to solve the 2D Burgers equation. During training, this model can use both function evaluation points, where the residual of the governing equations is sought to be minimized, and solution sample points, where the solution's value is known and training seeks to minimize the difference between the model's output and the reference data. The network was trained with different amounts of function evaluation points (n_f) and solution sample points (n_s), and the resulting models were compared.

By looking at the residual of the governing equations, we improved the models by increasing either n_f or n_s. Nonetheless, we have observed that this improvement happens in different manners for each variable. Increasing n_s causes the model to approximate the reference values quickly. However, only larger sample sizes can reach smooth curves, which more closely follow the governing equations. On the other hand, by setting n_s to zero and relying only on function evaluation points, the solution obtained is usually smooth, but it can only approach the actual solution for larger batch sizes ($n_f \geq 10000$ in our case).

These results can be beneficial for scenarios where the availability of reference data is limited. Adding function evaluation points allows one to improve the model without requiring additional data. Nonetheless, care must be taken so that enough function evaluation points are used. Otherwise, training may lead to solutions that do not follow the reference data, despite having lower residuals in the governing equations.

For future works, we suggest investigating how the balance between the physics-based loss and the data-based loss influences the resulting model. Perhaps different loss functions would be able to take advantage of the lowered governing equation residuals offered by adding function evaluation points without the downside of causing the model to drift away from the reference data, as we have observed at low values of n_f.

References

1. Beucler, T., Pritchard, M., Rasp, S., Ott, J., Baldi, P., Gentine, P.: Enforcing analytic constraints in neural networks emulating physical systems. Phys. Rev. Lett. **126**(9), 098302 (2021). https://doi.org/10.1103/PhysRevLett.126.098302
2. Fukami, K., Fukagata, K., Taira, K.: Machine-learning-based spatio-temporal super resolution reconstruction of turbulent flows. J. Fluid Mech. **909** (2020). https://doi.org/10.1017/jfm.2020.948
3. He, K., Zhang, X., Ren, S., Sun, J.: Deep residual learning for image recognition. In: 2016 IEEE Conference on Computer Vision and Pattern Recognition (CVPR), pp. 770–778 (2016). https://doi.org/10.1109/CVPR.2016.90
4. Karniadakis, G.E., Kevrekidis, I.G., Lu, L., Perdikaris, P., Wang, S., Yang, L.: Physics-informed machine learning. Nat. Rev. Phys. **3**(6), 422–440 (2021). https://doi.org/10.1038/s42254-021-00314-5
5. Kashinath, K., et al.: Physics-informed machine learning: case studies for weather and climate modelling. Philos. Trans. R. Soc. A: Math. Phys. Eng. Sci. **379**(2194) (2021). https://doi.org/10.1098/rsta.2020.0093
6. Lele, S.K.: Compact finite difference schemes with spectral-like resolution. J. Comput. Phys. **103**(1), 16–42 (1992). https://doi.org/10.1016/0021-9991(92)90324-R
7. Li, Z., et al.: Fourier neural operator for parametric partial differential equations. In: International Conference on Learning Representations (2021)
8. Nair, A.G., Yeh, C.A., Kaiser, E., Noack, B.R., Brunton, S.L., Taira, K.: Cluster-based feedback control of turbulent post-stall separated flows. J. Fluid Mech. **875**, 345–375 (2019). https://doi.org/10.1017/jfm.2019.469
9. Raissi, M., Perdikaris, P., Karniadakis, G.E.: Physics-informed neural networks: a deep learning framework for solving forward and inverse problems involving nonlinear partial differential equations. J. Comput. Phys. **378**, 686–707 (2019). https://doi.org/10.1016/j.jcp.2018.10.045

10. Read, J.S., et al.: Process-guided deep learning predictions of lake water temperature. Water Resour. Res. **55**(11), 9173–9190 (2019). https://doi.org/10.1029/2019WR024922

11. Sun, L., Gao, H., Pan, S., Wang, J.X.: Surrogate modeling for fluid flows based on physics-constrained deep learning without simulation data. Comput. Methods Appl. Mech. Eng. **361**, 112732 (2020). https://doi.org/10.1016/j.cma.2019.112732

12. Willard, J., Jia, X., Xu, S., Steinbach, M., Kumar, V.: Integrating scientific knowledge with machine learning for engineering and environmental systems **1**(1), 1–34 (2020)

13. Wu, M., Stefanakos, C., Gao, Z.: Multi-step-ahead forecasting of wave conditions based on a physics-based machine learning (PBML) model for marine operations. J. Mar. Sci. Eng. **8**(12), 1–24 (2020). https://doi.org/10.3390/jmse8120992

14. Xu, T., Valocchi, A.J.: Data-driven methods to improve baseflow prediction of a regional groundwater model. Comput. Geosci. **85**, 124–136 (2015). https://doi.org/10.1016/j.cageo.2015.05.016

Impact of Morphological Segmentation on Pre-trained Language Models

Matheus Westhelle, Luciana Bencke[ID], and Viviane P. Moreira [(✉)][ID]

Institute of Informatics, UFRGS, Porto Alegre, Brazil
{matheus.westhelle,lrbencke,viviane}@inf.ufrgs.br

Abstract. Pre-trained Language Models are the current state-of-the-art in many natural language processing tasks. These models rely on subword-based tokenization to solve the problem of out-of-vocabulary words. However, commonly used subword segmentation methods have no linguistic foundation. In this paper, we investigate the hypothesis that the study of internal word structure (*i.e.,* morphology) can offer informed priors to these models, such that they perform better in common tasks. We employ an unsupervised morpheme discovery method in a new word segmentation approach, which we call Morphologically Informed Segmentation (MIS), to test our hypothesis. Experiments with MIS on several natural language understanding tasks (text classification, recognizing textual entailment, and question-answering), in Portuguese, yielded promising results compared to a WordPiece baseline.

Keywords: Natural language processing · Computational linguistics · Morphology · Word representations

1 Introduction

Pre-trained language models based on transformers [24], such as BERT [7], represent the state-of-the-art in natural language processing, showing excellent performance in many different tasks. Segmentation of tokens into subwords is an essential element of these models, allowing them to handle out-of-vocabulary words, as well as learn to generalize on frequent character sequences. Some of the most popular segmentation techniques used in these models are Byte Pair Encoding [22] and WordPiece [27]. These techniques work very well empirically— however, they have no linguistic foundation and, as such, are not capable of encoding morphology [3,12]. This means that they would have trouble computing the meaning of new word formations, unseen in the training corpus.

Park *et al.* [19] also show that morphological complexity is a hindering element for language model training and that linguistically motivated segmentation methods are able to better deal with that complexity.

Hofmann *et al.* [11] showed that the use of segmentation with a morphological basis is beneficial in the case of complex words, *i.e.,* words that are created via affixation. Their work, however, is limited to the English language and focuses

© The Author(s), under exclusive license to Springer Nature Switzerland AG 2022
J. C. Xavier-Junior and R. A. Rios (Eds.): BRACIS 2022, LNAI 13654, pp. 402–416, 2022.
https://doi.org/10.1007/978-3-031-21689-3_29

on derivational morphology—the word-formation process where a word with a new meaning is created by the addition of affixes to a base word. Their approach leverages the WordPiece vocabulary of a BERT model without modifying it but changing the way it is used. Whenever possible, a word is split into its parts, with morpho-orthographical corrections based on simple rules; those parts are concatenated with hyphens so that a word such as *unquestionably* becomes *un-question-able-ly*; in this context, a "morpho-orthographical correction" means the recovery of the original morphemes (*ably* becomes *able-ly* after the correction). The use of English-specific morpho-orthographical correction rules means that it is not easy to reproduce this work in other languages, especially those with more complex morphology. In these cases, the list of necessary rules grows rapidly, such that experts are needed to create and curate them.

In this work, we raise a different hypothesis that is more compatible with languages with complex morphology: if we segment words according to their morphemes, is it possible to observe an improvement in the generated representations? Our final goal is to train a model that is capable of computing the meaning of words that are not part of the training corpus, through the composition of the meanings of their morphemes.

We evaluate our hypothesis on Brazilian Portuguese, which has a decidedly richer inflectional morphology when compared to English—inflectional morphology being the word-formation process in which a word is modified to express a difference in grammatical category (tense, case, number, gender, *etc.*.). To evaluate our hypothesis, we developed a segmentation strategy we call Morphologically Informed Segmentation (MIS). MIS relies on Morfessor, an unsupervised morpheme discovery model [25]. MIS was evaluated in a series of tasks: text classification, recognizing textual entailment (RTE), and question-answering natural language inference (QNLI). We compared it with another model trained using WordPiece. We pre-train two models from scratch: one using WordPiece segmentation, and another using our segmentation based on morphs obtained by a Morfessor model. We then perform fine-tuning of both models in four datasets: ASSIN RTE, representing the task of textual entailment recognition; a news dataset from the Folha newspaper and a dataset of true and fake news, Fake.Br [17], representing textual classification; and QNLI, from PLUE [9]. Our experiments show better F1-scores on three out of the four datasets we experimented on; we obtain more granular results by inspecting the confusion matrices of our classifiers and raise hypotheses that explain them.

The remainder of this paper is organized as follows: in Sect. 2, we lay down the theoretical framework for our work; in Sect. 3, we discuss similar work that explore the effect of morphological segmentation and show where our work stands out; Sect. 4 is where we present our experimental methodology; in Sect. 5, we present our results, raise hypotheses to explain them, and show the limitations in our work; finally, in Sect. 6, we discuss our conclusions, and offer future paths of research.

2   Background

This section introduces the fundamental concepts on which this work is based. We present a few basic concepts of morphology and present methods of automatic morphological segmentation

2.1   Morphs, Morphemes, and Allomorphs

Morphemes are commonly defined as the smallest unit of meaning within a word. The morpheme itself is an abstraction over morphs, which are the realization of morphemes. To illustrate, we use -s, Portuguese's morpheme for the formation of plurals: *casa + -s casas*. (In English, house → houses). However, when we consider the plural forms of *mês* (month) or *lápis* (pencil), we observe different morphs of the -s morpheme: -es, in *meses* (months), and ∅, in *lápis* (pencils)[1]. In this example, we see a phenomenon in which a morpheme shows multiple realizations; this phenomenon is called *allomorphy*.

2.2   Inflectional and Derivational Morphology

Inflectional morphology is the word-formation process in which words are formed by affixation to conform to a change in grammatical category, such as person, number, grammatical gender, or verb tense; in Portuguese, for example, the addition of the suffix -*ou* marks the simple past tense. Derivational morphology, on the other hand, is the word-formation process where affixation changes a word's meaning; as an example, take -*ção*, a suffix that forms deverbal nouns in Portuguese, such as *bater + -ção → bateção*—in English, *bater* means "to hit", and *bateção* would mean an act of continuously hitting something.

2.3   Morphological Segmentation

The task of morphological segmentation consists in breaking down a word into all the morphs that compose it. Let us take an example:

$$\text{superbizarra} \rightarrow \text{super-} + \text{bizarr} + \text{-a}$$

The word *superbizarra* can be broken into three morphs: the prefix *super-*; *bizarr*, the word's stem; and the gender desinence suffix -*a*.

Identifying morpheme boundaries within words is a task that requires linguistic knowledge of varying complexity across different languages. In isolating languages, *i.e.*, languages that present no inflection and where morphemes are (mostly) equivalent to words, the task is simple. Polysynthetic languages, however, present a bigger challenge, as a single word can present multiple stems and a high degree of affixation.

---

[1] A realization of a morpheme that does not manifest itself in a word is called a zero morph.

Portuguese is a fusional language. In fusional languages, it is common for a single inflectional morpheme to express multiple grammatical, syntactic, or semantic features. In *coma*, (singular imperative "eat"), *comer* + *-a*, *-a* expresses person (2nd person), number (singular), and mood (imperative).

2.4   Automatic Morphological Segmentation

Automatic morphological segmentation is a task that can be performed in several ways, each with its advantages and disadvantages. On one hand, a rule-based approach for identifying morphemes can be employed; a robust rule-based system is the most accurate form of automatic morphological segmentation. However, this approach is very costly, as the rules need to be handcrafted by linguists, which would require many hours of effort and would be specific to only one language. Another possible approach is to use a supervised learning algorithm and train it on a golden segmentation dataset; a model trained in such a fashion would then be able to segment new unseen words; this approach would not have perfect precision as a rule-based system would, and would still require the laborious construction of a dataset. We opted for a third alternative: using word segmentation based on an unsupervised morpheme discovery model [6]. The unsupervised nature of the method gives the flexibility to extend the method to low-resource languages: the only requirement is a corpus.

3   Related Work

Hofmann *et al.* [11] operate under the hypothesis that the BERT model is capable of learning good representations for words that are entirely in the model vocabulary (without having to be split), or whose meaning may have been captured through the co-occurrence of their segments, in which case it would not matter if the delimitation of these segments made linguistic sense. For example, *supera* + *##migo* ("superfriend" in English) has an invalid segmentation from a morphological point of view—as the correct one would be *super* + *##amigo*— but if these segments co-occurred frequently in pre-training, the model would be able to learn a good quality representation. However, for words that do not appear in the pre-training corpus, the model would then need to compute a representation from its segments, which, intuitively, would be simpler if these segments had a linguistic basis.

The segmentation used by Hofmann *et al.* [11] consists of iteratively removing affixes from a word, recovering the base through morpho-orthographic correction rules, and concatenating the found affixes to the root using hyphens to separate them. The affixes come from a list of known prefixes and suffixes that can also be found in WordPiece's vocabulary. In our work, we pre-train a language model by creating a vocabulary with morphs obtained by a Morfessor model, in order to create independence from the need for rules provided by linguists. Also unlike Hofmann *et al.* [11], we do not propose to pay special attention to derivational morphology, and so capturing all Portuguese morpho-orthographic adequacy rules to apply corrections becomes a high-cost undertaking. We take a simpler segmentation approach, using the segmentation provided by the Morfessor model and separating prefixes from a list of productive prefixes, when possible, into separate words; more details are presented in Sect. 4.

Nzeyimana and Rubungo [18] investigate the impact of morphological segmentation in Kinyarwanda. While they leverage a morphological analyzer and part-of-speech tags as features to their model, our approach is much less costly.

4   Materials and Methods

Training transformer-based language models can be prohibitive: the latest and greatest models, such as GPT-3 [4], are trained using high-scale computational resources—datasets of hundreds of Gigabytes, models using hundreds of billions of parameters, requiring clusters of GPUs for their training. Thus, this type of endeavor is not accessible to much of the academic community. With this in mind, we use the architecture of the ALBERT [13] model in our experiments, which is much simpler to train than the BERT model, but even so has comparable performance. ALBERT-base, the variant we use, only has 12M trainable parameters, compared to the 108M parameters of BERT-base. We also follow Liu *et al.* [14] in using only the Masked Language Modeling training objective, and we limited the size of our training dataset, in order to train models in a reasonable time. To perform the training of the models, both pre-training and fine-tuning, we use the Nvidia A100 GPUs available in the Google Colab environment [2].

Figure 1 shows the pipeline used in MIS. The input text is pre-processed by undergoing lowercasing, unicode normalization, and word-level tokenization. The words are then fed into a trained Morfessor model, which splits the words into their morphs. We then check whether the first morph appears in a known list of morphemes (shown in Table 1)—if it is, we treat it as a separate word. We explain with an example: take the word "superinteressante". Without treating the *super* prefix as a separate word, MIS would segment the word as *super* + *##interessa* + *##nte*. By treating it as a separate word, we get *super* + *interessa* + *##nte*. This way, we do not have to learn a separate representation for *##interessante*. We illustrate this example in Fig. 2.

The Portuguese Morfessor model used for segmentation was obtained via Polyglot [1]. For segmentation, we need to generate a vocabulary of morphs with a fixed size, which is necessary for the model to have a numerical representation for each token. We choose a size of 70,000 tokens, over double the size used in ALBERT's implementation—which was 30,000 tokens—to reduce Out-Of-Vocabulary tokens (OOVs) from the Morfessor model output. The code is available in our repository[2].

---

[2] https://gitlab.com/mwesthelle/putting-the-pieces-together.

(a) Pre-training Procedure

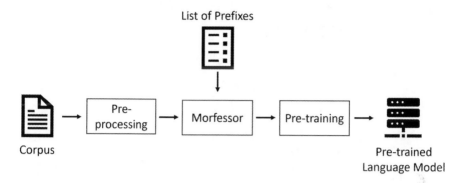

(b) Fine-tuning procedure

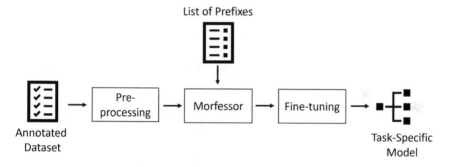

Fig. 1. MIS pipeline

4.1 Pre-training

The corpus used for pre-training the models was a random sample of 15% of a dump from Wikipedia[3] in Portuguese, composed of 48.5 million tokens. The data was split into test and validation sets, using a 9:1 ratio.

To perform the pre-training, we tokenized the training and validation sets in advance, using the WordPiece tokenizer trained by Souza *et al.* [23], included in the BERTimbau[4] model; and again using our tokenizer.

Following Liu *et al.* [14], we did not use the next sentence prediction (NSP) task in model training; we only used masking language modeling (MLM). In Devlin *et al.* [7], 90% of pre-training steps are performed using a sequence size of 128 tokens. In the remaining 10%, the sequence size used is 512 tokens. This was done to speed up training, as the attention mechanism has quadratic complexity

---

[3] https://dumps.wikimedia.org/.
[4] Available at https://huggingface.co/neuralmind/bert-base-portuguese-cased.

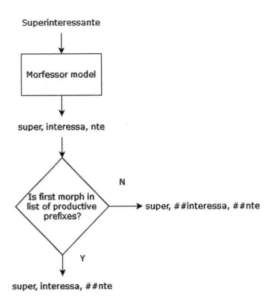

Fig. 2. A diagram depicting a flowchart of our segmentation method

Table 1. List of productive prefixes in Portuguese, compiled by the authors

a	pós	mono	es	tri
hiper	circum	retro	octa	hepta
pro	micro	em	super	pre
anti	pos	nano	ex	ultra
in	contra	sobre	pan	hexa
pró	mini	en	tetra	pré
bi	re	nonea	entre	
mega	des	sub	penta	

relative to the size of the sequence. We used a similar approach; the difference is that we trained the model using sequence size 128 for 5 epochs, which took two days for each model, and we increased the sequence size to 512 tokens and continue training for 1 epoch, which also took two days for each model. An epoch consists of 8,494 optimization steps, using batches of 256 examples each, for a total of 2,174,602 training sentences—the remaining instances that do not constitute a full batch size are discarded. We trained an ALBERT model, with *embeddings* of 128 dimensions, 12 hidden layers with 4096 dimensions, and 64 attention heads. Training was performed using mixed precision [16] and using the AdamW optimizer [15], with $\beta_1 = 0.9$, $\beta_2 = 0.999$, and $\epsilon = 1 \times 10^{-8}$. We use a learning rate of 5×10^{-5}.

4.2   Fine-Tuning

We fine-tune our pre-trained models on three natural language understanding tasks using four datasets in Portuguese. The datasets are described in detail in the following paragraphs.

Text Classification consists of associating text instances with labels. In our experiments, we addressed a binary classification task (*fake* vs. *true*) and a multi-class subject classification.

Fake.Br [17]. A fake news identification dataset with 7,200 news articles, equally distributed between two classes: fake and true.

Folha de São Paulo [21]. A dataset composed of 167,053 news stories from Folha de São Paulo. It is made available on the Kaggle platform and features 48 classes, many of which are difficult to map to a specific subject, *e.g. illustrated*, which probably alludes to the fact that the news article contains illustrations or images. In our experiments, we selected five classes with numbers of instances ranging between 17K and 22K whose labels are representative of the news subjects, namely: *daily life, sports, finance, world, politics*. These classes amount to a total of 96,819 instances.

Recognition of Textual Entailment and Paraphrase aim at, given a pair of sentences, to identify whether the second sentence can be entailed from the first, or whether both sentences can be inferred from one another, which categorizes a paraphrase. Thus, there are three possible labels for a pair of sentences: *entailment, paraphrase,* and *none*.

ASSIN [8]. A dataset of 10,000 pairs of sentences, half of which are in Brazilian Portuguese, while the other half are in European Portuguese.

There is a large class imbalance in this dataset. An overwhelming majority of sentence pairs, 7,316 out of the 10,000, are not related, belonging to the *none* class; 2,080 pairs are classified as *entailment*; and only 604 pairs are labeled as *paraphrase*.

Question Answering Natural Language Inference is the task of predicting whether, given a question and sentence pair, the sentence is a possible answer to the question.

PLUE/QNLI [9] is a dataset created by automatically translating the GLUE dataset [26] from English into Portuguese. It has 57,084 instances of each class, *entailment* and *not entailment*. The set also contains 5,740 unclassified instances that were discarded in our experiments (Table 2).

Table 2. Number of folds used for cross-validation (k) and Runtimes

Dataset	k	Max tokens	Time (min.)
ASSIN	5	128	27
Fake.Br	5	512	92
Folha de São Paulo	3	256	493
PLUE/QNLI	3	256	564

Fine-Tuning Procedure. The maximum sequence size we used varied according to the length of the instances in the dataset. For ASSIN, in which the instances are short, 128 was used. In Folha de São Paulo and PLUE/QNLI, we used sequence size of 256; and for Fake.Br, we used 512. Examples from the news datasets end up being truncated since they're very long. We can observe our segmentation method is more granular, so the examples are tokenized into more tokens and therefore suffer the effect of truncation to a greater degree. For illustration purposes, we use an example with a sequence size of 32 tokens. As can be seen below in an instance of the Fake.Br dataset, the sentence captured by our segmentation ends up being shorter: the bold text corresponds to the excess text that is captured by WordPiece but not captured by MIS. In Table 3, we can see how both segmenters break the text.

[CLS] violência policial segue sem freios no brasil, denuncia human rights watch. organização dos direitos humanos destacou **execuções extrajudiciais no** [SEP]

Table 3. Truncation in an instance from the Fake.br dataset (exceeding parts resulting from the less granular WordPiece segmenter are highlighted in bold)

WordPiece	*MIS*
[CLS] + violência + policial + segue + sem + fre + ##ios + no + bras + ##il + , + denuncia + human + rig + ##ht + ##s + wa + ##tch + . + organização + dos + direitos + humanos + destacou + **execu +** **##ções + extra + ##ju +** **##dici + ##ais + no + [SEP]**	[CLS] + viol + ##ência + policia + ##l + segue + s + ##em + fre + ##io + ##s + no + brasil + , + denuncia + human + right + ##s + wa + ##tch + . + organiza + ##ção + dos + dire + ##ito + ##s + human + ##os + desta + ##cou + [SEP]

4.3 Evaluation Metrics

Our results were evaluated with standard classification metrics, namely accuracy and macro-F1. Accuracy measures the proportion of the instances that were correctly classified. F1 is the harmonic mean between precision and recall. We use macro-averages to give the same weight to all classes. This is important for unbalanced datasets such as ASSIN.

5 Results

Our results, found in Table 4, show that MIS performs better than WordPiece in almost all cases, except for the Folha dataset. The disparity between the F1 macro metrics and accuracy in the ASSIN dataset can be explained by the large class imbalance. To evaluate whether the differences are statistically significant, we performed the McNemar test, a nonparametric paired test. The null hypothesis assumes that the probability of results for each classifier is the same. Using an α=0.01, all differences were considered significant (p-values $\ll$ 0.01).

We also report on the agreement between MIS and WordPiece using Cohen's kappa coefficient (κ) in Table 5. These results make sense with statistically different classifiers: annotation scores are very high when both classifiers perform well because there is little room for disagreement. However, when both classifiers perform poorly, such as in ASSIN RTE or QNLI, they will disagree on their mistakes, and the annotation agreement will be low (Tables 6, 7, 8 and 9).

Table 4. Experimental Results in Terms of macro-F1 and Accuracy

Dataset	Segmentation	macro-F1	Accuracy
ASSIN	WordPiece	0.484	$0.725 \pm 8.8 \times 10^{-3}$
	MIS	**0.499**	$\mathbf{0.739} \pm 5.3 \times 10^{-3}$
Folha	WordPiece	**0.925**	$\mathbf{0.925} \pm 9.2 \times 10^{-4}$
	MIS	0.921	$0.920 \pm 7.1 \times 10^{-4}$
Fake.Br	WordPiece	0.948	$0.948 \pm 5.9 \times 10^{-3}$
	MIS	**0.965**	$\mathbf{0.965} \pm 3.1 \times 10^{-3}$
QNLI	WordPiece	0.622	$0.622 \pm 2.1 \times 10^{-3}$
	MIS	**0.632**	$\mathbf{0.632} \pm 2.1 \times 10^{-3}$

Table 5. Cohen's kappa coefficient

Dataset	κ
ASSIN RTE	0.34
Folha	0.90
Fake.Br	0.88
QNLI	0.32

Our confusion matrices show some more interesting results. Our method performs slightly worse in the *Entailment* class of the ASSIN dataset, even though

Table 6. ASSIN confusion matrices

WordPiece

		Predicted		
		None	Entailment	Paraphrase
Actual	None	0.86	0.10	0.04
	Entailment	0.53	0.42	0.05
	Paraphrase	0.78	0.08	0.14

MIS

		Predicted		
		None	Entailment	Paraphrase
Actual	None	0.88	0.09	0.03
	Entailment	0.54	0.41	0.05
	Paraphrase	0.75	0.09	0.16

Table 7. Fake.Br confusion matrices

WordPiece

		Predicted	
		Fake	True
Actual	Fake	0.90	0.10
	True	0.01	0.99

MIS

		Predicted	
		Fake	True
Actual	Fake	0.96	0.04
	True	0.03	0.97

its overall results favor the model trained using our segmentation strategy; the same happens in the Fake.Br dataset, where our segmentation approach underperforms for the *True* class. As for the Folha dataset, our model shows slightly worse numbers for every class. Our hypothesis to explain the worse results is the truncation effect suffered by MIS. Fine-tuning on longer examples incurs two negative effects: (*i*) the model has less information to guess the correct classes and (*ii*) the model might have a harder time learning long-distance syntactical dependencies. We believe effect (*i*) may be responsible for the poorer performance on the Folha Dataset and effect (*ii*) may explain worse performance for the *Entailment* class in ASSIN.

Limitations
We use the ALBERT architecture, which allows us to train models faster. However, to the best of the authors' knowledge, there exists little in the way of probing methods that enable intrinsic evaluation, such as what exists for BERT models in the form of the works of Hewitt and Manning [10] or Chen *et al.* [5]. Such probing could give us insight into how our segmentation method affects the learning of syntax versus the WordPiece baseline.

Table 8. Folha confusion matrices

WordPiece

		Predicted				
		Daily Life	Sports	Finances	World	Politics
	Daily Life	0.904	0.011	0.027	0.018	0.039
	Sports	0.007	0.981	0.003	0.005	0.004
Actual	Finances	0.027	0.004	0.901	0.021	0.047
	World	0.019	0.06	0.028	0.932	0.014
	Politics	0.034	0.004	0.042	0.011	0.909

MIS

		Predicted				
		Daily Life	Sports	Finances	World	Politics
	Daily Life	0.902	0.013	0.031	0.015	0.039
	Sports	0.009	0.977	0.004	0.006	0.004
Actual	Finances	0.027	0.004	0.899	0.022	0.047
	World	0.024	0.08	0.034	0.919	0.014
	Politics	0.033	0.005	0.049	0.009	0.904

Table 9. QNLI confusion matrices

WordPiece

		Predicted	
		Entailment	Not Entailment
Actual	Entailment	0.63	0.37
	Not Entailment	0.39	0.61

MIS

		Predicted	
		Entailment	Not Entailment
Actual	Entailment	0.64	0.36
	Not Entailment	0.37	0.63

The approach to segmentation, while relying mostly on an unsupervised model, also leverages a handcrafted list of productive prefixes, which was deliberately not compiled by experts. Segmentation made by a morphological analyzer built by experts would provide the most accurate results. We experimented with a single list, so we were not able to investigate the relationship between the quality of the list of prefixes and the results of the segmentation.

We also argue that the truncation effect, seen at the end of Sect. 4, leads MIS to a disadvantage, as it effectively sees less information in examples with lengthier texts. The segmentation method, our independent variable, causes both truncation and the prediction of the fine-tuned model; truncation, caused by the segmentation method, also impacts the model's prediction. This is illustrated through a causal diagram [20], seen in Fig. 3.

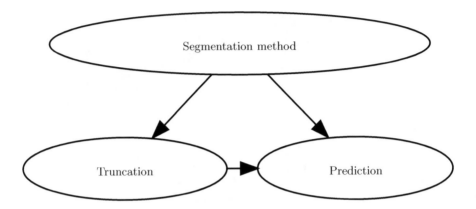

Fig. 3. Causal diagram illustrating the confounding effect of truncation.

6   Conclusion

The purpose of this work was to analyze the impact of applying a morphologically informed segmentation strategy to a pre-trained model based on Transformers. We proposed MIS, a segmentation method that relies on unsupervised morpheme discovery. We pre-trained language models using MIS and WordPiece (the traditional segmentation strategy used in language models) and applied them in three natural language understanding tasks across four datasets. Our results showed that MIS outperformed the baseline in three of those datasets.

In the future, we plan to pre-train BERT models instead of ALBERT, in order to have access to tools for probing linguistic properties, such as syntax, to be able to compare models trained using MIS and WordPiece in this aspect. We also plan to experiment with datasets composed strictly of short sentences, in order to eliminate the truncation variable in our experiments.

Our work explores how linguistic information can affect the performance of pre-trained models in some common tasks. In an era where these models grow increasingly in numbers, both in terms of parameters and in the data they are trained on, we believe that linguistic science can inform these models, and eventually help make them more computationally accessible. This work has shown that MIS is a competitive tokenization strategy that can be adopted in several tasks.

Acknowledgments. This work was partially supported by CNPq/Brazil and by CAPES Finance Code 001.

References

1. Al-Rfou, R.: Polyglot (2020). https://github.com/aboSamoor/polyglot
2. Bisong, E.: Google Colaboratory, pp. 59–64. Apress, Berkeley (2019). https://doi.org/10.1007/978-1-4842-4470-8_7
3. Bostrom, K., Durrett, G.: Byte pair encoding is suboptimal for language model pretraining. In: Findings of the Association for Computational Linguistics: EMNLP 2020, pp. 4617–4624. Online, November 2020
4. Brown, T., et al.: Language models are few-shot learners. In: Larochelle, H., Ranzato, M., Hadsell, R., Balcan, M.F., Lin, H. (eds.) Advances in Neural Information Processing Systems, vol. 33, pp. 1877–1901. Curran Associates, Inc. (2020)
5. Chen, B., et al.: Probing BERT in hyperbolic spaces. In: International Conference on Learning Representations (2021)
6. Creutz, M., Lagus, K.: Unsupervised discovery of morphemes. In: Proceedings of the ACL-02 Workshop on Morphological and Phonological Learning, pp. 21–30. Association for Computational Linguistics, July 2002
7. Devlin, J., Chang, M.W., Lee, K., Toutanova, K.: BERT: pre-training of deep bidirectional transformers for language understanding. In: Proceedings of the 2019 Conference of the North American Chapter of the Association for Computational Linguistics: Human Language Technologies, Volume 1 (Long and Short Papers), pp. 4171–4186, June 2019
8. Fonseca, E., Santos, L., Criscuolo, M., Aluisio, S.: Assin: Avaliacao de similaridade semantica e inferencia textual. In: Computational Processing of the Portuguese Language-12th International Conference, Tomar, Portugal, pp. 13–15 (2016)
9. GOMES, J.R.S.: Plue: Portuguese language understanding evaluation (2020). https://github.com/jubs12/PLUE
10. Hewitt, J., Manning, C.D.: A structural probe for finding syntax in word representations. In: NAACL (2019)
11. Hofmann, V., Pierrehumbert, J.B., Schütze, H.: Superbizarre is not superb: derivational morphology improves BERT's interpretation of complex words. In: ACL/IJCNLP (2021)
12. Klein, S., Tsarfaty, R.: Getting the ##life out of living: how adequate are word-pieces for modelling complex morphology? In: Proceedings of the 17th SIGMORPHON Workshop on Computational Research in Phonetics, Phonology, and Morphology, pp. 204–209. Association for Computational Linguistics, Online, July 2020
13. Lan, Z., Chen, M., Goodman, S., Gimpel, K., Sharma, P., Soricut, R.: AlBERT: a lite BERT for self-supervised learning of language representations. In: International Conference on Learning Representations (2020)
14. Liu, Y., et al.: RoBERTa: a robustly optimized BERT pretraining approach. arXiv abs/1907.11692 (2019)
15. Loshchilov, I., Hutter, F.: Decoupled weight decay regularization. In: International Conference on Learning Representations (2019)
16. Micikevicius, P., et al.: Mixed precision training. In: International Conference on Learning Representations (2018)
17. Monteiro, R.A., Santos, R.L.S., Pardo, T.A.S., de Almeida, T.A., Ruiz, E.E.S., Vale, O.A.: Contributions to the study of fake news in Portuguese: new corpus and automatic detection results. In: Villavicencio, A., et al. (eds.) PROPOR 2018. LNCS (LNAI), vol. 11122, pp. 324–334. Springer, Cham (2018). https://doi.org/10.1007/978-3-319-99722-3_33

18. Nzeyimana, A., Rubungo, A.N.: KinyaBERT: a morphology-aware Kinyarwanda language model. In: ACL (2022)
19. Park, H.H., Zhang, K.J., Haley, C., Steimel, K., Liu, H., Schwartz, L.: Morphology matters: a multilingual language modeling analysis. Trans. Assoc. Comput. Linguist. **9**, 261–276 (2021)
20. Pearl, J., Mackenzie, D.: The Book of Why: The New Science of Cause and Effect, 1st edn. Basic Books Inc., New York (2018)
21. Santana, M.: News of the site Folha de São Paulo (Brazilian Newspaper), Version 2. https://www.kaggle.com/datasets/marlesson/news-of-the-site-folhauol (2019). [Online; acessado em 24 de Novembro de 2021]
22. Sennrich, R., Haddow, B., Birch, A.: Neural machine translation of rare words with subword units. In: ACL, pp. 1715–1725, August 2016
23. Souza, F., Nogueira, R., Lotufo, R.: BERTimbau: pretrained BERT models for Brazilian Portuguese. In: Cerri, R., Prati, R.C. (eds.) BRACIS 2020. LNCS (LNAI), vol. 12319, pp. 403–417. Springer, Cham (2020). https://doi.org/10.1007/978-3-030-61377-8_28
24. Vaswani, A., et al.: Attention is all you need. In: Proceedings of the 31st International Conference on Neural Information Processing Systems. NIPS 2017, pp. 6000–6010. Curran Associates Inc., Red Hook (2017)
25. Virpioja, S., Smit, P., Grönroos, S.A., Kurimo, M.: Morfessor 2.0: Python implementation and extensions for Morfessor baseline (2013)
26. Wang, A., Singh, A., Michael, J., Hill, F., Levy, O., Bowman, S.: GLUE: a multitask benchmark and analysis platform for natural language understanding. In: EMNLP Workshop BlackboxNLP: Analyzing and Interpreting Neural Networks for NLP, pp. 353–355, November 2018
27. Wu, Y., et al.: Google's neural machine translation system: bridging the gap between human and machine translation. arXiv abs/1609.08144 (2016)

Learning Global Optimization by Deep Reinforcement Learning

Moésio Wenceslau da Silva Filho[✉], Gabriel A. Barbosa,
and Péricles B. C. Miranda

Federal Rural University of Pernambuco, Recife, Pernambuco 52171-900, Brazil
{moesio.wenceslau,gabriel.augusto,pericles.miranda}@ufrpe.br

Abstract. Learning to Optimize (L2O) is a growing field that employs
a variety of machine learning (ML) methods to learn optimization algorithms automatically from data instead of developing hand-engineered
algorithms that usually require hyperparameter tuning and problem-
specific design. However, there are some barriers to adopting those
learned optimizers in practice. For instance, they exhibit instability during training, poor generalization to problems outside the distribution,
and lack scalability. Current research efforts suggest either improving
L2O models or improving training techniques to overcome such hard-
ships. We focus on the latter and propose to train a Deep Reinforcement
Learning (Deep RL) agent to learn an optimization algorithm from training in a diverse set of benchmark functions. To this end, we propose a
general framework for learning to optimize by reinforcement learning,
which adapts training strategies used in other L2O approaches, such as
curriculum learning and input normalization. We investigate the importance of these strategies through an ablation study and show that even
though Deep RL, to the best of our knowledge, is not a well-explored
theme in L2O, it provides a direct framework to learn an optimizer able
to deal with the exploration-exploitation dilemma and that the applied
techniques improved stability and generalization.

Keywords: Learning to optimize · L2O · Deep Reinforcement
Learning

1 Introduction

Many problems in Computer Science can be formalized as optimization problems
[18], in which the best solution, for some criteria, must be selected from a set of
possible solutions. Thus, many optimization algorithms have been developed over
the years. However, the manual design of optimization algorithms is a laborious
process [4] that usually requires domain-specific knowledge and human experts
[13].

Learning to Optimize (L2O) [1, 4–7, 13–16, 19, 21] is a rising field of machine
learning (ML) that aims to replace hand-designed optimization algorithms with
learned optimizers. Usually, L2O methods learn a parameterized model that acts

J. C. Xavier-Junior and R. A. Rios (Eds.): BRACIS 2022, LNAI 13654, pp. 417–433, 2022.
https://doi.org/10.1007/978-3-031-21689-3_30

as an *optimizer* for a series of similar optimization problems called *optimizees* [5].

It is fairly common that the optimizees are learning problems [5], in which case, L2O can be viewed from a meta-learning perspective [1]. However, recent work considered other optimization problems that are not directly related to learning, such as benchmark functions [7], and protein docking [4].

The mainstream in L2O leverages recurrent neural networks (RNNs), typically long-short term memory (LSTM), as the model for the optimizer [1,4,14,21]. However, there are some barriers to adopting those learned optimizers in practice. For instance, training those optimizers is difficult [16], and they suffer from poor generalization [5]. Thus, the current effort suggests either improving L2O models, such as using hierarchical RNNs [21], or improving training [5,16].

We focus on the latter and train a Deep Reinforcement Learning (deep RL) agent to learn global optimization. Previous work with RL in L2O have considered slightly different formulations. For instance, in [7] the RL agent learned a component of the optimizer, while in [13] the agent was the optimizer. We argue that there is a need for a concise and flexible framework in applying Deep RL for learning to optimize, enabling us to use advances in other fields of RL, such as Multi-Task Reinforcement Learning and Meta Reinforcement Learning. To this end, we propose a general framework for learning to optimize by Deep Reinforcement Learning.

Our Contributions. We offer a framework for representing L2O problems from a Reinforcement Learning perspective, taking into account previous work and merging proposed strategies for improving training and stability of other learnable optimizers. The proposed framework is flexible and resembles the multi-task RL setting. We investigate the proposed framework to learn global optimization from training in set of 26 benchmark functions and obtain good preliminary results for 2-dimensional problems.

2   Preliminaries

In this section, we cover the basic concepts used throughout this paper. We review Deep Reinforcement Learning, POMDPs and Learning to Optimize (L2O).

2.1   Deep Reinforcement Learning

Deep Reinforcement Learning is a field that combines Reinforcement Learning (RL), which deals with sequential decision-making through an agent that takes actions in an environment, and Deep Learning, which employs Deep Neural Networks, enabling RL to scale to problems with high-dimensional state, and action spaces [2].

General RL problems can be defined as discrete-time stochastic control processes where an *agent* interacts with an *environment* to learn a behavior that optimizes a notion of *cumulative rewards*. The formal framework for the process depends on the task at hand. Markov Decision Processes (MDPs) and Partially Observable MDPs (POMDPs) are common approaches [2]. In the following paragraphs, we define POMDPs.

POMDPs are particularly useful for real-world applications since many decision-making problems are partially observable by nature, and issues with sensors (e. g., noise, data loss, occlusions) may limit the agent's perceptual abilities [11]. Another source of partial observability comes from the environment design, which might not fully capture the underlying states.

A POMDP is a tuple $(\mathcal{S}, \mathcal{A}, \mathcal{O}, F, U, R, b_0)$, where $\mathcal{S}$ is the state space, $\mathcal{A}$ is the action space, $\mathcal{O}$ is the observation space, $F(s_{t+1}|s_t, a_t)$ is the transition function (also called *dynamics* or *model*), $U(o_{t+1}|s_{t+1})$ is the emission function, $R(s_t, a_t, s_{t+1})$ is the reward function, and b_0 is the distribution over initial states s_0.

Under a POMDP, the agent-environment interaction is as follows: for every time step $t \in \mathbb{N}$, the environment is in a state $s_t \in \mathcal{S}$, the agent receives an observation $o_t \sim O(o_t|s_t)$ and takes an action $a_t \in \mathcal{A}$. Then, the environment transitions to a new state $s_{t+1} \sim F(s_{t+1}|s_t, a_t)$ and the agent receives a reward $r_{t+1} = R(s_t, a_t, s_{t+1})$.

In this formulation, the goal of the agent [11] is to learn a policy $\pi(a_t|o_{\leq t}, a_{<t})$, where $o_{\leq t} = (o_0, \ldots, o_t)$ and $a_{<t} = (a_0, \ldots, a_{t-1})$, that maximizes the expected return

$$\bar{R} = \mathbb{E}_{p(\tau)}\left[\sum_{t=1}^{T} \gamma^{t-1} r_t\right], \tag{1}$$

over trajectories $\tau = (s_0, a_0, \ldots, a_{T_1}, s_T)$ induced by π, where $0 \leq \gamma \leq 1$ is the discount factor, and T is the trajectory length which may vary between episodes.

Additionally, as in [17], we refer to s_t^o as the observable state and s_t^h as the hidden state. The observable state is the portion of s_t that can be directly unveiled by the observation o_t, while the hidden state is the remainder of s_t.

2.2 Problem Setup for L2O

In its more general form, L2O deals with the problem of learning an optimizer $\mathcal{U}(\cdot; \theta)$ parameterized by θ that is capable of optimizing functions $f(\mathbf{x})$, called *optimizees*, of a similar class [5]. To this end, $\mathcal{U}(\cdot; \theta)$ is trained to minimize an objective function $\mathcal{L}(\theta)$ over a distribution of optimizees $\mathcal{F}_{\text{train}}$. Then, the learned optimizer is used to iteratively update the optimizees' variables: $\mathbf{x}_{t+1} = \mathbf{x}_t + \mathcal{U}(\cdot; \theta)$.

However, this general form does not apply to all L2O approaches. For instance, [3] learned an optimizer by searching for a mathematical rule. For the sake of simplicity, we will consider the previous problem setup since it applies to many works in the field.

Table 1 summarizes different L2O approaches by comparing the choices of inputs features, optimizer architecture, and training/evaluation set of optimizees.

Table 1. Summary and comparison of different L2O approaches.

Reference	Architectures	Inputs	Optimizees
[1]	LSTM	$\nabla f(\mathbf{x})$	Quadratic functions; Neural networks;
[6]	LSTM; DNC	$f(\mathbf{x})$; $\mathbf{x}$	GPs; Benchmarks problems
[19]	LSTM	$f(\mathbf{x})$; $\mathbf{x}$	GMM; Benchmarks problems
[15]	LSTM	$\nabla f(\mathbf{x})$	Neural networks
[21]	Hierarchical RNN	g; γ; η	Benchmark problems; Neural networks
[4]	Population of LSTMs	$\nabla f(\mathbf{x})$; m; v; a;	Benchmark problems; Protein docking

g: scaled averaged gradients; m: gradient momentum;
γ: relative log gradient magnitudes; v: particle velocity;
η: relative log learning rate; a: particle attraction;

2.3   Strategies for Improving L2O Training

Most of the works in L2O propose strategies, techniques and tricks to improve learning, stability and generalization of learned optimizers by either improving the optimizer model [4,21] or improving training [6,15,16].

In the next paragraphs, we list some of the proposed strategies for improving the training of L2O approaches and discuss how they were implemented in different L2O RNN-based frameworks.

Augmented Training Set. One of the proposed techniques consists in augmenting the training set, that is, the optimizees distribution $\mathcal{F}_{\text{train}}$. [21] points out that previously learned optimizers have failed to generalize for functions outside $\mathcal{F}_{\text{train}}$, and a possibility to address this issue is to include a richer set of training functions that better capture the properties of commonly encountered loss landscapes. [5] suggests a similar approach; it is argued that a good optimizer needs to explore and experience various optimizees landscapes in order to generalize well.

Specifically, [21] proposed the $\mathcal{F}_{\text{train}}$ to have optimizees of five classes: (i) benchmark functions (e. g., Ackley, Rosenbrock, Beale, Booth); (ii) well-behaved convex problems (e. g., quadratic functions, logistic regressions); (iii) problems with noisy gradients and minibatches; (iv) slow convergence problems (e. g., oscillating valleys); and (v) transformed problems. Instead, [5] proposed to increase the number of sampled optimizees $f \sim \mathcal{F}_{\text{train}}$, and to re-use sampled optimizees but starting $\mathbf{x}_0$ at different locations.

Input Features Inspired on Optimization Algorithms. The choice of input features for a learnable optimizer is crucial for generalization and scalability [16]. [21] argues that choosing features inspired by other optimization algorithms is a way of incorporating useful knowledge in the optimizer. Thus, many works in L2O choose features related to other optimization algorithms.

For instance, [1] considered the gradients $\nabla f(\mathbf{x}_t)$ as input for the optimizer, taking inspiration from the *gradient descent* (GD) algorithm. [21] took inspiration from multiple optimization techniques (e. g., Nesterov momentum) and algorithms (e. g., RMSProp, ADAM), passing the scaled averaged gradients, the relative log gradient magnitudes, and the relative log learning rate as input for the optimizer. On the other hand, [4] proposed to consider features from both point-based optimization (gradient and momentum) and population-based optimization (velocity and attraction).

Table 2. Common loss functions for learnable optimizers.

Reference	No	$\mathcal{L}(\theta)$
[1,6]	1	$\mathbb{E}_f\left[f(\mathbf{x}^*)\right]$
[1,6]	2	$\mathbb{E}_f\left[\sum\limits_{t=1}^{T}\omega_t f(\mathbf{x}_t)\right]$
[6]	4	$-\mathbb{E}_{f,y_{1:T-1}}\left[\sum\limits_{t=1}^{T}\mathrm{EI}(\mathbf{x}_t\lvert y_{1:t-1})\right]$
[6]	5	$\mathbb{E}_{f,y_{1:T-1}}\left[\sum\limits_{t=1}^{T}\min\left\{f(\mathbf{x}_t)-\min\limits_{i<t}(f(\mathbf{x}_i)),0\right\}\right]$
[21]	6	$\mathbb{E}_f\left[\frac{1}{T}\sum\limits_{t=1}^{T}\left(\log(f(\mathbf{x}_t)+\epsilon)-\log(f(\mathbf{x}_0)+\epsilon)\right)\right]$

f: optimizee sampled from $\mathcal{F}_{\text{train}}$; $\mathbf{x}^*$: final optimizee parameters; ω_t: weight associated with time-step t; ϵ: constant value; $\mathrm{EI}(\cdot)$: expected posterior improvement of $\mathbf{x}_t$ given observations up to t;

Input Normalization. Another proposed technique for improving training stability and generalization of L2O is to apply some sort of input normalization. This can be achieved by either preprocessing inputs or using input features already normalized (e. g., scaled, averaged).

For instance, [1,19] used preprocessing functions to normalize the inputs. [1] proposed a gradient preprocessing formula using log and sign. Instead, [19] proposed a preprocessing formula to normalize inputs by considering the mean and variance of previously observed inputs. [15,21] used input features that are already normalized and did not need preprocessing.

Improved Loss (Objective) Function for the Learnable Optimizer. The objective function $\mathcal{L}(\theta)$ is crucial for learning a good optimizer. As such, many objective functions for the learnable optimizer have been proposed. Table 2 summarizes choices in the literature.

Curriculum Learning. A novel proposed strategy to further improve training is to use curriculum learning in L2O. [5] proposed to gradually unroll the optimizer more w.r.t the number of epochs. [5] argues that following a curriculum scheme enables the optimizer to start learning short-horizon trajectory patterns and gradually growing to recognize longer dependencies.

Imitation Learning. Another novel strategy is to apply imitation learning in L2O. [5] proposed to use analytical optimizers (e. g., ADAM) to stabilize training, prevent overfitting, and improve generalization.

2.4   Global Optimization

An unconstrained global optimization problem can be defined as:

$$\min F(\mathbf{x})$$

$$\text{subject to } L \leq x_i \leq U, \ i = 1, \ldots, D$$

where $F(\mathbf{x})$ is the objective function, $\mathbf{x} = [x_1, \ldots, x_D]^T$ is the vector of decision variables, L and U are the lower and upper bound, respectively.

However, such problems are usually noisy, multi-modal, non-convex, and non-separable, requiring methods to effectively explore the search space [18]. Thus, many evolutionary algorithms are employed. Another approach for solving global optimization problems is to learn to globally optimize [24].

3   Related Work

Initial works in learning to optimize are closely related to *meta-learning*, or *learning to learn* [1,6,13–16], which is the idea of acquiring knowledge or inductive bias to accelerate learning. In this sense, most of the *optimization tasks* used to learn an optimizer were learning tasks, such as learning the optimal weights for neural nets [1] and learning to solve control problems [6].

However, recent works have broadened the scope and started to consider optimization tasks that are not directly related to learning, such as benchmark functions [7,8,21], and other synthetic functions [24]. Still, learning tasks share similarities to many artificial landscapes, such as being non-convex, multi-modal, and noisy. In the following subsections, we briefly review some related work to our approach.

3.1 Learning to Optimize

Andrychowicz et al. [1] leverage an LSTM as a coordinate-wise optimizer, which takes the preprocessed gradients as input and outputs an update for the optimizee's variables. Chen et al. [6] also consider an LSTM, however using the optimizee's objective values and optimizee's variables as input. Wichrowska et al. [21] introduced a hierarchical RNN architecture for the optimizer. Cao et al. [4] proposed to further expand L2O by considering an algorithmic space of both point-based and population-based optimization algorithms. The authors in [5,15,16,19] proposed a wide range of techniques and tricks for improving learnable optimizers.

3.2 Learning to Optimize by Deep RL

The work proposed by Williams and Peng [22] was one of the firsts to consider RL for function optimization. The proposed approach consisted in training a neural network, through reinforcement learning, to generate better query points for the optimizee. Li and Malik [13] proposed to learn an optimization algorithm through reinforcement learning by using a history of previous gradients and objective values as input for the agent. In [14], the authors improved the framework proposed in [13] for learning to optimize shallow neural networks. Bello et al. [3] proposed another approach for L2O by considering the problem of learning a controller that generates mathematical update equations from primitive functions, the controller was trained by RL. Faury and Vasile [7] proposed another framework for L2O by splitting the optimizer into three sequential modules (update direction predictor, learning rate predictor, and resolution predictor); two were trained by RL in prototypical two-dimensional surfaces. Zhang et al. [24] proposed to learn a two-phase global optimization algorithm by deep learning and reinforcement learning. Silva-Filho [8] proposed to learn zeroth-order optimization algorithms by popular policy search algorithms.

3.3 Multi-Task Reinforcement Learning

Multi-task reinforcement learning is a subfield of reinforcement learning that deals with the problem of learning to solve multiple sequential-decision tasks at once [10,23]. It is related to L2O by Deep RL due to the characteristic of training a (Deep) RL agent in a distribution of similar tasks. Thus, we argue that L2O by Deep RL could benefit from the results of Multi-Task RL and vice-versa.

4 Learning Global Optimization by Deep RL

This section presents a framework for applying Deep RL to learn global optimization.

4.1   Problem Setup: L2O by Deep RL

In general, the problem setup is the same as the one discussed in 2.2. However, Deep RL requires a clear distinction between the agent and the environment. Furthermore, the environment can be formalized in different ways (e.g., POMDPs and MDPs).

Thus, we define the following problem setup for L2O by Deep RL:

- The agent is the optimizer $\mathcal{U}$;
- The environment is a distribution $\mathcal{P}_{\text{train}}$ of POMDPs;
- Each POMDP p in $\mathcal{P}_{\text{train}}$ represents the task of minimizing a function $f \sim \mathcal{F}_{\text{train}}$;
- For every $p_i, p_j \in \mathcal{P}_{\text{train}}$, the following properties hold:
  1. $\mathcal{A}_{p_i} = \mathcal{A}_{p_j}$, i. e., the action space is the same for all tasks;
  2. $\dim(o_t^{p_i}) = \dim(o_t^{p_j})$ for all $t \in \mathbb{N}$, i. e., all observations have the same dimensionality;
     □ Note that the dynamics, emission function, rewards, state space, and observation space do not need to be equal.
- The agent's goal is to maximize $\mathbb{E}_{p \sim \mathcal{P}_{\text{train}}} [\bar{R}]$, that is, the agent should behave to maximize the average expected return across all training tasks.

This setup is closely related to multi-task RL [10] and meta-RL [23]; however, they differ mostly due to the nature of the tasks (i.e., MDPs instead of POMDPs).

How Should Each Task $p \in \mathcal{P}_{\text{train}}$ **be Modelled?** Up to this point, we have not discussed how to cast the task of minimizing an optimizee $f \sim \mathcal{F}_{\text{train}}$ as a POMDP. Most of the previous work in L2O by a Deep RL agent considered slightly different designs, for instance:

- [8] considered p as a MDP where
  - $a_t = \Delta \mathbf{x}$;
  - $s_t = o_t = \mathbf{x}_t$;
  - $R(s_t, a_t, s_{t+1}) = -f(\mathbf{x}_{t+1})$;
- [14] considered p as a POMDP where
  - $a_t = \Delta \mathbf{x}$;
  - $s_t = \{\mathbf{x}_t, \phi(\cdot)\}$, where $\phi(\cdot)$ are features that depend on previous $\mathbf{x}_i$, $\hat{f}(\mathbf{x}_i)$ (noisy optimizee values), and $\nabla \hat{f}(\mathbf{x}_i)$ (noisy gradients);
  - $o_t = \Psi(\cdot|s_t)$, where $\Psi(\cdot|s_t)$ are features based on the state s_t;
  - $R(s_t, a_t, s_{t+1}) = f(\mathbf{x}_t)$, and the agent's goal is to minimize the cumulative rewards;

We propose a new task design based on previous work in L2O for learning global optimization. Following the general problem of L2O, we consider the actions as the update in the optimizees variables (i.e., $a_t = \Delta \mathbf{x}$).

For the states s_t, we acknowledge that, due to the nature of global optimization problems, it is difficult to choose features that fully describe the state of the environment for all possible optimizees. For instance, if the problem is continuous, convex, and smooth, one can argue that knowing the gradients at a time-step t fully describes the information needed to choose an optimal action. However, if the problem is non-convex and multimodal, then solely knowing the gradient might not be enough to choose an appropriate action.

Thus, we propose to use $s_t = s_t^h \cup s_t^o$, where $s_t^h = \{\mathbf{x}_t, f(\mathbf{x}_t)\} \cup \mathbb{U}$ and $s_t^o = \{\nabla f(\mathbf{x}_i), f(\mathbf{x}_i), \mathbf{x}_i\}_{i=0}^t$. That is, the hidden state consists of the optimizee's value ($f(\mathbf{x}_t)$), variables ($\mathbf{x}_t$), and other features $\mathbb{U}$ that might or might not be available (e. g., known global optima, high-order information). On the other hand, the observable state consists of past values of the gradients, values, and variables.

This approach enables us to define different dynamics and reward functions, which use s_t, to better suit a given training optimizee, while keeping the same observation structure for all tasks.

We propose to consider the observations o_t as $\{P(\nabla f(\mathbf{x}_t)), \boldsymbol{v}_t\}$, where $P(\cdot)$ is the gradient processing function proposed in [1], and $\boldsymbol{v}_t$ is the agent's average velocity, inspired in [4]. The next subsection discuss how these features can be obtained from s_t^o.

Lastly, we propose the following general reward function:

$$R(s_t, a_t, s_{t+1}) = -T(f(\mathbf{x}_{t+1})) \tag{2}$$

where $T : \mathbb{R} \to \mathbb{R}$ is a transformation to scale $f(\mathbf{x}_{t+1})$. This reward function is similar to those in [13,14], and [8]. We find it important for the rewards to be as close as possible to those of other tasks in $\mathcal{P}_{\text{train}}$. It is known in the multi-task RL setting that tasks with a greater expected return, in magnitude, are given more importance by the agent [10], thus individually scaling rewards is an important task. In the next section, we cover a possibility for T.

Since there are many choices of RL algorithms that either do not rely on the model or learn the model themselves [2], the dynamics are not described here. The proposed task design aims to be as flexible as possible while capturing essential elements of global optimization, enabling future practitioners to adapt and improve it.

4.2 Incorporating Strategies for Improving Training

Given the problem setup defined previously, we propose to adapt and incorporate some of the training strategies discussed in Sect. 2.3 to the Deep RL setting.

Augmented Training Set. This strategy can be directly applied to the training optimizee distribution $\mathcal{F}_{\text{train}}$. We propose to use benchmark functions for global optimization as the base training set, $\mathbf{B}_{\text{train}} = \{f_1, \dots, f_N\}$, and then define $\mathcal{F}_{\text{train}}$ as a distribution of these functions with some transformation parameters. That is, for $f, \phi \sim \mathcal{F}_{\text{train}}$, where $f \in \mathbf{B}$ and $\phi = \{\phi_0, \phi_1, \phi_2\} \in \mathbb{R}$, the optimizee is $\phi_0 f(\mathbf{x} + \phi_1) + \phi_2$ with $\phi_0, \phi_2 \in \mathbb{R}$ and $\phi_1 \in \mathbb{R}^n$.

Following this formulation, we can keep a small training set of benchmark functions with diverse characteristics, as proposed by [21], while being able to sample more optimizees, as proposed in [5].

Input Features Based on Other Optimizers. We propose to use two input features based on previous learned optimizers, and metaheuristics approaches.

The first input feature, $P(\nabla f(\mathbf{x}_t))$, describes the gradient at the current time-step t, where P maps each $\nabla_k = \frac{\partial f}{\partial x_k} \in \nabla f$ to

$$\begin{cases} \left(\frac{\log(\nabla_k)}{10}, \text{sgn}(\nabla_k)\right) & \text{if } |\nabla_k| \geq e^{-10} \\ \left(-1, e^{10}\nabla_k\right) & \text{otherwise} \end{cases}$$

which is the same gradient processing function proposed by [1].

The second input feature, inspired by [4] and metaheuristics approaches, describes the agent average velocity $\boldsymbol{v}_t$ up to the current time-step t. We define the average velocity as: $\boldsymbol{v}_0 = \mathbf{0}$, and $\boldsymbol{v}_t = \frac{\Delta \mathbf{x}}{\Delta t} = \frac{\mathbf{x}_t - \mathbf{x}_0}{t}$.

Normalization Through Scaling. We incorporate input normalization techniques directly into the input features, while $P(\nabla f(\mathbf{x}_t))$ uses log and sgn for normalization, $\boldsymbol{v}_t$ is bounded by the action space $\mathcal{A}$, which is shared between all optimizees. However, it is also important to normalize returns and rewards besides normalizing inputs.

We propose to use the bi-symmetric log transformation [20] to scale the optimizees values. Thus, (2) can be rewritten as:

$$R(s_t, a_t, s_{t+1}) = -\text{sgn}(y) \log_{10}(1 + |y \ln(10)|) \tag{3}$$

where $y = f(\mathbf{x}_{t+1})$, and ln is the natural logarithm. Perhaps, a more robust approach would be to adapt the RL algorithm to be scale invariant to the rewards magnitude, as proposed in [10], we leave this investigation to future work.

Curriculum Learning in a Distribution of POMDPs. We propose to incorporate, inspired in [5], a curriculum strategy where the agent learns each task $p \in \mathcal{P}_{\text{train}}$ in an ordered manner. That is, the agent starts by learning simpler tasks (optimizees) and progressively learns more complex ones.

Each task $p \in \mathcal{P}_{\text{train}}$, is ordered by its optimizee's modality and separability. We refer to the pair {modality, separability} as a property c of an optimizee f_p. Modality is defined as the number of ambiguous peaks in the function surface [12], unimodal functions are easier to solve, while multimodal functions are harder. Separability is another characteristic that can be used to measure the difficulty of an optimizee [12]. Fully separable functions are easier to solve when compared to their non-separable counterpart.

Thus, the proposed curriculum partitions the total training (N episodes) in K sub-training stages, with n_i episodes each ($\sum_{i=1}^{K} n_i = N$), of progressive difficulty. For each sub-training stage i, the agent trains in tasks $p_0, \ldots, p_j \sim \mathcal{P}_{\text{train}}$ whose optimizees f_{p_k} have properties c_i. In this formulation, if $j > k$ for any $j, k \in [1, K]$, then an optimizee with properties c_j is harder to optimize than an optimizee with properties c_k.

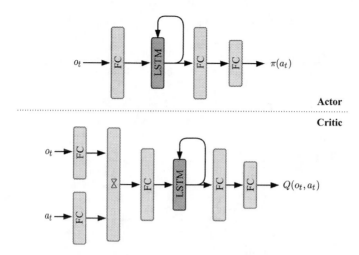

Fig. 1. Actor and Critic Networks. FC represents a fully connected layers, ⋈ is a concatenation, and LSTM represents a long short-term memory layer. All layers have `relu` activation, except for the last fully connected layer of the actor (`tanh`), and critic (`linear`).

In this work, we considered $K = 5$, and the following ordering: $c_1 = \{$unimodal, separable$\}$, $c_2 = \{$unimodal, partially-separable$\}$, $c_3 = \{$unimodal, non-separable$\}$, $c_4 = \{$multimodal, separable$\}$ and $c_5 = \{$multimodal, non-separable$\}$.

4.3 Recurrent TD3 for Learning to Global Optimize

To evaluate the proposed framework for learning global optimization, we selected the Twin Delayed DDPG (TD3) [9], a model-free actor-critic deep RL algorithm for solving MDPs, and a set of benchmark functions widely used in the optimization literature. We chose the algorithm TD3 due to its popularity, applicability in a variety of domains, and good preliminary results in previous L2O works [8].

In order to use TD3 to solve POMDPs, we needed to adapt its neural networks to learn to extract features from the past since the policies in POMDPs depend on past observations and actions (Subsect. 2.2). In the RL literature, a simple approach is to add a Recurrent Neural Network (RNN) to the existing algorithms [11]. Figure 1 shows the architecture for the actor and critic networks.

Table 3. Composition of the Training set.

No.	Properties	Functions
3	Separable, Unimodal	Schumer Steiglitz, Sum Squares, Powell Sum
8	Separable, Multimodal	Alpine 2, Csendes, Deb 1, Deb 3, Qing, Schwefel 2.26, W / Wavy, Weierstrass
2	Partially-separable, Unimodal	Chung Reynolds, Schwefel
6	Non-separable, Unimodal	Brown, Dixon Price, Schwefel 1.2, Schwefel 2.22, Schwefel 2.23, Streched V Sine Wave
7	Non-separable, Multimodal	Exponential, Mishra 2, Salomon, Sargan, Trigonometric 2, Whitley, Zakharov
Total: 26		

Table 4. List of evaluation functions.

Function	Properties	Search space	Global minimum
Sphere	Unimodal	$x_i \in [0.0, 10.0]$	0.0
Bent Cigar	Unimodal	$x_i \in [0.0, 10.0]$	0.0
Ackley	Multimodal	$x_i \in [-35.0, 35.0]$	0.0
Griewank	Multimodal	$x_i \in [-100.0, 100.0]$	0.0
Rastrigin	Multimodal	$x_i \in [-5.12, 5.12]$	0.0
Rosenbrock	Multimodal	$x_i \in [-30.0, 30.0]$	0.0

5   Experiments and Analysis

This section discusses the experiments and analysis of the proposed approach for learning global optimization.

Training Set. We consider a training set of 26 (Table 3) continuous, differentiable benchmark functions described in [12]. Each function is subject to its search space, and the optimizer must learn to optimize across different search spaces. The optimizee distribution $\mathcal{F}_{\text{train}}$ consists of those functions plus random transformations parameters ϕ.

Algorithm Hyperparameters. All hyperparameters have been empirically set by manual search. Unless stated otherwise, all results refer to the best-trained agent.

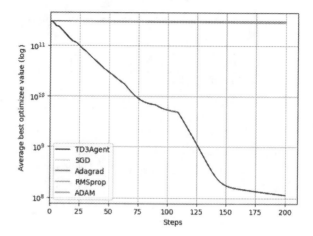

Fig. 2. Average best optimizee values over 200 steps for 100 sampled optimizees.

Evaluation. We first evaluate the learned optimizer in the training distribution, by sampling a 100 optimizees and comparing the average best value. Then, we evaluate the generalization of the optimizer in 6 benchmark functions (Table 4) not present in the training distribution. Unless stated otherwise, both training and evaluation considered 2-dimensional optimizees (i.e., $d = 2$, and $\mathbf{x} = [x_0, x_1]^T$), with sampled transformation parameters in the range $\phi_0 \in [0.5, 1.5]$, $\phi_1 \in [-1.5, 1.5]^d$, $\phi_2 \in [-5.0, 5.0]$.

Baselines. To compare the proposed approach with other optimizers, we selected 4 first-order analytical optimizers, namely, Stochastic Gradient Descent (SGD), Adagrad, RMSprop, and ADAM. We used the default parameters set in TensorFlow for all problems.

Implementation Details. We used Python 3.9, TensorFlow 2.7.0, and TF-Agent 0.11.0 in our implementations. Both training and evaluation were run in Google Colaboratory. The best learnt optimizer (agent) was trained for 2000 training episodes, with 75 steps each, with a training sequence length of 10 (i.e., size of sampled history from replay buffer). The curriculum strategy partitioned those 2000 episodes in: 200 episodes for c_1; 100 episodes for c_2; 100 episodes for c_3; 700 episodes for c_4; 900 episodes for c_5. During evaluation, the agent was given 200 steps to optimize the optimizees.

5.1 Comparison Against Baselines

Figure 2 compares the average best optimizee values, in log scale, from 100 optimizees sampled from $\mathcal{F}_{\text{train}}$ over 200 steps. We found that none of the analytical optimizers were able to achieve results better than the learned optimizer TD3Agent.

Table 5. Mean and standard deviation of best optimizee value over 100 independent runs for 2D problems with 200 steps.

Function	TD3Agent	SGD	Adagrad	RMSprop	ADAM
Sphere	**0.0**	0.0232	64.7831	70.5634	68.7703
	(0.0)	(0.0144)	(41.0723)	(39.3927)	(34.1719)
Bent Cigar	**0.0**	2.9464866e7	2.8709074e7	3.2879828e7	3.244124e7
	(0.0)	(2.830116e7)	(2.7833004e7)	(3.0206872e7)	(2.9399202e7)
Ackley	**16.9553**	19.0410	20.3046	19.4958	19.3892
	(5.4009)	**(1.5761)**	(2.4671)	(2.2098)	(2.3981)
Griewank	**1.5358**	1.9594	2.5994	2.4518	2.3464
	(1.2512)	(1.0968)	(1.2451)	(1.2879)	(1.1283)
Rastrigin	**6.1143**	14.0367	37.4525	22.0069	22.7056
	(3.3523)	(5.4853)	(15.0649)	(12.5299)	(12.9580)
Rosenbrock	**247.5643**	1.7007074e7	1.5635772e7	1.2053673e7	1.1696214e7
	(538.5479)	(2.1397274e7)	(2.0081116e7)	(1.850705e7)	(1.8787502e7)

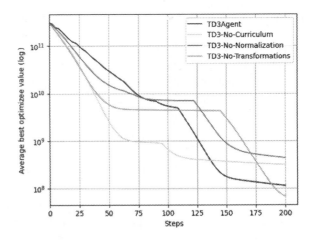

Fig. 3. Importance of different strategies to the learned optimizer.

Table 5 compares the best learned optimizer against the baselines, over a short horizon (200 steps), in the evaluation set. Since the evaluation functions were not available in the training set, we did not apply the transformations and evaluated the optimizers in the original function. We found that none of the algorithms were able to find the global optimum for the multimodal functions with precision; however, the TD3Agent found the best average solutions. It is also possible to see that the learned optimizer generalized well for the unimodal functions, but it could not fully generalize for the multimodal ones. We conjecture that no optimizee in the training set had a similar landscape to those in the evaluation set.

5.2 Ablation Study of Proposed Techniques

To evaluate the importance of the proposed training strategies, we train 3 other agents, where one of the strategies is missing. Figure 3 shows the performance of the learned optimizers in 100 optimizees sampled from $\mathcal{F}_{train}$. We found that the most significant strategies were normalizing the rewards and applying a curriculum scheme.

6 Conclusion

Learning to optimize (L2O) is an auspicious field that has the potential to break many barriers in optimization and machine learning however, there are some issues to address first. For instance, learned optimizers are usually unstable to train, generalize poorly, and lack scalability. The L2O community has proposed different means to deal with those problems, such as novel training strategies and more sophisticated models. To further contribute with those strategies, we propose casting the L2O problem as a Deep Reinforcement Learning task, in which an agent must learn to solve a distribution of POMDPs, representing a distribution of minimization tasks. To this end, we construct a general framework for applying Deep RL to L2O and integrate training strategies found to improve other learnable optimizers. We evaluate the proposed framework to learn global optimization from training in benchmark functions and find that the learned optimizer was able to achieve better results than popular analytical optimizers. Through an ablation study, we find that normalizing rewards and applying a curriculum scheme were the most important strategies. We hope the contributions of this work lay a solid ground for future works with Deep RL in L2O.

Acknowledgements. The authors thank the Brazilian National Council for Scientific and Technological Development (CNPq) for the help during the development of this work.

References

1. Andrychowicz, M., et al.: Learning to learn by gradient descent by gradient descent. Adv. Neural Inf. Process. Syst. **29**, 1–9 (2016)
2. Arulkumaran, K., Deisenroth, M.P., Brundage, M., Bharath, A.A.: Deep reinforcement learning: a brief survey. IEEE Signal Process. Mag. **34**(6), 26–38 (2017)
3. Bello, I., Zoph, B., Vasudevan, V., Le, Q.V.: Neural optimizer search with reinforcement learning. In: Proceedings of the 34th International Conference on Machine Learning. Proceedings of Machine Learning Research, vol. 70, pp. 459–468. PMLR (2017)
4. Cao, Y., Chen, T., Wang, Z., Shen, Y.: Learning to optimize in swarms. Adv. Neural Inf. Process. Syst. **32**, 1–11 (2019)
5. Chen, T., et al.: Training stronger baselines for learning to optimize. Adv. Neural Inf. Process. Syst. **33**, 7332–7343 (2020)

6. Chen, Y., et al.: Learning to learn without gradient descent by gradient descent. In: Proceedings of the 34th International Conference on Machine Learning. Proceedings of Machine Learning Research, vol. 70, pp. 748–756. PMLR (2017)
7. Faury, L., Vasile, F.: Rover descent: learning to optimize by learning to navigate on prototypical loss surfaces. In: Battiti, R., Brunato, M., Kotsireas, I., Pardalos, P.M. (eds.) LION 12 2018. LNCS, vol. 11353, pp. 271–287. Springer, Cham (2019). https://doi.org/10.1007/978-3-030-05348-2_24
8. Filho, M.S., Barbosa, G., Miranda, P., Nascimento, A., Mello, R.: Zeroth order policy search methods for global optimization problems: an experimental study. In: Anais do XVIII Encontro Nacional de Inteligência Artificial e Computacional, pp. 209–220. SBC (2021)
9. Fujimoto, S., van Hoof, H., Meger, D.: Addressing function approximation error in actor-critic methods. In: Proceedings of the 35th International Conference on Machine Learning. Proceedings of Machine Learning Research, vol. 80, pp. 1587–1596. PMLR (2018)
10. Hessel, M., Soyer, H., Espeholt, L., Czarnecki, W., Schmitt, S., van Hasselt, H.: Multi-task deep reinforcement learning with popart. In: Proceedings of the AAAI Conference on Artificial Intelligence, vol. 33, no. 01, pp. 3796–3803 (2019)
11. Igl, M., Zintgraf, L., Le, T.A., Wood, F., Whiteson, S.: Deep variational reinforcement learning for POMDPs. In: Proceedings of the 35th International Conference on Machine Learning. Proceedings of Machine Learning Research, vol. 80, pp. 2117–2126. PMLR (2018)
12. Jamil, M., Yang, X.S.: A literature survey of benchmark functions for global optimisation problems. Int. J. Math. Model. Numer. Optim. 4(2), 150–194 (2013)
13. Li, K., Malik, J.: Learning to optimize. In: 5th International Conference on Learning Representations (2017)
14. Li, K., Malik, J.: Learning to optimize neural nets. CoRR (2017)
15. Lv, K., Jiang, S., Li, J.: Learning gradient descent: better generalization and longer horizons. In: Proceedings of the 34th International Conference on Machine Learning. Proceedings of Machine Learning Research, vol. 70, pp. 2247–2255. PMLR (2017)
16. Metz, L., Maheswaranathan, N., Nixon, J., Freeman, D., Sohl-Dickstein, J.: Understanding and correcting pathologies in the training of learned optimizers. In: Proceedings of the 36th International Conference on Machine Learning. Proceedings of Machine Learning Research, vol. 97, pp. 4556–4565. PMLR (2019)
17. Ni, T., Eysenbach, B., Salakhutdinov, R.: Recurrent model-free RL is a strong baseline for many pomdps. CoRR (2021)
18. Nobile, M.S., Cazzaniga, P., Ashlock, D.A.: Dilation functions in global optimization. In: 2019 IEEE Congress on Evolutionary Computation (CEC), pp. 2300–2307 (2019)
19. TV, V., Malhotra, P., Narwariya, J., Vig, L., Shroff, G.: Meta-learning for blackbox optimization. In: Brefeld, U., Fromont, E., Hotho, A., Knobbe, A., Maathuis, M., Robardet, C. (eds.) ECML PKDD 2019. LNCS (LNAI), vol. 11907, pp. 366–381. Springer, Cham (2020). https://doi.org/10.1007/978-3-030-46147-8_22
20. Webber, J.B.W.: A bi-symmetric log transformation for wide-range data. Meas. Sci. Technol. 24(2), 027001 (2012)
21. Wichrowska, O., et al.: Learned optimizers that scale and generalize. In: Proceedings of the 34th International Conference on Machine Learning. Proceedings of Machine Learning Research, vol. 70, pp. 3751–3760. PMLR (2017)

22. Williams, R.J., Peng, J.: Function optimization using connectionist reinforcement learning algorithms. Connect. Sci. **3**(3), 241–268 (1991)
23. Yu, T., et al.: Meta-world: a benchmark and evaluation for multi-task and meta reinforcement learning. In: Proceedings of the Conference on Robot Learning. Proceedings of Machine Learning Research, vol. 100, pp. 1094–1100. PMLR (2020)
24. Zhang, H., Sun, J., Xu, Z.: Learning to be global optimizer. CoRR (2020)

A Frequency Learning Approach Based on the Hartley Transform for Texture Classification

Natalia Gil Canto[1]($\boxtimes$) ⓘ, José Augusto Stuchi[2]ⓘ, and Levy Boccato[1]ⓘ

[1] University of Campinas, Av. Albert Einstein, 400, Campinas, SP 13083-852, Brazil
n232881@dac.unicamp.br, lboccato@unicamp.br
[2] Phelcom Technologies, Rua José Missali, 820, São Carlos, SP 13562-405, Brazil
stuchi@phelcom.com.br

Abstract. Convolutional neural networks (CNNs) significantly impacted challenging real-world tasks, such as image and audio processing, giving rise to solutions with impressive results. Notwithstanding, in some scenarios, discriminative features may be more easily retrieved when data samples are represented in a different domain, and are processed with the aid of convenient operations in that domain, instead of the usual temporal/spatial convolution explored in CNNs. In this work, a learning model that operates entirely in the frequency domain with the aid of the discrete Hartley transform (DHT) is proposed. In particular, a frequency layer is developed based on the DHT property related to convolution, as well as a proper frequency pooling stage to reduce the number of parameters. The proposed DHT-based model was analyzed in the context of texture classification, which presents a natural appeal to the frequency domain, and it achieved competitive results in terms of accuracy with state-of-the-art CNNs, but with the advantage of requiring a much smaller number of trainable parameters, thus offering a promising and lightweight solution.

Keywords: Hartley transform · Image classification · Neural networks

1 Introduction

Technologies exploring artificial intelligence techniques are increasingly common nowadays, such as Alexa and Siri virtual assistants. In the context of computer vision, challenging tasks as image classification, object detection and semantic segmentation have greatly benefited from the development of deep learning models and experienced noticeable performance improvements [10, 40]. The main responsible for this success are the convolutional neural networks (CNNs), which process information spatially and learn to extract the most relevant data attributes at this domain. Since the pioneering deep model named AlexNet [19],

Supported by Deepmind.

J. C. Xavier-Junior and R. A. Rios (Eds.): BRACIS 2022, LNAI 13654, pp. 434–448, 2022.
https://doi.org/10.1007/978-3-031-21689-3_31

many modern architectures arose, such as ResNet [16], Xception [9], DenseNet [18], MobileNet [17], EfficientNet [33], TResNet [28] and NFNet [6].

However, in some scenarios, it may be less costly and easier to retrieve data-descriptive information in a different domain (e.g. the frequency domain). In this context, the design of a processing layer that naturally operates in the transformed domain emerges as a potential alternative for the convolution. Interestingly, many transformations (e.g. Fourier transform) present elegant properties associated with the temporal/spatial convolution, so that they are natural candidates to be employed and also suggest a structure for the processing layer.

This kind of perspective has already been studied in a few works of the literature [12,26,29,30] and, more recently, in [31], where the magnitude of the discrete Fourier transform (DFT) is passed on to a frequency filtering layer, which extracts relevant spectral features by multiplying the input spectrum by a trainable frequency filter. In addition, [31,32] proposed a frequency pooling scheme to reduce the number of adjustable parameters, as well as a multi-level block division to allow the network to extract both global and local features from the input images.

The model of [31,32] was analyzed in three scenarios of image classification, which clearly presented a strong appeal for the use of frequency domain information (e.g. retina image classification), and achieved performances comparable to those of state-of-the-art CNNs. Nonetheless, it is worth noticing that it only exploited the magnitude spectrum and completely discarded the phase spectrum, which could also bring valuable information to the classification task.

Therefore, taking inspiration from [31,32], we also propose a frequency learning model that can be used for image classification. In particular, instead of conceiving a framework to incorporate the Fourier phase information into a real-valued neural network, we propose to replace the DFT with the Hartley transform, since it yields a real-valued frequency-domain characterization for the data, which, thus, is ready to be fully used by standard layers (e.g. fully connected), and it also presents a relatively simple property related to convolution, so that a frequency filtering structure can be directly derived from it.

The chosen application for the proposed model is texture classification, where the frequency domain seems to be particularly pertinent as the involved classes typically present different spectral patterns. In this context, we compare the performance of our model with those of some well-known CNNs both in terms of accuracy and complexity, considering the number of free parameters and training time.

This paper is organized as follows: the theoretical elements associated with the Hartley transform are covered in Sect. 2, which are at the core of our proposal; recent works that explore the frequency domain along with deep models are outlined in Sect. 3; the frequency learning approach of [31,32] is presented in Sect. 4.1, which serves as the basis for the proposed method detailed in Sect. 4.2; finally, the experimental results in texture classification are exhibited and discussed in Sect. 5, whereas the main conclusions and future perspectives are presented in Sect. 6.

2   Theoretical Background: Hartley Transform

The Hartley transform maps a real function (in time or space) to a frequency-domain function that also has real values [25]. This transform was firstly defined by [15], but his contributions became better known from discussions held decades later [3–5,35–37].

2.1   Discrete-Time Hartley Transform

Given a sequence $x[n]$ of size N, the discrete Hartley transform (DHT) and its inverse (IDHT), can be defined as:

$$X_H(k) = \sum_{n=0}^{N-1} x[n] \operatorname{cas}\left(\frac{2\pi nk}{N}\right), \quad 0 \le k \le N-1 \tag{1}$$

and

$$x[n] = N^{-1} \sum_{k=0}^{N-1} X_H(k) \operatorname{cas}\left(\frac{2\pi nk}{N}\right), \quad 0 \le n \le N-1 \tag{2}$$

where $\operatorname{cas}(a) = \cos(a) + \operatorname{sen}(a)$.

It is important to mention that, according to [25], the Hartley transform is a more symmetric representation of the Fourier transform. Moreover, the DHT $X_H(k)$ can be obtained from the DFT $X(k)$ as follows:

$$X_H(k) = Re[X(k)] - Im[X(k)], \tag{3}$$

where $Re[\cdot]$ and $Im[\cdot]$ denote the real and imaginary parts of a complex function.

Given the interest of this work at image processing, it is also important to present the bidimensional (2D) DHT and IDHT, being valid the generalization for higher dimensions:

$$X_H(k_1, k_2) = \sum_{m=0}^{M-1} \sum_{n=0}^{N-1} x[m,n] \operatorname{cas}\left(2\pi k_1 m + 2\pi k_2 n\right), \tag{4}$$

$$x[m,n] = M^{-1}N^{-1} \sum_{k_1=0}^{M-1} \sum_{k_2=0}^{N-1} X_H(k_1, k_2) \operatorname{cas}\left(2\pi k_1 m + 2\pi k_2 n\right). \tag{5}$$

In this case, an image, $x[m,n]$, with dimension $M \times N$, has DHT of the same dimension whose values are also real.

2.2   Convolution Property

Analogously to the Fourier transform, the Hartley transform has an important property associated with the convolution operation. Let $x_1[n]$ and $x_2[n]$ be two sequences of size N, and $x_3[n]$ be the circular convolution[1] between them, i.e., $x_3[n] = x_1[n] * x_2[n]$. So, the DHT of $x_3[n]$ is given by

$$X_{H3}(k) = X_{H1}(k)X_{H2e}(k) + X_{H1}(-k)X_{H2o}(k), 0 \leq k \leq N - 1 \qquad (6)$$

where $X_{H3}(k)$, $X_{H1}(k)$ and $X_{H2}(k)$ represent the DHTs of $x_3[n]$, $x_1[n]$ and $x_2[n]$, respectively, and $X_{H2}(k) = X_{H2e}(k) + X_{H2o}(k)$ is written as the sum of its odd and even parts. The extension of this property to 2D signals is straightforward.

3 Related Works

Several papers suggested the implementation of convolution layers in the transformed domain with the purpose of building more efficient deep models. Most of these works explore the Fast Fourier Transform (FFT), given its advantage in terms of computational cost over a direct implementation of the spatial convolution commonly used in CNNs.

This is the case of recent works [8,21,23], but such idea was also discussed in earlier works, such as [1,2,13]. These studies have a common element regarding the network training: the successive use of the inverse FFT in order to return the processed data to the spatial domain, which ends up reducing the notion of learning how to extract and process spectral features.

The idea of carrying out the network training entirely in the frequency domain, which is one of the keystones of the approach of [31,32] and of our proposal, has also been investigated in other works. For instance, [26] developed a frequency layer that performs the element-wise product between an image in the transformed domain and a kernel of the same size. The authors observed gains in network training time compared to state-of-the-art CNNs for the MNIST and CIFAR10 datasets. However, the layer's poor scalability hampers the network training for larger images.

Other studies also investigated the use of different transforms within neural networks, such as the Discrete Cosine Transform (DCT) [11,14,34,38] and the DHT itself, the main subject of this research. In [41], the DHT is applied in the context of pooling layers on CNNs, whereas [22] suggests the transform usage based on its relationship with the DFT and its real characteristic. However, the network has the same difficulty to scale with the size of the images as noticed in [26], an issue also present in other recent works, such as [24,27,39].

4 Frequency Learning Approaches

Firstly, we revisit the model developed by [31,32] since our proposal is built upon the same main processing stages. In the sequence, we detail the modifications that constitute our proposal.

---

[1] The circular convolution can produce the same result of the linear convolution if $N \geq N_1 + N_2 - 1$, where N_1 and N_2 are the actual lengths of $x_1[n]$ and $x_2[n]$.

4.1   Frequency Training Through the DFT

The frequency learning approach elaborated by [31,32] is characterized by six distinct steps, which are illustrated in Fig. 1.

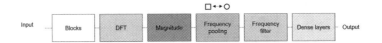

Fig. 1. Frequency learning structure proposed by [31,32].

The first step consists in decomposing the input image into blocks and aims at allowing the network to extract both global and local information from the original images. This block division can be performed up to an arbitrary number of levels, in such a way that the first level is related to the entire image, the second level yields the image divided into four equal blocks, while the third level takes the four blocks of the second level and further divides each of them into four equal sub-blocks, and so on. Hence, by adopting three levels, 21 blocks are produced, as can be seen in Fig. 2.

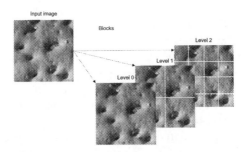

Fig. 2. Block division of an image considering three levels.

Then, these blocks are transformed to the frequency domain via 2D-DFT (Step 2), and only the magnitude spectra are retained and effectively explored by the network (Step 3). Given the DFT magnitude information, which presents a radial aspect (i.e., the frequencies increase from the center of the spectrum to the edges), a ring-shaped pooling is applied to each block i, which combines the magnitude information at frequencies that share the same radius r, according to Eq. (7), being R the distance from the center to the edge of the block and $C_i(r)$ the coefficient extracted from the elements for each radius.

$$C_i(r) = \sum_{r=1}^{R} A_i(r) \tag{7}$$

This type of pooling (Step 4) has the objective of reducing data dimensionality and, consequently, the number of trainable parameters in the frequency layer. Additionally, the width of each frequency ring can be selected, so that a larger width leads to less spectral coefficients $C_i(r)$ and, thus, a more compact representation for each image. As suggested by [31,32], circular or squared shaped rings can be explored depending on the application.

The next step introduces the first trainable layer of the network, the frequency layer, which implicitly exploits the Fourier transform convolution theorem. In this layer, weights learned by the network $W_i(r)$ are multiplied by the frequency pooling information $C_i(r)$. It is important to note that for each radius there is only one adjustable weight, given the dimensionality reduction produced by frequency pooling. Hence, the resulting product comprises the coefficients extracted from each ring. Then, by stacking the coefficients extracted from all blocks and from all rings, a feature vector is constructed and represents the input for the fully-connected (dense) network (Step 6) which, in the end, is responsible for generating the class prediction.

4.2 Frequency Training Through the DHT

The main idea underlying our proposal is to employ the Hartley transform to map the images to the frequency domain and, then, to explore the spectral information accordingly. The peculiarities of the DHT motivated a few adaptations in the frequency pooling and filtering stages. The entire DHT-based model is illustrated in Fig. 3.

Fig. 3. Structure for frequency learning based on the DHT.

Since the DHT yields a real-valued spectrum, with either positive and negative amplitudes, all the frequency content can be readily explored by standard neural network layers, such as fully-connected layers. Nevertheless, it is appropriate to apply data normalization to a suitable interval in order to facilitate information (and gradient) propagation through the layers.

Considering input images with pixel values between 0 and 255, the DHT produces frequency-domain images that contain a wide range of real values, that is, large positive and large negative pixel intensities, which motivates the use of an adequate function to normalize these data without information loss. The inverse hyperbolic sine emerged as an effective option to perform this operation.

Additionally, the presence of negative values in the transformed spectrum can lead to the annulment of pixel intensities if we consider the original frequency pooling scheme of Eq. (7), which could alter the expressiveness of each frequency band per radius. Hence, the DHT frequency pooling takes into account the magnitude of the normalized spectral components, as indicated in (8).

$$A_{Hi}(r) = \sum_{r=1}^{R} |\sinh^{-1}(X_{Hi})(r)| \tag{8}$$

Finally, the frequency filtering stage implements the spectral multiplications specified by the DHT convolution property, as defined in Eq. (6). Figure 4 illustrates this procedure. As we can observe, three operations are executed: (*i*) the input spectrum (obtained after frequency pooling) is element-wise multiplied by the even part of the frequency filter; (*ii*) the flipped input spectrum is multiplied by the odd part of the frequency filter; and (*iii*) the corresponding products are added.

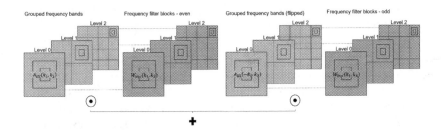

Fig. 4. Frequency filtering based on the convolution property of the DHT.

In the end, the filtered spectra for all blocks of the input image are stacked and propagated to the dense network.

5   Experimental Results

The proposed approach was contrasted with the frequency model of [31,32], as well as with modern CNNs, all facing the image classification problem under the same conditions, that is, being forced to learn from scratch using solely the target dataset samples.

For the experimental analysis, we decided to address two scenarios of texture classification, since, in this context, the frequency domain displays explicit and, to a certain extent, interpretable information about the data. In particular, two public datasets were explored: Kylberg Texture Dataset - KTD [20], composed by monochromatic images, and the Amsterdam Library of Textures - ALOT [7], which allows the method implementation in three color channels.

5.1   Kylberg Texture Dataset

For the first experiment, the Kylberg dataset, composed by 4480 images of size 576×576 pixels and divided in 28 classes, was split considering 70% of the images for training and 30% for testing. In the proposed model, three levels of image block division were considered, using rings of width equal to 1 pixel, which leads to a total of 2016 spectral coefficients for each image; this quantity also represents the size of the input vector of the fully connected network. Figure 5 displays the architecture defined for this dataset.

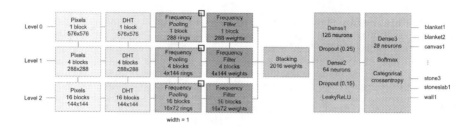

Fig. 5. Architecture for the Kylberg dataset

In this case, the overall procedure prior to the training stage involved the image block division, resulting in 21 blocks per image, the DHT calculation for each block and the frequency pooling of the pixel intensities considering square-shaped rings. This procedure is exemplified in Figs. 6 and 7 considering two input images belonging to classes 'rug1' and 'stone1', respectively.

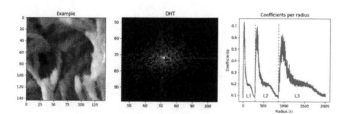

Fig. 6. Example of a third level block, its DHT and coefficient variation per radius for a sample of KTD class 'rug1'.

It is possible to observe that the images clearly present distinct Hartley spectra: while the sample from class 'rug1' has a frequency content more concentrated around the center, the spectrum of the 'stone1' sample is more spread. These differences led to quite distinct sets of coefficients after frequency pooling, as can be noticed at the rightmost graphics in Figs. 6 and 7.

The proposed model was trained with the aid of the Stochastic Gradient Descent optimizer (SGD), with momentum equal to 0.6 in its dense layers and 0.0 in the frequency layer. Furthermore, the initial learning rate was equal to 0.01 and was reduced according to a decay of 0.009 across all layers of the network. A batch size equal to 10 was used, and the architecture was trained

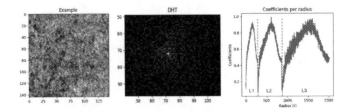

Fig. 7. Example of a third level block, its DHT and coefficient variation per radius for a sample of KTD class 'stone1'.

during 500 epochs. The adopted loss function was the categorical cross-entropy. The evolution of the loss and the accuracy during training is exhibited in Fig. 8.

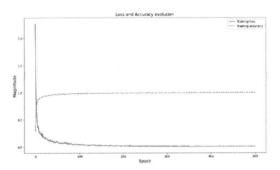

Fig. 8. Loss and accuracy evolution per training epoch.

As we can observe, the network training presented a uniform evolution, with little noise in both curves, which indicates an adequate weight adjustment over the epochs. It is also possible to notice a significant progress in the first 100 epochs, and a slower progression after this period. The model achieved in the end a test accuracy of 99.82%, which means that there were only 2 incorrect classifications.

Table 1 presents the performances and metrics describing the model complexity for the proposed approach and the original frequency approach of [31,32], as well as for DenseNet [18] and EfficientNet (V2S) [33]. The DHT-based network obtained a test accuracy slightly superior when compared to the model of [31,32], being also competitive with the CNNs. Interestingly, in terms of the number of trainable parameters, the frequency-domain approaches (including the DHT model) are significantly lighter, which certainly is a pertinent aspect having in view potential implementations on limited memory hardwares. The training time is also smaller, but not at the same proportion, which may be due to the lack of optimization and parallelization in the implemented code.

Finally, it is interesting to highlight the weights found in the frequency layer, given that they show certain symmetry, a characteristic of the Hartley transform

Table 1. Comparison between different networks and the proposed model for texture classification on KTD.

Method	Weights	Layers	Training time	Accuracy
FreqNet	0.280 M	4	7 m 22 s	99,73%
DenseNet	12.5 M	170	75 m 36 s	100%
EfficientNetV2S	20.2 M	171	52 m 06 s	98,48%
DHT-based model	**0.270 M**	**4**	**17 m 11 s**	**99,82%**

itself, as shown in Fig. 9. This format, moreover, indicates the three levels of block division that were defined for this dataset.

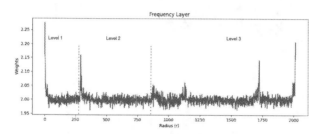

Fig. 9. Final configuration of the frequency layer weights for KTD.

5.2   Amsterdam Library of Textures

The second experiment considered the ALOT dataset divided into 50% of the data for training, 50% for testing. This dataset has 250 classes, each containing 100 color images (RGB), resized to 200×200 pixels. We once more adopted three levels of block division with square-shaped rings, but now with a width of 2 pixels, which leads to a total of 1026 spectral coefficients per image, and 21 blocks per image. The architecture of the employed network can be seen in Fig. 10.

An illustration of the DHT and the spectral coefficients obtained in frequency pooling is given in Figs. 11 and 12 considering two images from different classes. As we can notice, the first sample shows symmetrically scattered frequencies in all directions, whereas the second sample contains diagonal patterns. This behavior results in completely divergent profiles for the spectral coefficients, as we can notice in the rightmost graphics in Figs. 11 and 12. In this case, we can notice more peaks since we are stacking spectral information from three levels and from the three color channels of each image.

With respect to the training setup, the hyperparameters were the same as those used in the KTD, except by the maximum number of epochs, which here

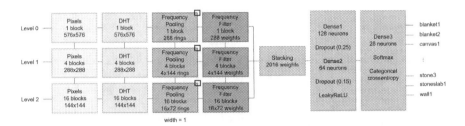

Fig. 10. Architecture for ALOT dataset.

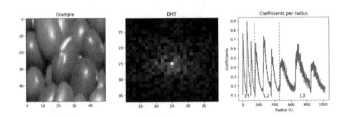

Fig. 11. Example of a third level block, its DHT and coefficient variation per radius for ALOT.

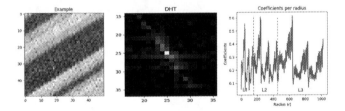

Fig. 12. Example of a third level block, its DHT and coefficient variation per radius for ALOT.

was equal to 1000. The evolution of the loss function and the accuracy during training also exhibited similar behaviors.

Table 2 compares the results obtained by the proposed model, the Fourier-based model of [31, 32] and some modern CNNs.

In terms of accuracy, the proposed approach obtained superior results when compared to the Fourier-based frequency model and MobileNetV2, reaching 96.29%, which is equivalent to 464 incorrect classifications out of a total of 12500 samples. The DenseNet, ResNet50V2 and EfficientNetV2S models were able to overcome it, but by a relatively small margin (up to 1.91%). On the other hand, the DHT-based network presents a huge reduction in the number of trainable parameters, which, consequently, reduces its training time.

Finally, as presented in Fig. 13, a certain symmetry of the frequency layer weights can also be seen in the current experiment. It is interesting to observe the curves profile regarding the number of splitting levels, given that, in this

Table 2. Comparison between different networks and the architecture proposed for texture classification on ALOT.

Method	Weights	Layers	Training time	Accuracy
FreqNet	0.181 M	4	52 m 34 s	92,98%
DenseNet	12.9 M	170	116 m 45 s	97,96%
MobileNetV2	2.5 M	54	129 m 33 s	96,00%
ResNet50V2	24 M	51	113 m 58 s	98,20%
EfficientNetV2S	20,5 M	171	140 m 33 s	97,23%
DHT-based model	**0.181 M**	**4**	**67 m 20 s**	**96,29%**

dataset, 3 color channels are considered, which justifies the triple of peaks in the frequency weights when compared to Fig. 9.

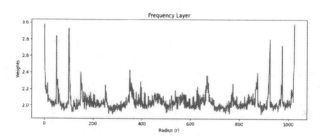

Fig. 13. Final configuration of the frequency layer weights for ALOT.

6   Conclusion

This work presented a frequency learning model for image classification, taking as inspiration the framework of [31,32], and proposed the use of the Hartley transform. The motivations for this idea are: (i) the real-valued character of the DHT, which allowed the exploration of the complete spectral information of the images by standard neural network models, and (ii) the existence of a convolution property for the DHT that also leads to multiplications in the frequency domain, which directly originated a simple structure for the frequency layer. Additionally, we also adopted a frequency pooling scheme, but introducing convenient modifications given the peculiarities of the DHT.

   The proposed model was analyzed in the context of texture classification and achieved competitive results when compared with modern CNNs. In the case of the KTD base, the network performance surpassed, in terms of accuracy, the Fourier-based model of [31] and EfficientNetV2S. Although the network has been surpassed by DenseNet, which reaches 100% of test accuracy, the DHT-based model, reaching 99.82% of accuracy, presented only 1.35% of the number of parameters of that network, with a 67% reduction in training time. In the second dataset (ALOT), the proposed model attained better results in comparison with the Fourier-based model of [31] and MobileNetV2. The DenseNet, ResNet50V2 and EfficientNetV2S networks outperformed the DHT-based model, but only by a maximum of 1.91% of test accuracy. Moreover, these deep networks required at least 12.9 million adjustable parameters, while the proposed models is much more lightweight.

Finally, as future work, it is pertinent to investigate different frequency pooling techniques that better exploit the original DHT information. Additionally, a more thorough sensitivity analysis regarding the main parameters of the frequency approach, such as the number of frequency filters, is certainly beneficial and may indicate potential points for improvements.

References

1. Ben-Yacoub, S.: Fast object detection using mlp and fft. Technical report, IDIAP (1997)
2. Ben-Yacoub, S., Fasel, B., Luettin, J.: Fast face detection using mlp and fft. In: Proceedings Second International Conference on Audio and Video-based Biometric Person Authentication (AVBPA 1999), pp. 31–36. No. CONF (1999)
3. Bracewell, R.N.: Discrete hartley transform. JOSA **73**(12), 1832–1835 (1983)
4. Bracewell, R.N.: The fast hartley transform. Proc. IEEE **72**(8), 1010–1018 (1984). https://doi.org/10.1109/PROC.1984.12968
5. Bracewell, R.N.: The Fourier Transform and its Applications, vol. 31999. McGraw-hill New York (1986)
6. Brock, A., De, S., Smith, S.L., Simonyan, K.: High-performance large-scale image recognition without normalization (2021). https://doi.org/10.48550/ARXIV.2102.06171
7. Burghouts, G.J., Geusebroek, J.M.: Material-specific adaptation of color invariant features. Pattern Recogn. Lett. **30**(3), 306–313 (2009)
8. Chitsaz, K., Hajabdollahi, M., Karimi, N., Samavi, S., Shirani, S.: Acceleration of convolutional neural network using fft-based split convolutions (2020). https://doi.org/10.48550/ARXIV.2003.12621
9. Chollet, F.: Xception: deep learning with depthwise separable convolutions (2016). https://doi.org/10.48550/ARXIV.1610.02357
10. Dai, Z., Liu, H., Le, Q.V., Tan, M.: Coatnet: marrying convolution and attention for all data sizes (2021). https://doi.org/10.48550/ARXIV.2106.04803
11. Ehrlich, M., Davis, L.: Deep residual learning in the jpeg transform domain (2018). https://doi.org/10.48550/ARXIV.1812.11690
12. El-Bakry, H.M., Zhao, Q.: Fast object/face detection using neural networks and fast fourier transform. World Acad. Sci. Eng. Technol. Int. J. Comput. Electr. Autom. Control Inf. Eng. **1**, 3748–3753 (2007)
13. Fasel, B.: Fast multi-scale face detection (1998). http://infoscience.epfl.ch/record/82495
14. Goldberg, K., Shapiro, S., Richardson, E., Avidan, S.: Rethinking fun: frequency-domain utilization networks (2020). https://doi.org/10.48550/ARXIV.2012.03357
15. Hartley, R.: A more symmetrical fourier analysis applied to transmission problems. Proc. IRE **30**(3), 144–150 (1942). https://doi.org/10.1109/JRPROC.1942.234333

16. He, K., Zhang, X., Ren, S., Sun, J.: Deep residual learning for image recognition (2015). https://doi.org/10.48550/ARXIV.1512.03385
17. Howard, A.G., et al.: Mobilenets: efficient convolutional neural networks for mobile vision applications (2017). https://doi.org/10.48550/ARXIV.1704.04861
18. Huang, G., Liu, Z., van der Maaten, L., Weinberger, K.Q.: Densely connected convolutional networks (2016). https://doi.org/10.48550/ARXIV.1608.06993
19. Krizhevsky, A., Sutskever, I., Hinton, G.E.: Imagenet classification with deep convolutional neural networks. In: Pereira, F., Burges, C., Bottou, L., Weinberger, K. (eds.) Advances in Neural Information Processing Systems, vol. 25. Curran Associates, Inc. (2012)
20. Kylberg, G.: The kylberg texture dataset v. 1.0 (2011). https://kylberg.org/datasets/
21. Lavin, A., Gray, S.: Fast algorithms for convolutional neural networks (2015). https://doi.org/10.48550/ARXIV.1509.09308
22. Li, J., You, S., Robles-Kelly, A.: A frequency domain neural network for fast image super-resolution. In: 2018 International Joint Conference on Neural Networks (IJCNN), pp. 1–8 (2018). https://doi.org/10.1109/IJCNN.2018.8489155
23. Lin, S., et al.: Fft-based deep learning deployment in embedded systems. In: 2018 Design, Automation & Test in Europe Conference & Exhibition (DATE), pp. 1045–1050 (2018). https://doi.org/10.23919/DATE.2018.8342166
24. Mozafari, S.H., Clark, J.J., Gross, W.J., Meyer, B.H.: Implementing convolutional neural networks using hartley stochastic computing with adaptive rate feature map compression. IEEE Open J. Circ. Syst. 2, 805–819 (2021). https://doi.org/10.1109/OJCAS.2021.3123899
25. Poularikas, A.D.: The Transforms and Applications Handbook, 2nd edn. CRC Press LLC, Boca Raton (2000)
26. Pratt, H., Williams, B., Coenen, F., Zheng, Y.: FCNN: fourier convolutional neural networks. In: Ceci, M., Hollmén, J., Todorovski, L., Vens, C., Džeroski, S. (eds.) ECML PKDD 2017. LNCS (LNAI), vol. 10534, pp. 786–798. Springer, Cham (2017). https://doi.org/10.1007/978-3-319-71249-9_47
27. Reis, E., Benlamri, R.: Accelerating convolutional neural network using discrete orthogonal transforms (2021). https://doi.org/10.36227/techrxiv.14593686.v1
28. Ridnik, T., Lawen, H., Noy, A., Baruch, E.B., Sharir, G., Friedman, I.: Tresnet: high performance gpu-dedicated architecture (2020). https://doi.org/10.48550/ARXIV.2003.13630
29. Rippel, O., Snoek, J., Adams, R.P.: Spectral representations for convolutional neural networks (2015). https://doi.org/10.48550/ARXIV.1506.03767
30. Sindhwani, V., Sainath, T.N., Kumar, S.: Structured transforms for small-footprint deep learning (2015). https://doi.org/10.48550/ARXIV.1510.01722
31. Stuchi, J.A.: Aprendizado em frequência para classificação de imagens. Ph.D. thesis, Faculdade de Engenharia Elétrica e de Computação, Universidade Estadual de Campinas (2020)
32. Stuchi, J.A., Boccato, L., Attux, R.: Frequency learning for image classification (2020). https://doi.org/10.48550/ARXIV.2006.15476
33. Tan, M., Le, Q.V.: Efficientnet: rethinking model scaling for convolutional neural networks (2019). https://doi.org/10.48550/ARXIV.1905.11946
34. Vien, A.G., Park, H., Lee, C.: Dual-domain deep convolutional neural networks for image demoireing. In: 2020 IEEE/CVF Conference on Computer Vision and Pattern Recognition Workshops (CVPRW), pp. 1934–1942 (2020). https://doi.org/10.1109/CVPRW50498.2020.00243

35. Wang, Z.D.: Harmonic analysis with a real frequency function-i. aperiodic case. Appl. Math. Comput. **9**(1), 53–73 (1981). https://doi.org/10.1016/0096-3003(81)90125-9

36. Wang, Z.D.: Harmonic analysis with a real function of frequency - ii. periodic and bounded cases. Appl. Math. Comput. **9**(3), 153–163 (1981). https://doi.org/10.1016/0096-3003(81)90026-6

37. Wang, Z.: Harmonic analysis with a real frequency function. iii. data sequence. Appl. Math. Comput. **9**(4), 245–255 (1981). https://doi.org/10.1016/0096-3003(81)90015-1

38. Xu, K., Qin, M., Sun, F., Wang, Y., Chen, Y.K., Ren, F.: Learning in the frequency domain (2020). https://doi.org/10.48550/ARXIV.2002.12416

39. Xue, S., Qiu, W., Liu, F., Jin, X.: Faster image super-resolution by improved frequency-domain neural networks. Signal Image Video Process. **14**(2), 257–265 (2019). https://doi.org/10.1007/s11760-019-01548-8

40. Yu, J., Wang, Z., Vasudevan, V., Yeung, L., Seyedhosseini, M., Wu, Y.: Coca: contrastive captioners are image-text foundation models (2022). https://doi.org/10.48550/ARXIV.2205.01917

41. Zhang, H., Ma, J.: Hartley spectral pooling for deep learning (2018). https://doi.org/10.48550/arXiv.1810.04028

How Resilient Are Imitation Learning Methods to Sub-optimal Experts?

Nathan Gavenski$^{(\boxtimes)}$, Juarez Monteiro, Adilson Medronha, and Rodrigo C. Barros

School of Technology, Pontifícia Universidade Católica do Rio Grande do Sul, Av. Ipiranga, 6681, Porto Alegre, RS 90619-900, Brazil
{nathan.gavenski,juarez.santos,adilson.medronha}@edu.pucrs.br, rodrigo.barros@pucrs.br

Abstract. Imitation Learning (IL) algorithms try to mimic expert behavior in order to be capable of performing specific tasks, but it remains unclear what those strategies could achieve when learning from sub-optimal data (faulty experts). Studying how Imitation Learning approaches learn when dealing with different degrees of quality from the observations can benefit tasks such as optimizing data collection, producing interpretable models, reducing bias when using sub-optimal experts, and more. Therefore, in this work we provide extensive experiments to verify how different Imitation Learning agents perform under various degrees of expert optimality. We experiment with four IL algorithms, three of them that learn self-supervisedly and one that uses the ground-truth labels (BC) in four different environments (tasks), and we compare them using optimal and sub-optimal experts. For assessing the performance of each agent, we compute two metrics: *Performance* and *Average Episodic Reward*. Our experiments show that IL approaches that learn self-supervisedly are relatively resilient to sub-optimal experts, which is not the case of the supervised approach. We also observe that sub-optimal experts are sometimes beneficial since they seem to act as a kind of regularization method, preventing models from data overfitting. You can replicate our experiments by using the code in our GitHub (https://github.com/NathanGavenski/How-resilient-IL-methods-are).

Keywords: Imitation learning · Self-supervised learning · Optimality analysis · Observation quality · Learning from observations

1 Introduction

Many species can learn by observing the actions of other individuals without being explicitly instructed on how to perform the actions. Learning by observation is a practice humans perform since childhood, and it can be done for learning many different tasks. For example, as human beings, we can learn how

---

N. Gavenski and J. Monteiro—These authors contributed equally to the work.

© The Author(s), under exclusive license to Springer Nature Switzerland AG 2022
J. C. Xavier-Junior and R. A. Rios (Eds.): BRACIS 2022, LNAI 13654, pp. 449–463, 2022.
https://doi.org/10.1007/978-3-031-21689-3_32

to dance by observing someone else dancing and then practicing. After understanding the specificities of the task, if the learning environment changes we can still execute the task since we have learned the intrinsic cognitive rules, and are not merely reproducing a specific motor action [3].

Imitation Learning (IL) is an artificial intelligence sub-area that seeks to learn a given task with the help of an expert. Methods of IL get inspiration from the human behavior so an agent is capable of learning by observing demonstrations of the task performed by an expert agent [1,16]. However, classical IL methods need explicitly-labeled data (annotation of each action performed by the expert) to teach an agent to display similar behavior, which is not the case of humans that can learn behaviors without further instructions (annotated data).

In more recent approaches, the community started exploring the potential of a different IL strategy called Imitation from Observation (IfO) [6,7,12,13,18]. In IfO, the agent does not need to access annotated actions. Instead, the idea is to create a model that predicts the correct action of a given state considering only random actions that are performed on-the-fly by the system. After this initial model is trained, it is used to annotate the proper actions taken by the expert when transitioning between states. A second model is then trained so the agent can learn to behave like the expert, now considering the recently-annotated actions. This two-model framework can be considered a self-supervised learning mechanism, since we do not need any prior annotated actions from the expert.

The focus of this paper is on IfO methods. More specifically, we want to verify how the current state-of-the-art IfO approaches behave when trying to learn policies from sub-optimal experts. By sub-optimal experts we mean those experts whose trajectories have smaller total reward than what is recommended or suggested by the environments. To the best of our knowledge, no other study in the literature attempt at verifying the performance of IfO agents when learning from sub-optimal data, and we do believe that is fundamental for understanding the current limitations of the area while opening new research directions.

The primary motivation of this study is to compare self-supervised agents trained with and without optimal experts. If the state-of-the-art methods can achieve similar performance when trained with either optimal or sub-optimal demonstrations, that will indicate that we do not need to seek for optimal solutions to generate solving policies for complex scenarios. On the other hand, IfO agents that degrade strongly with the decrease in demonstration quality point to the need of better solutions for cases in which it is not trivial (or cost-effective) to have access to an ideal expert whose trajectories are *optimal.*

For achieving our goal, we propose in this paper to perform a thorough set of experiments testing different approaches and environments to consolidate our findings. We formally formulate the problem in Sect. 2 while the methodology used in our experiments (including the baselines presented in the literature) is presented in Sect. 3. In Sect. 4, we present the results of our experiments, with an extensive discussion being performed in Sect. 5. Finally, we complete this paper by presenting our conclusions and future work directions in Sect. 6.

2 Problem Formulation

The problem of IL assumes an agent acting in a Markov Decision Process (MDP) represented by a five-tuple $M = \{S, A, T, r, \gamma\}$ [17], where S is the state-space, A is the action space, T is the transition model, r is the immediate reward function, and γ is the discount factor. Solving an MDP yields a stochastic policy $\pi(a|s)$ with a probability distribution over actions for an agent in state s that needs to take a given action a.

Imitation from observation [9] aims to learn the inverse dynamics $\mathcal{M}_a^{s_t, s_{t+1}} = P(a|s_t, s_{t+1})$ of the agent, *i.e.*, the probability distribution of each action a when the agent transitioned from state s_t to s_{t+1}. In this approach, the reward function is not explicitly defined and the actions performed by the expert are unknown, so we want to find an imitation policy from a set of state-only demonstrations of the expert $D = \{\zeta_1, \zeta_2, \ldots, \zeta_N\}$, where ζ is a state-only trajectory $\{s_0, s_1, \ldots, s_N\}$. Within the paradigm of learning from observations, there is the problem of finding solving policies self-supervisedly. The self-supervised learning paradigm is quite similar to supervised learning: one needs to train a model with data S_i and with a pseudo label $\hat{A}_i$, where A_i is an automatically-generated label by a pre-defined pretext task without involving any human annotation [10]. As long as the pseudo labels $\hat{A}$ are generated without involving human annotations, then the methods can be said to belong to the self-supervised learning paradigm.

3 Methodology

In this work, we want to test whether an IL algorithm is resilient to the quality of expert samples. In theory, when an agent learns the behavior from a sub-optimal trajectory, it should perform sub-optimally, i.e., with decreased performance when compared to learning from an optimal expert. However, we hypothesize that some IL algorithms can better withstand this gap in expert optimality. Thus, we look into the literature for various IL methods that do not use any self-experience with direct environment supervision, *e.g.*, reward signal. Despite the fact that much of the recent work with IL proposes hybrid approaches that exploit the benefits of reinforcement learning [4,11], we consider that using a direct signal from the environment regarding the optimality of actions would defeat the purpose of these experiments. Therefore, we choose not to employ studies such as MobILE [11] in our experimental methodology. We also exclude recent IL methods that require any kind of action information from the expert, such as OPOLO [19]. We present each of the four methods we have selected for our experimental analysis next.

3.1 Behavioral Cloning

Behavioral Cloning (BC) [15] is the most straightforward form of imitation learning from observation. It treats imitation learning as a supervised problem, where its objective is to predict the most likely action given a current state, $P(a \mid s)$.

Using samples comprised of the state at time t, the action, and the resulting state (s_t, a, s_{t+1}) from an expert, BC can learn how to reduce the gap between the agent's trajectory from the trajectory of the expert, approximating the unknown expert function. The drawback of such a simplistic approach is the dependence on the existence of (enough) expert annotated samples, which are not easy to come by, specially not in large amounts. For environments that are simpler to solve, one can create an agent, e.g., by creating a planner or by training a reinforcement learning policy, and then use it to create such a dataset. However, by doing so, it defeats the purpose of needing an imitation learning agent in the first place. Another possibility for creating the dataset is recording different trajectories, but that can become costly as the environment becomes more complex, since the BC algorithm will need exponentially more samples. BC is our (strong) baseline for comparison considering its nature of providing ground-truth labels (expert actions) to learn.

3.2   Generative Adversarial Imitation Learning

Generative Adversarial Imitation Learning (GAIL) [8] addresses the problem of needing a high number of expert trajectories by matching the state-action frequencies from the agent to those seen in the demonstrations. GAIL uses adversarial training to discriminate state-actions from either the agent or the expert while minimizing the difference between both. It pairs this adversarial training procedure with inverse reinforcement learning to create a generative model whose goal is to train generators to have similar behavior to the given expert, in a mini-max game:

$$\max_{\pi_\phi} \min_{\mathcal{DR}} -\mathbb{E}\pi_\phi[\log \mathcal{DR}(s)] - \mathbb{E}\pi_\varepsilon[\log(1 - \mathcal{DR}(s))], \tag{1}$$

where $\mathcal{DR}$ is a discriminator model and π_ϕ is the learned policy. GAIL is ultimately quite efficient in terms of expert data usage. However, it is not particularly efficient in terms of environment interactions during training, precisely due to the fact that it uses inverse reinforcement learning for training.

3.3   Imitating Latent Policies from Observation

Imitating Latent Policies from Observation (ILPO) [5] uses two different models to predict the next state of an expert, together with the most probable latent action for that transition. Edwards et al. [5] considers that there are a set of known actions and a set of latent actions for all environments. These two groups can be the same size, but since not all stationary transitions may be directly linked to the original action, ILPO empirically assumes that both sets differ. The first model in ILPO is responsible for learning the Latent Forward Dynamics. Considering that the model has no information regarding the action at this time, it tries to predict the next state conditioned to all possible latent actions. ILPO minimizes the difference between the current state and the next state for each action:

$$\mathcal{L}_{\min} = \min_{z} \| \Delta_t - G_\phi \left(E_p \left(s_t \right), z \right) \|^2, \tag{2}$$

where G_ϕ is the learned generative model, E_p the embedding that is trained concurrently, and z one of the possible latent actions. The second model in ILPO is trained to predict the action between the predicted next state and the current state. First, it learns to map the actions outside the environment (clustering the different latent actions), and then it maps to the actual environment actions. Even though ILPO addresses the need for expert labeled actions, the premise of exploring unknown latent actions (whose set size may differ from the one of the actual environment actions) creates the necessity of intense experimentation to calibrate hyperparameters, which can end up being quite costly.

3.4 Imitating Unknown Policies via Exploration

Imitating Unknown Policies via Exploration (IUPE) [6] uses a two-step iterative algorithm to train an agent in a self-supervised manner. During the first step, an Inverse Dynamics Model (IDM) learns to predict an action given a transition of state $P(a \mid s_i, s_{i+1})$. At first, these samples come all from a random agent that acts within the environment, but as the iterative process progresses the model starts receiving samples from a joint distribution of the random agent and the trained agent.

IUPE uses the IDM to create pseudo-labels for the expert dataset consisting of only trajectory states. With these self-labeled samples, it trains the policy in a supervised stationary manner $P(a \mid s_i)$, and then uses this policy in the environment to generate new samples for the IDM. IUPE also employs a sampling mechanism (Eq. 3) during this step, where it weights the random and policy samples to create a dataset more in line with the expert transitions.

$$P(A|E; \mathcal{I}^{\pi_\phi}) = \frac{\sum_{e=1}^{|E|} v_e \times P(A|e)}{|E|}, \tag{3}$$

where $\mathcal{I}^{\pi_\phi}$ are the trajectories created by the learned policy, E is a list of booleans indicating whether a trajectory reached the goal and A is the set of environment actions. Finally, IUPE employs an exploration mechanism that makes use of the softmax distribution over the logits to sample an action from both models. By not using the *maximum a posteriori* estimation it creates a stochastic policy capable of further exploring in early iterations, when the model displays higher uncertainty. The downside of using IUPE is its iterative nature, which can become costly depending on the complexity of the problem, making it very sample-inefficient.

3.5 Metrics and Environments

We measure each approach by using the average reward of hundred consecutive tries in each environment, as well as with the *Performance* [8] metric. *Performance* (Eq. 4) is the average reward for each run scaled to be within $[0, 1]$, where zero is a behavior compatible with a random policy (π_ξ) reward, and one a behavior compatible with the expert (π_ε).

$$\mathbb{P} = \frac{\sum_{i=1}^{E} \frac{\pi_\phi(e_i) - \pi_\xi(e_i)}{\pi_\varepsilon(e_i) - \pi_\xi(e_i)}}{E} \qquad (4)$$

A model can achieve scores lower than zero if it performs worst than what one would expect from a random policy, and higher than one if it performs better than the expert. Metrics such as accuracy are not used since achieving high accuracy in IL does not guarantee good results on solving the task.

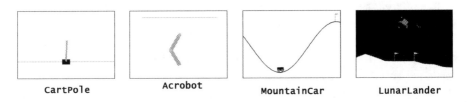

CartPole   Acrobot   MountainCar   LunarLander

Fig. 1. A single frame for each environment used in this work.

We evaluate the IL agents in the following environments. A single frame of each environment is presented in Fig. 1.

- **CartPole-v1** is an environment where an agent moves a car sideways, applying a force of +1 or −1. The goal is to prevent the pole from falling over. CartPole is a baseline environment in IL because simply an adaptive proportional integral derivative controller can model the expert. The action space consists of two actions: *left* and *right* movements. The space state has four dimensions:*car position, car velocity, pole angle,* and *pole velocity* at tips. The agent receives a single reward point every time the pole remains upright. Barto [2] describes solving CartPole as getting an average reward of 195 over 100 consecutive trials.
- **Acrobot-v1** is an environment where an agent has two joints and two links (or arms). The joint between the two links is actuated. In the beginning, the links are hanging downwards. The state space consists of: $\{\cos\theta_1, \sin\theta_1, \cos\theta_2, \sin\theta_2, \theta_1, \theta_2\}$, and the action space consists of the 3 possible forces. The goal is to move the end of the lower link up to a given height. Acrobot is an unsolvable task because it does not have a specified reward threshold.
- **MountainCar-v0** environment consists of a car situated in a valley. The agent needs to learn to leverage potential energy by driving up the opposite hill until completing the goal. The state-space has two continuous attributes: *velocity* and *position* and three discrete action spaces: *left, neutral,* and *right.* A reward of −1 is provided for every time step until the goal position of 0.5 is reached. The first state starts in a random position with no velocity. Moore [14] defines solving MountainCar as getting an average reward of −110 over 100 consecutive trials.

- **LunarLander-v2** is an environment where an agent needs to land on the moon under low gravity conditions. The state space is continuous, and the action space is discrete. There are four actions: *do nothing, move left, right,* and *reduce the falling velocity.* All actions have a reward of -1, except for *do nothing* state which is -0.3. A positive value is returned when the agent moves in the right direction (always at $0, 0$ coordinates). LunarLander-v2 is solved when the agent receives a reward of 200 over 100 constitutive trials.

For the expert samples, we train a different set of agents (mainly DQN and PPO) with different degrees of optimality. We define optimality in these environments as a threshold in the accumulated reward over 100 episodes. When training an agent to be the expert, if it adheres to the established threshold (see Table 1 for the specific values), we use its behavior for the (expert) dataset creation. Note that the AER values in Table 1 are decreasing, which means Expert[1] is better than Expert[2], and so on. The presented values of each expert in the corresponding environment are averages over $1,000$ episodes. We use the same amount of $1,000$ episodes per environment to train each IL method in the experimental analysis.

Table 1. Average Episodic Reward (AER) for experts with decreasing quality. Expert[1] is the optimal expert while Expert[5] is the worst-performing expert in our experimental analyses.

Algos	CartPole	Acrobot	MountainCar	LunarLander
Expert[1]	500 ± 0.00	-82 ± 22.46	-99 ± 8.60	228 ± 62.33
Expert[2]	435 ± 70.51	-97 ± 24.41	-129 ± 25.50	151 ± 106.18
Expert[3]	354 ± 137.07	-138 ± 58.15	-137 ± 25.89	98 ± 103.76
Expert[4]	220 ± 47.42	-199 ± 79.85	-149 ± 32.02	60 ± 119.35
Expert[5]	112 ± 7.50	-243 ± 136.82	-156 ± 47.76	4 ± 110.92

4   Results

In this experimental section, we focus on how different algorithms behave when receiving samples that are not optimal for each domain. We run each algorithm described in the previous section 10 times over the data of each expert for 100 epochs. We use the default topology for each approach, which is a multi-layer perceptron with two layers and 32 neurons on each layer.

Table 2 presents the average and standard deviation of both metrics for each algorithm using Expert[1] for each environment. AER values for the experts are also presented. We can clearly see that the easiest environment for all methods to learn was CartPole. All approaches reach a performance of 1 in that environment. The second most straightforward environment was Acrobot, where all algorithms reach an average of 0.865 performance points, with ILPO providing the largest

Table 2. Performance ($\mathbb{P}$) and Average Episodic Reward (AER) for all algorithms on all environments using the optimal expert.

Algos	Metrics	CartPole	Acrobot	MountainCar	LunarLander
Random	AER	18.7 ± 0	-482.6 ± 0	-200 ± 0	-182.72 ± 0
	$\mathbb{P}$	0 ± 0	0 ± 0	0 ± 0	0 ± 0
Expert[1]	AER	500 ± 0	-82 ± 22.46	-99 ± 8.60	228 ± 62.33
	$\mathbb{P}$	1 ± 0	1 ± 0	1 ± 0	1 ± 0
BC	AER	$\mathbf{500.0 \pm 0.0}$	-93.6 ± 18.5	-200.0 ± 0.0	$\mathbf{-80.9 \pm 188.15}$
	$\mathbb{P}$	$\mathbf{1 \pm 0}$	0.97 ± 0.0	0.0 ± 0.0	$\mathbf{0.25 \pm 0.03}$
GAIL	AER	$\mathbf{500.0 \pm 0.0}$	-286.23 ± 90.86	-200.0 ± 0.0	-92.26 ± 114.67
	$\mathbb{P}$	$\mathbf{1 \pm 0}$	0.48 ± 0.15	0.0 ± 0.0	0.22 ± 0.13
ILPO	AER	$\mathbf{500.0 \pm 0.0}$	$\mathbf{-75.65 \pm 12.85}$	-184.54 ± 10.06	-98.46 ± 56.54
	$\mathbb{P}$	$\mathbf{1 \pm 0}$	$\mathbf{1.02 \pm 0.0}$	0.15 ± 0.31	0.2 ± 0.07
IUPE	AER	$\mathbf{500.0 \pm 0.0}$	-87.26 ± 22.19	$\mathbf{-166.97 \pm 18.34}$	-81.34 ± 74.5
	$\mathbb{P}$	$\mathbf{1 \pm 0}$	0.99 ± 0.05	$\mathbf{0.38 \pm 0.15}$	0.25 ± 0.25

reward of -75.42 (outperforming the expert), and the lowest being GAIL with -290.57 reward points. A point worth of notice is that the results provided by IUPE in the LunarLander environment, even though not close to the expert, reach a performance similar to BC—a strong baseline that has access to the actions performed by the expert at any state, i.e., ground-truth labels. When contrasting the results of CartPole and Acrobot with those in MountainCar and LunarLander, where the average performance for all algorithms was ≈ 0.095 and ≈ 0.2425, respectively, we can hypothesize that: (i) precise overall trajectories in both MountainCar and LunarLander highly correlate to high rewards, and (ii) in environments where trajectories can be noisy, as long as a few actions are properly performed, agents that only act locally (without any additional degree of exploration) will perform better than exploratory agents, hence the results seen in Acrobot and Cartpole.

In Table 3 we show results for all approaches with Expert[2]. We see that CartPole remains as being the easiest environment for all methods, except for BC that cannot reach 1 in performance. Considering that the CartPole environment considers a reward of 195 as solving the environment, we expect that all other algorithms will remain with similar results throughout the upcoming sub-optimal experts. With an average of 0.905 performance points, we can see that the non-punitive nature of random actions in Acrobot makes all IL approaches have little to no decrease in performance when compared to the optimal expert. These results further corroborate our second conclusion from Table 2.

For the MountainCar environment, we observe a decrease in the results for all approaches. We expect this to happen since building momentum is crucial for solving the task. A single non-optimal action could result in a significant deviation from the optimal trajectory, and recovering from unseen states is

Table 3. Performance ($\mathbb{P}$) and Average Episodic Reward (AER) for all algorithms on all environments using Expert[2].

Algos	Metrics	CartPole	Acrobot	MountainCar	LunarLander
Random	AER	18.7 ± 0	-482.6 ± 0	-200 ± 0	-182.72 ± 0
	$\mathbb{P}$	0 ± 0	0 ± 0	0 ± 0	0 ± 0
Expert[2]	AER	435 ± 70.51	-97 ± 24.41	-129 ± 25.50	151 ± 106.18
	$\mathbb{P}$	1 ± 0	1 ± 0	1 ± 0	1 ± 0
BC	AER	415.84 ± 81.46	-103.36 ± 18.0	-200.0 ± 0.0	$\mathbf{32.45 \pm 63.39}$
	$\mathbb{P}$	0.95 ± 0.04	0.98 ± 0.0	0.0 ± 0.0	$\mathbf{0.64 \pm 0.01}$
GAIL	AER	$\mathbf{500.0 \pm 0.0}$	-253.55 ± 84.78	-199.26 ± 2.73	-100.21 ± 99.02
	$\mathbb{P}$	$\mathbf{1.16 \pm 0.0}$	0.61 ± 0.17	0.0 ± 0.1	0.23 ± 0.14
ILPO	AER	$\mathbf{500.0 \pm 0.0}$	$\mathbf{-76.07 \pm 13.48}$	-192.7 ± 2.63	-89.06 ± 76.45
	$\mathbb{P}$	$\mathbf{1.16 \pm 0.0}$	$\mathbf{1.05 \pm 0.0}$	0.0 ± 0.4	0.26 ± 0.11
IUPE	AER	489.61 ± 9.06	-120.36 ± 36.35	$\mathbf{-190.26 \pm 11.03}$	-57.93 ± 91.75
	$\mathbb{P}$	1.16 ± 0.24	0.98 ± 0.16	$\mathbf{0.12 \pm 0.22}$	0.35 ± 0.22

usually hard for IL algorithms [9]. On the other hand, for the LunarLander environment, results are quite surprising. Even though the expert result decreased 50 reward points, transitioning from trajectories that solved the environment to those that do not caused an increase in performance for BC and little to no decrease for the remaining approaches. This behavior shows us that despite the fact that trajectories from LunarLander are highly correlated to the final reward, having a sub-optimal expert might actually help with generalization. With trajectories a little worse than those that do solve the environment, the IL agent does not overfit to strict behaviors, possibly learning to deviate from the landing positions seen during training, with a surprising beneficial effect in terms of generalization.

Table 4 shows the results for Expert[3]. In this scenario, we see IUPE decreasing in terms of AER and performance alongside BC in the CartPole environment. It seems that IUPE relies much more on expert quality than GAIL and ILPO, which are capable of keeping their results at the environment maximum (500 reward points). For the Acrobot environment, all algorithms keep their performance with little to no degradation in reward, and the standard deviations are also all very similar. IUPE keeps reaching the best performance in MountainCar, with -172.92 reward points (close to the result of the optimal expert). Even though IUPE underperforms when compared to ILPO, when we analyze the stability of IUPE (see the standard deviation values), it outperforms ILPO in most environments, except for CartPole. The LunarLander results in Table 4 further show that when considering an environment with strict trajectories (e.g., land in-between the flags), having fewer optimal experts can help IL algorithms to better generalize. Nevertheless, note that achieving a good performance here (behavior close to the expert) does not mean much, considering that the expert is faulty, which means achieving a performance of 1 does not correlate with optimal behavior anymore.

Table 4. Performance ($\mathbb{P}$) and Average Episodic Reward (AER) for all algorithms on all environments using Expert[3].

Algos	Metrics	CartPole	Acrobot	MountainCar	LunarLander
Random	AER	18.7 ± 0	-482.6 ± 0	-200 ± 0	-182.72 ± 0
	$\mathbb{P}$	0 ± 0	0 ± 0	0 ± 0	0 ± 0
Expert[3]	AER	354 ± 137.07	-138 ± 58.15	-137 ± 25.89	98 ± 103.76
	$\mathbb{P}$	1 ± 0	1 ± 0	1 ± 0	1 ± 0
BC	AER	181.99 ± 78.5	-130.94 ± 25.4	-200.0 ± 0.0	$\mathbf{107.48 \pm 101.49}$
	$\mathbb{P}$	0.49 ± 0.02	1.02 ± 0.0	0.0 ± 0.0	$\mathbf{1.03 \pm 0.03}$
GAIL	AER	$\mathbf{500.0 \pm 0.0}$	-248.78 ± 82.66	-199.96 ± 1.6	-96.88 ± 106.57
	$\mathbb{P}$	$\mathbf{1.44 \pm 0.0}$	0.66 ± 0.14	0.0 ± 0.03	0.29 ± 0.19
ILPO	AER	500.0 ± 0.0	$\mathbf{-75.63 \pm 14.05}$	-199.82 ± 4.36	-90.88 ± 68.94
	$\mathbb{P}$	1.44 ± 0.0	$\mathbf{1.18 \pm 0.0}$	0.0 ± 0.32	0.33 ± 0.06
IUPE	AER	177.73 ± 85.75	-85.59 ± 22.59	$\mathbf{-173.5 \pm 14.55}$	-190.7 ± 89.16
	$\mathbb{P}$	0.63 ± 0.38	1.15 ± 0.07	$\mathbf{0.43 \pm 0.3}$	0.12 ± 0.46

Table 5. Performance ($\mathbb{P}$) and Average Episodic Reward (AER) for all algorithms on all environments using Expert[4].

Algos	Metrics	CartPole	Acrobot	MountainCar	LunarLander
Random	AER	18.7 ± 0	-482.6 ± 0	-200 ± 0	-182.72 ± 0
	$\mathbb{P}$	0 ± 0	0 ± 0	0 ± 0	0 ± 0
Expert[4]	AER	220 ± 47.42	-199 ± 79.85	-149 ± 32.02	60 ± 119.35
	$\mathbb{P}$	1 ± 0	1 ± 0	1 ± 0	1 ± 0
BC	AER	372.76 ± 120.85	-179.18 ± 26.72	-200.0 ± 0.0	$\mathbf{71.48 \pm 136.87}$
	$\mathbb{P}$	1.76 ± 0.05	1.07 ± 0.0	0.0 ± 0.0	$\mathbf{1.04 \pm 0.05}$
GAIL	AER	498.28 ± 16.08	-316.42 ± 79.66	-200.0 ± 0.37	-88.32 ± 91.24
	$\mathbb{P}$	2.39 ± 0.04	0.53 ± 0.2	0.0 ± 0.0	0.39 ± 0.16
ILPO	AER	$\mathbf{500.0 \pm 0.0}$	$\mathbf{-75.78 \pm 13.8}$	-190.47 ± 5.25	-103.39 ± 80.0
	$\mathbb{P}$	$\mathbf{2.39 \pm 0.0}$	$\mathbf{1.43 \pm 0.0}$	0.0 ± 0.67	0.32 ± 0.09
IUPE	AER	357.65 ± 61.64	-338.1 ± 40.02	$\mathbf{-161.05 \pm 20.11}$	-79.54 ± 110.0
	$\mathbb{P}$	1.84 ± 0.69	0.24 ± 0.64	$\mathbf{0.8 \pm 0.51}$	0.49 ± 0.2

Table 5 shows results for Expert[4]. These results are the middle way of solving each environment, except for the CartPole environment (195 reward points). When executing these experiments, we expected that IUPE and BC would keep degrading in Acrobot and CartPole. However, this was the case only for the Acrobot environment. For CartPole, we can observe that ILPO and GAIL kept the maximum reward as expected, but we observe an increase in the reward for both BC and IUPE. For BC, we also notice an increase in the standard deviation of the ten runs. We observe that IUPE keeps showing good results for MountainCar, even though the expert optimality decreases. These results, coupled with those of ILPO on Acrobot, make us conclude that this behavior occurs due to the exploration nature of the approach. While ILPO only sees the expert and some random samples, IUPE continuously receives different samples for its inverse dynamics model. A fair assumption would be that self-supervised methods with exploration mechanisms can learn more dynamic models (hence the MountainCar results), while those without exploration only do better in more stochastic environments.

Table 6 shows results for the worst expert, Expert[5]. In this scenario, none of the experts solve the task but still comfortably outperform the random agent. All algorithms have a high level of degradation in their performance for the Cart-Pole, Acrobot, and MountainCar environments, except for ILPO in the first two. ILPO manages to maintain its Acrobot result consistent throughout the different experts, which corroborates our conclusion that self-supervised IL methods without exploration are more effective in environments that rely less on the construction of a trajectory (performing an action in Acrobot impacts less in the overall trajectory than in MountainCar, for instance). We also observe that IUPE maintains its results with almost no change when degrading the expert samples. This behavior substantiates our conclusion that self-supervised IL methods with exploration mechanisms can help IL agents create smoother actions in environments more susceptible to divergence in trajectories (the momentum in MountainCar, for instance). Furthermore, as expected in the LunarLander environment, all methods had decreasing results in this last scenario.

Table 6. Performance ($\mathbb{P}$) and Average Episodic Reward (AER) for all algorithms on all environments using Expert[5].

Algos	Metrics	CartPole	Acrobot	MountainCar	LunarLander
Random	AER	18.7 ± 0	-482.6 ± 0	-200 ± 0	-182.72 ± 0
	$\mathbb{P}$	0 ± 0	0 ± 0	0 ± 0	0 ± 0
Expert[5]	AER	112 ± 7.50	-243 ± 136.82	-156 ± 47.76	4 ± 110.92
	$\mathbb{P}$	1 ± 0	1 ± 0	1 ± 0	1 ± 0
BC	AER	155.96 ± 71.82	-178.82 ± 55.38	-200.0 ± 0.1	$\mathbf{-6.03 \pm 93.79}$
	$\mathbb{P}$	1.46 ± 0.05	1.27 ± 0.02	0.0 ± 0.0	$\mathbf{0.96 \pm 0.02}$
GAIL	AER	484.22 ± 40.29	-331.85 ± 84.55	-199.94 ± 2.14	-60.28 ± 101.21
	$\mathbb{P}$	5.11 ± 0.31	0.61 ± 0.26	0.0 ± 0.03	0.77 ± 0.4
ILPO	AER	$\mathbf{500.0 \pm 0.0}$	$\mathbf{-75.93 \pm 15.15}$	-192.58 ± 7.65	-96.57 ± 76.11
	$\mathbb{P}$	$\mathbf{5.16 \pm 0.0}$	$\mathbf{1.7 \pm 0.0}$	0.0 ± 0.64	0.41 ± 0.14
IUPE	AER	134.72 ± 22.51	-259.57 ± 23.58	$\mathbf{-178.24 \pm 23.54}$	-176.33 ± 85.52
	$\mathbb{P}$	1.33 ± 0.55	1.33 ± 0.82	$\mathbf{0.6 \pm 0.36}$	0.14 ± 0.57

In Fig. 2, we can see the result for all approaches in the four environments throughout all five experts. The lines display the tendency of each algorithm when sample optimality is reduced, where the blue line represents the expert.

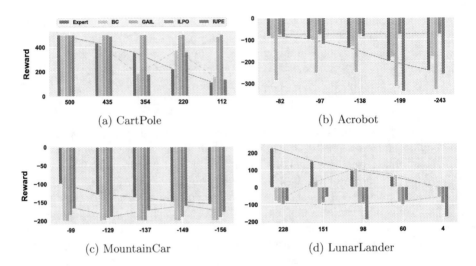

(a) CartPole

(b) Acrobot

(c) MountainCar

(d) LunarLander

Fig. 2. Results for all environments, using all five different experts for each environment and all four algorithms. The "x" axis is the expert reward for that group of experiments, while the "y" axis is the reward accumulated over hundred runs for each agent. The lines on each graph display the tendency of the expert and one or more algorithms with a different behavior.

For the CartPole environment (Fig. 2a), we observe that BC has a linear decrease in performance, even though it had access to all labels from the expert. IUPE follows the behavior of BC, while GAIL and ILPO are fairly robust throughout the entire process of sample-quality degradation.

Next, we analyze the behavior in the Acrobot (Fig. 2b) and MountainCar (Fig. 2c) environments. In Acrobot, ILPO is capable of keeping its performance throughout sample-quality degradation. This shows that ILPO has learned the dynamics of the environment, while the expert only works as a guide to its objective. In the MountainCar environment, we see the same pattern for IUPE, whose performance was rather stable with some correlation to the expert.

Finally, in the LunarLander (Fig. 2d) environment, we observe that BC had the best results overall, GAIL the most consistent/robust, and IUPE the best result in 3 out of 5 experts, regarding those without access to the ground-truth labels. Overall, receiving sub-optimal trajectories allows the approaches to learn the dynamics of the environment more properly and achieve better results. This does not happen in all environments, however. We hypothesize that perhaps LunarLander presents a better scenario to test generalization for IL approaches since simply learning to mimic the trajectory of the expert with no knowledge on how and where to land does not translate into good performance, considering that the final goal changes according to the chosen seeds.

5   A Note on Evaluation Metrics

In this work, similarly to the main studies of the area, we use the *Performance* metric [8] to evaluate results, which is perhaps the most common metric when working with IL. Explained in Sect. 3.5, this metric is the normalization of the agent's performance—average reward over 100 executions—by that of the expert and the one expected by a random policy. Therefore, an agent that performs better than the expert can achieve results higher than 1, while one that performs poorly may achieve negative results.

We would like to discuss the fact that this metric may not convey the correct information, or at least not indicate what people may think it does. Firstly, the metric inherits the same issues from linear normalization procedures when dealing with skewed data. Even though we do not use it for optimizing classification or regression, it can misrepresent how the agent behaves in an environment.

For example, let us take a look at the experiments in MountainCar under two scenarios: (i) when the expert reward is -160 and the random reward is -200 (the lowest reward an agent could achieve); and (ii) when the expert reward is -110 (the threshold considered for solving the task) and the random reward is again -200. In the first scenario, when an agent achieves the expert behavior, it will score a performance of 1, while in the second scenario the same reward would result in a performance of ≈ 0.44. This example shows the problem of assuming as a premise that the expert is an optimal policy, also seen in Tables 5 and 6. If the selected expert samples are not optimal, the performance metric will not accurately represent how good the agent is. In this example, the agent is 50 reward points from solving the task, though the metric says that the agent is optimal. Hence, there is a need of knowing *a priori* the optimality level of the expert, which can be *per se* a complex problem in several application domains. On the other hand, if an agent achieves a reward of -100 in the same example, the performance will be 2.5 and 1.11 for the first and second scenarios, respectively. This example shows that (i) the samples might not be ideal (as were most of the samples from this work), and (ii) the policy might not have learned the exact behavior from the expert. For both hypotheses, the results show that the method learned from (and even transcended) the expert.

We can also conclude that the reward function does not accurately represent the trajectory of the expert. Let us imagine an environment where an agent must drive a car from point A to point B and then pick up a passenger. If the reward function only tracks the distance driven by the agent and not the act of picking up a passenger, the reward of the agent that does not pick up its passenger and that of the expert will be the same, resulting in a performance of 1. The same can happen if the reward function only considers the act of picking up a passenger and not the distance driven. If the agent takes a longer path than the expert, performance will similarly be 1, which was supposed to be optimal. This example applies to the LunarLander environment, where the agent is highly rewarded for landing in-between flags. Even by taking some time to reach its destiny, the agent can have a performance close to 1.

In addition, we can discuss how performance does not convey information regarding generalization. When using classic control environments, IL can easily force the expert's trajectory to be as close as possible to the expert's, requiring no effort to map unseen states correctly. We can see this problem by analyzing how ILPO keeps its results over the multiple sub-optimal experts in Fig. 2b. Even though the expert degraded consistently, ILPO learned to map a trajectory correctly. This behavior is excellent for all cases where the environment task does not require any generalization over time, such being the case for MountainCar. When we compare the behavior from Figs. 2c and 2d, we can observe that these algorithms perform close to the random policy in environments where a minor level of generalization is required. And note that, still, performance will yield good results with suboptimal agents, a significant concern for anyone who is using the metric without really taking into account its flaws.

6   Conclusion and Future Work

In this work, we experiment with four different IL algorithms in scenarios with varied levels of expert quality. More specifically, we employed five different degrees of optimality for these four approaches, and we analyzed how the decrease in quality impacted them when solving different tasks. ILPO and IUPE had a better performance with less correlation to the expert than the other two approaches, BC and GAIL. Using approaches where the agent first needs to learn to classify the transition between states so it can later learn the expert policy helps them being more resilient to different degrees of sample quality. Even though IUPE does not use the same model for classifying these transitions, we believe that its iterative nature helps the model with generalization since it receives different labels for the same state samples throughout its training. We also discovered that some environments are good in showing a clear trade-off between optimality and generalization capability of IL agents. However, by reducing the expert reward in the LunarLander environment, we observed an increase in the performance of the self-supervised IL approaches, which was a surprise to say the least. Since this environment correlates its final reward with its goal, less-optimal experts seem to help the IL agents see more states, further helping them at generalization while acting as regularizers. As future work, we want to test how different methods interact with expert samples when using partial observations. Expert samples in the wild are not easy to come by, so creating methods that are resilient to missing information is of great importance. We also want to check how current IL methods perform in domain-shift scenarios. Finally, we think proposing new evaluation metrics for IL is probably important, specially with the assumption that experts may be sub-optimal.

Acknowledgment. This paper was achieved in cooperation with Banco Cooperativo Sicredi.

References

1. Argall, B.D., Chernova, S., Veloso, M., Browning, B.: A survey of robot learning from demonstration. Robot. Auton. Syst. **57**(5), 469–483 (2009)
2. Barto, A.G., Sutton, R.S., Anderson, C.W.: Neuronlike adaptive elements that can solve difficult learning control problems. IEEE Trans. Syst. Man Cybern. **1**(5), 834–846 (1983)
3. Burke, C.J., Tobler, P.N., Baddeley, M., Schultz, W.: Neural mechanisms of observational learning. Proc. Natl. Acad. Sci. U. S. A. **107**(32), 14431–14436 (2010)
4. Ciosek, K.: Imitation learning by reinforcement learning. arXiv preprint arXiv:2108.04763 (2021)
5. Edwards, A., Sahni, H., Schroecker, Y., Isbell, C.: Imitating latent policies from observation. In: International Conference on Machine Learning, pp. 1755–1763. PMLR (2019)
6. Gavenski, N., Monteiro, J., Granada, R., Meneguzzi, F., Barros, R.C.: Imitating unknown policies via exploration. arXiv preprint arXiv:2008.05660 (2020)
7. Gavenski, N.S.: Self-supervised imitation learning from observation. Master's thesis, Pontifícia Universidade Católica do Rio Grande do Sul (2021)
8. Ho, J., Ermon, S.: Generative adversarial imitation learning. In: Proceedings of the 30th Conference on Neural Information Processing Systems (NIPS 2016), NIPS 2016, pp. 4565–4573 (2016)
9. Hussein, A., Gaber, M.M., Elyan, E., Jayne, C.: Imitation learning: a survey of learning methods. ACM Comput. Surv. (CSUR) **50**(2), 1–35 (2017)
10. Jing, L., Tian, Y.: Self-supervised visual feature learning with deep neural networks: a survey. IEEE Trans. Pattern Anal. Mach. Intell. **1**(01), 1–24 (2019). https://doi.org/10.1109/TPAMI.2020.2992393
11. Kidambi, R., Chang, J.D., Sun, W.: Mobile: model-based imitation learning from observations alone (2021)
12. Liu, Y., Gupta, A., Abbeel, P., Levine, S.: Imitation from observation: learning to imitate behaviors from raw video via context translation. In: Proceedings of ICRA 2018, pp. 1118–1125 (2018)
13. Monteiro, J., Gavenski, N., Granada, R., Meneguzzi, F., Barros, R.C.: Augmented behavioral cloning from observation. In: Proceedings of the 2020 International Conference on Neural Networks, IJCNN 2020, pp. 1–8. IEEE, July 2020. https://arxiv.org/abs/2004.13529
14. Moore, A.W.: Efficient memory-based learning for robot control. Ph.D. thesis, University of Cambridge (1990)
15. Pomerleau, D.A.: ALVINN: an autonomous land vehicle in a neural network. In: Proceedings of the 1st Conference on Neural Information Processing Systems, NIPS 1988, pp. 305–313 (1988)
16. Schaal, S.: Learning from demonstration. In: Proceedings of NIPS 1996, pp. 1040–1046 (1996)
17. Sutton, R.S., Barto, A.G.: Introduction to Reinforcement Learning, vol. 2. MIT Press, Cambridge (1998)
18. Torabi, F., Warnell, G., Stone, P.: Behavioral cloning from observation. In: Proceedings of IJCAI 2018, pp. 4950–4957 (2018)
19. Zhu, Z., Lin, K., Dai, B., Zhou, J.: Off-policy imitation learning from observations. Adv. Neural. Inf. Process. Syst. **33**, 12402–12413 (2020)

To Answer or Not to Answer? Filtering Questions for QA Systems

Paulo Pirozelli[1,4]($\boxtimes$)(ID), Anarosa A. F. Brandão[2,4](ID), Sarajane M. Peres[3,4](ID), and Fabio G. Cozman[2,4](ID)

[1] Instituto de Estudos Avançados, São Paulo, Brazil
paulo.pirozelli.silva@usp.br
[2] Escola Politécnica, São Paulo, Brazil
{anarosa.brandao,sarajane,fgcozman}@usp.br
[3] Escola de Artes, Ciências e Humanidades, São Paulo, Brazil
[4] Center for Artificial Intelligence (C4AI), São Paulo, Brazil

Abstract. Question answering (QA) systems are usually structured as strict conditional generators, which return an answer for every input question. Sometimes, however, the policy of always responding to questions may prove itself harmful, given the possibility of giving inaccurate answers, particularly for ambiguous or sensitive questions; instead, it may be better for a QA system to decide which questions should be answered or not. In this paper, we explore dual system architectures that filter unanswerable or meaningless questions, thus answering only a subset of the questions raised. Two experiments are performed in order to evaluate this modular approach: a classification on SQuAD 2.0 for unanswerable questions, and a regression on Pirá for question meaningfulness. Despite the difficulties involved in the tasks, we show that filtering questions may contribute to improve the quality of the answers generated by QA systems. By using classification and regression models to filter questions, we can get better control over the accuracy of the answers produced by the answerer systems.

Keywords: Question answering · Answer triggering · Dual system · Question filtering

1 Introduction

A question answering (QA) system may be thought as conditional generator that predicts an answer given a question, often with the support of some context. In other words, for every input question, the system returns an answer. In practice, however, no QA system is able to answer any possible question, even over a

This work was carried out at the Center for Artificial Intelligence (C4AI-USP), with support by the São Paulo Research Foundation (FAPESP grant #2019/ 07665-4) and by the IBM Corporation. Fabio G. Cozman thanks the support of the National Council for Scientific and Technological Development of Brazil (CNPq grant #312180/2018-7).

J. C. Xavier-Junior and R. A. Rios (Eds.): BRACIS 2022, LNAI 13654, pp. 464–478, 2022.
https://doi.org/10.1007/978-3-031-21689-3_33

restricted domain, except when questions are restricted to a strict format. The reasons for this limitation are varied: from the lack of necessary information, to malformed questions, ambiguity, and tacit assumptions.

The policy of always answering questions may be a detrimental one in some contexts. This is particularly true for high-risk AI systems, where there are "significant risks to the health and safety or fundamental rights of persons" [6]. In such domains, it is often better for a QA system to confine itself to questions it is strongly certain of and avoid answering sensitive or dubious requests. Deciding which questions should move through the QA system is important to guarantee safety and factual grounding [23].

If it is the case that some questions should not be answered at all, then a QA system has to understand which questions should receive an answer and which should not. Two main approaches can be taken for that purpose. First, a QA system may be trained directly on datasets containing answerable and unanswerable questions, simultaneously learning *when* and *what* to respond. Second, a QA system may have a dual composition, in which a first component filters inadequate questions and the other module answers the selected questions.

In this paper, we investigate QA systems of the latter type; in particular, we analyze the connection, in those dual systems, of question filtering and QA quality. Our aim is to understand: i) how accurate can a classifier/regressor be on question answerability and meaningfulness; and ii) how do filtering systems affect the quality of the answering system. Although end-to-end systems have produced state-of-the-art results for answer triggering datasets [5,11,15], by identifying answerable questions as part of the training process, and have been under recent scrutiny as regards their self-evaluation awareness [9], our goal here is to quantify the relation between the level of answerability and meaningfulness of a question and the quality of the generated responses. By using a dual system architecture, in which a model previously identifies inappropriate questions, it is possible to modularize a critical step of a QA system, assuring a better control of what is being answered.

This paper is organized as follows. Section 2 provides an overview of the technical literature and describes the data used in our experiments. Two main tasks are conducted by us: first, we consider a traditional (discrete) answer triggering approach, in which the problem is to figure out which questions have an answer (Sect. 3); then, we explore a regression system in which we measure a question's degree of meaningfulness (Sect. 4). In both cases, we explore the effectiveness of filtering systems and how they affect the outcome of answerer models. In Sect. 5 we discuss the results of our investigation as well as limitations of the current approaches and future directions for research. Finally, we conclude with a few remarks on dual QA systems (Sect. 6).[1]

---

[1] In order to assure reproducibility, codes, dataset partitions, and trained models are made available at the project's GitHub repository: https://github.com/C4AI/Pira/tree/main/Triggering.

2   Background

Answer triggering is the task of deciding whether a question should be answered or not. By allowing some questions not to have an answer, models are required to learn *when* they should answer a given question. In Sect. 2.1, we briefly present the main architectures for QA systems, such as rule-based, end-to-end, and modular approaches. Section 2.2 reviews the datasets available for answering triggering and related tasks. Section 2.3 describes the two datasets used in our experiments, SQuAD 2.0 and Pirá.

2.1   Question Answering Systems

QA systems can have many different architectures. Before the popularization of deep learning, dialogue systems usually employed a mixture of rule-based approaches and feature-based classifiers, often intertwined in complex architectures, as in the Watson DeepQA system [7].

More recently, neural approaches came to dominate the field, at least for research purposes. Popular among these are end-to-end systems, such as T5 [17], and decoder (e.g., BERT [5]) and encoder-based models (e.g., GPT [3,16]), adapted for question answering tasks. There are also QA systems that combine different specialized mechanisms within the same training process. It is the case, for example, of RAG (Retrieval-Augmented Generation) [13], which uses a neural retriever, DPR [10], and a language generator, BART [12].

Finally, modular systems combine independent models that execute specific functions in the QA pipeline, without end-to-end training. DrQA [4], for instance, has a document retriever, based on bigram hashing and TF-IDF matching, and a document reader, which uses an achitecture of bidirectional LSTMs.

In this paper, we study a modular architecture for QA systems with two components, which we refer to as dual system. It consists of a filtering model that assess which questions should be answered and an answerer model that responds only to the selected questions.

2.2   Answer Triggering

Answer triggering was first defined by Yang et al. [26], together with a purposefully-developed dataset, WikiQA. Questions in WikiQA were based on Bing query logs, and the summary of the associated Wikipedia pages were used to determine if questions had an answer or not. SeqAL [8] was also based on Wikipedia, but using a larger number of questions from more domains and using the full entry pages. Answer triggering datasets grew out in popularity with SQuAD 2.0 [18], which added a large number of unanswerable questions to the original reading compreenhsion SQuAD dataset [19]. More importantly, unanswerable questions in SQuAD 2.0 were deliberately produced to have putative candidate answers. Although not a strict answer triggering dataset, Pirá [2] brings a number of human assessment on question meaningfulness that has a similar shape.

It is not always clear whether a question can be answered or not. Questions can be ambiguous or poorly structured, and whether or not a question has an answer may lay on a gray area, depending on contextual information that is not readily available. Some reading comprehension datasets try to overcome this difficulty by including a third outcome signaling uncertainty. ReCO [24] is a dataset of opinion-based queries in Chinese which uses three candidate answers for annotation: a positive one like Yes, a negative one like No, and an undefined one in case the question cannot be answered with the given documents. QuAIL [21] is a multi-choice dataset developed to include three degrees of certainty: answerable questions (given a context), unanswerable questions (even with context and world knowledge), and partially certain questions (when a good guess can be made).

2.3 Datasets

Two datasets are used in our experiments, SQuAD 2.0 and Pirá. Table 1 depicts their main statistics.[2]

Table 1. Number of QA sets for different splits of SQuAD 2.0 and Pirá.

Model	# QA instance (%)			
	Train	Validation	Test	Total
SQuAD 2.0	130319 (91.65%)	5936 (4.17%)	5937 (4.17%)	142192 (100%)
Pirá	1755 (80.28%)	215 (9.83%)	216 (9.88%)	2186 (100%)

SQuAD 2.0. SQuAD 2.0 is an extractive reading comprehension dataset. It combines the original SQuAD dataset [19], a reading comprehension resource with 100K+ questions, with approximately 53K unanswerable questions (marked as empty strings). To produce the unanswerable questions, annotators were asked to create questions over paragraphs that could not be correctly answered from these texts only. To avoid that questions unrelated to the context were created, annotators were instructed to produce questions that were relevant to the context and which contained plausible answers in the paragraph (such as the name of a person for a Who-type question). These plausible answers serve as effective distractors to questions, making it harder to realize what questions are in fact unanswerable. In total, SQuAD 2.0 contains around 151K questions, of which approximately 35.5% do not have answers. Another aspect of the dataset is that answerable questions present multiple answers, made by different annotators; for our experiments, we use only the first answer for each question as the ground

---

[2] In Pirá, only QA sets with meaningful evaluations were used. For the original dataset, the numbers would be: train: 1896 (79.98%), validation: 225 (9.96%), test: 227 (10%), total: 2258 (100%).

truth answer. The test set for this dataset is not publicly available; we thus break the original validation set into two equally-sized partitions to get our validation and test sets (which explains the smaller number of QA sets described in Table 1 as compared to the total number of QA sets of SQuAD 2.0).

Pirá. Pirá [2] is a bilingual question answering dataset on the ocean, the Brazilian coast, and climate change. QA sets in Pirá are based on two corpora of supporting texts: one composed of scientific abstracts on the Brazilian Coast, and the other of small excerpts of two United Nations reports on the ocean. The dataset generation process comprised an assessment phase in which QA sets were manually evaluated in a number of aspects. Among these evaluations, participants were asked as to whether the QA sets were meaningful, based on a Likert scale (1 - Strongly disagree, 2 - Disagree, 3 - Neither agree nor disagree, 4 - Agree, 5 - Strongly agree). Figure 1 displays the distribution of QA instances in the test set by level of question meaningfulness. We also use the human validation answers produced in the assessments phase for our second experiment. Pirá contains 2248 QA sets in total. To conduct the experiments described in this paper, the dataset was splitted into three random partitions: training (80%), validation (10%), and test (10%) sets.

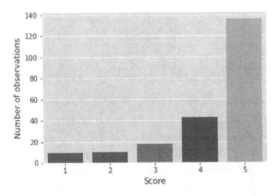

Fig. 1. Number of QA sets in the test set of Pirá by question meaningfulness level.

As regards the experiments conducted in this paper, SQuAD 2.0 and Pirá differ in important aspects. First, SQuAD 2.0 is an answering triggering dataset, meaning that some questions in it may have an answer while others may not, whereas in Pirá all questions are associated with answers. In addition, the former uses a qualitative ordinal (binary) variable, while the latter uses a numerical discrete variable (1–5). Finally, SQuAD 2.0 is concerned with answerability whereas Pirá is concerned with question meaningfulness. Those differences will be relevant to the experiments described above.

3   Answer Triggering

As a first contribution, we are interested in testing the usefulness of filtering questions based on answerability. As our answerer system, we use a DistilBERT-base model [22], fine-tuned on SQuAD 1.1 (a dataset where all questions have answers); context and question are concatenated and used as input. Three different scenarios are compared to measure the effects of question filtering on answer quality:

- questions from SQuAD 2.0 are passed indistinctly to the DistilBERT answerer system;
- questions are first grouped by answerability labels based on ground truth classifications and then passed to the answerer system; and
- questions are first grouped by answerability labels based on a classification model and then passed to the answerer system.

These three possibilities are illustrated in Fig. 2.

When generated answers are compared to the actual, manually-created ones, the QA system achieves a F1-score of 38.70 in the full test set (Fig. 2a).[3] Table 2 brings the results for this and the following tests. Furthermore, when only answerable questions are selected (based on real labels), there is a considerable increase in the quality of answers, with the F1-score going up to 78.25, a gain of 102.19% (Fig. 2b). This difference is due to the attempt, in the first case, to answer questions that have no answer whatsoever; when restricted solely to questions that do have answers, the average quality of answers improves.

Table 2. F1-score for a DistilBERT answerer model fine-tuned on SQuAD 1.1, when applied to the test set of SQuAD 2.0; the F1-score (0–100) is obtained by comparing the predicted answers to the (first) ground truth answers. Real labels are obtained from the annotated SQuAD 2.0 dataset (where unanswerable questions are presented as empty strings); predicted labels are obtained from three classification models: DistilBERT, RoBERTa, and ALBERT, all fine-tuned on SQuAD 2.0. Results for real and predicted labels are divided by answerable (Answ.) and unanswerable (Unansw.) questions. The F1-score of an empty answer (i.e., an unanswerable question) is by definition 0. In bold, the best result for answerable questions based on the predicted labels.

Model	Total	Real label		Predicted label	
		Answ.	Unansw.	Answ.	Unansw.
DistilBERT	38.70	78.25	0	39.42	18.53
RoBERTa				46.08	33.13
ALBERT				**63.54**	**6.81**

Hence, a filtering procedure that was able to filter answerable questions could in theory improve the quality of the answers generated by the answerer module.

---

[3] F1-score is implemented with the official SQuAD script. Available at: https://rajpurkar.github.io/SQuAD-explorer/.

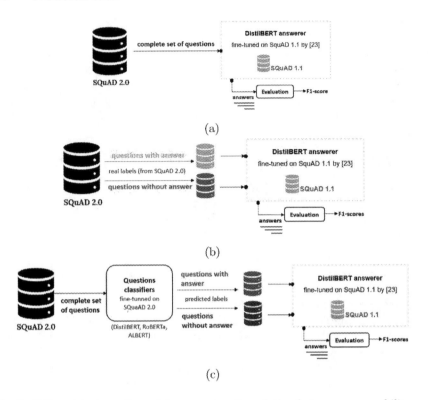

(a)

(b)

(c)

Fig. 2. Different tests performed for assessing the relation between answerability and answer quality. From top to bottom: (a) questions are passed indistinctly to the answerer model; (b) questions are first grouped by answerability labels based on ground truth labels before going through the answerer model; and (c) questions are first grouped by answerability labels obtained from a classifier before going through the answerer model. The answers generated with the answerer system are then compared to the actual answers from SQuAD 2.0 using F1-score as an agreement metric.

In order to test this hypothesis, we perform a classification task on SQuAD 2.0's test set for question answerability. Three transformer models are used for the task: DistilBERT [22], RoBERTa [15], and ALBERT [11]; all of them fine-tuned on SQuAD 2.0 (since we want a model that already knows some information regarding answerability). A concatenation of context and question is used as input. All models are trained for 8 epochs in the train set, and the best log is chosen based on the validation set. Accuracy and F1-score for the three classifiers, as well as the number of predicted labels, are shown in Table 3.

After training the classifiers, we predict answerability labels for the questions in the test set of SQuAD 2.0 based on each of the models. Next, we calculate the F1-score for answerable or unanswerable separately, according to the predicted labels (Fig. 2c). As can be seen from Table 2, there is a considerable difference

Table 3. **Left**: Distribution of predicted labels for DistilBERT, RoBERTa, ALBERT, and ground truth in the test set (Answ. = Answerable, Unansw. = Unanswerable). **Right**: Accuracy and F1-score for DistilBERT, RoBERTa, ALBERT in the answer triggering task. Best result in bold.

Model	# Predicted labels		Results	
	Answ.	Unansw.	Accuracy	F1-score
DistilBERT	5731 (96.53%)	206 (3.47%)	51.03	37.90
RoBERTa	2553 (43.00%)	3384 (57.00%)	57.84	57.59
ALBERT	**3337 (56.21%)**	**2600 (43.79%)**	**84.08**	**84.03**
Test set	3001 (50.55%)	2936 (49.45%)		

in the quality of answers when answerability is taken into account.[4] When only questions that are predicted to have an answer are considered, the F1-score goes up to 39.42 (+1.87%) with DistilBERT, to 46.08 (19.07+%) with RoBERTa, and to 63.54 with ALBERT (64.19+%); as regards to questions predicted as having no answer, F1-score goes down to 18.53 (−52.12%), 33.13 (−14.39%), and 6.18 (−82.38%), respectively. The unintuitive fact that RoBERTa achieves better results than DistilBERT in both answerable and unanswerable questions is explained by a base rate problem: the DistilBERT model classifies the majority of questions as answerable (96.53%), whereas the other two models classify only 43.00% and 56.21% of the questions as answerable, respectively; a statistics closer to actual percentage of answerable questions in the test set (50.55%).

4 Continuous Answering Triggering

Traditionally, answering triggering is understood as in our previous experiment: a binary classification task on whether a question can be answered or not. In reality, though, the answerability of a question is often a complex affair. Although many questions can be undoubtedly categorized as having an answer or not, others lay on the middle part of the spectrum.

Therefore, as a second contribution, we explore whether more fine-grained information on questions can help to achieve better QA systems. For this task, we work with the English part of Pirá, a reading comprehension dataset on the ocean and the Brazilian coast (cf. Sect. 2.3). Contrary to answer triggering datasets *tout court* (cf. Sect. 2.2), Pirá does not possess explicit features indicating unanswerability or certainty degrees. Instead, we use its manual evaluations on question meaningfulness as proxies for answerability: questions with a low value for meaningfulness are treated as having a lower degree of answerability.

---

[4] Both the classifiers described in this section and the regressors trained in the next use random initializations that may resul in slightly different predictions. To ensure the consistency of results, we repeated the same experiment 10 times each. The results described here are, therefore, representative of the trained models.

The Likert scale (1–5) scores used in the assessments provide a detailed level of analysis of answerability, more so than a binary or three-point alternative; even better, it permits us to treat question meaningfulness as an ordinal variable. Based on that, we reframe our answer triggering problem as a regression task, in which we aim to predict the degree of meaningfulness of a question in a 1 to 5 scale.

To see whether our meaningfulness regressor is indeed useful, we pair it again with a QA system. In theory, a QA system that only answers high-quality questions should give superior answers overall. Thus, we conduct a number of experiments to measure the quality of the QA system when questions are filtered by their degree of meaningfulness. First, we fine-tune a DistilBERT, ALBERT, and RoBERTa models on Pirá, using a concatenation of question and context as input. Models were trained for a total of 8 epochs in the training set, and evaluations were performed on the validation test. Similarly to the previous experiment, the ALBERT-based approach achieved the smallest loss and Root Mean Square Error in the validation set; for this reason, it was chosen as our regressor system. For the QA systems, we use two DistilBERT models fine-tuned for question answering on SQuAD 1.1 and SQuAD 2.0, respectively.

After training the regressor models, we predict the degree of meaningfulness for the questions in the test set. Questions are then grouped in 10 progressively smaller partitions, based on the predictions made with the regressor. For our first test, we measure the quality of the answers given by the QA system for these different partitions. As smaller partitions select questions evaluated better according to our regressor, we expect that the answers generated for them to be comparatively better. To measure the quality of answers, we rely again on F1-score; the original answer in Pirá serves as the ground truth.

Figure 3(a) shows the results for both QA models. The two graphs exhibit a similar trend. In both cases, F1-score goes up when smaller partitions of the test set feed the QA system. In this as in other tests, results for both QA models are similar—something expected, given that the F1-score between the answers generated with these two models is 70.03. Furthermore, as in the other tests discussed above, the F1-score for SQuAD 1.1 is usually higher than for SQuAD 2.0. Finally, the high spike in the last partitions may not be as significant as it appears; rather, it is likely due to randomness, given its small size, with only 21 observations.

F1-score is a metric based on the presence of the same tokens in the ground and predicted answers. It is well known, however, that automatic metrics may not correlate well with human evaluations [14]. There is also a more straightforward shortcoming of F1-score: this metric is not able to identify subtler similarity phenomena between answers, involving paraphrasing. For this reason, we decided to check the similarity between predicted and ground truth answers based on vector representations. Embeddings for both the original and the generated answer were produced with Sentence-BERT [20], and cosine dissimilarity (1 - cosine distance) served as a measure of semantic similarity (rather than word similarity, as in the case of F1-score).

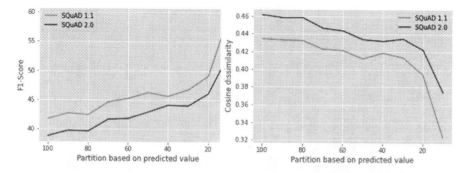

Fig. 3. Left: F1-score for different partitions of the test set (based on the predicted values of a RoBERTa regressor), comparing the ground truth answers in Pirá with answers generated by two DiltilBERT models fine-tuned on SQuAD 1.1 and SQuAD 2.0, respectively. **Right:** osine dissimilarity for different partitions of the test set (based on the predicted values of a RoBERTa regressor), comparing the ground truth answers in Pirá with answers generated by two DiltilBERT models fine-tuned on SQuAD 1.1 and SQuAD 2.0, respectively.

Figure 3(b) shows the results for both QA models. Answer dissimilarity, as measured by the cosine distance of sentence embeddings, tends to fall for smaller partitions; in other words, answers get better when more meaningful questions are selected, similarly to what was observed for F1-score. As was the case for F1-score, SQuAD 1.1 performs better than SQuAD 2.0.

The results obtained here are considerably worse than the results of the original SQuAD 1.1 and SQuAD 2.0 datasets. As reported in the original papers, a F1-score of 51 can be achieved with a strong logistic regression model for SQuAD 1.1 [19], and neural models can achieve a F1-score of 86 on SQuAD 1.1 and 66 on SQuAD 2.0 [18]. What explains the worse results for Pirá 2.0? Part of the gap may be explained by the non-extractive nature of its answers and the technical nature of the supporting texts. Another hypothesis is that our regressor is unable to detect levels of answerability. In order to test this possibility, we used the ground truth evaluations of question meaningfulness from Pirá to partition the dataset, instead of the predictions based on the regressor. Although this information is never present in real applications, this analysis may point to shortcomings derived from our prediction process. Figure 4(a) shows the results in F1-score for both QA models, for each level of meaningfulness.

It seems counter-intuitive that lower quality questions (according to the annotators' evaluations) achieve higher F1-scores. One reason for that may be a problem with human evaluations, perhaps due to a flawed instruction process. Nonetheless, we must also consider the small number of examples of low meaningful questions (cf. Fig. 1). One of the reasons our regressor may perform badly is because our regression model did not have access to many questions with a low degree of meaningfulness. For the larger group of questions evaluated from 3 to 5, F1-score seems to work more or less as expected.

474   P. Pirozelli et al.

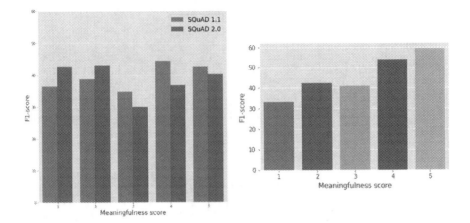

Fig. 4. Left: Average F1-score for each level of question meaningfulness (based on ground truth evaluations), comparing the original answers from Pirá and answers generated by two DistilBERT answerer models fine-tuned on SQuAD 1.1 and SQuAD 2.0, respectively. **Right:** Average F1-score for each level of question meaningfulness (based on ground truth evaluations), comparing the original and validation answers from Pirá.

As a final test, we evaluated whether part of the explanation for the low F1-score we got was not also caused by limitations in answerer models. In order to assess that, we tested the agreement, measured by F1-score, between answers given in the QA creation phase and those given in the evaluation phase. Again, we used real assessments of question meaningfulness as the criterion for partitioning the test set. Figure 4(b) presents the results for this test. A few facts can be observed. First, F1-score is considerably higher here than in previous tests, in which the generated answers were taken into account. Second, except for a slight oscillation for intermediary values, the F1-score demonstrates a consistent behavior, achieving larger values as the level of meaningfulness grows.

5 Discussion

The two experiments run in this work have shown that filtering out inadequate questions leads to better QA systems. Developing models that decide which questions to answer can help to achieve greater control over the quality of the answers. Results, however, were less than ideal, as the two trained models—the classifier and the regressor—were only relatively successful in selecting which questions should be passed to the answerer system. Therefore, if a dual system is to be implemented, better filtering models are highly needed.

For our first experiment on classification, the difficulty seems to derive from the nature of SQuAD 2.0, which has purposely-generated plausible unanswered questions. Unswerability appears to involve subtle elements that are not always captured by language models restricted to word correlations. More generally, common causes that affect the performance of answer triggering systems are related to syntactic bias (paying more attention to the structure of an answer than to its content); the presence of irrelevant information within the target answer; and lexical ambiguities [1].

As for the second experiment with Pirá, the limitations seem to be caused by a non-systematic annotation process. That feeling is strengthened by qualitative analysis of the dataset. In particular, when evaluating a question's meaningfulness, a number of aspects were often conflated by annotators: grammaticality, answerability, and context.

Our filtering system has been focused on finding low-quality questions, understood as those questions that cannot be correctly answered or that are ill-formulated. This filtering process, however, could be extended to a number of other situations. In particular, developing question filtering models is a real necessity for high-risk AI systems, since sensitive contexts demand that QA models avoid answering some questions. More importantly, these systems require a strict control over answer certainty. A separate module for filtering questions may, thus, provide a modular and inspectable tool.

Finally, as the small number of datasets available show, more answer triggering resources are needed. Particularly valuable would be datasets containing fine-grained annotations beyond simple answerability (binary) labels, such as annotations focused on the sources of low-quality in questions—e.g., grammar issues, lack of contextual information, ambiguity. Furthermore, it is important to develop filtering systems that can classify questions with respect to features other than accuracy, such as language toxicity [25], or based on conversational attributes, such as sensibleness, specificity, and interestingness [23].

6   Conclusion

In this paper, we have explored whether filtering models can contribute to control the quality of answers generated by answerer models. Two experiments were conducted: a classification task, with the aim of finding answerable questions; and a regression task, in which we predicted the degree of meaningfulness of questions. For both tasks, results showed a correlation between the ability to filter some questions and the quality of the answers generated.

The analysis conducted in this paper is a first step in the attempt to investigate modular approaches to QA systems and, in particular, on detached models that can select questions and control answer quality. In the future, we wish to expand this investigation in a number of directions. First, we want to develop better QA filtering systems, perhaps with the employment of specifically-developed architectures. Second, we want to train these models in multiple datasets, hoping that information from multiple sources can assist the task of discovering more general clues on answerability. Finally, we intend to explore filtering system where the task is to avoid answering sensitive questions and where high confidence in responses is needed.

References

1. Acheampong, K.N., Tian, W., Sifah, E.B., Opuni-Boachie, K.O.-A.: The emergence, advancement and future of textual answer triggering. In: Arai, K., Kapoor, S., Bhatia, R. (eds.) SAI 2020. AISC, vol. 1229, pp. 674–693. Springer, Cham (2020). https://doi.org/10.1007/978-3-030-52246-9_50
2. Paschoal, A.F.A., et al.: Pirá: a bilingual portuguese-english dataset for question-answering about the ocean. In: 30th ACM International Conference on Information and Knowledge Management (CIKM 2021) (2021). https://doi.org/10.1145/3459637.3482012
3. Brown, T.B., et al.: Language models are few-shot learners. CoRR abs/2005.14165 (2020). https://arxiv.org/abs/2005.14165
4. Chen, D., Fisch, A., Weston, J., Bordes, A.: Reading Wikipedia to answer open-domain questions. In: Barzilay, R., Kan, M. (eds.) Proceedings of the 55th Annual Meeting of the Association for Computational Linguistics, ACL 2017, Vancouver, Canada, 30 July–4 August, Volume 1: Long Papers, pp. 1870–1879. Association for Computational Linguistics (2017). https://doi.org/10.18653/v1/P17-1171
5. Devlin, J., Chang, M., Lee, K., Toutanova, K.: BERT: pre-training of deep bidirectional transformers for language understanding. In: Burstein, J., Doran, C., Solorio, T. (eds.) Proceedings of the 2019 Conference of the North American Chapter of the Association for Computational Linguistics: Human Language Technologies, NAACL-HLT 2019, Minneapolis, MN, USA, 2–7 June 2019, Volume 1 (Long and Short Papers), pp. 4171–4186. Association for Computational Linguistics (2019). https://doi.org/10.18653/v1/n19-1423
6. European-Commission: Proposal for a regulation laying down harmonised rules on artificial intelligence (artificial intelligence act) and amending certain union legislative acts (2021). https://eur-lex.europa.eu/legal-content/EN/TXT/HTML/?uri=CELEX:52021PC0206&from=EN#footnote8
7. Ferrucci, D.A.: Introduction to "this is watson". IBM J. Res. Dev. **56**(3), 1 (2012). https://doi.org/10.1147/JRD.2012.2184356
8. Jurczyk, T., Zhai, M., Choi, J.D.: SelQA: a new benchmark for selection-based question answering. In: 28th IEEE International Conference on Tools with Artificial Intelligence, ICTAI 2016, San Jose, CA, USA, 6–8 November 2016, pp. 820–827. IEEE Computer Society (2016). https://doi.org/10.1109/ICTAI.2016.0128
9. Kadavath, S., et al.: Language models (mostly) know what they know (2022). https://arxiv.org/abs/2207.05221
10. Karpukhin, V., et al.: Dense passage retrieval for open-domain question answering. In: Webber, B., Cohn, T., He, Y., Liu, Y. (eds.) Proceedings of the 2020 Conference on Empirical Methods in Natural Language Processing, EMNLP 2020, Online, 16–20 November 2020, pp. 6769–6781. Association for Computational Linguistics (2020). https://doi.org/10.18653/v1/2020.emnlp-main.550
11. Lan, Z., Chen, M., Goodman, S., Gimpel, K., Sharma, P., Soricut, R.: ALBERT: a lite BERT for self-supervised learning of language representations. In: 8th International Conference on Learning Representations, ICLR 2020, Addis Ababa, Ethiopia, 26–30 April 2020. OpenReview.net (2020). https://openreview.net/forum?id=H1eA7AEtvS
12. Lewis, M., et al.: BART: denoising sequence-to-sequence pre-training for natural language generation, translation, and comprehension. In: Jurafsky, D., Chai, J., Schluter, N., Tetreault, J.R. (eds.) Proceedings of the 58th Annual Meeting of the Association for Computational Linguistics, ACL 2020, Online, 5–10 July 2020, pp.

7871–7880. Association for Computational Linguistics (2020). https://doi.org/10.18653/v1/2020.acl-main.703

13. Lewis, P.S.H., et al.: Retrieval-augmented generation for knowledge-intensive NLP tasks. In: Larochelle, H., Ranzato, M., Hadsell, R., Balcan, M., Lin, H. (eds.) Advances in Neural Information Processing Systems, vol. 33, Annual Conference on Neural Information Processing Systems 2020, NeurIPS 2020, 6–12 December 2020, virtual (2020)

14. Liu, C., Lowe, R., Serban, I., Noseworthy, M., Charlin, L., Pineau, J.: How NOT to evaluate your dialogue system: an empirical study of unsupervised evaluation metrics for dialogue response generation. In: Su, J., Carreras, X., Duh, K. (eds.) Proceedings of the 2016 Conference on Empirical Methods in Natural Language Processing, EMNLP 2016, Austin, Texas, USA, 1–4 November 2016, pp. 2122–2132. The Association for Computational Linguistics (2016). https://doi.org/10.18653/v1/d16-1230

15. Liu, Y., et al.: RoBERTa: a robustly optimized BERT pretraining approach. CoRR abs/1907.11692 (2019). http://arxiv.org/abs/1907.11692

16. Radford, A., Narasimhan, K., Salimans, T., Sutskever, I., et al.: Improving language understanding by generative pre-training (2018)

17. Raffel, C., et al.: Exploring the limits of transfer learning with a unified text-to-text transformer. J. Mach. Learn. Res. **21**, 140:1–140:67 (2020). http://jmlr.org/papers/v21/20-074.html

18. Rajpurkar, P., Jia, R., Liang, P.: Know what you don't know: unanswerable questions for squad. In: Gurevych, I., Miyao, Y. (eds.) Proceedings of the 56th Annual Meeting of the Association for Computational Linguistics, ACL 2018, Melbourne, Australia, 15–20 July 2018, Volume 2: Short Papers, pp. 784–789. Association for Computational Linguistics (2018). https://doi.org/10.18653/v1/P18-2124

19. Rajpurkar, P., Zhang, J., Lopyrev, K., Liang, P.: Squad: 100, 000+ questions for machine comprehension of text. In: Su, J., Carreras, X., Duh, K. (eds.) Proceedings of the 2016 Conference on Empirical Methods in Natural Language Processing, EMNLP, Austin, Texas, USA, 1–4 November 2016, pp. 2383–2392. The Association for Computational Linguistics (2016). https://doi.org/10.18653/v1/d16-1264

20. Reimers, N., Gurevych, I.: Sentence-BERT: sentence embeddings using Siamese BERT-networks. In: Inui, K., Jiang, J., Ng, V., Wan, X. (eds.) Proceedings of the 2019 Conference on Empirical Methods in Natural Language Processing and the 9th International Joint Conference on Natural Language Processing, EMNLP-IJCNLP 2019, Hong Kong, China, 3–7 November 2019, pp. 3980–3990. Association for Computational Linguistics (2019). https://doi.org/10.18653/v1/D19-1410

21. Rogers, A., Kovaleva, O., Downey, M., Rumshisky, A.: Getting closer to AI complete question answering: a set of prerequisite real tasks. In: The Thirty-Fourth AAAI Conference on Artificial Intelligence, AAAI 2020, The Thirty-Second Innovative Applications of Artificial Intelligence Conference, IAAI 2020, The Tenth AAAI Symposium on Educational Advances in Artificial Intelligence, EAAI 2020, New York, NY, USA, 7–12 February 2020, pp. 8722–8731. AAAI Press (2020). https://ojs.aaai.org/index.php/AAAI/article/view/6398

22. Sanh, V., Debut, L., Chaumond, J., Wolf, T.: DistilBERT, a distilled version of BERT: smaller, faster, cheaper and lighter. CoRR abs/1910.01108 (2019). http://arxiv.org/abs/1910.01108

23. Thoppilan, R., et al.: LaMDA: language models for dialog applications (2022)

24. Wang, B., Yao, T., Zhang, Q., Xu, J., Wang, X.: ReCO: a large scale Chinese reading comprehension dataset on opinion. CoRR abs/2006.12146 (2020). https://arxiv.org/abs/2006.12146

25. Welbl, J., et al.: Challenges in detoxifying language models. In: Findings of the Association for Computational Linguistics: EMNLP 2021, pp. 2447–2469. Association for Computational Linguistics, November 2021. https://doi.org/10.18653/v1/2021.findings-emnlp.210

26. Yang, Y., Yih, W.T., Meek, C.: WikiQA: a challenge dataset for open-domain question answering. In: Proceedings of the 2015 Conference on Empirical Methods in Natural Language Processing, pp. 2013–2018. Association for Computational Linguistics, Lisbon, September 2015. https://doi.org/10.18653/v1/D15-1237

Deep Learning-Based Abstractive Summarization for Brazilian Portuguese Texts

Pedro H. Paiola[✉][iD], Gustavo H. de Rosa[iD], and João P. Papa[iD]

Department of Computing, São Paulo State University, Bauru, SP, Brazil
{pedro.paiola,gustavo.rosa,joao.papa}@unesp.br

Abstract. Automatic summarization captures the most relevant information and condenses it into an understandable text in natural language. Such a task can be classified as either extractive or abstractive summarization. Research on Brazilian Portuguese-based abstractive summarization is still scarce. This work explores abstractive summarization in Portuguese-based texts using a deep learning-based approach. The results are relatively satisfactory considering the ROUGE measurements and the quality of the generated summaries. Still, there are some problems regarding coherence, readability, and grammar. We strongly believe they are linked to the inherent complexity of generating an abstract and the degradation of text quality by the translation steps. These results should be seen as preliminary, serving as a basis for future research.

Keywords: Natural language processing · Machine learning · Summarization · Abstractive summarization · Brazilian Portuguese

1 Introduction

Text summarization aims at furnishing outlines from source texts, describing their most valuable information in just a few sentences. A summary depicts the primary information of a source text and assists humans in deciding whether such a text is relevant or not to their reading. Additionally, one can perceive that summarization is extremely useful due to the increasing data growth, where it attempts to diminish effort and time when searching for pertinent information.

The advance of some research areas, such as Natural Language Processing (NLP), has enabled improvements of automatic summarization methods. Nevertheless, such a process is not straightforward since the most relevant information must be correctly captured from a text and condensed into an understandable natural language. Furthermore, such a task does not have an optimal answer as humans can produce completely different summaries when analyzing the same text.

Recently, the literature has proposed to classify summarization methods in two categories: (i) extractive summarization, which identifies the most important sentences from the source text and composes the summary using them,

© The Author(s), under exclusive license to Springer Nature Switzerland AG 2022
J. C. Xavier-Junior and R. A. Rios (Eds.): BRACIS 2022, LNAI 13654, pp. 479–493, 2022.
https://doi.org/10.1007/978-3-031-21689-3_34

and (ii) abstractive summarization, which generates new sentences based on the most relevant information from the source text [23]. Abstractive summarization poses a more complex task due to the difficulty in generating natural language; however, it can produce texts closer to human-based writing.

Regarding English-based summarization, Raffel et al. [31] proposed the T5 (Text-to-Text Transfer Transformer) framework, which fine-tunes a pre-trained model on various downstream tasks, such as summarization, question answering and text classification. Furthermore, Zhang et al. [44] proposed a BERT pre-training stage with an abstractive summarization-tailored objective and achieved better effectiveness and efficiency, while Song et al. [37] improved the quality of abstract summaries by controlling the number of verbatim copies.

On the other hand, Portuguese-based automatic summarization is scarce, where most works are focused on extractive summarization [28,32,33], specially multi-document extractive summarization [11,36]. In particular, very few abstractive summarization methods were found, mainly on sentence compression [21,25,29], which can be applied to produce abstractive summaries, and opinion summarization based on a template-based approach [8] or on a AMR (Abstract Meaning Representation) based approach [14]. In this work, we use a deep learning-based approach to perform abstractive summarization, applied to Portuguese datasets, such as TeMário [27] and CSTNews [17], and multilingual datasets that include Portuguese texts, such as WikiLingua [16] and XL-Sum [13].

Therefore, the main contributions of this paper are two-fold: (i) to explore abstractive summarization in Portuguese texts, and (ii) to apply deep learning approach to Portuguese-based abstractive summarization, obtaining reasonable results, even considering the low amount of resources in Portuguese datasets. Section 2 presents a literature review concerning the main topic addressed here, and Sect. 3 discusses the methodology considered in this work. Experiments are detailed in Sect. 4, and conclusions and future works are stated in Sect. 5.

2   Literature Review

Extractive summarizers have implicit limitations as they cannot generate new sentences; hence, they may face a series of problems, such as cohesion, readability, and lack of quality. On the other hand, abstractive summarizers can generate new sentences and overcome such difficulties, yet, they pose as more complex tasks when compared to extractive-based techniques.

The most common approach to performing abstract summarization concerns deep learning (DL) architectures, which constitute end-to-end approaches that learn how to abstract essential information without resorting to middleware tasks, such as information extraction, content selection, and sentence generation. Nevertheless, when working with deep learning, one has less control over the learning and generation processes, making it difficult to precisely identify what the model is learning and how it is extracting/encoding text information [19]. Additionally, some recent challenges are how to define the level of abstraction and the length of the final summary, i.e., when to stop generating text.

Most DL-based approaches use Encoder-Decoder models, such as the standard Seq2Seq architecture. Both encoder and decoder are neural networks, where the former is responsible for converting words into vectors and capturing the context, while the latter predicts the next token based on previous ones [12]. Rush et al. [34] proposed the first abstractive summarization work using such an approach, which is also based on attention mechanisms and denoted as Attention-Based Summarization (ABS). Recently, Raffel et al. [31] proposed an alternative to abstractive summarization denoted as T5 (Text-to-Text Transfer Transformer), which employs transfer learning to fine-tune downstream tasks, such as automatic summarization, question answering, text classification and translation, among others.

The rise of pre-trained models, such as BERT [9], has provided a great benefit to abstractive summarization methods. Zhang et al. [44], for instance, proposed a BERT-based system denoted as PEGASUS, which conducts a pre-training step similar to the summarization task and allows a better and faster fine-tuning procedure. In practice, the authors use BERT's masking words technique to complete the sentences and enable the model to identify the gaps. Additionally, the authors performed an experimental evaluation over six different datasets, achieving state-of-the-art results with only $1,000$ samples, showing that pre-trained models are interesting alternatives to overcome the abstractive summarization task.

A key problem of automatic summarization is how to evaluate a certain method, determining the quality of its candidate summaries. The evaluation measures most used in the literature are those belonging to the ROUGE (Recall-Oriented Understudy for Gisting Evaluation) package [18], which consists of a set of content-based measures, calculated from the number of overlapping n-grams between the candidate summary (system generated summary) and the reference summary (human written summary). Although ROUGE is the most used measure, it has a series of limitations and problems. For example, as the calculation of the ROUGE score is performed from the overlapping n-grams, if a summary presents the same content as the reference summary, containing the same ideas, but using different expressions, the final score should not be very high, despite the quality of the summary. Therefore, it suffers especially in the evaluation of abstractive summaries [12]. For this reason, there are proposals for several other summary evaluation measures [30,39,43,45,46]; however, they are still little used for various reasons such as computational cost, lack of an evaluation protocol and difficulty in comparing them with each other, especially in real scenarios, different from those used in the original experiments [10].

2.1 Automatic Summarization in Brazilian Portuguese

Although one can refer to some state-of-the-art research concerning English-based abstractive summarization, few works deal with such a task when applied to Brazilian Portuguese. The main reason lies in the small number of Portuguese-annotated datasets compared to English-based ones. Most of these works focus on sentence compression task [21,25,29]. The method presented by Condori and Pardo [8] uses a template-based approach for summarizing opinions, a specific domain of multi-document summarization. Other method presented by Inácio [14] also proposes an opinion summarization model, but AMR-based [1].

On the other hand, several works on Portuguese-based extractive summarization can be found, especially considering multi-document summarization. One of the first Portuguese-based extractive summarization works, denoted as Gist-Summ, was proposed by Pardo et al. [28]. The idea represents the text with a unique sentence (gist-sentence) and the text information that complements it. To determine the relevance degree of each sentence, GistSumm provides two options: (i) keyword matching [3], and (ii) TF-ISF (Term Frequency-Inverse Sentence Frequency) [24]. The former method employs a score relative to each word's occurrences in the text and scores a sentence using its words' scores sum, while the latter method uses a score based on the number of times a word has occurred in the sentence and the inverse number of sentences in which the word has appeared.

Rino et al. [32] proposed the SuPor, which uses a Bayesian classifier to estimate the relevance of sentences based on a set of attributes, such as sentence length, word frequency, sentence or paragraph location, and the occurrence of proper nouns. Moreover, SuPor uses lexical chains [2], and a map of relationships [35] to maintain the summary cohesion. A more recent work proposed by Rocha et al. [33], denoted as PragmaSUM, introduces an extractive summarization method that allows users to personify summaries through keywords, seeking to improve their accuracy and performance.

Sodre et al. [36] introduced a set of regression algorithms to estimate an importance score for sentences in a text considering the task of multi-document summarization. The authors also used several pre-processing techniques, such as Part-of-Speech tagging, named entity recognition, and removal of stopwords. Their experimental results showed that the Bayesian regression algorithm obtained the best ROUGE-1 metrics across the CSTNews dataset. Some additional works that deal with multi-document summarization are the CST-Summ [5] and RC-4 [6].

2.2   Cross-Lingual Summarization

As presented earlier, the most common approach to performing automatic summarization is based on deep learning. However, these models are heavily data-driven, i.e., a large number of texts annotated with summaries is required to train them effectively. For this reason, most summarization works are centered around the English language, due to the availability of large datasets. [13]. In this sense, cross-lingual summarization can provide promising means to explore the performance of text summarization in other languages, such as Portuguese, where the amount of available data is scarce.

The cross-lingual summarization process consists of generating a summary in the target language from the given document in a different source language. This task could be performed by combining a monolingual summarization system with an machine translation system, but both of which are unsolved natural language processing tasks, which makes cross-lingual summarization even more challenging. From this pipeline, we can describe two different approaches [42]: summarize-then-translate and translate-then-summarize. The first approach is preferable, since the translation is applied to summary, i.e., to a smaller number of sentences, avoiding a higher rate of errors resulting from the translation and requiring less computational effort. However, this approach is only applicable when there is a high-resource summary database available for the source text language. Otherwise, the translate-then-summarize approach becomes the only viable option [26].

3 Methodology

This section presents the proposed approach, the datasets and methodology used for training and evaluating the summarization models.

3.1 Datasets

One of the most well-known Portuguese corpora focused on summarization is the TeMário dataset [27], which is composed of journalistic text and their corresponding summaries. The summaries were written by a professional summarizer, a teacher, and a text editor consultant. Additionally, TeMário is composed of 100 documents and $61,412$ words, whose annotated summaries correspond to approximately 25–30% of the source text sizes. In 2006, this dataset was extended to TeMário 2006 [22], which adds roughly 150 new texts to the original corpus.

Another benchmark dataset, yet focused on multi-document summaries, concerns the CSTNews [5,17], which is composed of 50 text collections, where each collection corresponds to a particular subject and has roughly 4 documents. Additionally, each collection is annotated with a summary and meta-information, while each document is annotated with a reference summary.

More recently, new multilingual dataset that includes Portuguese texts have also been proposed: WikiLingua [16] and XL-Sum [13]. The first one includes texts in 18 languages, with 141,457 articles in English and 81,695 in Portuguese, each corresponding to some English article. WikiLingua's texts consist of tutorials taken from the WikiHow page. XL-Sum, in turn, comprises texts in 44 languages, with 301,444 samples in English and 23,521 in Portuguese (later the authors made available a dataset only with texts in Portuguese, containing 71,752 samples), in which the texts consist of news extracted from the British Broadcasting Corporation (BBC) page. A great advantage of these corpora, for Portuguese-based summarization studies, is the amount of samples annotated with summaries, considerably higher in relation to previous corpora.

3.2 Proposed Approach

Considering the reported performance of pre-trained models in other summarization systems, some of them trained with datasets with few resources, this approach was chosen for training abstractive summarization models. The pre-trained model selected was the PTT5 [7], which consists of the T5 model pre-trained with the corpus brWaC [41]. This approach is illustrated by Fig. 1.

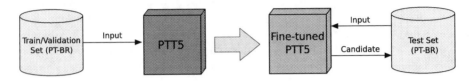

Fig. 1. Pipeline used to conduct Portuguese-based abstractive summarization through the fine-tuning of the PTT5 model.

With the pre-trained PTT5 model, a fine-tuning was performed on each of the chosen datasets. The models fine-tuned in the WikiLingua and XL-Sum datasets also underwent a second fine-tuning in the TeMário and CSTNews databases. The idea of this second fine-tuning is to verify, considering the small amount of samples from these last two datasets, if the models are able to adapt the "knowledge" they acquired in the larger datasets to obtain better results in the low-resources datasets.

The training of the models was implemented using the Python language and the Transformers and PyTorch modules. For the optimization, the Adam algorithm [15] was used, varying the learning rate between 3×10^{-5} and 3×10^{-4}. The models were trained on an NVidia K80 GPU, with 16 GB of RAM, for 30 epochs. Regarding the maximum number of input and output tokens, the values 512 and 150 were used, respectively, for the CSTNews, WikiLingua and XL-Sum databases, and 1024 and 512 for TeMário. The process of splitting the text into tokens, identifying text units, especially words, was performed using the tokenizer of the PTT5 model itself. It is important to highlight that the parameters, in general, were defined empirically, based on the parameters used in other studies, on the characteristics of the datasets and on the limitations of available time and resources. With the models already fine-tuned, the generation of candidate summaries was performed using the beam search algorithm. In this work, $k = 5$ was used as beam width[1].

A problem for the evaluation of these models in TeMario and CSTNews corpora is the absence of a baseline for Abstractive Summarization. For this reason, in an attempt to obtain a guide for comparison, a cross-lingual training was also carried out using the pre-trained T5 [31] model, that allows to perform the abstractive summarization of English texts. Therefore, the translate-then-summarize approach was used, translating TeMário and CSTNews texts into English and fine-tuning the T5 model with these texts, as illustrated in Fig. 2. We have used the Lite-T5 Translation [20] to accomplish the translation between English and Portuguese texts. The candidate summaries produced by the models were evaluated by the set of measures ROUGE.

---

[1] Code and models available at: https://github.com/pedropaiola/ptt5-summ.

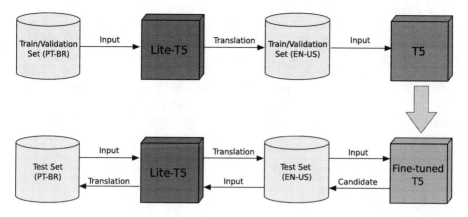

Fig. 2. Pipeline used to conduct Portuguese-based abstractive summarization using cross-lingual training with the T5 model.

4   Experimental Results

In this section, we present the experimental results concerning the methodology proposed in the manuscript. The results were divided into two subsections: the first refers to the WikiLingua and XL-Sum datasets, which are more recent and have a greater amount of annotated data; and the second refers to the TeMário and CSTNews datasets, which have few annotated samples, but are more traditional in automatic summarization research in Portuguese.

4.1   WikiLingua and XL-Sum

The great advantage of the WikiLingua and XL-Sum datasets over TeMário and CSTNews is the fact that they have a large number of samples, which is a particularly important feature for training deep learning models. Table 1 presents the results of the evaluation of the models fine-tuned on these datasets, based on the experiments described in the methodology.

Table 1. Evaluation of models fine-tuned with the WikiLingua and XL-Sum datasets, according to the measures ROUGE-1 (R1), ROUGE-2 (R2) and ROUGE-L (RL)

Dataset	R1	R2	RL
WikiLingua (PTT5)	33.00	12.58	25.39
XL-Sum [13]	37.17	15.90	28.56
XL-Sum (PTT5)	35.42	14.21	26.25

For the WikiLingua dataset, no previous results were found for the Portuguese language. As for XL-Sum, the authors of the dataset present the results of mT5 model fine-tuned to this corpus, performing training with all languages at the same time. For this reason, the trained model provided by the authors was used in this work, and the training was not replicated. The results of the monolingual model fine-tuned in this work are slightly lower than in the original article. This result is reasonable, since, on the one hand, several studies show that models pre-trained in only one language present better results in this same language than models pre-trained in multilingual corpora [4,38,40], an example being the PTT5 [7] itself, on the other hand, multilingual fine-tuning for a given task can lead to better results, especially for low-resources languages, as presented in the paper referring to the XL-Sum corpus [13] itself.

4.2   TeMario and CSTNews

Unlike WikiLingua and XL-Sum datasets, Temário and CSTNews have few resources, which makes it difficult for deep learning models to learn. Table 2 shows the evaluations of the summaries generated by the PTT5 models fine-tuned in the TeMário corpus, as well as by the T5 model applied to the translated texts of this corpus, according to the ROUGE measures. The PTT5-A and PTT5-B models were fine-tuned directly on the TeMário dataset, and they differ from each other only by the size of the summaries generated, with the second model generating longer summaries. The PTT5-C and PTT5-D models were previously fine-tuned on the WikiLingua and XL-Sum datasets, respectively, and then underwent a second fine-tuning in the TeMário dataset.

Table 2. Results of models fine-tuned on the TeMário dataset, evaluated with the measures ROUGE-1 (R1), ROUGE-2 (R2) and ROUGE-L (RL)

Model	R1	R2	RL
T5	43, 38	14, 26	24, 47
PTT5-A	43, 90	19, 15	27, 11
PTT5-B	48, 78	20, 45	29, 26
PTT5-C (WikiLingua)	**49, 91**	**20, 96**	**29, 84**
PTT5-D (XL-Sum)	47, 95	19, 32	27, 81

The PTT5-C model obtained the best results in all measurements used. However, the differences are not very significant for the other PTT5 models, especially between the PTT5-B and PTT5-C models. The greatest difference was the evaluation of the PPT5-A model by the ROUGE-1 measure, which obtained a value between 4.05 to 6.01 lower than the other models.

Now, for the CSTNews dataset, the Table 3 presents the evaluations of the summaries generated by the models fine-tuned in this corpus, similarly to the presentation of the results for TeMário.

As for the models fine-tuned in TeMário, the results of the PTT5 models do not differ much from each other. However, in this case, the best measurements

Table 3. Results of models fine-tuned on the CSTNews dataset, evaluated with the measures ROUGE-1 (R1), ROUGE-2 (R2) and ROUGE-L (RL)

Model	R1	R2	RL
T5	44, 56	19, 16	31, 83
PTT5-E	52, 48	**35, 62**	**41, 78**
PTT5-F	52, 64	34, 04	40, 74
PTT5-G (WikiLingua)	**54, 15**	34, 53	41, 01
PTT5-H (XL-Sum)	52, 34	33, 33	38, 42

obtained do not correspond to a single model. The PTT5-E was the best evaluated by ROUGE-2 and ROUGE-L and the PTT5-G by ROUGE-1. Also, as for TeMário, all PTT5 models performed better than the cross-lingual summarization model using the T5.

To better understand these results, one could evaluate the level of compression and abstractness of the summaries produced by these models. These results were omitted in this article, due to page limitations, but in general they point out that ROUGE measures benefit more the models that present a lower abstractness and a compression closer to the compression of the reference summaries.

To more conclusively determine the quality of each of these models, it would be necessary to carry out a qualitative evaluation of the candidate summaries of each one, which would require more time and human effort. Trying to somehow make up for the lack of an adequate qualitative analysis, below is an example of a text from CSTNews with their respective candidate and reference summaries. The analysis of this case does not allow to obtain deeper conclusions about the quality of the models, but it can help in the understanding of their functioning.

Summarization Example in the CSTNews Dataset. Below is an example of the source text and its reference summary, present in the CSTNews, followed by the candidate summaries produced by each of the models presented above.

Source Text

O Parlamento da Turquia aprovou por ampla maioria (507 votos contra 19), nesta quarta-feira, um pedido do governo para permitir que tropas do país cruzem a fronteira para o norte do Iraque, a fim de combater rebeldes separatistas curdos refugiados na região montanhosa. A medida fez com que o preço do petróleo disparasse no cenário internacional, mas a Petrobras garantiu que isso não interferirá no mercado de combustíveis brasileiro.

Pouco antes de o Congresso dar o sinal verde à operação militar, o primeiro-ministro da Turquia, o islamita Recep Tayyip Erdogan, disse que "a paciência do povo turco se esgotou" com as ações dos guerrilheiros separatistas curdos do Partido dos Trabalhadores do Curdistão (conhecido como PKK) que estão refugiados no Norte do Iraque.

A possibilidade de incursão militar da Turquia, que é membro da Otan (organização militar que reúne 26 países, entre eles EUA, Grã-Bretanha, França e Alemanha), no Iraque está deixando a Casa Branca em estado de alerta. O presidente dos EUA,

George W. Bush, pediu nesta quarta-feira que o Exército turco busque uma solução diplomática para a questão.

Washington teme que uma incursão turca possa desestabilizar a mais pacífica região iraquiana e, provavelmente, toda a região do Oriente Médio, levando o Irã, seu arqui-inimigo, a intervir.

A Comissão Européia, por sua vez, exortou a Turquia a respeitar a integridade do território iraquiano. [...]

- É crucial que a Turquia continue a atacar esse problema pela cooperação entre as autoridades relevantes - declarou Krisztina Nagy, porta-voz da Comissão Européia.

Erdogan deu de ombros às preocupações de aliados da Otan:
- O que importa é o que o Parlamento diz.

O premier está sob forte pressão interna por causa de uma série de ataques cometidos por guerrilheiros curdos que usam o Norte do Iraque como base. Em Istambul, maior cidade turca, professores e estudantes realizaram grande manifestação contra o terrorismo e a política externa dos EUA.

Reference Summary
O Parlamento da Turquia aprovou um pedido do governo para permitir que tropas do país cruzem a fronteira do Iraque, a fim de combater rebeldes separatistas curdos. O presidente dos EUA, George W. Bush, pediu que o Exército turco busque uma solução diplomática para a questão sob o risco de uma invasão iraniana nessa região do Iraque. A Comissão Européia, por sua vez, exortou a Turquia a respeitar a integridade do território iraquiano. No entanto, o premier turco, Edorgan, que está sob forte pressão devido aos ataques dos guerrilheiros curdos na fronteira, deu de ombros às preocupações de aliados da Otan.

T5 Candidate Summary
O parlamento da Turquia adotou um pedido de autorização de tropas do país para atravessar a fronteira ao norte do Iraque, com o objetivo de combater as rebeliões dos refugiados caribenhos na região serrana. A medida provocou a pressão do petróleo para desencadear o cenário internacional, mas a petroBRA garantiu que isso não interferisse no mercado brasileiro de combustíveis. A possibilidade de uma incursão na Turquia está deixando o centro de atenção e o presidente norte-americano George W. Bush, na quarta-feira, pediu a ação turca para buscar a solução diplomática para o tema.

PTT5-E Candidate Summary
O parlamento da Turquia aprovou por ampla maioria (507 votos contra 19), nesta quarta-feira, um pedido do governo para permitir que tropas do país cruzem a fronteira para o norte do Iraque, a fim de combater rebeldes separatistas curdos refugiados na região montanhosa. A medida fez com que o preço do petróleo disparasse no mercado internacional, mas a Petrobras garantiu que isso não interferirá no abastecimento de combustíveis brasileiro. Pouco antes de o congresso dar o sinal verde para a operação militar, o primeiro-ministro dos EUA, Tayyip Erdogan, disse que "a paciência do

PTT5-F Candidate Summary

O parlamento da Turquia aprovou por ampla maioria (507 votos contra 19), nesta quarta-feira, um pedido do governo para permitir que tropas do país cruzem a fronteira para o norte do Iraque, a fim de combater rebeldes separatistas curdos refugiados na região montanhosa. A medida fez com que o preço do petróleo disparasse no mercado internacional, mas a Petrobras garantiu que isso não interferirá no abastecimento de combustíveis brasileiro. Pouco antes de o congresso dar o sinal verde para a operação militar, o primeiro-ministro dos EUA, Tayyip Erdogan, disse que "a paciência do povo turco se esgotou" com as ações dos guerrilheiros do partido dos trabalhadores do curdistão (conhecido como PKK) que estão refugiados no norte. O exército turco teme que uma incursão turca possa desestabilizar a mais pacífica região do Oriente Médio, levando o Irã, seu arquiinimigo, à intervir. as autoridades

PTT5-G (WikiLingua) Candidate Summary

O parlamento da Turquia aprovou por ampla maioria (507 votos contra 19), nesta quarta-feira, um pedido do governo para permitir que tropas do país cruzem a fronteira para o norte do Iraque, a fim de combater rebeldes separatistas curdos refugiados na região montanhosa. O presidente dos EUA, George W. Bush, pediu para que o exército turco busque uma solução diplomática para a questão. A comissão européia, por sua vez, exortou o governo a respeitar a integridade do território iraquiano.

PTT5-H (XL-Sum) Candidate Summary

O parlamento da Turquia aprovou, por ampla maioria, um pedido do governo para permitir que tropas do país cruzem a fronteira para o norte do Iraque, a fim de combater rebeldes separatistas curdos que estão refugiados na região montanhosa. O presidente dos EUA, George W. Bush, pediu nesta quarta-feira que o exército turco busque uma solução diplomática para a questão. A comissão européia exortou o primeiro-ministro e o premier a atacar esse problema pela cooperação entre as autoridades.

Analysis of Summaries

Analyzing the T5 model, it is possible to observe very clearly the effect of text quality degradation resulting from the translation phases. The candidate summary has several errors in sentences, sometimes presenting errors of fact, such as referring to "rebeldes separativas curdos" as "refugiados caribenhos". However, in general, the model is capable of summarizing the source text, bringing some of its main information.

One of the first facts that can be noticed about the PTT5 models is that although the first fine-tuning with the WikiLingua or XL-Sum datasets did not produce great differences in the evaluation of the models, the difference in the way the summaries are generated is remarkable.

The PTT5-E and PTT5-F models are almost limited to copying the source text. PTT5-F only at the end of the text omits a few sentences (the third paragraph of the source text) and makes a few changes, which are incorrect, referring to Tayyip Erdogan as prime minister of the US, not Turkey, and replacing "Washington" by "exército turco" in the last sentence of the summary.

The last two models present a better performance, generating smaller candidates and all their sentences correspond to the information highlighted in the reference summary. Both models also demonstrate their capacity for abstraction by making certain changes to sentences, such as PTT5-G suppressing the date of George Bush's request, and PTT5-H removing the date and amount of votes from the Turkish Parliament. The only problem identified was in the last sentence of the summary of PTT5-H, in which the prime minister and the premier are referred to as if they were different people.

However, it is important to point out that these last two models do not always produce summaries with this level of quality, and in other texts they also present a higher level of factual errors and hallucinations, for example.

5   Conclusions

The results obtained by the experiments described in this paper are promising, considering there is a scarcity of other works that explore abstractive summarization in Portuguese, mainly according to a deep learning-based approach. Training on the larger WikiLingua and XL-Sum datasets yielded satisfactory results. XL-Sum, in particular, there is a baseline from the work of the authors of the corpus. Our model did not outperform the original results, but remained close.

On the other hand, training with the TeMário and CSTNews datasets, more traditional in automatic summarization studies in Portuguese, imposed more challenges, mainly due to the small number of annotated samples. Even so, the results were reasonably satisfactory considering the ROUGE measures and when analyzing the summaries produced themselves.

The fine-tuned models presented in this paper still present a series of problems, mainly in relation to coherence and correspondence with the facts brought by the source text. However, these are challenges inherent to abstractive summarization, to the best of our knowledge these are the first results of abstractive summarization in the TeMário and CSTNews datasets using deep learning. Henceforth, this work may become a starting point for new studies.

References

1. Banarescu, L., et al.: Abstract meaning representation for sembanking. In: Proceedings of the 7th Linguistic Annotation Workshop and Interoperability with Discourse, pp. 178–186 (2013)
2. Barzilay, R., Elhadad, M.: Using lexical chains for text summarization. In: Mani, I., Maybury, M.T. (eds.) Advances in Automatic Text Summarization, pp. 111–121. The MIT Press, Cambridge (1999)
3. Black, W.J., Johnson, F.C.: A practical evaluation of two rule-based automatic abstraction techniques. Expert Syst. Inform. Manage. 1(3), 159–177 (1988)
4. Canete, J., Chaperon, G., Fuentes, R., Ho, J.H., Kang, H., Pérez, J.: Spanish pre-trained bert model and evaluation data. In: PML4DC at ICLR 2020 (2020)
5. Cardoso, P.C., et al.: CSTNews-a discourse-annotated corpus for single and multi-document summarization of news texts in Brazilian Portuguese. In: Proceedings of the 3rd RST Brazilian Meeting, pp. 88–105 (2011)

6. Cardoso, P.C., Pardo, T.A.: Multi-document summarization using semantic discourse models. Procesamiento del Lenguaje Natural **56**, 57–64 (2016)
7. Carmo, D., Piau, M., Campiotti, I., Nogueira, R., Lotufo, R.: Ptt5: pretraining and validating the t5 model on Brazilian Portuguese data. arXiv preprint arXiv:2008.09144 (2020)
8. Condori, R.E.L., Pardo, T.A.S.: Opinion summarization methods: comparing and extending extractive and abstractive approaches. Expert Syst. Appl. **78**, 124–134 (2017)
9. Devlin, J., Chang, M.W., Lee, K., Toutanova, K.: Bert: pre-training of deep bidirectional transformers for language understanding (2018). arXiv preprint ArXiv: 1810.04805
10. Fabbri, A.R., Kryscinski, W., McCann, B., Xiong, C., Socher, R., Radev, D.: SummEval: re-evaluating summarization evaluation (2020). arXiv preprint ArXiv: 2007.12626
11. Gomes, L., Oliveira, H.T.A.: A multi-document summarization system for news articles in Portuguese using integer linear programming. In: Anais do XVI Encontro Nacional de Inteligência Artificial e Computacional, pp. 622–633. Sociedade Brasileira de Computação, Salvador (2019)
12. Gupta, S., Gupta, S.K.: Abstractive summarization: an overview of the state of the art. Expert Syst. Appl. **121**, 49–65 (2019)
13. Hasan, T., et al.: XL-Sum: large-scale multilingual abstractive summarization for 44 languages. In: Findings of the Association for Computational Linguistics: ACL-IJCNLP 2021, pp. 4693–4703. Association for Computational Linguistics, Online, August 2021. https://doi.org/10.18653/v1/2021.findings-acl.413, https://aclanthology.org/2021.findings-acl.413
14. Inácio, M.L.: Sumarização de Opinião com base em Abstract Meaning Representation. Ph.D. thesis, Universidade de São Paulo (2021)
15. Kingma, D.P., Ba, J.: Adam: a method for stochastic optimization (2014). https://doi.org/10.48550/ARXIV.1412.6980, https://arxiv.org/abs/1412.6980
16. Ladhak, F., Durmus, E., Cardie, C., McKeown, K.: WikiLingua: a new benchmark dataset for cross-lingual abstractive summarization. In: Findings of the Association for Computational Linguistics: EMNLP 2020, pp. 4034–4048. Association for Computational Linguistics, Online, November 2020. https://doi.org/10.18653/v1/2020.findings-emnlp.360, https://aclanthology.org/2020.findings-emnlp.360
17. Leixo, P., Pardo, T.A.S., et al.: CSTNews: um corpus de textos jornalísticos anotados segundo a teoria discursiva multidocumento cst (cross-document structure theory). Série de Relatórios Técnicos do Instituto de Ciências Matemáticas e de Computação, Universidade de São Paulo NILC-TR-08-05 (2008). http://repositorio.icmc.usp.br//handle/RIICMC/6761
18. Lin, C.Y.: ROUGE: a package for automatic evaluation of summaries. In: Text Summarization Branches Out: Proceedings of the ACL-04 Workshop, pp. 74–81. Association for Computational Linguistics, Stroudsburg (2004)
19. Lin, H., Ng, V.: Abstractive summarization: a survey of the state of the art. In: Proceedings of the AAAI Conference on Artificial Intelligence, vol. 33, no. 01, pp. 9815–9822 (2019)
20. Lopes, A., Nogueira, R., Lotufo, R., Pedrini, H.: Lite training strategies for Portuguese-English and English-Portuguese translation. In: Proceedings of the Fifth Conference on Machine Translation, pp. 833–840. Association for Computational Linguistics, Online (2020)

21. Martins, A.F., Smith, N.A.: Summarization with a joint model for sentence extraction and compression. In: Proceedings of the Workshop on Integer Linear Programming for Natural Language Processing, pp. 1–9 (2009)
22. Maziero, E.G., Uzêda, V., Pardo, T.A.S., Nunes, M.d.G.V.: Temário 2006: Estendendo o córpus temário. Série de Relatórios Técnicos do Instituto de Ciências Matemáticas e de Computação, Universidade de São Paulo NILC-TR-07-06 (2007)
23. Nenkova, A., McKeown, K.: Automatic summarization. In: Foundations and Trends in Information Retrieval, vol. 5, pp. 103–233. Now Publishers Inc, Delft (2011)
24. Larocca Neto, J., Santos, A.D., Kaestner, C.A.A., Freitas, A.A.: Generating text summaries through the relative importance of topics. In: Monard, M.C., Sichman, J.S. (eds.) IBERAMIA/SBIA -2000. LNCS (LNAI), vol. 1952, pp. 300–309. Springer, Heidelberg (2000). https://doi.org/10.1007/3-540-44399-1_31
25. Nóbrega, F.A.A., Pardo, T.A.S.: Investigating machine learning approaches for sentence compression in different application contexts for Portuguese. In: Silva, J., Ribeiro, R., Quaresma, P., Adami, A., Branco, A. (eds.) PROPOR 2016. LNCS (LNAI), vol. 9727, pp. 245–250. Springer, Cham (2016). https://doi.org/10.1007/978-3-319-41552-9_25
26. Ouyang, J., Song, B., McKeown, K.: A robust abstractive system for cross-lingual summarization. In: Proceedings of the 2019 Conference of the North American Chapter of the Association for Computational Linguistics: Human Language Technologies, Volume 1 (Long and Short Papers), Minneapolis, Minnesota, pp. 2025–2031. Association for Computational Linguistics, June 2019. https://doi.org/10.18653/v1/N19-1204, https://aclanthology.org/N19-1204
27. Pardo, T.A.S., Rino, L.H.M.: Temário: Um corpus para sumarização automática de textos. Série de Relatórios Técnicos do Instituto de Ciências Matemáticas e de Computação, Universidade de São Paulo NILC-TR-03-09 (2003)
28. Pardo, T.A.S., Rino, L.H.M., Nunes, M.G.V.: GistSumm: a summarization tool based on a new extractive method. In: Mamede, N.J., Trancoso, I., Baptista, J., das Graças Volpe Nunes, M. (eds.) PROPOR 2003. LNCS (LNAI), vol. 2721, pp. 210–218. Springer, Heidelberg (2003). https://doi.org/10.1007/3-540-45011-4_34
29. Nóbrega, F.A.A., Jorge, A.M., Brazdil, P., Pardo, T.A.S.: Sentence compression for Portuguese. In: Quaresma, P., Vieira, R., Aluísio, S., Moniz, H., Batista, F., Gonçalves, T. (eds.) PROPOR 2020. LNCS (LNAI), vol. 12037, pp. 270–280. Springer, Cham (2020). https://doi.org/10.1007/978-3-030-41505-1_26
30. Passonneau, R.J., Chen, E., Guo, W., Perin, D.: Automated pyramid scoring of summaries using distributional semantics. In: Proceedings of the 51st Annual Meeting of the Association for Computational Linguistics (Volume 2: Short Papers), pp. 143–147 (2013)
31. Raffel, C., et al.: Exploring the limits of transfer learning with a unified text-to-text transformer (2020). arXiv preprint ArXiv: 1910.10683
32. Rino, L.H.M., Módolo, M.: SuPor: an environment for AS of texts in Brazilian Portuguese. In: Vicedo, J.L., Martínez-Barco, P., Muñoz, R., Saiz Noeda, M. (eds.) EsTAL 2004. LNCS (LNAI), vol. 3230, pp. 419–430. Springer, Heidelberg (2004). https://doi.org/10.1007/978-3-540-30228-5_37
33. Rocha, V.J.C.: PragmaSUM: novos métodos na utilização de palavras-chave na sumarização automática. Master's thesis, Universidade Federal dos Vales do Jequitinhonha e Mucuri, Diamantina (2017)
34. Rush, A.M., Chopra, S., Weston, J.: A neural attention model for abstractive sentence summarization (2015). arXiv preprint ArXiv: 1509.00685

35. Salton, G., Singhal, A., Mitra, M., Buckley, C.: Automatic text structuring and summarization. Inform. Process. Manage. **33**(2), 193–207 (1997)
36. Sodré, L.C., Oliveira, H.T.A.: Evaluating regression algorithms for automatic text summarization in Brazilian Portuguese. In: Anais do XV Encontro Nacional de Inteligência Artificial e Computacional. pp. 634–645. Sociedade Brasileira de Computação (2019)
37. Song, K., Wang, B., Feng, Z., Liu, R., Liu, F.: Controlling the amount of verbatim copying in abstractive summarization. In: Proceedings of the AAAI Conference on Artificial Intelligence, vol. 34, no. 05, pp. 8902–8909 (2020)
38. Souza, F., Nogueira, R., Lotufo, R.: Portuguese named entity recognition using BERT-CRF (2020)
39. Vadapalli, R., Kurisinkel, L.J., Gupta, M., Varma, V.: SSAS: semantic similarity for abstractive summarization. In: Proceedings of the Eighth International Joint Conference on Natural Language Processing (Volume 2: Short Papers), pp. 198–203 (2017)
40. Virtanen, A., et al.: Multilingual is not enough: BERT for finnish (2019)
41. Wagner Filho, J.A., Wilkens, R., Idiart, M., Villavicencio, A.: The brWaC corpus: a new open resource for Brazilian Portuguese. In: Proceedings of the Eleventh International Conference on Language Resources and Evaluation (LREC 2018). European Language Resources Association (ELRA), Miyazaki, Japan, May 2018
42. Wan, X., Li, H., Xiao, J.: Cross-language document summarization based on machine translation quality prediction. In: Proceedings of the 48th Annual Meeting of the Association for Computational Linguistics, pp. 917–926 (2010)
43. Yang, Q., Passonneau, R., De Melo, G.: PEAK: pyramid evaluation via automated knowledge extraction. In: Proceedings of the AAAI Conference on Artificial Intelligence, vol. 30 (2016)
44. Zhang, J., Zhao, Y., Saleh, M., Liu, P.J.: PEGASUS: pre-training with extracted gap-sentences for abstractive summarization (2019). arXiv preprint ArXiv: 1912.08777
45. Zhang, T., Kishore, V., Wu, F., Weinberger, K.Q., Artzi, Y.: BERTscore: evaluating text generation with BERT. In: International Conference on Learning Representations (2020). https://openreview.net/forum?id=SkeHuCVFDr
46. Zhao, W., Peyrard, M., Liu, F., Gao, Y., Meyer, C.M., Eger, S.: MoverScore: text generation evaluating with contextualized embeddings and earth mover distance (2019). arXiv preprint ArXiv: 1909.02622

Interact2Vec: Neural Item and User Embedding for Collaborative Filtering

Pedro R. Pires[✉] and Tiago A. Almeida

Department of Computer Science, Federal University of São Carlos, Sorocaba, Brazil
pedro.pires@dcomp.sor.ufscar.br, talmeida@ufscar.br

Abstract. Recommender systems gained great popularity in the last decade. However, despite the significant advances, they still have open problems, such as high data dimensionality and sparseness. Among several alternatives proposed to address these problems, the state-of-the-art solutions aim to represent items and users as dense vectors in a reduced dimensionality space. In this context, one of the most contemporary techniques is neural embeddings-based models, i.e., distributed vector representations generated through artificial neural networks. Many of the latest advances in this area have shown promising results compared to established approaches. However, most existing proposals demand complex neural architectures or content data, often unavailable. This paper presents the Interact2Vec, a new neural network-based model for concomitantly generating a distributed representation of users and items. It has the main advantage of being computationally efficient and only requires implicit user feedback. The results indicate a high performance comparable to other neural embeddings models that demand more significant computational power.

Keywords: Recommender systems · Collaborative filtering · Distributed vector representation · Embedding-based models

1 Introduction

With the development of technology and the ease of providing and accessing content, an ever-expanding amount of data is created and shared daily. This scenario has brought several advances to the modern world. However, with this enormous amount of information, only a small portion is of interest to each user. To alleviate this problem, Recommender Systems (RS) emerged in the 1990s and have become increasingly present in our digital lives [2]. Among different RS, Collaborative Filtering (CF) is the most popular. Simplicity is the main reason for the high popularity of CF since it does not demand additional data, only an interaction matrix indicating whether users consumed a given item [2].

This study was financed by the Coordenação de Aperfeiçoamento de Pessoal de Nível Superior – Brasil (CAPES) Finance Code 88882.426978/2019-01, and Fundação de Amparo à Pesquisa do Estado de São Paulo (FAPESP) grant #2021/14591-7.

J. C. Xavier-Junior and R. A. Rios (Eds.): BRACIS 2022, LNAI 13654, pp. 494–509, 2022.
https://doi.org/10.1007/978-3-031-21689-3_35

The pioneer CF recommender systems use the concept of neighborhood. Users are represented as vectors of consumed items and receive recommendations according to the items consumed by other nearest users. However, due to the accelerated growth in the number of users and items, neighborhood-based algorithms face some limitations related to sparsity and scalability, since modern RS deal with an ever-growing number of items and users but with a much smaller relative fraction of interactions [14]. Many studies have proposed representing users and items in a reduced dimensional space to circumvent these problems. In this context, matrix factorization algorithms have gained popularity, using matrix decomposition techniques to generate low-dimensional arrays of latent factors for both users and items [15].

Recently, a new approach has gained ground in the RS literature. Strongly inspired by state-of-the-art Natural Language Processing (NLP) techniques [16], artificial neural networks have been trained to represent items as neural embeddings, i.e., dense vectors with low and fixed dimensions that carry intrinsic meaning. As it reduces scalability and sparsity problems, neural embeddings are attractive in recommendation problems. The first NLP-based neural embedding models in the context of recommendation were Prod2Vec, User2Vec [10], and Item2Vec [1]. Those models are adaptations of neural networks commonly used to learn word embeddings and achieve results comparable to established algorithms. However, despite many advances and new proposals concerning this strategy, they often consist of training complex neural networks or demand additional content, making their application in different scenarios infeasible.

This paper extends the recent studies on applying distributed vector representation models learned by neural networks in collaborative filtering RS. Aiming to offer a straightforward application approach with low computational demand, we designed the Interact2Vec, a method to generate vector representations of items and users in the same low-dimensional vector space jointly and efficiently, which can then be used for top-N recommendation. We employed state-of-the-art strategies commonly used by NLP models to optimize the model's training phase and enrich the final embeddings. After training the model, we consumed the embeddings using different strategies to yield recommendations and analyzed the outcome in a top-N ranking task. Its utmost quality is the high efficiency, allowing training even in scenarios of scarce computational resources without compromising the quality of the generated recommendations.

2   Related Work

Collaborative filtering is the most widely used approach among existing recommendation systems because it requires only a matrix of user-item interactions to generate recommendations [2]. However, due to scalability and sparsity problems [14], established neighborhood-based algorithms have been replaced by matrix factorization-based approaches [15].

Although matrix factorization techniques offer recognized quality, they are computationally expensive and have limitations in sparse datasets [2, 24]. New methods inspired by state-of-the-art Natural Language Processing (NLP) techniques have recently arisen to overcome these problems by learning neural embeddings for items or users. Neural embeddings are dense vector representations of low and fixed dimensionality, which carry intrinsic meaning and are computed by artificial neural networks.

Neural embeddings gained great visibility in the NLP area with the success of Word2Vec, a set of neural models for generating context-based word embeddings, which proved to be powerful without demanding much computational effort [16]. Currently, neural embedding is one of the main strategies for solving many problems in different domains besides NLP [3].

In the recommender systems area, one of the earliest uses of neural models to generate item embeddings is the Prod2Vec [10]. The model was heavily inspired by Skip-gram [16], achieving higher accuracy than other heuristic recommenders used as a baseline in a scenario of recommendation via e-mail. In the same study, the authors also presented User2Vec, the first approach to compute user and item neural embeddings concomitantly, by feeding the model with a composition of the vector representation of the user and certain consumed products.

In the following year, Item2Vec was proposed [1], an adaptation of Skip-gram's architecture with a reformulated concept of context: any two items purchased by the same user are related, thus using a window of variable size to capture correlated items. Item2Vec was superior to matrix factorization models in several intrinsic evaluation tasks.

Both Prod2Vec and Item2Vec are pure collaborative filtering methods based on implicit feedback, i.e., the models learn only with the consumption of user-item implicit interactions. The subsequent research sought to consider a hybrid filtering scenario with the consumption of descriptive content to enrich the embeddings, adapting the previous embedding-based recommenders [8,22] or feeding item metadata to different neural architectures [11,24].

Other studies employed more complex neural networks, with a dominant strategy converting the recommendation problem to a sequence forecasting problem and applying convolutional [20] or recurrent neural networks [13,19]. Deep learning models were also used to learn the embeddings [17,23]. Although new proposals have suggested using complex neural architectures, much of the recent research focuses on training simpler models inspired by Word2Vec [9,21] or applying NLP models directly over textual information of items [5,12].

The literature shows that most recent studies have focused on using content information to enrich the representation. Although the achieved results are competitive, they have the disadvantage of not being easily applicable since they depend on additional data that may not be available. Additionally, most proposals use neural models only to generate item embeddings, ignoring user embeddings or learning them through simple heuristics. In more recent proposals, it is also common to use very complex neural models, which are difficult to apply in scenarios where computational resources are scarce.

Inspired by Item2Vec and User2Vec, two collaborative filtering shallow neural networks that require small computational effort, we propose a new neural model for learning embeddings in recommender systems, which we named Interact2Vec. Although computationally more efficient, our model has a similar network architecture to Item2Vec, but a similar objective to User2Vec, simultaneously learning embeddings of items and users.

3   Interact2Vec

The Interact2Vec is a novel neural model that generates user and item embeddings simultaneously. We have designed it to *(i)* generate low dimensionality and dense embeddings, thus avoiding the problem of high sparsity; *(ii)* have a computational cost equal to or less than other neural embeddings-based methods; and *(iii)* require only implicit feedback without demanding content data, being easy to apply in different scenarios. The following subsections explain how Interact2Vec works, its neural architecture and objective function, techniques used during the learning phase, and different strategies for yielding recommendations using the embeddings. In the end, we present an analysis of its computational complexity compared with the baseline neural embeddings models.

3.1   Neural Architecture and Objective Function

Interact2Vec is a shallow artificial neural network with an architecture inspired by Item2Vec [1] and an objective function inspired by User2Vec [10]. The network has three layers: an input layer $\mathcal{J}$, a hidden layer $\mathcal{H}$, and an output layer $\mathcal{O}$, as illustrated in Fig. 1.

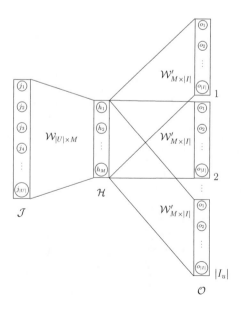

Fig. 1. Interact2Vec's neural architecture

First, we will define a recommender system as a set R of interactions between two main entities: a set U of $|U|$ users and a set I of $|I|$ items. R is composed of elements r_{ui} that represent the interaction between a user $u \mid u \in U$ and an item $i \mid i \in I$. Thus, if user u has previously interacted with item i, we have that $r_{ui} \in R$; otherwise, $r_{ui} \notin R$. We will also denote the subset of items consumed by u as $I_u = \{i \in I : r_{ui} \in R_u\}$, and the subset of users who consumed i as $U_i = \{u \in U : r_{ui} \in R_i\}$. Consequently, $|I_u|$ represents the amount of items consumed by user u, and $|U_i|$ the amount of users who interacted with item i.

The input layer $\mathcal{J}$ consists of a vector of size $|U|$ representing a target user u as a one-hot encoded vector. $\mathcal{H}$ has size M, corresponding to the number of dimensions desired for the final embeddings. It is connected to $\mathcal{J}$ by a weight matrix $\mathcal{W}$ of shape $|U| \times M$, thus $\mathcal{H} = \mathcal{J} \cdot \mathcal{W}$. Finally, $\mathcal{O}$ contains $|I_u|$ vectors of size $|I|$ (number of items), representing the items consumed by user u, also one-hot encoded. Each of the vectors is connected to $\mathcal{H}$ by the same weight matrix $\mathcal{W}'$ of shape $M \times |I|$ and a softmax activation function. Thus $\mathcal{O} = softmax(\mathcal{H}^T \cdot \mathcal{W}')$.

Similar to User2Vec, Interact2Vec learns user and item embeddings by consuming user-item relationships. However, in opposition to the other model, which trains the network by combining user and item embeddings as input, Interact2Vec's input layer is fed only with user embeddings. Given a user u as input, its main objective is to predict all items i previously consumed by u, i.e., $i \in I_u$, maximizing Eq. 1:

$$\frac{1}{|U|} \sum_{u \in U} \left(\frac{1}{|I_u|} \sum_{i \in I_u} \log \sigma(u, i) \right) \tag{1}$$

in which σ is the softmax activation function described in Eq. 2:

$$\sigma(u, i) = \frac{e^{(\mathcal{W}_u \mathcal{W}_i'^T)}}{\sum_{j \in I} e^{(\mathcal{W}_u \mathcal{W}_j'^T)}} \tag{2}$$

in which $\mathcal{W}_u$ and $\mathcal{W}_i'^T$ contains user u and item i embeddings, respectively.

We compute the error as the sum of the differences between the expected one-hot vectors and the predicted outputs for each epoch, as in a traditional classification problem. We then update the network weight matrices by backpropagation. After training, the rows of $\mathcal{W}$ will contain the user embeddings, while the columns of $\mathcal{W}'$ will contain the item embeddings.

3.2   Strategies to Optimize Network Training

Like other neural embedding models based on NLP models, Interact2Vec employs several techniques during the learning stage to increase its generalization power and reduce its computational cost; This allows the method to better adapt to the application domain and require less processing power. In the following, we present each of these techniques.

Subsampling of Frequent Items. In NLP applications, performing a subsampling of frequent words prior to training can improve the generalization power of the model and improve its performance [16]. For this, we adopted a similar strategy, removing a portion of the interactions of popular items. We have followed the probability function given by Eq. 3 for selecting the interactions to be removed.

$$P(\text{discard} \mid i) = \left(\sqrt{\frac{|U_i|}{\rho}} + 1 \right) \cdot \frac{\rho}{|U_i|} \tag{3}$$

in which ρ corresponds to a hyperparameter used for adjusting the subsampling rate. An increase in the value of ρ increases the probability of removing the interaction.

Negative Sampling. Predicting scores for every possible user-item pair is computationally demanding, with a quadratic growth as new users and items are added. To alleviate this problem, we employed negative sampling to reduce the number of comparisons [16]. The weight matrices are updated considering only a small subset G of "negative" items (i.e., the ones the user has not interacted with), randomly selected for each "positive" item ($i \in I_u$) at each epoch. Therefore, the objective function previously expressed by Eq. 1 becomes the function presented in Eq. 4, which is also maximized.

$$\frac{1}{|U|} \sum_{u \in U} \left(\frac{1}{|I_u|} \sum_{i \in I_u} \left(\log \sigma(u, i) - \sum_{j \in G} \log \sigma(u, j) \right) \right) \tag{4}$$

The random selection of G follows a probability distribution expressed by Eq. 5, where $z(i)$ represents the number of interactions item I has, that is, $|U_i|$, and γ is a hyperparameter that balances the probability of selection between more or less popular items.

$$P(i) = \frac{z(i)^\gamma}{\sum_{j \in I} z(j)^\gamma} \tag{5}$$

Regularization. To avoid over-sampling and improve generalization, we applied L2 regularization (Ridge regression) in both weight matrices $\mathcal{W}$ and $\mathcal{W}'$ of Interact2Vec. The objective function can then be expressed by Eq. 6:

$$\frac{1}{|U|} \sum_{u \in U} \left(\frac{1}{|I_u|} \sum_{i \in I_u} \left(\log \sigma(u, i) - \sum_{j \in G} \log \sigma(u, j) \right) \right) - \lambda \sum_{i \in I} ||\mathcal{W}'^T_i||^2 - \lambda \sum_{u \in U} ||\mathcal{W}_u||^2 \tag{6}$$

in which λ is a hyperparameter that adjusts the impact of the regularization in the content of the embeddings.

3.3   Recommender Algorithms

Like Item2Vec and User2Vec, Interact2Vec is not a recommender algorithm itself. Instead, its main goal is to learn vector representations for users and items that other algorithms can use to generate the final recommendation. Since we can use the same low dimensionality vector space to represent users and items, we can yield the final recommendation using similarity-based recommenders and even more computationally cost methods. Here we propose five techniques to use Interact2Vec's embeddings for a top-N recommendation, described below.

User-Item Similarity. Since related users and items are closer in the embeddings vector space, it is possible to generate a top-N ranking for a particular user by simply retrieving the N closest embeddings of items the user has not interacted with. Therefore, given a user u, we calculate the cosine similarity, between the user u and every item i he/she has not interacted, i.e., $sim(u, i) \forall i \mid i \notin I_u$.

Item-Item Similarity. A second possible approach is to ignore the vector representation of users and calculate only the similarities between items, a common strategy used for top-N ranking [7]. Then, we can compute the recommendation using the similarities between items consumed by the target user and new items. In this recommender, the algorithm still computes the similarity between users and items. However, this is calculated using the average between the interacted items and every other, thus ignoring the user embedding.

Weighted Similarities. In many cases, the position of items and users in the vector space can cause divergences between the output of the two methods explained above. Thus, it may be interesting to combine them so that the final recommendation is built through a weighted vote, as shown in Fig. 2.

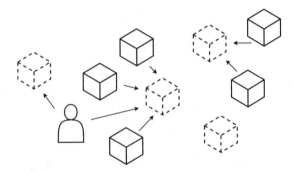

Fig. 2. Recommendation by the weighted similarity between user-item and item-item similarities. Dashed edge cubes represent items the user has not interacted with.

In this approach, we can calculate the similarity $sim_w(u, i)$ using Eq. 7, i.e., calculating the weighted average between the user-item similarity $sim_u(u, i)$, explained in Sect. 3.3, and the item-item similarity $sim_i(u, i)$, explained in Sect. 3.3. β and μ are constants used to define the weight that each recommendation method will have in the final recommendation.

$$sim_w(u, i) = \frac{\beta \times sim_u(u, i) + \mu \times sim_i(u, i)}{\beta + \mu} \tag{7}$$

Combination of the Embeddings. This strategy consists of recommending through item-item similarity, but using new embeddings generated by the combination of user and item embeddings so that a single representation vector carries information of both entities.

We perform this combination by concatenating the average value of multiple user embeddings with the item embedding. Therefore, we can represent an item i as $\left[\mathcal{W}'^T_i, \frac{\sum_{u \in U_i} W_u}{|U_i|} \right]$, i.e., the concatenation of the original embedding for i and the average value of the embeddings for every user that has consumed i ($u \in |U_i|$). Additionally, to avoid outliers, it is possible to restrict only to the K users nearest to i in the vector space instead of using every user embedding.

Recommender Ensemble. Finally, since every method mentioned above has a particular strategy to yield the recommendation, it is interesting to compose the final top-N recommendation using a voting mechanism so that the most recommended items among every method are selected.

For a given user u, each method m must yield a top-L ranking $s_m(u, L)$, in which $L \geq N$. Being S the set with every top-L recommendation, we can then compute the final recommendation through voting among the selected items in every $s_m(u, L) \in S$. Additionally, the votes of each method can be weighted according to its performance, or for each item, given its position in the ranking.

3.4 Algorithm Efficiency Analysis

To analyze the computational complexity of Interact2Vec, we can break its training procedure into five levels: *(i)* propagation of a single sample; *(ii)* every sample of an item; *(iii)* every item of a user; *(iv)* every user of an epoch; *(v)* every epoch. In this analysis, we will not consider the optimization phase when addressing the efficiency since it depends on the adopted optimization algorithm, and we can use the same algorithm for every neural model.

The propagation of a single sample, i.e., a user-item pair, consists of a query on a lookup table containing the embeddings, followed by a vector multiplication. Using an indexed table, the query used to retrieve the embedding content can be done with $O(1)$ complexity. The vector multiplication is proportional to the embedding size. Therefore, we can represent its complexity as $O(2M)$, or $O(M)$, where M is the dimension for the embeddings.

This operation is performed for a single item i and then repeated for every negative item $i \in G$. That way, the network will perform $O(|G| \times M)$ operations. Since the network is adjusted for every item consumed by a user and for every user, we can say that the operation mentioned above is repeated for every interaction $r \in R$. Finally, the network is trained over C epochs. Therefore, we can represent its final complexity as $O(C \times |R| \times |G| \times M)$, i.e., Interact2Vec's complexity is tied to the number of epochs, interactions, negative samples, and the dimensionality of the embedding. In practice, however, the number of interactions is expressively more significant than the number of other factors ($|R| \gg \{M, |G|, C\}$), so we can say that the number of operations performed by Interact2Vec grows linearly to the number of interactions in the dataset, having $O(|R|)$.

With this behavior, Interact2Vec is more efficient – or at least similar – to the baseline neural embedding-based methods. User2Vec [10] operates in the same manner as Interact2Vec, performing $O(|R|)$ operations, but its aggregation step performed over user and item embeddings can impact its performance compared to Interact2Vec. On the other hand, Item2Vec [1] is more costly than Interact2Vec, presenting $O(C \times |R| \times (|R| - 1) \times |G| \times M) \approx O(|R|^2)$ complexity in the worst-case scenario since it iterates over multiple combinations of item-item pairs consumed by the same user.

4   Experiments and Results

To compare the Interact2Vec with other neural embeddings models, we conducted a top-N recommendation task, as described below.

4.1   Datasets and Preprocessing

We conducted the experiments over the datasets shown in Table 1. All datasets are widely used in literature, have public access, and consist of different application domains. Columns $|U|$, $|I|$ and $|R|$ contain, respectively, the number of users, items and interactions. Column S contain the sparsity rate (i.e., $S = 1 - \frac{|R|}{|U| \times |I|}$). Finally, column "Type" indicates if the interactions of the dataset are explicit (E), implicit (I) or a combination of both (E+I).

During preprocessing, all duplicated interactions were removed, keeping only one occurrence. For inconsistent interactions, every interaction was removed. For datasets with different types of interaction, we used only the one that better indicates the interest for an item, i.e., "listen" for Last.FM and "buy" for RetailRocket. We considered every interaction as positive for datasets containing explicit feedback, no matter the associated rating.

4.2   Experimental Protocol

We split the datasets into train, validation, and test set, following an 8:1:1 rate, and trained the models using grid-search cross-validation. Due to computational power limitations, for MovieLens and NetflixPrize datasets, we used only a random subset of interactions, respectively 10% and 5% during the hyperparameter adjustment phase and 100% and 25% during the final experiment. Additionally,

Table 1. Datasets used in the experiments.

Dataset	$|U|$	$|I|$	$|R|$	S	Type
Anime[a]	37,128	10,697	1,476,495	99.63%	E+I
BestBuy[b]	1,268,702	69,858	1,862,782	99.99%	I
Book-Crossing[c]	59,517	246,724	716,109	99.99%	E+I
CiaoDVD[d]	17,615	16,121	72,345	99.97%	E
DeliciousBookmarks[c]	1,867	69,223	104,799	99.92%	I
Filmtrust[d]	1,508	2,071	35,494	98.86%	E
Last.FM[c]	1,892	17,632	92,834	99.72%	I
MovieLens[c]	162,541	59,047	25,000,095	99.74%	E
NetflixPrize[e]	480,189	17,770	100,480,507	98.82%	E
RetailRocket[f]	11,719	12,025	21,270	99.98%	I

[a] Anime Recommendations dataset. Available at: www.kaggle.com/ CooperUnion/anime-recommendations-dataset
[b] Data Mining Hackathon on BIG DATA (7GB). Available at: www.kaggle. com/c/acm-sf-chapter-hackathon-big
[c] GroupLens - Datasets. Available at: www.grouplens.org/datasets/
[d] CiaoDVD dataset and Filmtrust. Available at: www.github.com/caserec/ Datasets-for-Recommender-Systems
[e] Netflix Prize data. Available at: www.kaggle.com/netflix-inc/netflix-prize-data
[f] Retailrocket recommender system dataset. Available at www.kaggle.com/ retailrocket/ecommerce-dataset

we removed items consumed by only one user and users who consumed only one item since the compared methods can be trained only with users who interacted with two or more items. Since we did not want to address the cold-start problem, unknown users and items were removed from the validation and test datasets.

We compared the Interact2Vec with two state-of-the-art neural embedding algorithms that rely solely on implicit feedback, Item2Vec (ITM2V) [1] and User2Vec (USR2V) [10]. We implemented all algorithms in Python3, and tuned its hyperparameters using a grid-search approach. ITM2V and USR2V were tuned according to insights proposed in [4], with the number of epochs C ranging in $\{50, 100, 150\}$, negative exponent γ for the negative sampling in $\{-1.0, -0.5, 0.5, 1.0\}$, and the subsampling factor ρ in $\{10^{-5}, 10^{-4}, 10^{-3}\}$. Finally, we used fixed values for the learning rate ($\alpha = 0.25$), embeddings size ($M = 100$), and number of negative samples ($|G| = 5$). For Interact2Vec (INT2V), considering that exhaustive testing of every parameter combination is computationally infeasible, we conducted a study to assess the impact of parameter selection. We found that some values tend to present better results for the learning rate ($\alpha = 0.25$), the number of epochs ($C = 50$), subsampling rate of frequent items ($\rho = 10^{-6}$), and regularization factor ($\lambda = 0.1$), which were used during the experiments. At the same time, the size of the embeddings M

ranged in $\{50, 100, 150\}$, the number of negative samples G in $\{5, 10, 15\}$ and the negative exponent γ for the negative sampling in $\{-1.0, -0.5, 0.5, 1.0\}$.

In addition to the parameters tuned during the embeddings learning phase, we also adjusted the parameters for the recommender algorithms that consume the embeddings and generate the final recommendation. For ITM2V and USR2V, we used item-item and user-item similarity, respectively. For INT2V, we tested every algorithm listed in Sect. 3.3. For the weighted similarities, we ranged β and μ in $\{0.1, 0.25, 0.5, 0.75, 0.9\}$, for the combination of the embeddings we tested values $\{1, 5, 10, 15, |U_i|\}$ for K, and for the recommender ensemble we tested values $\{15, 30, 45\}$ for L and weighted the votes as described in the method. We selected the recommender algorithm for each dataset using a grid search according to its performance in the validation set. Their performance varied widely among the different datasets, without a proper consensus on the best recommender algorithm. Even so, preliminary results point to the superiority of the recommendation using weighted similarities, which we aim to investigate in future works.

To evaluate the algorithms, we calculated the F1-score and NDCG in a top-N recommendation scenario, with N ranging between 1 and 20. The models showed similar behavior for different values of N, with little variations in their relative position among each other. With that in mind, we focused our analysis on a top-15 scenario, a value commonly used in the literature. Results are shown in the grayscale Table 2. The darker the cell, the better the result for that specific dataset and metric, with the best result highlighted in **bold**.

Table 2. F1-score and NDCG achieved by each algorithm in each dataset.

Dataset	F1@15			NDCG@15		
	ITM2V	USR2V	INT2V	ITM2V	USR2V	INT2V
Anime	**0.0877**	0.0072	0.0752	**0.1275**	0.0084	0.1267
BestBuy	**0.0170**	0.0049	0.0127	**0.0557**	0.0160	0.0435
Book-Crossing	**0.0078**	0.0012	0.0043	**0.0131**	0.0014	0.0076
CiaoDVD	0.0120	0.0031	**0.0192**	0.0277	0.0061	**0.0457**
DeliciousBookmarks	0.0393	0.0129	**0.0544**	0.0969	0.0235	**0.1615**
Filmtrust	**0.2779**	0.1270	0.2697	**0.5721**	0.1948	0.5663
Last.FM	**0.1047**	0.0157	0.1040	**0.1894**	0.0229	0.1737
MovieLens	**0.0975**	0.0003	0.0593	**0.1211**	0.0004	0.0683
NetflixPrize	**0.0537**	0.0007	0.0291	**0.0645**	0.0014	0.0357
RetailRocket	**0.0184**	0.0062	0.0169	**0.0829**	0.0133	0.0663

The recommenders behaved similarly in both metrics, i.e., methods that achieve good results for F1@15 tend to achieve good results for NDCG@15. In both metrics, Item2Vec and Interact2Vec were the best or second-best models for every dataset. On the other hand, User2Vec achieved the worst results in all experiments. We believe this is due to the aggregation step performed during training, which can result in information loss. The performance of Item2Vec was more consistent, being the best model in 80% of the datasets. Even so, Interact2Vec presented very similar results, achieving the best F1-Score and NDCG on two of the datasets.

To evaluate the computational efficiency of Interact2Vec in practice, we have compared the elapsed time for training the embeddings for Item2Vec and Interact2Vec. For this, we have implemented both models using the Keras library, with the same optimization techniques and fixed values for every hyperparameter, thus being comparable. In addition, we have tested sets of samples from Last.FM dataset incrementally, training the models three times for each dataset variation. Finally, we calculated the average elapsed time for each model, depicted in Fig. 3. The results show that the greater the number of interactions, the more discrepant is the superiority of Interact2Vec. The proposed model could train the embeddings more than 300% faster than Item2Vec while presenting an NDCG only 5% lower on average, a slight drawback considering the significant gains in computational efficiency.

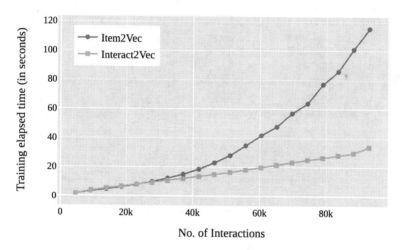

Fig. 3. Comparison of the elapsed time for training Last.FM embeddings using Item2Vec and Interact2Vec when increasing the number of interactions.

To properly compare Interact2Vec with the other methods, we conducted a statistic test using a ranking constructed with the results for the NDCG@15. First, we calculated a nonparametric Friedman test to check whether there are significant differences between the performance of the methods [6]. Results indicated that the models are statistically different, with 95% of confidence ($X_r^2 = 16,80$). Thus, we conducted a post-hoc Bonferroni-Dunn test to perform a pairwise comparison among Interact2Vec and the two other methods [6], as shown in Fig. 4. Considering the critical difference calculated by the test

(CD = 1.00), we can conclude that Interact2Vec is statistically superior to User2Vec, and there is no statistical evidence that Interact2Vec is superior or inferior to Item2Vec.

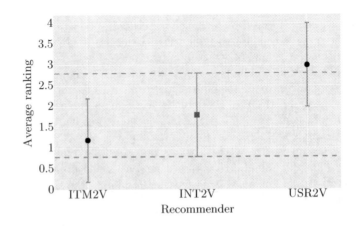

Fig. 4. Graphical representation of the *post-hoc* Bonferroni-Dunn test

In conclusion, we cannot state that the performance obtained by Interact2Vec is statistically superior to that of Item2Vec. However, the proposed approach is computationally much more efficient, presenting a pseudo-linear computational complexity. User2Vec also shares this quality, but its results are disappointing. Thus, our method offers low computational complexity and is capable of learning item and user embeddings simultaneously during training. Moreover, it does not suffer significant losses in the quality of the final recommendation. Therefore, Interact2Vec is a good alternative as a neural embedding model for recommender systems based on implicit feedback, especially in scenarios with computational limitations, such as lack of resources or need for fast training.

5   Conclusions and Future Work

In this paper, we proposed Interact2Vec, a new neural model capable of concurrently learning user and item embeddings for recommender systems. It has the advantage of being computationally efficient and without requiring content data. These characteristics allow us to apply the model in scenarios with a shortage of computational resources and when the system only records implicit feedback.

First, we compared the number of operations performed by Interact2Vec with other neural embeddings methods. We then showed how the complexity of Interact2Vec scales practically linearly according to the number of interactions. Finally, to assess the quality of the model, we evaluated it in a top-N ranking task. The model achieved superior results to User2Vec and competitive results compared with Item2Vec, being more computationally efficient than the latter.

Interact2Vec achieved the best values for both F1-score and NDCG for datasets CiaoDVD and DeliciousBookmarks. In future works, we intend to investigate this behavior further because understanding why the datasets were favorable to the proposed method may lead to insights of improvements, possibly allowing Interact2Vec to beat Item2Vec in other datasets as well. Additionally, we also aim to analyze the quality of each recommender algorithm proposed in Sect. 3.3 to detect if there is a correlation between the type of recommender algorithm and the characteristics of the consumed data.

Since Interact2Vec does not consume explicit feedback, i.e., user ratings, it is only suitable for top-N recommendations. For future work, we suggest studying strategies for adapting the model to consume explicit feedback, thus allowing it to perform rating prediction tasks. Two possible strategies are: (i) to adapt the objective function to compute the error according to the given rating; and (ii) using new recommendation methods that weighted the similarities between the embeddings according to the ratings.

Based on evidence from the literature [8,22], we also consider that we can improve the quality of the embeddings by consuming content data, especially for problems that demand intrinsic knowledge, which would make its application more difficult but would improve its recommending quality.

Finally, we suggest a broader and more complete study to address the intrinsic quality of the embeddings generated by Interact2Vec compared to the other embedding-based models. In this study, we focused on extrinsic evaluation, i.e., the recommendation itself. However, we believe that a complete understanding of the model's capabilities would be possible when the embeddings are applied in other experiments, such as auto-tagging and item clustering [1,18].

References

1. Barkan, O., Koenigstein, N.: Item2Vec: Neural item embedding for collaborative filtering. In: IEEE 26th International Workshop on Machine Learning for Signal Processing, Piscataway, NJ, USA, pp. 1–6. MLSP 2016. IEEE (2016). https://doi.org/10.1109/MLSP.2016.7738886
2. Bobadilla, J., Ortega, F., Hernando, A., Gutiérrez, A.: Recommender systems survey. Knowl.-Based Syst. **46**, 109–132 (2013). https://doi.org/10.1016/j.knosys.2013.03.012
3. Camacho-Collados, J., Pilehvar, M.T.: From word to sense embeddings: a survey on vector representations of meaning. J. Artif. Intell. Res. **63**(1), 743–788 (2018). https://doi.org/10.1613/jair.1.11259
4. Caselles-Duprés, H., Lesaint, F., Royo-Letelier, J.: Word2Vec applied to recommendation: hyperparameters matter. In: Proceedings of the 12th ACM Conference on Recommender Systems, pp. 352–356. RecSys 2018. Association for Computing Machinery, New York (2018). https://doi.org/10.1145/3240323.3240377
5. Collins, A., Beel, J.: Document embeddings vs. keyphrases vs. terms for recommender systems: a large-scale online evaluation. In: Proceedings of the 2019 ACM/IEEE Joint Conference on Digital Libraries, pp. 130–133. JCDL 2019. IEEE, New York (2019). https://doi.org/10.1109/JCDL.2019.00027

6. Demšar, J.: Statistical comparisons of classifiers over multiple data sets. J. Mach. Learn. Res. **7**, 1–30 (2006). https://doi.org/10.5555/1248547.1248548

7. Deshpande, M., Karypis, G.: Item-based top-N recommendation algorithms. ACM Trans. Inform. Syst. **22**(1), 143–177 (2004). https://doi.org/10.1145/963770.963776

8. FU, P., hua LV, J., long MA, S., jie LI, B.: Attr2Vec: a neural network based item embedding method. In: Proceedings of the 2nd International Conference on Computer, Mechatronics and Electronic Engineering, pp. 300–307. CMEE 2017. DEStech Publications, Lancaster (2017). https://doi.org/10.12783/dtcse/cmee2017/19993

9. Grbovic, M., Cheng, H.: Real-time personalization using embeddings for search ranking at Airbnb. In: Proceedings of the 24th ACM SIGKDD International Conference on Knowledge Discovery and Data Mining, pp. 311–320. KDD 2018. Association for Computing Machinery, New York (2018). https://doi.org/10.1145/3219819.3219885

10. Grbovic, M., Radosavljevic, V., Djuric, N., Bhamidipati, N., Savla, J., Bhagwan, V., Sharp, D.: E-commerce in your inbox: Product recommendations at scale. In: Proceedings of the 21th ACM SIGKDD International Conference on Knowledge Discovery and Data Mining, pp. 1809–1818. KDD 2015. Association for Computing Machinery, New York (2015). https://doi.org/10.1145/2783258.2788627

11. Greenstein-Messica, A., Rokach, L., Friedman, M.: Session-based recommendations using item embedding. In: Proceedings of the 22nd International Conference on Intelligent User Interfaces, pp. 629–633. IUI 2017. Association for Computing Machinery, New York (2017). https://doi.org/10.1145/3025171.3025197

12. Hasanzadeh, S., Fakhrahmad, S.M., Taheri, M.: Review-based recommender systems: a proposed rating prediction scheme using word embedding representation of reviews. Comp. J. 1–10 (2020). https://doi.org/10.1093/comjnl/bxaa044

13. Hidasi, B., Karatzoglou, A., Baltrunas, L., Tikk, D.: Session-based recommendations with recurrent neural networks. In: Proceedings of the International Conference on Learning Representations, pp. 1–10. ICLR 2016. OpenReview, Amherst (2016)

14. Khsuro, S., Ali, Z., Ullah, I.: Recommender systems: issues, challenges, and research opportunities. In: Proceedings of the 7th International Conference on Information Science and Applications, pp. 1179–1189. ICISA 2016. Springer Science+Business Media, Heidelberg (2016). https://doi.org/10.1007/978-981-10-0557-2_112

15. Koren, Y., Bell, R., Volinsky, C.: Matrix factorization techniques for recommender systems. Computer **42**(8), 30–37 (2009). https://doi.org/10.1109/MC.2009.263

16. Mikolov, T., Sutskever, I., Chen, K., Conrado, G., Dan, J.: Distributed representations of words and phrases and their compositionality. In: Proceedings of the 26th International Conference on Neural Information Processing Systems, pp. 3111–3119. NIPS 2013. Curran Associates Inc., Red Hook (2013). https://doi.org/10.5555/2999792.2999959

17. Sidana, S., Trofimov, M., Horodnytskyi, O., Laclau, C., Maximov, Y., Amini, M.-R.: User preference and embedding learning with implicit feedback for recommender systems. Data Min. Knowl. Disc. **35**(2), 568–592 (2021). https://doi.org/10.1007/s10618-020-00730-8

18. Song, Y., Zhang, L., Giles, C.L.: Automatic tag recommendation algorithms for social recommender systems. ACM Trans. Web **4**(1), 4:1–4:31 (2011). https://doi.org/10.1145/1921591.1921595

19. Tan, Y.K., Xu, X., Liu, Y.: Improved recurrent neural networks for session-based recommendations. In: Proceedings of the 1st Workshop on Deep Learning for Recommender Systems, pp. 17–22. DLRS 2016. Association for Computing Machinery, New York (2016). https://doi.org/10.1145/2988450.2988452

20. Tang, J., Wang, K.: Personalized top-n sequential recommendation via convolutional sequence embedding. In: Proceedings of the 11th ACM International Conference on Web Search and Data Mining. pp. 565–573. WSDM 2018. Association for Computing Machinery, New York (2018). https://doi.org/10.1145/2939672.2939673

21. Valcarce, D., Landin, A., Parapar, J.: Álvaro Barreiro: collaborative filtering embeddings for memory-based recommender systems. Eng. Appl. Artif. Intell. **85**, 347–356 (2019). https://doi.org/10.1016/j.engappai.2019.06.020

22. Vasile, F., Smirnova, E., Conneau, A.: Meta-Prod2Vec: product embeddings using side-information for recommendation. In: Proceedings of the 10th ACM Conference on Recommender Systems, pp. 225–232. RecSys 2016. Association for Computing Machinery, New York (2016). https://doi.org/10.1145/2959100.2959160

23. Zarzour, H., Al-Sharif, Z.A., Jararweh, Y.: RecDNNing: a recommender system using deep neural network with user and item embeddings. In: Proceedings of the 10th International Conference on Information and Communication Systems. ICICS 2019. IEEE, New York (2019). https://doi.org/10.1109/IACS.2019.8809156

24. Zhang, F., Yuan, N.J., Lian, D., Xie, X., Ma, W.Y.: Collaborative knowledge base embedding for recommender systems. In: Proceedings of the 22nd ACM SIGKDD International Conference on Knowledge Discovery and Data Mining, pp. 353–362. KDD 2016. Association for Computing Machinery, New York (2016). https://doi.org/10.1145/2939672.2939673

Deep Learning-Based COVID-19 Screening Using Photographs of Chest X-Rays Displayed in Computer Monitors

Pedro Silva[ID], Eduardo Luz[ID], Larissa Silva, Caio Gonçalves, Dênis Oliveira, Rodrigo Silva[ID], and Gladston Moreira[(✉)][ID]

Universidade Federal de Ouro Preto, Ouro Preto-MG, Brazil
{silvap,eduluz,rodrigo.silva,gladston}@ufop.edu.br

Abstract. Several recent research papers have shown the usefulness of Deep Learning (DL) techniques for COVID-19 screening in Chest X-Rays (CXRs). To make this technology accessible and easy to use, a natural path is to leverage the widespread use of smartphones. In these cases, the DL models will inevitably be presented with photographs taken with such devices from a computer monitor. Thus, in this work, a dataset of CXR digital photographs taken from computer monitors with smartphones is built and DL models are evaluated on it. The results show that the current models are not able to correctly classify this kind of input. As an alternative, we build a model that discards pictures of monitors such that the COVID-19 screening module does not have to cope with them.

Keywords: Deep learning · Covid-19 · Chest X-Ray · EfficientNet

1 Introduction

In the late months of 2019, a new coronavirus, named SARS-CoV-2 quickly spread to various countries becoming a pandemic. In February of 2020, the World Health Organization (WHO) named the disease caused by SARS-CoV-2 as COVID-19. The COVID-19 infection may manifest itself as a flu-like illness potentially progressing to an acute respiratory distress syndrome [4]. The disease severity resulted in global public health measures to contain person-to-person viral spread [7]. In most countries, these measures involve social distancing and large-scale vaccination and testing for early disease detection and isolation of sick patients.

The Reverse-Transcriptase Polymerase Chain Reaction (RT-PCR) is, currently, the gold standard for the diagnosis of COVID-19 [4]. However, effective exclusion of COVID-19 infection requires multiple negative tests [2]. Tests which, due to the pandemic, became scarce and expensive. The high cost and scarcity of test kits has driven efforts to the search for alternative diagnostic methods and many researchers have turned to Artificial Intelligence (AI) for help.

Given the success of AI, in particular, Deep Learning (DL), in tasks of pattern recognition, the application of these techniques to Chest X-Ray (CXR)

J. C. Xavier-Junior and R. A. Rios (Eds.): BRACIS 2022, LNAI 13654, pp. 510–522, 2022.
https://doi.org/10.1007/978-3-031-21689-3_36

based screening of COVID-19 has become very popular [1,13,18,21]. To fit these models, labeled training data is required. One of the main sources of COVID-19 CXR images is the repository made available by Cohen et al. [6] which was used, for instance, in [10,11,13,19]. In [18] a protocol to build a more comprehensive dataset to make the models capable of classifying various types of respiratory diseases was proposed. This dataset, named COVIDx, merges five CXR databases and contains images from healthy patients as well as patients with multiple variants of pneumonia caused by different bacteria and viruses, including the SARS-CoV-2.

In COVIDx, the vast majority of CRXs belonging to non-COVID-19 patients were provided by the National Institute of Health (NIH) [20]. All these images are in DICOM[1] format and were collected by mining the NIH's own PACS[2].

Despite being the most adequate file format, DICOM is not widely used in the majority of the developing regions which tend to use film [3,16]. Hence, not by coincidence, the COVID-19 CXRs images come from much more heterogeneous sources composed of public sources as well as indirect collection from hospitals and physicians from all over the world [6,19].

In a time in which social distancing is recommended and mobility is restricted, an appealing approach to scale data collection and the deployment of DL models is to leverage the widespread use of smartphones. It is clear that mobile applications which allow healthcare practitioners to share information with DL researchers and use the produced models would be useful. In this scenario, one of the easiest ways to capture CXRs either for sharing or running them through the DL models would be via cellphone photographs. In this context, the goal of this work, in particular, is to investigate the behavior of existing models, trained with the COVIDx dataset when they are presented with photographs taken with smartphones from a computer monitor. This monitor could be, for instance, attached to a PACS or simply to a hospital computer which stores digital photos of chest films.

As can be seen in Fig. 1, this procedure may generate distortions and add noise to the images. Thus, the question of whether these photographs can be used in combination with deep learning models to produce accurate COVID-19 detection arises. To address this question, we split it into the following hypotheses: (i) a DL model for CXR based diagnosis of COVID-19 misclassifies smartphone photographs from computer monitors; (ii) augmenting the training dataset with smartphone pictures of displayed CXRs gives the model the ability to produce accurate results even with this noisy data input method; and (iii) assuming that smartphone pictures of displayed CXRs do not make the cut for the screening process, it is possible to build a model that distinguishes them from proper CXR images and discards them automatically.

---

[1] Digital Imaging and Communications in Medicine.

[2] PACS (Picture Archiving and Communication System) is a medical imaging technology that provides economical storage, retrieval, management, distribution, and presentation of medical images.

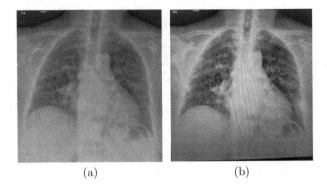

(a)   (b)

Fig. 1. COVIDx X-ray and a monitor picture of the same image. (a) COVIDx Image: Publicly available at https://github.com/ieee8023/covid-chestxray-dataset/. (b) A picture of the same image taken of a computer monitor.

To run in a edge device such as a cellphone, the DL model must consume as little computational resources as possible. Currently, the EfficientNet [17] family is among the most efficient models (i.e. requiring least memory and FLOPS for inference) that reaches state-of-the-art accuracy on both imagenet [8] and common image classification transfer learning tasks [9,17]. For these reasons, this work, focuses on adaptations of these models to the COVID-19 screening problem.

Overall, the results show that the test models are far from being able to correctly classify most of the pictures taken of monitors. However, data augmentation with these photographs or automatically discarding them may be workarounds. The results reported here have important implications when considering turning the DL models into a web or mobile app. If not taken into account they may lead to very frustrating use of the technology in the real world.

The remainder of this paper is organized as follows: In Sect. 2, the EfficientNet-C19 is defined. In Sect. 3, the COVIDx dataset is described and the new dataset created for this work is presented. In Sect. 4, the quality metrics used to evaluate the DL models are defined. In Sect. 5, the computational experiments designed to test the hypothesis above are described and the results are reported. Finally, in Sect. 6 the conclusions and final remarks are presented.

2   EfficientNet-C19

The EfficientNet-C19 neural network [13] extends the family of EfficientNets [17] for the CXR based COVID-19 screening problem. The EfficientNet family has as its basic building block the architecture shown in Table 1. Its main component, the Mobile Inverted Bottleneck Conv Block, MBconv [15], is depicted in Fig. 2.

The idea behind the EfficientNet family is to start from the high-quality yet compact baseline model presented in Table 1 and uniformly scale each of its

Table 1. EfficientNet baseline network: B0 architecture.

Stage	Operator	Resolution	#channels	#layers
1	Conv3 × 3	224 × 224	32	1
2	MBConv1, k3 × 3	112 × 112	16	1
3	MBConv6, k3 × 3	112 × 112	24	2
4	MBConv6, k5 × 5	56 × 56	40	2
5	MBConv6, k3 × 3	28 × 28	80	3
6	MBConv6, k5 × 5	14 × 14	112	3
7	MBConv6, k5 × 5	14 × 14	192	4
8	MBConv6, k3 × 3	7 × 7	320	1
9	Conv1 × 1/Pooling/FC	7 × 7	1, 280	1

Fig. 2. MBConv Block [15]. DWConv stands for depthwise Conv, k3 × 3/k5 × 5 defines the kernel size, BN is batch normalization, $HxWxF$ represents the tensor shape (height, width, depth), and x1/2/3/4 is the multiplier for a number of repeated layers.

dimensions systematically with a fixed set of scaling coefficients. The different scaling factors give rise to the different members of the family.

An EfficientNet is defined by three dimensions: (i) depth; (ii) width; and (iii) resolution as illustrated in Fig. 3. Starting from the baseline model, called B0, in Table 1 each dimension is scaled by the parameter ϕ according to Eq. 1 where, $\alpha = 1.2$ $\beta = 1.1$ and $\gamma = 1.1$ are constants obtained experimentally using a grid search. By varying ϕ, one obtains new architectures of the EfficientNet family. For instance, $\phi = 1$ gives rise to the EfficientNet B1, $\phi = 2$ gives rise to the EfficientNet B2, and so on.

According to [17], Eq. 1 provides a nice balance between performance and computational cost.

$$depth = \alpha^\phi \quad width = \beta^\phi \quad resolution = \gamma^\phi,$$
$$\text{s.t. } \alpha \cdot \beta^2 \cdot \gamma^2 \approx 2 \qquad \alpha \geq 1, \beta \geq 1, \gamma \geq 1, \tag{1}$$

In [12], as shown in Table 2, the authors add four new blocks to the baseline model to improve the EfficientNet performance on the COVID-19 screening problem. Here, this model will be called EfficientNet-C19 B0. For the complete discussion on the rationale behind these new blocks, see [13].

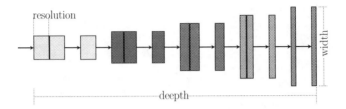

Fig. 3. Efficient net compound scaling on three parameters. (Adapted from [17])

Table 2. EfficientNet-C19 baseline model or EfficientNet-C19 B0. (NC = Number of Classes).

Stage	Operator	Resolution	#channels	#layers
1–9	EfficientNet B0	224 × 224	32	1
10	BN/Dropout	7 × 7	1280	1
11	FC/BN/Swich/Dropout	1	512	1
12	FC/BN/Swich	1	128	1
13	FC/Softmax	1	NC	1

To obtain other models from the EfficientNet-C19 family, one changes the EfficientNet layers. That is, in Table 2, if instead of the EfficientNet B0, one uses the EfficientNet B3 in the first stages, the model becomes the EfficientNet-C19 B3.

Since the main question addressed in this paper has arisen from a smartphone application, it makes sense to test a model that would fit well in a mobile app. For reference, the COVID-Net presented in [19] requires 2.1 GB of memory while the EfficientNet-C19 B3 requires only 134 MB.

3   Data Set Augmentation with Photographs of CXRs Displayed in Computer Monitors

To investigate whether smartphone photographs of CXRs displayed in monitors are suitable for COVID-19 identification in CXRs, a new dataset of such photographs must be built. Thus, in Sect. 3.1 we describe the COVIDx dataset which is the biggest CXR dataset for the COVID-19 screening problem. Then, in Sect. 3.2, we describe the procedure used to build a photograph dataset from COVIDx.

3.1   The COVIDx Dataset

The COVIDx dataset combines five data repositories and has been built to leverage the following types of patient cases from each of the data repositories [19]: (i) COVID-19 cases from the COVID-19 Image Data Collection [6], the COVID-19 Chest X-ray Dataset Initiative[3], the ActualMed COVID-19 Chest X-ray Dataset Initiative[4], and COVID-19 radiography database [5]; (ii) patient cases who have no pneumonia (i.e., normal) from the RSNA Pneumonia Detection Challenge dataset [14] and the COVID-19 Image Data Collection [6]; and (iii) non-COVID19 pneumonia patient cases from RSNA Pneumonia Detection Challenge dataset [6].

The COVIDx was designed to represent a classification with three classes: (i) *normal* - for healthy patients; (ii) *COVID-19* - for patients with COVID-19; and (iii) *pneumonia* - for patients with non-COVID-19 pneumonia.

The majority of the instances which belong to the normal and pneumonia classes come from the RNSA dataset [14]. The COVID-19 class instances come from multiple sources. The COVIDx has a total of 13,800 images from 13,645 individuals and is split into two partitions, one for training purposes and one for testing (model evaluation). The distribution of images between the partitions is shown in Table 3. The source code to reproduce the dataset is publicly available.[5]

Table 3. COVIDx Images distribution among classes and partitions.

Type	Normal	Pneumonia	COVID-19	Total
Training	7966	5421	152	13569
Test	100	100	31	231

3.2   The COVID-19 Dataset of CRXs Displayed in Monitors (C19-CRX-M) Dataset

As shown in Table 3, the number of COVID-19 images for training is 152 images. The normal and pneumonia classes have a huge number of samples when compared to the COVID-19. It is impractical to take photos of all images from pneumonia and normal classes (13,387 images). In that sense, we only select 152 random images of normal samples and 152 random images of pneumonia samples from the COVIDx dataset.

To generate the dataset of screen photographs, the selected images from the COVIDx dataset were displayed on different computer screens of which photographs were taken with different smartphones. The selection process can be summarized as follows:

---

[3] https://github.com/agchung/Figure1-COVID-chestxray-dataset.
[4] https://github.com/agchung/Actualmed-COVID-chestxray-dataset.
[5] https://github.com/lindawangg/COVID-Net.

- For C19-CRX-M training set: 152 Normal images randomly selected from the COVIDx training set, 152 Pneumonia images randomly selected from the COVIDx training set, and all the 152 COVID-19 images are available in the COVIDx training set.
- For the C19-CRX-M test set: All the images are available in the COVIDx test set.

The C19-CRX-M class distribution is shown in Table 4. The detailed information about the selected images and used devices is available at github.

Table 4. C19-CRX-M Images distribution among classes and partitions.

Type	Normal	Pneumonia	COVID-19	Total
Training	152	152	152	456
Test	100	100	31	231

After describing the datasets, in the next section, we define the metrics used to assess the quality of the models.

4   Evaluation Metrics

Following the methodology in [13] and [19], in this work, three metrics are used to evaluate models: accuracy (Acc), COVID-19 sensitivity (Se_C), and COVID-19 positive prediction ($+P_C$), i.e.,

$$Acc = \frac{TP_N + TP_P + TP_C}{\#samples} \qquad Se_C = \frac{TP_C}{TP_C + FN_C} \qquad + P_C = \frac{TP_C}{TP_C + FP_C} \qquad (2)$$

where: TP_N is the number of normal samples correctly classified; TP_P is the number of Pneumonia (Non-COVID-19) samples correctly classified; TP_C is the number of COVID-19 samples correctly classified; FN_C is the number of COVID-19 samples classified as normal or Pneumonia (non-COVID-19); FP_C is the number of Pneumonia (non-COVID-19) and normal samples classified as COVID-19.

5   Computational Experiments and Discussion

In this section, the experiments implemented to test each of the hypotheses raised in Sect. 1 are presented along with results and implications.

5.1   Misclassification of Photographs of Displayed CXRs

This experiment tackles the following hypothesis: *A DL model for CXR based diagnosis of COVID-19 misclassify smartphone photographs of Displayed CXRs.*

Setup. The EffcientNet-C19 B3 of [13] is used to classify the test images from the C19-CRX-M dataset. Then, accuracy, positive prediction, and sensitivity metrics as defined in Sect. 4 were computed. To verify how this setup would affect a larger model, the exact same procedure is performed with the COVIDNet Large of [19] which is more than 2GB larger than EffcientNet-C19 B3.

Results. Table 5, presents the results. It is possible to observe that both approaches fail to appropriately classify the CXR photographs. As can be seen in the confusion matrices in Fig. 4, the majority of the images are classified as COVID-19. This explains the high sensitivity with and low positive prediction for the COVID-19 class.

Table 5. Evaluation of deep learning model on the C19-CRX-M dataset

Approach	Acc	Se_C	$+P_C$
COVIDNet - Wang *et al.* [19]	16.88%	100.00%	13.90%
EfficientNet-C19 - Luz *et al.* [13]	16.02%	100.00%	15.27%

Since both models were trained in the same dataset, we conjecture that these results may have occurred because of the way the COVIDx is built. In COVIDx the majority of pneumonia and normal images come from the same source, that is, the NIH Clinic Center PACS system [14]. Meanwhile, the COVID-19 images come from very heterogeneous sources including donations from physicians. Hence, the COVID-19 set is more subject to external noise than its pneumonia and normal counterparts. This might have induced the DL models to "think" that the screen photographs belonged to the COVID-19 class. Figure 4 presents the confusion matrix for both models which supports the above claims.

5.2   Effect of Dataset Augmentation

Once one is aware of the problem with the CXR photographs, a natural step is to add data like this to the training dataset, as a data augmentation technique. Thus, in this section, the following hypothesis is tested: *Augmenting the training dataset with smartphone photographs of displayed CXRs gives the model the ability to produce accurate results even with this noisy data input method.*

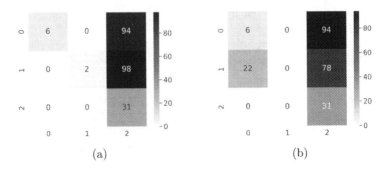

(a)   (b)

Fig. 4. Confusion matrices: (a) EfficientNet-C19, (b) COVIDNet. 0 is normal samples, 1, pneumonia and 2, COVID-19.

Setup. Due to its effectiveness and suitability for smartphone applications, in this experiment, the focus is on two variants of the EfficientNet-C19 [13], the B0 and B3.

Both neural networks are trained with a combination between the C19-CRX-M dataset and the COVIDx images used to generate the C19-CRX-M. Thus, the models see the original and screen versions of every image in the training and dataset.

As shown in Table 6, the images used by both architectures consist of the C19-CRX-M dataset plus the images from the COVIDx dataset used to produce the C19-CRX-M. Furthermore, we also vary the resolution of the input images which can be 224×224 (EfficientNet B0 default input size [17]), 300×300 (EfficientNet B3 default input size [17]), and 448×448.

Table 6. Distribution of images from the combination of the original images and the C19-CRX-M dataset

Type	Source	Normal	Pneumonia	COVID-19	Total
Training	Screen photograph	152	152	152	456
	Original image	152	152	152	456
Test	Screen photograph	100	100	31	231
	Original image	100	100	31	231

Results. Table 7 presents the results for the three quality metrics defined in Sect. 4.

Table 7. Results for the EfficientNet based models on the smartphone photographs, original imagens and a merge of both. (EF = EfficienNet-C19; ORI = COVIDx Original Images; CAM = C19-CRX-M Images)

Model	Test data	Acc	Se_C	$+P_C$
EFB0 224 × 224	CAM	51.52%	83.87%	22.41%
	ORI	90.91%	90.32%	80.00%
	ORI + CAM	77.21%	87.10%	35.76%
EFB3 300 × 300	CAM	74.46%	87.10%	43.55%
	ORI	90.04%	87.10%	87.10%
	ORI + CAM	82.25%	87.10%	58.06%
EFB0 448 × 448	CAM	57.14%	96.77%	31.91%
	ORI	91.77%	96.77%	96.77%
	ORI + CAM	74.46%	96.77%	48.00%
EFB3 448 × 448	CAM	65.80%	90.32%	37.33%
	ORI	91.77%	100.00%	91.18%
	ORI + CAM	78.79%	95.16%	54.13%

The first point to highlight is the increase in both accuracy and positive prediction of COVID-19 screen photographs when compared with the results in Table 5. Nevertheless, this improvement remains far from the results obtained on the COVIDx images.

Increasing the input image size from 224 × 224 to 448 × 448 was beneficial for the EfficientNet-C19 B0 but it was not beneficial the EfficientNet-C19 B3. We conjecture that the B3 version is more sensitive to noise than the B0 version. Thus, for B3, having a higher rate of compression in the input decreases this effect. On the other hand, since B0 is already robust to noise, having a larger input image gave it more information to exploit.

Figure 5 shows the confusion matrices for the four tested models. It is possible to see that, with the augmented dataset, the model mistakes get more diversified and the bias towards COVID-19 observed in the previous experiment (Fig. 4) is not as extreme anymore.

Overall, the augmented dataset did significantly improve the accuracy of the models. Even so, the models still struggle to correctly classify the smartphone photographs of the displayed CXRs and the overall accuracy remains unacceptable for the intended application. Thus, for the presented setting, the augmented dataset did not solve the problem satisfactorily. Nevertheless, given how the augmentation changed the distribution of the errors, a bigger and more varied dataset may improve the results even further.

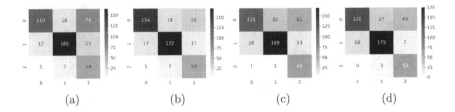

Fig. 5. Confusion matrices for the four models tested on the C19-CRX-M dataset. 0 is normal samples, 1, pneumonia and 2, COVID-19. (a) is the EfficientNet B0 224 × 224, (b) is the EfficientNet B3 300 × 300, (c) is the EfficientNet B0 448 × 448 and (d) is the EfficientNet B3 448 × 448.

5.3   Discarding Photographs of Displayed CXRs Automatically

Having verified the inability of the models in coping with the CXR screen photographs, in this section, we test the following hypothesis: *It is possible to build a model that distinguishes photographs of displayed CXRs from proper CXR images and discards them automatically before the diagnosis process.*

Setup. In this experiment, we train the EfficientNet-C19 B0 on the dataset presented in Table 6 to verify if it can distinguish between the CXR photographs and proper CXR images. Hence, the task becomes a two-class classification problem. One class represents the proper images obtained from the COVIDx dataset and the other class represents the photographs in the C19-CRX-M dataset.

As shown in Table 6, the training set is balanced. Thus, it has been decided not to perform any data augmentation and use only the data available.

Results. The confusion matrix obtained with the proposed setup is depicted in Fig. 6. It can be seen that the proposed approach reached an accuracy of 100%. Thus, this methodology may be used as a previous step to COVID-19 classification in which the signals are classified as good (proper images) or not (photographs of displayed CXRs).

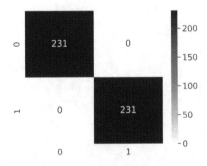

Fig. 6. Confusion matrix for discarding CXRs screen photographs automatically. 0 is the original image and 1 is screen pictures.

6   Conclusion

Deep Learning applied to CXR based COVID-19 screening has shown a lot of promise, in particular, in a scenario of worldwide test kit shortage. Thus, having a mobile app embedding such technology would be an important step in order to make the technology really useful and accessible. In such an application, a natural input would be a picture taken from the smartphone itself often from the monitor attached to the PACS. In order to study the effect of such inputs in the DL models, the C19-CRX-M dataset was created by taking pictures of CXR images displayed on computer monitors.

The results show that the models trained on COVIDx fail to classify the CXR pictures and tend to classify the majority of them as COVID-19. We conjecture that this phenomenon might be due to the nature of the COVIDx dataset, in which COVID-19 images are from a different distribution when compared to the normal and pneumonia ones which are mostly DICOM files from NIH PACS.

We have also evaluated a data augmentation strategy in which the CXR pictures are merged with the original images. In this scenario, an overall reduction is observed in the accuracy, COVID-19 positive prediction, and COVID-19 sensitivity when compared with a scenario with the original images only. However, there is an improvement in the screen picture classification, from 16.88% and 13.90% to 88.25% and 58.06% of accuracy and COVID-19 positive prediction, respectively.

Despite the improvement, a 58.06% COVID-19 positive prediction remains too low for a real-world application. Because of that, an approach to filter the CXR pictures out of the COVID-19 classification pipeline has also been proposed. Since the noise is visually quite significant, the proposed method had no difficulty in filtering the pictures. The proposed methodology has presented 100% effectiveness which makes the system as whole much more reliable.

Overall, the results show that the tested models are far from being able to correctly classify most of the pictures taken of monitors. Thus, researchers and practitioners must be aware of these limitations, especially, when planning to put these models to production and embed them into a web service or mobile app. On the other hand, these same neural network architectures found it easy to distinguish these pictures from regular images. Having a model like that to discard screen pictures might be a workaround while the datasets are not big and comprehensive enough to allow for the construction of a reliable solution.

References

1. Abbas, A., Abdelsamea, M.M., Gaber, M.M.: Classification of COVID-19 in chest X-ray images using Detrac deep convolutional neural network. Appl. Intell. **51**(2), 854–864 (2021)
2. American College of Radiology: ACR recommendations for the use of chest radiography and computed tomography (CT) for suspected COVID-19 infection. ACR website. (2020)
3. Andronikou, S., et al.: Paediatric radiology seen from Africa. Part I: providing diagnostic imaging to a young population. Pediatric Radiol. **41**(7), 811–825 (2011)

4. Araujo-Filho, J.D.A.B., Sawamura, M.V.Y., Costa, A.N., Cerri, G.G., Nomura, C.H.: COVID-19 Pneumonia: what is the role of imaging in diagnosis? Jornal Brasileiro de Pneumologia 46 (2020)
5. Chowdhury, M.E.H., et al.: Can AI help in screening viral and COVID-19 pneumonia? (2020)
6. Cohen, J.P., Morrison, P., Dao, L.: COVID-19 image data collection. arXiv preprint arXiv:2003.11597 (2020)
7. Davarpanah, A.H., et al.: Novel screening and triage strategy in Iran during deadly coronavirus disease 2019 (COVID-19) epidemic: value of humanitarian teleconsultation service. J. Am. College Radiol. 17(6), 1 (2020). https://doi.org/10.1016/j.jacr.2020.03.015
8. Deng, J., Dong, W., Socher, R., Li, L.J., Li, K., Fei-Fei, L.: ImageNet: a large-scale hierarchical image database. In: CVPR09 (2009)
9. Fu, Y.: Image classification via fine-tuning with EfficientNet (2020). https://bit.ly/3AG4hQ6
10. Hemdan, E.E.D., Shouman, M.A., Karar, M.E.: COVIDX-Net: a framework of deep learning classifiers to diagnose COVID-19 in X-ray images. arXiv preprint arXiv:2003.11055 (2020)
11. Li, T., Han, Z., Wei, B., Zheng, Y., Hong, Y., Cong, J.: Robust screening of COVID-19 from chest X-ray via discriminative cost-sensitive learning. ArXiv abs/2004.12592 (2020)
12. Luz, E., Moreira, G., Junior, L.A.Z., Menotti, D.: Deep periocular representation aiming video surveillance. Pattern Recogn. Lett. 114, 2–12 (2018)
13. Luz, E., et al.: Towards an effective and efficient deep learning model for COVID-19 patterns detection in X-ray images. Res. Biomed. Eng. 38(1), 149–162 (2021). https://doi.org/10.1007/s42600-021-00151-6
14. RSNA: Radiological Society of North America. RSNA pneumonia detection challenge. https://www.kaggle.com/c/rsna-pneumonia-detection-challenge/data. Accessed 01 Apr 2020
15. Sandler, M., Howard, A., Zhu, M., Zhmoginov, A., Chen, L.C.: MobileNetV2: inverted residuals and linear bottlenecks. In: Proceedings of the IEEE Conference on Computer Vision and Pattern Recognition, pp. 4510–4520 (2018)
16. Schwartz, A.B., et al.: The accuracy of mobile teleradiology in the evaluation of chest X-rays. J. Telemed. Telecare 20(8), 460–463 (2014). https://doi.org/10.1177/1357633X14555639
17. Tan, M., Le, Q.V.: EfficientNet: rethinking model scaling for convolutional neural networks. arXiv preprint arXiv:1905.11946 (2019)
18. Wang, L., Lin, Z.Q., Wong, A.: COVID-Net: a tailored deep convolutional neural network design for detection of COVID-19 cases from chest X-ray images. Sci. Rep. 10, 19549 (2020). https://doi.org/10.1038/s41598-020-76550-z
19. Wang, L., Wong, A.: COVID-Net: a tailored deep convolutional neural network design for detection of COVID-19 cases from chest radiography images. arXiv preprint arXiv:2003.09871 (2020)
20. Wang, X., Peng, Y., Lu, L., Lu, Z., Bagheri, M., Summers, R.M.: ChestX-ray8: hospital-scale chest X-ray database and benchmarks on weakly-supervised classification and localization of common thorax diseases. In: 2017 IEEE Conference on Computer Vision and Pattern Recognition (CVPR) (2017). https://doi.org/10.1109/cvpr.2017.369, https://doi.org/10.1109/CVPR.2017.369
21. Xue, Y., Onzo, B.M., Mansour, R.F., Su, S.: Deep convolutional neural network approach for COVID-19 detection. Comput. Syst. Sci. Eng. 42(1), 201–211 (2022)

Artificial Neural Networks to Analyze Energy Consumption and Temperature of UAV On-Board Computers Executing Algorithms for Object Detection

Renato de Sousa Maximiano[1]([✉]) [iD],
Valdivino Alexandre de Santiago Júnior[1] [iD], and Elcio Hideiti Shiguemori[2] [iD]

[1] Instituto Nacional de Pesquisas Espaciais (INPE), São José dos Campos,
SP 12227-010, Brazil
{renato.maximiano,valdivino.santiago}@inpe.br
[2] Instituto de Estudos Avançados (IEAV), Trevo Coronel Aviador José Alberto
Albano do Amarante 01 - Putim, São José dos Campos, SP 12228-001, Brazil
elcio@ieav.cta.br

Abstract. When incorporating object detection models into unmanned aerial vehicles (UAVs) on-board computers, two aspects are relevant aspects. Firstly, the energy consumption required by the computer on board the UAV during the mission, since low-cost electric UAVs currently have low flight autonomy. Moreover, during the mission, the computer's processor may suffer overheating caused by the running algorithm, which may directly impair the continuity of a given task or burn the computer. In this study, we aim to estimate the energy consumption and make temperature predictions of a computer embedded in UAVs for missions involving object detection. We propose a method, Analyzing Energy Consumption and Temperature of On-board computer of UAVs via Neural Networks (ETOUNN), which uses a multilayer perceptron (MLP) network to estimate the energy consumption and a long short-term memory (LSTM) network for predicting temperature. Our experiment relied on a Raspberry Pi 4 8 GB computer running nine popular models of object detectors (deep neural networks): eight of which are pre-trained models of the YOLO family, and one Mask R-CNN network. Regarding energy consumption, we compared our method to multivariate and simple regression-based on two metrics: mean squared error (MSE) and the R^2 regression score function. As for temperature prediction and considering the same metrics, ETOUNN was compared to the Autoregressive Integrated Moving Average (ARIMA), the Neural Basis Expansion Analysis for interpretable Time Series forecasting (N-BEATS), and a gated recurrent unit (GRU) network. In both comparisons, our method presented superior performances, showing that it is a promising strategy.

Keywords: UAVs · Artificial neural networks · Deep learning · Object detection · Energy consumption · Temperature

© The Author(s), under exclusive license to Springer Nature Switzerland AG 2022
J. C. Xavier-Junior and R. A. Rios (Eds.): BRACIS 2022, LNAI 13654, pp. 523–538, 2022.
https://doi.org/10.1007/978-3-031-21689-3_37

1 Introduction

Unmanned aerial vehicles (UAVs) can be classified as aircraft without humans on board, remotely piloted by individuals on the ground or in-flight [17]. Currently, UAVs have had a significant range of applications, in various sectors, such as construction/infrastructure [30], agriculture [22], transport and logistics [14], surveillance and security [26], public health related to the COVID-19 pandemic [2], and for the aerospace sector [12].

In many missions involving UAVs, computational vision techniques [19] [38] are used. Object detection is an important task within computational vision as it allows not only classifying an image into a single object of interest but also several objects, detailing each object via the delimitation of coordinates [28]. Currently, there are different models for object detection tasks where they can be divided into single-stage detectors, such as Single Shot MultiBox Detector (SSD) and You Only Look Once (YOLO) [5], and two-stage ones such as R-Convolutional Neural Network (R-CNN) and Mask R-CNN [20]. The detector algorithms can be executed in computers embedded in the UAVs. Raspberry Pi is a computer widely used for this type of task [36] [34], as it has small geometric dimensions and it is not heavy.

Two important factors must be considered when choosing to incorporate object detection models into an on-board computer. Firstly, the energy consumption required by the embedded computer of the UAV must be taken into account. Currently, most low-cost electric UAVs only fly up to 30 min [11]. Mathematical models for estimating energy consumption in UAVs take into account factors such as the energy needed to overcome air drag, rotors, and power supply to the UAV's electronics [23]. While some of these factors can be estimated with good accuracy, the power supply part for the UAV's electronics is a little more difficult to estimate.

One of the reasons for this difficulty is that the same UAV can run different software into its electronics/computer, and this can demand more or less energy. Hence, characterizing which techniques/algorithms, implemented in software and embedded in the on-board computer of a UAV, demand greater energy consumption, and also the magnitude of this greater demand, becomes relevant. The second factor refers to the temperature of the embedded computer's processor. During the mission, the on-board computer processor may overheat caused by the on-board algorithm and this may impact the continuity of the mission, decrease the life of the equipment, or even may cause the board to burn out. Thus, making predictions of the processor temperature during the mission is important to maintain the life of the embedded computer and avoid problems during the mission.

In this article, we aim to estimate energy consumption and predict the temperature of a computer's processor embedded in UAVs. We relied on a Raspberry Pi 4 computer and nine popular object detectors. We propose a method, Analyzing Energy Consumption and Temperature of On-board computer of UAVs via Neural Networks (ETOUNN), which uses a multilayer perceptron (MLP) [13] network to estimate energy consumption and long short-term memory (LSTM)

[15] network for predicting temperature. In its first stage, our method proposes the creation of several MLP models, by varying the values of hyper-parameters, capable of estimating the energy consumption of the algorithms used during the flight, in addition to assess the impacts of such energy consumption related to the UAV. In The second step, ETOUNN aims to predict the temperature of the Raspberry Pi 4 processor, and we also suggest several LSTM models by selecting various values of hyper-parameters.

Our experiment considered nine models of object detectors, deep neural networks (DNNs): two YOLOv3 models, three YOLOv4 models, three YOLOv4-Tiny models, and a Mask R-CNN model. Regarding energy consumption, we compared our method to multivariate and simple regression based on two metrics: mean squared error (MSE) and the R^2 regression score function. As for temperature prediction and considering the same metrics, ETOUNN was compared to the Autoregressive Integrated Moving Average (ARIMA) [27], the Neural Basis Expansion Analysis for interpretable Time Series forecasting (N-BEATS) [29], and a gated recurrent unit (GRU) [8] network.

The contributions of this study are: i) we propose a method that addresses two important aspects for embedding objection detection models into a UAV's on-board computer: energy consumption and temperature prediction; ii) we perform an extensive evaluation to compare our method to several other approaches to show the feasibility of our proposal.

This article is organized as follows. Section 2 presents relevant related studies. Section 3 presents our method and describe the experiment we conducted. Results and discussion are presented in Sect. 4. Section 5 presents conclusions and future directions.

2   Related Work

2.1   Energy Consumption

In [37], the energy consumption of convolutional neural networks for word detection is analyzed using a Raspberry Pi, where energy measurements are obtained through a USB meter. The results of this research show a high correlation between inference time and model accuracy with energy consumption. The work, proposed by [6], does something similar working with computational vision algorithms, reaching the same conclusion of the strong correlation between inference time and model accuracy with energy consumption. [18] aims to measure the performance and power consumption of OpenCV programs on the Raspberry Pi, where programs run by varying the execution frequency. The results show significant differences in performance and power consumption when varying the algorithm used and the operating frequency. Both works cited above to perform an analysis of energy consumption when artificial intelligence algorithms are executing, the analyses are performed by directly evaluating the performance of the algorithms [3], on the other hand, investigates how the Raspberry Pi's energy consumption is affected by the main functionalities that can be performed by end users on the platform, the study also compares the Raspberry Pi with other devices such as cell phones, tablets, and desktops, noting that when compared to these devices, the Raspberry Pi has better energy efficiency. In general, the works cited focus only on the analysis of energy consumption, seeking an answer to the factors that impact energy consumption. For these analyses, the algorithm itself is not isolated, obtaining global answers for energy consumption (Algorithm + Computer). Our work focuses on filling this gap, focusing not only on energy consumption analysis but also on estimating consumption. In addition to also being able to isolate the power consumption of the algorithm and the power consumption of the computer.

2.2   Temperature

Increasing the Raspberry Pi's efficiency can lead to a considerable temperature rise. In [4] and [31], the computer overheats when running computational vision algorithms, compromising the life of the computer and possibly leading to a total loss of the board depending on the temperature hit. In line with these observations, the work proposed by [24] aims to analyze techniques to lower the temperature of the Raspberry Pi during maximum processor workload. For the work, 3 cases were analyzed, without refrigeration, with refrigeration, and with active refrigeration, where only the last case showed an improvement in the operating conditions of the equipment. However, even with the use of active refrigeration, in some cases the temperature exceeded 70 °C. In [16] and [25] are also used, cooling techniques to avoid compromises on the Raspberry Pi. The works cited above show a critical problem of overheating on the Raspberry Pi when a task of high complexity is demanded, and in general, the solution applied to this problem is the use of cooling. The use of cooling does not guarantee 100% that the board will not degrade or burn at high temperatures. Our methodology can, through AI techniques, predict the overheating of the computer when using computational vision algorithms, contributing to the life of the equipment and avoiding catastrophic losses.

3   The ETOUNN Method and Experiment Description

The ETOUNN method can be divided in 6 steps as shown in Fig. 1. We detail each step below. Moreover, in order to better explain how our method work in practice, we also describe here how we instantiated each step of our method regarding the experiment we carried out.

3.1   Initial Tests and Configurations

The first step is to verify that the selected computational vision algorithms work correctly when running on the Raspberry Pi processor. Thus, it is necessary to adjust the versions of the libraries and enable the Raspberry Pi camera functions. Examples of model activation can be seen in Fig. 2.

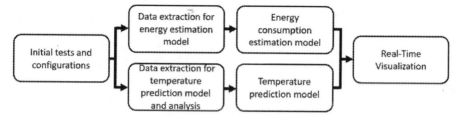

Fig. 1. The ETOUNN method.

Fig. 2. Examples of results obtained with detection algorithms when activated on the Raspberry Pi.

We considered networks pre-trained with the COCO dataset [7]. The models used were: i) YOLO family [1], with different input sizes at activation (YOLOv3 320×320, YOLOv3 416×416; YOLOv4 320×320, YOLOv4 416×416, YOLOv4 512×512; YOLOv4 -tiny 320×320, YOLOv4 -tiny 416×416 YOLOv4 -tiny 512×512); ii) Mask-R-CNN [10]. Even if we have currently newer versions of YOLO detectors, we decided to rely on YOLOv3 and YOLOv4 models since they are very representative approaches of this family of detectors. The OpenCV version used was 4.5.0 running on a Raspberry Pi 4 8 GB.

3.2   Data Extraction for Energy Estimation Model

To train the energy consumption estimation model, data must be extracted from the Raspberry Pi during task execution. Data were extracted from processor temperature, percentage of CPU usage, memory usage, and electrical current, while performing various tasks (Raspberry Pi at rest, browsing the web, running the YOLO and Mask-R-CNN algorithms). A total of 2,323 points were extracted, with a time interval of 1 s between them, totaling approximately 40 min of use. The idea was to obtain several values of these variables, with the objective that the model could obtain good results regardless of the situation of use of the Raspberry Pi. To extract the processor temperature (TEMP), CPU usage percentage (CPU), and memory usage (MEM), the "vcgencmd" command was used, a feature of the Raspberry Pi operating system. A USB-Um34c [35] current meter was used to extract the electric current demand while using the Raspberry Pi. Figure 3 illustrates the organization of the collected data, where CURR means electric current.

	TEMP	CPU	MEM	CURR
0	42.8	3.0	180.1	0.625
1	42.8	3.0	180.4	0.616
2	42.8	3.5	180.2	0.639
3	43.3	3.5	180.2	0.659
4	42.8	4.2	180.1	0.651

Fig. 3. Samples for estimating energy consumption.

3.3   Energy Consumption Estimation Model

The purpose of the first model is to estimate the energy consumption of the Raspberry Pi. As the voltage is constant at 5.15 V, it is necessary to estimate the electric current in order to calculate the electric power (P) as show in Eq. 1:

$$P = U * i \tag{1}$$

where i is the electric current (CURR) and U is the electric voltage. Since electrical energy is roughly defined as electrical power × time, we can estimate the energy consumption by estimating CURR.

The first process is to evaluate the data collected in the previous step and verify the correlation between the variables. As for this study, the correlation results for the electric current variable were: 0.89 for temperature, 0.96 for CPU, and 0.69 for memory.

An MLP network is used to estimate the energy consumption of the Raspberry Pi. To find a model with good effectiveness, an exhaustive search was performed. The following hyper-parameters were varied: number of layers, number of neurons, and dropout after the first layer. Some hyper-parameters such as activation function, optimizer and batch size were fixed. In addition, three-variable input configurations were used: i) Removing the variable with the highest correlation with the electrical current, i.e. CPU; ii) Removing the variable with the lowest correlation with the electrical current, i.e. MEM; and iii) Keeping all variables.

A total of 1,488 points were selected for training, 371 for validation and 464 for testing. Fixed and changed hyper-parameters can be seen below. **As for the models it was fixed:**

- Optimizer: Adam;
- Activation function: Relu;
- Loss: MSE;
- Epochs: 100, Patience: 10;
- Batch size: 12.

As for the models it was varied:

- Number of layers: {1, 2, 3, 4, 5};
- Neurons per layer: {128, 256, 512};
- Dropout: {0, 0.2, 0.4}.

Altogether 3,267 different models were analyzed.

3.4 Data Extraction for Temperature Prediction Model and Analysis

The data to train the Raspberry Pi processor temperature prediction model were collected from simulations of the Raspberry Pi executing object detection algorithms. We considered the flight characteristics of Phantom 4, a commercial UAV developed by Dà-Jiang Innovations Science and Technology (DJI) [9]. This UAV has a battery of 89.2 Wh (Watt-hour) and autonomy of 30 min. Ten simulations of 30 min each were performed for every selected algorithm configuration. Therefore, in total, 90 tables were extracted with 1,800 points of processor temperature and percentage of CPU usage, with a time step equal to 1 s. This amounts 45 h of simulation.

3.5 Temperature Prediction Model

It is recommended to operate the Raspberry Pi 4 at temperatures below 70C, to maintain the equipment's useful life. Moreover, it is important to avoid temperatures close to 80 C in order to not permanently damage the board [32]. With the high temperatures reached in the Raspberry Pi processor running computational vision algorithms, temperature prediction is important. Based on an LSTM model, the goal is to predict the future 15 s of processor temperature as it is considered a safe time frame for making decisions, such as an algorithm pause or an algorithm change during flight before the system overheats.

The process of choosing the model was carried out via a search in the space of hyper-parameters, changing the number of layers, number of neurons, dropout and batch size of the input data of the network.

The data captured in the first 8 simulations of each algorithm configuration were used as training data, in which 20% of the data were randomly separated for validation. And the data from the ninth and tenth simulation of each configuration were used for testing.

Fixed and changed hyper-parameters can be seen below. **As for the models it was fixed:**

- Optimizer: Adam;
- Activation function: Hyperbolic tangent;
- Recurrence function: Sigmoid;
- Loss: MSE;
- Epochs: 100, Patience: 10;
- Batch size: 4;
- Forecast points: 15.

As for the models it was varied:

- Number of layers: $\{1, 3, 5\}$;
- Neurons per layer: $\{32, 64, 128\}$;
- Dropout: $\{0, 0.3\}$;
- Points before: $\{15, 30\}$;

Twenty different LSTM models were analyzed.

3.6   Real-Time Visualization

After obtaining the best models for estimating energy consumption and forecasting the temperature of the embedded computer's processor, our method proposes to execute both models in a ground station (communication via network) [33], visualizing the results in real-time. Thus, the operator can perceive the results and make the proper decisions based on them. We believe that this is more feasible since adding more algorithms into the UAV's computer would almost certainly imply an increase in the two variables of interest (energy and temperature).

4   Results and Discussion

4.1   MLP for Estimating Energy Consumption

Firstly, all collected data and developed code can be accessed online[1].After running the 1,089 models for each input data configuration and obtaining the results for each configuration, the best models were separated by number of layers configuration and input data configuration and, as we have already mentioned, considering the following settings: i) Removing the variable with the highest correlation with the electrical current, i.e. CPU; ii) Removing the variable with the lowest correlation with the electrical current, i.e. MEM; and iii) Keeping all variables. The results illustrated in Table 1 show that the addition of layers

---

[1] https://github.com/RenatoMaximiano/ETOUNN.Accesson:August30,2022.

caused a significant improvement in the results, with the 5-layer model being the best configuration in both data entry configurations. An improvement in the results is observed when removing the lowest correlation data from the input data. The model with the best results (in **bold**) had as input the variables of Temperature and CPU, with 5 layers, 256 neurons in the first hidden layer, a dropout of 0.2, and then 4 more hidden layers, with 256, 128, 256 and 512 neurons, respectively. This model got an MSE of 0.00054.

Table 1. Energy consumption: Results with the best MLP models by layer and input.

Input	layer-1	Dropout	layer-2	layer-3	layer-4	layer-5	MSE	R2
i)	256	0.2	x	x	x	x	0.00579	0.83552
i)	256	0.4	128	x	x	x	0.00538	0.84737
i)	128	0.2	128	256	x	x	0.00512	0.85472
i)	512	0.4	512	128	128	x	0.00512	0.85474
i)	128	0.2	128	256	128	256	0.00511	0.85550
ii)	128	0.4	x	x	x	x	0.00102	0.97114
ii)	256	0.4	256	x	x	x	0.00095	0.97307
ii)	256	0.4	512	128	x	x	0.00067	0.98104
ii)	256	0.4	128	256	128	x	0.00058	0.98338
ii)	**256**	**0.2**	**256**	**128**	**256**	**512**	**0.00054**	**0.9847**
iii)	128	0.2	x	x	x	x	0.00095	0.9728
iii)	256	0.2	512	x	x	x	0.00068	0.9807
iii)	128	0.4	256	512	x	x	0.00076	0.97835
iii)	256	0.2	512	128	128	x	0.00060	0.98121
iii)	128	0.4	128	256	128	256	0.00056	0.98331

We compared the best MLP network to multivariate regression models [21]. Three multivariate regression models were analyzed where the input data for the regression models considered the three configurations of the input data of the MLP models: i) ; ii) and iii). In addition, a simple regression model is also compared, iv) With one variable with the highest correlation with the electrical current, (CPU).

Results can be seen in Table 2. The best regression model obtained a mean square error of 0.00263, that is, the MLP network has an error 4.8 times smaller. Thus, our method was highly superior than these approaches justifying the need of an neural network approach.

Table 2. MLP vs regression.

Input	Model	MSE	R2
ii)	**MLP**	**0.00054**	**0.98470**
i)	Multivariate regression	0.00526	0.85063
ii)	Multivariate regression	0.00282	0.91986
iii)	Multivariate regression	0.00263	0.92522
iv)	Simple regression	0.00288	0.91818

4.2   Energy Consumption Analysis

The energy consumption estimation model was applied to all 90 simulations. Equation 2 shows the energy consumption Wh, where $\overline{W_t}$ is the average energy used by the board + algorithm, t is the runtime in hours, and Wh_{uav} is the energy supplied by the UAV's battery. It is possible to verify a consumption (Raspberry Pi + Algorithm) of up to 3.37% of the UAV's battery power, that is, 3 Wh of consumption. This results in a 68 s decrease in the UAV's total autonomy. When considering only the algorithm, the values are 1.64% of the UAV's battery power consumption, resulting in a 33 s decrease in the UAV's total autonomy. It is also possible to observe that the detector algorithms consume a maximum of 48.67% of the consumption generated by the Raspberry Pi, and it can be noted that more robust versions of YOLO consume more energy, along with the Mask-R-CNN algorithm. The results for the simulations of each configuration with the highest percentage of energy consumption and the seconds consumed of the total autonomy of the drone, as well as the respective percentages of the Raspbeery Pi and the algorithms can be seen in Table 3.

$$Wh(\%) = \left(\frac{\overline{W_t} \cdot t \cdot 100}{Wh_{uav}} \right) \tag{2}$$

Table 3. Simulation results for energy consumption.

Algorithm	Wh%	Time(s)	%Rasp	%Algorithm
Y.v3-320-1	3.09	62.44	55.98	44.02
Y.v3-416-9	3.21	64.81	53.93	46.07
Y.v4t-320-2	2.85	57.57	60.71	39.29
Y.v4t-416-0	2.86	57.69	60.59	39.41
Y.v4t-512-7	3	60.63	57.65	42.35
Y.v4.-320-1	3.08	62.21	56.18	43.82
Y.v4.-416-2	3.25	65.61	53.28	46.72
Y.v4.-512-5	3.37	68.09	51.33	48.67
Mask-7	3.29	66.4	52.64	47.36

4.3   LSTM for Processor Temperature Prediction

After running 20 models and obtaining the results for each configuration, the best models by number of layers were separated. The results illustrated in Table 4 show the best configuration. The 5-layer model, with 128 neurons in the first hidden layer, dropout of 0.3, 64 neurons in the second and third layers, 32 neurons in the fourth and fifth layers, and an input size equal to 30 time steps, had an error root mean square equal to 2.67673. This was the best model which is highlighted in **bold**.

Table 4. Temperature prediction with input equal to 30-time steps: LSTM results.

layer-1	Dropout	layer-2	layer-3	layer-4	layer-5	MSE	R2
64	0.3	x	x	x	x	2.69371	0.76151
128	0.3	64	32	x	x	2.71590	0.78037
128	**0.3**	**64**	**64**	**32**	**32**	**2.67673**	**0.78642**

We compared the best LSTM network with other techniques used for time series forecasting: ARIMA, N-BEATS and a GRU network. For the model and GRU, we ran 20 different configurations, changing the number of layers and neurons as previously done for the LSTM network. The same was done for the N-BEATS model, analyzing together the configuration proposed in [29]. The best GRU model followed the same configuration as the best LSTM model. The best model for the N-Beats was with only one hidden layer, composed of 128 neurons. The results can be seen in Fig. 4 and in Table 5. Again, our ETOUNN method and its proposed LSTM model performed better than the other time series forecasting techniques, as shown in **bold**.

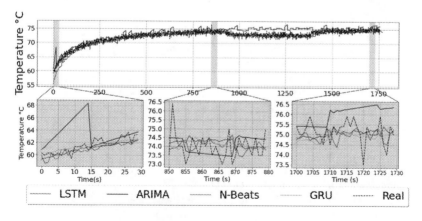

Fig. 4. Raspberry Pi 4 processor temperature forecast over 30 min.

Table 5. Comparison of forecast models.

Model	MSE	R2
LSTM	**2.67673**	**0.78642**
ARIMA	4.48777	0.72865
N-Beats	2.73033	0.77484
GRU	2.68513	0.77267

Note that the second best technique with results close to ours was GRU which is also a sort of recurrent neural network, followed by the N-Beats and ARIMA model.

4.4   Average and Maximum Values for Processor Temperature and CPU Usage (%)

The average and maximum values of processor temperature and CPU usage (%) for each algorithm run can be seen in Table 6. When analyzing the average and maximum results of the Raspberry Pi processor temperature, it is possible to see high temperatures when running the detector algorithms, exceeding the recommended temperature of 70 C to avoid degradation and getting very close to the extreme temperature of 80 C.

Table 6. Average and maximum values for processor temperature and CPU usage (%).

Algorithm	Avg. Temp	Max. Temp	Avg. CPU	Max. CPU
yolov3-320	71.17 σ 4.92	78.4	87.78 σ 7.02	99.0
yolov3-416	71.42 σ 4.40	78.4	90.00 σ 7.95	99.0
yolov4-tiny-320	70.01 σ 3.92	75.9	87.73 σ 8.23	99.3
yolov4-tiny-416	69.27 σ 3.66	77.4	89.60 σ 8.68	98.7
yolov4-tiny-512	70.30 σ 4.13	77.9	92.34 σ 10.02	99.3
yolov4-320	68.49 σ 3.15	74.5	81.96 σ 1.64	86.6
yolov4-416	68.95 σ 3.05	74.0	84.42 σ 2.83	89.0
yolov4-512	68.12 σ 2.81	73.0	86.75 σ 4.02	98.0
Mask	67.31 σ 2.72	72.5	89.29 σ 7.43	100.0

Forecast of Points in Sequence Above 70 °C. The main purpose of the prediction model is to predict computer overheating trends. This occurs when the Raspberry Pi starts to run constantly in temperatures above 70 C red line in Fig. 5. An evaluation was then performed to estimate the accuracy of the prediction of overheating trends. Thus, three-point trends were defined in a sequence above 70 C, five points or more in a sequence above 70 C, in addition to isolated points above 70 C. The results are very promising, we managed to get 85.69 (for sequence = 1), 96.38 (for sequence = 3) and 98.43 (for sequence >= 5).

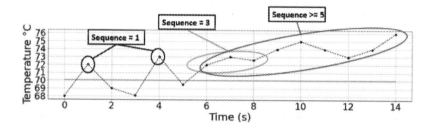

Fig. 5. Tendencies.

5   Conclusions

In this article, we analyzed the energy consumption and temperature prediction of a computer embedded in UAVs for missions involving object detection. The motivation to fulfill these objectives comes from two important factors that should be considered when incorporating object detection models into an on-board computer: energy consumption of the computer and temperature prediction of the computer's processor.

To achieve this goal, the ETOUNN method is proposed to estimate the energy consumption of a Raspberry Pi 4 8 GB computer, and to predict the temperature of its processor when executing computational vision algorithms for object detection. We relied on an exhaustive approach to select an MLP to address the energy consumption and a search to find the most suitable LSTM network to achieve the processor temperature prediction.

Results are quite optimistic where our method got a mean square error of 0.00054 for estimating energy consumption and 2.67673 for predicting the processor temperature. We compared the MLP-based energy consumption approach to multivariate and simple regression. As for temperature prediction, our method was compared to ARIMA, a traditional technique, N-BEATS, a recent DNN approach, and a GRU network. In both comparisons, our method presented superior performances showing that it is a promising approach for practitioners. The results show that the processor temperature prediction model was able to predict with 98.43% a board overheating trend.

We have already started the implementation of the real-time visualization task of our method. As for the future, we will finish such an implementation. We will also consider automated tuning of hyper-parameters to realize whether there are any advantages over our strategy which is based on a manual process. We will compare the temperature prediction part of our method to other techniques such as Prophet and CNN-1D. Moreover, we will investigate the possibility to create a multi-tasking learning approach where we will create a single model to address both tasks (energy consumption and temperature prediction).

Acknowledgments. This research was developed within the **IDeepS** project which is supported by LNCC via resources of the SDumont supercomputer. This research was also supported by CAPES, grant #88887.610576/2021-00.

References

1. AlexeyAB (2021). https://github.com/AlexeyAB/darknet. Accessed 4 Feb 2022
2. Anggraeni, S., et al.: The deployment of drones in sending drugs and patienblood samples covid-19. Indonesian J. Sci. Technol., 18–25 (2020)
3. Bekaroo, G., Santokhee, A.: Power consumption of the raspberry pi: a comparative analysis. In: 2016 IEEE International Conference on Emerging Technologies and Innovative Business Practices for the Transformation of Societies (EmergiTech), pp. 361–366. IEEE (2016)
4. Benoit-Cattin, T., Velasco-Montero, D., Fernández-Berni, J.: Impact of thermal throttling on long-term visual inference in a cpu-based edge device. Electronics **9**(12), 2106 (2020)
5. Bochkovskiy, A., Wang, C.Y., Liao, H.Y.M.: Yolov4: optimal speed and accuracy of object detection. arXiv preprint arXiv:2004.10934 (2020)
6. Canziani, A., Paszke, A., Culurciello, E.: An analysis of deep neural network models for practical applications. arXiv preprint arXiv:1605.07678 (2016)
7. in Context, C.O. (2021). https://cocodataset.org/home. Accessed 4 Feb 2022
8. Dey, R., Salem, F.M.: Gate-variants of gated recurrent unit (gru) neural networks. In: 2017 IEEE 60th International Midwest Symposium on Circuits and Systems (MWSCAS), pp. 1597–1600. IEEE (2017)
9. DJI (2021). https://www.dji.com/br. Accessed 25 Feb 2022
10. ESCOLADEESTUDANTES (2021). https://github.com/escoladeestudantes/opencv/tree/min/22_ObjectDetection_Mask-RCNN_Inception_v2_COCO. Accessed 4 Nov 2021
11. FILMORA (2021). https://filmora.wondershare.com/drones/drones-with-longest-flight-time.html. Accessed 25 Oct 2021
12. Fornari, G., de Santiago Júnior, V.A., Shiguemori, E.H.: A self-adaptive approach for autonomous UAV navigation via computer vision. In: Gervasi, O., Murgante, B., Misra, S., Stankova, E., Torre, C.M., Rocha, A.M.A.C., Taniar, D., Apduhan, B.O., Tarantino, E., Ryu, Y. (eds.) ICCSA 2018. LNCS, vol. 10961, pp. 268–280. Springer, Cham (2018). https://doi.org/10.1007/978-3-319-95165-2_19
13. Gardner, M.W., Dorling, S.: Artificial neural networks (the multilayer perceptron)-a review of applications in the atmospheric sciences. Atmos. Environ. **32**(14–15), 2627–2636 (1998)
14. Gonzalez-R, P.L., Canca, D., Andrade-Pineda, J.L., Calle, M., Leon-Blanco, J.M.: Truck-drone team logistics: a heuristic approach to multi-drop route planning. Transp. Res. Part C Emerging Technol. **114**, 657–680 (2020)
15. Hochreiter, S., Schmidhuber, J.: Long short-term memory. Neural Comput. **9**(8), 1735–1780 (1997)
16. Joseph, F.J.J.: Iot based weather monitoring system for effective analytics. Int. J. Eng. Adv. Technol. **8**(4), 311–315 (2019)
17. Jr., J.D.A.: Fundamentos de Engenharia Aeronautica (2015)

18. Kadota, K., Taniguchi, I., Tomiyama, H.: Measurement of performance and energy consumption of opencv programs on raspberry pi. Bull. Networking Comput. Syst. Softw. **9**(1), 35–39 (2020)
19. Kanellakis, C., Nikolakopoulos, G.: Survey on computer vision for uavs: current developments and trends. J. Intell. Robot. Syst. **87**(1), 141–168 (2017)
20. Kassim, Y.M., Byrne, M.E., Burch, C., Mote, K., Hardin, J., Larsen, D.R., Palaniappan, K.: Small object bird detection in infrared drone videos using mask r-cnn deep learning. Electronic Imaging **2020**(8), 85–1 (2020)
21. Katipamula, S., Reddy, T.A., Claridge, D.E.: Multivariate regression modeling (1998)
22. Kulbacki, M., et al.: Survey of drones for agriculture automation from planting to harvest. In: 2018 IEEE 22nd International Conference on Intelligent Engineering Systems (INES), pp. 000353–000358. IEEE (2018)
23. Langelaan, J.W., Schmitz, S., Palacios, J., Lorenz, R.D.: Energetics of rotary-wing exploration of titan. In: 2017 IEEE Aerospace Conference, pp. 1–11. IEEE (2017)
24. Machowski, J., Dzieńkowski, M.: Selection of the type of cooling for an overclocked raspberry pi 4b minicomputer processor operating at maximum load conditions. J. Comput. Sci. Inst. **18**, 55–60 (2021)
25. Manganiello, F.: Computer vision on raspberry pi. In: Computer Vision with Maker Tech, pp. 159–225. Springer (2021)
26. Marin, L.: The humanitarian drone and the borders: unveiling the rationales underlying the deployment of drones in border surveillance. In: Custers, B. (ed.) The Future of Drone Use. ITLS, vol. 27, pp. 115–132. T.M.C. Asser Press, The Hague (2016). https://doi.org/10.1007/978-94-6265-132-6_6
27. Morettin, P.A., Toloi, C.M.d.C.: Análise de séries temporais (2004)
28. Morimitsu, H.: Uma abordagem estrutural para detecção de objetos e localização em ambientes internos por dispositivos móveis. Ph.D. thesis, Universidade de São Paulo (2011)
29. Oreshkin, B.N., Carpov, D., Chapados, N., Bengio, Y.: N-beats: neural basis expansion analysis for interpretable time series forecasting. arXiv preprint arXiv:1905.10437 (2019)
30. Phung, M.D., Quach, C.H., Dinh, T.H., Ha, Q.: Enhanced discrete particle swarm optimization path planning for uav vision-based surface inspection. Autom. Constr. **81**, 25–33 (2017)
31. Prathaban, T., Thean, W., Sazali, M.I.S.M.: A vision-based home security system using opencv on raspberry pi 3. In: AIP Conference Proceedings, vol. 2173, p. 020013. AIP Publishing LLC (2019)
32. RASPBERRY-PI (2022). https://www.raspberrypi.com/products/raspberry-pi-4-model-b/. Accessed 25 Feb 2022
33. RASPBERRY-PI (2022). https://www.raspberrypi.com/documentation/computers/remote-access.html. Accessed 25 Feb 2022
34. Safadinho, D., Ramos, J., Ribeiro, R., Filipe, V., Barroso, J., Pereira, A.: Uav landing using computer vision techniques for human detection. Sensors **20**(3), 613 (2020)
35. SUPEREYES (2021). https://supereyes.ru/img/instructions/Instruction_UM34(C).pdf. Accessed 4 Oct 2021
36. Szolga, L.A.: On flight real time image processing by drone equipped with raspberry pi4. In: 2021 IEEE 27th International Symposium for Design and Technology in Electronic Packaging (SIITME), pp. 334–337. IEEE (2021)

37. Tang, R., Wang, W., Tu, Z., Lin, J.: An experimental analysis of the power consumption of convolutional neural networks for keyword spotting. In: 2018 IEEE International Conference on Acoustics, Speech and Signal Processing (ICASSP), pp. 5479–5483. IEEE (2018)
38. Van Beeck, K., Ophoff, T., Vandersteegen, M., Tuytelaars, T., Scaramuzza, D., Goedemé, T.: Real-time embedded computer vision on UAVs: In: Bartoli, A., Fusiello, A. (eds.) ECCV 2020. LNCS, vol. 12538, pp. 665–674. Springer, Cham (2020). https://doi.org/10.1007/978-3-030-66823-5_40

FastContext: Handling Out-of-Vocabulary Words Using the Word Structure and Context

Renato M. Silva[1,3]([✉]), Johannes V. Lochter[2,3], Tiago A. Almeida[1], and Akebo Yamakami[2]

[1] Department of Computer Science, Federal University of São Carlos (UFSCar), Sorocaba, São Paulo, Brazil
talmeida@ufscar.br
[2] Department of Systems and Energy, University of Campinas (UNICAMP), Campinas, São Paulo, Brazil
akebo@dt.fee.unicamp.br
[3] Department of Computer Engineering, Facens University, Sorocaba, São Paulo, Brazil
{renato.silva,johannes.lochter}@facens.br

Abstract. Languages are dynamic, and new words or variations of existing ones appear over time. Also, the dictionary used by the distributed text representation models is limited. Therefore, methods that can handle unknown words (i.e., out-of-vocabulary – OOV) are essential for the quality of natural language processing systems. Although some techniques can handle OOV words, most of them are based only on one source of information (e.g., word structure or context) or rely on straightforward strategies unable to capture semantic or morphological information. In this study, we present FastContext, a method for handling OOV words that improves the embedding based on subword information returned by the state-of-the-art FastText through a context-based embedding computed by a deep learning model. We evaluated its performance using tasks of word similarity, named entity recognition, and part-of-speech tagging. FastContext performed better than FastText in scenarios where the context is the most relevant source to infer the meaning of the OOV words. Moreover, the results obtained by the proposed approach were better than the ones obtained by state-of-the-art OOV handling techniques, such as HiCE, Comick, and DistilBERT.

1 Introduction

As people get used to communicating over the Internet, the number of new users increases fast each year. The volume of text messages on social networks and blogs has also been growing increasingly. As human analysis on large volumes of data becomes unfeasible, natural language processing (NLP) techniques have become increasingly important. For automating processes usually executed by humans, such as reading messages and capturing their semantic relations, NLP

J. C. Xavier-Junior and R. A. Rios (Eds.): BRACIS 2022, LNAI 13654, pp. 539–557, 2022.
https://doi.org/10.1007/978-3-031-21689-3_38

systems need to transform unstructured data into some structure using text representation methods. The text representation adopted by computer systems for many years was distributive, such as bag-of-words. However, it has known issues, such as high dimensional representation, word locality loss, and inability to capture the semantic meaning, especially in short and noisy texts [17].

Due to common issues of distributive representations, distributed representation has arisen. Popular methods such as continuous bag-of-words (CBOW), skip-gram (SG) [20], and FastText [3], are trained by exploring each word's neighborhood in messages from a large corpus to capture its semantic relations into a fixed-length vector, known as word embedding. The representation model is a collection of word embeddings with an entry for each word of the vocabulary.

When a word was not observed when training the text representation model, it is known as an out-of-vocabulary (OOV) word. Since it does not have an embedding representation associated, the predictive model can not use it, which can degrade its performance. Some straightforward techniques are commonly used to represent OOV words in distributed text representation, such as a random or a zero vector [33]. Both techniques provide information about the presence of an OOV word in the message but none or little information about the OOV and its semantic role in the message is given.

In order to properly handle OOV words providing semantic information to a learning method, there are two primary sources of information to compute the representation: (a) morphological structures of the OOV words, such as suffix, prefix, and radicals; and (b) the context, corresponding to the set of the words surrounding the OOV in the message. Mimick and FastText uses only morphological information to compute an OOV embedding. On the other side, more advanced text representation methods are more focused on context, such as deep neural networks based on Transformer architecture [31] (e.g., BERT, DistilBERT, and RoBERTa). Recently, some approaches were proposed to explore both morphology and context, such as Comick [9] and HiCE [11].

Some studies evaluated OOV handling methods in different NLP tasks. For example, [18] compared some OOV handling methods in text categorization, named entity recognition (NER), and part-of-speech (POS) tagging. According to the results, the methods that employ both morphological and context information to infer the embedding for a given OOV word obtained good results in all evaluated tasks. However, FastText was the best method in NER and POS-tagging tasks, even using only one source of information to handle OOV words: its subwords (morphological information). Despite the high performance of FastText, it has a disadvantage in scenarios where the context is relevant. The same subwords can form many different words. In this case, only the context could help to select the best candidate. Also, for some OOV words, the only useful source of information is the context, as they may contain subwords that are not related to any other word seen by the model during its training.

Based on the results reported by [18], we raised the hypothesis that an OOV handling method based on subwords and context information could preserve the performance of FastText while being a good candidate for a greater variety of NLP tasks. Based on this hypothesis, we propose in this study an OOV handling method called FastContext. It improves the OOV embedding computed by FastText by using a context-based embedding learned by a deep learning model.

The remainder of this paper is organized as follows. Section 2 briefly describes the main existing OOV handling methods. Section 3 details our proposed method. Section 4 presents the experiments with their methodology and discussion over found results. Finally, we offer our main conclusions and guidelines for future work in Sect. 5.

2   OOV Handling

Unknown words can harm the performance of predictive models in text processing tasks. Therefore, OOV handling is often necessary to find an appropriate representation for these words. Otherwise, the sentence representation may ignore the information regarding unknown words in the text message [10].

The more traditional and commonly employed methods in the literature for OOV handling in distributed representation are also simple in their proposals and assumptions. They do not use learning methods to infer the representation or find a substitute word for the unknown term. For example, instead of ignoring the OOV words, leaving no trace of their existence for a given learning method, it is possible to associate all of them to a random vector [10]. Another strategy described by [10] is to represent each unknown word by a different vector of random values. According to [33], the OOV word can also be represented by a vector of zeros to inhibit activation in a neural network, making the network understand there is something there, instead of ignoring it.

As many OOV are misspelled words, [25] suggests handling them by finding the expected word when misspelled. The author proposes to compute a general translation vector, which is the average distance between the canonical version and its misspelled word. In this way, we can find the canonical form by summing the general translation vector to the misspelled word embedding calculated from its subword information. Thus, we can use the resulting vector to find the closest words in the representation model, where the canonical form is expected to be.

Another effective strategy to handle OOV words is the one adopted by Fast-Text, which uses embeddings based on character n-grams. For instance, considering $n = 3$ and the input word book, FastText represents it as the subwords $<bo, boo, ook, ok>$. Angle brackets represent the beginning and end of words, so that $<ook>$ and ook are two different words. Also, $<book>$ is included as a word in the representation model. When a word is not in the vocabulary, the model can use its n-grams to represent it. For example, $<booking>$ could be represented by the sum of $<bo, boo, ook$ if the n-grams ing and $ng>$ do not exist in the vocabulary. Its capacity of representing a word by its n-grams uses morphological information to find a representation for an OOV if any subword is available in the trained FastText model.

Another method for OOV handling is Mimick [22]. It is a neural network architecture proposed to learn the relationship between the words' characters in the vocabulary and the word embeddings from an existing representation model. Each character is represented by a fixed-length vector named character embedding, adjusted through the training phase using a Bidirectional LSTM. As its name suggests, the network mimics the embedding for a given word through the embedding for each character, minimizing the Euclidean distance between the network output and the target word embedding.

FastText and Mimick are examples of OOV handling methods capable of finding a representation for an OOV using its subword information, solely based on morphological structure. However, these methods cannot deal with OOV words that have different meanings in different contexts. If morphological information is the only source to generate a representation, then an OOV word will always have the same representation, regardless of the context in which it appears.

Although several methods can handle OOV using only morphological structure, the context information can also be important. For instance, [12] suggest representing an OOV by the mean of the embeddings of adjacent words in the sample. Although this method does not analyze the semantics of the sample or the OOV's morphology, the authors noticed that this strategy achieved better results than replacing the OOV with a zero or a random vector.

Comick [9] is an extension of Mimick that besides receiving the OOV characters as input, it also receives context information from words adjacent to the OOV in the text message. Comick has three inputs: left context, OOV, and right context. Both contexts are fed into the network as a collection of words, so they are represented by word embeddings. In contrast, the OOV word is segmented by characters and represented by character embeddings. Contexts share the same pre-trained word embedding model, while characters have their own representation model, learned through the training phase. Each part is processed using a Bidirectional LSTM. A concatenated output is generated from the output of each of these parts, which is projected into the network output.

As an alternative to Comick, HiCE [11] was proposed using modern network implementations such as attention mechanisms to encode the input and generate an approximate output for the OOV. In this architecture, a sliding window is employed to analyze the context several times. It employs attention weights layers to define the importance of each window. The result is concatenated to a character-cnn block responsible for analyzing the morphological information of the OOV words. A dense layer projects the concatenation, generating the vector representation for the OOV word.

Another strategy to handle OOV words is through deep language models. Although they have obtained state-of-the-art results in several NLP tasks, some of them demand intensive memory consumption. Some proposals aim to compact these models while keeping their performance as high as possible. For instance,

DistilBERT [27] has a size 40% smaller than BERT, but retains its capabilities as a language understanding model, and it is faster.

As there are several alternatives to deal with the OOV words, [18] evaluated and compared the state-of-the-art methods (FastText [3], DistilBERT [27], GPT2 [23], Electra [5], LSTM [28], Transformer [31], RoBERTa [16], Comick [9], and HiCE [11]) in intrinsic and extrinsic evaluations using text categorization tasks, such as named entity recognition (NER) and part-of-speech (POS) tagging. According to the authors, although none of them obtained the best performance in all tasks, Comick, in general, achieved higher performance while FastText stood out in the experiments with NER e POS tagging. Based on these results, we can conclude that the strategy used by Comick of combining morphological and contextual information of the OOV words might generate better results in a greater variety of NLP tasks. Furthermore, given the outstanding results of FastText in NER and POS tagging tasks reported by [18], we hypothesized that it is possible to provide an OOV handling method by extending the FastText to extract information from both morphology and context in a more effective way than Comick and HiCE.

Based on this hypothesis, in the following section we present FastContext. This OOV handling method uses a context-based embedding created by a deep learning model to improve the OOV embedding learned by FastText. This method aims to extend FastText to use the context and character structure while preserving its performance and making it more general.

3   FastContext

We introduce the FastContext as an extension of FastText [3], aiming to consider the context information in addition to the morphological data. FastContext consists of two parts: (1) a deep neural network architecture to generate a reference vector for the OOV word based on its morphological structure and the context information; and (2) an algorithm to select the most appropriate representation based on the reference vector. In the following, we introduce the deep neural network architecture and explain how we used it to handle OOV.

3.1   Deep Neural Network Architecture

Although some studies proposed deep neural networks to learn good representations for OOV words [9,11], these methods may not perform well in tasks with short text messages [18]. To address this gap, we designed the deep neural network architecture presented in Fig. 1 as an essential part of FastContext.

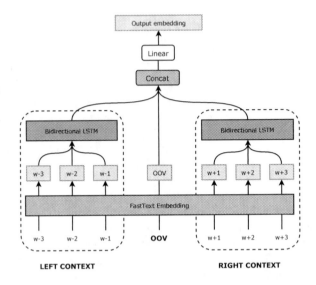

Fig. 1. Deep neural network architecture.

The proposed architecture handles its input in three different channels: the left context, the OOV, and the right context. A pre-trained FastText embedding represents every word from the input (the OOV and the words from both contexts). FastContext demands a good representation for each word, mainly for the OOV, because the architecture does not have a character-rnn or character-cnn module like Mimick [22].

After each part of the input is represented by FastText, a bidirectional LSTM cell handles each context (left and right). Although both cells have the same structure, they do not share weights. The output vectors from these cells are concatenated with the OOV representation returned by FastText. The concatenated vector resulting from the previous step is then connected to a dense layer and projected into a vector space similar to the original pre-trained embedding model, which generates its output.

We train the FastContext using a sliding window over a corpus. First, we separate each window into three parts: the left context, the central word, and the right context. The central word is scrambled by inverting the position of the two central letters, generating an OOV word. The left and the right context and the OOV are used as input to the network during training.

The objective function is to minimize the cosine distance between the central word embedding and the network's output, which we expect to generate an appropriate embedding for an OOV word. We call the network output the reference vector because we used it in the next step: the selection algorithm.

3.2 Selection Algorithm

FastContext selects the most appropriate word from a list of candidates from FastText. Figure 2 shows this selection algorithm.

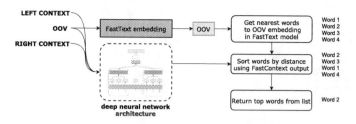

Fig. 2. FastContext method.

The input of the algorithm is the left and right contexts and the OOV word itself. The output is the most suitable word to replace the OOV obtained from a pre-trained FastText embedding. To find the most appropriate word, we fed the input information into the deep neural network architecture, which returns a reference vector inferred by morphological and context information. Simultaneously, the OOV is embedded, and a list with the words closest to its embedding is returned. Then, we sort the elements of this list by the cosine similarity to the reference vector. Higher similarity words are closer to the top of the list returned by this sorting phase. Finally, we select the word at the top of the list as the most suitable to replace the OOV. In resume, FastContext combines morphological information with the context, using the selection algorithm (Fig. 2) to approximate the FastText output to the reference vector returned by the deep neural network architecture (Fig. 1).

To illustrate how FastContext works, Table 1 presents (i) a text sample, (ii) the OOV for the given embedding model, (iii) the list of the words closest to the vector returned by FastText when embedding the OOV, and (iv) the same list of words but sorted by the cosine similarity with the reference vector.

Table 1. FastContext example of usage.

Sample	OOV	FastText	FastContext
Caterpillar inc was awarded an army	Reduce	Troduce	Produce
Contract option valued at number		Froduce	Imtroducing
Million to roduce a high speed		Indroduce	Repoduce
Rubber tracked bulldozer		Inroduce	Capatalize
		Itroduce	Accommidate
		⋮	Manupulate
		Produce	⋮
		⋮	Supaproducer
		Accommidate	Roducer
		Producerx	Coproduce

In the example presented in Table 1, FastContext receives the three words to the left, the other three to the right, and the OOV (the central word). The OOV "roduce" from this sample is the result of a typo. Its left context is "valued number million"[1] and its right context is "high speed rubber". The expected word to replace "roduce" is "produce".

FastContext processes both contexts and the OOV by a trained neural network and generates the reference vector. Next, the OOV is embedded by a pre-trained FastText embedding model, and a list of the closest words to its embedding is retrieved. Table 1 presents the nearest words to the embedding of the OOV "roduce". The most immediate word is "troduce", which is not our expected candidate. Then, FastContext sorts this list of words using the cosine similarity to the reference vector. The column *FastContext* presents the sorted list. In this case, our expected word is at the top of the sorted list ("produce"). Although the third and fourth positions, "repoduce" and "capatalize", are typos, they are more interesting to replace the OOV word than any of the first options from Fastext, since they are related to production in the context of finance contracts.

This example shows how using the context through the reference vector returned by the deep neural network helped improve the result of FastText. Using morphological information alone as done by FastText is often insufficient to generate useful quality embeddings. FastContext increases the probability of returning better embeddings for the OOV words while being more generic than FastText and a better candidate for scenarios where context is relevant.

4   Experiments

As is traditionally done in the literature, we carry out two types of experiments to assess FastContext's performance: an intrinsic and extrinsic evaluation. In the intrinsic evaluation, we evaluate FastContext in a word similarity task using a benchmark misspelling dataset. Finally, we conduct a comprehensive extrinsic evaluation in two established tasks that can be significantly affected by OOV words: named entity recognition (NER) and part-of-speech (POS) tagging.

In all experiments, to generate the vector representation of the documents, we used FastText word embeddings [3] trained on Twitter7 (T7) [32], a corpus of tweets posted from June to December 2009. We removed the retweets and empty messages of this corpus and selected only the English-language text samples. In the end, we used the remaining 364,025,273 messages to train the embeddings. The word embedding size is 200.

We use the FastText model trained on T7 to train the FastContext deep neural network architecture (Sect. 3.1) and selection algorithm (Sect. 3.2). First,

---

[1] We remove any word shorter than three characters.

we trained its architecture using 10% of the messages of the T7 dataset. We built the LSTM cells using the PyTorch[2] repository with its default parameters, except for the number of epochs, which we set to 10. We padded or truncated the messages to 200 words and used a vector of zeros to represent the padding words. Finally, we set the size of the list of words to 50 in the selection algorithm.

We compared the performance of FastContext with baseline techniques that apply strategies with different levels of complexity to handle OOV words. Some of them make simple substitutions; others use information from the morphological structure of the OOV word, or infer the OOV word based on its context. Below, we present the baseline techniques evaluated.

- **Zero**: the OOV is represented by a vector of zeros.
- **Random**: all OOV words are represented by the same random vector generated at the beginning of the experiment.
- **Sum**: the OOV is represented by the sum of the embeddings of the words in the document.
- **Average**: the OOV is represented by the average of the embeddings of the words in the document.
- **FastText**: the OOV is represented by the vector obtained by the FastText [3].
- **DistilBERT**: we used the original model available in the `transformers`[3] library for Python 3, identified by the keyword `'distilbert-base-cased'`.
- **HiCE**: we trained the model random sampling 10% of the T7 dataset using the default parameters of the official implementation[4]. The morphological information flag was set to true, thus it uses the word structure to predict embeddings.
- **Comick**: we trained the model random sampling 10% of the T7 dataset using the default parameters on the private implementation obtained from [9].

4.1 Word Similarity

We performed an intrinsic evaluation on the word similarity task to analyze how well it captures the semantic similarity between an OOV word and its gold standard counterpart. We used the benchmark TOEFL-Spell dataset, which contains annotations of misspellings from essays written by non-native speakers of English [8]. To evaluate the OOV handling methods, we selected only the correctly spelled words that are not OOV and the misspellings that are OOV words for the FastText model. In the end, 606 valid words of the TOEFL-Spell dataset remained with one or more corresponding misspellings.

---

[2] PyTorch Github. Available at https://bit.ly/2B7LS3U, accessed on November 14, 2022.

[3] Transformers. Available at https://huggingface.co/transformers, accessed on November 14, 2022.

[4] HiCE. Available at https://github.com/acbull/HiCE, accessed on November 14, 2022.

We searched for an occurrence of each correctly spelled word in one of the first ten thousand messages on T7. In the end, we selected a message for each of the 486 correct words in this subset of T7. We replaced the correctly spelled words with one of the respective misspellings (chosen at random). Then, we computed the embedding for the misspelled word using each of the OOV handling methods. Finally, we calculated the cosine similarity between the OOV embedding and the gold standard embedding of the correctly spelled word.

Table 2 presents the average cosine similarity obtained by each OOV handling method. We did not evaluate the zero and random approaches because as they generate the same vector for all OOV words, the cosine similarity would always be the same.

Table 2. Results obtained in the word similarity task.

Method =>	FastText	FastContext	Average	Sum	HiCE	DistilBERT	Comick
Avg. cosine similarity =>	0.47	0.41	0.40	0.40	0.29	0.26	0.07

The average cosine similarity obtained by FastContext was better than HiCE and Comick, two baselines that also use information from the word structure and context to handle OOV words. Concerning Comick, the performance of FastContext was 485% higher. DistilBERT, which uses data only from the context, also obtained a much lower average similarity than FastContext (36% lower).

Interestingly, the straightforward methods (sum and average) obtained a higher average similarity than other more complex approaches based on artificial neural networks (HiCE, DistilBERT, and Comick). The short and noise messages used to generate the text representation model and to train HiCE and Comick may have affected their learning.

The best method in the task of word similarity was FastText. FastContext was the second-best one, but it has the advantage of being more generic because it uses information from subwords and the context to infer embedding for OOV words. When the OOV word characters are not sufficient to infer its embedding, FastContext tends to be better than FastText because it also uses information from the context. To provide further evidence for this hypothesis, we compared FastText and FastContext in a task that simulates a scenario with new words with semantic similarity to known words but whose characters have no relation to any other known word. For that, we used the well-known benchmark Chimera dataset [15].

In this dataset, two, four, or six sentences are used to determine the meaning of a novel concept, called chimera, whose meaning is a combination of the meanings of two existing words. Each chimera is represented by a nonce word, whose morphological structure is not related to the two words on which its meaning is based. For each chimera, the dataset provides a set of six probing words, and the human-annotated similarities between the probing words and the Chimera [15]. To generate the vector representation for each sentence in the Chimera dataset, we also used the FastText word embeddings trained on T7.

To compare FastContext and FastText, we used them to infer an embedding for a given chimera based on each sentence (two, four, or six sentences) that forms its meaning. Six nonces can represent each chimera. We discard nonces that are not an OOV word and select one of the remaining nonces at random to represent the chimera in the sentences that form its meaning. For each method, the final embedding for the chimera is the average of the vectors obtained for each sentence. For each chimera, we calculated the cosine similarity between its embedding and the probe words. Then, we used the Spearman correlation to measure the agreement between the human annotations and the results obtained by FastContext and FastText.

Table 3. Average Spearman correlation obtained in the Chimera Dataset.

	FastContext	FastText
2 sentences	0.05	0.04
4 sentences	0.08	0.04
6 sentences	0.06	0.03

The results corroborate with our hypothesis that FastContext is more generic than FastText because it uses the OOV's context in addition to its morphology. In scenarios where the context is relevant, FastContext inferred better OOV embeddings. In both experiments, the context was important for FastContext to infer higher quality embeddings than those obtained by FastText.

4.2   Downstream Tasks

The phenomenon of OOV words may severely impair machine learning methods in downstream tasks such as NER and POS-tagging. It is challenging to identify the grammatical group or the named entity without a known vector representation. To evaluate FastContext in these tasks, we performed experiments with the well-known datasets presented in Table 4.

First, we converted all documents to lowercase. As the samples are provided separated by their terms with each one having an associated label (entity or POS), it was unnecessary to perform tokenization. Then, we processed each term using Ekphrasis [2], a tool to handle text from social media, such as emojis, URLs, email addresses, numbers, monetary values, dates, and user mentions.

Table 4 presents the main statistics about the datasets, where $|D|$ is the number of documents, and $|V|$ is the number of unique terms (vocabulary). Moreover, $\mathcal{M}^t$ and $\mathcal{I}^t$ are the median and the interquartile range of the number of terms per document.

Table 4. Basic statistics about the datasets for NER and POS tagging.

Dataset	$|D|$	$|V|$	$\mathcal{M}^t$	$\mathcal{I}^t$
GENIA-POS [29]	18,546	21,495	24.00	14.00
Treebank-POS [19] (from NLTK)	3,914	12,408	25.00	16.00
Tweebank-POS [14]	918	4,479	12.00	12.00
Twitter-POS [24]	787	4,766	20.00	12.00
Anatomical-NER [21]	4,697	13,232	23.00	19.00
BIO-NER [13]	22,402	25,103	24.00	15.00
CoNLL2003-NER [30]	22,137	30,289	9.00	16.00
GUM-NER [4]	3,495	9,786	16.00	15.00
Rare-NER [7]	5,690	20,773	17.00	13.00
SEC-NER [26]	1,475	4,168	24.00	40.00
WikiGold-NER [1]	1,841	8,504	19.00	16.00

Evaluation. We carried out the NER and POS tagging experiments using a Bidirectional LSTM with a time distributed dense layer. We built it using Keras[5] on top of TensorFlow[6]. All the documents were padded to 200 words. A vector of zeros represented the padding words and the OOV words not handled. We set the number of epochs to 10, and used the RMSProp optimizer with the default learning rate of Keras. We did not perform any parameter optimization for the neural network because this study's objective is not to obtain the best possible result but to analyze the ability of FastContext to handle OOV words.

We performed the experiments using a holdout validation with 70% of the documents in the training set and 30% in the test set. To compare the results in the NER task, we employed the entity level F-measure. In the experiments with POS-tagging, we evaluated the prediction performance using token accuracy.

Results. Table 5 presents the results. For each dataset, the method that obtained the best F-measure (NER) or the best accuracy (POS-tagging) received rank 1, while the worst one got rank 9.

---

[5] Keras. Available at https://keras.io/. Accessed on November 14, 2022.
[6] TensorFlow. Available at https://www.tensorflow.org/. Accessed on November 14, 2022.

Table 5. Performance considering all words.

	Zero	Random	Sum	Average	FastText	HiCE	Comick	DistilBERT	FastContext
GENIA-POS	0.96	0.96	0.96	0.96	0.98	0.96	0.96	0.95	0.97
NLTKTreebank-POS	0.93	0.94	0.93	0.93	0.94	0.92	0.93	0.91	0.94
Tweebank-POS	0.80	0.80	0.80	0.80	0.80	0.79	0.79	0.80	0.80
Twitter-POS	0.76	0.76	0.75	0.76	0.77	0.76	0.76	0.76	0.77
Anatomical-NER	0.61	0.62	0.57	0.61	0.61	0.61	0.62	0.59	0.61
Bio-NER	0.63	0.63	0.61	0.61	0.66	0.60	0.63	0.57	0.65
CONLL2003-NER	0.87	0.88	0.88	0.88	0.88	0.88	0.88	0.87	0.88
GUM-NER	0.33	0.34	0.33	0.33	0.34	0.33	0.33	0.34	0.34
Rare-NER	0.43	0.43	0.43	0.44	0.43	0.42	0.44	0.42	0.44
SEC-NER	0.78	0.78	0.78	0.78	0.79	0.79	0.78	0.78	0.79
WikiGold-NER	0.52	0.54	0.53	0.56	0.55	0.53	0.53	0.54	0.56
Avg rank	6.00	4.14	6.32	4.82	2.86	6.27	5.18	6.82	2.59

In general, FastContext obtained better results than all the other baselines that use information from the context to handle OOV words (HiCE, Comick, and DistilBERT). It also obtained the best average ranking and the best performance in 8 of the 11 datasets.

The best overall baseline was FastText, which obtained the second-best average ranking. Although it achieved a lower average ranking than FastContext, their results were similar. From our point of view, this is an excellent result for FastContext, as it was not our goal to be superior to FastText but to be competitive with it and, at the same time, to be more generalist. Apart from the good results in NER e POS-tagging tasks compared to FastText, FastContext has the advantage of being more generic because it uses the OOV context in addition to its morphological structure.

To complement the analysis, we also calculated the performance measures considering only the OOV words with more than two characters and at least one alphanumeric character. In this new analysis, we did not consider all the other words when calculating the performance measures. As the percentage of OOV words per document, in general, is low, we believe that this analysis can better capture the performance concerning the tags or entities exclusively of the OOV words. We hypothesize that if a particular technique properly handled the OOV, it is likely that LSTM will detect the OOV tag or entity correctly. Table 6 presents the results of this analysis.

Table 6. Performance considering only the OOV words.

	Zero	Random	Sum	Average	FastText	HiCE	Comick	DistilBERT	FastContext
GENIA-POS	0.77	0.77	0.76	0.76	**0.93**	0.75	0.75	0.66	0.86
NLTKTreebank-POS	0.81	0.85	0.80	0.83	**0.92**	0.74	0.79	0.56	0.88
Tweebank-POS	0.20	0.38	0.36	0.21	**0.45**	0.26	0.23	0.12	0.30
Twitter-POS	0.22	0.21	0.18	0.23	**0.54**	0.28	0.18	0.15	0.39
Anatomical-NER	0.40	0.48	0.37	0.22	**0.49**	0.47	0.42	0.29	0.37
Bio-NER	0.68	0.69	0.64	0.67	**0.76**	0.66	0.67	0.61	0.72
CONLL2003-NER	0.86	0.92	0.91	0.91	0.92	0.92	0.92	0.83	**0.93**
GUM-NER	0.32	**0.44**	0.36	0.30	0.42	0.39	0.32	0.42	**0.44**
Rare-NER	0.04	0.02	0.07	0.00	**0.26**	0.18	0.11	0.08	0.25
SEC-NER	0.29	0.29	0.00	0.29	**0.73**	0.67	0.25	0.29	0.44
WikiGold-NER	0.30	0.32	0.37	0.23	**0.48**	0.32	0.25	0.18	0.46
Avg rank	5.86	3.86	6.09	6.64	**1.45**	4.68	6.14	7.73	2.55

The results show that, again, FastContext presented superior results over almost all baselines and a much more significant difference. For example, in the results shown in Table 5, the performance obtained by FastContext was, on average, superior to Comick by 0.009. Still, when considering only the OOV words, the difference increases to 0.10. Compared to DistilBERT, the performance obtained by FastContext was higher, on average, 3.19% considering all words, and 79.97% considering only the OOV words. The results obtained by FastContext were also considerably higher than zero, random, sum, average, and HiCE when only the classes of the OOV words were counted for the performance calculation. As a result, the average ranking obtained by FastContext was the second best.

FastText was the only baseline that achieved a better result than FastContext when considering only the OOV words. We can safely conclude that FastText is very effective in NER and POS-tagging tasks. It obtained the best performance in both standard evaluation and when considering only the OOV words. However, FastText can only be effectively applied in scenarios where the subwords of the OOV words are sufficient to infer the embeddings. In many texts, the context is more important than the morphological structure of the OOV words or may even be the only source of information that can infer the meaning of the OOV words. Therefore, the strategy used by FastContext to combine data from the OOV structure and its context tends to be more effective for a wider variety of scenarios.

For a more reliable comparison between FastContext and the baseline methods, we performed a statistical analysis using the non-parametric Friedman test [6]. For a significance level $\alpha = 0.05$, the Friedman test rejected the null hypothesis and indicated statistically significant differences between the methods.

We then performed a pairwise comparison using the Bonferroni-Dunn post hoc test to analyze whether there is statistical evidence indicating that FastContext was superior to any baselines. This test states that the performance of two methods differs significantly if the difference between their ranks is greater than or equal to a critical difference [6]. Figure 3 illustrates the statistical analysis of the results using a significance level $\alpha = 0.05$.

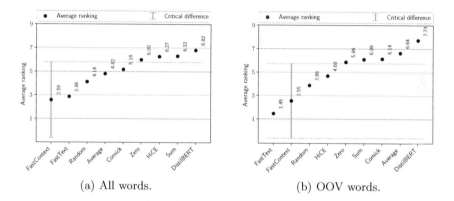

(a) All words.   (b) OOV words.

Fig. 3. Average rankings and critical differences calculated using the Bonferroni-Dunn post-hoc test.

In Fig. 3, methods above the upper red dotted line are considered statistically inferior to FastContext. The proposed method obtained a better average ranking than all baselines and there is statistical evidence to state that its performance is superior to Zero, HiCE, Sum, and DistilBERT when all the words were considered (Fig. 3a). Considering only the OOV words (Fig. 3b), there is enough evidence that FastContext is better than Zero, Sum, Comick, Average, and DistilBERT.

On the other hand, there was not enough statistical evidence to state that the performance of FastContext was superior to FastText, Random, Average, and Comick when all the words were considered (Fig. 3b). Moreover, there is not enough evidence that FastContext is superior to FastText, Random, and HiCE when only the OOV words were used to calculate the performance measures (Fig. 3b).

In addition to the excellent performance shown by the statistical analysis, FastContext has the advantage of being more generic than FastText, which uses only information about subwords to infer a vector for a given OOV word. It is also more generic than DistilBERT, which uses only the context. The results also show that FastContext better combines the morphological and contextual information than HiCE and Comick since it presented better results in the performed experiments.

5   Conclusions

The performance of NLP downstream tasks greatly depends on the quality of text representation. One of the widely used approaches for representing text documents is the distributed text representation that maps words into a low-dimensional continuous space to capture semantic and syntactic information. As a model cannot create a representation for OOV words, it is essential to use approaches that properly handle them and prevent the quality of text representation from being compromised.

Some studies handle OOV words using techniques that generate static vectors (e.g., zero or random vector) or use information about its morphology or context. Using isolated information is generally inefficient because the text is dynamic, and a given document can have OOV words from different sources. Using words known by the text representation model, it is possible to infer some OOV words, mainly when generated through spelling errors, the formation of acronyms, addition of suffixes, or other means. However, often only the context or a combination of the morphological and contextual information is effective to infer the meaning of a given OOV word.

This study presented FastContext, a novel method that extends the state-of-the-art FastText for handling OOV words based on information from both word structure and surrounding context. The proposed approach uses a context based embedding learned by a Bidirectional LSTM to improve the OOV embedding created by FastText.

FastContext presented a performance superior to most baselines in the task of word similarity. FastText was the best baseline in the word similarity task, obtaining the results closest to those of FastContext. However, we showed that in scenarios where the context is more relevant than the subwords of the OOV word, FastContext obtained better results.

We also performed an extrinsic evaluation of FastContext in NER and POS-tagging tasks, employing datasets often used in related studies. In general, FastContext obtained a performance similar to FastText at the same time that it is more generic since the use of context makes it capable of inferring the vector of OOV words even in scenarios where their structure is not sufficient. Moreover, FastContext obtained better results than all other baselines, both when we analyzed all classes and when we considered only the classes predicted for the OOV words.

In future research, we intend to analyze FastContext in text documents from other languages, such as Portuguese, Spanish, French, and Italian. We also plan to evaluate it in other NLP tasks, such as fake news, hate speech detection, spam detection, and text summarization.

Acknowledgments. We gratefully acknowledge the support provided by the São Paulo Research Foundation (FAPESP; grant #2018/02146-6).

References

1. Balasuriya, D., Ringland, N., Nothman, J., Murphy, T., Curran, J.R.: Named entity recognition in Wikipedia. In: Proceedings of the 2009 Workshop on The People's Web Meets NLP: Collaboratively Constructed Semantic Resources (People's Web), pp. 10–18. Association for Computational Linguistics, Suntec, Singapore, August 2009. https://www.aclweb.org/anthology/W09-3302
2. Baziotis, C., Pelekis, N., Doulkeridis, C.: DataStories at SemEval-2017 task 4: Deep LSTM with attention for message-level and topic-based sentiment analysis. In: Proceedings of the 11th International Workshop on Semantic Evaluation (SemEval-2017), pp. 747–754. Association for Computational Linguistics, Vancouver, Canada, August 2017. https://doi.org/10.18653/v1/S17-2126, https://www.aclweb.org/anthology/S17-2126
3. Bojanowski, P., Grave, E., Joulin, A., Mikolov, T.: Enriching word vectors with subword information. Trans. Assoc. Comput. Linguist. **5**, 135–146 (2017)
4. Bos, J., Basile, V., Evang, K., Venhuizen, N., Bjerva, J.: The groningen meaning bank. In: Ide, N., Pustejovsky, J. (eds.) Handbook of Linguistic Annotation, vol. 2, pp. 463–496. Springer (2017). https://doi.org/10.1007/978-94-024-0881-2_18
5. Clark, K., Luong, M.T., Le, Q.V., Manning, C.D.: ELECTRA: pre-training text encoders as discriminators rather than generators. In: ICLR, pp. 1–18 (2020)
6. Demšar, J.: Statistical comparisons of classifiers over multiple data sets. J. Mach. Learn. Res. **7**, 1–30 (2006)
7. Derczynski, L., Nichols, E., van Erp, M., Limsopatham, N.: Results of the WNUT2017 shared task on novel and emerging entity recognition. In: Proceedings of the 3rd Workshop on Noisy User-generated Text, pp. 140–147. Association for Computational Linguistics, Copenhagen, Denmark, September 2017. https://doi.org/10.18653/v1/W17-4418
8. Flor, M., Fried, M., Rozovskaya, A.: A benchmark corpus of English misspellings and a minimally-supervised model for spelling correction. In: Proceedings of the Fourteenth Workshop on Innovative Use of NLP for Building Educational Applications, pp. 76–86. Association for Computational Linguistics, Florence, Italy, August 2019. https://doi.org/10.18653/v1/W19-4407
9. Garneau, N., Leboeuf, J.S., Lamontagne, L.: Predicting and interpreting embeddings for out of vocabulary words in downstream tasks. In: Proceedings of the 2018 EMNLP Workshop BlackboxNLP: Analyzing and Interpreting Neural Networks for NLP, pp. 331–333. Association for Computational Linguistics, Brussels, Belgium, November 2018. https://doi.org/10.18653/v1/W18-5439
10. Goldberg, Y., Hirst, G.: Neural Network Methods in Natural Language Processing. Morgan & Claypool Publishers (2017)
11. Hu, Z., Chen, T., Chang, K.W., Sun, Y.: Few-shot representation learning for out-of-vocabulary words. In: Proceedings of the 57th Annual Meeting of the Association for Computational Linguistics, ACL 2019, Florence, Italy, Jul 2019
12. Khodak, M., Saunshi, N., Liang, Y., Ma, T., Stewart, B., Arora, S.: A la carte embedding: cheap but effective induction of semantic feature vectors. In: Proceedings of the 56th Annual Meeting of the Association for Computational Linguistics (Volume 1: Long Papers), pp. 12–22. Association for Computational Linguistics, Melbourne, Australia, July 2018. https://doi.org/10.18653/v1/P18-1002

13. Kim, J.D., Ohta, T., Tsuruoka, Y., Tateisi, Y., Collier, N.: Introduction to the bio-entity recognition task at JNLPBA. In: Proceedings of the International Joint Workshop on Natural Language Processing in Biomedicine and Its Applications, pp. 70–75. JNLPBA 2004. Association for Computational Linguistics, Stroudsburg, PA, USA (2004). http://dl.acm.org/citation.cfm?id=1567594.1567610

14. Kong, L., Schneider, N., Swayamdipta, S., Bhatia, A., Dyer, C., Smith, N.A.: A dependency parser for tweets. In: Proceedings of the 2014 Conference on Empirical Methods in Natural Language Processing (EMNLP), pp. 1001–1012. Association for Computational Linguistics, Doha, Qatar, October 2014. https://doi.org/10.3115/v1/D14-1108, https://www.aclweb.org/anthology/D14-1108

15. Lazaridou, A., Marelli, M., Zamparelli, R., Baroni, M.: Compositionally derived representations of morphologically complex words in distributional semantics. In: Proceedings of the 51st Annual Meeting of the Association for Computational Linguistics (Volume 1: Long Papers), pp. 1517–1526. Association for Computational Linguistics, Sofia, Bulgaria, August 2013. https://www.aclweb.org/anthology/P13-1149

16. Liu, Y., et al.: RoBERTa: a robustly optimized BERT pretraining approach. CoRR arXiv:1907.11692 (2019)

17. Lochter, J.V., Pires, P.R., Bossolani, C., Yamakami, A., Almeida, T.A.: Evaluating the impact of corpora used to train distributed text representation models for noisy and short texts. In: 2018 International Joint Conference on Neural Networks (IJCNN), pp. 1–8, July 2018

18. Lochter, J.V., Silva, R.M., Almeida, T.A.: Deep learning models for representing out-of-vocabulary words. In: Proceedings of the 9th Brazilian Conference on Intelligent Systems (BRACIS 2020), pp. 418–434. Springer International Publishing, Rio Grande, RS, Brazil, October 2020. https://doi.org/10.1007/978-3-030-61377-8_29

19. Marcus, M.P., Marcinkiewicz, M.A., Santorini, B.: Building a large annotated corpus of English: The Penn treebank. Comput. Linguist. **19**(2), 313–330 (1993)

20. Mikolov, T., Sutskever, I., Chen, K., Corrado, G., Dean, J.: Distributed representations of words and phrases and their compositionality. In: Proceedings of the 26th International Conference on Neural Information Processing Systems (NIPS 2013), pp. 3111–3119. Curran Associates Inc., Lake Tahoe, Nevada, USA (2013)

21. Ohta, T., Pyysalo, S., Tsujii, J., Ananiadou, S.: Open-domain anatomical entity mention detection. In: Proceedings of the Workshop on Detecting Structure in Scholarly Discourse, pp. 27–36. ACL 2012. Association for Computational Linguistics, Jeju Island, Korea, July 2012

22. Pinter, Y., Guthrie, R., Eisenstein, J.: Mimicking word embeddings using subword RNNs. CoRR arXiv:1707.06961 (2017)

23. Radford, A., Wu, J., Child, R., Luan, D., Amodei, D., Sutskever, I.: Language models are unsupervised multitask learners. OpenAI Blog (2019)

24. Ritter, A., Clark, S., Mausam, Etzioni, O.: Named entity recognition in tweets: an experimental study. In: Proceedings of the 2011 Conference on Empirical Methods in Natural Language Processing, pp. 1524–1534. Association for Computational Linguistics, Edinburgh, Scotland, UK, July 2011

25. Rushton, E.: A simple spell checker built from word vectors (2018). https://blog.usejournal.com/a-simple-spell-checker-built-from-word-vectors-9f28452b6f26

26. Alvarado, J.C.S., Verspoor, K., Baldwin, T.: Domain adaption of named entity recognition to support credit risk assessment. In: Proceedings of the Australasian Language Technology Association Workshop 2015, pp. 84–90, Parramatta, Australia, December 2015

27. Sanh, V., Debut, L., Chaumond, J., Wolf, T.: Distilbert, a distilled version of BERT: smaller, faster, cheaper and lighter (2019)
28. Sundermeyer, M., Schlüter, R., Ney, H.: LSTM neural networks for language modeling. In: INTERSPEECH, pp. 1–4 (2012)
29. Tateisi, Y., Tsujii, J.I.: Part-of-speech annotation of biology research abstracts. In: Proceedings of the Fourth International Conference on Language Resources and Evaluation (LREC 2004). European Language Resources Association (ELRA), Lisbon, Portugal, May 2004
30. Sang, E.F.T.K., De Meulder, F.: Introduction to the CoNLL-2003 shared task: language-independent named entity recognition. In: Proceedings of the Seventh Conference on Natural Language Learning at HLT-NAACL 2003 - Volume 4, pp. 142–147. CONLL 2003. Association for Computational Linguistics, USA (2003). https://doi.org/10.3115/1119176.1119195
31. Vaswani, A., et al.: Attention is all you need. In: Guyon, I., Luxburg, U.V., Bengio, S., Wallach, H., Fergus, R., Vishwanathan, S., Garnett, R. (eds.) Advances in Neural Information Processing Systems 30, pp. 5998–6008. Curran Associates, Inc. (2017). http://papers.nips.cc/paper/7181-attention-is-all-you-need.pdf
32. Yang, J., Leskovec, J.: Patterns of temporal variation in online media. In: Proceedings of the Fourth ACM International Conference on Web Search and Data Mining, pp. 177–186. WSDM 2011. ACM, New York, NY, USA (2011)
33. Yang, X., Macdonald, C., Ounis, I.: Using word embeddings in twitter election classification. Inf. Retr. 21(2–3), 183–207 (2018). https://doi.org/10.1007/s10791-017-9319-5

A Wrapper Approach for Video Anomaly Detection Applying Light Gradient Boosting Machine in a Multiple Instance Learning Setting

Silas Santiago Lopes Pereira[1,2(✉)] (ID) and José Everardo Bessa Maia[1] (ID)

[1] Universidade Estadual do Ceará - UECE, Fortaleza, CE 60714-903, Brazil
jose.maia@uece.br
[2] Federal Institute of Education, Science and Technology of Ceará - IFCE, Aracati, CE 62800-000, Brazil
silas.santiago@ifce.edu.br

Abstract. The automatic detection of video anomalies is a challenging task due to problems such as the subjectivity of the anomaly definition and the sparseness and diversity of anomalous events with the consequent difficulty in obtaining discriminative features. Furthermore, labeling videos is a laborious and expensive task. Multiple instance learning (MIL), by labeling videos instead of frames, has become a solution to mitigate this last challenge. This work presents a wrapper-based MIL approach applying LightGBM for video anomaly detection. From the evaluation with a challenging dataset, we found that our model is competitive against other published methods which used the same test setup.

Keywords: Video anomaly · Multiple instance learning · LightGBM

1 Introduction

Video anomaly detection (VAD) in intelligent surveillance systems contributes to minimize the manual and laborious work of live monitoring. The goal of video anomaly detection (VAD) is to localize spatially or temporally anomalous events in videos [6]. Abnormal behavior detection in video surveillance is an essential task for public safety and monitoring. In human-based surveillance systems, the challenge is that it requires constant human attention and focus by human operators to track surveillance streams continuously. In this sense, automatic anomalous event detection is of great importance. Another challenging aspect in abnormal event detection is the scarceness of labelled information [1].

An important motivation for the application of weakly supervised video anomaly detection is because the obtention of video labels is more realistic and capable to produce more reliable results than unsupervised approaches. There are two classifications for existing weakly supervised video anomaly detection methods, i.e. encoder agnostic and encoder-based methods. The encoder-agnostic

© The Author(s), under exclusive license to Springer Nature Switzerland AG 2022
J. C. Xavier-Junior and R. A. Rios (Eds.): BRACIS 2022, LNAI 13654, pp. 558–573, 2022.
https://doi.org/10.1007/978-3-031-21689-3_39

methods estimate anomaly scores by using task-agnostic video features obtained from a feature encoder, such as C3D or I3D. These methods train only the classifier. Encoder-based approaches performs simultaneously the training of feature encoder and classifier [6].

Multiple Instance Learning (MIL) is a variation of supervised learning for problems with incomplete knowledge about the labels of training instances. The data is then treated as a set of bags where each bag corresponds to a set of individual instances [7]. Different works have addressed the MIL problem to mitigate anomaly detection in video surveillance scenarios [6,8,18–20].

Gradient-boosting decision tree (GBDT) is a widely used approach in which the algorithm has achieved state-of-the-art results in various machine learning problems. The emergency of big data brings computational complexities to GBDT in recent years. As the number of features and instances increases to big data, conventional implementations of GBDT becomes very timing consuming and the trade-off between accuracy and efficiency becomes challenging [9]. LightGBM [9] was released by Microsoft in 2017 as an approach for iterative and parallel training with weak classifiers (decision trees). This is a method for parallel optimization known for fast training speed, high accuracy, memory consumption and support to distributed processing. [22]

The conception of a video anomaly detection model remains challenging, although this research area has been studied for years, once the model needs to be able to understand the differences between abnormal and normal events, especially in situations where events with anomalies are rare and substantially diversified [6]. To mitigate these challenges, we present in this work a new wrapper-based multiple instance learning approach for short-term video anomaly detection that applies a LightGBM model built with publicly available deep features constructed with a clip-based instance generation strategy. The main contributions of this work are summarized as follows:

1. We extend the study published in [16] by the employment of a short-term video anomaly detection approach based on LightGBM method for binary classification under MIL perspective. We also compare the results against other commonly used methods and with the state-of-the-art literature. The results are promising in terms of Area under ROC Curve (AUC);
2. We evaluate the performance results of our approach at frame, segment and video levels. We advocate that analyzing model performance at different levels of granularity is relevant in evaluating multi-instance approaches, mainly in the case of short-term video anomaly detection;
3. We analyze the performance impact of highly correlated features in the generalization capability of LightGBM model;

This work is organized as follows: Sect. 2 reviews some works directly related to this research. Section 3 presents the necessary background. Section 4 describes the methodology and results of our performance evaluation experiments. Section 5 concludes the article.

2   Related Work

There is a considerable number of research studies in the literature on video anomaly detection. A comprehensive survey that expand the coverage of this section can be found in [15].

[20] introduces the AR-NET (Anomaly Regression Net), which is a clip-based video anomaly detection approach. To ensure that training stage only takes into account video-label labels, they train an anomaly regression network for segment-level classification under multiple instance learning paradigm. The authors propose and evaluate to learning functions, to known, Dynamic Multiple-Instance Learning Loss (DMIL) and Center Loss. The feature extractor uses the pre-trained neural network model Inception-v1 I3D (Inflated 3D), which is fed by RGB appearance and optical flow motion data. According to the authors, these features were generated with a clip-based instance generation strategy so that the approach is suitable for short-term video anomaly detection. From the evaluation with the challenging benchmark dataset ShanghaiTech, the proposed AR-NET approach overcomes compared state-of-the-art techniques in performance.

In [6], the authors present the multiple instance self-training framework (MIST) to address the weakly supervised video anomaly detection problem. The proposed framework aims to refine task-specific discriminative representations with only video-level weak labels. The authors argue that existing approaches have not contemplated build a task-specific encoder in an efficient manner to offer discriminative representations for events under surveillance scenes. The framework is structured as a two-stage self-training procedure since this one is composed of a multiple instance pseudo label generator and a self-guided attention boosted feature encoder. This generator module is intended to produce more reliable clip-level pseudo labels by the adaptation of a sparse continuous sampling strategy to adapt to the variation in duration of untrimmed videos and class imbalance. The experiments were based on two different feature encoders (C3D and I3D) and demonstrated the proposed approach is able to create a task-specific feature encoder. From the evaluation on two public benchmark datasets, the authors demonstrated the proposed method is competitive in relation to other compared weakly supervised methods. For the ShanghaiTech dataset, the approach obtained a frame-level AUC of 94.83%.

In [25], the authors conduct a supervised learning task following the binary-classification paradigm under noise labels to address the weakly supervised anomaly detection problem, on which training data contains only video-level anomaly labels. The authors design a graph convolutional network (GNC) for noisy label correction as a previous step for training an action classifier. The main intuition is to clean away label noise and then apply fully supervised action classifiers to weakly supervised anomaly detection. Experiments were conducted on three distinct anomaly detection datasets (UCF-Crime, Shang-haiTech and UCSD-Peds) with two types of action classifiers. The achieved frame-level AUC score for UCF-Crime, ShanghaiTech and UCSD-Peds datasets were 82.12%, 84.44% and 93.2% respectively. According to authors, the effectiveness and versatility of proposed approach is evidenced by the competitive performance results.

In [19], The authors propose a segment-based approach named Robust Temporal Feature Magnitude (RTFM) Learning to address video anomaly detection under MIL paradigm. The proposed approach is based on temporal feature magnitude of video snippets, in which features with high and low magnitude represents anomalous and normal snippets, respectively. The method is able to learn a temporal feature magnitude function which detects rare anomalous snippets from anomalous videos composed of many normal snippets, and a large margin between abnormal and normal snippets are guaranteed. The authors validate the proposed method on four multi-scene benchmark datasets (ShanghaiTech, UCF-Crime, XD-Violence and UCSD-Peds), created for weakly supervised video anomaly detection tasks. By the use of distinct pre-trained features (such as I3D and C3D), the authors demonstrate that the proposed approach achieves high AUC rates of 97.21%, 84.30%, 77.81% for ShanghaiTech, UCF-Crime and XD-Violence datasets, respectively, which is better benchmark results when compared to state-of-art.

In our study, we compared our proposed approach with the results of [20] and other related approaches [18,23,25] also evaluated by them. We verify the impact of using a wrapper-based multiple instance learning approach which employs LightGBM binary classifier for short-term video anomaly detection.

3   Background

3.1   Multiple Instance Learning (MIL)

The Multiple Instance Learning (MIL) problem in the binary classification context can be formally specified as the follows: Consider a instance space $X = \mathbb{R}^d$ and a set of labels $Y = \{0, 1\}$. A model is then built from a dataset with m bags $\beta = \{\beta_1, \beta_2, \ldots, \beta_m\}$. Each bag $\beta_i = \{\mathbf{x}_{i1}, \ldots, \mathbf{x}_{ij}, \ldots, \mathbf{x}_{in_i}\}$ is a set with n_i instances and $\mathbf{x}_{ij} \in X$. During the training step, each bag β_i has only the information about the associated bag label $\mathbf{y}_i \in Y$, but instance labels are unknown. The learning goal is to predict the label of an unseen bag and also predict the label of its instances [24].

In multiple instance learning, a convenient mode to build multiple instance classifiers from single-instance learners is from a wrapper for a single-instance algorithm that acts as an interface between the instance and bag levels. Firstly, each instance in a bag receives its bag label. Second, a single-instance classifier at instance level is built from training data and is used to label instances of a unseen bag. The bag label is obtained from the application of a multiple instance assumption over instance labels [7]. In MIL, a positive bag is composed at least by one positive instance and a negative bag contains only negative instances [20]. In the context of video surveillance under MIL approach, each video can be treated as a bag, and video segments (clips) or even frames can be treated as instances in this bag.

3.2 LightGBM

LightGBM is a novel Gradient-boosting decision tree (GBDT) algorithm that deals with the high number of instances and features with the employment of two approaches named Gradient-based One-Side Sampling (GOSS) and Exclusive Feature Bundling (EFB) [9]. GOSS is a sampling technique for GBDT for down-sampling data instances and seeks to retain the accuracy of information gain estimation. The method can maintain the accuracy for learned decision trees and obtain good balance between the number of instances in data. The method performs random sampling on data instances with small gradients and keeps all the instances with high gradients. EFB is a lossless approach for feature dimensionality reduction. The optimal bundling problem is transformed into a graph coloring problem in EFB, which is then solved using a greedy method with a fixed approximation ratio.

4 Experimental Planning

This section details the main steps for data preparation, modeling, and evaluation of our proposed video anomaly detection scheme. We briefly describe our experiment workflow in the following subsections and discuss the main relevant results. We present our experiment workflow in Fig. 1.

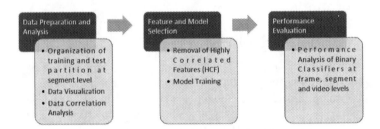

Fig. 1. Experiment workflow

The next subsections detail all the necessary steps to the construction of our proposed scheme. We first detail the adopted benchmark dataset and the available deep features constructed with a clip-based instance generation strategy that are used to train our classifier. Then we perform a data analysis procedure for better understanding of training features. We then create a procedure for removal of high correlated features occurrences. Finally, we present a performance comparison of our proposed approach with other binary classifiers and state-of-the-art results.

4.1 Data Preparation and Analysis

Data Preparation. We evaluate our proposed approach with the ShanghaiTech dataset [12], which contains untrimmed videos with variable durations, contents, and scenes. The dataset includes video captures taken at the ShanghaiTech University and describes various lighting conditions and viewpoints. This challenging dataset is originally proposed for unary classification (since all training video data are normal) and contains 130 anomalous events in 13 scenes of 437 videos. In [25], the authors proposed a split of this dataset to allow the modeling and evaluation of binary classification-based approaches. In this split, there are 238 and 199 training and testing video instances, respectively. In the training partition, there are 175 normal videos and 63 anomalous ones. In the test partition, there are 155 normal videos and 44 anomalous ones. Table 1 presents the number of instances in training and testing splits for the considered dataset. The table also presents the class distribution at the video, segment, and frame levels. There are two categories in this dataset: Normal (N) and Anomaly (A).

Table 1. Class distribution at video, segment and frame level

	# videos		# segments		# frames	
Train	238 (54.46%)		10734 (55%)		171744 (55%)	
	N	A	N	A	N	A
	175	63	9299	1435	148784	22960
Test	199 (45.54%)		8781 (45%)		140496 (45%)	
	N	A	N	A	N	A
	155	44	7702	1079	123232	17264
Total	437		19515		312240	

In [20] the authors used the pre-trained deep neural network Inflated 3D (I3D) as a feature extractor. The generated features represent the junction of appearance (RGB) and movement (optical flow) data. We use the pre-processed Inflated 3D (I3D) deep features of the considered dataset in our experiments. These I3D features are publicly available at this link[1]. The processed version of the ShanghaiTech dataset as I3D features contains the same number of video instances. Each video instance in this dataset is represented as a matrix with dimension $n \times 2048$ or $n \times 1024$, where n is a variable number of existing segments and the number of attributes is 1024 (when only appearance features or movement information are considered individually) or 2048 (when both appearance and movement information are considered). It is important to note that these features were created by a clip-based instance generation strategy. According to the authors in [20], this approach consists of divide videos into clips with a fixed number of frames and is more suitable to detect short-term anomalies. This is

---

[1] https://github.com/wanboyang/Anomaly_AR_Net_ICME_2020.

distinct for segment-based methods, where each video is divided in a fixed number of segments. The latter approach lacks the capability to detect short-term anomalies once features of anomalous frames may be overwhelmed by normal ones in a segment.

In our experiments, we consider both I3D features generated from RGB and Optical flow data. Since we use the features preprocessed by [20] in a clip-based instance generation strategy, our approach is also suitable for short-term video anomaly detection. The following ground truths are provided for performance evaluation: For each processed video, there is a corresponding category label (normal or anomaly) and there are also the labels of each existing frame of this video. In our research, we applied these features to build and evaluate binary classification models for the anomaly detection task. We can comprehend each video instance x_i is illustrated as shown in Fig. 2.

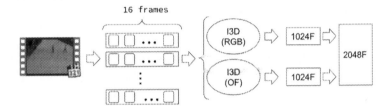

Fig. 2. I3D feature composition of preprocessed dataset

We describe the data preparation for modeling and performance evaluation as follows. Initially, we load the dataset of videos $\mathbf{D} = \{(X_i, y_i, yf_i)\}_{i=1}^N$. Each instance X_i is a matrix $n \times 2048$, where n is a variable number of segments in a given video, $y_i \in \{0, 1\}$ is the video label and $yf_i = [yf_i^1, \ldots, yf_i^k]$ is a sequence of k frame labels existing in the video. In the last expression, yf_i^j is the label of frame j in video i, $yf_i^j \in \{0, 1\}$ and k is a variable number of frames. Then, we organize $\mathbf{D}$ into training and test datasets using the split provided by [25] for binary classification as described in Table 1. We represent these training and test partitions as $\mathbf{D}_{train} = \{\mathbf{D}_N^{train}, \mathbf{D}_A^{train}\}$ and $\mathbf{D}_{test} = \{\mathbf{D}_N^{test}, \mathbf{D}_A^{test}\}$. Then, we rearrange the training partition to build a segment-level machine learning estimator. Each video in $\mathbf{D}_{train}$ is transformed into n new segments with 2048 deep features per segment. The new training segment partition is described as $\mathbf{S}_{train} = \{(S_i, y_i)\}$, where S_i is a video segment and y_i is the corresponding segment class, which is the same label as the video containing this clip. The resulting model is then evaluated at video, segment and frame level.

Data Analysis. Exploratory data analysis is a relevant initial step to inspect a new dataset and understand its characteristics and nature [13].

We initially explore some statistical properties of the selected dataset for a better data understanding and appropriate applicability of machine learning techniques. We performed exploratory data analysis on the I3D features available for the ShanghaiTech dataset to verify the quality of predictive variables by statistical measurements and graphics visualization. This procedure aims to prevent overfitting and biased models.

The t-Distributed Stochastic Neighbor Embedding (TSNE) technique [11] is a common dimensionality-reduction non-linear manifold algorithm for visualizing high-dimensional datasets. This method helps to visualize the structure among high dimensionality data points in non-linear data. By the employment of this technique through the implementation in this link[2], the training and testing splits could be explored and visualized. We set the perplexity hyperparameter in TSNE to 500, as recommended in the package documentation for large datasets. We can understand this parameter as the balance between preserving the local and global structure of the data. We could observe that the scatter plot contains similar patterns between the two classes, which makes binary classification problem a challenging task. We perform data dimensionality reduction by TSNE from 2048 deep I3D features (complete dataset) for only two features in order to plot the Fig. 3.

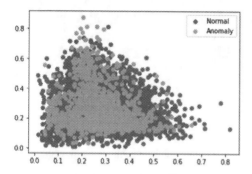

Fig. 3. Visualization of training data points through TSNE non-linear manifold technique

Data Correlation Analysis. In sequence, we show the Pearson correlation matrix for the training and testing splits in Fig. 4. This technique helps to examine the presence of a relationship among variables in the dataset, indicating how strong one attribute is associated with the other one. These matrices are computed with the Pearson Correlation Coefficient (PCC) in Eq. (1), where n is the number of samples, x_i and y_i are individuals samples of two different attributes, $\bar{x}$ and $\bar{y}$ its respective averages [17].

$$r(x,y) = \frac{\sum_{i=1}^{n}(x_i - \bar{x})(y_i - \bar{y})}{\sqrt{\sum_{i=1}^{n}(x_i - \bar{x})^2}\sqrt{\sum_{i=1}^{n}(y_i - \bar{y})^2}} \tag{1}$$

---

[2] https://github.com/pavlin-policar/openTSNE.

Frequency of Frame Counts in the Segments of Anomalous Videos.
We present the frequency of frame counts in the segments of anomalous videos
for the train split in Table 2. Since the segment inherits the label of the video
that contains it and since usually, an anomalous video could contain normal
and abnormal segments. The number of anomalous frames in each 16-size frame
sequence will vary between 0 and 16 anomalous frames in a segment.

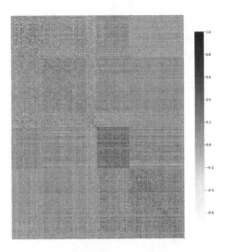

Fig. 4. Correlation matrix of training partition

Table 2. Count of anomalous frames in the segments of anomalous videos

Anomalous frame counts	0	1	2	3	4	5	6	7	8	9	10	11	12	13	14	15	16
Number of segments	781	15	6	7	6	9	9	11	6	10	10	13	12	9	15	25	491

For the training split, there are 781 anomalous segments (54.43%) with no
anomalous frame inside these segments and 438 anomalous segments (34.22%)
where all frames inside these ones are anomalous. This means that a video originally labeled as an anomaly is composed of normal and abnormal segments. This
is a common situation since an anomaly event can occur in specific moments of
the video timeline. Under the MIL paradigm, since video label is replicated to
their segments, this label noise is inevitably propagated, which makes binary
classification a challenging task.

4.2   Feature and Model Selection

Feature Selection. This study noticed that there are highly correlated deep
features in these splits. According to [2], there are various feature selection methods that consider correlated features as redundant information and therefore
need to be removed. In this sense, in our study, we also consider the removal

of the higher correlated features in the experiments. From the computation and analysis of Pearson correlation matrix of training data at segment level, we could remove the most highly correlated features. According to [14], variables whose absolute value is higher than 0.70 can be considered highly correlated.

We adopt the following procedure to exclude of highly correlated features (HCF): we first select upper triangle of correlation matrix and then find the feature columns with correlation greater than a given threshold. For each column i of this matrix, we check if there is a pair of variables (i, j), with $i \neq j$, where the absolute value is higher than this threshold. If affirmative, the column i is marked to be removed. A new version of training and test splits are used for an additional experiment. It is important to note that we also empirically verify this threshold as the most adequate for the target classifier adopted and evaluated in the next subsection. With this threshold, we reduced feature space from 2048 to 1923 features in our complementary experiment.

Model Selection. For the evaluation at the frame level, we describe the test segment partition by $\mathbf{S}_{test} = \{(S_i, yfs_i)\}$, where yfs_i is a sequence of 16 frame labels obtained from ground truth variable yf_i. Since we build the generated models at the segment level, we mapped each predicted test segment output to the corresponding output frame sequence (each video clip corresponds to a sequence of 16 frames) to allow evaluation at the frame level and comparison with state-or-art literature. For the evaluation at the segment level, we consider the video ground truths in the comparison with each segment-level model output. Finally, for the evaluation of the video level, we average the segment estimates contained in each video to form the prediction for the video (bag).

We propose the combination of a light gradient boosting machine model and the representation power of I3D deep features to build a robust and competitive classifier for short-term video anomaly detection with a wrapper multiple instance learning approach. A general overview of our proposal is displayed in Fig. 5, where c is a class (normal or anomaly), X_{new} is a new unseen video, S_i is a segment of this video and n is the number of segments in this video This approach is categorized as wrapper in MIL literature [7] since it adequate the structure of multi-instance dataset to a single-instance representation to use a single instance-learning algorithm (in our case, LGBM) without modification.

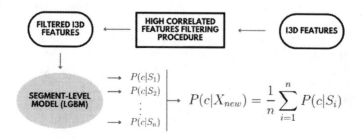

Fig. 5. Overview of our proposed approach

According to [7], although this heuristic can cause biased probability estimates, it performs surprisingly well for different datasets. With this procedure, the video label is obtained by the wrapper based on the video's segment labels. Such as [20], we consider the video anomaly detection problem from a weakly supervised perspective, and we apply binary classification since we have normal and abnormal data in the training set. We consider only the video label ground truths to build the machine learning model. We assume the MIL assumption that a positive video (bag) contains at least one instance of a positive event, and a negative video consists of only negative examples.

To evaluate the generalization capability of compared models for the video surveillance anomaly detection task, we consider the following evaluation metrics: balanced accuracy ($BACC = \frac{TPR+TNR}{2}$), precision of anomalies ($PREC = \frac{TP}{TP+FP}$), false-positive rate ($FPR = \frac{FP}{FP+TN}$), true-positive rate ($recall = \frac{TP}{TP+FN}$), the harmonic mean of precision and recall F1-Score $F1 = \frac{precision \cdot recall}{precision + recall}$ and AUC (Area Under the ROC Curve) as evaluation metrics in each experimented video.

4.3   Performance Evaluation

In this subsection, we present the performance evaluation of the LGBM [9] method in front of other well-known techniques in other to validate our approach. We executed our experiments from the cloud computing service Google Colab[3]. We utilize the algorithm implementations in the packages *Scikit-learn* available for Python[4] language. In our research we adopt the binary classification paradigm for the video anomaly classification problem. Let's consider a dataset with n videos as $X = \{x_i\}_{i=1}^n$ where each video x_i in the dataset has a temporal duration t_i in a way that $T = \{t_i\}_{i=1}^n$ is the temporal duration of the whole dataset. We represent the binary labels for each video in dataset X as $Y = \{y_i\}_{i=1}^n$. A predictive model receives a given video x_{test} and produces an output as a score, class or probability [20].

Comparison Among Binary Classifiers. We guide the performance experiment as follows: Firstly, we analyze the training partition at the segment level to best understand the underlying properties of the considered dataset. Second, we apply a holdout procedure to train and evaluate the predictive models with the training and test partitions, respectively. Third, we evaluate the built models with the test set with well-known evaluation metrics in the video anomaly detection research field. We measured and evaluated the performance of supervised classifiers, to know, LGBM [9], eXtreme Gradient Boosting (XGBoost) [4], Random Forest [5], Multilayer Perceptron (MLP) [10], and Support Vector Machine (SVM) [3] for the binary classification task under the MIL paradigm. Specifically for the LGBM technique, we also evaluate the performance impact

---

[3] https://colab.research.google.com/.
[4] https://www.python.org/.

in the absence of highly correlated features (HCF) in training and test splits. We summarize in Tables 3, 4 and 5 the performance results of the different adopted machine learning models in three levels of granularity (video, segment of video, and frame).

Table 3. Performance evaluation of binary classification at video level

	AUC	FPR	BACC	PREC	REC	F1
LGBM (no HCF)	0.958211	0.019355	0.774413	0.892857	0.568182	**0.694444**
LGBM	0.956745	0.019355	0.774413	0.892857	0.568182	**0.694444**
MLP (1L, 256N)	**0.962317**	0.006452	**0.826320**	0.966667	**0.659091**	0.783784
SVM RBF (C = 0.1)	0.948827	**0.000000**	0.522727	**1.000000**	0.045455	0.086957
Random Forest	0.951613	0.006452	0.701320	0.947368	0.409091	0.571429
XGBOOST	0.963343	0.006452	0.758138	0.958333	0.522727	0.676471

Table 4. Performance evaluation of binary classification at segment level

	AUC	FPR	BACC	PREC	REC	F1
LGBM (no HCF)	**0.942827**	0.016619	0.809114	0.842558	0.634847	0.724101
LGBM	0.940852	0.016230	0.811626	0.846626	0.639481	**0.728617**
MLP (1L, 256N)	0.925965	0.033757	**0.828812**	0.741551	**0.691381**	0.715588
SVM RBF (C = 0.1)	0.895105	**0.000649**	0.559916	**0.962963**	0.120482	0.214168
Random Forest	0.916029	0.008310	0.720590	0.883424	0.449490	0.595823
XGBOOST	0.934727	0.014022	0.795584	0.858081	0.605190	0.709783

Table 5. Performance evaluation of binary classification at the frame level

	AUC	FPR	BACC	PREC	REC	F1
LGBM (no HCF)	**0.924980**	0.061932	0.771480	0.368850	0.604892	0.458262
LGBM	0.922219	0.060861	0.782983	0.381288	0.626828	**0.474156**
MLP (1L, 256N)	0.905006	0.080165	**0.804660**	0.339774	**0.689486**	0.455219
SVM RBF (C = 0.1)	0.897680	**0.009256**	0.554184	**0.431944**	0.117625	0.184899
Random Forest	0.907402	0.041874	0.682858	0.368056	0.407590	0.386815
XGBOOST	0.915088	0.058047	0.739320	0.356175	0.536687	0.428183

We could note that the achieved results for the evaluated approaches are approximate. For instance, with a network with one single layer and 256 neurons, we achieve an AUC of approximately 96.23%, 92.59% and 90.50% for the evaluations at video, segment and frame levels, respectively. As the parameter C acts as a regularization parameter and its value can be determined either analytically or experimentally [21], we experiment with three distinct values for parameter C

in SVM optimization (0.1, 0.5 and 1.0). We also perform experiments for MLP with one and two layers and alternating 256 and 2048 hidden neurons per layer. For the LGBM method, we adopt 5000 estimators once we verify empirically that this configuration provided the highest AUC in our testbeds.

The predominance of the LGBM algorithm as the best technique for the evaluated dataset becomes evident when we look for AUC metric. The LGBM algorithm obtained the highest values for AUCROC when we consider the removal of highly correlated features by Pearson correlation, with 92.49%, approximately.

Comparison with SOTA Results. In our study, we compared our proposed machine learning scheme with the state-of-the-art research [20] and other related approaches [18,23,25] also evaluated by them, as shown in Table 6. We use the same I3D features of [20], where there is a Github repository[5] of proposed approach AR-Net of Wan et al. (2020) where a link for previously preprocessed I3D features can be obtained. According to the authors, the extracted features are not fine-tuned and the optical flow frames were obtained from a TV-L1 algorithm with $\alpha = 4$ for the ShanghaiTech dataset. The Deep networks I3D and C3D are currently state-of-the-art in pre-trained deep video feature extractors. It is necessary to segment the whole video into video snippets to employ these neural networks for feature extraction. The recent works in video anomaly detection with multiple instance learning settings adopt two different approaches for video segmentation: clip-based (where each segment fixed segment size) or segment-based (where training video is fragmented into a fixed number of segments). In the last approach the segment size will vary among the videos in the training set. Although this approach exhibits better performance in recent studies, we understand that the first approach is more applicable in practice. Thus, we adopt the first approach. In this sense, we only compare our proposal with works that also adopt this same approach for feature representation.

Table 6. Comparison with literature. * indicates that these results [18,23,25] are provided in [20]

Approach	AUC (%)	FPR (%)
[18] Sultani et al. (2018)*	86.30	0.15
[23] Zhang et al. (2019)*	82.50	0.10
[25] Zhong et al. (2019)*	84.44	–
[20] Wan et al. (2020) - (MIL Loss + Center Loss)	91.24	0.10
[20] Wan et al. (2020) - (MIL Loss)	89.10	0.21
Proposed approach (LGBM with no HCF)	**92.49**	**6.19**

Although other works have proposed and evaluated approaches with the same dataset [6,8,19,25], there may be differences in the necessary preprocessing phase

---

[5] https://github.com/wanboyang/Anomaly_AR_Net_ICME_2020.

to extract video characteristics with a deep feature extractor, such as the type of feature extractor (I3D, C3D and so forth), the optical flow method and its params, and the procedure for video fragmentation. For this reason, we only compare our approach with [20] as we use the exactly same I3D features. As [20], we also adopt a clip-based approach where videos are partitioned into clips with a fixed number of frames. This is a different approach for segment-based methods [18,19,23], where each video is divided in a fixes number of segments. According to [20], as an anomalous event can represent a tiny part of a whole video, the features in anomalous frames may be overwhelmed by normal ones in a segment for the segment-based approach. The consequence of this situation is that clips with anomalies inside it tend to be related to normal patterns.

We could note that our proposed approach is able to overcome the frame-level results of the literature in terms of the AUC metric, although our method suffers from a high false positive rate. Although the compared SOTA models are built over sophisticated learning schemes, our approach directly applies a machine learning method traditionally used for a binary classification task and roughly adapts it for the MIL task, which could explain the high number of false alarms. Despite that, the results indicate our approach as promising once we achieved competitive results.

5   Conclusion

We present a multi-instance learning scheme based on the LGBM classifier to detect video anomalies with competitive performance in AUC in the data set chosen for testing. For pre-processed I3D features, we could see that combining an LGBM classifier with a filter method applied to highly correlated I3D features slightly improved our results in terms of AUC. These results position our proposed approach as effective and competitive.

Future directions include the evaluation of the proposed approach in other video surveillance datasets, the analysis of instance and feature selection approaches to mitigate the dimensionality problem in training models on large-scale datasets and tackling the problem of FPR which is still unsatisfactory. To analyze the proposed approach in different scenarios, we also aim to create different versions of the applied preprocessed dataset.

References

1. Asad, M., Jiang, H., Yang, J., Tu, E., Malik, A.A.: Multi-stream 3D latent feature clustering for abnormality detection in videos. Appl. Intell. **52**(1), 1126–1143 (2022)
2. Braytee, A., Anaissi, A., Kennedy, P.J.: Sparse feature learning using ensemble model for highly-correlated high-dimensional data. In: Cheng, L., Leung, A.C.S., Ozawa, S. (eds.) ICONIP 2018. LNCS, vol. 11303, pp. 423–434. Springer, Cham (2018). https://doi.org/10.1007/978-3-030-04182-3_37
3. Cervantes, J., Garcia-Lamont, F., Rodríguez-Mazahua, L., Lopez, A.: A comprehensive survey on support vector machine classification: applications, challenges and trends. Neurocomputing **408**, 189–215 (2020)

4. Chen, T., et al.: XGBoost: extreme gradient boosting. R package version 0.4-2 1(4), pp. 1–4 (2015)
5. Cutler, A., Cutler, D.R., Stevens, J.R.: Random forests. In: Zhang, C., Ma, Y. (eds.) Ensemble Machine Learning, pp. 157–175. Springer, Boston (2012). https://doi.org/10.1007/978-1-4419-9326-7_5
6. Feng, J.C., Hong, F.T., Zheng, W.S.: MIST: multiple instance self-training framework for video anomaly detection. In: Proceedings of the IEEE/CVF Conference on Computer Vision and Pattern Recognition, pp. 14009–14018 (2021)
7. Herrera, F., et al.: Multiple instance learning. In: Herrera, F., et al. (eds.) Multiple Instance Learning, pp. 17–33. Springer, Cham (2016). https://doi.org/10.1007/978-3-319-47759-6_2
8. Kamoona, A.M., Gosta, A.K., Bab-Hadiashar, A., Hoseinnezhad, R.: Multiple instance-based video anomaly detection using deep temporal encoding-decoding. arXiv preprint arXiv:2007.01548 (2020)
9. Ke, G., et al.: LightGBM: a highly efficient gradient boosting decision tree. In: Advances in Neural Information Processing Systems 30 (2017)
10. Kubat, M.: Neural networks: a comprehensive foundation by Simon Haykin, Macmillan, 1994, ISBN 0-02-352781-7. Knowl. Eng. Rev. 13(4), 409-412 (1999)
11. Liu, S., Maljovec, D., Wang, B., Bremer, P.T., Pascucci, V.: Visualizing high-dimensional data: advances in the past decade. IEEE Trans. Visual. Comput. Graph. 23(3), 1249–1268 (2016)
12. Luo, W., Liu, W., Gao, S.: A revisit of sparse coding based anomaly detection in stacked RNN framework. In: Proceedings of the IEEE International Conference on Computer Vision, pp. 341–349 (2017)
13. Milo, T., Somech, A.: Automating exploratory data analysis via machine learning: an overview. In: Proceedings of the 2020 ACM SIGMOD International Conference on Management of Data, pp. 2617–2622 (2020)
14. Mukaka, M.: Statistics corner: a guide to appropriate use of correlation in medical research. Malawi Med. J. 24(3), 69–71 (2012)
15. Nayak, R., Pati, U.C., Das, S.K.: A comprehensive review on deep learning-based methods for video anomaly detection. Image Vis. Comput. 106, 104078 (2021)
16. Pereira, S.S., Maia, J.B.: Uma abordagem baseada em redes neurais, multiple instance learning e pca para detecção de anomalias em videovigilância. In: Anais do XLVIII Seminário Integrado de Software e Hardware, pp. 123–130. SBC (2021)
17. Sedgwick, P.: Pearson's correlation coefficient. BMJ 345, 4483 (2012)
18. Sultani, W., Chen, C., Shah, M.: Real-world anomaly detection in surveillance videos. In: Proceedings of the IEEE Conference on Computer Vision and Pattern Recognition, pp. 6479–6488 (2018)
19. Tian, Y., Pang, G., Chen, Y., Singh, R., Verjans, J.W., Carneiro, G.: Weakly-supervised video anomaly detection with robust temporal feature magnitude learning. arXiv preprint arXiv:2101.10030 (2021)
20. Wan, B., Fang, Y., Xia, X., Mei, J.: Weakly supervised video anomaly detection via center-guided discriminative learning. In: 2020 IEEE International Conference on Multimedia and Expo (ICME), pp. 1–6. IEEE (2020)
21. Wu, X., Kumar, V.: The Top Ten Algorithms in Data Mining. CRC Press, Boca Raton (2009)
22. Yi, C., Wu, S., Xi, B., Ming, D., Zhang, Y., Zhou, Z.: Terrorist video detection system based on faster R-CNN and LightGBM. In: Proceedings of the 4th International Conference on Computer Science and Application Engineering, pp. 1–8 (2020)

23. Zhang, J., Qing, L., Miao, J.: Temporal convolutional network with complementary inner bag loss for weakly supervised anomaly detection. In: 2019 IEEE International Conference on Image Processing (ICIP), pp. 4030–4034. IEEE (2019)
24. Zhang, W.: Non-IID multi-instance learning for predicting instance and bag labels using variational auto-encoder. arXiv preprint arXiv:2105.01276 (2021)
25. Zhong, J.X., Li, N., Kong, W., Liu, S., Li, T.H., Li, G.: Graph convolutional label noise cleaner: train a plug-and-play action classifier for anomaly detection. In: Proceedings of the IEEE Conference on Computer Vision and Pattern Recognition, pp. 1237–1246 (2019)

PAN RAM Bootstrapping Regressor - A New RAM-Based Architecture for Regression Problems

Starch Melo de Souza[1]([⊠]) [ID], Kelly Pereira de Lima[2] [ID],
Anthony José da Cunha Carneiro Lins[3] [ID], Adriano Fabio Querino de Brito[4] [ID],
and Paulo J. L. Adeodato[1] [ID]

[1] Universidade Federal de Pernambuco, Recife, Brazil
starch.souza@gmail.com, pjla@cin.ufpe.br
[2] In Forma Software, Recife, Brazil
[3] Universidade Católica de Pernambuco, Recife, Brazil
[4] Secretaria de Estado da Fazenda - PB, João Pessoa, Brazil

Abstract. RAM-based neural networks have been used a few decades before MultiLayer Perceptrons. Despite their implementability in hardware and speed, they have some drawbacks compared to more recent techniques, particularly related to continuous input variables, which kept them out of mainstream research. About a decade ago, the PAN RAM was an attempt to handle continuous inputs with a polynomial approximator neuron in the n-tuple architecture applied to binary decision problems. Constraints on applications and data preparation still remained. This paper presents an evolution of the PAN RAM neuron that can do regression and a single-layer architecture that is dynamically built based on bootstrapping. The proposed system was benchmarked against the Multilayer Perceptron on three regression problems using the Abalone, White Wine, and California Housing datasets from the UCI repository. In the unicaudal paired t-test carried out on a 10-fold cross-validation comparison measuring the Mean Absolute Error (MAE), the proposed system performed better than the Multilayer Perceptron (MLP) on the abalone and white wine datasets. In contrast, for the California dataset there was no significant improvement, all at a 0.05 significance level.

Keywords: RAM-based neuron · Polynomial approximation · Bootstrapping · Regression

1 Introduction

RAM-based neural networks were on the market [1] long before MLP became popular [2], but for various reasons they never became very popular. For many researchers, one reason is that it was not biologically inspired by the McCulloch-Pitts neuron.

© The Author(s), under exclusive license to Springer Nature Switzerland AG 2022
J. C. Xavier-Junior and R. A. Rios (Eds.): BRACIS 2022, LNAI 13654, pp. 574–587, 2022.
https://doi.org/10.1007/978-3-031-21689-3_40

RAM-based networks had a substantial disadvantage in handling continuous input variable representation. The PAN RAM neuron [3] overcame this drawback, which was a severe problem, by proposing a continuous addressing scheme to the binary memory sites, which produced a RAM-based neuron capable of implementing a polynomial approximation function.

The paper [3] also applied the neuron in a modified version of the n-tuple adapted by Adeodato and Oliveira Neto for binary classification [6]. The resulting system combines the power of the Polynomial Approximation Neuron (PAN) with the subspace sampling of the n-tuple classifier.

This paper presents a bootstrapping PAN RAM regressor, an evolution of the RAM-based neuron proposal [3]. The proposed approach overcomes the difficulty to handle true continuous variables and applies statistical techniques of data resampling based on bootstrapping to create the architecture. For the selection of the best neurons, a separatrix measure was used, and the decile with the best on a validation set was chosen (lowest Mean Absolute Error performance metric).

The statistical comparison of the bootstrapping PAN RAM regressor against the MLP on a 10-fold cross-validation experiment on three datasets available in the UCI repository [4] proved that the proposed approach is successful. For the Abalone and White Wine datasets, the bootstrapping PAN RAM regressor performed better than the MLP (significant paired t-test with p-value < 0.05). For the California dataset, despite the better result, the proposed regressor improvement compared to the MLP was not statistically significant at a 0.05 significance level.

The paper is organized into four more sections. Section 2 describes the adaptation of the PAN RAM neuron and the bootstrapping architecture associated with it in the regression context. Section 3 details the public datasets used, the experimental design, and the metrics adopted in the performance evaluation. Section 4 presents interprets and discusses the empirical results comparing the performance between PAN RAM bootstrapping and the MLP neural network in regression problems. Finally, Sect. 5 presents the concluding remarks on applicability, limitations, and future research.

2 The Proposed PAN RAM Model

This paper proposes an adaptation of the PAN RAM neuron [3] to allow solving regression issues through a dynamically built single-layer architecture based on bootstrapping. The neuron PAN RAM receives a set of n input values normalized between zero (0) and one (1) which access the addresses of a RAM memory with n inputs.

2.1 PAN RAM Adapted Neuron

The PAN RAM neuron [3] was adapted to 1) eliminate the class-balancing step of the training set classes used in the supervised learning approach of binary classification, 2) make it extensible to solve regression problems, and 3) it presents a scientifically sound strategy for architecture optimization.

These adaptations were possible due to the adoption of the replacement of the value 0.5, usually set as an initial value in each site of RAM-based neurons by the average value of the target class. The 0.5 value was initially conceived in the Probabilistic Logic Neuron - PLN [5] to represent the maximum uncertainty in the neuron' s initial learning state. For binary classification, that level of uncertainty required balancing the training data according to the target class in the binary domain.

The improved learning algorithm of [3] in a single PAN RAM neuron, called **"improved PAN RAM"**, as seen in the Algorithm 1.

---

1 Prepare the training dataset;
2 Set the pair of accumulators of all your 2^n memory sites (m) with values equal to zero;
3 Start training;
4 **repeat**
5 | Select a labeled pattern (p) and present it to neuron inputs;
6 | Calculate the address weight (w) for each memory site;
7 | Calculate the contribution of the target class weighted by its address weight for each memory site;
8 | Sum the address weight contributions at each memory site;
9 | Sum the binary target contributions weighed by the address weight at each memory site;
10 | /* All patterns are used only once in any sequence.   */
11 **until** *all training patterns are used*;
12 Divide the sum of the weighted target contributions by the sum of the address weights for each memory site;
13 /* Each memory site not addressed during training will be populated with the average value of the target class on the training data set. This is an improvement that turns class-balancing unnecessary. These are the learned parameters stored in each memory site (m).   */
14 End the training

Algorithm 1: PAN RAM Neuron

The main idea behind the Polynomial Approximation Neuron (PAN) is that a set of n continuous values normalized between zero (0) and one (1) can access the binary address memory sites of an n-input RAM memory [3].

A unitary address intensity of a single pattern is distributed for each binary memory site, with a weight defined according to how similar the continuous corresponding coordinate is to the binary address of a memory position [3].

The terms of the inner product below will refer to as address weights [3] from now on w_{ij} is

$$w_{i_1 i_2} = b_1 b_2 . x_1 x_2 \tag{1}$$

$$w_{i_1\overline{i_2}} = b_1\overline{b_2}x_1\overline{x_2} \tag{2}$$

$$w_{\overline{i_1}i_2} = \overline{b_1}b_2.\overline{x_1}x_2 \tag{3}$$

$$w_{\overline{i_1}\overline{i_2}} = \overline{b_1}b_2.\overline{x_1}\overline{x_2}. \tag{4}$$

where $\bar{x}$ is the complementary value of a variable x ($\bar{x} = 1 - x$), binary memory addresses (b_1b_2) and normalized continuous addressing (x_1x_2). This address weight computation is valid both for training the memory sites and for recalling their contents to produce the neuron's polynomial response to a pattern.

Formally, α stored after training the p patterns, for example, in the memory site whose binary is i_1i_2, is calculated by the formula in [3]:

$$\alpha_{i_1i_2} = \frac{\displaystyle\sum_{j=1}^{p} y_j w_{i_1i_2}}{\displaystyle\sum_{j=1}^{p} w_{i_1i_2}} \tag{5}$$

where y_j is the target associated with the jth labeled pattern

The "improved PAN RAM" neuron implemented by the training and pattern recognition process is a polynomial approximation of the input variables. The "improved PAN RAM" neuron implements the function.

$$\hat{y} = \alpha_{00}.w_{00} + \alpha_{01}.w_{01} + \alpha_{10}.w_{10} + \alpha_{11}.w_{11} \tag{6}$$

being $m_{ij} = \alpha_{ij}.w_{ij}$ and where α_{ij} are the parameters learned in the training process, presented in Table 1. The mathematical formulation of the PAN RAM neuron was described in Subsection II.B - "The Proposed PAN Model" in reference [3].

Table 1 illustrates the training process for a 2-input neuron with four training patterns, showing the address weights w_{ij} (which add up to one by definition) and the target contribution per site (the memory contents) for each of the four memory sites m_{ij}. After the presentation of the entire training dataset, the learned network parameters α_{ij} were obtained by simply dividing the total target contribution and the full address weight per memory site, shown in bold.

In the pattern recognition phase, any input pattern produces an address weight decomposition according to the same procedure as above. The neuron's response is simply the sum of the multiplication of its memory contents (α_{ij}) by the address weights (w_{ij}) on each site (internal product). Table 2 presents the process of recognizing 4 patterns of memory content for each of the 4 memory sites shown in Table 1 to produce neuron responses ($\hat{y}$).

Table 1. Training process

Patt_ID				Address weight per site			
	x_1	x_2		w_{00}	w_{01}	w_{10}	w_{11}
p_1	0.25	0.25		0.56	0.19	0.19	0.06
p_2	0.25	0.75		0.19	0.56	0.06	0.19
p_3	0.75	0.25		0.19	0.06	0.56	0.19
p_4	0.75	0.75		0.06	0.19	0.19	0.56
			Total	1,00	1,00	1,00	1,00
Patt_ID				Target contribution per site			
	x_1	x_2	Target	m_{00}	m_{01}	m_{10}	m_{11}
p_1	0.25	0.25	2.37	1.34	0.45	0.45	0.15
p_2	0.25	0.75	4.62	0.87	2.60	0.29	0.87
p_3	0.75	0.25	3.12	0.59	0.20	1.76	0.59
p_4	0.75	0.75	5.87	0.37	1.10	1.10	3.30
			Total	3.17	4.35	3.60	4.91
			Mem	α_{00}	α_{01}	α_{10}	α_{11}
			α	**3.17**	**4.35**	**3.60**	**4.91**

Table 2. Test process

Patt_ID	Address weight per site						
	x_1	x_2	w_{00}	w_{01}	w_{10}	w_{11}	
t_1	0.30	0.20	0.56	0.14	0.24	0.06	
t_2	0.20	0.80	0.16	0.64	0.04	0.16	
t_3	0.70	0.30	0.21	0.09	0.49	0.21	
t_4	0.80	0.70	0.06	0.14	0.24	0.56	
Patt_ID	Response per site						
	x_1	x_2	m_{00}	m_{01}	m_{10}	m_{11}	$\hat{y}$
t_1	0.30	0.20	1.77	0.61	0.86	0.29	3.53
t_2	0.20	0.80	0.50	2.78	0.14	0.78	4.21
t_3	0.70	0.30	0.66	0.39	1.76	1.03	3.84
t_4	0.80	0.70	0.19	0.61	0.86	2.75	4.41

2.2   Proposed Bootstrapping PAN RAM Regression

The relaxation in the class-balancing requirement with the storage of the class-prior in non-addressed sites motivated the use of the new PAN RAM neuron to store the average of continuous target values to apply it to regression problems.

Another problem to be overcome with the new PAN RAM neuron was that traditional architectures, such as the n-tuple with random sampling of the input variables, would lead to performing polynomial approximations. Considering that discretely set neuron connections to the variables, sampling were necessary. That was when the bootstrapping procedure came into play as a scientifically sound re-sampling technique, widely used in various statistical situations. The technique is based on obtaining a "new" dataset by re-sampling the original dataset [7].

This algorithm comprises bootstrapping the modeling set to train each neuron individually (one at a time), connected by random sampling to the input variables. At each bootstrap B cycle, the neuron is training with the performance indicators being measured in the validation set (data not selected in the bootstrap sample) and the architectures and their results are stored. New neurons are added to the network and sorted by their median performance, considering their bootstrapping cycles.

From the moment the network reaches the total of T neurons, it will order the performance of each generated neuron in ascending order, from the best performance (lowest error) to the worst performance (highest error) among the T neurons in the network. In the end, it will compose the network of the top quantiles of the best performing neurons generated (median). In this paper, the threshold was set at the top performing neurons' decile.

In the single-layer architecture, the score-response of the network is simply the average of the responses of each of the selected top performing neurons. It is important to emphasize that the performance is measured on the non-sampled data during the process of each bootstrap cycle and that the median performance is chosen for robustness.

The PAN RAM bootstrapping regressor learning algorithm can be presented in the following steps:

---

1 Select a neuron;
2 **repeat**
3   Randomly allocate the variables to its k inputs and save the configuration;
4   **repeat**
5   Draw the bootstrap;
6   Train the neuron with the training set;
7   Test the neuron with the validation set;
8   **until** *draw of B bootstrap cycles*;
9   Save the connection map and memory contents of the median performing neuron on the validation set ;
10 **until** *reaching T neurons in the network, sorted in ascending order by performance on the validation set*;
11 Select the decile of the best performing neurons generated and discard the others

Algorithm 2: PAN RAM bootstrapping regressor

In the training phase, the bootstrap PAN RAM regressor follows the strategy below:

1. The data sets must be composed of a random sample, with the condition that this sample represents the population to be analyzed according to the context of the problem.
2. Define the architecture of the bootstrap PAN RAM regressor:
   (a) Total number of neurons in the network
   (b) Number of inputs per neuron
   (c) Number of bootstrap cycles
3. Train all PAN RAM bootstrapping neurons as specified by the algorithm in Subsection II.B of [3]
4. Save network architecture and learned parameters (connection map and memory contents)

Once the bootstrap PAN RAM regressor is trained, the pattern recognition process (recall) follows the sequence below:

1. Load the network architecture (number of neurons in the network, number of inputs per neuron)
2. Load acquired knowledge for each neuron (connection map and learned memory contents, α_i)
3. Present a test set of unknown patterns to have their response estimated.
   (a) Present a pattern at the regressor inputs
   (b) Compute the average of all top decile neurons as the regression response for the pattern

3   Experimental Setup

This cross-section will present the dataset, ten-fold cross validation technique, regression performance metrics, Bootstrapping PAN regressor and MLP neural networks.

3.1   Public Datasets

Table 3 lists the databases used in the regression benchmarking process. The White Wine Quality dataset, Abalone dataset and California Housing dataset can be found in the UCI repository [8], [9] and [10], respectively.

The dataset White Wine Quality Data Set [6] contains a sample of the physicochemical and sensory analysis for 4898 white wines. The first 11 attributes are physicochemical tests (e.g. pH, alcohol, density, etc.) and the last is the wine quality attribute labelled by a human expert based on sensory tests. The quality of the wine varies between 0 (poor) and 10 (excellent).

According to [11], three types of models are presented; the first is an MLP neural network, the second is a multiple regression, and finally an SVM (Support Vector Machine) to estimate the quality and taste of wines. To evaluate the selected models, 20 cross-validation runs of 5-folds were adopted, in a total of 100 experiments for each tested configuration.

Table 3. Dataset analysis with sample number, target average and number of attributes

Data set	Number of examples	# attributes (numeric + categorical)	Target average
White Wine data set	4898	11 (11 + 0)	5.87
Abalone data set	4177	8 (7 + 1)	9.93
California Housing	20460	8 (8 + 0)	207341.60

The Abalone dataset [9] has 4177 examples with a total of 8 attributes, 7 being numeric and corresponding to physical measurements (for example, length, diameter, height, etc.) and 1 sex attribute that is categorical. The age of the abalone (a genus of gastropod mollusks) is determined by cutting the shell through the cone, coloring it, and counting the number of rings under a microscope - a tedious and time-consuming task.

According to [12], MLP, Mixture of MLP regressions (MoMR), Expectation-Maximization (EM), Backpropagation (BP) and Backpropagation quasi-Newton (BPQ) are used to predict the age of abalone from physical measurements. In addition, they performed the comparison using the Bayesian Information Criterion (BIC) measure and used the coefficient of determination to verify the goodness of fit. And they concluded that MoMR worked well for the dataset.

The California Housing database contains information from the 1990 California census and was initially presented by [10]. It has an easy-to-understand list of variables, with a sample of 20460 examples with 8 numerical attributes (for example, longitude, latitude, total rooms, total bathrooms, etc.) and the target class.

3.2 Ten-Fold Cross Validation

Cross-validation is a technique used to compare machine learning algorithms and has been widely used as a criterion for model selection [13] and [14]. Despite the so-called "big data" era, the amount of data available in real-world applications is generally quite limited. This condition makes data resampling, such as bootstrapping, or data partitioning, such as k-fold cross-validation, strategies necessary to evaluate the performance of algorithms.

In k-fold cross-validation, data are partitioned into k folds, with $(k-1)$ folds applied to the construction of the machine learning model. The leftover fold, known as hold-out, is applied to test the model developed [14]. The process repeats k times, leaving out each fold for testing once. This procedure gives the model building a greater emphasis than its testing, but keeps statistical independence on the test sets. For this work, the number of folds defined was k = 10. The k-fold cross-validation strategy can be applied in machine learning algorithms for different tasks, such as classification or regression.

For the validity of the statistics of the comparison between the methods, it is necessary to evaluate the performance of a sampling process for each regression problem. Thus, a single-capacity paired t-statistic test was performed to evaluate the performance of the two algorithms.

In this work, k = 10 was chosen with simple random sampling. Each test fold produced a set of mean absolute error (MAE) performance metrics that had their mean, standard deviation and coefficient of variation calculated for each regressor.

Thus, to assess whether there was a significant difference in performance between the regressors, the comparison was made in a ten fold cross-validation process and the confidence level was set at 95 % in a paired one-tailed t test for each fold the difference in performance was measured.

3.3   Regression Performance Metric

A widely accepted performance metric in regression problem was chosen to compare the three approaches, namely, mean absolute error. The mean absolute error (MAE) is taken as the main metric of interest, since, for many regression problems, studying the quality of the uncertainty estimate is of great interest.

According to [15], the MAE would be a good indicator of the average performance of a model for regression problems. In this paper, the MAE metric was used for assessing the performance of each system on the experiment datasets. For a data set, it is calculated as follows $MAE = \dfrac{1}{n} \sum_{i=1}^{n} |y_i - \hat{y}_i|$ where n is the sample size, y_i is the observed value (fact), $\hat{y}_i$ is the value of the prediction (hypotheses).

The MAE is in a range between 0 and infinity and returns the magnitude of the error, so the smaller the value, the better the prediction.

3.4   Bootstrapping PAN RAM Regressor

In the experiment with the proposed bootstrapping PAN RAM regressor and in [3], the cost of RAM memory and the computational cost are exponential 2^n according to the number of inputs per neuron (n).

The paper [3] chose 10 inputs per neuron, while in this research we have varied this parameter from 6 to 14 inputs per neuron (6, 8, 10, 12 and 14). The connection strategy chosen was random allocation with replacement to obtain polynomials with varying degrees on each sampled variable. This allows a very large functional diversity in the space of polynomial hypotheses up to order fourteen (14). The number of bootstrap cycles equal to 31 ($n > 30$) was adopted as a constant value, by the Central Limit Theorem (CLT) it explains a sample distribution approximated by a normal distribution. Thus, n = 31 was chosen to have the median directly (the median as the central value of the numerical set).

The experimental design consisted of a 3×5 factorial analysis scheme, in which the total number of neurons varied (200, 300, 400) in the network and the number of inputs per neuron (6, 8, 10, 12 and 14), totaling 15 experiments.

Based on the experimental design as described in the Algorithm 2, the main goal was to select the best performing neuron according to the median bootstrap cycles applied on the validation set.

For the comparisons performed in this work (against MLP) the entire configuration was the same for both approaches. The same randomly sampled datasets with 9 modeling folds (out of 10) were used for training (75%) and for validation (25%).

As for the data sets are modelled with the bootstrap sampled training set (about 63%) of labeled distinct data, the validation set with the bootstrap leftover (about 37%) and a data sample for the test suite.

Data were normalized to values between 0 (zero) and 1 (one). Before normalization, data were winsorized at $\frac{\alpha}{2} = 0.05$ to circumvent problems with outliers. Winsorizing is a statistical technique for reducing the influence of outliers on the mean and variance. It consists of squashing the values on the tails of the data distribution beyond $\frac{\alpha}{2}$ to the extreme upper and lower quantiles. This paper uses winsorizing, considering the 5th and the 95th percentiles as limits for normalization.

3.5 MLP Neural Networks

Among the different architectures of artificial neural networks, feedforward networks have been used with some frequency when dealing with applications with nonlinear regression problems.

The MLP architecture with a single hidden layer is heavily applied to handle nonlinear regression [16]. As part of the analytical process of the regressor model, this paper analyzed some hyperparameters to evaluate the best configuration for each problem. The parameters analyzed were the number of neurons in the hidden layer, the learning rate and the momentum, all the others assuming the software default values. The implementation was carried out through the MLPREG function of the fdm2id package [17] in the R programming language.

The parameters adjustments lead to more adequate configurations to the scope of each problem, represented in the analyzed datasets. The neuron activation function for neurons in the hidden and output layers was the Logistic (or Sigmoid) function, which produces values in the interval between $[0, 1]$ [18]. That representation is well suited to all three problems, which present only positive outcomes.

The MLP had a single hidden layer with varying number of neurons. The training process used the following parameters: learning rate $= 10^{-3}$, an absolute convergence tolerance $= 10^{-4}$ and relative convergence tolerance $= 10^{-8}$, constants with the optimization process based on the BFGS algorithm (Broyden-Fletcher-Goldfarb-Shanno) [19]. These experimental parameters were chosen by the 3×5 factorial analysis scheme, with variation on the number of neurons trained in the hidden layer, observing the best results with 4 neurons in the hidden layer.

A paired t-test statistic was performed for the performance level of the MAE metric and comparison between the proposed algorithm and the MLP, with the best experimental performance settings for the 2 algorithms. The significance level was set to 0.05 in the test to detect any different performance.

4   Experimental Results and Interpretation

Figure 1 below shows the graphical representation of the interaction between the number of inputs per neuron and the number of neurons for the Abalone dataset.

It can be seen from Fig. 1 that increasing the number of inputs per neuron reduces the MAE performance indicator. However, the total number of neurons for selection of the best decile does not seem to cause much difference in performance.

So, the following question arises: does the increase in the number of inputs per neuron decrease the MAE? As the solution to the problem is exponential growth, the possible combinations of the number of inputs per neuron would be 2^n such as 2^{14} and 2^{28}. In this way, a possible solution to circumvent this cost of exponential growth in this problem would be Quantum Computing.

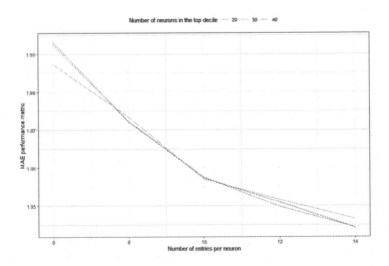

Fig. 1. Plots of the performance error (MAE) of the PAN RAM as a function of the number of inputs per neuron for 20, 30 and 40 top decile neurons on the abalone dataset problem.

By analyzing the first decile, one can observe the number of times a variable was connected the neuron. In the Abalone dataset problem, for example, the variables 10 and 7 are the most frequently sampled as inputs to the top decile

(10%). A more detailed analysis of the decile made it possible to visualize the degree of variables in the polynomial of each neuron. Subsequently, an evolution of the algorithm is to associate a sample distribution for each variable, and thus allow a boost in connection sampling. In this experiment, all dataset variables were used.

Table 4 presents statistics with the performance of the average algorithms based on the 10-fold cross-validation of the MLP and the proposed PAN RAM bootstrapping regressor.

Table 4. Descriptive analysis of algorithm performance of the MAE metric.

Dataset	Model	Size	Mean sample	Standard deviation	Coefficient of variation
Abalone	PAN RAM	10	1.944	0.115	0.059
	MLP	10	3.129	0.929	0.296
White Wine	PAN RAM	10	0.637	0.021	0.034
	MLP	10	1.135	0.342	0.301
California Housing	PAN RAM	10	76793	2678	0.035
	MLP	10	81631	9634	0.118

Table 5 shows the result of the unicaudal paired t-test at the 95% confidence level and shows that the differences in the performance of the MAE metric that is significant for the Abalone and White Wine dataset (p-value shown in bold), that is, the proposed model presents a better performance in relation to the MLP. As for the California dataset, we can see that this metric is not significant, so there is equality between the averages of the algorithms.

Table 5. Descriptive analysis of algorithm performance.

Dataset	Mean difference	p-value
Abalone data set	1.185	**0.004**
White Wine quality data set	0.498	**0.001**
California Housing	4838.447	0.203

For statistical analyses, the lower the MAE value, the better the forecast. The results achieved with the proposed model, for the tests on the Abalone and White Wine data sets, present lower MAE values compared to the MLP, as well as a greater precision of the coefficient of variation, see Table 4. The PAN RAM model also obtains a confidence level of 95% in the Abalone and White Wine datasets.

Regarding the results obtained with the California Housing dataset, despite the equivalence, the proposed model has the advantage of presenting the lowest average for the MAE performance metric and greater precision, as can be seen by the coefficient of variation in Table 4.

5   Concluding Remarks

This paper has presented a new PAN RAM-based neural network, with an improved version of the PAN RAM neuron, which proved to be well suited for classification and regression problems. It inherits the capability of the PAN RAM neuron to handle continuous input variables and adds three main improvements on the previous n-tuple PAN RAM classifier: 1) suppresses the need of class-balancing for classification problems, 2) it can solve regression problems, and 3) it presents a scientifically sound strategy for architecture optimization via bootstrapping on the training phase.

The most relevant contribution is the ability to handle regression problems through a dynamically built single layer architecture based on bootstrapping. This process of constructing a single-layer architecture with simple modules by using bootstrapping may be extended to any type of function approximator.

The comparison performed on 10-fold cross-validation against the MLP trained with the BFGS algorithm showed the bootstrapping PAN RAM Regressor performed better in 2 out 3 public dataset problems found in the UCI repository. A unicaudal paired t-test proved that the improvement was statistically significant ($p < 0.05$) for the Abalone and White Wine datasets while, for the California Housing dataset, the improvement wasn't statistically significant.

The performance improvement over the MLP is motivating and opens up new perspectives yet to be explored. The exponential growth of computational cost with the increase in the degree of the polynomials is a limiting aspect that leads to further investigation in terms of sampling the appropriate variables with their corresponding degrees. Despite the exponential cost increase with the mathematical functional capability, the simplicity of the operations involved in this one-shot learning process may render it amenable to be solved with quantum computing, but that is a giant leap which needs deeper investigation.

References

1. Bledsoe, W.W., Browning, I.: Pattern recognition and reading by machine. In: Proceedings of The Eastern Joint Computer Conference, pp. 225–232 (1959)
2. Rumelhart, D.E., Hinton, G.E., Williams, G.E.: Learning internal representations by error propagation. In: Rumelhart, D.E., McClelland, J.L. (eds.) Parallel Distributed Processing, vol. 1. MIT Press, Cambridge (1986)
3. Adeodato, P. J. L., Oliveira Neto, R. F.: Polynomial approximation RAM neuron capable of handling true continuous input variables. In: International Joint Conference on Neural Networks (IJCNN), pp. 76–83 (2016). https://doi.org/10.1109/IJCNN.2016.7727183.4
4. Dua, D., Graff, C.: UCI Machine Learning Repository]. School of Information and Computer Science, University of California, Irvine, CA (2019). http://archive.ics.uci.edu/ml
5. Myers, C., Aleksander, I.: Learning algorithms for probabilistic neural nets. Neural Netw. 1(1 SUPPL), 205 (1988). https://doi.org/10.1016/0893-6080(88)90242-0

6. Adeodato, P.J.L., Oliveira Neto, R. F.: pRAM n-tuple Classifier-a new architecture of probabilistic RAM neurons for classification problems. In: The 2010 International Joint Conference on Neural Networks (IJCNN), pp. 1–7 (2010)

7. Efron, B., Tibshirani, R.J.: An Introduction to the Bootstrap. CRC Press, Boca Raton (1994)

8. Dua, D., Graff, C.: UCI machine learning repository: wine quality data set. https://archive.ics.uci.edu/ml/datasets/wine+quality. Accessed 25 Apr 2022

9. Dua, D., Graff, C..: UCI machine learning repository: Abalone data set. https://archive.ics.uci.edu/ml/datasets/Abalone. Accessed 25 Apr 2022

10. Pace, R.K., Ronald, B.: Sparse spatial autoregressions. Stat. Probab. Lett. **33**(3), 291–297 (1997)

11. Cortez, P., Cerdeira, A., Almeida, F., Matos, T., Reis. J.: Modeling wine preferences by data mining from physicochemical properties. In: Decision Support Systems, pp. 547–553. Elsevier (2009)

12. Nakano, R., Satoh, S.: Mixture of multilayer perceptron regressions. In: ICPRAM, pp. 509–516 (2019)

13. Jung, Y.: Multiple predicting K-fold cross-validation for model selection. J. Nonparametr. Stat. **30**(1), 197–215 (2018). https://doi.org/10.1080/10485252.2017.1404598

14. Arlot, S., Celisse, A.: A survey of cross validation procedures for model selection. Stat. Surv. **4**, 40–79 (2010). https://doi.org/10.1214/09-SS054

15. Chai, T., Draxler, R.R.: Root mean square error (RMSE) or mean absolute error (MAE)? - arguments against avoiding RMSE in the literature. Geosci. Model Dev. **7**(3), 1247–1250 (2014)

16. Rynkiewicz, J.: General bound of overfitting for MLP regression models. Neurocomputing **90**, 106–110 (2012). https://doi.org/10.1016/j.neucom.2011.11.028

17. Alexandre, B.: fdm2id: Data Mining and R Programming for Beginners. R package version 0.9.5. https://CRAN.R-project.org/package=fdm2id. Accessed 25 Apr 2022

18. Turian, J., Bergstra, J., Bengio, Y.: Quadratic features and deep architectures for chunking. In: Proceedings of Human Language Technologies: The 2009 Annual Conference of the North American Chapter of the Association for Computational Linguistics, pp. 245–248 (2009)

19. Venables, W.N., Ripley, B.D.: Modern Applied Statistics with S, 4th edn. Springer, New York (2002). https://doi.org/10.1007/978-0-387-21706-2

ConveXplainer for Graph Neural Networks

Tamara A. Pereira[1(✉)], Erik Jhones F. Nascimento[1], Diego Mesquita[2],
and Amauri H. Souza[1]

[1] Federal Institute of Ceará, Fortaleza, Brazil
tamaraarrudap@gmail.com, erikjhonesf@gmail.com, amauriholanda@ifce.edu.br
[2] Getulio Vargas Foundation, Rio de Janeiro, Brazil
diego.mesquita@aalto.fi

Abstract. Graph neural networks (GNNs) have become the most
prominent framework for representation learning on graph-structured
data. Nonetheless, cue to its black-box nature, they often suffer from
the same plague that afflicts many deep learning systems: lack of interpretability. To mitigate this issue, many recent approaches have been
proposed to explain GNN predictions. In this paper, we propose a simple
explanation method for graph neural networks. Drawing inspiration from
recent works showing that GNNs can often be simplified without any
impact on performance, we propose distilling GNNs into simpler (linear)
models and explaining the latter instead. After distillation, we extract
explanations by solving a convex optimization problem which identifies
the most relevant nodes for a given node-level prediction. Experiments
on synthetic and real-world benchmarks show that our method is competitive with, if not outperforms, state-of-the-art explainers for GNNs.

Keywords: Graph neural networks · Explainability · Model
distillation

1 Introduction

In the last decade, deep learning has taken over artificial intelligence (AI)
research, driving breakthroughs in applications such as face recognition [2,23],
self-driving cars [3,21], language modeling [4], game play [24], and algorithmic
stock trading [28]. Nonetheless, the predictive power of deep learning often comes
at the cost of limited interpretability. The black-box nature of these methods
makes it hard to diagnose whether model predictions are, e.g., riddled by con-
founders or align well with domain expert knowledge.

To overcome these shortcomings of deep models, there is a growing interest
in developing methods to explain neural network predictions, leading to the
renaissance of the eXplainable AI (XAI) [7] field. Although methods for xAI can
come in many flavors, a significant portion seeks to identify which input elements
(e.g., features) are most relevant/salient to the corresponding predictions.

© The Author(s), under exclusive license to Springer Nature Switzerland AG 2022
J. C. Xavier-Junior and R. A. Rios (Eds.): BRACIS 2022, LNAI 13654, pp. 588–600, 2022.
https://doi.org/10.1007/978-3-031-21689-3_41

Understanding model predictions is especially important for high-stake applications such as drug design and personalized medicine, in which inputs are structured and usually given as graphs. In particular, graph neural networks (GNNs) [22] are the gold standard for supervised learning over graph-structured data, with notable applications in molecular property prediction [8], fake-news detection [18,19], and content recommendation [5,30]. Not surprisingly, a flurry of recent works has focused on explaining GNN predictions [16,26,31]

Notably, several recent works [10,17,25,27] show that GNNs are often more complex than they need to—especially for node-level prediction tasks—, counting on expandable model components. That is, it is possible to simplify GNNs without loss of predictive performance, and still benefit from the lower computational cost and greater interpretability of simplified models. These findings naturally lead to the following question:

— *Can we build simpler explanatory models for graph neural networks?*

In this work, we propose ConveX, a simple explanation strategy for GNNs. More specifically, we first distill the (possibly complex) GNN we want to explain into a simpler one. Then, we generate explanations for our simplified model solving a convex optimization problem that allows identifying which nodes/edges of the input graph are most relevant for a given prediction.

Experiments with synthetic and real-world datasets show that, despit its simplicity, ConveX achieves competitive results when compared to state-of-the-art models, such as GNNExplainer [31] and PGMExplainer [26].

The remaining of this paper is organized as follows. Section two provides a brief background on GNNs. Section 3 discusses related works on explanations for node classification. Section 4 proposes ConveX, a novel explanation strategy that leverages knowledge distillation. Section 5 compares ConveX against the state-of-the-art (SOTA) in a variety of explainability benchmarks. Finally, Sect. 6 draws conclusions and discusses future works.

2   Background

Notation. We define a graph $G = (\mathcal{V}, \mathcal{E})$, with a set of nodes $\mathcal{V} = \{1, \ldots, n\}$ and a set of edges $\mathcal{E} \subseteq \mathcal{V} \times \mathcal{V}$. We denote the adjacency matrix of G by $\mathbf{A} \in \mathbb{R}^{n \times n}$, i.e., A_{ij} is one if $(i,j) \in \mathcal{E}$ and zero otherwise. Let $\mathbf{D}$ be the diagonal degree matrix of G, i.e., $D_{ii} := \sum_j A_{ij}$. We also define the *normalized* adjacency matrix as $\tilde{\mathbf{A}} = \mathbf{D}^{-1/2}(\mathbf{A} + \mathbf{I})\mathbf{D}^{-1/2}$, where $\mathbf{I}$ is the n-dimensional identity matrix. Furthermore, let $\mathbf{X} \in \mathbb{R}^{n \times d}$ be a matrix of d-dimensional node features. Throughout this work, we also often denote a graph G using the pair $(\mathbf{A}, \mathbf{X})$.

2.1   Graph Neural Networks

Graph neural networks (GNNs) have gained traction over the last few years due to their potential to extract meaningful graph representations while still preserving invariances (e.g., to node permutations). In general, modern GNNs apply a series of convolutions over the node states (initially equal to node features), after which we have refined representations for each node. Then, we can use these representations for arbitrary downstream tasks.

The output of a (fully-convolutional) GNN after ℓ layers can be written as a function $\boldsymbol{H}^{(\ell)} = f(\boldsymbol{H}^{(\ell-1)}, \boldsymbol{A})$, where $\boldsymbol{H}^{(\ell)}$ is matrix with n rows, one for each node in $\mathcal{V}$. Specific GNNs differ essentially in how they define $f(\cdot, \cdot)$. After a suitable number of layers, say L, we can apply a multi-layer perceptron (MLP) on top of node embeddings to get predictions. If we consider node classification, the logits for all nodes are given by $\boldsymbol{Y} = \mathrm{MLP}(\boldsymbol{H}^{(L)})$, where $\boldsymbol{Y} \in \mathbb{R}^{n \times C}$ and C is the number of classes in our task.

The remaining of this subsection covers two GNN models: graph convolutional networks (GCNs) [12] and simplified graph convolutions (SGCs) [27]. The former is arguably the most popular GNN in the literature and is used profusely throughout our experiments. The latter is a linear graph model, which will be an asset for our explanation method.

Graph Convolutional Networks (GCNs) [12] are multi-layer architectures in which nodes repeatedly gather their neighbors' states, subsequently combining them using a symmetric weighting scheme. Then, each node updates its state in a recurrent fashion using the result from neighborhood aggregation. Similarly to conventional feedforward networks, GCNs can be seen as a sequence of linear transformations followed by non-linear activation functions (e.g. ReLU). Denoting the weights of the ℓ-th GCN layer by $\boldsymbol{\Theta}^{(\ell)}$ and the activation function as σ, we can write compactly the output of said layer as:

$$\boldsymbol{H}^{(\ell)} = \sigma\left(\tilde{\boldsymbol{A}}\boldsymbol{H}^{(\ell-1)}\boldsymbol{\Theta}^{(\ell)}\right), \tag{1}$$

where $\boldsymbol{H}^{(\ell-1)}$ is the output of the previous layer and $\boldsymbol{H}^{(0)}$ equals the original features, i.e., $\boldsymbol{H}^{(0)} = \boldsymbol{X}$.

Simple Graph Convolution (SGC) [27] is a simplification of GCN. We can derive SGC by removing the activation functions from intermediate layers and subsequently collapsing all weight matrices into one. To make it more concrete, recall the we can use the recursion in Eq. (1) to write the output of an ℓ-layer GCN as:

$$\boldsymbol{H}^{(\ell)} = \sigma\left(\tilde{\boldsymbol{A}}\boldsymbol{H}^{(\ell-1)}\boldsymbol{\Theta}^{(\ell)}\right), \tag{2}$$

$$= \sigma\left(\tilde{\boldsymbol{A}}\sigma\left(\cdots\sigma\left(\tilde{\boldsymbol{A}}\sigma\left(\tilde{\boldsymbol{A}}\boldsymbol{X}\boldsymbol{\Theta}^{(1)}\right)\boldsymbol{\Theta}^{(2)}\right)\cdots\right)\boldsymbol{\Theta}^{(\ell)}\right) \tag{3}$$

Removing the intermediate non-linear activations from the equation above leaves us with:

$$\boldsymbol{H}^{(\ell)} = \sigma\left(\tilde{\boldsymbol{A}}\cdots\tilde{\boldsymbol{A}}\tilde{\boldsymbol{A}}\boldsymbol{X}\boldsymbol{\Theta}^{(1)}\boldsymbol{\Theta}^{(2)}\cdots\boldsymbol{\Theta}^{(\ell)}\right) \tag{4}$$

$$= \sigma\left(\tilde{\boldsymbol{A}}^{\ell}\boldsymbol{X}\boldsymbol{\Theta}^{(1)}\boldsymbol{\Theta}^{(2)}\cdots\boldsymbol{\Theta}^{(\ell)}\right). \tag{5}$$

To finish the derivation, we substitute the product $\Theta^{(1)}\Theta^{(2)}\cdots\Theta^{(\ell)}$ by a single weight matrix Θ. Therefore, we wind up with the node embeddings for an L-layer SGC:

$$H = \sigma\left(\tilde{A}^L X \Theta\right). \tag{6}$$

Notably, Wu *et al.* [27] showed that SGC often performs similarly to or better than GCN in a variety of node classification tasks. On top of that, training SGCs is computationally more than GCNs andd SGC models comprise significantly fewer parameters.

3 Related Works: Explanaining Node Predictions

Despite the intuitive nature of graph convolutions, stacking GNN layers—in hope of achieving superior performance—leads to an undesirable side effect: lack of interpretability. These explanations might be crucial to, e.g., validate decisions in critical applications or to help experts validate the model. To mitigate this issue, there is a growing literature proposing instance-level explanations for node prediction. Notably, the predominant approach behind SOTA methods is to create auxiliary models (explainers) capable of identifying which input elements (e.g., nodes or edges) are most relevant to the prediction of the GNN we want to explain. The rationale behind this choice is that members of a class usually share common structures, e.g., mutagenic compounds often comprise telltale chemical sequences such as NO_2 (a pair of oxygen atoms together with a nitrogen atom). Consequently, checking which patterns are most relevant to a GNN prediction can be instrumental for domain experts and may help us debug spurious correlations.

GNNExplainer [31] was one of the first methods to explain GNN predictions. The method is perturbation-based and generates explanations by learning masks for edges and node attributes that allow it to remove information that does not impact GNN's predictions. The masks are randomly initialized and treated as trainable variables. Then, GNNExplainer combines the masks with the original graph G, thus generating a subgraph G_s and a subset of attributes of nodes X_s that contains important information for the prediction. The idea is to learn these masks by maximizing the mutual information between the possible explanatory subgraph (G_s, X_s) and the GNN prediction y, that is

$$\max_{G_s} \mathrm{MI}(y, (G_s, X_s)) = H(y) - H(y|G = G_s, X = X_s). \tag{7}$$

The entropy term $H(y)$ is constant as the GNN to be explained Φ is fixed after training. So, maximizing the mutual information between the predicted label distribution y and the explanation (G_s, X_s) is equivalent to minimizing the conditional entropy $H(y|G = G_s, X = X_s)$, which can be expressed as follows:

$$H(y|G = G_s, X = X_s) = -\mathbb{E}_{y|G_s, X_s}[\log P_\Phi(y|G = G_s, X = X_s)]. \tag{8}$$

In practice, the program in Eq. (7) is an intractable combinatorial optimization problem. To circumvent this limitation, Ying *et al.* [31] relax the problem by learning a soft mask $M \in [0,1]^{n \times n}$ that weighs the edges of the input graph G.

PGM-Explainer [26] builds on probabilistic graphical models to obtain instance - level explanations for GNNs. Its explanation is an interpretable Bayesian network that approximates the GNN's prediction. Its process of generating explanations has three main steps: 1. Data generation, this step consists of generating, pre-processing, and recording a set of input-output pairs, called sampled data, of the prediction to be explained. 2. Variable selection, eliminates unimportant variables from sampled data to improve the runtime and encourage compact explanations. For this step, PGM-Explainer needs to identify which variables are important and avoid eliminating them, PGM-Explainer addresses this problem by observing that important variables to GNN's prediction are in the Markov-blanket of prediction. 3. Structure learning, takes the filtered data from the previous step and generates an explanation.

While outside the scope of our work, it is worth mentioning that, besides instance-level, there are other works focusing on model-level explanations. These works aim to identify which graph patterns impact the most the overall behavior of a GNN [32].

4   ConveX

We now introduce ConveX—a new method for node-level explanation of graph neural networks. ConveX follows a two-step procedure: i) we first fit a simple GNN to approximate the predictions of the model to be explained (distillation phase); ii) then, we explain the simplified GNN by solving an optimization problem that has a simple loss landscape (i.e., it is convex if the GNN is linear).

Hereafter, we denote the GNN to be explained by Φ. The matrix $\hat{Y} = \Phi(G)$ comprises the predictions for all nodes in G—the i-th row of $\hat{Y}$ contains the class predictions of node i. Given the GNN Φ and its predictions $\hat{Y}$, the interest is in finding an explainer model capable of identifying the most influential information for the prediction y_i from Φ to node i. In this work, the GNN Φ is considered a black-box model, that is, the explainer model does not have access to any internal information, such as parameters or hidden representations of the model, but only to the input and output of the GNN.

4.1   Knowledge Distillation

Despite the success of deep learning models, most of these models have high complexity due to the need to adjust a large number of parameters. With that in mind, the approach called knowledge distillation [9] arose, in which the objective is to distill the knowledge of a complex network through a simple and interpretable model. The use of knowledge distillation for models of neural networks in graphs has been addressed in recent works [29,33] that validate the efficiency of these strategies.

In this work, we use SGC [27] to approximate the predictions obtained with the GNN Φ. Formally, the distilled model (SGC), here denoted by Ψ, receives the input graph $G = (A, X)$ and provides class predictions $\hat{Y}^{(\Psi)} = \Psi(G) =$ softmax$(\tilde{A}^L X \Theta)$, where Θ is the matrix of model parameters, L is the number of layers of the GNN Φ, and the softmax function acts row-wise.

The distillation process consists of adjusting the parameters Θ of the SGC model Ψ so that it approximates the predictions of the network to be explained Φ. This can be achieved by minimizing the Kullback-Leibler divergence KL between the predictions of Φ and Ψ_Θ. Consider that $\hat{y}_i^{(\Psi_\Theta)}$ and $\hat{y}_i^{(\Phi)}$ denote the class predictions for node i from the Ψ_Θ and Φ models, respectively. More concisely, our distillation process consists in solving:

$$\min_\Theta \left\{ \sum_i \text{KL}\left(\hat{y}_i^{(\Phi)}, \hat{y}_i^{(\Psi_\Theta)}\right) = \sum_{i \in \mathcal{V}} \sum_{c=1}^C \hat{y}_{ic}^{(\Phi)} \log \frac{\hat{y}_{ic}^{(\Phi)}}{\hat{y}_{ic}^{(\Psi_\Theta)}} \right\}. \tag{9}$$

4.2 Obtaining Node-Level Explanations

Intuitively, finding a good explanation $\mathcal{E}$ for a prediction $\hat{y}_i$—Φ's prediction for node $i \in \mathcal{V}$ given a graph G—can be seen as finding the smallest subgraph $G_\mathcal{E}$ of G containing the nodes that influence the most that prediction. That being said, we define $\mathcal{E}$ as an n-dimensional vector of indicator variables, one for each node in G's vertex set $\mathcal{V}$.

Since we focus on explaining Ψ as a surrogate of Φ, we start off by formulating our problem as finding the explanation $\mathcal{E}$ the minimizes a discrepancy between output $\hat{y}_i^{(\Psi)}$ of Ψ given the original graph and the prediction using only the graph induced by $\mathcal{E}$:

$$\min_{\mathcal{E} \in \{0,1\}^n} \| \tilde{A}_i^L \text{diag}(\mathcal{E}) X \Theta - \tilde{A}_i^L X \Theta \|_2^2, \tag{10}$$

where $\tilde{A}_i^L$ denotes the i-th row of the matrix $\tilde{A}^L$. Nonetheless, the formulation in Eq. (10) has a major issue: it does not impose any budget on our node selection, admitting trivial solutions like $\mathcal{E} = \{1\}^n$. To solve this and simultaneously avoid binary optimization, we replace the search space by the simplex $\Delta = \{r \in \mathbb{R}^n : \sum_i r_i = 1, \forall_i r_i \geq 0\}$. Implementing this change and re-arranging computations, we wind up with:

$$\min_{\mathcal{E} \in \Delta} \left\| \tilde{A}_i^L \left(\text{diag}(\mathcal{E}) - I_n\right) X \Theta \right\|_2^2, \tag{11}$$

where I_n is the n-dimensional identity matrix. Notably, Δ is a convex set. It is also easy to prove the objective function in Eq. (11) is a quadratic program. To this end let us denote the objective function above by f. Then, it follows that:

$$
\begin{aligned}
f(\boldsymbol{\mathcal{E}}) &= \left\| \widetilde{\boldsymbol{A}}_i^L \left(\mathrm{diag}(\boldsymbol{\mathcal{E}}) - \boldsymbol{I}_n \right) \boldsymbol{X}\boldsymbol{\Theta} \right\|_2^2 \\
&= \left\| \widetilde{\boldsymbol{A}}_i^L \mathrm{diag}(\boldsymbol{\mathcal{E}})\boldsymbol{X}\boldsymbol{\Theta} \right\|_2^2 - 2 \left(\boldsymbol{\mathcal{E}}^{\mathsf{T}} \mathrm{diag} \left(\left(\widetilde{\boldsymbol{A}}_i^L \right)^{\mathsf{T}} \right) \boldsymbol{X}\boldsymbol{\Theta}^{\mathsf{T}} \widetilde{\boldsymbol{A}}_i^L \boldsymbol{X}\boldsymbol{\Theta} \right) + \delta \\
&= \left\| \widetilde{\boldsymbol{A}}_i^L \mathrm{diag}(\boldsymbol{\mathcal{E}})\boldsymbol{X}\boldsymbol{\Theta} \right\|_2^2 + \boldsymbol{\mathcal{E}}^{\mathsf{T}}\boldsymbol{c} + \delta \\
&= \boldsymbol{\mathcal{E}}^{\mathsf{T}} \mathrm{diag} \left(\left(\widetilde{\boldsymbol{A}}_i^L \right)^{\mathsf{T}} \right) \boldsymbol{X}\boldsymbol{\Theta}\boldsymbol{\Theta}^{\mathsf{T}}\boldsymbol{X}^{\mathsf{T}} \mathrm{diag} \left(\left(\widetilde{\boldsymbol{A}}_i^L \right)^{\mathsf{T}} \right) \boldsymbol{\mathcal{E}} + \boldsymbol{\mathcal{E}}^{\mathsf{T}}\boldsymbol{c} + \delta \\
&= \boldsymbol{\mathcal{E}}^{\mathsf{T}}\boldsymbol{Q}\boldsymbol{\mathcal{E}} + \boldsymbol{\mathcal{E}}^{\mathsf{T}}\boldsymbol{c} + \delta
\end{aligned}
$$

which is the cannonic quadratic form with δ being a constant and

$$
\boldsymbol{c} = -2\mathrm{diag} \left(\left(\widetilde{\boldsymbol{A}}_i^L \right)^{\mathsf{T}} \right) \boldsymbol{X}\boldsymbol{\Theta}^{\mathsf{T}} \widetilde{\boldsymbol{A}}_i^L \boldsymbol{X}\boldsymbol{\Theta},
$$

$$
\boldsymbol{Q} = \mathrm{diag} \left(\left(\widetilde{\boldsymbol{A}}_i^L \right)^{\mathsf{T}} \right) \boldsymbol{X}\boldsymbol{\Theta}\boldsymbol{\Theta}^{\mathsf{T}}\boldsymbol{X}^{\mathsf{T}} \mathrm{diag} \left(\left(\widetilde{\boldsymbol{A}}_i^L \right)^{\mathsf{T}} \right),
$$

and since $\boldsymbol{Q}$ has the form $\boldsymbol{P}^{\mathsf{T}}\boldsymbol{P}$, it is positive semidefinite, and our optimization problem in Eq. (11) is convex.

Since a conventional GNN layer uses first order information (i.e., the immediate neighborhood) to update node representations, only nodes at distance $\leq L$ influence each other's prediction in a GNN with depth L. Therefore, $G_{\mathcal{E}}$ must be a subgraph of the graph induced by i and its L-neighborhood in G. For this reason, we mask out nodes outside this neighborhood, holding their importance at zero. For ease of implementation, we solve Eq. (11) in the unconstrained $\mathbb{R}^n$, mapping vectors from $\mathbb{R}^n$ to Δ using the softmax function. After optimizing for $\boldsymbol{\mathcal{E}}$, the values in $\boldsymbol{\mathcal{E}}$ serve as a ranking for the importance of each node.

5   Experiments

In this section, we validate the efficacy of ConveX on artificial and real-world benchmarks. We have implemented all experiments using PyTorch [20]. The code and data used in this work are available[1].

5.1   Datasets

Synthetic Datasets. We consider six popular synthetic datasets for node-level explanation of GNNs: BA-House-Shapes, BA-Community, BA-Grids, Tree-Cycles, Tree-Grids, and BA-Bottle-Shaped. We note that these datasets are available in [31] and [26].

Each dataset consists of a single graph comprised of multiple copies of the same motif (i.e., subgraph with a specific structural pattern) connected

---

[1] https://github.com/tamararruda/ConveX.

to base subgraphs. For the datasets, BA-House-Shapes, BA-Community, BA-Grids, and BA-Bottle-Shaped the base subgraphs are randomly generated using the Barabási- Albert (BA) [1] model. For datasets Tree-Cycles and Tree-Grids, the base subgraphs are an 8-level balanced binary tree. The class of each motif-node depends only on elements belonging to the same motif, and consequently, the explanation associated with any node must include only motif elements, i.e., it cannot include base nodes. Therefore, the base subgraphs denote information irrelevant to the prediction of any node.

Real-World Datasets. We also use two real-world datasets: Bitcoin-Alpha and Bitcoin-OTC [13,14]. These datasets denote networks in which nodes correspond to user accounts that trade Bitcoin. A directed edge (u, v) (between users u and v) denotes the degree of reliability assigned by u to v, i.e., each edge has an associated score denoting the degree of trust. The Bitcoin-Alpha and Bitcoin-OTC networks have 3783 and 5881 accounts, respectively. Platform members rate other members on a scale from -10 (total distrust) to $+10$ (total trust). Each account is labeled as trusted or untrusted based on the ratings of other members. In addition, accounts have features that capture account output information, such as the average rate or normalized number of votes the account has taken. Target explanations for each node are provided by experts.

5.2 Experimental Setup

We compare ConveX against three explainers: GNNExplainer [31], and PGMExplainer [26] and an extension of Shapley Additive explanations (SHAP) [15] to GNNs—SHAP is an additive feature attribution method. To ensure a valid comparison, we closely follow guidelines and the evaluation setup from the original works. Following the setup in [26], the GNN to be explained consists of a 3-layer GCN [12] with ReLU activation. We use an 80%/10%/10% (train/val/test) split for all datasets. Moreover, the GCN model is trained for 10000 epochs using early stopping with patience of 100 epochs.

For the distillation phase in ConveX, we use a SGC [27] model with 3 layers. During model distillation, predictions from all nodes are used such that the distiller model better fits the model to be explained. We use learning rate of 0.1 with a weight decay of 5.0×10^{-6} for 10000 epochs. To obtain node-level explanations, ConveX applies gradient descent with learning rate of 0.1 for a maximum number of iterations equal to 100. For the synthetic benchmarks, which do not count on node features, we train the SGCs using one-hot node features that indicate each node's degree.

All implementations were developed using the PyTorch [20] and Torch Geometric [6] libraries. In addition, in all experiments, we use Adam [11] optimizer.

Our evaluation setup closely follows that from [26]. In particular, we report accuracy for the synthetic datasets as "true" explanations are available. Importantly, the models only aim to explain predictions for motif-nodes. An explanation consists of a rank of n nodes, where n is the number of nodes in the corresponding motif. For Bitcoin-Alpha and Bitcoin-OTC, we use precision as

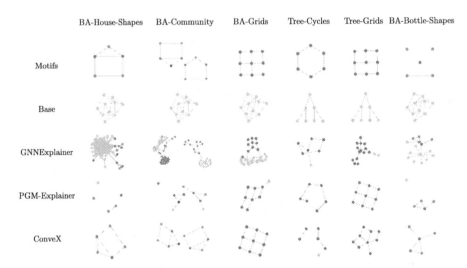

Fig. 1. Illustration of how synthetic datasets are assembled with their motifs and base nodes. The node labels are represented by colors. Furthermore, to evaluate how each explainer behaves, examples of explanations extracted from GNNExplainer, PGM-Explainer, and ConveX for the same prediction in each dataset are shown. (Color figure online)

evaluation metric. The explanation methods generate a fixed number of nodes n as explanations (with $n \in \{3, 4, 5\}$) as true explanations for these datasets have varying sizes. Lastly, we do not provide errorbars (std. deviations) to allow comparison with the numbers reported in the original works [26,31].

5.3   Results

The results achieved with the Ψ distiller for the eight datasets are shown in the Table 1. The evaluation metric used was the accuracy between the model to be explained and the distiller model. Table 1 reports the mean and standard deviation calculated over 10 independent runs.

Table 1. Distillation accuracy.

BA-House	BA-Community	BA-Grids	Tree-Cycles	Tree-Grids	BA-Bottle	Bitcoin-Alpha	Bitcoin-OTC
94.2 ± 1.2	86.6 ± 0.1	99.9 ± 0.1	97.7 ± 0.2	98.0 ± 0.2	98.5 ± 0.2	90.4 ± 0.1	89.1 ± 0.2

In general, the results show that the distiller Ψ manages to closely approximate the model to be explained Φ since for most datasets we obtain accuracy above 90%. Interestingly, even when poor distillation results occur (e.g., for the BA-community dataset), ConveX achieves significantly higher results than other state-of-the-art explainers (as we will observe in Table 2). One possible explanation for this counter-intuitive result is that the distiller can differentiate between motif and base nodes, and this suffices to obtain good explanations as we are only interested in explaining motif nodes. Figure 2 reports the confusion matrix for the BA-community dataset. Despite the low distillation accuracy (86.6%), the model correctly predicts base nodes (classes 1 and 5). Therefore, the model achieves high accuracy for the binary classification problem of distinguishing motif and base nodes, supporting our hypothesis.

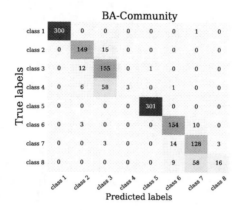

Fig. 2. Confusion matrix for the BA-Community dataset. The classes 1 and 5 correspond to base nodes. Note that the distiller is able to differentiate well between motif- and base-nodes.

Table 2 reports the results for the synthetic datasets. The results show that ConveX generated better explanations than all the explainers on four out of six datasets: BA-House, BA-Community, BA-Grids and BA-Bottle. PGMExplainer achieves the highest accuracy on Tree-Cycles and Tree-Grids.

Figure 1 shows motifs, base subgraphs and explanations provided from different explainers for the synthetic datasets. Overall, ConveX is the model that better captures the motif structure on BA-House, BA-Community, BA-Grids and BA-Bottle, validating its higher accuracy on these benchmarks.

Table 2. Performance (accuracy) of explanatory models for synthetic datasets. ConveX is the best performing model on 4/6 datasets.

	BA-House	BA-Community	BA-Grids	Tree-Cycles	Tree-Grids	BA-Bottle
SHAP	0.947	0.741	0.872	0.884	0.641	0.741
GNNExplainer	0.925	0.836	0.741	0.948	0.875	0.612
PGM-Explainer	0.965	0.926	0.885	**0.954**	**0.878**	0.953
ConveX	**0.979**	**0.951**	**0.896**	0.836	0.805	**0.994**

Table 3. Performance (precision) of explanatory models for real-world datasets.

	Bitcoin-Alpha			Bitcoin-OTC		
	Top 3	Top 4	Top 5	Top 3	Top 4	Top 5
SHAP	0.537	0.498	0.465	0.607	0.587	0.566
GNNExplainer	0.375	0.332	0.307	0.385	0.338	0.312
PGM-Explainer	0.873	0.857	**0.848**	0.833	0.817	**0.808**
ConveX	**0.912**	**0.879**	0.823	**0.885**	**0.835**	0.775

Table 3 shows the results for the Bitcoin-Alpha and Bitcoin-OTC datasets. ConveX outperforms GNNExplainer and SHAP by a large margin. Notably, ConveX is the best performing model for top-3 and top-4 predictions while PGM-Explainer achieves the highest precision for top-5.

6   Conclusion

In this work, we focused on finding simpler formulations for models that explain graphs neural networks and we proposed ConveX, a convex model for generating explanations for predictions of GNNs. ConveX seeks to identify which information is relevant to GNN predictions in a simple way. The proposed model uses knowledge distillation to condense the knowledge of a possibly complex network into a simpler and more interpretable model. To explain node predictions, ConveX computes a node importance vector (weights) that preserves the predictions of the distilled net. To emphasize the notion that we must prioritize nodes, ConveX further restricts the importance vector to lie in the simplex.

We evaluated ConveX using eight datasets and compared it against three baseline explainers. The results show that ConveX generates better explanations in most cases. Overall, our assessment provides evidence towards a positive answer to our initial research question: it is possible to build simpler explainers for graph neural networks.

References

1. Barabási, A.L., Albert, R.: Emergence of scaling in random networks. Science **286**, 509–512 (1999)
2. Cao, Q., Shen, L., Xie, W., Parkhi, O.M., Zisserman, A.: VGGFace2: a dataset for recognising faces across pose and age. In: 2018 13th IEEE International Conference on Automatic Face and Gesture Recognition (FG 2018), Los Alamitos, CA, USA, pp. 67–74 (2018)
3. Chen, X., Ma, H., Wan, J., Li, B., Xia, T.: Multi-view 3D object detection network for autonomous driving, pp. 6526–6534 (2017)
4. Devlin, J., Chang, M.W., Lee, K., Toutanova, K.: BERT: pre-training of deep bidirectional transformers for language understanding. In: Proceedings of the Conference of the North American Chapter of the Association for Computational Linguistics (2019)

5. Fan, W., et al.: Graph neural networks for social recommendation. In: The World Wide Web Conference, WWW 2019, pp. 417–426. ACM, New York (2019)
6. Fey, M., Lenssen, J.E.: Fast graph representation learning with PyTorch Geometric. In: ICLR Workshop on Representation Learning on Graphs and Manifolds (2019)
7. Fong, R., Vedaldi, A.: Interpretable explanations of black boxes by meaningful perturbation, pp. 3449–3457 (2017)
8. Gilmer, J., Schoenholz, S.S., Riley, P.F., Vinyals, O., Dahl, G.E.: Neural message passing for quantum chemistry, pp. 1263–1272 (2017)
9. Hinton, G.E., Vinyals, O., Dean, J.: Distilling the knowledge in a neural network, vol. abs/1503.02531 (2015)
10. Huang, Q., He, H., Singh, A., Lim, S., Benson, A.: Combining label propagation and simple models out-performs graph neural networks. In: International Conference on Learning Representations (ICLR) (2021)
11. Kingma, D., Ba, J.: Adam: a method for stochastic optimization. In: International Conference on Learning Representations (ICLR 2015) (2015)
12. Kipf, T.N., Welling, M.: Semi-supervised classification with graph convolutional networks. In: International Conference on Learning Representations (ICLR) (2017)
13. Kumar, S., Hooi, B., Makhija, D., Kumar, M., Faloutsos, C., Subrahmanian, V.: REV2: fraudulent user prediction in rating platforms. In: Proceedings of the Eleventh ACM International Conference on Web Search and Data Mining, pp. 333–341. ACM (2018)
14. Kumar, S., Spezzano, F., Subrahmanian, V., Faloutsos, C.: Edge weight prediction in weighted signed networks. In: 2016 IEEE 16th International Conference on Data Mining (ICDM), pp. 221–230. IEEE (2016)
15. Lundberg, S., Lee, S.I.: A unified approach to interpreting model predictions. In: Proceedings of the 31st International Conference on Neural Information Processing Systems, NIPS 2017 (2017)
16. Luo, D., et al.: Parameterized explainer for graph neural network. In: Larochelle, H., Ranzato, M., Hadsell, R., Balcan, M.F., Lin, H. (eds.) Advances in Neural Information Processing Systems, vol. 33, pp. 19620–19631 (2020)
17. Mesquita, D., Souza, A.H., Kaski, S.: Rethinking pooling in graph neural networks. In: Advances in Neural Information Processing Systems (NeurIPS) (2020)
18. Noorshams, N., Verma, S., Hofleitner, A.: TIES: temporal interaction embeddings for enhancing social media integrity at Facebook, pp. 3128–3135 (2020)
19. Pacheco, D., Hui, P.M., Torres-Lugo, C., Truong, B.T., Flammini, A., Menczer, F.: Uncovering coordinated networks on social media: methods and case studies. In: Proceedings of International AAAI Conference on Web and Social Media (ICWSM), vol. 15, pp. 455–466 (2021)
20. Paszke, A., et al.: PyTorch: an imperative style, high-performance deep learning library, pp. 8024–8035 (2019)
21. Sallab, A.E., Abdou, M., Perot, E., Yogamani, S.K.: Deep reinforcement learning framework for autonomous driving. S&T Electronic Imaging, Autonomous Vehicles and Machines 2017 abs/1704.02532 (2017)
22. Scarselli, F., Gori, M., Tsoi, A.C., Hagenbuchner, M., Monfardini, G.: The graph neural network model. EEE Trans. Neural Netw. **20**, 61–80 (2009)
23. Schroff, F., Kalenichenko, D., Philbin, J.: FaceNet: a unified embedding for face recognition and clustering. In: 2015 IEEE Conference on Computer Vision and Pattern Recognition (CVPR), pp. 815–823 (2015)
24. Silver, D., et al.: Mastering the game of Go with deep neural networks and tree search. Nature **529**(7587), 484–489 (2016)

25. Chen, T., Bian, S., Sun, Y.: Are powerful graph neural nets necessary? A dissection on graph classification. CoRR abs/1905.04579 (2019)
26. Vu, M., Thai, M.T.: PGM-explainer: probabilistic graphical model explanations for graph neural networks. In: Advances in Neural Information Processing Systems, pp. 12225–12235 (2020)
27. Wu, F., Souza, A., Zhang, T., Fifty, C., Yu, T., Weinberger, K.: Simplifying graph convolutional networks. In: Proceedings of the 36th International Conference on Machine Learning (ICML), pp. 6861–6871 (2019)
28. Xu, Y.L., Konstantinidis, K., Mandic, D.P.: Multi-graph tensor networks. In: The First Workshop on Quantum Tensor Networks in Machine Learning, 34th Conference on Neural Information Processing Systems (NeurIPS) (2020)
29. Yang, Y., Qiu, J., Song, M., Tao, D., Wang, X.: Distilling knowledge from graph convolutional networks. In: Proceedings of the IEEE/CVF Conference on Computer Vision and Pattern Recognition, pp. 7074–7083 (2020)
30. Ying, R., He, R., Chen, K., Eksombatchai, P., Hamilton, W.L., Leskovec, J.: Graph convolutional neural networks for web-scale recommender systems. In: Proceedings of the 24th ACM SIGKDD International Conference on Knowledge Discovery; Data Mining, KDD 2018, pp. 974–983. ACM, New York (2018)
31. Ying, Z., Bourgeois, D., You, J., Zitnik, M., Leskovec, J.: GNNExplainer: generating explanations for graph neural networks. In: Wallach, H., Larochelle, H., Beygelzimer, A., d'Alché-Buc, F., Fox, E., Garnett, R. (eds.) Advances in Neural Information Processing Systems, vol. 32 (2019)
32. Yuan, H., Tang, J., Hu, X., Ji, S.: XGNN: towards model-level explanations of graph neural networks. In: Proceedings of the 26th ACM SIGKDD International Conference on Knowledge Discovery; Data Mining, pp. 430–438. ACM, New York (2020)
33. Zhou, S., et al.: Distilling holistic knowledge with graph neural networks. In: Proceedings of the IEEE/CVF International Conference on Computer Vision (ICCV), pp. 10387–10396 (2021)

Extreme Learning Machine to Graph Convolutional Networks

Thales Gonçalves[(✉)][iD] and Luis Gustavo Nonato[iD]

Institute of Mathematics and Computer Sciences,
University of São Paulo (ICMC-USP), São Carlos, Brazil
thalesogoncalves@usp.br, gnonato@icmc.usp.br

Abstract. Graph Convolutional Network (GCN) is a powerful model to deal with data arranged as a graph, a structured non-euclidian domain. It is known that GCN reaches high accuracy even when operating with just 2 layers. Another well-known result shows that Extreme Learning Machine (ELM) is an efficient analytic learning technique to train 2 layers Multi-Layer Perceptron (MLP). In this work, we extend ELM theory to operate in the context of GCN, giving rise to ELM-GCN, a novel learning mechanism to train GCN that turns out to be faster than baseline techniques while maintaining prediction capability. We also show a theoretical upper bound in the number of hidden units required to guarantee the GCN performance. To the best of our knowledge, our approach is the first to provide such theoretical guarantees while proposing a non-iterative learning algorithm to train graph convolutional networks.

Keywords: Graph convolutional network · Extreme learning machine · Graph machine learning

1 Introduction

The interest to extend machine learning methods to operate on graph-structured data has increased considerably in the last few years. Graph Convolutional Network (GCN) [13] is of particular importance in this context. GCN can be seen as an extension of the well-known Convolutional Neural Network [15] (which handles grid-structured data) to graph-structured data. GCN has demonstrated its effectiveness in a wide range of tasks, including classification [13], link prediction [31], graph encoding [14], recommendation systems [27], traffic forecasting [33], action recognition [25], and crime forecasting [12].

One interesting characteristic of GCN is that it can present quite good performance even when configured as a 2-layer network [3,7,12–14,20,33]. Indeed, the oversmoothing effect [16] is well-known to degrade GCN performance as it gets deeper. These facts raise the question of whether well-established mechanisms such as Extreme Learning Machine (ELM) [10] and Regularized Extreme Learning Machine (RELM) [6], which are designed to train 2-layer neural networks, can be extended to train 2-layer GCNs. ELM and RELM are analytical

J. C. Xavier-Junior and R. A. Rios (Eds.): BRACIS 2022, LNAI 13654, pp. 601–615, 2022.
https://doi.org/10.1007/978-3-031-21689-3_42

training schemes that have proven to be effective in applications ranging from computer vision [8,17] to medical data classification [2]. Since ELM and RELM are not iterative methods, they tend to be much faster than gradient descent techniques such as backpropagation and its variants [1].

In this work, we show that ELM and RELM can indeed be extended to the context of GCN. In fact, we extend the main theoretical results of ELM [9] to 2-layer GCN. We also show the effectiveness of the proposed analytical training mechanisms, called ELM-GCN and RELM-GCN, in several experiments and comparisons involving synthetic and real graph datasets.

In summary, the main contributions of this work are:

– ELM-GCN and RELM-GCN, the extension of ELM and RELM to the context of graph convolutional network;
– A theoretical upper bound in the number of hidden units to guarantee that a GCN trained with the proposed ELM-GCN algorithm results in controlled training error;
– A number of experiments involving synthetic and real graph datasets, showing the effectiveness of RELM-GCN when compared against other GCN training approaches.

2   Related Works

In recent years, many works have been proposed to generalize machine learning techniques originally designed to handle Cartesian data (or grid-structured) to operate on graph-structured domains. Examples of such techniques include neural network architectures for graph embedding [14], graph-based spatial-temporal analysis [19], attention mechanisms on graphs [22] and graph convolutional neural networks [13]. To better contextualize our work, we focus this section on works that address training mechanisms for graph neural networks. A more comprehensive review of graph neural network techniques can be found in the recent survey by Wu et al. [24].

A main issue in the context of graph neural networks is the time spent to train the models, specially in problems involving large graphs. A number of different strategies have been proposed to tackle this issue. Hamilton et al. [7], for instance, propose GraphSAGE, a training mechanism that relies on an aggregation function to sample the neighborhood of nodes. Cluster-GCN [4] is a learning algorithm that applies graph cluster to restrict the neighborhood search to a subgraph identified by a graph cluster algorithm. GraphACT [29] builds upon CPU-FPGA heterogeneous systems to boost the training process. L-GCN [28] is a layer-wise training algorithm for GCN that learns the weight matrix in each layer in a sequential manner. The Simple Graph Convolution [23] method reduces the complexity of GCNs by removing nonlinearities, collapsing the result into a single linear transformation. A technique that has gained great attention in recent years is the fastGCN proposed by Chen et al. [3], which interprets graph convolution as integral transforms of embedding functions under probability measures, evaluating the integrals through Monte Carlo method.

The methods discussed above rely on iterative gradient descent based algorithms to update the weights in each layer. In contrast, the method proposed in this work computes the weights of GCNs analytically, exhibiting comparable performance to other GCN training mechanisms while being more efficient in terms of computational times.

Regarding studies of shallow versus deep GCNs, Kipf and Welling [13] concludes that for the datasets they considered, GCN with more than 3 layers always had its performance degraded. The best accuracy they found was when GCN was configured with 2 layers in the majority of cases. Li et al. [16] showed that feature vectors among nodes become more similar as more GCN layers are stacked, because of the message-passing Laplacian-like step in each layer. This well-known effect is regarded as the oversmoothing effect and in particular Li et al. [16] proved that if the number of layers grows indefinitely, every node of a connected graph would present the same feature vector, being impossible for a downstream classification layer to distinguish between nodes of different classes.

Graph Convolutional Extreme Learning Machine (GCELM) [32] is a training methodology that closely relates to the proposed RELM-GCN. However, our approach, RELM-GCN, differs from GCELM in two main aspects: first, RELM-GCN has message passing mechanism in the second layer, which GCELM has not. This leads to the important consequence that each vertex in our model gathers information from both 1- and 2-hop neighbors, while GCELM only considers information of adjacent nodes. Second, Zhang et al. [32] conduct experiments only on non-graph machine learning datasets, i.e., they derive a graph from correlations present on the data used in their experiments. Therefore, the graph structure and the fracture vectors associated to the nodes are closely correlated, being hard to assess whether the good reported results are a consequence of their training mechanism or due to the bias they introduced when generating the graph. Finally, we formulate and prove theorems to establish theoretical guarantees to our approach and such theoretical results are not present in GCELM.

3   Background

In this section, we provide some basic concepts about GCN and ELM that will be important to understand the proposed ELM-GCN and RELM-GCN.

GCN. Let $G = (V, E)$ be a graph, where V is the set of N vertices (or nodes) and E is the set of edges, where each edge in E connects two vertices in V. Supposing A the adjacency matrix of G, Kipf and Welling [13] propose a spectral interpretation of the convolution operation that, after some algebraic manipulation, defines a convolution layer as:

$$f(A, X) = \sigma\big(\hat{A}X\Theta\big) \tag{1}$$

where X is the input data matrix, Θ is the layer weight matrix, σ is the layer non-linear activation function, and $\hat{A} \in \mathbb{R}^{N \times N}$ is a normalization of A given by:

$$\hat{A} = \tilde{D}^{-1/2}\tilde{A}\tilde{D}^{-1/2}, \quad \tilde{D} = \mathrm{diag}\left(\sum_j \tilde{A}_{i,j}\right), \quad \tilde{A} = A + I, \tag{2}$$

where $I \in \mathbb{R}^{N \times N}$ is the identity matrix.

A Graph Convolutional Network - GCN is defined as a stack of convolution layers, i.e. a nested sequence composition of Eq. 1 according to the number of layers. In particular, a 2-layer GCN model is mathematically given by:

$$Y = \sigma_2\left(\hat{A}\,\sigma_1\left(\hat{A}X\Theta^{(1)}\right)\Theta^{(2)}\right) \tag{3}$$

In this context, we call the first and second layers as hidden and output layers, respectively. In Eq. 3, X is a C-dimensional signal in G, i.e., a function $X : V \to \mathbb{R}^C$ that assigns a C-dimensional feature vector to each vertex in G. X can also be written as a matrix in $\mathbb{R}^{N \times C}$. $\Theta^{(1)} \in \mathbb{R}^{C \times H}$ and $\Theta^{(2)} \in \mathbb{R}^{H \times F}$ are the hidden and output layers weight matrices, respectively (parameters that are calibrated by a learning algorithm). H is the number of units in the hidden layer (a hyperparameter) and F is the number of possible classes in a classification problem. σ_1 and σ_2 are the hidden and output layers activation functions, respectively.

The task of a GCN model is to predict $T \in \mathbb{R}^{N \times F}$, the target matrix that assigns an one-hot-encoding label to each vertex based on the input node features X and on the topological structure of G encoded in $\hat{A}$. Notice that the number of nodes N in the graph, the number of node features C and the number of classes F are all determined by the input graph-structured dataset. Thus, the only "free" hyperparameter in a 2-layer GCN architecture is the number of hidden units H.

ELM. Consider a 2-layer Multi-Layer Perceptron (MLP) network with linear output activation function and no biases. Such MLP archictecture can be mathematically stated as:

$$Y = \sigma\left(X\Theta^{(1)}\right)\Theta^{(2)} \tag{4}$$

The key idea of Extreme Learning Machine-ELM [10] is that even if $\Theta^{(1)}$ is randomly settled (and kept **unchanged**), $\Theta^{(2)}$ can still be analytically computed so as to minimize the error between the predicted Y and the targets T. Precisely, suppose $\Theta^{(1)}$ a $C \times H$ matrix with entries drawn from a probability distribution and consider $Y_h = \sigma(X\Theta^{(1)})$ the (random) $N \times H$ non-linear mapping of X resulting from the hidden layer. Since the output layer is linear ($Y = Y_h\Theta^{(2)}$), if Y_h (a random mapping) is an invertible matrix then $\Theta^{(2)}$ can be computed as $\Theta^{(2)} := Y_h^{-1}T$, making the network output matches perfectly the target labels.

An interesting result proven by Huang et al. [10] is that if the number of hidden units H matches the number of data samples, then Y_h is invertible with probability one, thus $\Theta^{(2)} := Y_h^{-1}T$ gives a network with null training error. Moreover, Huang et al. [10] also show that one can upper bound the training error by properly tunning the number of units H in the hidden layer. In this latter case, the inverse matrix Y_h^{-1} must be replaced by the Moore-Penrose pseudo-inverse $Y_h^{\dagger}$.

A variant of ELM is the so-called Regularized Extreme Learning Machine (RELM) proposed by Deng et al. [6]. RELM relies on a formulation where the norm of the weight matrix $\Theta^{(2)}$ is penalized during optimization. With some algebraic manipulation, the regularized weight matrix $\Theta^{(2)}$ can be computed as:

$$\Theta^{(2)} := \left(\frac{1}{\gamma} I + Y_h^T Y_h \right)^{\dagger} Y_h^T T, \tag{5}$$

where γ is a regularization hyperparameter and $I \in \mathbb{R}^{H \times H}$ is the identity matrix.

4 ELM-GCN and RELM-GCN

It is well known that a GCN with exactly two layers performs quite well as a classification model [13]. As discussed in Sect. 3, ELM is an efficient learning algorithm to train 2-layer MLP models [10]. In the following, we show how to extend ELM to operate (train) on 2-layer GCNs with linear output activation function.

Given a 2-layer GCN, we assume that $\Theta^{(1)}$ (see Eq. 3) is a matrix with entries randomly sampled from a continuous probability distribution ψ and that $\Theta^{(1)}$ is fixed during the whole training process. Let Y_h be the output of the hidden layer given the input graph signal X, that is:

$$Y_h = \sigma(\hat{A} X \Theta^{(1)}). \tag{6}$$

It is not difficult to see that the output of the GCN is linear, i.e., $Y = \hat{A} Y_h \Theta^{(2)}$. Therefore, if $(\hat{A} Y_h)$ is an invertible matrix, we can analytically compute the output weight matrix as $\Theta^{(2)} := (\hat{A} Y_h)^{-1} T$, ensuring a perfect match between the predicted and target labels, i.e., $Y = T$. The question now is: under

---

Algorithm 1 . Extreme Learning Machine to Graph Convolutional Network (ELM-GCN) – case H = N

Input: $\hat{A}$, X, T, σ, ψ
Output: $\Theta^{(1)}$, $\Theta^{(2)}$

$\rightarrow \Theta^{(1)} \sim \psi$
$\rightarrow Y_h = \sigma(\hat{A} X \Theta^{(1)})$
$\rightarrow \Theta^{(2)} = (\hat{A} Y_h)^{-1} T$

Algorithm 2 . Extreme Learning Machine to Graph Convolutional Network (ELM-GCN)

Input: $\hat{A}$, X, T, σ, ψ
Output: $\Theta^{(1)}$, $\Theta^{(2)}$

$\rightarrow \Theta^{(1)} \sim \psi$
$\rightarrow Y_h = \sigma(\hat{A} X \Theta^{(1)})$
$\rightarrow \Theta^{(2)} = (\hat{A} Y_h)^{\dagger} T$

which circumstances is $(\hat{A}Y_h)$ invertible? Considering that the number of hidden units H is set to be the same as the number N of nodes in G, we can prove Theorem 1 (the proof is in Appendix), which guarantees that $(\hat{A}Y_h)$ is invertible with probability one and thus, the output weight matrix $\Theta^{(2)}$ can be analytically computed to ensure no training error.

Theorem 1 *(ELM-GCN – case H = N)*:
Let $\sigma : \mathbb{R} \to \mathbb{R}$ be an infinitely differentiable activation function in any interval, G a graph with N nodes, non-negative edge weights and invertible matrix $\tilde{A}$. Let $\hat{X} = \hat{A}X \in \mathbb{R}^{N \times C}$ be a convolved graph signal matrix with distinct rows and $T \in \mathbb{R}^{N \times F}$ be the target labels. Then, if a single hidden layer GCN with N hidden units has its hidden weights $\Theta^{(1)}$ randomly sampled according to any continuous probability distribution ψ, then the convolved hidden mapping $(\hat{A}Y_h)$ is, with probability one, invertible and thus there exists $\Theta^{(2)}$ such that $\|\hat{A}Y_h\Theta^{(2)} - T\| = 0$.
Obs:. $\Theta^{(2)} := (\hat{A}Y_h)^{-1}T$

Theorem 1 shows that, under certain conditions, one can analytically train the output layer weights of a GCN given a random hidden layer weights matrix, resulting in a network with no training error. Note that the random weights can be drawn from any continuous probability distribution ψ, which includes, but is not limited to, the uniform (in an arbitrary interval) and normal (with arbitrary mean and standard deviation) distributions. Algorithm 1 shows the learning steps to train a 2-layer GCN using the ELM-GCN scheme described above.

The number of nodes in a graph dataset is usually large, which means that Algorithm 1 would demand a network with an unpractical number of hidden units. Moreover, null error in the training phase is not usually desired since it indicates overfitting. Therefore, Theorem 1 actually provides an upper bound in the number of hidden units to guarantee zero training error. To the best of our knowledge, this is the first work to provide the maximum number of hidden units in a GCN to ensure zero training error.

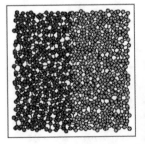

Fig. 1. Synthetic data

Algorithm 3 . Regularized Extreme Learning Machine to Graph Convolutional Network (RELM-GCN)

Input: $\hat{A}$, X, T, σ, ψ, γ
Output: $\Theta^{(1)}$, $\Theta^{(2)}$

$\to \Theta^{(1)} \sim \psi$
$\to Y_h = \sigma(\hat{A}X\Theta^{(1)})$
$\to \Theta^{(2)} = \left(\frac{1}{\gamma} I + (\hat{A}Y_h)^T (\hat{A}Y_h) \right)^{\dagger} (\hat{A}Y_h)^T T$

As shown in Theorem 2, it is possible to train a GCN with less than N hidden units, with the trade-off that training error is not guaranteed to be null anymore, but it can still be upper bounded. The alternative approach not only requires less hidden units, but also alleviates the overfitting problem. Moreover, Theorem 2 shows it is possible to tune the number of hidden units to ensure a training error not larger than a given threshold.

Theorem 2 *(ELM-GCN):*
Let $\sigma : \mathbb{R} \to \mathbb{R}$ be an infinitely differentiable activation function in any interval, $\epsilon > 0$ an arbitrary scalar, G a graph with N nodes, non-negative edge weights and invertible matrix $\tilde{A}$. Let $\hat{X} = \hat{A}X \in \mathbb{R}^{N \times C}$ be a convolved graph signal matrix with distinct rows and $T \in \mathbb{R}^{N \times F}$ be the target labels. Then, there exists $H \leqslant N$ such that if a single hidden layer GCN with H hidden units has its hidden weights $\Theta^{(1)}$ randomly sampled according to any continuous probability distribution ψ, then, with probability one, there is $\Theta^{(2)}$ such that $\|\hat{A}Y_h\Theta^{(2)} - T\| < \epsilon$.
Obs:. $\Theta^{(2)} := (\hat{A}Y_h)^\dagger T$

Algorithm 2 shows the ELM-GCN algorithm that computes the weights of the network for any number of hidden units H. Note that Algorithm 2 is similar to Algorithm 1, but replacing the inverse $(\hat{A}Y_h)^{-1}$ by the pseudo-inverse $(\hat{A}Y_h)^\dagger$ operator. Moreover, Algorithm 2 is a generalization of Algorithm 1, since in the special case when $H = N$, the matrix $(\hat{A}Y_h)$ is square (and invertible with probability one), making the pseudo-inverse $(\hat{A}Y_h)^\dagger$ to be equal to $(\hat{A}Y_h)^{-1}$.

We have also adapted RELM algorithm to the context of GCN, resulting in a new expression to compute $\Theta^{(2)}$, as shown in Algorithm 3. The regularized version of our algorithm is called Regularized Extreme Learning Machine to Graph Convolutional Network (RELM-GCN) and we also prove that ELM-GCN is a special case of RELM-GCN when the hyperparameter $\gamma \to \infty$ (Appendix).

5 Experiments

Synthetic Data. This first experiment relies on a simple but illustrative synthetic dataset that allows us to assess whether the ELM-GCN and RELM-GCN algorithms behave as expected when training a GCN.

Consider a graph G derived from a 30×30 regular grid, that is, nodes are placed in the center of each grid cell and each node is connected by an edge to its left, right, top, and bottom neighbors. Gaussian noise is added to the x and y coordinates of the nodes and the perturbed coordinates are assigned as a two-dimensional feature vector to the nodes in G (see Fig. 1). A binary label (0 or 1) is associated to each node depending on whether the node comes from the left or right half of the grid, that is, the left half of the nodes are labeled as 0 and the right half as 1, as depicted in Fig. 1. Although this graph dataset gives rise to a simple classification task, it is able to reveal whether the proposed algorithms behave as expected when training 2-layer GCNs with different hidden layer configurations.

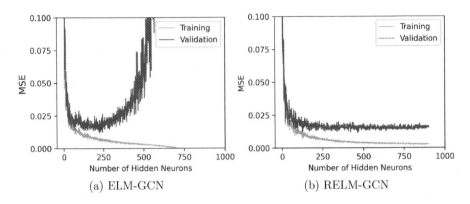

(a) ELM-GCN   (b) RELM-GCN

Fig. 2. Performance of GCN trained with ELM-GCN and RELM-GCN in the graph of Fig. 1.

We divide the graph nodes randomly into training (80%), validation (10%), and test (10%) subsets. A GCN is then trained with both ELM-GCN and RELM-GCN strategies keeping the subsets fixed, but varying the number of hidden units H from 1 to 900, the last being the number of nodes in the graph. For RELM-GCN, we set the regularization parameter γ as $\{10^{-8}, 10^{-7}, \ldots, 10^8\}$ for each H value. Figure 2a shows the Mean Square Error (MSE) of ELM-GCN in terms of the number of hidden units. In Fig. 2b, the MSE corresponds to the smallest error for all γ in each H value.

ELM-GCN was trained with 900 hyperparameter configurations ($H \in \{1, 2, \ldots 900\}$). Similarly, RELM-GCN had more than 15,000 distinct set ups ($\gamma \in \{10^{-8}, 10^{-7}, \ldots, 10^8\}$ for each H). Therefore, it would be intractable to employ this amount of trainings in reasonable time with some standard iterative learning algorithm.

Notice in Fig. 2a that the training error tends to decrease when the number of hidden neurons H increases. Validation error, in contrast, drops quickly until a certain point, when it starts to increase, indicating overfitting. In contrast, validation and training errors for RELM-GCN follow the same decreasing tendency, indicating that the regularization mechanism minimizes overfitting. Those classical behaviors show that both ELM-GCN and RELM-GCN perform as expected and similar to other non-regularized and regularized learning techniques. Moreover, the ELM-GCN training error vanishes when the number of hidden units reaches 720 (the number of graph training nodes), matching the upper bound stated in Theorem 1.

Real Data. We assess the performance of ELM-GCN and RELM-GCN when training GCNs on four well-known graph datasets: Cora, Citeseer, Pubmed and Reddit. The first three datasets are citation networks and the goal is to categorize documents. For the fourth dataset, the model should predict posts categories from Reddit community, a social network. Cora, Citeseer and Pubmed are avail-

Table 1. Statistics and split of each dataset.

Dataset	Nodes	Edges	Features	Classes	Split (Train./Val./Test)
Cora	2,708	5,429	1,433	7	1,208/500/1,000
Citeseer	3,327	4,732	3,703	6	1,827/500/1,000
Pubmed	19,717	44,338	500	3	18,217/500/1,000
Reddit	232,965	11,606,919	602	41	153,932/23,699/55,334

able in https://github.com/tkipf/gcn and the Reddit dataset can be obtained from http://snap.stanford.edu/graphsage/. Similarly to Chen et al. [3], for the citation networks we build the validation and test subsets as in Kipf and Welling [13], employing the remaining nodes for training. In the case of Reddit, we split the dataset as in Chen et al. [3]. Table 1 shows the dataset statistics and how the split has been done.

We compare the proposed ELM-GCN/RELM-GCN against the classical GCN [13], which we call Backpropagation (BP), and the fastGCN proposed by Chen et al. [3]. Baseline implementations were downloaded from https://github. com/tkipf/gcn and https://github.com/matenure/FastGCN, respectively.

The hyperparameters for BP and fastGCN are settled as proposed in the baseline implementation. Specifically, in the citation networks, BP [13] is configured with 16 hidden units, $5 \cdot 10^{-4}$ L_2 as regularization parameter, 0.01 as learning rate, dropout equal to 0.5, 200 epochs and 10 patience iteration (i.e., optimization is early stopped if accuracy in the validation does not increase over 10 consecutive iterations). GCN is not trained with BP for Reddit dataset, as it runs out of memory for large graphs. For fastGCN [3], the number of hidden units is 16 for Cora and Pubmed and 128 for Reddit, L_2 regularization parameter is $5 \cdot 10^{-4}$ for Cora and Pubmed and $1 \cdot 10^{-4}$ for Reddit, learning rate ranges in $\{0.01, 0.001, 0.0001\}$, no dropout is used and 200 epochs is employed for all datasets, setting 10 patience iteration for Cora and Pubmed and 30 for Reddit. The sample size is 400 for Cora and Reddit and 100 for Pubmed, batch size is 256 for Cora and Reddit and 1024 for Pubmed. We use importance sampling for fastGCN, since Chen et al. [3] report better accuracies with this configuration. Since Chen et al. [3] do not conduct experiments on Citeseer dataset, we configured all hyperparameters for this dataset to be the same as in Cora.

It is well known that classical ELM requires more hidden units when compared to Backpropagation [10]. Therefore, for our techniques, we have run experiments with $\{128, 256, 512, 750, 1000, 1250, 1500\}$ hidden units. The regularization parameter γ ranges in $\{10^{-8}, 10^{-7}, ... , 10^8\}$ and no dropout was used. We select hyperparameters that led to the best accuracy during validation.

For each learning configuration, we train the networks based on both transductive and inductive paradigms, as proposed by Yang et al. [26]. In the transductive paradigm the whole graph is assumed to be known for the training step and the task is to predict labels from the features associated to the nodes of the graph, training labels, and the graph topology. In the inductive paradigm, the model learns from a subgraph made up of training nodes only. After training, the full graph is presented to the network and the task becomes to predict labels from the whole structure. For each dataset, training paradigm and learning algorithm, 10 executions are performed. The results shown in Tables 2 and 3 are the average of these executions. We ran experiments in a single machine with 4-core 1.99GHz Intel Core i7 and 16G RAM.

Figure 3 depicts graphically the content of Tables 2 and 3. From Fig. 3 it is possible to observe that the classical GCN (BP), fastGCN, ELM-GCN and RELM-GCN present similar performance in terms of accuracy for all datasets in both paradigms. Regarding training time, both ELM-GCN and its regularized version turn out to be at least one order of magnitude faster than BP and fastGCN in three out of four datasets (Cora, Citesser, and Reddit). In the Pubmed dataset, RELM-GCN is also one order of magnitude faster than BP, while being 15% faster than fastGCN. Therefore, we can see that our proposed schemes are competitive training alternatives for 2-layer GCNs in terms of accuracy, while presenting a considerable gain in the training time.

We also note that ELM-GCN and RELM-GCN demand more hidden units to reach an accuracy comparable to the baseline techniques (all selected configurations contain at least 256 neurons). In fact, this is an expected behavior, since the classical ELM presents the same characteristic [6,10]. The intuition behind this is that both ELM-GCN and its regularized version assume the weights in the hidden layer to be random and fixed during the whole training process. Therefore, in order to increase the probability of discrimination in the output layer, the latent space associated to the hidden layer must be of high dimension, pushing up the number of hidden units. Despite this larger configuration, the analytical computation of output weights still ensures a considerable gain in terms of training time.

Table 2. Accuracy and training time with transductive paradigm.

Dataset	Accuracy				Time (s)			
	BP	fastGCN	ELM-GCN	RELM-GCN	BP	fastGCN	ELM-GCN	RELM-GCN
Cora	.8633	.8386	.8283	**.8687**	15.33	16.77	**0.15**	0.42
Citeseer	**.7772**	.7529	.7405	.7734	17.43	49.42	**0.51**	0.66
Pubmed	.8685	.8628	.8713	**.8774**	152.64	4.85	4.48	**4.20**
Reddit	NA	**.9383**	.9194	.9196	NA	911.38	136.64	**65.41**

Table 3. Accuracy and training time with inductive paradigm.

Dataset	Accuracy				Time (s)			
	BP	fastGCN	ELM-GCN	RELM-GCN	BP	fastGCN	ELM-GCN	RELM-GCN
Cora	.8317	.8462	.7858	**.8718**	7.20	11.23	**0.10**	0.46
Citeseer	.7782	**.7849**	.7010	.7749	13.28	42.81	**0.17**	0.91
Pubmed	.8664	.8665	.8730	**.8733**	147.78	6.22	11.65	**5.15**
Reddit	NA	**.9336**	.9102	.9250	NA	831.01	90.95	**47.61**

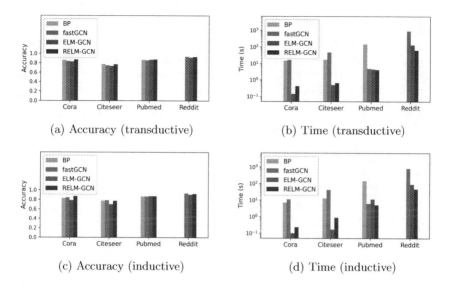

(a) Accuracy (transductive) (b) Time (transductive)

(c) Accuracy (inductive) (d) Time (inductive)

Fig. 3. Accuracy and training times for both transductive and inductive paradigms.

6 Conclusion

In this work we presented ELM-GCN and RELM-GCN, two analytical learning algorithms to train 2-layer GCNs. The proposed extreme learning machine algorithms, defined for graph-structured domains, come with solid theoretical foundations, providing an upper bound in the number of hidden units needed to reach a desired training error.

The experiments involving synthetic and real graph datasets show that RELM-GCN is able to reach an accuracy similar to competing methods, but reducing the training time considerably. In fact, the proposed approach turned out to be at least one order of magnitude faster in most of our experiments.

One of the limitations of the proposed approach is that it is constrained to 2-layer GCN. However, this architecture has been a popular choice in many recent works [3,7,12–14,20,33], thus ELM-GCN and RELM-GCN turn out to be useful in many application scenarios.

Researches focused on other extensions of the classical ELM are still booming [11,18,21,30]. Generalizing the new achievements while proposing new ones for graph-structured data is a research path we plan to follow.

Acknowledgments. This work was supported by grant #2018/24516-0, São Paulo Research Foundation (FAPESP). The opinions, hypotheses and conclusions or recommendations expressed in this material are those of responsibility of the author(s) and do not necessarily reflect FAPESP's view.

Appendix 1. Proofs

In this appendix we present the proofs of Theorems 1 and 2, which support the theory of Extreme Learning Machine to Graph Convolutional Networks. We also show that RELM-GCN matches ELM-GCN when $\gamma \to \infty$.

Theorem 1

Proof. We interpret the convolved graph signal matrix $\hat{X}$ rows as the input samples of classic ELM Theorem (Theorem 2.1 from [10]). Since the hypotheses that rows of $\hat{X}$ are distinct, σ is an infinitely differentiable activation function, and $\Theta^{(1)}$ is randomly sampled from some continuous probability distribution, we conclude the hypothesis of the classic ELM Theorem is satisfied, thus $\sigma(\hat{X}\Theta^{(1)}) = \sigma(\hat{A}X\Theta^{(1)}) =: Y_h$ is invertible with probability one.

Since the edge weights of G are non-negative, all the elements in matrix $\tilde{A}$ (Eq. 2) are also non-negative. Moreover, diagonal elements of $\tilde{A}$ are positive. Thus, diagonal elements of $\tilde{D}$ (Eq. 2) are also positive and hence $\tilde{D}$ and $\tilde{D}^{-1/2}$ are invertible matrices. Furthermore, from the hypothesis that $\tilde{A}$ is invertible, Eq. 2 shows that $\hat{A}$ must also be an invertible matrix. Therefore, with probability one, $(\hat{A}\,Y_h)$ is invertible and by defining $\Theta^{(2)} := (\hat{A}Y_h)^{-1}T$ we have $\|\hat{A}Y_h\Theta^{(2)} - T\| = 0$, concluding the proof of the Theorem.

Theorem 2

Proof. Following exactly the same proof of classic ELM Theorem (Theorem 2.2 from [10]), the validity of the Theorem comes from the fact that, otherwise, one could choose $H = N$ which makes $\|\hat{A}Y_h\Theta^{(2)} - T\| = 0 < \epsilon$ according to Theorem 1.

Now we show that ELM-GCN is a special case of RELM-GCN when $\gamma \to \infty$.

Proof. When $\gamma \to \infty$ we have $\frac{1}{\gamma}I \to 0$. Thus the analytical assignment to $\Theta^{(2)}$ by RELM-GCN (last instruction of Algorithm 3) becomes:

$$
\begin{aligned}
\Theta^{(2)} &= \left(\frac{1}{\gamma}I + (\hat{A}Y_h)^T(\hat{A}Y_h)\right)^\dagger (\hat{A}Y_h)^T\,T = \left((\hat{A}Y_h)^T(\hat{A}Y_h)\right)^\dagger (\hat{A}Y_h)^T\,T \\
&= (\hat{A}Y_h)^\dagger \left((\hat{A}Y_h)^T\right)^\dagger (\hat{A}Y_h)^T\,T = (\hat{A}Y_h)^\dagger \left((\hat{A}Y_h)^\dagger\right)^T (\hat{A}Y_h)^T\,T \\
&= (\hat{A}Y_h)^\dagger \left((\hat{A}Y_h)(\hat{A}Y_h)^\dagger\right)^T\,T = (\hat{A}Y_h)^\dagger(\hat{A}Y_h)(\hat{A}Y_h)^\dagger\,T = (\hat{A}Y_h)^\dagger\,T
\end{aligned}
$$

which is the assignment to $\Theta^{(2)}$ given by ELM-GCN (last instruction of Algorithm 2).

Appendix 2. Additional Experiment Details

In the following, we further validate the results obtained in the experiments involving real data. Specifically, we analyse the different runs that produced Fig. 3 using Wilcoxon Signed-Rank Test [5]. This hypothesis test is a nonparametric statistical test that compares two samples that are paired. Precisely, the test compares accuracy and training time produced by either ELM-GCN or RELM-GCN against the ones resulting from the other two algorithms. First, we consider the null hypothesis that one of our approaches and competing algorithms generate results according to the same distribution. If the null hypothesis is rejected, we proceed to the next step which considers another null hypothesis that ELM-GCN or its regularized version performs worst (i.e. lower accuracy or higher training time) than the other learning techniques. In all tests we use significance of 99.9%.

Regarding ELM-GCN, the Wilcoxon test rejected the hypothesis that this technique produces output at least as accurate as BP or fastGCN. However in terms of training time, the null hypothesis that ELM-GCN comes from same distribution as its competitors is rejected. Moreover, the Wilcoxon test also rejects the hypothesis that ELM-GCN has higher training time than BP or fastGCN.

Comparing RELM-GCN with BP, the Wilcoxon test could not reject the null hypothesis that both techniques produce the same accuracy. However, when RELM-GCN is compared against fastGCN, we get an interesting outcome. The null hypothesis can not be rejected when both learning algorithms are compared in the inductive paradigm, but the hypothesis is rejected in the transductive scenario. Moreover, the hypothesis that RELM-GCN is less accurate than fast-GCN in the same paradigm is rejected. Indeed, a careful analysis of Fig. 3a shows that RELM-GCN consistently outperforms fastGCN on the first 3 datasets while performing comparably on Reddit.

Furthermore, the Wilcoxon test rejected the null hypothesis that RELM-GCN is as fast as competing techniques, regardless of the algorithm and paradigm chosen to compare. Moreover, the second step of the test showed that we should also reject the hypothesis that RELM-GCN is slower than the other algorithms in any learning paradigm. Conclusions provided by the Wilcoxon test are consistent with training times shown in Fig. 3, since RELM-GCN outperforms the competing algorithms in most datasets, being only comparable with fastGCN in Pubmed.

References

1. Baydin, A.G., Pearlmutter, B.A., Radul, A.A., Siskind, J.M.: Automatic differentiation in machine learning: a survey. J. Mach. Learn. Res. **18** (2018)
2. Baykara, M., Abdulrahman, A.: Seizure detection based on adaptive feature extraction by applying extreme learning machines. Traitement du Signal **38**(2), 331–340 (2021)
3. Chen, J., Ma, T., Xiao, C.: Fastgcn: fast learning with graph convolutional networks via importance sampling. arXiv preprint arXiv:1801.10247 (2018)

4. Chiang, W.L., Liu, X., Si, S., Li, Y., Bengio, S., Hsieh, C.J.: Cluster-gcn: an efficient algorithm for training deep and large graph convolutional networks. In: Proceedings of the 25th ACM SIGKDD International Conference on Knowledge Discovery & Data Mining, pp. 257–266 (2019)

5. Demšar, J.: Statistical comparisons of classifiers over multiple data sets. J. Mach. Learn. Res. **7**, 1–30 (2006)

6. Deng, W., Zheng, Q., Chen, L.: Regularized extreme learning machine. In: 2009 IEEE Symposium on Computational Intelligence and Data Mining, pp. 389–395. IEEE (2009)

7. Hamilton, W.L., Ying, R., Leskovec, J.: Inductive representation learning on large graphs. arXiv preprint arXiv:1706.02216 (2017)

8. He, B., Xu, D., Nian, R., van Heeswijk, M., Yu, Q., Miche, Y., Lendasse, A.: Fast face recognition via sparse coding and extreme learning machine. Cogn. Comput. **6**(2), 264–277 (2014)

9. Huang, G.B., Wang, D.H., Lan, Y.: Extreme learning machines: a survey. Int. J. Mach. Learn. Cybern. **2**(2), 107–122 (2011)

10. Huang, G.B., Zhu, Q.Y., Siew, C.K.: Extreme learning machine: theory and applications. Neurocomputing **70**(1–3), 489–501 (2006)

11. Inaba, F.K., Teatini Salles, E.O., Perron, S., Caporossi, G.: DGR-ELM - Distributed Generalized Regularized ELM for classification. Neurocomputing **275**, 1522–1530 (2018)

12. Jin, G., Wang, Q., Zhu, C., Feng, Y., Huang, J., Zhou, J.: Addressing crime situation forecasting task with temporal graph convolutional neural network approach. In: 2020 12th International Conference on Measuring Technology and Mechatronics Automation (ICMTMA), pp. 474–478. IEEE (2020)

13. Kipf, T.N., Welling, M.: Semi-supervised classification with graph convolutional networks. arXiv preprint arXiv:1609.02907 (2016)

14. Kipf, T.N., Welling, M.: Variational graph auto-encoders. arXiv preprint arXiv:1611.07308 (2016)

15. Krizhevsky, A., Sutskever, I., Hinton, G.E.: Imagenet classification with deep convolutional neural networks. In: Advances in Neural Information Processing Systems, pp. 1097–1105 (2012)

16. Li, Q., Han, Z., Wu, X.M.: Deeper insights into graph convolutional networks for semi-supervised learning. In: Thirty-Second AAAI Conference on Artificial Intelligence (2018)

17. Lv, Q., Niu, X., Dou, Y., Xu, J., Lei, Y.: Classification of hyperspectral remote sensing image using hierarchical local-receptive-field-based extreme learning machine. IEEE Geosci. Remote Sens. Lett. **13**(3), 434–438 (2016)

18. Martínez-Martínez, J.M., Escandell-Montero, P., Soria-Olivas, E., Martín-Guerrero, J.D., Magdalena-Benedito, R., Gómez-Sanchis, J.: Regularized extreme learning machine for regression problems. Neurocomputing **74**(17), 3716–3721 (2011). https://doi.org/10.1016/j.neucom.2011.06.013. https://linkinghub.elsevier.com/retrieve/pii/S092523121100378X

19. Seo, Y., Defferrard, M., Vandergheynst, P., Bresson, X.: Structured sequence modeling with graph convolutional recurrent networks. In: Cheng, L., Leung, A.C.S., Ozawa, S. (eds.) ICONIP 2018. LNCS, vol. 11301, pp. 362–373. Springer, Cham (2018). https://doi.org/10.1007/978-3-030-04167-0_33

20. Shchur, O., Mumme, M., Bojchevski, A., Günnemann, S.: Pitfalls of graph neural network evaluation. arXiv preprint arXiv:1811.05868 (2018)

21. da Silva, B.L.S., Inaba, F.K., Salles, E.O.T., Ciarelli, P.M.: Outlier robust extreme machine learning for multi-target regression. Expert Syst. Appl. **140**, 112877 (2020)

22. Veličković, P., Cucurull, G., Casanova, A., Romero, A., Lio, P., Bengio, Y.: Graph attention networks. arXiv preprint arXiv:1710.10903 (2017)
23. Wu, F., Souza, A., Zhang, T., Fifty, C., Yu, T., Weinberger, K.: Simplifying graph convolutional networks. In: International Conference on Machine Learning, pp. 6861–6871. PMLR (2019)
24. Wu, Z., Pan, S., Chen, F., Long, G., Zhang, C., Philip, S.Y.: A comprehensive survey on graph neural networks. IEEE Trans. Neural Networks Learn. Syst. (2020)
25. Yan, S., Xiong, Y., Lin, D.: Spatial temporal graph convolutional networks for skeleton-based action recognition. In: Thirty-Second AAAI conference on Artificial Intelligence (2018)
26. Yang, Z., Cohen, W., Salakhudinov, R.: Revisiting semi-supervised learning with graph embeddings. In: International Conference on Machine Learning, pp. 40–48. PMLR (2016)
27. Ying, R., He, R., Chen, K., Eksombatchai, P., Hamilton, W.L., Leskovec, J.: Graph convolutional neural networks for web-scale recommender systems. In: Proceedings of the 24th ACM SIGKDD International Conference on Knowledge Discovery & Data Mining, pp. 974–983 (2018)
28. You, Y., Chen, T., Wang, Z., Shen, Y.: L2-gcn: layer-wise and learned efficient training of graph convolutional networks. In: Proceedings of the IEEE/CVF Conference on Computer Vision and Pattern Recognition, pp. 2127–2135 (2020)
29. Zeng, H., Prasanna, V.: Graphact: accelerating gcn training on cpu-fpga heterogeneous platforms. In: Proceedings of the 2020 ACM/SIGDA International Symposium on Field-Programmable Gate Arrays, pp. 255–265 (2020)
30. Zhang, K., Luo, M.: Outlier-robust extreme learning machine for regression problems. Neurocomputing 151, 1519–1527 (2015)
31. Zhang, M., Chen, Y.: Link prediction based on graph neural networks. arXiv preprint arXiv:1802.09691 (2018)
32. Zhang, Z., Cai, Y., Gong, W., Liu, X., Cai, Z.: Graph convolutional extreme learning machine. In: 2020 International Joint Conference on Neural Networks (IJCNN), pp. 1–8. IEEE (2020)
33. Zhao, L., et al.: T-gcn: a temporal graph convolutional network for traffic prediction. IEEE Trans. Intell. Transp. Syst. (2019)

Sequence Labeling Algorithms for Punctuation Restoration in Brazilian Portuguese Texts

Tiago B. De Lima[1] , Pericles Miranda[1], Rafael Ferreira Mello[1],
Moesio Wenceslau[1(✉)], Ig Ibert Bittencourt[2], Thiago Damasceno Cordeiro[2],
and Jário José[2]

[1] Universidade Federal Rural de Pernambuco, Rua Dom Manuel de Medeiros, Recife,
Pernambuco 52171-900, Brazil
{tiago.blima,rafael.mello,moesio.wenceslau,pericles.miranda}@ufrpe.br
[2] Universidade Federal de Alagoas, Av. Lourival Melo Mota, S/N - Cidade
Universitária, Maceió, AL 57072-970, Brazil
{ig.ibert,thiago,jjsj}@ic.ufal.br

Abstract. Punctuation Restoration is an essential post-processing task of text generation methods, such as Speech-to-Text (STT) and Machine Translation (MT). Usually, the generation models employed in those tasks produce unpunctuated text, which is difficult for human readers and might degrade the performance of many downstream text processing tasks. Thus, many techniques exist to restore the text's punctuation. For instance, approaches based on Conditional Random Fields (CRF) and pre-trained models, such as the Bidirectional Encoder Representations from Transformers (BERT), have been widely applied. In the last few years, however, one approach has gained significant attention: casting the Punctuation Restoration problem into a sequence labeling task. In Sequence Labeling, each punctuation symbol becomes a label (e.g., COMMA, QUESTION, and PERIOD) that sequence tagging models can predict. This approach has achieved competitive results against state-of-the-art punctuation restoration algorithms. However, most research focuses on English, lacking discussion in other languages, such as Brazilian Portuguese. Therefore, this paper conducts an experimental analysis comparing the Bi-Long Short-Term Memory (BI-LSTM) + CRF model and BERT to predict punctuation in Brazilian Portuguese. We evaluate those approaches in the IWSLT2 2012-03 and OBRAS dataset in terms of precision, recall, and F_1-score. The results showed that BERT achieved competitive results in terms of punctuation prediction, but it requires much more GPU resources for training than the BI-LSTM + CRF algorithm.

1 Introduction

Punctuation Restoration, also called Punctuation Prediction [14], is the task to insert missing punctuation marks in a sequence of unpunctuated text [19,22]. It is an important step in the post-processing of Speech-To-Text (STT), which

J. C. Xavier-Junior and R. A. Rios (Eds.): BRACIS 2022, LNAI 13654, pp. 616–630, 2022.
https://doi.org/10.1007/978-3-031-21689-3_43

usually does not take punctuation into account [2], and other text-generation techniques, such as Machine Translation (MT) [28]. Thus, various methods have been considered in the last years for solving this problem, including traditional Machine Learning (ML) algorithms, Deep Learning techniques [22], and pre-trained methods, such as the Bidirectional Encoder Representations from Transformers (BERT) [7].

The recent literature characterises the punctuation restoration problem as a Sequence Labelling task [19,22,29]. In this approach, every token is assigned to one of the possible labels [29], which usually represents the existence of a punctuation mark (e.g., COMMA, PERIOD, QUESTION) or no punctuation at all (e.g., EMPTY). This approach has achieved state-of-the-art results when combined with Neural Networks [22]. However, it is also possible to apply this approach with other techniques, such as Bidirectional encoders [26], Conditional Random Fields (CRF) [16], and pre-trained models (e.g., BERT) [22].

Although sequence labeling has obtained good results in punctuation restoration, the analysis of text produced in languages other than English is not well explored in the literature. Specifically, sequence labeling approaches for punctuation restoration in Brazilian Portuguese are still a gap in the community.

Thus, this paper explores different sequence labeling methods for punctuation restoration in Brazilian Portuguese texts. More specifically, we compare the performance of the BI-LSTM with CRF model [23] against the BERT, pre-trained in Portuguese, model [24] in two different datasets: the International Workshop on Spoken Language Translation (IWSLT) 2012, which consists of TED talks transcripts, and OBRAS, a corpus of Brazilian Portuguese literature texts. We compare the models' performance in terms of precision, recall, and F_1-score.

The results show that sequence labelling with the pre-trained BERT model is a promising approach for punctuation restoration in Brazilian Portuguese texts, surpassing the BI-LSTM+CRF model in most cases of the IWSLT 2012 dataset. When tested in the out-of-domain dataset OBRAS, the BERT model reached competitive results compared to other approaches in the literature.

The rest of the paper is structured as follows: Sect. 2 provides an overview of deep learning techniques applied to punctuation restoration; Sect. 3 discusses related works in the literature; Sect. 4 describes the datasets, algorithms, and experimental settings; Sect. 5 details the experimental results; and, lastly, Sect. 6 presents the conclusions and future research directions.

2 Preliminaries

There are a variety of approaches for solving the punctuation restoration task, ranging from rule-based methods to deep learning techniques [22]. This section covers some learning algorithms applied to punctuation restoration over the years.

Deep learning (DL) has become increasingly popular over the last years, gaining significant attention as part of many Natural Language Processing (NLP) tasks and frameworks [8]. In this context, Sequence to Sequence Neural Networks [25] are a promising approach for NLP tasks due to the range of their applications, such as Machine Translation (MT) [30], Text Simplification (TS) [4], and Question Answer (QA) [5]. Furthermore, they can be adapted to other domains and are the building blocks of Deep Encoder representations [27].

For punctuation restoration, the Deep Learning approach has played an important role recently, gaining significant attention and leading with state-of-art results [22]. Specifically, BI-LSTM [21] and, more recently, BERT [2] are two viable and promising approaches. Therefore, we will briefly explore those algorithms in the following subsections.

2.1   BI-LSTM

The Bidirectional LSTM (BI-LSTM) is a Recurrent Neural Network (RNN) that can learn both forward and backward temporal information from an input sequence [10]. This characteristic improved learning in many tasks, such as Machine Translation [13] and Sequence Labeling [10].

However, BI-LSTMs suffer from learning in big datasets due to high memory requirements [27]. Thus, Attention Mechanisms are an alternative to mitigate those issues by allowing the network to focus on capturing only essential information for the task, improving learning and stability [27].

Furthermore, it is also possible to combine BI-LSTMs with CRF networks, resulting in a BI-LSTM-CRF network, which boosts accuracy in some sequence labeling tasks [10].

2.2   BERT and Self-attention

The Bidirectional Encoder Representation from Transformers (BERT) is a pre-trained language model [7] that has achieved state-of-art results in many NLP tasks by simply appending extra output layers to the original model, and fine-tuning to the task [7,13,21]. BERT is built on top of an attention mechanism known as Self-Attention [7] and can extract patterns and features by conditionally masking and predicting tokens in a large set of corpus [7]. In the following paragraphs, we explain BERT's input/output representation and its attention mechanisms.

In BERT, the input consists of a series of tokens, and the word encoding process is as follows [7]: First, three distinct embedding strategies, namely token encoding, sentence encoding, and positional encoding, process the input. Then, the output is the sum of those encodings for each token. Figure 1 depicts this process.

As aforementioned, BERT is built on top of an attention mechanism called Self-Attention, which relates different positions of a sequence to represent the sequence better [27]. In general, attention is achieved through attention functions mapping a query (Q, a vector) and a set of key-value pairs (K and V, respectively, both vectors) to an output [27]. A simple attention function is the Scaled Dot-Product Attention [27] shown in Eq. 1, where d_k is the number of dimensions of the key. Specifically, in self-attention layers, Q, K, and V are from the previous

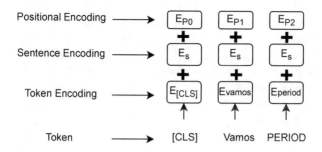

Fig. 1. A simple BERT encoder layer.

layer of the network, which enables the network to account for all sequence positions processed by previous layers [27].

$$\text{Attention}(Q, K, V) = \text{softmax}\left(\frac{QK^T}{\sqrt{d_k}}\right) V \qquad (1)$$

3 Related Works

Speech-to-text and other text-generation tasks procedures often fail to produce grammatically correct and readable text outputs from a punctuation point of view [12,26], motivating the development of algorithms to perform the restoration of the missing punctuation [22].

One of the most successful strategies for handling punctuation restoration is to consider the problem as a sequence labeling task [19,22], whose objective is to classify tokens in the sequence to pre-defined labels or classes [6]. For punctuation restoration, the classes indicate if a given token should have a punctuation mark inserted after it [22].

Table 1 shows an example of punctuation restoration through label prediction in a text sequence where the classes are COMMA, PERIOD, QUESTION, and O (i.e., no punctuation, also referred to as the EMPTY class).

Table 1. Example of punctuation restoration by sequence labelling.

Input	Carlos	could	you	please	come	here
Prediction	COMMA	O	COMMA	COMMA	O	QUESTION
Output	Carlos,	could	you,	please,	come	here?

However, there are other possible approaches for punctuation restoration that do not necessarily rely on sequence labelling. For instance, there are deterministic rule-based alternatives [22], N-gram language models [22], and Machine Translation (MT) approaches [26].

Furthermore, even in the sequence labeling approach, there are slight variations in the applied methods. For instance, [16] considered Conditional Random Fields (CRF), achieving good results in both English and Chinese languages. However, CRF relies on minimal linguistics assumptions, which might not be satisfied in all applications. On the other hand, ML and Deep Learning classifiers have been extensively considered [22] and have almost no linguistic assumptions. For ML methods, both single model approaches, such as BI-LSTM [26], and multi-model approaches, such as BI-LSTM with CRF layers [10], are common in the literature.

However, deep learning-based algorithms are far the preferred approach for punctuation restoration in the last years, leading with state-of-the-art results by applying sequence labeling to punctuation restoration [22]. Table 2 summarises popular ML, and Deep Learning approaches for Punctuation Restoration present in the literature. In the following paragraphs, we briefly overview some of these methods.

Table 2. Popular ML and deep learning approaches for punctuation restoration.

Reference	Method	Dataset	Language	Metrics
[26]	BI-LSTM	IWSLT2011	English, Estonian	Precision, Recall, F_1-score, slot error rate (SER)
[11]	LSTM	MGB Challenge dataset (MGB-1)	English	Precision, Recall, F_1-score, Perplexity
[16]	Factorial CRF	IWSLT09	English, Chinese	Precision, Recall, F_1-score
[18]	BERT + BI-LSTM + CRF	IWSLT2012	English	Precision, Recall, F_1-score
[14]	Multilingual LSTM	SpeechRecognition TV show	43 Languages	Precision, Recall, F_1-score
[19]	BERT	IWSLT2012	English, Hugarian	Precision, Recall, F_1-score
Our	BERT BI-LSTM+CRF	IWSLT2012 OBRAS	Brazilian Portuguese	Precision, Recall, F_1-score

Tilk and Alumäe [26] considered a BI-LSTM with attention for punctuation restoration both in English and Estonian. The results showed that Global Vectors for Word Representation (GloVe) [20], an unsupervised algorithm for obtaining vector representations of worlds, significantly improved the performance of the model.

Ondřej et al. [11] present a different approach by casting the punctuation restoration problem as a Machine Translation task of translating non-punctuated text to punctuated text.

Makhija et al. [18] used minimal annotated data with a BI-LSTM + CRF model combined with BERT embedding mechanisms, providing contextual information to the sequence tagging task.

Li and Lin [14] present a new approach: multilingual punctuation restoration. The main idea was to use byte-pair encoding, which allows sharing of information across different related languages. They considered a set of 43 languages, including English, Spanish, France, Italian, and Portuguese, and achieved good results. Specifically, the model achieved more than 80% F_1-score in Portuguese.

Nagy et al. [19] considered BERT, trained with the IWSLT 2012-03 dataset, for the English and treebank for the Hungarian language. It achieved competitive results with the state-of-the-art models, showing the potential of BERT, a pretrained model, to address punctuation restoration for different languages.

However, although there are works considering languages other than English, few addressed the punctuation prediction for Brazilian Portuguese, and Portuguese [14]. Thus, to fill these gaps in the community, we address punctuation restoration for Brazilian Portuguese texts. Specifically, we investigate learning algorithms (BERT and BI-LSTM + CRF) for punctuation restoration, as a sequence labeling task, in Brazilian Portuguese. Table 2 summarizes all related work and contrasts them with the current research (last line).

4 Materials and Methods

This work assesses the BI-LSTM + CRF and BERT algorithms for punctuation restoration in Brazilian Portuguese texts. The algorithms were chosen due to their promising results in other languages [18,19,26], and the lack of works applying them to Brazilian Portuguese.

In order to evaluate those algorithms, we first define an annotated corpus for training and evaluation. Details of such corpus are explained in Subsect. 4.1. Afterward, we configure and train the algorithms for the task. Hyperparameters and details are explained in Subsect. 4.2. Lastly, we explain the evaluation metrics and critical difference analysis in Subsect. 4.3.

4.1 Datasets

In the experiments, we considered two datasets: the IWLST 2012-03 dataset[1], and the OBRAS corpus[2]. Following a sequence labeling design [19], each token (word) of the datasets are annotated according to the following classes:

○ COMMA, for commas, and dash marks;
○ PERIOD, for periods, semicolons, and exclamation marks;
○ QUESTION, for question marks;
○ O, for no punctuation (i.e., the EMPTY class).

---

[1] Available at: https://wit3.fbk.eu/2012-03.
[2] Available at: https://www.linguateca.pt/OBRAS/OBRAS.html.

The IWLST 2012-03 dataset comprises speech-to-text transcripts of TED talk presentations, including a Brazilian Portuguese version. We used the NLTK tokenize package to obtain words after applying the following punctuation conversions: (i) semicolons to periods; (ii) exclamation marks to periods; and (iii) dash marks to commas. Additionally, all words were converted to lower case to avoid bias in the prediction [19], and each document was considered unique to build the TRAIN, DEV, and TEST sets. Table 3 shows the number of sentences, words, and labels for the IWLST dataset for each set (TRAIN, DEV, or TEST).

Table 3. Number of sentences, words, and labels for the IWLST dataset.

Labels	TRAIN	DEV	TEST
O	1,929,873	14,069	22,208
COMMA	169,384	1,169	2,270
PERIOD	147,379	935	1,721
QUESTION	11,595	87	152
Sentences	139,653	1,570	887
Words	2,258,231	16,260	26,351

The OBRAS dataset contains a range of different Brazilian Portuguese literature texts available in the open domain. The tokenization process was analogous to that applied in the IWLST data, also using the NLTK tokenize package. Besides, we also converted all words to lower case. It is worth mentioning that this dataset was unavailable during the training phase of the algorithms. That is the reason we considered it an out-of-domain dataset. Table 4 shows the number of sentences, words, and labels of the OBRAS dataset.

Table 4. Number of sentences, words, and labels for the OBRAS dataset.

Labels	Count
O	2,298,811
COMMA	303,424
PERIOD	202,573
QUESTION	15,380
Sentences	193,236
Words	2,820,188

4.2   Compared Algorithms

The BI-LSTM + CRF with pre-trained embedding and the BERT model are two famous and promising approaches for Punctuation Restoration in the literature

[22]. Nonetheless, the performance of these algorithms has yet to be investigated for punctuation restoration in Brazilian Portuguese texts. In this work, we evaluate those two algorithms using the CRF model as a baseline. In the following paragraphs, we explain their configurations.

CRF: We consider the CRF as a baseline algorithm for sequence labeling and punctuation restoration, as done in [16,17]. We used the same features as in [17], all hyperparameters were set empirically and are shown in Table 5.

Table 5. Hyperparameters for CRF.

Hyperparameter	Value
Algorithm	L-BFGS
c_1	0.1
c_2	0.1
Max iterations	100
All possible transitions	TRUE

BI-LSTM: The BI-LSTM model was trained with Word2Vec skip-gram 300 (BI-LSTM+Skip$_s$300) [9] and early stopping. The hyperparameters were set empirically, and are shown in Table 6. We used the implementation present in the FLAIR Framework [1].

Table 6. Hyperparameters and training configuration for the BI-LSTM.

Hyperparameter	Value
Learning rate	0.1
Max epochs	100
Mini-batch size	32
Patience	3
Annealing factor	0.5
Shuffle	TRUE
Training with DEV	FALSE
Batch growth annealing	FALSE

BERT: The experiments used the pre-trained BERT model present in the Simple Transformers Framework[3]. For the fine-tuning phase of BERT, the hyperparameters were set empirically and are shown in Table 7.

---

[3] https://simpletransformers.ai/.

4.3 Evaluation

We evaluated the performance of the algorithms in terms of Precision (P), Recall (R), and F_1-score. Those evaluation metrics are defined as follows:

Table 7. Hyperparameters and model setup for BERT.

Parameter	Value
Early stopping	TRUE
Num. train epochs	12
Train batch size	16
Eval batch size	8

$$\text{Precision} = \frac{TP}{(TP + FP)}, \tag{2}$$

$$\text{Recall} = \frac{TN}{(TN + FN)}, \tag{3}$$

$$F_1 = \frac{2 \times \text{Recall} \times \text{Precision}}{\text{Recall} + \text{Precision}} \tag{4}$$

where TP are true positives, TN are true negatives, FP are false positives and FN are false negatives.

We decided to use those metrics to evaluate the capacity of each model to not only predict correct punctuation (precision) but also to recall missing predictions in the original text. Except when stated otherwise, the results refer to a single run of the model in the respective dataset. All experiments were run in the Google Colaboratory.

5 Results and Discussion

In this section, we present and discuss the results. From here on, except when stated otherwise, we will refer to the models by their algorithms' name, that is, we refer to BERT-BASE as BERT, and BI-LSTM+Skip$_s$300 by BI-LSTM.

In Subsect. 5.1, we present and discuss the performance of the algorithms in the IWLST 2012-03 dataset. Additionally, in Subsect. 5.2, we evaluate the performance of the algorithms in the out-of-domain dataset OBRAS, and provide a cost analysis of each algorithm in Subsect. 5.3.

5.1 Evaluation on IWLST 2012-03 Dataset

Table 8 presents the obtained results in each evaluation metric for every class in the task. As it can be seen, the BERT algorithm outperformed all other competitors in recall (R) and F_1-score. Besides, BERT also achieved superior precision for COMMA and QUESTION.

Table 9 presents the overall results, called *micro average metrics*, reached by the models. The BERT model achieved better average performance for all metrics, with 0.833 precision, 0.789 recall, and 0.810 F_1-score.

Table 8. Precision, Recall and F_1-score, in a single run, for all classes representing punctuation marks.

	COMMA			PERIOD			QUESTION		
	P	R	F_1	P	R	F_1	P	R	F_1
CRF	0.556	0.306	0.395	0.869	0.836	0.852	0.318	0.046	0.080
BI-LSTM+Skip$_s$300	0.670	0.530	0.592	**0.924**	0.842	0.881	0.750	0.572	0.649
BERT-BASE	**0.770**	**0.719**	**0.744**	0.911	**0.887**	**0.899**	**0.844**	**0.711**	**0.771**

Table 9. Micro average metrics, in a single run, over the IWLST 2012-03 dataset.

Model	Precision	Recall	F_1-score
CRF	0.738	0.525	0.614
BI-LSTM+Skip$_s$300	0.792	0.667	0.724
BERT-BASE	**0.833**	**0.789**	**0.810**

On the other hand, the BI-LSTM + CRF outperformed BERT in precision for PERIOD, while achieving similar precision to BERT in COMMA. Thus, the BI-LSTM + CRF may be a viable alternative when question marks are not part of the language. In any case, the results suggest that the BI-LSTM + CRF struggles to handle unbalanced datasets.

It is worth mentioning that the baseline, the CRF algorithm, was surpassed by both models when comparing the results for each class. However, it achieved similar results to both BI-LSTM and BERT for COMMA. In opposition, it achieved poor results to QUESTION. Since it uses hand-crafted features, we conjecture that CRF depends on cased information to predict the punctuation, as suggested by [17], and deals poorly with unbalanced datasets.

In summary, the BERT model achieved an overall better performance than the BI-LSTM + CRF model and CRF algorithm, regarding all considered classes. We believe that BERT's bidirectional encoder procedure is able to capture meaningful information better than other contextual embedding strategies.

5.2   Out-of-Domain Evaluation

Cross-domain evaluation is important when one wants to guarantee the method can be applied/tested in different domains, especially when data can hardly be available for some domains [15]. Hence, testing models in a different domain they were once trained is extremely valuable.

The results presented in Sect. 5.1 showed that BERT, pre-trained in the IWLST 2012-03 dataset, achieved better overall results when compared to the other models. Thus, we evaluated the BERT model in the out-of-domain OBRAS dataset, and the results are shown in Table 10.

Table 10. Evaluation results (precision, recall, and F_1-score) of the BERT-BASE model in the OBRAS dataset.

Label	P	R	F_1
COMMA	0.697	0.608	0.649
PERIOD	0.877	0.865	0.871
QUESTION	0.626	0.427	0.508
Micro averages	0.771	0.703	0.735

The results clearly show that the BERT model reached a good precision in all classes and on the micro averages. However, the recall metric dropped significantly for QUESTION labels, which could impact Automatic Speech Recognition (ASR) by missing punctuation marks that should be predicted. In any case, the overall results indicate that the model's predictions are mostly correct.

5.3   Cost Analysis

Experimental Setup: The BERT and BI-LSTM algorithms were trained in a Tesla P100-PCIE 16 GB memory. For the BERT algorithm, the ADAM with Weight Decay optimiser was used, while for the BI-LSTM algorithm, the SGD with Weight Decay was used.

We conducted computational cost analysis in terms of GPU resources to understand how much resources must be allocated to train a BERT model and a BI-LSTM + CRF model in the IWLST 2012-03 dataset. We used the Weights & Biases (W&B) framework [3] to collect the data. Figure 2 shows the GPU memory access, GPU utilization, and GPU memory allocation requests.

We found that the BI-LSTM + CRF algorithm had lower GPU time and memory consumption than the BERT algorithm, being easier for training when GPU resources are scarce. Furthermore, the pre-trained BERT model has 110 million parameters, surpassing the BI-LSTM + CRF model, requiring more resources during evaluation.

Thus, although the BERT model achieves better results in punctuation restoration for Brazilian Portuguese, it has high resource requirements for training and prediction. It might make it difficult for deployment in small devices that

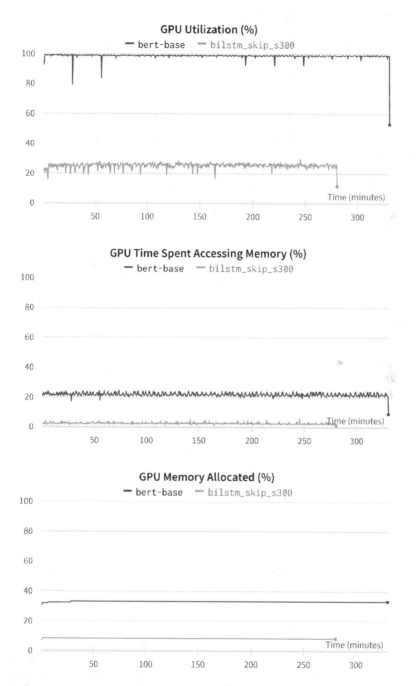

Fig. 2. Consumption of GPU resources for training both BI-LSTM +CRF and BERT.

need to perform speech-to-text in real-time without relying on an internet connection. For such scenarios, the BI-LSTM + CRF model appears to be a better option, which balances both processing performance and prediction precision.

6 Conclusion

Punctuation Restoration is a relevant topic that has been widely investigated in the last few years since punctuation information is important for many NLP tasks and facilitates human understanding. However, there is still a gap in the literature investigating punctuation restoration in languages other than English, for instance, for Brazilian Portuguese language. Thus, to help mitigate this gap, in this work, we explored state-of-art ML algorithms applied for punctuation restoration of Brazilian Portuguese texts.

As with most of the recent literature, we also treat the punctuation restoration problem as a sequence labeling task. We performed an experimental analysis of the BERT and BI-LSTM + CRF algorithms in two Brazilian Portuguese datasets: the IWLST 2012-03 (Brazilian translated version) dataset and the OBRAS corpus.

The results showed that BERT is a promising approach, surpassing the BI-LSTM + CRF algorithm in most cases of the IWLST 2012-03 dataset. It also achieved good performance in the out-of-domain OBRAS dataset, suggesting robustness for cross-domain applications. However, through a computation cost analysis, we found that the BERT algorithm requires much more GPU resources for training than the BI-LSTM + CRF algorithm.

In any case, we hope our findings contribute to pursuing the state-of-the-art and enriching the literature for punctuation restoration in Brazilian Portuguese. In future works, we intend to investigate multilingual models to address the problem of punctuation restoration in different languages and consider more datasets and models.

References

1. Akbik, A., Bergmann, T., Blythe, D., Rasul, K., Schweter, S., Vollgraf, R.: FLAIR: an easy-to-use framework for state-of-the-art NLP. In: NAACL 2019, Annual Conference of the North American Chapter of the Association for Computational Linguistics (Demonstrations), pp. 54–59 (2019)
2. Alam, T., Khan, A., Alam, F.: Punctuation restoration using transformer models for high-and low-resource languages. In: Proceedings of the 6th Workshop on Noisy User-generated Text (W-NUT 2020), pp. 132–142 (2020)
3. Biewald, L.: Experiment tracking with weights and biases (2020)
4. Botarleanu, R.-M., Dascalu, M., Crossley, S.A., McNamara, D.S.: Sequence-to-sequence models for automated text simplification. In: Bittencourt, I.I., Cukurova, M., Muldner, K., Luckin, R., Millán, E. (eds.) AIED 2020. LNCS (LNAI), vol. 12164, pp. 31–36. Springer, Cham (2020). https://doi.org/10.1007/978-3-030-52240-7_6

5. Chandra, Y.W., Suyanto, S.: Indonesian chatbot of university admission using a question answering system based on sequence-to-sequence model. Procedia Comput. Sci. **157**, 367–374 (2019)
6. Chiticariu, L., Krishnamurthy, R., Li, Y., Reiss, F., Vaithyanathan, S.: Domain adaptation of rule-based annotators for named-entity recognition tasks. In: Proceedings of the 2010 Conference on Empirical Methods in Natural Language Processing, pp. 1002–1012 (2010)
7. Devlin, J., Chang, M.W., Lee, K., Toutanova, K.: Bert: pre-training of deep bidirectional transformers for language understanding. arXiv preprint. arXiv:1810.04805 (2018)
8. Guo, J., He, H., He, T., Lausen, L., Li, M., Lin, H., Shi, X., Wang, C., Xie, J., Zha, S., et al.: GluonCV and GluonNLP: deep learning in computer vision and natural language processing. J. Mach. Learn. Res. **21**(23), 1–7 (2020)
9. Hartmann, N., Fonseca, E., Shulby, C., Treviso, M., Rodrigues, J., Aluisio, S.: Portuguese word embeddings: evaluating on word analogies and natural language tasks. arXiv preprint. arXiv:1708.06025 (2017)
10. Huang, Z., Xu, W., Yu, K.: Bidirectional LSTM-CRF models for sequence tagging. CoRR abs/1508.01991 (2015)
11. Klejch, O., Bell, P., Renals, S.: Punctuated transcription of multi-genre broadcasts using acoustic and lexical approaches. In: 2016 IEEE Spoken Language Technology Workshop (SLT), pp. 433–440 (2016)
12. Kolár, J., Lamel, L.: Development and evaluation of automatic punctuation for French and English speech-to-text. In: Interspeech, pp. 1376–1379 (2012)
13. Li, W., Gao, S., Zhou, H., Huang, Z., Zhang, K., Li, W.: The automatic text classification method based on bert and feature union. In: 2019 IEEE 25th International Conference on Parallel and Distributed Systems (ICPADS), pp. 774–777. IEEE (2019)
14. Li, X., Lin, E.: A 43 language multilingual punctuation prediction neural network model. In: International Speech Communication Association, pp. 1067–1071 (2020)
15. Liu, Z., et al.: Crossner: evaluating cross-domain named entity recognition. In: Proceedings of the AAAI Conference on Artificial Intelligence, vol. 35, pp. 13452–13460 (2021)
16. Lu, W., Ng, H.T.: Better punctuation prediction with dynamic conditional random fields. In: Proceedings of the 2010 Conference on Empirical Methods in Natural Language Processing, pp. 177–186 (2010)
17. Lui, M., Wang, L.: Recovering casing and punctuation using conditional random fields. In: Proceedings of the Australasian Language Technology Association Workshop 2013 (ALTA 2013), pp. 137–141 (2013)
18. Makhija, K., Ho, T.N., Chng, E.S.: Transfer learning for punctuation prediction. In: 2019 Asia-Pacific Signal and Information Processing Association Annual Summit and Conference (APSIPA ASC), pp. 268–273 (2019)
19. Nagy, A., Bial, B., Ács, J.: Automatic punctuation restoration with BERT models (2021)
20. Pennington, J., Socher, R., Manning, C.D.: Glove: global vectors for word representation. In: Empirical Methods in Natural Language Processing (EMNLP), pp. 1532–1543 (2014)
21. Pires, T., Schlinger, E., Garrette, D.: How multilingual is multilingual bert? arXiv preprint. arXiv:1906.01502 (2019)
22. Păiş, V., Tufiş, D.: Capitalization and punctuation restoration: a survey. Artif. Intell. Rev. **55**(3), 1681–1722 (2021). https://doi.org/10.1007/s10462-021-10051-x

23. Souza, F., Nogueira, R., Lotufo, R.: Portuguese named entity recognition using bert-crf. arXiv preprint. arXiv:1909.10649 (2019)
24. Souza, F., Nogueira, R., Lotufo, R.: BERTimbau: pretrained BERT models for Brazilian Portuguese. In: Cerri, R., Prati, R.C. (eds.) BRACIS 2020. LNCS (LNAI), vol. 12319, pp. 403–417. Springer, Cham (2020). https://doi.org/10.1007/978-3-030-61377-8_28
25. Sutskever, I., Vinyals, O., Le, Q.V.: Sequence to sequence learning with neural networks. In: Advances in Neural Information Processing Systems, vol. 27 (2014)
26. Tilk, O., Alumäe, T.: Bidirectional recurrent neural network with attention mechanism for punctuation restoration. In: Interspeech, pp. 3047–3051 (2016)
27. Vaswani, A., et al.: Attention is all you need. In: Advances in Neural Information Processing Systems, vol. 30 (2017)
28. Wang, F., Chen, W., Yang, Z., Xu, B.: Self-attention based network for punctuation restoration. In: 2018 24th International Conference on Pattern Recognition (ICPR), pp. 2803–2808 (2018)
29. Yi, J., Tao, J., Bai, Y., Tian, Z., Fan, C.: Adversarial transfer learning for punctuation restoration. arXiv preprint. arXiv:2004.00248 (2020)
30. Zheng, Z., Zhou, H., Huang, S., Chen, J., Xu, J., Li, L.: Duplex sequence-to-sequence learning for reversible machine translation. In: Advances in Neural Information Processing Systems, vol. 34, pp. 21070–21084. Curran Associates, Inc. (2021)

Neural Architecture Search Applied to Hybrid Morphological Neural Networks

Victor Alexandre Gomes Weil$^{(\boxtimes)}$ and Joao Batista Florindo

University of Campinas, Campinas, SP 13083-872, Brazil
v264861@dac.unicamp.br, florindo@unicamp.br

Abstract. This work addresses a way to train morphological neural network differentially using backpropagation. The proposed algorithm can also learn whether to use erosion or dilation, based on the data being processed. Finally, we apply architecture search techniques in order to find the best architecture that may include classical and/or morphological operations. The proposed method coupled with architecture search techniques shows significant improvements on the evaluated data sets.

Keywords: Neural networks · Mathematical morphology · Neural architecture search

1 Introduction

Machine learning algorithms are widely used in different applications such as pattern recognition, image and speech classification. These algorithms are a branch of Artificial Intelligence (AI) and computer science that improves its performance through the leverage of data and learn to make specific and more accurate predictions [19]. In particular, the computing system called *neural network* has grown popularity in recent years due to its high capacity of generalization and feature extraction. Automating machine learning techniques [25] are also a popular research field in recent times, called Neural Architecture Search (NAS) [9]. These techniques automate the process of searching and optimizing the hyperparameters of architectures.

Mathematical morphology deals with nonlinear filtering of images [22] through the computing of maximum and minimum operations. Because of the similarity between neuron operations and the elementary morphological operations such as dilation and erosion, combining the use of nonlinear operations in neural network neurons could lead to better results.

In this study, we introduce and evaluate two morphological dense layers that can be trained through backpropagation in neural network architectures on several classification tasks. In order to find the best architecture that fits the

Supported by Coordenação de Aperfeiçoamento de Pessoal de Nível Superior (CAPES).

morphological operations used, NAS techniques were employed to find the best hyperparameters and structure of architectures in distinct problems.

Three major contributions of our work are the following ones:

- Two morphological dense layers that learn maximum and minimum operations (dilation and erosion) through backpropagation were proposed;
- The evaluation of the proposed operations in several data sets with different complexities;
- The use of NAS techniques with morphological operations in order to automatically build network architectures and improve accuracy on evaluated data sets.

In the following sections we first show the related works that are useful for the general understanding of the work (Sect. 2), a brief review of relevant concepts is also made in Sect. 3, we propose our method in Sect. 4, then describe the experiments in Sect. 5, show the results in Sect. 6 and present concluding remarks in Sect. 7.

2   Related Works

Neural networks are applied to a wide variety of problems and, in many of those problems, they are part of what is called *deep learning* [17]. In early 2011, works such as [6,15] brought attention back to the neural networks due to their results and the increasing computing power that made it possible to train large neural networks in a timely manner.

Several works [1,11,14,18,20] already explored the use of morphological operations in neural networks. For example, in [18] a *p-convolution* (PConv) morphological layer was proposed. This layer was able to approximate dilation, erosion and classical convolution. Works such as [14] and [11] introduce multiple morphological layers that can learn to reproduce the morphological operations and the structuring element of a dilation and an erosion through backpropagation, but there were no applications of these layers in classification problems.

In [20] the authors proposed a trainable morphological network using dilation and erosion operators as neurons in a dense layer. It was also shown at their theoretical results that, in conjuction with linear combinations, these operators represent a sum of hinge functions. Although they show different applications, their approach restricts dilation and erosion operators to different neurons and, in counterpart, our work will use dilation and erosion operators in the same neuron.

Furthermore, in recent years, multiple works explore the automation in architecture construction. The first works aimed at doing this automation were [3,29], where reinforcement learning were used in order to design architectures for speech recognition and image classification. However, these methods had a high computational cost. Recent works [21,27] explore other approaches to the task of finding the optimal with lower computational cost.

One of the few works that approaches the use of NAS techniques with morphological operations included in their search space is [13].

3   Review of Relevant Concepts

This section provides a brief review of the concepts needed to understand this work. Definitions of morphological neurons are presented and we also relate those definitions to the concepts of dilation and erosion present in mathematical morphology.

3.1   Dilation and Erosion

The most basic operations of mathematical morphology are dilation and erosion. In previous works their definitions may vary [14, 20, 23] and, in some of them, they resemble convolutions. Below we present their generic definitions considering these operations as convolutions in images:

Definition 1 (Dilation [23]). *Let* $f : E \subset \mathbb{R}^{m \times n} \to \mathbb{R}$ *be an input element with* $x \in E$ *being its coordinates and* w *a real-valued structuring element, then*

$$(f \oplus w)(x) := \sup_{z \in E}(f(z) + w(z - x)) \tag{1}$$

Definition 2 (Erosion [23]).

$$(f \ominus w)(x) := \inf_{z \in E}(f(z) - w(x - z)) \tag{2}$$

Although these definitions are restricted to $\mathbb{R}^{m \times n}$ (images), it is also possible to define them in $\mathbb{R}^n$ [4], being similar to the definitions presented above. In particular, when considering an input element $f \in \mathbb{R}^n$ and a structuring element $w \in \mathbb{R}^n$, the following equations are obtained as a result:

$$(f \oplus w) := \sup_j (f + w)_j \tag{3}$$

$$(f \ominus w) := \inf_j (f - w)_j \tag{4}$$

3.2   Morphological Neurons

One of the main differences between perceptron and morphological neurons is the algebraic operation performed on each one [7]. While in perceptrons we have summations of multiplications, the basic morphological neurons can be defined as follows:

Definition 3 (Morphological Neurons [7]). *Let* m_i^l *be the output of the i-th morphological neuron on the* $l - th$ *layer, this output can be defined as:*

$$m_i^l := \max_j \left\{ h_j^{l-1} + w_{ij}^l \right\} \tag{5}$$

also, not often used,

$$m_i^l := \min_j \left\{ h_j^{l-1} - w_{ij}^l \right\}, \tag{6}$$

where w_{ij}^l *is the structuring element (synaptic weight) of l-th layer and* h_j^{l-1} *is the j-th element of the output vector of the previous layer* $l - 1$.

This distinct algebraic computation performed between perceptrons and morphological neurons causes the existence of a nonlinearity in layers containing these types of neurons due to the use of maximum and minimum operations. It is also important to notice that (5) and (6) are similar to the particular cases of dilation and erosion ((3) and (4)), respectively.

In addition to these operations, in [26] the notion of multiplicative maximum and minimum is defined as follows

Definition 4 (Maximum (Minimum) Multiplicative). *Let* $a, b \in (\mathbb{R}^n)_\infty^{\geq 0}$, *then the maximum multiplicative is computed as follows:*

$$a \vee b := \max_j \ (a_j b_j) \tag{7}$$

and the minimum multiplicative

$$a \wedge b := \min_j \ (a_j b_j) \tag{8}$$

Despite the restrictions imposed to compute the maximum (minimum) multiplicative, its definition resembles the equation of a perceptron, where, instead of using a summation, the maximum (minimum) operation is used.

4   Proposed Method

Most of the studies in the related works section explore the use of mathematical morphology operators and train their network with fixed dilation and erosion hyperparameters. One of the few works that use dilation and erosion operations as parameters to be learned by the network is Kirszenberg *et al.* [14], where the sum and multiplication operations in the classic convolution are replaced by dilation and erosion operations using max/min operators.

This work introduces another definition for a morphological layer that uses (7) and (8). Inspired by the method proposed by [14] this work explores, through *softmax* function, an approximation of maximum and minimum operators presented in **Definition** 3 and using them as a learnable feature.

4.1   Soft Morphological Neuron

During backpropagation only the gradients of a single maximum (minimum) value specified in the maximum (minimum) function is updated and the remaining gradients are equal to 0, which is the problem found when using Equations (5) and (6) (morphological neurons). As a result, training through backpropagation, especially in dense architectures, usually takes a long time to converge since there are several weights to be updated on each neuron for a network to generate a satisfactory result in classification problems.

To solve that problem, we propose the use of α-*softmax* [16] function to obtain a smooth approximation of maximum and minimum operators, similar to what is done in [14] on convolutional layers.

Definition 5 (α-softmax). *Let $x \in \mathbb{R}^n$ and $\alpha \in \mathbb{R}$, then*

$$S_\alpha(x) = \frac{\sum_{i=1}^{n} x_i e^{\alpha x_i}}{\sum_{i=1}^{n} e^{\alpha x_i}} \qquad (9)$$

According to Lange *et al.* [16], this function has the following properties:

(a) *If $\alpha \to \infty$ then $S_\alpha(x) \to \max_i x_i$*

(b) *If $\alpha \to -\infty$ then $S_\alpha(x) \to \min_i x_i$*

(c) *If $\alpha \to 0$ then $S_\alpha(x) \to \frac{\sum_{i=1}^{n} x_i}{n}$.*

With (a) and (b) we conclude that S_α will approximate the nonlinear equations of maximum and minimum present in morphological neurons. As an example, let h^{l-1} be an output vector on the $(l-1)$-th layer and w^l the structuring element (or synaptic weights) of the l-th layer, then:

$$\lim_{\alpha \to \infty} S_\alpha(h_j^{l-1} + w_j^l) = \max_j \left(h_j^{l-1} + w_j^l \right) = \left(h_j^{l-1} \oplus w_j^l \right), \qquad (10)$$

$$\lim_{\alpha \to -\infty} S_\alpha(h_j^{l-1} + w_j^l) = \min_j \left(h_j^{l-1} + w_j^l \right) = \left(h_j^{l-1} \ominus (-w_j^l) \right). \qquad (11)$$

Therefore, through this approach we can include morphological neurons in the dense layers of a neural network architecture. Moreover, an important detail is that the hyperparameter α in α-softmax is also differentiable. Hence, we can use two strategies: to keep it fixed and consider it as having the same value for each neuron or training it through the use of *backpropagation*. In this work, for dense layer neurons, α was considered as a trainable parameter together with the network weights during *backpropagation*, i.e., the morphological neurons will learn during training if an erosion (minimum operation) or dilation (maximum operation) will be performed in their computation.

In practice, the case in which $\alpha \to \infty$ ($\alpha \to -\infty$) does not occur. Each morphological neuron will be soft-morphological and they will perform a soft-dilation (soft-erosion). Moreover, a neural network architecture that contains at least one layer of soft-morphological neurons will be called *Soft Morphological Network* (SM-Net).

Figure 1 shows a comparison between two morphological neurons from the morphological addition performing operations with fixed α and a perceptron-type neuron. In some cases, we call SM-Net (Add) and SM-Net (Mul) as the SM-Net architecture that uses only one type of morphological neurons, which is defined by (12) and (13), respectively.

Definition 6 (Soft Morphological Dense Layer (Addition)). *Let h_i^l be the output of the layer, then the i - th neuron in Soft Morphological Dense Layer (Addition) will compute the following operation*

$$h_i^l = \frac{\sum_{j=1}^{n} \left(h_j^{l-1} + w_{ij}^l \right) e^{\alpha \left(h_j^{l-1} + w_{ij}^l \right)}}{\sum_{i=j}^{n} e^{\alpha \left(h_j^{l-1} + w_{ij}^l \right)}} + b_i^l, \qquad (12)$$

where w_{ij}^l is the structuring element (or synaptic weights) and b_i^l is a bias of the l-th layer and h_j^{l-1} is the j-th component of the output element on the (l − 1)-th layer.

Definition 7 (Soft Morphological Dense Layer (Multiplication)). *Let h_i^l be the output of the layer, then the $i - th$ neuron in Soft Morphological Dense Layer (Multiplication) will compute the following operation*

$$h_i^l = \frac{\sum_{j=1}^n \left(h_j^{l-1} w_{ij}^l\right) e^{\alpha\left(h_j^{l-1} w_{ij}^l\right)}}{\sum_{i=j}^n e^{\alpha\left(h_j^{l-1} w_{ij}^l\right)}} + b_i^l \tag{13}$$

where w_{ij}^l is the structuring element (or synaptic weights) and b_i^l is a bias of the l-th layer and h_j^{l-1} is the j-th component of the output element on the (l − 1)-th layer.

It is important to notice that **Definition** 7 is based on the multiplicative maximum (minimum) as defined in (7) and (8). Equally important, due to the properties of the S_α function, when $\alpha \to 0$ we approximate a perceptron.

The initialization of the weights on both of the morphological dense layers follows a uniform random distribution both for α and w. The bias b will be initialized with zeros. The uniform random distribution on α is done to ensure that each neuron is able learn different operations (soft-dilation or soft-erosion) during *backpropagation*.

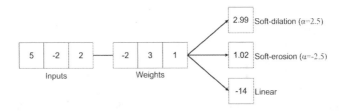

Fig. 1. Example of the proposed SM-Net (Add) dense operation.

4.2   Hybrid Architecture

To apply our proposed soft-morphological layer, first an architecture should be defined. Due to the results presented by Mondal et al. [20], where it was shown that a single morphological layer followed by another composed of perceptrons (called morphological block) can represent a sum of hinge functions [24], we use a similar hybrid architecture where in some cases morphological layers will be preceded or followed by perceptron layers.

In order to show the generalizability of our morphological network, we exemplify in Fig. 2 a simple SM-Net architecture using a single morphological block similar to what is proposed by [20] and it was used for classification in a synthetic dataset of 3 circles with different radii, each one representing a class. The results presented in Fig. 3 are the comparison between SM-Net and a classical neural network where the morphological neurons in the hidden layer are replaced by perceptrons using *tanh* as an activation function.

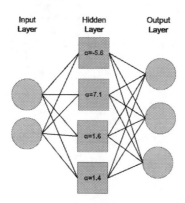

Fig. 2. Hybrid neural network architecture, where squares denote a morphological neuron and α the learned operation (soft-dilation or soft-erosion) for each neuron.

On this first synthetic problem, with a small amount of neurons in the hidden layer, the SM-Net suited better than a classical neural network, even though it did not use an activation function. This is possibly due to the non-linearity present by definition on the morphological layer, and the result proven in [20]. The most relevant difference between their approach and ours was the fact that through our morphological layer in (12) the neurons could learn which operation (soft-dilation or soft-erosion) should be computed.

In the experiments section of this work we will select several sets to classify through the use of these operations. Similar to the architectures proposed by [12,20], the morphological layers of this work are preceded or succeeded by a perceptron layer. The difference in our architecture will be that, based on the dataset, more than one morphological layer can be used and the morphological operations are learned during training.

4.3   NAS and Morphology

There are few works that use morphological operations in the *search space* of NAS [13] or optimize the hyperparameters present in the architecture of a morphological network through hyperparameter optimization techniques [12]. As a consequence, the literature lacks references to the combined use of these techniques. Therefore, in this work we aim to optimize neural architectures with the morphological operations proposed above in NAS *search space* as a way to expand the possibilities for the choice of architectures. With a *search strategy* that combines the use of *Bayesian Optimization* and *Hyperband*, we will use

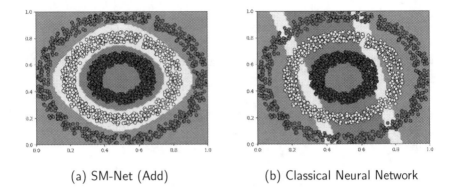

(a) SM-Net (Add)   (b) Classical Neural Network

Fig. 3. (a) Decision boundary generated by SM-Net. (b) Decision boundary generated by a plain neural network using perceptrons.

the algorithm proposed in [10] to optimize network's hyperparameters, such as: dense layer type (linear or morphologic), activation function after each layer, number of layers, neurons and feature maps in morphological layers.

5 Experiment

In this section we explained details about the experiment done to evaluate the layers proposed above in classification tasks.

5.1 Datasets

In order to properly evaluate our hybrid architectures, we need to define datasets with different complexities, from two-dimensional to N-dimensional data. In particular, we started using synthetic nonlinear sets like 3 spirals, 2 looped spirals and the XOR problem. As these sets can have only 2 characteristics, they can be visualized in Fig. 4.

Detailed information about each of the chosen datasets are shown in Table 1, where we distinguish real world data from artificial data. Most of the real world datasets were chosen among the databases found in [8]. Also, all datasets were split into 60% for training and 20% for validating and testing.

5.2 Dense Hybrid Networks

On this experiment, we intend to test our SM-Net, hybrid network with the morphological layers defined in (12) and (13), on the datasets presented in Table 1, and create the hybrid architectures empirically. The objective is to achieve the highest accuracy in each of the datasets with the smallest amount of parameters on validation samples and compare our hybrid network with a densely connected architecture of perceptrons built also through trial and error. Since each dataset

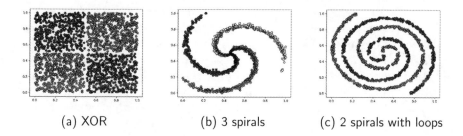

(a) XOR   (b) 3 spirals   (c) 2 spirals with loops

Fig. 4. Synthetic datasets for classification in hybrid networks where each color represents a class.

Table 1. Details about datasets used in the Experiment.

| | Dataset names | Number of | | | | |
		Features (dimension)	Classes	Train samples	Validation samples	Test samples
Artificial data	XOR	2	2	1200	400	400
	Spirals with loops	2	2	720	240	240
	3 spirals	2	3	720	240	240
Real world	Vertebral column	6	2	186	62	62
	TicTacToe	9	2	574	192	192
	Wine quality (white) [5]	11	10	2940	979	979
	Letter recognition	16	26	12000	4000	4000
	Wine	13	3	137	47	47
	Diabetic retinopathy debrecen [2]	19	2	691	230	230
	Default of credit cards clients [28]	24	2	18000	6000	6000
	Teaching assistant evaluation	5	3	89	31	31

requires a different training configuration to achieve optimal accuracy, we will also show the training configurations that are used both in the hybrid network and in the classical neural network on this experiment and, since there are a lot of different datasets, we will not explicitly show the architecture for each one.

Furthermore, we separate each morphological operation into different architectures, where SM-Net (Add) contain only the morphological operation defined by (12) and SM-Net (Mul) is created using (13). Both architectures can contain classical neurons. This separation was done with the aim of evaluating their accuracy in different datasets.

Finally, based on the results found empirically, NAS with BOHB search strategy were applied to the datasets with margin for test accuracy improvement in order to have automatic construction of dense architectures, considering both of the presented morphological operations in its search space. In addition, the criterion for choosing the best architecture in each dataset was to obtain a architecture with smaller number of parameters and the highest validation accuracy. After the best achitecture was found, we used the train and validation set to train and then evaluate the accuracy of the test set.

Table 2 shows the *search space* that was considered for all datasets. It is noteworthy that the number of hidden layers and neurons were restricted in order to limit the number of architectures available to be searched with NAS, thus reducing the time and computational cost to find the optimal architecture for each dataset.

Table 2. Algorithm search space.

Search space	
Hyperparameter	Search choices
Number of hidden layers	{1, 2, 3}
Number of neurons	Integer values in $[12, 150]$
Layer type	{Perceptron, MorphAdd, MorphMul}
Layer activation	{Identity, Tanh, ReLU, LeakyReLU}
Learning rate	Values in a uniform range from 0.0001 to 0.01

6   Results

We present in Table 3 the training configuration empirically found that leads to the results displayed in Table 4. As previously described, two morphological operations of addition (Add) and multiplication (Mul) were split into different architectures on the table to also compare their performances. It is clear that both operations have their advantages relying on the dataset and, moreover, both SM-Net architectures have similar or superior accuracies if compared to perceptron networks (MLPs) shown on that table. Particulary, with fewer parameters, the SM-Net achieved the same or better accuracy than the MLP.

Table 3. Best configuration found empirically.

	Name	Training configuration			
		Optimization algorithm	Learning rate	Epochs	Batch size
Artificial data	XOR	Adam	0.002	500	100
	Spirals with loops	Adam	0.005	1500	100
	3 spirals	Adam	0.005	1500	100
Real world	Vertebral column	Adam	0.001	1500	32
	TicTacToe	Adam	0.01	1000	64
	Wine quality (white)	Adam	0.005	2000	250
	Letter recognition	Adam	0.005	1200	512
	Wine	Adam	0.005	1000	10
	Diabetic retinopathy debrecen	Adam	0.001	3000	32
	Default of credit cards clients	Adam	0.001	1000	2048
	Teaching assistant evaluation	Adam	0.005	2000	16

Table 4. Empirical Results Found in Multiple Datasets showing the SM-Net Performance and the Comparison Between MLP Architectures.

	Dataset	Multilayer Perceptron (MLP)				SM-Net (Add/Mul)			
	Name	Number of parameters	Number of hidden layers	Test accuracy	Training time	Number of parameters (Add/Mul)	Number of hidden layers	Test accuracy (Add/Mul)	Training time (Add/Mul)
Artificial data	XOR	53	2	1	18 s	50/55	2/2	0.85/1	20 s/23 s
	Spirals with loops	867	2	1	40 s	206/242	2/2	0.99/1	39 s/41 s
	3 spirals	58	2	0.99	43 s	63/63	2/2	1/0.99	45 s/50 s
Real world	Vertebral column	2594	2	0.87	34 s	820/820	2/2	0.87/0.90	45 s/41 s
	TicTacToe	554	1	0.95	33 s	314/314	1/1	0.99/0.97	41 s/46 s
	Wine quality (white)	23510	2	0.59	95 s	18010/20810	2/2	0.61/0.63	170 s/192 s
	Letter recognition	14426	2	0.95	190 s	14526/11601	2/2	0.96/0.97	276 s/307 s
	Wine	428	1	1	24 s	240/294	1/1	1/1	26 s/27 s
	Diabetic retinopathy debrecen	7152	2	0.71	165 s	1152/2332	1/2	0.71/0.75	185 s/190 s
	Default of credit cards clients	35162	2	0.77	245 s	3422/1682	2/1	0.77/0.81	259 s/235 s
	Teaching assistant evaluation	2223	2	0.51	52 s	1248/693	2/2	0.51/0.54	63 s/40 s

On Fig. 5 we show the decision boundary learned by the SM-Net architectures and how well they generalize on each of the synthetic datasets with fewer parameters than an MLP, as stated in Table 4. The training time, however, remained similar. When evaluating just the 3 synthetic datasets, it is noticeable that the SM-Net with MorphMul layer had a slightly superior performance in comparison to MorphAdd and the MLP. The decision boundaries of the MLP architecture can be seen through Fig. 6.

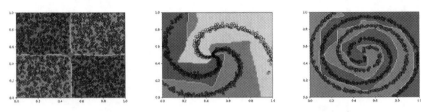

(a) XOR with SM-Net (Mul) architecture

(b) 3 spirals with SM-Net (Add) architecture

(c) 2 spirals with loops using SM-Net (Mul) architecture

Fig. 5. Decision boundaries learned for each synthetic dataset using a morphological operation in at least one layer (SM-Net).

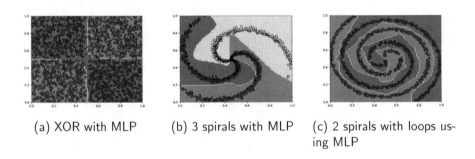

(a) XOR with MLP

(b) 3 spirals with MLP

(c) 2 spirals with loops using MLP

Fig. 6. Decision boundaries learned for each synthetic dataset using classical perceptrons in the architecture (MLP).

As several datasets have already obtained accuracy greater than 0.98, we applied NAS algorithm only on the following datasets: *Vertebral Column, Wine Quality (White), Diabetic Retinopathy Debrecen* and *Teaching Assistant Evaluation*.

Table 5 shows the results that were obtained through the use of NAS and, on each dataset, at least one of the morphological operations were chosen on the optimal architecture, where MorphAdd and MorphMul stand for the operations defined in (12) and (13), respectively.

There were minor improvements in accuracy on all chosen datasets. Particularly, in the *Teaching Assistant Evaluation* dataset, the NAS algorithm chose an architecture composed only of morphological operations. In *Vertebral Column* the optimal model also uses a MorphMul operation in combination with a classical perceptron output layer.

In datasets such as *Wine Quality* and *Diabetic Retinopathy Debrecen* the MorphAdd was chosen in between classical perceptron layers, which might give an idea that it is the best way to place this custom layer. The minor improvements found on the evaluated datasets may have occurred due to insufficient NAS training time or the lack of data in some of them. However, in larger and more complex datasets the improvements could be significant.

Table 5. Architectures found through NAS and their respectives results

	Dataset			
	Vertebral column	Wine quality (white)	Diabetic retinopathy debrecen	Teaching assistant evaluation
Number of hidden layers	1	3	2	1
Layer types	MorphMul Perceptron	Perceptron MorphAdd Perceptron Perceptron	Perceptron MorphAdd Perceptron	MorphMul MorphMul
Number of hidden neurons	28	123 58 108	28 85	110
Hidden layer activation	Tanh	Tanh Tanh Tanh	Tanh ReLU	Tanh
Learning rate	0.0006	0.0045	0.0079	0.0043
Number of parameters	14910	15861	3282	1106
Epochs trained (NAS)	600	2000	750	600
Total NAS runtime	20 h 17 min	23 h 40 min	21 h 17 min	19 h 23 min
Number of architectures trained	1671	530	704	1655
Test accuracy	0.82	0.65	0.74	0.55

7 Conclusion

In this work we introduced two new layers with nonlinearity included in their equation using morphological operations and trained them with backpropagation, which is usually avoided due to the non-differentiability of these operations. We show that, in the evaluated data, the combined use of morphological operations and classical perceptrons can lead to better generalization compared to using just classical perceptrons. On top of that, the use of NAS techniques improved even further the accuracy of the evaluated datasets in comparison with the empirically created architectures and, in their final architecture, morphological operations were included.

In futher works, we expect to evaluate these dense operations in bigger and more complex problems such as image and time series classification. Moreover, we are going to evaluate the convolutional morphological operation proposed in [11,14] on classification problems, which their work does not account for.

References

1. Angulo, J.: Pseudo-morphological image diffusion using the counter-harmonic paradigm. In: Blanc-Talon, J., Bone, D., Philips, W., Popescu, D., Scheunders, P. (eds.) ACIVS 2010. LNCS, vol. 6474, pp. 426–437. Springer, Heidelberg (2010). https://doi.org/10.1007/978-3-642-17688-3_40
2. Antal, B., Hajdu, A.: An ensemble-based system for automatic screening of diabetic retinopathy. Knowl.-Based Syst. **60**, 20–27 (2014)
3. Baker, B., et al.: Designing neural network architectures using reinforcement learning. arXiv e-prints arXiv:1611.02167 (2016)
4. Bloch, I., Heijmans, H., Ronse, C.: Mathematical morphology. In: Aiello, M., Pratt-Hartmann, I., Van Benthem, J. (eds.) Handbook of Spatial Logics, pp. 857–944. Springer, Dordrecht (2007). https://doi.org/10.1007/978-1-4020-5587-4_14
5. Cortez, P., Cerdeira, A., Almeida, F., Matos, T., Reis, J.: Modeling wine preferences by data mining from physicochemical properties. Decis. Support Syst. **47**(4), 547–553 (2009)
6. Dahl, G., et al.: Context-dependent pre-trained deep neural networks for large-vocabulary speech recognition. IEEE Trans. Audio Speech Lang. Process. **20**(1), 30–42 (2011)
7. Davidson, J.L., Hummer, F.: Morphology neural networks: an introduction with applications. Circuits Syst. Signal Process. **12**(2), 177–210 (1993). https://doi.org/10.1007/BF01189873
8. Dua, D., Graff, C.: UCI machine learning repository (2017). http://archive.ics.uci.edu/ml
9. Elsken, T., Metzen, J.H., Hutter, F.: Neural architecture search: a survey. J. Mach. Learn. Res. **20**(1), 1997–2017 (2019)
10. Falkner, S., Klein, A., Hutter, F.: BOHB: robust and efficient hyperparameter optimization at scale. In: International Conference on Machine Learning, pp. 1437–1446. PMLR (2018)
11. Hermary, R., Tochon, G., Puybareau, É., Kirszenberg, A., Angulo, J.: Learning grayscale mathematical morphology with smooth morphological layers. J. Math. Imaging Vis. **64**, 1–18 (2022). https://doi.org/10.1007/s10851-022-01091-1

12. Hernández, G., Zamora, E., Sossa, H., Téllez, G., Furlán, F.: Hybrid neural networks for big data classification. Neurocomputing **390**, 327–340 (2020)
13. Hu, Y., Belkhir, N., Angulo, J., Yao, A., Franchi, G.: Learning deep morphological networks with neural architecture search (2021). https://doi.org/10.48550/ARXIV.2106.07714. https://arxiv.org/abs/2106.07714
14. Kirszenberg, A., Tochon, G., Puybareau, É., Angulo, J.: Going beyond p-convolutions to learn grayscale morphological operators. In: Lindblad, J., Malmberg, F., Sladoje, N. (eds.) DGMM 2021. LNCS, vol. 12708, pp. 470–482. Springer, Cham (2021). https://doi.org/10.1007/978-3-030-76657-3_34
15. Krizhevsky, A., et al.: ImageNet classification with deep convolutional neural networks. Adv. Neural. Inf. Process. Syst. **25**, 1097–1105 (2012)
16. Lange, M., Zühlke, D., Holz, O., Villmann, T., Mittweida, S.G.: Applications of lp-norms and their smooth approximations for gradient based learning vector quantization. In: ESANN, pp. 271–276. Citeseer (2014)
17. LeCun, Y., Bengio, Y., Hinton, G.: Deep learning. Nature **521**(7553), 436–444 (2015)
18. Masci, J., Angulo, J., Schmidhuber, J.: A learning framework for morphological operators using counter–harmonic mean. In: Hendriks, C.L.L., Borgefors, G., Strand, R. (eds.) ISMM 2013. LNCS, vol. 7883, pp. 329–340. Springer, Heidelberg (2013). https://doi.org/10.1007/978-3-642-38294-9_28
19. Mitchell, T.M.: Artificial neural networks. Mach. Learn. **45**(81), 127 (1997)
20. Mondal, R., Mukherjee, S.S., Santra, S., Chanda, B.: Morphological network: how far can we go with morphological neurons? arXiv preprint arXiv:1901.00109 (2019)
21. Pham, H., et al.: Efficient neural architecture search via parameters sharing. In: International Conference on Machine Learning, pp. 4095–4104. PMLR (2018)
22. Serra, J.: Introduction to mathematical morphology. Comput. Vis. Graph. Image Process. **35**(3), 283–305 (1986)
23. Sternberg, S.R.: Grayscale morphology. Comput. Vis. Graph. Image Process. **35**(3), 333–355 (1986). https://doi.org/10.1016/0734-189X(86)90004-6, https://www.sciencedirect.com/science/article/pii/0734189X86900046
24. Wang, S., Sun, X.: Generalization of hinging hyperplanes. IEEE Trans. Inf. Theory **51**(12), 4425–4431 (2005)
25. Waring, J., Lindvall, C., Umeton, R.: Automated machine learning: review of the state-of-the-art and opportunities for healthcare. Artif. Intell. Med. **104**, 101822 (2020)
26. Wilson, J.N., Ritter, G.X.: Handbook of Computer Vision Algorithms in Image Algebra. CRC Press, Boca Raton (2000)
27. Xia, X., Xiao, X., Wang, X., Zheng, M.: Progressive automatic design of search space for one-shot neural architecture search (2020). https://doi.org/10.48550/ARXIV.2005.07564, https://arxiv.org/abs/2005.07564
28. Yeh, I.C., Lien, C.H.: The comparisons of data mining techniques for the predictive accuracy of probability of default of credit card clients. Expert Syst. Appl. **36**(2), 2473–2480 (2009)
29. Zoph, B., Le, Q.: Neural architecture search with reinforcement learning. arXiv preprint arXiv:1611.01578 (2016)

Extending the Universal Approximation Theorem for a Broad Class of Hypercomplex-Valued Neural Networks

Wington L. Vital[ID], Guilherme Vieira[ID], and Marcos Eduardo Valle$^{(\boxtimes)}$[ID]

Universidade Estadual de Campinas, Campinas, Brazil
w265003@dac.unicamp.br, {vieira.g,valle}@ime.unicamp.br

Abstract. The universal approximation theorem asserts that a single hidden layer neural network approximates continuous functions with any desired precision on compact sets. As an existential result, the universal approximation theorem supports the use of neural networks for various applications, including regression and classification tasks. The universal approximation theorem is not limited to real-valued neural networks but also holds for complex, quaternion, tessarines, and Clifford-valued neural networks. This paper extends the universal approximation theorem for a broad class of hypercomplex-valued neural networks. Precisely, we first introduce the concept of non-degenerate hypercomplex algebra. Complex numbers, quaternions, and tessarines are examples of non-degenerate hypercomplex algebras. Then, we state the universal approximation theorem for hypercomplex-valued neural networks defined on a non-degenerate algebra.

Keywords: Hypercomplex algebras · Neural networks · Universal approximation theorem

1 Introduction

Artificial neural networks are computational models created to emulate the behavior of biological neural networks. Their origins are tied back to the pioneer works of McCulloch and Pitts [24], and Rosenblatt [28]. Since then, many applications have emerged in various fields, such as computer vision, physics, control, pattern recognition, economics, and many applications in the medical field. Neural networks are known for being approximators with adjustable capability. Thus, a major interest in the topic of neural networks is that of approximating a generic class of functions with arbitrary precision. The approximation capability

This work was supported in part by the National Council for Scientific and Technological Development (CNPq) under grant no 315820/2021-7, the São Paulo Research Foundation (FAPESP) under grant no 2022/01831-2, and the Coordenação de Aperfeiçoamento de Pessoal de Nível Superior - Brasil (CAPES) - Finance Code 001.

J. C. Xavier-Junior and R. A. Rios (Eds.): BRACIS 2022, LNAI 13654, pp. 646–660, 2022.
https://doi.org/10.1007/978-3-031-21689-3_45

of neural networks was initially motivated by representation theorems and the need to provide its theoretical justification [13,23].

As far as we know, the starting point of the approximation theory for neural networks was the *universal approximation theorem* formulated by Cybenko in the late 1980s [12]. In a few words, Cybenko showed that a single hidden layer real-valued multilayer perceptron (MLP) equipped with a sigmoid activation function could approximate continuous function to any desired precision in a compact set. A few years later, Cybenko's universal approximation theorem was generalized to real-valued MLP models with any non-constant bounded activation function [19]. Recently, many researchers addressed the approximation capabilities of neural networks, including deep and shallow models based on piece-wise linear activation functions such as the widely used rectified linear unit ReLU [27].

In the 1990s, Arena et al. extended the universal approximation theorem for complex and quaternion-valued single hidden layer feedforward networks with the so-called split activation functions [3,4]. This significant breakthrough was vital in formulating universal approximation theorems for other hypercomplex-valued neural networks, such as the hyperbolic and tessarine-valued networks [6,9]. In particular, the universal approximation theorem has been successfully extended for neural networks defined on Clifford algebras by Buchholz and Sommer in the early 2000s [7].

Despite the results mentioned above, there is a lack of a more general version of the universal approximation theorem. This work extends the universal approximation theorem to a broad class of hypercomplex algebras. Indeed, we consider a broad framework for hypercomplex numbers, which includes the most widely used algebras as particular instances [10,21]. Then, we address the problem of approximating a continuous hypercomplex-valued function on a compact subset by a hypercomplex-valued multilayer perceptron (ℍMLP). The theoretical results present in this paper justifies some recent successfull applications of neural networks based on hypercomplex algebras beyond complex numbers and quaternions [14,15,30,32,33].

The paper is organized as follows: Sect. 2 briefly reviews concepts regarding hypercomplex algebras. Section 3 reviews the MLP architecture and the existing universal approximation theorems. The main result of this work, namely, the universal approximation theorem for a broad class of hypercomplex-valued neural networks, is given in Sect. 4. We would like to point out that we omitted the results' proofs due to the page limit. The paper finishes with some concluding remarks in Sect. 5.

2   A Brief Review of Hypercomplex Algebras

Let us start by recalling the basic theory of hypercomplex algebras [10,21]. This theory is of paramount importance to the main results of this work, which will be detailed further in Sect. 4.

The hypercomplex algebras considered in this paper are defined over the field ℝ, but it is worth mentioning that it is possible to work with such algebras over any field. For a more general extensive approach to hypercomplex algebra concepts, please refer to [10,21].

A hypercomplex number x has a representation in the form

$$x = x_0 + x_1 i_1 + \ldots + x_n i_n, \tag{1}$$

where $x_0, x_1, \ldots, x_n \in \mathbb{R}$. The elements $i_1, i_2, \ldots, i_n$ are called hyperimaginary units.

The addition of hypercomplex numbers is done component by component, that is,

$$x + y = (x_0 + y_0) + (x_1 + y_1)\, i_1 + \ldots + (x_n + y_n)\, i_n, \tag{2}$$

for hypercomplex numbers $x = x_0 + x_1 i_1 + \ldots + x_n i_n$ and $y = y_0 + y_1 i_1 + \ldots + y_n i_n$.

The multiplication of two hypercomplex numbers is performed distributively using the product of the hyperimaginary units. Precisely, the product of two hypercomplex units is defined by

$$i_\alpha i_\beta := p_{\alpha\beta,0} + p_{\alpha\beta,1} i_1 + \ldots + p_{\alpha\beta,n} i_n. \tag{3}$$

for all $\alpha, \beta = 1, \ldots, n$ and $p_{\alpha\beta,\gamma} \in \mathbb{R}$ with $\gamma = 0, 1, \ldots, n$. In this way, the multiplication of the hypercomplex numbers $x = x_0 + x_1 i_1 + \ldots + x_n i_n$ and $y = y_0 + y_1 i_1 + \ldots + y_n i_n$ is computed as follows

$$
\begin{aligned}
xy = {} & \left(x_0 y_0 + \sum_{\alpha,\beta=1}^{n} x_\alpha y_\beta p_{\alpha\beta,0} \right) \\
& + \left(x_0 y_1 + x_1 y_0 + \sum_{\alpha,\beta=1}^{n} x_\alpha y_\beta p_{\alpha\beta,1} \right) i_1 + \ldots \\
& + \left(x_0 y_n + x_n y_0 + \sum_{\alpha,\beta=1}^{n} x_\alpha y_\beta p_{\alpha\beta,n} \right) i_n.
\end{aligned} \tag{4}
$$

A hypercomplex algebra, which we will denote by $\mathbb{H}$, is a hypercomplex number system equipped with the addition (2) and the multiplication (4).

We would like to remark that the product of a hypercomplex number $x = x_0 + x_1 i_1 + \cdots + x_n i_n$ by a scalar $\alpha \in \mathbb{R}$, given by

$$\alpha x = \alpha x_0 + \alpha x_1 i_1 + \cdots + \alpha x_n i_n, \tag{5}$$

can be derived from (4) by identifying $\alpha \in \mathbb{R}$ with the hypercomplex number $\alpha + 0 i_1 + \cdots + 0 i_n \in \mathbb{H}$. As a consequence, a hypercomplex algebra $\mathbb{H}$ is a vector space with the addition and scalar product given by (2) and (5). Moreover, $\tau = \{1, i_1, \ldots, i_n\}$ is the canonical basis for $\mathbb{H}$. The canonical basis τ yields a one-to-one correspondence between a hypercomplex number $x = x_0 + x_1 i_1 + \cdots + x_n i_n$ and a vector $[x]_\tau = (x_0, x_1, \ldots, x_n) \in \mathbb{R}^{n+1}$. Using the such correspondence, we define the absolute value $|x|$ of a hypercomplex number $x \in \mathbb{H}$ as the Euclidean norm of $[x]_\tau$, that is,

$$|x| := \|[x]_\tau\|_2 = \sqrt{x_0^2 + x_1^2 + \cdots + x_n^2}. \tag{6}$$

Concluding, there exists an isomorphism between $\mathbb{H}$ and $\mathbb{R}^{n+1}$. However, beyond its vector space structure, an hypercomplex algebra $\mathbb{H}$ is equipped with a multiplication given by (4).

Complex numbers ($\mathbb{C}$), quaternions ($\mathbb{Q}$), and octonions ($\mathbb{O}$) are examples of hypercomplex algebras. Hyperbolic numbers ($\mathbb{U}$), dual numbers ($\mathbb{D}$), and tessarines ($\mathbb{T}$) are also hypercomplex algebras. The following examples illustrate further some hypercomplex algebras.

Example 1. Complex, hyperbolic, and dual numbers are hypercomplex algebras of dimension 2, i.e., the elements of these algebras are of the form $x = x_0 + ix_1$. They differ in the value of i^2. The most well-known of these 2-dimensional (2D) hypercomplex algebras is the complex numbers where $i^2 = -1$. Complex numbers play a key role in physics, electromagnetism, and electrical and electronic circuits. In contrast, hyperbolic numbers have $i^2 = 1$ and have important connections with abstract algebra, ring theory, and special relativity [10]. Lastly, dual numbers are a degenerate algebra in which $i^2 = 0$.

Example 2. Quaternions are a 4D hypercomplex algebra denoted by $\mathbb{Q}$. The quaternion elements are $x = x_0 + x_1 i + x_2 j + x_3 k$, where $i \equiv i_1$, $j \equiv i_2$, $k \equiv i_3$ are the hyperimaginary units. The quaternion product is associative and anticommutative, and is of particular interest to describe rotations in the 3D Euclidean space $\mathbb{R}^3$. Formally, we have:

$$i^2 = j^2 = k^2 = -1, \quad ij = k, \quad \text{and} \quad ji = -k. \tag{7}$$

Together with complex numbers, quaternion is one of the most well-known hypercomplex algebras. Quaternions has seen applications in many fields ranging from physics to computer vision and control due to the intrinsic relation between movement in the 3D space and quaternion product.

Example 3. Cayley-Dickson algebras are a family of hypercomplex algebras that contains the previously mentioned complex and quaternions as particular instances. The Cayley-Dickson algebras are produced by an iterative parametric process [1] that generates algebras of doubling dimension, i.e., these algebras always have a dimension equal to a power of 2. Cayley-Dickson algebras have been successfully used to implement efficient neural network models for color image processing tasks [33].

Example 4. The tessarines $\mathbb{T}$ are a commutative 4D algebra similar to the quaternions, hence they are often referred to as *commutative quaternions* [11]. The tessarines elements are $x = x_0 + x_1 i + x_2 j + x_3 k$, where $i \equiv i_1, j \equiv i_2, k \equiv i_3$ are the hyperimaginary units. Unlike the quaternions, we have:

$$i^2 = -1, \ j^2 = 1, \ k^2 = -1, \quad \text{and} \quad ij = ji = k. \tag{8}$$

Like the quaternions, tessarines have been used for digital signal processing [2,26]. A recent paper by Senna and Valle addressed tessarine-valued deep neural networks, which outperformed real-valued deep neural networks for image processing and analysis tasks [29].

Example 5. The Klein four-group $\mathbb{K}_4$ is a 4D hypercomplex algebra whose imaginary unit are self-inverse, i.e. $i^2 = j^2 = k^2 = 1$ and $ij = k$. Besides the theoretical studies in symmetric group theory [20], the Klein four-group has been used for the design of hypercomplex-valued Hopfield neural networks [22].

Example 6. Besides quaternions, tessarines, and the Klein four-group, the hyperbolic quaternions are a 4D non-associative and anticommutative hypercomplex algebra whose hypercomplex units satisfy

$$i^2 = j^2 = k^2 = 1, \ ij = k = -ji, \ jk = i = -kj, \ \text{and} \ ki = j = -ik. \quad (9)$$

Among others 4D hypercomplex algebras, the hyperbolic quaternions have been used to design a servo-level robot manipulator controller by Takahashi [30].

Example 7. Clifford algebras are an important family of hypercomplex algebras with interesting geometric properties and a wide range of applications [5,17]. A Clifford algebra is generated from the vector space $\mathbb{R}^n$ equipped with a quadratic form $Q : \mathbb{R}^n \to \mathbb{R}$ [8,31]. Precisely, the Clifford algebra $C\ell_{p,q,r}$, where p, q, and r are non-negative integers such that $p + q + r = n$, is constructed from an orthonormal basis $\{e_1, e_2, \ldots, e_n\}$ of $\mathbb{R}^n$ such that

$$Q(e_i + e_j) = Q(e_i) + Q(e_j) \quad \text{and} \quad Q(e_i) = \begin{cases} +1, & 1 \leq i \leq p, \\ -1, & p+1 \leq i \leq q, \\ 0, & p+q+1 \leq i \leq n. \end{cases} \quad (10)$$

In particular, the Clifford algebra $C\ell_{0,1,0}$ is equivalent to the complex numbers, $C\ell_{1,0,0}$ is equivalent to the hyperbolic numbers, and $C\ell_{0,2,0}$ is equivalent to the quaternions. A Clifford algebra is degenerate if $r > 0$. A non-degenerate Clifford algebra $C\ell_{p,q,0}$ is also denoted by $C\ell_{p,q}$, that is, $C\ell_{p,q} \equiv C\ell_{p,q,0}$.

The examples above present a handful of algebras with different sets of properties or lack thereof. While complex, hyperbolic, dual numbers, tessarines and the Klein group are commutative, the quaternions and general Clifford algebras are not. The hyperbolic quaternions and the octonions, a well-known Cayley-Dickson 8D hypercomplex algebra, are not associative. The hyperbolic numbers present non-null zero divisors. Only a few properties are observed across all hypercomplex number systems $\mathbb{H}$. Notably, the identity $(\omega x)(\eta y) = (\omega \eta)(xy)$ holds for all $x, y \in \mathbb{H}$ and $\omega, \eta \in \mathbb{R}$. Also, we have distributivity as $x(y + w) = xy + xw$ and $(y + w)x = yx + wx$, for all $x, y, z \in \mathbb{H}$.

3   Some Approximation Theorems from the Literature

A multilayer perceptron (MLP) is a feedforward artificial neural network architecture with neurons arranged in layers. Each neuron in a layer is connected to all neurons in the previous layer, hence this model is also known as fully-connected or dense. The feedforward step through a MLP with a single hidden-layer with M neurons can be described by a finite linear combination of the hidden neurons outputs. Formally, the output of a single hidden-layer MLP network $\mathcal{N}_{\mathbb{R}}(\boldsymbol{x})$ is given by

$$\mathcal{N}_{\mathbb{R}}(\boldsymbol{x}) = \sum_{i=1}^{M} \alpha_i \phi(\boldsymbol{y}_i^T \cdot \boldsymbol{x} + \theta_i), \tag{11}$$

where $\boldsymbol{x} \in \mathbb{R}^N$ represents the input to the neural network, $\boldsymbol{y}_i \in \mathbb{R}^N$ and $\alpha_i \in \mathbb{R}$ are the weights between input and hidden layers, and hidden and output layers, respectively. Moreover, $\theta_i \in \mathbb{R}$ is the bias terms for the ith neuron in the hidden layer and $\phi : \mathbb{R} \to \mathbb{R}$ is the activation function.

The class of all functions that can be obtained using a MLP with activation function ϕ will be denoted by

$$\mathcal{H}_\phi = \left\{ \mathcal{N}_{\mathbb{R}}(\boldsymbol{x}) = \sum_{i=1}^{M} \alpha_i \phi(\boldsymbol{y}_i^T \cdot \boldsymbol{x} + \theta_i) : M \in \mathbb{N}, \boldsymbol{y}_i \in \mathbb{R}^N, \alpha_i, \theta_i \in \mathbb{R} \right\}. \tag{12}$$

Sigmoid functions are widely used activation functions and include the logistc function defined by

$$\sigma(x) = \frac{1}{1 + e^{-x}}, \quad \forall x \in \mathbb{R}, \tag{13}$$

as a particular instance. Besides sigmoid functions, modern neural networks also use the rectified linear unit ReLU as activation function, which is defined as follows for all $x \in \mathbb{R}$:

$$\text{ReLU}(x) = \begin{cases} x, & \text{if } x > 0, \\ 0, & \text{if } x \le 0. \end{cases} \tag{14}$$

The key interest in the usage of activation functions is to discriminate inputs. We review this key property below, in which we denote by $\mathcal{C}(K)$ the class of all continuous functions on a compact subset $K \subset \mathbb{R}^N$.

Definition 1 (Discriminatory Function). *Consider a real-valued function $\phi : \mathbb{R} \to \mathbb{R}$ and let $K \subset \mathbb{R}^N$ be a compact. The function ϕ is said to be discriminatory if, for a finite signed regular Borel measure μ on K, the following holds*

$$\int_K \phi(\boldsymbol{y}^T \cdot \boldsymbol{x} + \theta) d\mu(\boldsymbol{x}) = 0, \quad \forall \boldsymbol{y} \in \mathbb{R}^N \text{ and } \forall \theta \in \mathbb{R}, \tag{15}$$

if, and only if, μ is the zero measure, i.e., $\mu = 0$.

The sigmoid and ReLU functions defined above are examples of discriminatory activation functions [12,16]. More generally, Hornik showed that bounded non-constant real-valued functions are discriminatory [19].

The next theorem, published in 1989, establishes the universal approximation property for real-valued networks. Note that Definition 1 plays a key role in establishing the result proved by Cybenko [12].

Theorem 1 (Universal Approximation Theorem [12]). *Consider a compact $K \subset \mathbb{R}^N$ and let $\phi : \mathbb{R} \to \mathbb{R}$ be a continuous discriminatory function. The class of all real-valued neural networks defined by (12) is dense in $\mathcal{C}(K)$, the set of all real-valued continuous functions on K. In other words, given a real-valued continuous-function $f_{\mathbb{R}} : K \to \mathbb{R}$ and $\epsilon > 0$, there is a single hidden-layer MLP network given by (11) such that*

$$|f_{\mathbb{R}}(\boldsymbol{x}) - \mathcal{N}_{\mathbb{R}}(\boldsymbol{x})| < \epsilon, \quad \forall \boldsymbol{x} \in K. \tag{16}$$

Over the following decades, the universal approximation property was proven for neural networks with values in several other algebras. We highlight some of these works in the remainder of this section.

3.1   Complex-Valued Case

The structure of a complex-valued MLP ($\mathbb{C}$MLP) is equivalent to that of a real-valued MLP, except that input and output signals, weights and bias are complex numbers instead of real values. Additionally, the activation functions are complex-valued functions [4]. Note that the logistic function given by (13) can be generalized to complex parameters using Euler's formula $e^{xi} = \cos(x) + i \sin(x)$ as follows for all $x \in \mathbb{C}$:

$$\sigma(x) = \frac{1}{1 + e^{-x}}. \tag{17}$$

However, in 1998, Arena *et al.* noted that the universal approximation property in the context of the $\mathbb{C}$MLP network with the activation function (17) is generally not valid [4]. Nonetheless, they proved that the split activation function

$$\sigma(x) = \frac{1}{1 + e^{-x_0}} + i\frac{1}{1 + e^{-x_1}} \tag{18}$$

for $x = x_0 + ix_1 \in \mathbb{C}$ is discriminatory. Moreover, they generalized Theorem 1 for $\mathbb{C}$MLP networks with split sigmoid activation functions [4].

3.2   Quaternion-Valued Case

In the same vein, Arena *et al.* also defined quaternion-valued MLP ($\mathbb{Q}$MLP) by replacing the real input and output, weights and biases, by quaternion numbers. They then proceeded to prove that $\mathbb{Q}$MLPs with a single hidden layer and split sigmoid activation function

$$\sigma(x) = \frac{1}{1 + e^{-x_0}} + i\frac{1}{1 + e^{-x_1}} + j\frac{1}{1 + e^{-x_2}} + k\frac{1}{1 + e^{-x_3}}, \tag{19}$$

for $x = x_0 + ix_1 + jx_2 + kx_3 \in \mathbb{Q}$, are universal approximators in the set of continuous quaternion-valued functions [3].

3.3 Hyperbolic-Valued Case

In the year 2000, Buchholz and Sommer introduced a MLP based on hyperbolic numbers, the aptly named hyperbolic multilayer perceptron (𝕌MLP). This network equipped with a split logistic activation function given by (18) is also a universal approximator [6]. Buchholz and Sommer provided experiments highlighting that the 𝕌MLP can learn tasks with underlying hyperbolic properties much more accurately and efficiently than ℂMLP and real-valued MLP networks.

3.4 Tessarine-Valued Case

Recently, Carniello *et al.* experimented with networks with inputs, outputs and parameters in the tessarine algebra [9]. The researchers proposed the 𝕋MLP, a MLP architecture similar to the complex, quaternion and hyperbolic MLPs mentioned above but based on tesarines. The authors then proceeded to show that the proposed 𝕋MLP is a universal approximator for continuous functions defined on compact subsets of 𝕋 with sigmoid and the ReLU activation functions. Experiments show that the tessarine-valued network is a powerful approximator, presenting superior performance when compared to the real-valued MLP in a task of approximating tessarine functions [9].

3.5 Clifford-Valued Case

In 2001, Buchholz and Sommer worked with a class of neural networks based on Clifford algebras [7]. They found that the universal approximation property holds for MLPs based on non-degenerate Clifford algebra. In addition they pointed out that degenerate Clifford algebras may lead to models without universal approximation capability.

It is worth noting that Buchholz and Sommer considered sigmoid activation functions. However, it is possible to show that the split ReLU activation function is discriminatory in a Clifford algebra. Hence, Clifford MLPs are universal approximators with the split ReLU activation function as well.

4   Universal Approximation Theorem for Hypercomplex-Valued Neural Networks

This section deals with the extension of the universal approximation theorem to a wide class of artificial neural networks with hypercomplex values. This is the main result of this work, which is based on the concept of non-degenerate hypercomplex algebra.

4.1 Non-degenerate Hypercomplex Algebras

Let us start by introducing preliminary results and some core definitions that lead us to the main result. This subsection relies on the hypercomplex algebra concepts detailed in Sect. 2 and linear algebra [18].

A linear operator on a hypercomplex algebra $\mathbb{H}$ is an operator $T : \mathbb{H} \to \mathbb{H}$ such that $T(\alpha x + y) = \alpha T(x) + T(y)$ for all $x, y \in \mathbb{H}$ and $\alpha \in \mathbb{R}$ [21].

A bilinear form on $\mathbb{H}$ is a mapping $B : \mathbb{H} \times \mathbb{H} \to \mathbb{R}$ such that

$$B(c_1 x_1 + c_2 x_2, v) = c_1 B(x_1, v) + c_2 B(x_2, v), \tag{20}$$

and

$$B(x, d_1 v_1 + d_2 v_2) = d_1 B(x, v_1) + d_2 B(x, v_2), \tag{21}$$

hold true for any $x_1, x_2, v_1, v_2, x, v \in \mathbb{H}$ and $c_1, c_2, d_1, d_2 \in \mathbb{R}$. In words, a bilinear form is linear in both its arguments.

The following preliminary result consists of a theorem linking the hypercomplex algebra product given by (4) to bilinear forms. This result also leads to matrix representations of (4).

Theorem 2. *Let $\mathbb{H}$ be a hypercomplex algebra. The product of x by y in $\mathbb{H}$ given by (4) satisfies the identity:*

$$xy = B_0(x, y) + \sum_{j=1}^{n} B_j(x, y) \boldsymbol{i}_j \tag{22}$$

where $B_0, B_1, \dots, B_n : \mathbb{H} \times \mathbb{H} \to \mathbb{R}$ are bilinear forms whose matrix representations in the canonical base $\tau = \{1, \boldsymbol{i}_1, \cdots, \boldsymbol{i}_n\}$ are

$$\left[\mathcal{B}_0 \right]_\tau = \begin{bmatrix} 1 & 0 & \cdots & 0 \\ 0 & p_{11,0} & \cdots & p_{1n,0} \\ \vdots & \vdots & \ddots & \vdots \\ 0 & p_{n1,0} & \cdots & p_{nn,0} \end{bmatrix} \in \mathbb{R}^{(n+1)\times(n+1)}, \tag{23}$$

and, for $j = 1, \dots, n$,

$$\left[\mathcal{B}_j \right]_\tau = \begin{bmatrix} 0 & 0 & 0 & \cdots & 1 & \cdots & 0 \\ 0 & p_{11,j} & p_{12,j} & \cdots & p_{1j,j} & \cdots & p_{1n,j} \\ \vdots & \vdots & \vdots & \vdots & \vdots & & \vdots \\ 1 & p_{j1,j} & p_{j2,j} & \cdots & p_{jj,j} & \cdots & p_{jn,j} \\ \vdots & \vdots & \vdots & \vdots & \vdots & & \vdots \\ 0 & p_{n1,j} & p_{n2,j} & \cdots & p_{nj,j} & \cdots & p_{nn,j} \end{bmatrix} \in \mathbb{R}^{(n+1)\times(n+1)}. \tag{24}$$

We note that the matrices in Theorem 2 depend on the choice of basis τ. Moreover, the numbers $p_{\alpha\beta,j}$ depend on the hyperimaginary unit products (3), which ultimately define the algebra $\mathbb{H}$.

Next we define non-degeneracy of hypercomplex algebras. From linear algebra, we have that a bilinear form is said to be non-degenerate if the following hold true $B(u, v) = 0, \ \forall u \in \mathbb{H} \iff v = 0_\mathbb{H}$ and $B(u, v) = 0, \ \forall v \in \mathbb{H} \iff u = 0_\mathbb{H}$. A bilinear form that fails this condition is degenerate. Equivalently, given the canonical basis τ, a bilinear form B is non-degenerate if and only if the matrix $[B]_\tau$ is invertible. Borrowing the terminology from linear algebra, we introduce the following definition:

Definition 2 (Non-degenerate Hypercomplex Algebra). *A hypercomplex algebra* $\mathbb{H}$ *is non-degenerate if the matrices* $[\mathcal{B}_j]_\tau$ *associated with the bilinear form of the product of* $\mathbb{H}$ *are all invertible (see Theorem 2 above). Otherwise* $\mathbb{H}$ *is said to be degenerate.*

We provide examples of Theorem 2 and Definition 2 with well-known 2D hypercomplex algebras, namely the complex, hyperbolic, and dual numbers.

Example 8. Consider a hyperimaginary algebra $\mathbb{H}$ of dimension 2. This algebra possesses a single hyperimaginary unit, whose product is

$$i_1^2 = a_{11,0} + a_{11,1} i_1$$

By computing the product of $x = x_0 + x_1 i_1$ and $y = y_0 + y_1 i_1$ in $\mathbb{H}$, we obtain

$$xy = x_0 y_0 + x_1 y_1 a_{11,0} + (x_1 y_1 a_{11,1} + x_0 y_1 + x_1 y_0) i_1.$$

Let $\tau = \{1, i_1\}$ be the canonical basis of $\mathbb{H}$. From Theorem 2, the product in $\mathbb{H}$ can be written as follows

$$xy = [x]_\tau^T [\mathcal{B}_0]_\tau [y]_\tau + [x]_\tau^T [\mathcal{B}_1]_\tau [y]_\tau i_1.$$

where $[x]_\tau$ and $[y]_\tau$ are the vector representation of x and y with respect to the canonical basis τ and the matrices of the bilinear forms are

$$[\mathcal{B}_0]_\tau = \begin{bmatrix} 1 & 0 \\ 0 & a_{11,0} \end{bmatrix} \quad \text{and} \quad [\mathcal{B}_1]_\tau = \begin{bmatrix} 0 & 1 \\ 1 & a_{11,1} \end{bmatrix}.$$

In particular, we have the matrices of the bilinear forms associated with the product of complex numbers if $a_{11,0} = -1$ and $a_{11,1} = 0$. Similarly, if $a_{11,0} = 1$ and $a_{11,1} = 0$, we obtain the matrices of the bilinear forms associated with the product of hyperbolic numbers. Because the matrices $[\mathcal{B}_0]_\tau$ and $[\mathcal{B}_1]_\tau$ are both non-singular for either complex or hypercomplex numbers, these two algebras are notably non-degenerate. In contrast, we have $a_{11,0} = a_{11,1} = 0$ in the product of dual numbers and, in this case, the matrix $[\mathcal{B}_0]_\tau$ is singular. Thus, the dual numbers is a degenerate hypercomplex algebra. More generally, note that $[\mathcal{B}_1]_\tau$ is non-singular regardless of the value $a_{11,1}$. Thus, the condition for a 2D hypercomplex algebra to be non-degenerate is that $[\mathcal{B}_0]_\tau$ is invertible, i.e., $a_{11,0} \neq 0$.

The next example addresses 4D hypercomplex algebras and include quaternions, tessarines, hyperbolic quaternions, and Klein four-group as particular instances.

Example 9. Consider a 4D hypercomplex algebra $\mathbb{H}$ in which the product of hyperimaginary units satisfies

$$i_\alpha i_\beta = a_{\alpha\beta,0} + a_{\alpha\beta,1} i_1 + a_{\alpha\beta,2} i_2 + a_{\alpha\beta,3} i_3 \tag{25}$$

for all $\alpha, \beta \in \{1, 2, 3\}$. Let us take $x = x_0 + x_1 i_1 + x_2 i_2 + x_3 i_3$ and $y = y_0 + y_1 i_1 + y_2 i_2 + y_3 i_3$ in $\mathbb{H}$, and the canonical basis of $\mathbb{H}$ as $\tau = \{1, i_1, i_2, i_3\}$. Then, the product of x by y can be represented by bilinear forms whose matrices are given by

$$
\left[\mathcal{B}_0\right]_\tau = \begin{bmatrix} 1 & 0 & 0 & 0 \\ 0 & a_{11,0} & a_{12,0} & a_{13,0} \\ 0 & a_{21,0} & a_{22,0} & a_{23,0} \\ 0 & a_{31,0} & a_{32,0} & a_{33,0} \end{bmatrix}, \quad
\left[\mathcal{B}_1\right]_\tau = \begin{bmatrix} 0 & 1 & 0 & 0 \\ 1 & a_{11,1} & a_{12,1} & a_{13,1} \\ 0 & a_{21,1} & a_{22,1} & a_{23,1} \\ 0 & a_{31,1} & a_{32,1} & a_{33,1} \end{bmatrix},
$$

$$
\left[\mathcal{B}_2\right]_\tau = \begin{bmatrix} 0 & 0 & 1 & 0 \\ 0 & a_{11,2} & a_{12,2} & a_{13,2} \\ 1 & a_{21,2} & a_{22,2} & a_{23,2} \\ 0 & a_{31,2} & a_{32,2} & a_{33,2} \end{bmatrix}, \quad
\left[\mathcal{B}_3\right]_\tau = \begin{bmatrix} 0 & 0 & 0 & 1 \\ 0 & a_{11,3} & a_{12,3} & a_{13,3} \\ 0 & a_{21,3} & a_{22,3} & a_{23,3} \\ 1 & a_{31,3} & a_{32,3} & a_{33,3} \end{bmatrix}.
$$

Therefore, an arbitrary 4D hypercomplex algebra is non-degenerate if, and only if, the above matrices are invertible. In particular the hypercomplex algebras of quaternions, tessarines, hyperbolic quaternions and Klein four-group are non-degenerate.

4.2   Universal Approximation Theorem to a Broad Class of Hypercomplex-valued Neural Networks

In the previous sections we have presented a few universal approximation theorems. A common theme among them is the requirement for the activation function to be discriminatory. We have also defined degeneracy of hypercomplex algebras. The main result of this work, namely, the Universal Approximation Theorem for a broad class of hypercomplex-valued neural networks is achieved by combining these concepts and properties. In this section we formalize a few definitions and notations before stating our result in Theorem 3.

We start off by recalling that a split activation function $\psi_\mathbb{H} : \mathbb{H} \to \mathbb{H}$ is defined based on a real function $\psi : \mathbb{R} \to \mathbb{R}$ by

$$
\psi_\mathbb{H}(x) = \psi(x_0) + i_1 \psi(x_1) + i_2 \psi(x_1) + \cdots + i_n \psi(x_2) \tag{26}
$$

for all $x = x_0 + x_1 i_1 + \cdots x_n i_n \in \mathbb{H}$. In this work, the activation functions chosen are the split ReLU and the split sigmoid, both well-known from applications and from the literature of other approximation theorems.

We define an $\mathbb{H}$MLP as a MLP model in which inputs, outputs, and trainable parameters are hypercomplex numbers instead of real numbers. By making such a general definition we encompass previously known models such as complex, quaternion, hyperbolic, tessarine, and Clifford-valued networks as particular cases, thus resulting in a broader family of models. In the following definition we highlight that in hypercomplex-valued MLPs the feedforward step can also be seen as a finite linear combination.

Definition 3 (ℍMLP). *Let* ℍ *be a hypercomplex algebra. A hypercomplex-valued multilayer perceptron (*ℍ*MLP) can be described by*

$$\mathcal{N}_{\mathbb{H}}(\boldsymbol{x}) = \sum_{i=1}^{M} \alpha_i \psi(\boldsymbol{y}_i^T \cdot \boldsymbol{x} + \theta_i), \forall \boldsymbol{x} \in \mathbb{H}^N, \qquad (27)$$

where $\boldsymbol{x} \in \mathbb{H}^N$ *represents the input to the neural network,* $\mathcal{N}_{\mathbb{R}}(\boldsymbol{x}) \in \mathbb{H}$ *is the output,* $y_i \in \mathbb{H}^N$ *and* $\alpha_i \in \mathbb{H}$ *are the weights between input and hidden layers, and hidden and output layers, respectively,* $\theta_i \in \mathbb{H}$ *are the biases for the neurons in the hidden layer, and* $\psi : \mathbb{H} \to \mathbb{H}$ *is the activation function. The number of neurons in the hidden layer is* M.

This definition is analogous to the real-valued MLP described in Sect. 3. Now, we have the necessary components and can state the main result of this work: the extension of the universal approximation theorem to neural networks defined in non-degenerate hypercomplex algebras.

Theorem 3. *Consider a non-degenerate hypercomplex algebra* ℍ *and let* $K \subset$ $\mathbb{H}^N$ *be a compact. Also, consider a real-valued continuous discriminatory function* $\psi : \mathbb{R} \to \mathbb{R}$ *such that* $\lim_{\lambda \to -\infty} \psi(\lambda) = 0$ *and let* $\psi_{\mathbb{H}} : \mathbb{H} \to \mathbb{H}$ *be the split function associated to* ψ *by means of* (26). *Then, the class*

$$\mathcal{H}_\psi = \left\{ \mathcal{N}_{\mathbb{H}}(\boldsymbol{x}) = \sum_{i=1}^{M} \alpha_i \psi(\boldsymbol{y}_i^T \cdot \boldsymbol{x} + \theta_i) : M \in \mathbb{N}, \boldsymbol{y}_i \in \mathbb{H}^N, \alpha_i, \theta_i \in \mathbb{H} \right\}, \qquad (28)$$

is dense in the set $\mathcal{C}(K)$ *of all hypercomplex-valued continuous functions on* K. *In other words, given a hypercomplex-valued continuous function* $f_{\mathbb{H}} : K \to \mathbb{H}$ *and* $\epsilon > 0$, *there exists a* ℍ*MLP network* $\mathcal{N}_{\mathbb{H}} : \mathbb{H}^N \to \mathbb{H}$ *given by* (27) *such that*

$$|f_{\mathbb{H}}(\boldsymbol{x}) - \mathcal{N}_{\mathbb{H}}(\boldsymbol{x})| < \epsilon, \quad \forall \boldsymbol{x} \in K, \qquad (29)$$

where $| \cdot |$ *denotes the absolute value of hypercomplex numbers defined by* (6).

The Theorem 3 extends the existing universal approximation theorems [3, 4,6,7,9] and strengthens neural networks models on the broad family of non-degenerate hypercomplex algebras.

5   Concluding Remarks

The universal approximation theorem asserts that a single hidden layer neural network can approximate continuous functions with arbitrary precision. This essential theoretical result was first proven for real-valued networks in the late 1980s [12]. In the years that followed, the universal approximation theorem was also proven for neural networks based on well-known hypercomplex algebras, such as complex [4], quaternions [3], and Clifford algebras [7]. However, each of these results was derived individually, meaning there is a lack of generality in the proofs of universal approximation theorems. In this work, we investigate the existing theorems and tie the universal approximation property of hypercomplex-valued networks to two main factors: an appropriate activation function choice and the underlying algebra's degeneracy. By identifying these objects, we review the definitions of discriminatory activation functions and introduce the concept of non-degenerate hypercomplex algebras. Finally, we give sufficient conditions for a neural network to be a universal approximator in a broad class of hypercomplex-valued algebras. Specifically, we formulate the universal approximation theorem: hypercomplex-valued single hidden layer neural networks with discriminatory split activation functions are dense in the set of continuous functions on a compact subset of the Cartesian product of a non-degenerate hypercomplex algebra.

The universal approximation theorem formulated in this paper serves many purposes, including the following items:

1. It consolidates the results regarding the universal approximation property of many well-known algebras, thus eliminating the need to prove this property for each algebra individually. In particular, the class of non-degenerate hypercomplex algebras includes the complex and hyperbolic numbers, quaternions, tessarines, and Clifford algebras, all of which have particular results of their own, as mentioned in previous sections.
2. Many algebras that have not had this result proven are now directly known as the basis for neural networks with universal approximation property. That is the case for the Klein group and the octonions, among others.
3. This result further promotes the use of hypercomplex-valued networks. Indeed, hypercomplex-valued networks are known to perform well in problems involving multidimensional signals such as images, video, and 3D movement [25,33]. The property of universal approximators strengthens these models' applications, posing them as strictly better than real-valued models for a wider variety of applications.

References

1. Albert, A.A.: Quadratic forms permitting composition. Ann. Math. **43**(1), 161–177 (1942)
2. Alfsmann, D.: On families of 2 n-dimensional hypercomplex algebras suitable for digital signal processing. In: 2006 14th European Signal Processing Conference, pp. 1–4. IEEE (2006)
3. Arena, P., Fortuna, L., Muscato, G., Xibilia, M.: Multilayer perceptrons to approximate quaternion valued functions. Neural Netw. **10**(2), 335–342 (1997)
4. Arena, P., Fortuna, L., Muscato, G., Xibilia, M.G.: Neural Networks in Multidimensional Domains: Fundamentals and New trends in Modeling and Control. Springer, London (1998). https://doi.org/10.1007/BFb0047683
5. Breuils, S., Tachibana, K., Hitzer, E.: New applications of Clifford's geometric algebra. Adv. Appl. Clifford Algebras **32**(2), 1–39 (2022). https://doi.org/10.1007/S00006-021-01196-7,https://link.springer.com/article/10.1007/s00006-021-01196-7

6. Buchholz, S., Sommer, G.: A hyperbolic multilayer perceptron. In: Proceedings of the IEEE-INNS-ENNS International Joint Conference on Neural Networks, IJCNN 2000. Neural Computing: New Challenges and Perspectives for the New Millennium, vol. 2, pp. 129–133. IEEE (2000)

7. Buchholz, S., Sommer, G.: Clifford algebra multilayer perceptrons. In: Sommer, G. (ed.) Geometric Computing with Clifford Algebras, pp. 315–334. Springer, Heidelberg (2001). https://doi.org/10.1007/978-3-662-04621-0_13

8. Buchholz, S., Sommer, G.: On Clifford neurons and Clifford multi-layer perceptrons. Neural Netw. **21**(7), 925–935 (2008). https://doi.org/10.1016/j.neunet.2008.03.004

9. Carniello, R., Vital, W., Valle, M.: Universal approximation theorem for tessarine-valued neural networks. In: Anais do XVIII Encontro Nacional de Inteligência Artificial e Computacional, pp. 233–243. SBC, Porto Alegre (2021). https://doi.org/10.5753/eniac.2021.18256, https://sol.sbc.org.br/index.php/eniac/article/view/18256

10. Catoni, F., Boccaletti, D., Cannata, R., Catoni, V., Nichelatti, E., Zampetti, P.: The Mathematics of Minkowski Space-Time. Birkhäuser Basel (2008). https://doi.org/10.1007/978-3-7643-8614-6

11. Cerroni, C.: From the theory of congeneric surd equations to Segre's bicomplex numbers. Hist. Math. **44**(3), 232–251 (2017). https://doi.org/10.1016/j.hm.2017.03.001, https://www.sciencedirect.com/science/article/pii/S0315086017300241

12. Cybenko, G.: Approximation by superpositions of a sigmoidal function. Math. Control Signals Syst. **2**(4), 303–314 (1989), https://link.springer.com/article/10.1007/BF02551274

13. Givental, A.B., et al. (eds.): On Functions of Three Variables, pp. 5–8. Springer, Heidelberg (2009). https://doi.org/10.1007/978-3-642-01742-1_2

14. Grassucci, E., Mancini, G., Brignone, C., Uncini, A., Comminiello, D.: Dual quaternion ambisonics array for six-degree-of-freedom acoustic representation (2022). https://doi.org/10.48550/ARXIV.2204.01851

15. Grassucci, E., Zhang, A., Comminiello, D.: Lightweight convolutional neural networks by hypercomplex parameterization (2022). https://openreview.net/forum?id=S5qdnMhf7R

16. Guilhoto, L.F.: An overview of artificial neural networks for mathematicians (2018)

17. Hitzer, E., Nitta, T., Kuroe, Y.: Applications of Clifford's geometric algebra. Adv. Appl. Clifford Algebras **23**(2), 377–404 (2013). https://doi.org/10.1007/s00006-013-0378-4

18. Hoffman, K.: Linear Algebra. Prentice-Hall, Englewood Cliffs (1971)

19. Hornik, K.: Approximation capabilities of multilayer feedforward networks. Neural Netw. **4**(2), 251–257 (1991). https://doi.org/10.1016/0893-6080(91)90009-T, https://www.sciencedirect.com/science/article/pii/089360809190009T

20. Huang, J.S., Yu, J.: Klein four-subgroups of lie algebra automorphisms. Pac. J. Math. **262**(2), 397–420 (2013)

21. Kantor, I., Solodovnikov, A.: Hypercomplex Numbers: An Elementary Introduction to Algebras, vol. 302. Springer, New York (1989)

22. Kobayashi, M.: Hopfield neural networks using Klein four-group. Neurocomputing **387**, 123–128 (2020). https://doi.org/10.1016/j.neucom.2019.12.127, https://www.sciencedirect.com/science/article/pii/S0925231220300850

23. Kolmogorov, A.N.: On the representation of continuous functions of many variables by superposition of continuous functions of one variable and addition. In: Doklady Akademii Nauk. vol. 114, pp. 953–956. Russian Academy of Sciences (1957)

24. McCulloch, W.S., Pitts, W.: A logical calculus of the ideas immanent in nervous activity. Bull. Math. Biophys. **5**(4), 115–133 (1943). https://link.springer.com/article/10.1007/BF02478259

25. Parcollet, T., Morchid, M., Linarès, G.: A survey of quaternion neural networks. Artif. Intell. Rev. **53**(4), 2957–2982 (2020)

26. Pei, S.C., Chang, J.H., Ding, J.J.: Commutative reduced biquaternions and their Fourier transform for signal and image processing applications. IEEE Trans. Signal Process. **52**(7), 2012–2031 (2004). https://doi.org/10.1109/TSP.2004.828901

27. Petersen, P., Voigtlaender, F.: Optimal approximation of piecewise smooth functions using deep relu neural networks. Neural Networks **108**, 296–330 (2018). https://doi.org/10.1016/j.neunet.2018.08.019, https://www.sciencedirect.com/science/article/pii/S0893608018302454

28. Rosenblatt, F.: The perceptron: a probabilistic model for information storage and organization in the brain. Psychol. Rev. **65**(6), 386–408 (1958). https://link.springer.com/article/10.1007/BF02551274

29. Senna, F., Valle, M.: Tessarine and quaternion-valued deep neural networks for image classification. In: Anais do XVIII Encontro Nacional de Inteligência Artificial e Computacional, pp. 350–361. SBC, Porto Alegre (2021). https://doi.org/10.5753/eniac.2021.18266, https://sol.sbc.org.br/index.php/eniac/article/view/18266

30. Takahashi, K.: Comparison of high-dimensional neural networks using hypercomplex numbers in a robot manipulator control. Artif. Life Robot. **26**(3), 367–377 (2021)

31. Vaz, J., da Rocha, R.: An Introduction to Clifford Algebras and Spinors. Oxford University Press, Oxford (2016)

32. Vieira, G., Valle, M.E.: Acute lymphoblastic leukemia detection using hypercomplex-valued convolutional neural networks (2022). https://doi.org/10.48550/ARXIV.2205.13273

33. Vieira, G., Valle, M.E.: A general framework for hypercomplex-valued extreme learning machines. J. Comput. Math. Data Sci. **3**, 100032 (2022)

Author Index

Printed in the United States
by Baker & Taylor Publisher Services